NOT JUST HAPPY TOGETHER: THE TURTLES FROM A-Z
(AM RADIO TO ZAPPA)

NOT JUST HAPPY TOGETHER: THE TURTLES FROM A-Z

(AM RADIO TO ZAPPA)

by Mark Arnold and Charles F. Rosenay!!!

Milwaukee Wisconsin USA

NOT JUST HAPPY TOGETHER:
THE TURTLES FROM A-Z (AM RADIO TO ZAPPA)
by Mark Arnold and Charles F. Rosenay!!!

© 2024 Mark Arnold and Fun Ideas Productions and Charles F. Rosenay!!!

All rights to The Turtles and Flo & Eddie are trademarks of Mark Volman and Howard Kaylan.
All rights to Frank Zappa, The Mothers of Invention are trademarks of The Frank Zappa Estate.
All rights to Strawberry Shortcake, The Care Bears, G.I. Joe, Gumby, and all other characters represented in this book are owned by their respective copyright and trademark holders.

The material used in this book is used for historical purposes and literary criticism and review and is used by permission and is used as Fair Use to be illustrative for the text contained herein. It is not intended to plagiarize or in any other way infringe on the copyright or in any other way infringe on the copyrights of any copyrighted materials contained herein.

The opinions contained within the interviews contained in this book are those of the person being interviewed and do not necessarily reflect the opinion of the authors.

Every effort has been made to present the details accurately and as precisely as possble. If you find an error, please email Charles Rosenay!!! at NotJustHappyTogether@gmail.com for correction in future editions.

First printing.
All Rights Reserved.

Reproduction in whole or in part without the author's permission is strictly forbidden. Permission is granted to other publications or media to excerpt the contents contained herein for review purposes provided that the correct credit and copyright information is included for any materials reproduced.

For information, contact:
Genius Book Publishing
PO Box 250380
Milwaukee, Wisconsin 53225 USA
GeniusBookPublishing.com

Cover photographs by Henry Diltz, used with permission.

Typesetting and layout by Steven W. Booth.

Published in the USA by Genius Book Publishing.

Library of Congress Cataloging-in-Publication Data
Arnold, Mark, and Rosenay, Charles .
Not Just Happy Together: The Turtles from A-Z (AM Radio To Zappa)
by Mark Arnold and Charles F. Rosenay!!!
Includes index.
ISBN - 978-1-958727-22-5

240101-4 Letter

BOOKS BY MARK ARNOLD

The Best of The Harveyville Fun Times!
Created and Produced by Total TeleVision productions
If You're Cracked, You're Happy, Part Won and Part Too
Mark Arnold Picks on The Beatles
Frozen in Ice: The Story of Walt Disney Productions 1966-1985
Think Pink: The DePatie-Freleng Story
Pocket Full of Dennis the Menace
The Harvey Comics Companion
Long Title: Looking for the Good Times; Examining the Monkees' Songs (with Michael A. Ventrella)
Aaaaalllviiinnn: The Story of Ross Bagdasarian, Sr., Liberty Records, Format Films and The Alvin Show
Headquartered: A Timeline of The Monkees Solo Years (with Michael A. Ventrella)
The Comedy of Jack Davis
The Comedy of John Severin
Pac-Man: The First Animated TV Show Based Upon a Video Game
The TTV Scrapbook (with Victoria Biggers)
The Stars of Walt Disney Productions

BOOKS BY CHARLES F. ROSENAY!!!

Monsters, Celebrities, Actors, Athletes & Rock Stars: The Book of Top 10 Horror Lists
True Ghost Stories of Connecticut
Celebrities Actors Athletes Mods & Rockers: The Book of Top 10 Beatles Lists

ACKNOWLEDGMENTS

Mark Arnold and Charles F. Rosenay!!! would like to thank the various members of The Turtles and their friends for their time and their memories. Their words and input are greatly appreciated. Special thanks also go out to Steven and Leya Booth, Kim Cooper, Daniel Coston, Ron Dante, George Dassinger, Henry Diltz, Roger Dilernia, Lee Hester, JoAnn Kassoff, Steve Ludwig, Cathy Lynch, Al Pereira, Plastic EP, Edd Raineri, Kelly Kuvo Richardson, Andrew Sandoval, Gary Strobl, Fred Velez, Michael A. Ventrella, Goldmine Magazine, Rhino Records, and to Turtles fans and collectors worldwide.

Apologies if we have forgotten anyone.

TURTLES DEDICATION

John "Jonny" Barbata (born April 1, 1945)
Chip Douglas (born Douglas Farthing Hatlelid) (born August 27, 1942)
Howard Kaylan (born Howard Kaplan) aka Eddie (born June 22, 1947)
Joel Larson (born April 29, 1947)
Donald Ray Murray (November 8, 1945 – March 22, 1996)
Gilbert Allan Nichol (born March 31, 1946)
W. James Pons (born March 14, 1943)
Charles "Chuck" Portz (born March 28, 1945)
John L. Seiter (born August 17, 1947)
James Tucker (October 17, 1946 – November 12, 2020)
Mark Volman aka The Phlorescent Leech or Flo (born April 19, 1947)

INTERVIEWS CONDUCTED FOR THIS BOOK

Andy Cahan - February 9, 2021
Dinky Dawson - February 20, 2021
John Barbata - February 20, 2021
Ron Dante - March 6, 2021
Elaine "Spanky" McFarlane - March 6, 2021
Rick "Squid" Guidotti - April 7, 2021
Artie Kornfeld - April 12, 2021
Bob Lind - April 29, 2021
Ron Nevison - May 1, 2021
Gary Puckett - June 6, 2021
Jerry Yester - July 23, 2021
Godfrey Townsend - October 18, 2021
Chip Douglas - December 3, 2021
Greg Hawkes - December 4, 2021
Henry Diltz - April 18, 2022
Howard Kaylan - April 19, 2022
Jimmy Hunter - April 25, 2022
Steve Boone - June 22, 2022
Mitch Weissman - January 11, 2023

TABLE OF CONTENTS

FOREWORD by Gary Puckett 1

THE TURTLES AND ME by Charles F. Rosenay!!! 2

FORGET THE MONKEES, WHY THE HELL AREN'T THE TURTLES IN THE ROCK AND ROLL HALL OF FAME?!?
A Rant and Historical Discussion by Mark Arnold 4

IN A (NUT)SHELL: A HISTORY OF THE TURTLES by Mark Arnold 8

THE TURTLES A-Z (including THE CROSSFIRES)
Comments by Mark and Charles 22

A BRIEF HISTORY OF FRANK ZAPPA'S MOTHERS by Mark Arnold 148

FRANK ZAPPA'S MOTHERS A-Z Comments by Mark and Charles 151

A BRIEF HISTORY OF FLO & EDDIE by Mark Arnold 209

FLO & EDDIE A-Z (including CHECKPOINT CHARLIE)
Comments by Mark and Charles 212

A BRIEF HISTORY OF HOWARD AND MARK'S CHILDREN ALBUMS
by Mark Arnold 303

CHILDREN'S ALBUMS A-Z Comments by Mark and Charles 306

THE TURTLES REUNION 2003 by Mark Arnold 317

INTERVIEWS WITH TURTLES AND FRIENDS
by Mark, Charles and others 319

DISCOGRAPHY 434

BIBLIOGRAPHY 439

INDEX 440

ABOUT THE AUTHORS 456

Charles F. Rosenay!!!, Mark Volman, Gary Puckett, June 10, 2023
(Photo: Katherine McCabe)

FOREWORD
by Gary Puckett

The Turtles.... Who are they, anyway?

Teen idols? Maybe. Quintessential pop/rock band? Absolutely! Funny, rude, and irreverent? For sure! Disc jockeys? Yes, that too! I didn't know the other original members of the group, but I sure have known Flo and Eddie well.

We've been on the road and worked together for many years. Like you, I always loved their recordings, including their work with Frank Zappa, Bruce Springsteen, Alice Cooper, and T-Rex.

Read on. There's a lot about these guys that you'll be interested to know.

I'm proud to have them as friends.

THE TURTLES AND ME
by Charles F. Rosenay!!!

My family moved from The Bronx, NY to New Haven, CT when I was about 10 years old. My parents weren't exactly on the younger side, but they were cool, and we always listened to Top 40 AM radio in the car—never the news or sports (unless the Mets were on, then my dad and I would listen to baseball). Although we left New York and were physically New Englanders, we were still New Yorkers at heart. My dad didn't miss Brooklyn as much, but my mom, a Bronxite all her life, never got fully acclimated to Connecticut. So we visited our relatives "in the city"... every weekend! The 90-minute ride was often spent singing songs. We sang Beatles, Monkees, Four Seasons, Supremes, Hermans Hermits, Dave Clark Five, Gary Puckett, Gary Lewis and the Playboys, Bee Gees, and all the rest. At some point, they bought me a personal cassette deck to record our warbling. They also bought me a few cassette tapes to play in case our voices got tired. Knowing I already had every Beatles and Monkees record, and played them constantly, they thought, correctly, that I'd want to play another band. They figured they couldn't go wrong with another act that had a name from the animal kingdom, so they got me a Turtles tape. What a great choice! Obviously, we loved "Happy Together" (who didn't?!), which was one of the songs we sang regularly, and I found every single track to be great. There was never a "are we there yet?" as The Turtles became our go-to travel buddies.

They brought joy to my family then, and still bring a smile to my face now. In fact, that was the other magic of The Turtles—making fans smile. And laugh! These guys weren't just wonderful music makers, they were funny too. One of the things I loved so much about The Beatles and The Monkees was that they didn't just give us great songs, they gave us personality and humor. Well, so did The Turtles!

In preparing for this book, I learned a great deal about these Turtles that I'd never known. Like so many others, as I grew older and became more knowledgeable about music, at some point there was the discovery that many of our favorite acts used studio musicians... even The Beach Boys! The Turtles, however, were fine musicians who played their own instruments. Whereas so many groups sounded exactly the same on all their songs, The Turtles were unique and ever evolving. But they could also sound just like their contemporaries when they wanted to, or artists that came before them. Read my reviews in this book and listen (or re-listen) to the tracks and you'll note my comparisons to The Beatles, The Rolling Stones, The Animals, The Who, The Kinks, the aforementioned Beach Boys, The Ventures, and so many others. Heck, there are some recordings where they even sounded like bands that didn't even exist yet (like ELO and The Raspberries)!

If you're reading this, you're probably already a Turtles fan, so it's likely I'm not telling you anything you don't already know [except my personal history of how I became a fan traveling in the back seat of my dad's Dodge Coronet either on the Connecticut Turnpike (I-95) or on the Merritt Parkway, (Route 15)]. If you're not already a fan, and somehow found this book, I know the commentary will get you interested, and perhaps you'll seek out the songs.

I do hope you'll enjoy my mini-reviews, observations, commentaries, and ramblings ("Rambling Rosenay!!!") of their recordings. I've tried to present serious critiques, but more often added humor for entertainment sake. You know what they say about opinions. Everyone has 'em, or something like that (gotta keep it clean). Like Mark and Howard, in some cases, I chose humor over seriousness—in their case it was in their performances; in my case it was in my reviews or comments. My goal, like The Turtles, is to entertain.

These Turtles. They're not teenagers (anymore), they're not ninjas, they're not mutants (that last one may be up for argument), but they were part of the soundtrack of our lives, and because of their music, they're the only Turtles that will live on forever.

They were and always will be more than "Happy Together."

Charles F. Rosenay!!! and Mark Volman show off their respective books. *Photo: Katherine McCabe*

FORGET THE MONKEES, WHY THE HELL AREN'T THE TURTLES IN THE ROCK AND ROLL HALL OF FAME?!?

A Rant and Historical Discussion by Mark Arnold

This may shock anyone who's reading this, but I've been a Turtles fan longer than I have been a Monkees fan. I just didn't know it. Anyone who has read my two Monkees books or has listened to my *Fun Ideas Podcast* probably knows my history with The Monkees. In short, I didn't like them when I first encountered them as a child on Saturday morning TV reruns in the early 1970s. That all changed with Michael Nesmith's *Elephant Parts* in 1980, when I suddenly discovered that there actually was some talent and creativity there in the bunch. I began collecting the group's records, and realized there was more to them than just the typical teeny-bopper flash-in-the-pan group.

In the meantime, I had already encountered on TV the two crazy hippies colloquially known as Flo & Eddie. I was already a fan of comedian Martin Mull, thanks to the comedic soap opera *Mary Hartman, Mary Hartman* and its spinoff talk show parody called *Fernwood 2-Night* (later called *America 2-Night*). I discovered that Mull also sang humorous songs and eventually hosted an episode of *The Midnight Special* in 1978 that featured Flo & Eddie as his special guests. I think somewhere along the line I saw this and Mull's 1976 appearance on *Soundstage* that also featured Flo & Eddie. Mull was really the attraction for me. In fact, I saw him live on stage in 1977, my first actual concert. Flo & Eddie also had a certain charm for me, and I liked that they actually could sing despite their hairy facades.

Around this same time, I became aware of a fledgling record label called Rhino Records, that loved to reissue rarities and obscurities of rock and roll and comedy. One of their earliest releases was a picture disc featuring (what seemed to me at the time) a bunch of fat guys going by the name The Turtles. This turned out to be a 12" EP that featured two previously unreleased songs, a demo, and a long out-of-print song bearing the title *1968*. As the songs and the group seemed unfamiliar to me, I didn't purchase this disc until about a decade later when I was already a certified Turtles fan.

I soon discovered that a tune I did know from just hearing it on the radio called "Happy Together" was done by this mysterious group known as The Turtles. Well, I liked that song... a lot... but I still wasn't willing to plop down good money on four songs I didn't know at all.

Rhino Records had a lot of faith in these Turtles, and by the early to mid-1980s, they had reissued the group's music in a number of configurations including a compilation, some of their original 1960s LPs, and even a turtle-shaped EP on green vinyl. The most fascinating of these was a three-record box set called *The History of Flo & Eddie and The Turtles*. I was gobsmacked. I mean, why the hell were these crazy singers named Flo & Eddie even remotely combined with the group that sang the angelic "Happy Together?" This was worthy of further investigation.

Strangely, I did not go out and purchase Rhino's 14 track *Turtles Greatest Hits* collection from 1982, which would have been the obvious choice, or even this three-record set, which I deemed too pricey for my teenage income.

Eventually, I was rummaging through those cheapie cut-out bins that had various LPs and audio cassettes with drill holes in them. I came across a different *Turtles Greatest Hits* on cassette that had more tracks than the Rhino one and was a release from France. I think it was 99 cents, if memory serves, which was the perfect price if *Happy Together* turned out to be the only good track on the tape.

I went home and played it. The first song was "She'd Rather Be with Me," and it immediately captivated me as much as "Happy Together" did. I discovered that this song, too, was almost a number one record. Now The Turtles were no longer one hit wonders to me.

The track that followed, however, "You Don't Have to Walk in the Rain," was very strange sounding to my ears and it took me years to actually like it and appreciate it.

The next song was "You Know What I Mean," followed by "Elenore," both winners to me, although "Elenore" did have some pretty silly lyrics.

Next up was "Grim Reaper of Love." Like "You Don't Have to Walk in the Rain," this one also took me a while to warm up to. The tally so far: four hits (counting "Happy Together") and two misses.

"Lady-O" was sung very sweetly, and "It Ain't Me Babe" was my first encounter with the Bob Dylan song, as I wasn't much of a Dylan fan, apart from the covers done by The Byrds and Jimi Hendrix. So now we were at six hits and two misses. Not bad. I kept listening.

"Sound Asleep" was very strange upon first listen. In fact, I would have to say that I didn't like it much, although it was kind of neat to hear a tree being sawed and felled in stereo. Overall, I thought it was, even more than "Elenore," more of a rip-off of "Happy Together."

"You Baby" and "Let Me Be" were both decent rockers, so I gave them high grades. Next was "Happy Together" followed by "Guide for the Married Man," another winner.

"The Story of Rock and Roll" followed and was kind of meh, but I really liked the rest of the tracks: "She's My Girl," "You Showed Me," "Me About You," "Outside Chance," and "Can I Get to Know You Better?"

My final tally for the 18 tracks: 14 hits and 4 misses. Not bad for a greatest hits collection of songs I hadn't heard before apart from one. I liked The Turtles and I played that tape over and over and over again. Eventually I came around and liked the four songs I initially wasn't too crazy about.

In the meantime, Rhino started reissuing the rest of The Turtles catalog, including *The Turtles Present the Battle of the Bands*, *Turtle Soup*, and *Wooden Head*. The first of these three really intrigued me as I had heard about this concept album wherein The Turtles pretended to be a bunch of other bands in various styles and "competed" in a Battle of the Bands, something The Turtles (and their precursor The Crossfires) actually did—compete in Battle of the Bands competitions in the formative years of their career.

I already knew "You Showed Me" and "Elenore," but when I played the rest of the album, EVERY track was glorious and was filled with many treasures. I loved the stylistic differences with the country-sounding "Chicken Little Was Right" and "Too Much Heartsick Feeling," but it was the humor that put me over the edge with tracks like "Oh, Daddy!," "I'm Chief Kamanawanalaya" and especially, "Food."

I honestly felt that The Turtles had out-Beatled The Beatles, coming up with a better concept album than *Sgt. Pepper's Lonely Hearts Club Band* and their upcoming *The Beatles* aka *The White Album*.

Equally surprising and also baffling was that despite *The Battle of the Bands* having two Top 10 hits for The Turtles, the album only charted at a paltry #128! That must have been quite a disappointment!

Indeed it was, as Howard Kaylan revealed in his autobiography much more recently. He actually left The Turtles for a time between *Battle of the Bands* and *Turtle Soup*. He didn't claim that *Battle*'s lousy chart performance was the reason, but I speculate that it had something to do with it. It also explains why *Turtle Soup* features the other Turtles taking on lead vocals on some tracks.

Eventually, I got all The Turtles' other albums. To me, *Happy Together* is their only LP that comes close to *Battle of the Bands* as far as overall consistency. *Turtle Soup* still kind of leaves me cold, but knowing that Howard left for a time and producer Ray Davies from The Kinks really didn't know how to produce The Turtles, it's amazing that it hangs together as well as it does.

The leftover tracks that would have become *Shell Shock* and eventually be rerecorded and issued as Flo & Eddie tracks leads me to believe that had The Turtles not broken up and were somehow able to wrangle themselves from the clutches of White Whale Records, they might have had greater chart success in the 1970s.

As it was, and as the story goes, The Turtles broke up in early 1970, and Howard Kaylan and Mark Volman (and soon Jim Pons) had joined Frank Zappa's reformed Mothers of Invention by March. Now simply known as The Mothers, they basically went on tour together through the end of 1971, when two significant events ended their progress: the fire in Switzerland at Montreux that destroyed their instruments and was the inspiration for Deep Purple's "Smoke on the Water" on December 4, and six days later, on December 11, when a jealous fan pushed Zappa into the orchestra pit in London, where the band was now playing with rented instruments.

Zappa was so prolific a performer that a studio album, a soundtrack double album, and three live albums (one released by John Lennon and Yoko Ono) came out during 1971-72, with many more years later.

Flo & Eddie bid their time while Zappa recovered from his fall into the orchestra pit, creating their own albums starting in 1972. Zappa did recover by 1973, but decided to transition into a more jazz fusion stage where he created some of his highest charting albums of his career: *Over-Nite Sensation* and *Apostrophe*. Zappa, Kaylan, and Volman remained friends, and OCCASIONALLY worked with each other professionally again.

Flo & Eddie had secured the rights to The Turtles music by 1974, and quickly issued a double-LP compilation called *Happy Together Again!* In November.

Throughout the rest of the '70s, Mark Volman and Howard Kaylan continued to tour and release albums under the Flo & Eddie moniker, as well as sing backup on some of rock and roll's biggest songs, including "Hungry Heart" by Bruce Springsteen and "Get it On (Bang a Gong)" by T. Rex.

In the 1980s, Flo & Eddie released the last of their studio LPs as well as a number of children's albums featuring the characters of Strawberry Shortcake, the Care Bears, and G.I. Joe. They continued touring as The Turtles featuring Flo & Eddie and released a live album in the 1990s that was reissued and repackaged many times.

Also by the 1980s, many, many, many Turtles compilations hit the shelves with varying success and with occasional rarities and outtakes. As a fan and collector, I cherry-picked the best ones, getting all of The Turtles, The Mothers, and Flo & Eddie, but cautiously avoiding the children's albums and totally missing bizarre pet projects like Checkpoint Charlie and most of The Rhythm Butchers releases, which are admittedly best forgotten.

I've seen The Turtles a number of times and have gotten both Howard's and Mark's autographs. I've also eagerly purchased Howard's only solo album and wished there were more.

As I got more and more interested in The Monkees during this same time period, I realized that there was a growing public outcry demanding why The Monkees were not in the Rock and Roll Hall of Fame.

While I feel that The Monkees SHOULD be in the Rock and Roll Hall of Fame, I can somewhat see the reasoning of why they aren't, namely due to how they were formed and packaged... at least for their TV series and first two albums. This would mean that other "fictional" groups like the Chipmunks, The Beagles, The Banana Splits, the Globetrotters, The Partridge

Family, The Hardy Boys, The Archies, Josie and the Pussycats, the Cattanooga Cats, the Groovie Goolies, The Bugaloos, and others could all theoretically also be in consideration for the Rock and Roll Hall of Fame, which arguably could tarnish the image and meaning of the Hall.

But none of this applies to The Turtles! The Turtles were created organically the way a rock band is arguably supposed to, originally as The Crossfires (and other names). The Turtles played their own instruments from the start mainly because they *had* to. White Whale was cheap. Even Howard and Mark honked their way into the group with their saxophones before becoming singers and clowns. The Turtles did use outside writers for their songs, but so did The Beatles. Also like John Lennon and Paul McCartney of The Beatles, Howard, Al Nichol, and Chuck Portz were all writing original songs from the beginning.

Eventually, The Turtles were writing and performing all of their own music and had as many Top 40 hits as The Monkees.

Additionally, Flo & Eddie have done a few rap parodies in concert over the years. While I feel that rap has no place in a Rock and Roll Hall of Fame, this alone should help qualify them.

So, why *aren't* The Turtles in the Rock and Roll Hall of Fame? Politics. Grrrr!

Note from co-author Charles: Let's get this book—and Mark Arnold's valid argument—into the hands of the powers-to-be at the Rock & Roll Hall of Fame so the oversight of The Turtles' omission can be rectified.

Mark Arnold interviewing Turtles Producer Jerry Yester, July 23, 2021.

IN A (NUT)SHELL:
A HISTORY OF THE TURTLES
by Mark Arnold

The 16-page booklet in 1983's *The History of Flo & Eddie and The Turtles* was the first attempt in trying to tell The Turtles' story. This printed version was expanded in 1989, and was expanded yet again when Rhino Records interviewed members of The Turtles and their various associates for the direct-to-video documentary *The Turtles: Happy Together,* which was originally released in January 1991. The details were discussed again when Howard Kaylan released his autobiography *Shell Shocked: My Life with the Turtles Flo & Eddie and Frank Zappa etc.* in 2013, as well as in Harold Bronson's *The Rhino Records Story*, released the same year. There have also been interviews with multiple Turtles over the years about their songs with their comments which have been included in such collections as *Solid Zinc: The Turtles Anthology* (2003) and *All the Singles* (2016). In virtually every case, The Turtles' story has been told from the inside. This book tells the story from the outside: from observers, analysts, and fans.

The story of The Turtles is one identified with Westchester, California, as that is where the first Turtles performance began. Howard Kaplan, Mark Volman, Al Nichol, and Chuck Portz were all members of The Westchester High School A Capella Choir, conducted by Robert Wood. Photos exist of these four standing next to each other in the choir, and a recording actually exists of them singing their alma mater song with the rest of the choir, which was released on *The Story of Flo & Eddie and The Turtles* in 1983.

Amazingly, this isn't the first recording of anyone who was in The Turtles. In Kaylan's autobiography called *Shell Shocked: My Life with The Turtles, Flo & Eddie and Frank Zappa, etc.*, he explains that he used to use those recording booths on Coney Island and recorded his first single, which he still possesses to this day: "Radar" backed with (b/w) "High Tide." Unfortunately, these recordings remain unreleased to the general public. In that same book, Kaylan also reveals the first songs he ever wrote: "Let the Cold Winds Blow," "Wanderin' Kind," plus "Almost There" with his then-girlfriend, Nita Garfield.

One interesting fact is that none of the four were born in Westchester, nor were any of the other Turtles. Kaplan/Kaylan was born in The Bronx. Nichol was born in Winston-Salem, North Carolina. Portz was born in Santa Monica, California. Volman was born in Los Angeles and lived in Redondo Beach before his family settled in Westchester.

Evidently, this version of the school's choir was highly successful and they won all sorts of city competitions as The Crosswind Singers. This led to Kaplan (as tenor sax), Nichol (on guitar), and Portz (on bass) forming their own group called The Belvederes, which became The Nightriders with a fourth member, Glen Wilson (on drums). The Nightriders lasted from approximately October 1961 through December 31, 1962.

Wilson was replaced by avid surfer and drummer Don Murray from neighboring Inglewood High, and the band changed its name to The Crossfires on January 1, 1963. Then they added Dale Walton on rhythm guitar, and Volman, who was initially a roadie, eventually joined on alto sax. Walton was replaced with Tom Stanton, and Jim Tucker would replace Stanton. The resulting six of Kaplan, Nichol, Portz, Murray, Volman, and Portz would eventually become The Turtles.

Ironically, even though blessed with vocal expertise, The Crossfires were essentially an instrumental band playing surf music, both original and covers. Despite the eventual leadership of Kaplan and Volman, business cards at this time referred to Al Nichol and Don Murray as the leaders of the band. It was during this time that The Crossfires entered and won a number of battle of the bands competitions, and had their own fan club called The Chunky Club.

The Crossfires also cut their first 15 tracks during 1963 and 1964, despite only four being released as singles, which were only sold at concerts: "Dr. Jekyll and Mr. Hyde" b/w "Fiberglass Jungle" (August 1963) and "One Potato Two Potato" b/w "That'll Be the Day" (February 1965) actually charted in a local San Bernardino chart. The rest of the tracks save "Santa and the Sidewalk Surfer" (released in 1974) didn't see official release until 1981 on Rhino Records. Drummer Terry Hand substituted for Murray on a couple of these early recorded tracks.

Though in no way intentionally following The Beatles in those days—as they were still unknown to the U.S.—it is quite ironic that The Turtles' first single as The Crossfires and The Beatles' first single as The Quarrymen both featured a rendition of "That'll Be the Day." Also, the lewd and lascivious behavior of The Crossfires in Westchester was strongly reminiscent of The Beatles' behavior during their time in Hamburg, so much so that each band was kicked out of their respective locations.

In November 1963, The Crossfires became the house band at local DJ Reb Foster's Revelaire Club at 312 South Catalina Avenue in Redondo Beach. Foster loved them so much that he became their first manager and producer, and introduced them to the guys who started White Whale Records. Incidentally, Foster's cousin was Bill Utley, and Foster and Utley became The Turtles' first managers essentially because they told them they were.

At the Revelaire, The Crossfires played virtually every Friday and Saturday night well into 1965. The sextet played during their last two years of high school, but after graduating in June 1965, the band found themselves suddenly struggling and not making enough to support themselves, especially when two of the band members were already married—Al Nichol and Don Murray. Murray had married his high school girlfriend, Kathy Koontz, and they would go on to have a daughter named Jenny. On their last scheduled night at the Revelaire, they planned to break up the band. Ironically, they were approached by Ted Feigin and Lee Lasseff on that same night and signed to their new label, which was unnamed at the time but eventually became White Whale Records. The label was christened by Feigin who was a huge fan of *Moby Dick*, and he named the production company Ishmael after Moby Dick's chief protagonist.

Feigin and Lasseff wanted to mold The Crossfires into a folk rock act and demanded a group name change. The Crossfires offered The Half Dozen and The Six Pack (a band name I actually kind of like), but ended up deciding upon Reb Foster's suggestion of The Tyrtles, though not immediately. According to Kaplan, they laughed at and despised this new moniker, thinking it was suggesting that they were slow or dimwitted. Foster explained that animal names were all the rage and that if they had one similar to The Animals and The Beatles, they might be confused for a British band, as they had been before. In fact, however, when they announced this name change, their audience booed them.

Eventually, the band came 'round to calling themselves The Turtles sans the alternate Byrds-like spelling. The "y" instead went to replace the "p" in Kaplan's last name. Kaylan explains in his autobiography that he initially wanted to change his name from Kaplan to Kaylan in childhood and did it informally with the band first and then officially in 1967.

Soon, The Turtles WERE confused for a British band. Kaylan himself took to impersonating Gerry Marsden of Gerry and the Pacemakers, because who the hell knew what all of the Pacemakers' names were, much less what they looked like.

White Whale quickly got The Turtles into the studio to record their first single: *"It Ain't Me Babe"* b/w *"Almost There,"* and it was released in June 1965, less than one month after their signing and name change. "It Ain't Me Babe" was a Bob Dylan song from *Another Side of Bob Dylan*. The B-side "Almost There" was a Kaylan original. The single of the A-side was an immediate hit and peaked at #8 on the *Billboard* and *Cashbox* charts. It went to #3 in Canada, where The Turtles would routinely chart better than in the U.S.

It must be said that unlike most of The Turtles' contemporaries like The Beach Boys, The Monkees, The Byrds, The Mamas & the Papas, Sonny & Cher, Simon & Garfunkel, etc., The Turtles rarely used the services of The Wrecking Crew, who performed as backup band for all these artists and many more. The reason was that the White Whale label was too cheap to hire their services, so The Turtles had to play their own songs. This worked to their advantage as it proved they were a tight-knit group, especially after all their years of stage performances.

The newly christened Turtles made their non-Revelaire Club debut in Disneyland's Fantasyland Theatre on July 13, 1965 with The Dixie Cups, Gayle Harris, The Mustangs, and the Humdinger dancers, and then opened for Herman's Hermits at the Rose Bowl in Pasadena on August 7th with The Lovin' Spoonful, The Bobby Fuller Four, The Guilloteens, The Midnighters, and The Great Scots also on the bill. This performance in front of 50,000 people was their very first taste of stardom.

It was during this time that The Turtles made their very first major TV appearances on *Shivaree* on July 31 and October 23. *Shivaree* was a Los Angeles-based music show similar to *Shindig* that aired from 1965-1968 locally and in syndication in 150 markets in the U.S. and seven other countries. The show was The Turtles' first national TV exposure. Videos exist on YouTube of them singing "Almost There." It was no *Ed Sullivan Show*, but it was a start.

Next, the Turtles appeared on *The Lloyd Thaxton Show* on August 12, where they performed "It Ain't Me Babe" and "Wanderin' Kind." They would return to the show twice in 1966.

On August 15, The Turtles flew from Los Angeles to join Dick Clark's *Caravan of Stars*. The Turtles were very lucky as they were a last-minute replacement for Van Morrison's group Them on a tour that was supposed to have Peter and Gordon, Tom Jones, Them, The Shirelles, Ronnie Dove, Mel Carter, Brian Hyland, Billy Joe Royal, Jimmy Ford and the Executives, Jimmy Rice, and Timothy Rice. The Turtles joined the tour as it was already underway on August 17th in Chicago. The Turtles would continue with the tour through September 9th. For The Turtles, this was immediate stardom, despite the fact that they only had one single and their first album wouldn't be released until October. The Turtles would continue to perform various random Northern and Southern California dates throughout the rest of 1965 in a tour called "Wrap Up '65."

Next they appeared for the first of seven times on *Where the Action Is*. They sang "Almost There" and "It Ain't Me Babe" on August 20 and "It Ain't Me Babe" again on September 1.

They also appeared twice on *Shindig*. Once on September 30 performing "We'll Meet Again," "It Ain't Me Babe," and "Needles and Pins" (This was not one of their regular songs!). They played "Your Maw Said You Cried" and "Let Me Be" on their second and final appearance on that show, which aired on November 13. Videos exist of "It Ain't Me Babe," "Let Me Be," and "Needles and Pins."

The Turtles also appeared on "Hollywood a Go-Go" on October 23, 1965, performing "It Ain't Me Babe" and "Let Me Be." Videos exist of both performances.

It was during 1965 that The Turtles played at the Phone Booth in New York, and met the writer of "It Ain't Me Babe," Bob Dylan. Dylan was in some sort of catatonic state when they were introduced to him, and after seeing them perform their set, Dylan was reported to have said about their version of "It Ain't Me Babe": "That's a great last song; it should be on [a] record," apparently unaware that this was a Turtles' cover of his own composition that they had just had a hit with and had sold over 550,000 copies! Ah well, everybody must get stoned...

By the time of the release of their first album, also titled *It Ain't Me Babe*, which peaked at #98 on *Billboard* and #35 on *Cashbox*, The Turtles released their second single. "Let Me Be" b/w

"Your Maw Said You Cried" became a quick hit in August 1965, reaching #29 on *Billboard*, #26 on the *Cashbox* charts, and #14 in Canada. With two hits under their belt, The Turtles eventually graduated from show opener to headliner on tour, again similar to The Beatles' rise in stardom. The Turtles on tour was like Beatlemania with girls, girls, and more girls, plus a mugging and some dislike of the longhaired weirdos coming to their towns.

After P.F. Sloan's "Let Me Be" became a hit, the Turtles considered releasing his "Eve of Destruction" as a single, but The Turtles vetoed it in favor of Sloan's "I Get Out of Breath." "Eve" was eventually released by The Turtles, after their breakup and against their will, in June of 1970, with another Kaylan original "Wanderin' Kind" as the B-side. (More on that later.) Ironically, this was also the B-side of "You Baby," their eventual third single, which was written by Sloan with Steve Barri. It was released in January 1966 and peaked at #20 on *Billboard*, #15 on *Record World*, and #17 on *Cashbox*.

"You Baby" also hit #11 in Canada. With The Turtles' ongoing success in Canada, they actually issued an additional single of "It Was a Very Good Year" b/w "Let the Cold Winds Blow," which made it to #7. Amazingly, the single was not released at all in the U.S., probably because Frank Sinatra had recently had a U.S. hit with the same song and they didn't want to alienate young listeners with what would appear to be a cover of something by "old" Sinatra.

With "You Baby" becoming a hit, it dictated a more pop direction for the group, so plans to do a follow-up single of "I Get Out of Breath" were shelved. The song was recorded, but remained unreleased until the "odds and sods" compilation of *Wooden Head* in 1970.

Also, with "You Baby" becoming a hit, it necessitated The Turtles calling their second album *You Baby*. They also repeated "Let Me Be" from "It Ain't Me Babe" for good measure. The *You Baby* LP did not chart at all on *Billboard*, but made it to #71 on *Cashbox*.

Like The Monkees' second album, *More of The Monkees*, a visit to J.C. Penney's was in order to change their outfits to a more clean-cut image than that of grungy, anti-establishment folk rockers. The dramatic change of The Turtles from album to album showed their flexibility, but it also showed their ongoing identity crisis. Were they folk rockers? Were they pop stars? Were they purveyors of psychedelic music? Each album and year for The Turtles was more dramatically different than even The Beatles!

After "You Baby," the honchos at White Whale allowed The Turtles to record one of their own compositions for a single. This was not because they were tested songwriters, even though Howard Kaylan's song "A Walk in the Sun" had become a minor hit for The Angry, and he was allowed four original compositions on *It Ain't Me Babe*, three on *You Baby*, and two B-sides. It was more that because White Whale could reap more benefits from their publishing division called Ishmael, as well as capitalizing on the fad of a pop group writing all of their own material rather than relying solely on cover tunes.

The quirky "Grim Reaper of Love" b/w "Come Back" was selected as The Turtles' fourth single, released in May 1966, and reaching #81 on *Billboard*, #61 on *Cashbox,* and #61 in Canada. It was probably chosen because it was the best original they had written at the time. "Reaper" was from the writing team of Nichol and Portz who composed many of The Turtles' songs when they were still The Crossfires, despite the fact that many of them remained unreleased at this point. "Come Back" was another Kaylan original, but he continued to be relegated to The Turtles' B-sides despite his current productivity.

The Turtles toured virtually non-stop during 1965 and 1966 to the point where Don Murray left the group abruptly, citing exhaustion and the apparent dislike of The Turtles' musical direction from a surfing band to a folk rock band to a pop band. Some sources say that he was fired due to his unwillingness to improve upon the same drumming he had been doing since he was 15. Others say that he merely quit due to going berserk and becoming paranoid and fighting with other members of the band. By his own admission he was also a bit of a perfectionist and continued to strive to top himself. In any case, he was a popular member of the band, but was gone by May 1966, leaving during the middle of a recording session at Western Recorders (probably for "LIke the Seasons" or "Makin' My Mind Up"). He was initially replaced by iconic Wrecking Crew drummer Hal Blaine, and then by Joel Larson.

Larson appeared on very few of The Turtles' records, such as "We'll Meet Again," as his tenure with the band lasted only a few days. Over the years, he was the drummer for The Grass Roots, The Merry-Go-Round, and for artist Lee Michaels. He was soon permanently replaced by drummer John Barbata by July 1966, at the suggestion of The Byrds' Gene Clark.

Murray eventually joined Paul Williams' psychedelic folk group, The Holy Mackerel, and he played with The Surfaris for many years. He was interviewed for the 1990 Turtles documentary *The Turtles: Happy Together* about his years with The Crossfires and The Turtles.

On January 1, 1996, 50-year-old Murray went surfing for the final time. Two days later, he was admitted to the hospital for a routine ulcer surgery and died from postoperative complications on March 22, 1996. He was in the process of reforming The Crossfires with Tom Stanton at the time of his death.

Meanwhile, The Turtles continued their hectic touring pace throughout 1966. Tour highlights included a return appearance on *The Lloyd Thaxton Show* on February 7 to sing "Let Me Be," and in July to sing "Outside Chance," "Flying High," and "We'll Meet Again."

On Dick Clark's *Where the Action Is*, The Turtles sang "It Ain't Me Babe" on February 11, "Grim Reaper of Love" and "You Baby" on July 8, "Grim Reaper of Love" on September 13, "Can I Get to Know You Better?" on December 9, and "Can I Get to Know You Better?" and "You Baby" on December 12. The group was also scheduled to be on Dick Clark's *Caravan of Stars* during 1966, but their Canadian appearances were canceled, cited as having "visa problems." There were probably other behind-the-scenes shenanigans, as there were always shady deals going on with The Turtles that weren't always public knowledge. Plus, The Turtles' behavior while on the road could be classified as somewhat decadent.

Also in 1966, The Turtles made an appearance on *Hullabaloo* performing "You Baby" on March 7, introduced by Pat Boone; *The Clay Cole Show* on March 26; the Hollywood Bowl on April 2; the Cow Palace on April 4-5; The Fillmore on July 6; *American Bandstand* (to perform "You Baby"), "Outside Chance" on July 23; and another major TV appearance on *Hollywood Palace* on December 10. This last performance was filmed on August 29-31, where they performed "Can I Get to Know You Better?" after being introduced by host Jimmy Durante. This was a color performance; their first for television.

The Turtles performed "She'll Come Back" in the B-picture called *Out of Sight*, which was released on April 25. It would be The Turtles' only onscreen appearance in a feature film and their first color performance. The film was released by Universal Pictures in response to the many beach party movies released by American International. The film itself is a loose secret agent caper parody about a plot to disrupt a concert. It features cameos by many of the top pop artists of the day and stars Jonathan Daly, who appeared in numerous Disney pictures and would go on to co-star on the TV series *CPO Sharkey* in the mid-1970s. The Turtles just perform their one song but take no part in the action of the film. "She'll Come Back" was included on the Decca soundtrack album and eventually appeared on *Wooden Head*.

Desperate for a good follow-up hit after "Grim Reaper" basically stiffed, The Turtles recorded and almost released "So Goes Love" b/w "On a Summer's Day" in July 1966. Both songs suffered different fates, as "So Goes Love" ended up as a bonus track on *Golden Hits* in 1967 and "On a Summer's Day" was finally released on 1970's *Wooden Head*.

The nod for The Turtles' fifth single release instead went to "We'll Meet Again" b/w "Outside Chance." Still hoping for another hit, everyone was alarmed that this upbeat version of the Vera

Lynn classic totally stiffed and didn't hit the *Billboard* charts at all. *Record World* charted it at #106 and *Cashbox* at #116.

"Outside Chance" was written by Warren Zevon (writing as Lyme) and Glenn Crocker. It was drummer John Barbata's debut with the group. The sudden flop of "We'll Meet Again" caused White Whale to do a limited rush release of Jack Dalton and Gary Montgomery's "Makin' My Mind Up" in September 1966, which did chart in Seattle's Top 10, but did nothing nationally. The single sported the same B-side as "We'll Meet Again."

Released in October 1966, "Can I Get to Know You Better?" b/w "Like the Seasons" did do a little better, charting at #89 on *Billboard* and #97 on *Cashbox*. The A-side was another Sloan and Barri composition, which they chose to release next just to play it safe. Warren Zevon and Violet Santangelo were responsible for the B-side, which was credited to Lyme and Cybelle. They had, in fact, recorded their version of the song prior to this under that moniker, and it was also released on White Whale.

The Turtles' eighth single was their game changer that brought them international fame and also hastened their demise. The song "Happy Together" was based on a demo by Garry Bonner and Alan Gordon that was passed over by every musical artist in town due to its primitive sound of a guy slapping his legs for rhythm and for its marginal singing.

The acetate actually became worn out due to so many plays and rejections, and The Turtles were able to see a hit through this amateurish production. Bonner and Gordon were formerly from a group called The Magicians, but would now find greater success as songwriters, particularly for The Turtles. "Happy Together" b/w "Like the Seasons" became a #1 for three weeks in January 1967. Chart peaks worldwide included #2 in New Zealand and Canada, #3 in South Africa, #5 in Holland, #6 in Rhodesia, #11 in Finland, #12 in the UK, #19 in Ireland, and #20 in Sweden.

Additional success of this single was due to Gene Clark group's Chip Douglas, who produced, arranged, sang, and played bass on the record, and even became a member of The Turtles after Chuck Portz threw in the towel in October 1966. Some sources say Portz was fired from the band, but he cited similar issues to the previously-departed Don Murray, and claimed it was an amicable parting. Portz went back to school and eventually retired on Catalina Island in California where he became an abalone diver. Portz quit prior to "Happy Together," feeling that The Turtles were over after three flops in a row, despite remaining a wildly popular live act on tour. He was later interviewed for *The Turtles: Happy Together* in 1990.

There was a promotional film made for "Happy Together," believed to be their first. It showed The Turtles romping around a la The Monkees. Promotional films were still quite rare in the 1960s, but came to prominence after The Monkees' TV show made its debut in September 1966, and also due to The Beatles creating these films in lieu of touring and personal appearances.

Seeing The Turtles performing at the Whisky a Go-Go in early 1967 prompted The Monkees' Michael Nesmith to ask Chip Douglas to work with The Monkees. Douglas left in February 1967 and was replaced by bassist Jim Pons of The Leaves. Douglas did return in 1968 to produce *The Turtles Present the Battle of the Bands* after The Monkees decided to produce all their own material.

Major TV appearances started to rack up at this point, most always with The Turtles performing "Happy Together" and perhaps one other song. These appearances included *The Smothers Brothers Comedy Hour* on February 12 and March 19, 1967; one final *Where the Action Is* where they performed "Can I Get to Know You Better?" and "You Baby" on March 29, *American Bandstand* on April 1; *The Ed Sullivan Show* on May 14 and November 12 (repeat footage); *The Clay Cole Show* on June 3, July 15, and December 9; *Dee Time* on June 6; *The Tonight Show Starring Johnny Carson* on June 30 (where Johnny waved them over after their performance, a sign of Carson's approval); *The Groovy Show* on July 18; *Top of the Pops* on July 27; *Malibu U* on August 11; and *Hullabaloo* on October 29.

The Turtles followed up their great success of "Happy Together" with "She'd Rather Be with Me," another Bonner and Gordon original and the group's ninth single. This was backed with "The Walking Song," a Howard Kaylan/Al Nichol original, and the first group original on a single since "Grim Reaper." This single was released in April of 1967 and peaked at #3 on *Billboard*, #2 on *Cashbox*, and #1 on *Record World*. Chip Douglas was already gone by this point. He went on to produce The Monkees, including their biggest hit "Daydream Believer." "She'd Rather Be with Me" was also an international hit, peaking at #1 in Canada and South Africa, #3 in Denmark and Ireland, and #4 in the UK.

This was followed by the theme song of Gene Kelly's *A Guide for the Married Man*. The Turtles do not appear in this film, but their version of the song plays over the film's title credits. "Guide for the Married Man" b/w "Think I'll Run Away" became the group's 10th single, but like "Makin' My Mind Up," it was only released in limited quantities as the record was recalled shortly after release in May 1967 due to White Whale's erratic record distribution. "Guide for the Married Man" was written by film composers John Williams and Leslie Bricusse while "Think I'll Run Away" was another Turtles original by Kaylan and Volman.

The Turtles' third album, titled *Happy Together*, was released on April 29, 1967. It was comprised of the previously-released "Makin' My Mind Up," which added some brass to the arrangement for this album version, "Guide for the Married Man," "The Walking Song," "Happy Together," "She'd Rather Be with Me," "Like the Seasons," and five others. The album reached #25 on the *Billboard* charts and #15 on *Cashbox*, their highest charting album of original material. The album sold over 500,000 units and became a gold record.

Due to the worldwide success of "Happy Together," The Turtles embarked on their first European tour, commencing in June 1967. They traveled to England, Denmark, France, Germany, Belgium, and Holland. It was on this tour that The Turtles met The Beatles. It was also on this tour that The Turtles recorded three tracks live for the UK BBC radio show *Saturday Club*: "Happy Together," "She'd Rather Be with Me," and "You Baby." The live recordings were all eventually released between 1983 and 1994.

By July 1967, Jim Tucker had left the group. He was not replaced and the six pack remained at five members with no official rhythm guitarist for the rest of their career. It was rumored that Tucker left due to his meeting John Lennon not going as expected, but according to Tucker, it was simply another matter of not wanting to do it any longer and being exhausted from the touring grind, similar to what Murray and Portz had cited. Tucker went back to Grass Valley, California and became an electrical engineer, but he continued to play music with popular Arizona country-rock act Mogollon at the Nevada County Fair. He also was interviewed for the 1990 *The Turtles: Happy Together* documentary from Rhino. He passed away on November 12, 2020, leaving behind two daughters and three grandchildren.

At this same time, The Turtles released their 11th single, "You Know What I Mean" b/w "Rugs of Woods and Flowers." "You Know What I Mean" was Bonner and Gordon's third single for the group, and it ended up charting at a respectable #12 on both *Billboard* and *Cashbox*, and as high as #6 in Canada. "Rugs of Woods and Flowers" was the first item released by The Turtles that gives a hint as to their Rhythm Butchers alter ego, and written by Kaylan and Nichol.

Though the remaining Turtles seemed to still be a close-knit bunch, the beginning of the end was already at hand with bad managers, embezzlement, adultery, and underhanded dealings with their record label that they became slaves to.

It was around this time, late 1967, that The Turtles' road manager Dave Krambeck was telling them that Bill Utley and Reb Foster were screwing them over. Krambeck proceeded to take over their management by working out a deal to buy out the current management for $250,000 of The Turtles' own money. Then Krambeck sold half of the management to Martin Phillips Management aka Michael Philips Management for $13,000. Finally, Krambeck missed the next payment to Foster and ran off to Mexico with Jim Pons' wife. Rick Soderland and Charlie Galvin soon became new road managers for The Turtles. Galvin had recently married Elaine "Spanky" McFarlane of the band Spanky and Our Gang.

Of course, none of The Turtles were businessmen. They were barely out of high school and just turning 20 years old. The complete saga is somewhat complicated to explain, so we humbly refer you to the final minutes of the 1990 Turtles documentary *The Turtles: Happy Together* where Kaylan and Volman explain exactly what happened during the ending of their career.

The Turtles finished up their 1967 single releases with their 12th single "She's My Girl" b/w "Chicken Little Was Right." "She's My Girl" was Bonner and Gordon's fourth and final single for The Turtles, as The Turtles decided to do the majority of the song composing from this point forward. This single also had a respectable showing, peaking at #14 on *Billboard* and #15 on *Cashbox*. It was released in October 1967. "Chicken Little Was Right" was later redone for *The Turtles Presents the Battle of the Bands*.

"She's My Girl" also became the second Turtles single to get the promo film treatment.

In November, 1967, The Turtles released their first compilation called *Golden Hits*. It featured all of their charting hits from "It Ain't Me Babe" through "You Know What I Mean," curiously leaving off the recent "She's My Girl," and adding the previously-unreleased "So Goes Love" and "Is It Any Wonder?" The album became The Turtles' highest charting album, hitting #7 on *Billboard* and #5 on *Cashbox*, and earning another gold record.

As The Turtles entered 1968, they looked forward to the prospect of an even bigger hit album and bigger hit singles. They notched off two more hit singles for their efforts. Touring continued throughout most of that year, with small breaks taken for recording, particularly in March and May. Concerts remained inside of the U.S. as their international fame had waned since 1967. Of note, their April 5th concert in Chicago was canceled due to the civil unrest following the assassination of Martin Luther King, Jr. in Memphis the day before.

The Turtles appeared on *American Bandstand* on January 6, 1968, and *The Woody Woodbury Show* on February 2, playing "She's My Girl." They appeared on *The Mike Douglas Show* on February 26 where they played "Happy Together" and "She'd Rather Be with Me," and appeared again on October 2nd. They appeared on *The Joey Bishop Show* three times, on July 21, September 2, and November 18. They were on *Kraft Music Hall* on July 24, where they performed "The Battle of the Bands," "Elenore," and "The Story of Rock and Roll."

They made an appearance as themselves in a musical comedy TV show called *That's Life* on September 24, which also featured Robert Morse, E.J. Peaker, George Burns, and Tony Randall. They appeared on *The Steve Allen Show* on November 6, and they returned to *Top of the Pops* on November 28.

Around this time, The Turtles' wives wanted to open a boutique so locations were scoured on Sunset in L.A.. Some sources say a shop was rented and opened in the former Thee Experience nightclub location at 7551 Sunset in January 1968, while others say no shop ever opened. In any case, it was not a success.

Then, in February 1968, The Turtles released their 13th single, "Sound Asleep" b/w "Umbassa and the Dragon." Both sides were highly "way out" and were a result of The Turtles wanting to wrestle control of the writing and producing of their music. The result was a somewhat dismal #57 on the *Billboard* charts and #32 on *Cashbox*. The songs themselves are highly creative and even humorous, especially the B-side which was another example of their Rhythm Butchers alter ego coming to the surface again on a record release.

"Sound Asleep" would appear on *More Golden Hits* in 1970, while the B-side would elude inclusion on a Turtles' LP until 1987's catch-all album *Chalon Road*. It actually made its album debut before that, on Rhino's *World's Worst Records* collection in 1983.

The Turtles wanted to follow "Sound Asleep" with an even further out single of "To See the Sun" b/w "The Owl," but White Whale put their foot down and the songs remained incomplete. They did see release in their incomplete form in October 1978 on the Rhino picture disc EP titled *1968*.

It was around this same time that The Turtles did an actual illegal move, which was to shop around for another label while still being signed to an existing label. According to Kaylan, they were working out a deal to sign with RCA, but nothing ever happened with it because they were still contractually obligated to White Whale.

"The Story of Rock and Roll" b/w "Can You Hear the Cows?" became The Turtles' 14th single, released in May 1968. White Whale was taking no chances and again stopped The Turtles from writing and producing their own material, as they were still seeking another "Happy Together." "Story of Rock and Roll" was written by Harry Nilsson, and both sides of the new single were produced by Chip Douglas, who was brought back precisely for The Turtles to have another "Happy Together." It didn't work, and "The Story of Rock and Roll" only crept up to #48 on the *Billboard* charts and #37 on *Cashbox*. It had nice piano playing by Douglas, however, and landed on *More Golden Hits* in 1970. The B-side was another of The Turtles' madness, and eluded album inclusion until 1987's *Chalon Road*.

The White Whale executives kept chanting, "Give us another 'Happy Together!' Give us another 'Happy Together!'" In frustration and desperation, Howard Kaylan locked himself in his hotel room to give White Whale what they wanted. He analyzed "Happy Together" and basically rewrote it, hoping that they would see the error of their ways and tell The Turtles to get more progressive. Instead, White While embraced the new song with lyrics like "pride and joy, etc." Kaylan's plan backfired. "Elenore" b/w "Surfer Dan" became their 15th single in September and hit #6 on the *Billboard* charts and #5 on *Cashbox*.

"Elenore" also performed well internationally, reaching #4 in Canada, #6 in Ireland, and South Africa, #7 in the UK, #3 in Australia, and #1 in New Zealand.

"Surfer Dan" was billed as being by The Cross Fires on *The Battle of the Bands* album as a nod to their old surfing band. The sixth member pictured on the picture sleeve and in the album's centerspread wearing the scuba gear is presumably producer Chip Douglas.

On November 1, all of the efforts The Turtles had been making since February 1968 came to fruition with the release of their ambitious fourth studio album and fifth overall, *The Turtles Present the Battle of the Bands*.

The Turtles Present the Battle of the Bands should have been a chart-topper since it included two Top 10 hits, "Elenore" and "You Showed Me." Unfortunately, it landed at a paltry #128 on *Billboard*. It did quite a bit better on *Cashbox*, but still stalled at #43.

No other Turtles besides Kaylan appeared on "Christmas is My Time of Year" b/w "Will You Still Believe in Me," except Barbata on drums. The single was released in November under the artist name The Christmas Spirit, and featured Gram Parsons, Linda Ronstadt, Chip Douglas, and Bobby Kimmel, in addition to Kaylan. Ronstadt and Douglas were dating at the time, hence her inclusion. She had just left The Stone Poneys, of which Kimmel was also a member, for a solo career. Douglas remembers Volman on it, but Volman claims he was not. The A-side was written by Kaylan and Douglas; Kimmel the B.

Red Rhodes is also on it, playing steel guitar. He would become known for being in Michael Nesmith's First National Band after Nesmith left The Monkees. Of course, Nesmith also wrote Ronstadt's "Different Drum," The Stone Poneys' biggest hit. Small world.

Meanwhile, The Turtles' 16th single and second from *The Battle of the Bands* album was released in December. Like "Elenore," it also peaked at #6 on *Billboard*, #4 on *Cashbox*, and #1 on *Record World*. It was "You Showed Me" b/w "Buzzsaw." The A-side was a Byrds composition, while the B was completely original. The song performed well internationally, peaking at #13 in Canada, #20 in New Zealand, and #8 in France. The Byrds' version had a much faster tempo. It was remembered by Chip Douglas who attempted to play the tune for The Turtles, but he had to do it at a much slower pace as his organ bellows were broken. They said they would record it only if they could do it at the slower tempo.

From this point, The Turtles were burdened with various lawsuits hanging over their heads. They hired Rosalie Morton to sort everything out and she suggested that The Turtles stop hiring their friends to manage them, and instead get some professional management through Campbell-Silver-Cosby, co-owned by comedian Bill Cosby. It would be co-owner Roy Silver who actually wound up briefly managing The Turtles.

Third co-owner Bruce Post Campbell ran Tetragrammaton Records, whose most famous act was Deep Purple. Tetragrammaton also issued one Bill Cosby album and distributed the infamous album *Unfinished Music No. 1 - Two Virgins, which* featured the nude album sleeve of John Lennon and Yoko Ono. Soon, the gas ran out of this arrangement, as Cosby left the team, and Morton revealed herself to be a loose cannon who didn't help The Turtles' interests. The Turtles would be signed with Jeff Wald and Ron De Blasio by 1969.

By far the most interesting appearance The Turtles made in late 1968 was for an unaired game show pilot called "The Generation Gap." On it, The Turtles performed "Elenore." The resulting series aired from February 7 to May 23, 1969 with no additional Turtles appearances.

The Turtles continued to tour into 1969, starting the year off in Canada, but much of the rest of 1969 left a lot to be desired. Gone were the huge stadium shows with the great line-ups of top bands.

Drummer Barbata had left by February, 1969 and was replaced by John "The Chief" Seiter. Barbata initially left to drum for Crosby, Stills and Nash (and later, Young), and also appeared on "The Dating Game." When CSNY was winding down in 1971, Barbata's career led him to Jefferson Airplane, later Jefferson Starship. He probably would have continued with that group if not for a massive car accident in October 1978 that broke his neck, arm, and jaw. He recovered from his injuries and still performs music to this day. He is now living in Oklahoma.

Seiter, meanwhile, had most recently been with Spanky and Our Gang, a group that had broken up in 1968 after the death of their lead guitarist Malcolm Hale.

In 1968, Chip Douglas also left for the second and final time, eventually retiring in Hawaii after years of doing more production work for the likes of The Monkees, Davy Jones, Linda Ronstadt, The Modern Folk Quartet (his band), and many others. The Turtles had dreams for who they wanted as a new producer. They briefly considered George Martin, who was assumed unavailable, but then settled on The Kinks' Ray Davies who had just finished producing his band's *Village Green Preservation Society* album. The majority of the singles and the album *Turtle Soup* were the results of his work. The Turtles thought Davies would turn them into The Kinks or, in other words, a real band. Davies thought he would turn The Turtles into an orchestra, which The Turtles hated.

"House on the Hill" b/w "Come Over" were the first recordings released from the Ray Davies sessions, and the A-side became The Turtles 17th single in April 1969. Unfortunately, despite being very good songs, they did not chart. Both songs would end up on *Turtle Soup* later in the year.

With the "House on the Hill" single failing, the follow-up single of "How You Love Me" was left unissued, and "You Don't Have to Walk in the Rain" b/w "Come Over" was released instead in

May as their 18th single. It fared somewhat better that "House on the Hill" and made it to #51 on *Billboard*, #52 on *Cashbox*, and #40 in Canada. These songs all ended up on *Turtle Soup* as well.

TV appearances in 1969 included *The Mike Douglas Show* on April 29, where they performed "House on the Hill" and "Elenore," *American Bandstand* on November 22, where they performed "Lady-O," and *The 1969 Miss Teen USA Pageant* hosted by Dean Jones with the Miss Teen Lovelies on November 29, where The Turtles performed a medley of their hits.

Kaylan briefly left the group after a performance at a private party went badly. This performance was set up by their co-manager Jeff Wald, who would go on to make his wife Helen Reddy a major success by 1971. This event was the Tricia Nixon Private Party held at The White House in Washington, DC on May 10, 1969. The Temptations were also on the bill. There are many tales about this performance with stories about the FBI and cocaine and a drunk Volman trying to pick up Luci Baines Johnson that have been told in great detail in *The Turtles: Happy Together* documentary, but overall the performance went well for the group. That private party started a chain of other private party appearances by The Turtles.

The last straw was at a party in Burlingame, California, for the daughter of the President of U.S. Steel. After five songs, Kaylan got fed up and essentially left the stage mid-song during "She'd Rather Be with Me." He was essentially sick of performing to all of these entitled brats who weren't responding. He reacted by throwing lounge equipment and umbrellas into their pool, then storming off and quitting the band.

Two months later, on June 24, Kaylan was back in the group to finish up *Turtle Soup*. While Kaylan was gone, the other band members had taken over lead vocals on certain songs and were not willing to relinquish them once he returned. It seemed like The Turtles were being more diplomatic on vocals on *Turtle Soup*, when in reality it was due to Kaylan's disappearance and the rest of the band deciding to carry on.

"Love in the City" b/w "Bachelor Mother" became The Turtles 19th single, released in September. It reached #91 on *Billboard*, #61 on *Cashbox*, #48 on *Record World*, and #46 in Canada. Both songs were also included on *Turtle Soup*.

Finally, after three singles released during the course of the year, The Turtles' fifth studio album and sixth overall was released in October 1969. *Turtle Soup* reached #117 on *Billboard* and #105 on *Cashbox*. Produced by Ray Davies with quality music and material, it fared worse in the long run than any of their other albums, save *You Baby*.

At the same time as all of these personnel changes, The Turtles signed another multi-year record deal on October 27, 1969, which was over by 1970. This deal included starting their own label called Blimp. The Beatles had Apple, so The Turtles had Blimp. This logo only graced their singles released in 1969 in conjunction with *Turtle Soup* and the "Lady-O" single.

After *Turtle Soup*, The Turtles immediately began working on yet another album, tentatively titled *Shell Shock*, as they agreed that they wanted to make a better album. They recorded a few songs, but the entire Turtle enterprise was crashing down due to the lawsuits, the fatigue, and the larceny. White Whale wanted Kaylan and Volman to fly to Memphis with producer Chips Moman to record over some pre-recorded backing tracks. They found the idea repulsive and did not cooperate. The Turtles had had enough, but they didn't want to leave White Whale on such a bad note, so as a final parting gesture they recorded one more good song.

That song was "Lady-O" b/w "Somewhere Friday Night," released in November. It became their 20th and final truly authorized single. It hit #78 on *Billboard*, #67 on *Cashbox*, and #59 in Canada. Composer Judee Sill was hired by Blimp at $35 a week to write songs for their publishing company. She was recommended by Jim Pons, who knew her back when he was in The Leaves. The B-side was yet another track from *Turtle Soup*.

The Turtles filmed a promotional clip for "Lady-O" with them riding horses, high on more than life. It's a sweet video, but there were many behind-the-scenes problems like a burr under the saddle of one of the horses and the fact that our stoned riders had never ridden before.

Despite the fact that "Lady-O" was supposed to be the final new Turtles recording, sessions for *Shell Shock* continued after that date, and live performances continued into 1970. The Turtles re-signed with Bill Utley and Reb Foster in January 1970 and threw out their lawsuit. The Turtles also paid off Martin Phillips Management aka Michael Philips Management and the sessions with Jerry Yester continued.

It makes sense that memories were confused or missing as there was so much turmoil going on with the group and with White Whale, but here are the songs that The Turtles were working on at the end: "We Ain't Gonna Party No More," "Goodbye Surprise," "There You Sit Lonely," "Like it Or Not," "Marmendy Mill," "Strange Girl," "If We Only Had the Time," "Teardrops," and "Gas Money."

Recordings continued until White Whale locked the group out of the studio. They refused to open unless The Turtles agreed to record "Who Would Ever Think That I Would Marry Margaret?" which they finally, albeit reluctantly, agreed to do weeks later. According to Jerry Yester, they didn't put up much of a fight and were actually happy to record it. In either case, they did record it, but resented the fact that White Whale thought it would make a great hit single.

Many of the songs intended for *Shell Shock* were re-recorded and issued on *The Phlorescent Leech and Eddie* in 1972 and *Flo & Eddie* in 1973. Rhino Records tried to reconstruct what would have been The Turtles' version of *Shell Shock* in 1987, but they added some tracks that may have not made the final cut and left off some that could have.

The last documented tour date for an original Turtles concert was December 28, 1969 at Miami-Hollywood Speedway as part of the Miami Rock Festival—the last rock festival of the '60s.

"Teardrops" b/w "Gas Money" was to be The Turtles' 21st single release in February 1970, but instead came out as by The Dedications. Apparently, only promo copies featuring the A-side went out. The B-side would remain unreleased until 1974's *Happy Together Again!* compilation.

"Who Would Ever Think That I Would Marry Margaret?" b/w "We Ain't Gonna Party No More" was released in March, and hit #123 on *Record World*. It ended up being The Turtles' 21st single and last single to feature all-new material.

More Golden Hits was the second compilation and seventh album overall for The Turtles, released in March 1970. All single A-sides from "Sound Asleep" through the latest "Margaret"/"Party" single appear, except for "House on the Hill" and "Teardrops," plus a 1967 leftover of "Cat in the Window" made its debut. It peaked at #146 on *Billboard*.

Their next and last known booking was for *The Barbara McNair Show* and aired on April 19, 1970. They performed "Somewhere Friday Night" and "Lady-O." This seems to be their last gasp for the original group that is documented since Kaylan and Volman split up The Turtles in early May 1970 and had joined Frank Zappa's Mothers of Invention by May 15. Sessions for *Shell Shock* abruptly ended with Jerry Yester being let go, unpaid for his services, and White Whale halting any additional new recordings as they were winding down to close.

Al Nichol briefly joined the reformed Leaves with Jim Pons, which lasted from 1970-1971. Then he moved to Nevada and later became a member of Turtle Park. Pons reformed The Leaves for a year and then joined Kaylan and Volman with Zappa's Mothers, continued with Flo & Eddie's first two albums and, by 1973, was moving on and eventually working for the New York Jets football team, a completely different field.

John Seiter had joined Jerry Yester's band, Rosebud, in 1970, and they released one album in 1971. Rosebud ended when Yester's relationship with Judy Henske also ended. Jim Pons later brought along Seiter to work for the New York Jets as well.

Pons retired in 2000 and now lives in Jacksonville, Florida, where he does game day videos for the Jacksonville Jaguars and plays upright bass in a bluegrass gospel band called Deep Creek.

"Is it Any Wonder?" b/w "Wanderin' Kind" came out in April 1970 as The Turtles' 22nd single but did not chart. From this point forward, White Whale was calling the shots and reissuing pre-Blimp tracks on singles.

"Eve of Destruction" b/w "Wanderin' Kind" followed in June as their 23rd single. Amazingly, the five-year-old track hit #100 on *Billboard* and #105 on *Cashbox*.

The Turtles were apparently on the bill for the Festival for Peace on August 6 at Shea Stadium, but their names do not appear on the poster. This would have been after they had broken up, and after Kaylan and Volman joined Frank Zappa's Mothers of Invention, but it is entirely possible that they fulfilled this date as it may have been a contractual obligation. If anyone knows, please tell us.

"Me About You" b/w "Think I'll Run Away" was then released in October 1970. It made it to #105 on *Billboard* and #96 on *Record World*. It was the 25th and final Turtles single released on White Whale.

In November 1970, *Wooden Head* became The Turtles' eighth and final original album released on White Whale, long after the group broke up. The album consisted of B-sides and rarities up to that point, all pre-Blimp. Of all the tracks released as singles in recent times, only "Wanderin' Kind" made the album.

White Whale Records finally folded in 1971 and the following demos written by The Turtles were copyrighted July 9, 1971: "John's Medley," "Can I Go On?," "I've Been Gone Too Long," "Kathleen's Brain," "Let's Pack and Beat it," "Marmendy Mill," "On the Inside," "Saturday Movie," "Strange Girl," and "You Want to Be a Woman." To date, "Can I Go On?," "Marmendy Mill," "Strange Girl," and "You Want to Be a Woman" have been released. It is uncertain if the other songs exist or are actually working titles for other Turtles songs. They have not been included in this discography if they cannot be heard.

The Turtles' assets were sold at auction in 1974 for $50,000, by which point Kaylan and Volman had won the rights to the Turtles' master recordings. They reissued The Turtles on a two-record compilation from Sire called *Happy Together Again!*, which also featured a few unreleased tracks. In October 1978, more unreleased tracks surfaced on a 12" EP picture disc called *1968*, and The Turtles established an extensive reissue campaign with Rhino Records.

Over the years, additional unreleased tracks have surfaced as part of updated compilations. Two catch-all compilations appeared in 1987 from Rhino: *Chalon Road* and a re-creation of *Shell Shock*. These basically scooped up all B-sides and outtakes that had not been on albums previously.

The rest of the White Whale catalog is currently controlled by Concord Music's Craft Recordings under Varese Sarabande.

After Feigin and Lasseff folded White Whale, they created Anthem Records, a label that lasted until 1973. Some latter-day White Whale acts were transferred to this new label.

Kaylan and Volman tried using The Turtles' name again in 1975, but were forbidden to do so. They would not earn the rights to their own names or The Turtles' name until 1983, after which they usually toured as The Turtles, Flo & Eddie and The Turtles, or The Turtles featuring Flo & Eddie. Kaylan and Volman set up both East Coast and West Coast touring versions of their backing group, which remained with fairly consistent line-ups from the 1980s to the 2010s.

The closest the original Turtles came to fully reuniting was for a fundraiser for the David Center on September 6, 2003 in Hempstead New York. John Seiter, Howard Kaylan, Jim Pons, and Mark Volman performed.

Kaylan and Volman continued with their Happy Together Tour until Howard Kaylan retired from touring in 2018. He was replaced by The Archies' Ron Dante, leaving Mark Volman as the final original Turtles member on tour as of this writing.

THE TURTLES A-Z (including THE CROSSFIRES)

ALL ACCESS (compilation) by The Turtles
Turtles involvement: Live tracks (except Medley and BBC): See *The Turtles Featuring Flo & Eddie Captured Live.*
"Turtles Hits Medley" and Live BBC: See *The History Of Flo & Eddie And The Turtles.*
Studio tracks: See individual Turtles tracks
Additional personnel: See individual Turtles tracks
Recording dates: 1965 - 1970 and December 31, 1991
Highest chart position: Did not chart
Original release date: March 29, 2008

You Baby (live 1991)
It Ain't Me Babe (live 1991)
She's My Girl (live 1991)
Let Me Be (live 1991)
You Showed Me (live 1991)
Goodbye Surprise (live 1991)
Elenore (live 1991)
She'd Rather Be With Me (live 1991)
Happy Together (live 1991)
Eve of Destruction
Outside Chance
Can I Get to Know You Better
Like A Rolling Stone
Turtles Hits Medley: It Ain't Me Babe / You Baby / Happy Together / She'd Rather Be With Me / Elenore (live 1969)
Guide for the Married Man
Gas Money
Happy Together (live 1967 BBC radio)

This CD was only sold at concerts and features live and original studio tracks. The live tracks from 1991 are the same ones from *The Turtles Featuring Flo & Eddie Captured Live*. The Medley is the same live one from "The 1969 Miss Teen USA Pageant."

—

ALL MY PROBLEMS (Lee Lasseff, Ted Feigin) by The Turtles
Turtles involvement: Mark Volman—vocal harmony, tambourine; Howard Kaylan—lead vocals; Al Nichol—vocal harmony, lead guitar, organ; Jim Tucker—rhythm guitar; Chuck Portz—bass guitar; Don Murray—drums
Additional personnel: Lee Lasseff and Ted Feigin—executive producers; Bones Howe—production, sound, engineering; Dwight Tunji Trio (Howe, Feigin & Lasseff)—percussion, special effects
Recording dates: October 1965 - January 1966 at Western Recorders, Hollywood, California

Highest chart position: Did not chart from *You Baby*
Original release date: April 1966
Significant other versions: Bob Gibson, Cynthia Gooding, Billy Faier, Erik Darling, Joan Baez, Dick and Dee Dee, Ray Stevens, Paul McCartney, Harry Belafonte, Pete Seeger, Dave Van Ronk, Anita Carter, The Seekers, Peter, Paul and Mary, Nick and Gabrielle Drake, Cerys Matthews, The Kingston Trio, The Shadows, The Brandywine Singers, Mickey Newbury, Elvis Presley, Lindsey Buckingham

Mark: Not the song from Smile Empty Soul. Is this the same song as "All My Trials," "All My Sorrows," and "Bahamian Lullaby"? I think it is the same with different lyrics. Such is the case with old folk songs. People take these old songs, give them new lyrics and then take writer and publishing credits for them. See the excellent 2019 documentary on the history of "The Lion Sleeps Tonight" called *Remastered: The Lion's Share* for what I am referring to on the subject of folk song theft.

As for The Turtles version, they do an acceptable version in order to keep their folk rock credentials intact on their second album. Personally, I like Joan Baez's or Paul McCartney's version best.

Charles: With spot-on double-tracked harmonies right from the start, it would sound like this would be a winner, but the recording falls short, sounding more like an unfinished composition. Does it bother anyone else that the letter T in the word forgotten is so over-pronounced? All my problems... soon forgotten—just like this track. Stick to some of the other versions (Elvis! Belafonte! McCartney!).

—

ALL THE SINGLES (compilation) by The Turtles
Turtles involvement: See individual Turtles tracks
Additional personnel: See individual Turtles tracks
Recording dates: 1965 - 1970
Highest chart position: Did not chart
Original release date: August 19, 2016

It Ain't Me Babe
Almost There
Let Me Be
Your Maw Said You Cried
You Baby

Wanderin' Kind
Grim Reaper of Love
Come Back
So Goes Love
On a Summer's Day
We'll Meet Again
Outside Chance
Makin' My Mind Up
Can I Get to Know You Better
Like The Seasons
Happy Together
She'd Rather Be With Me
The Walking Song
Guide For the Married Man
Think I'll Run Away
You Know What I Mean
Rugs of Woods and Flowers
She's My Girl
Chicken Little Was Right
Pepsi Ad (unlisted bonus track)
Sound Asleep
Umbassa and the Dragon
The Story of Rock and Roll
Can't You Hear the Cows
Elenore
Surfer Dan
Christmas is My Time of Year
You Showed Me
Buzzsaw
House on the Hill
Come Over
How You Loved Me
You Don't Have to Walk in the Rain
Love in the City
Bachelor Mother
Lady-O
Somewhere Friday Night
Teardrops
Gas Money
Who Would Ever Think That I Would Marry Margaret?
We Ain't Gonna Party No More
Is It Any Wonder?
Eve of Destruction
Me About You
Camaro Ad (unlisted bonus track)

This 50-track 2-CD set compiles all of The Turtles A-sides and B-sides in their original mono or stereo form and includes some unreleased and rare versions. This is the edition to add to one's collection as it is the only place to get some of these in original mono form and in their original single mixes and lengths—all in one collection. Plus, it's all nicely remastered and has a nifty little booklet with commentary by almost all of The Turtles including the elusive Al Nichol.

—

ALMOST THERE (Howard Kaylan) by The Turtles
Turtles involvement: Mark Volman—guitar, tambourine, vocals; Howard Kaylan—keyboards, lead vocals; Al Nichol—lead guitar, keyboards, vocals, bass guitar; Jim Tucker—rhythm guitar, vocals; Chuck Portz—bass guitar, vocals; Don Murray—drums
Additional personnel: Lee Lasseff and Ted Feigin—executive producers; Bones Howe—production, sound, engineering
Recording dates: mid-1965 at Western Recorders, Hollywood, California
Highest chart position: Single did not chart; B-side of "It Ain't Me, Babe:" Did not chart from *You Baby*
Original release date: July 1965 for single; April 1966 for album

Mark: "Almost There" is credited as the first Turtles song ever recorded. I always felt that this was kind of a reworking of "Twenty Flight Rock" with a countdown of how many miles it takes for Howard to get to his baby, instead of climbing up flights of stairs. "I knock upon her door!" and a double drum tap and he's THERE!! Hmmm, I wonder what will happen next? Insert your own lewd, lascivious thoughts here.
Charles: Even better than the best of the mid-sixties garage band hits, "Almost There" rocks more on the level of The Kinks, The Who, or (mostly) The Outsiders. It also boasts a harmonica break, and a countdown motif which drives the song to a satisfying (not dead) end. Beep beep yeah!

—

BACHELOR MOTHER (The Turtles) by The Turtles
Turtles involvement: Mark Volman—lead vocal, percussion, occasional guitars; Howard Kaylan—vocals, occasional percussion, organ; Al Nichol—vocals, guitars, keyboards, six string bass; Jim Pons—vocals, bass, occasional guitars; John Seiter—vocals, drums, occasional piano
Additional personnel: Ray Davies—producer; Chuck Britz—engineer
Recording dates: April - July 1969 at United Records, Hollywood, California

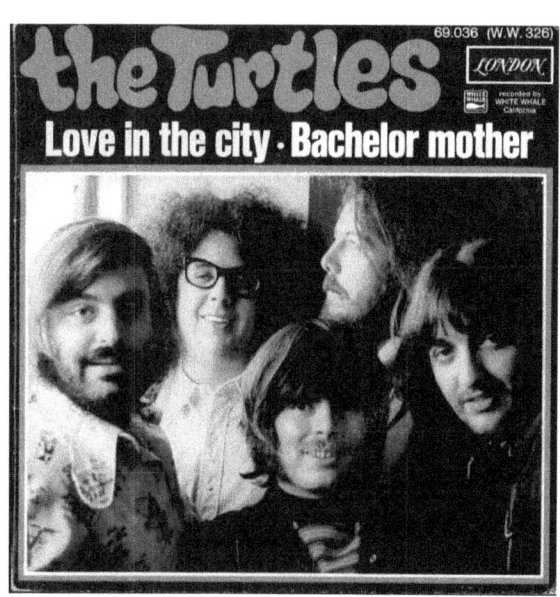

Highest chart position: Single did not chart; B-side to "Love in the City:" #117 from *Turtle Soup*
Original release date: September 1969 for single; October 1969 for album

Mark: This is another song that actually comes across as a Kinks song, so Ray Davies was somewhat successful in pulling off what The Turtles actually wanted, which was to make them sound like a real band. Unfortunately, for them, that real band would be The Kinks! Oh, well. Points for trying?

Charles: It's hootenanny time with this bouncy offering. Gets happy with hand claps and that feel-good feel, but it's missing a strong chorus. Biggest drawback of this is that the "and I'll make love to you" refrain is clearly a direct steal from Buddy Knox's "Party Doll."

—

BATTLE OF THE BANDS, THE aka BATTLE OF THE BANDS (Harry Nilsson, Chip Douglas) by The U.S. Teens featuring Raoul
Turtles involvement: Mark Volman—vocals, special effects; Howard Kaylan—lead vocals; Al Nichol—guitars, organ, Moog synthesizer, vocals; Jim Pons—bass, vocals; John Barbata—drums, percussion, vocals
Additional personnel: Chip Douglas—producer: Jim Hilton, Armin Steiner—engineers; Bob Jenkins—bongos; Chip Douglas, Harry Nilsson—piano
Recording dates: May - June 1968 at Gold Star Studios, Hollywood, California; Western Recorders, Hollywood, California; T.T.G./Sunset-Highland Recording Studios, Hollywood, California
Highest chart position: #128 from *The Turtles Present the Battle of the Bands*
Original release date: November 1, 1968

Mark: Nilsson's best contribution for The Turtles. It's a jaunty, upbeat, enthusiastic dance tune. Strangely, the mix always sounded a bit muddy, but perhaps that was intentional. Nice brass, bongos, and screams throughout. I always love the apparent vocal mistake at about 1:53. There's a live version from the "Kraft Music Hall" where host Ed McMahon introduces The Turtles as "Grumpy, Dopey, Sneezy, Sleepy, and Bashful."

Charles: It's interesting to watch the YouTube video of The Turtles performing this. Mark and Howard are in sync trying to get the audience pumped, who are looking at them like they're aliens from another planet—or actual performing turtles. They don't care—they're giving it their all for national television. The band is embellished by a bongo player, but the star of the whole song may be John Barbata, drumming like his life depended on it. During the instrumental break, the guys put down their mics to try and get the stoic crowd to clap along, and they finally succeed to an extent, before they pick back up their mics and sing again. A classic clip.

Throw in some additional points for Harry Nilsson playing piano on this track.

BATTLE OF THE BANDS RADIO SPOT a.k.a **BATTLE OF THE BANDS ALBUM COMMERCIAL** (unknown) by The Turtles
Turtles involvement: See individual Turtles tracks
Additional personnel: The "Real" Don Steele—announcer
Recording dates: 1968
Highest chart position: Did not chart from *The History Of Flo & Eddie And The Turtles*
Original release date: 1968 for radio; 1983 for album

Mark: This sounds like some mock ad that would appear in a Quentin Tarantino film, but it is the real deal announced by the very "Real" Don Steele (1936-1997), who was working at Los Angeles' infamous KHJ-AM radio from 1965-1973 that Tarantino does feature prominently in his **Once Upon a Time in Hollywood**. The ad includes clips from "Elenore," "You Showed Me," and "The Battle of the Bands."
Charles: White Whale Records presents a cool and kitsch radio promo spot that sounds like it's a spoof of commercials but is actually legit. If "you can't believe your ears," listen again. It's hysterical. With a few snippets of songs, this will "knock rock & sock it to ya."

BEST OF THE TURTLES, THE (compilation) by The Turtles
Turtles involvement: See individual Turtles tracks
Additional personnel: See individual Turtles tracks
Recording dates: 1965 - 1970
Highest chart position: Did not chart
Original release date: 1981

Elenore
It Ain't Me Babe
She's My Girl
Happy Together

She'd Rather Be With Me
You Baby
You Showed Me
Let Me Be

Reissue label Lost-Nite issued this peculiar compilation as a 10" on red vinyl, which those features are probably the only drawing point. It also came out on 10" black vinyl.

—

BEST OF THE TURTLES, THE (compilation) by The Turtles
Turtles involvement: See individual Turtles tracks
Additional personnel: See individual Turtles tracks
Recording dates: 1965 - 1970
Highest chart position: Did not chart
Original release date: February 1994

It Ain't Me Babe
Let Me Be
You Baby
You Know What I Mean
She's My Girl
Happy Together
She'd Rather Be With Me
Elenore
You Showed Me
You Don't Have to Walk in the Rain

Yet another short weight collection of Turtles tracks released by Rhino. If you ever pick up a Turtles greatest hits compilation and it's less than 15 tracks like this one, put it back. There are many better, more robust collections out there.

—

BEST OF THE TURTLES, THE (GOLDEN ARCHIVE SERIES) (compilation) by The Turtles
Turtles involvement: See individual Turtles tracks
Additional personnel: See individual Turtles tracks
Recording dates: 1965 - 1970
Highest chart position: Did not chart
Original release date: 1987

It Ain't Me Babe
Let Me Be
You Baby
She's My Girl
Can I Get to Know You Better
Love in the City
Elenore

Happy Together
She'd Rather Be With Me
You Know What I Mean
Sound Asleep
You Don't Have to Walk in the Rain
You Showed Me
The Story of Rock and Roll

This vinyl compilation was the one promoted when "Happy Together" was re-released as a single to publicize the movie called *Making Mr. Right*. It's essentially a reissue of Rhino's 1982 compilation.

—

BUZZSAW aka **BUZZ SAW** (The Turtles) by The Fabulous Dawgs
Turtles involvement: Mark Volman—vocals, special effects; Howard Kaylan—lead vocals; Al Nichol—guitars, organ, piano, Moog synthesizer, vocals; Jim Pons—bass, vocals; John Barbata—drums, percussion, vocals
Additional personnel: Chip Douglas—producer: Jim Hilton, Armin Steiner—engineers
Recording dates: May - June 1968 at Gold Star Studios, Hollywood, California; Western Recorders, Hollywood, California; T.T.G./Sunset-Highland Recording Studios, Hollywood, California
Highest chart position: Single did not chart; B-side of "You Showed Me;" #128 from *The Turtles Present the Battle of the Bands*
Original release date: November 1, 1968 for album; December 1968 for single

Mark: Essentially an instrumental, with an occasional "buzz saw" stated, which I'm pretty sure by Pons. Also are some fine James Brown-type screams courtesy of Howard. That great buzz saw sound on the guitar is something the great Al NIchol was able to achieve due to his many years of being a surf guitarist here and on the next track "Surfer Dan." A brief bit of it appears on "Medley #2" on *The History Of Flo & Eddie And The Turtles.*
Charles: This bluesy organ-driven party fest is a tour de force instrumental, with the only actual words being "buzz saw" (think "Tequila" by the Champs). Maybe Pitbull got his "Fireball" from this song and just added all the rapping. Probably not. Fine as a B-side. Put it in your Spotify playlist after the obscure track "Buzz Buzz" by the forgotten Connecticut band, The Dirty Angels (look em up!).

—

CALIFORNIA GOLD—HAPPY TOGETHER, AGAIN (compilation) by The Turtles
Turtles involvement: Live tracks (except "Medley" and BBC): See *The Turtles Featuring Flo & Eddie Captured Live*.
"Turtles Hits Medley" and Live BBC: See *The History Of Flo & Eddie And The Turtles*.
Studio tracks: See individual Turtles tracks
Additional personnel: See individual Turtles tracks
Recording dates: 1965 - 1970 and December 31, 1991
Highest chart position: Did not chart
Original release date: 1994

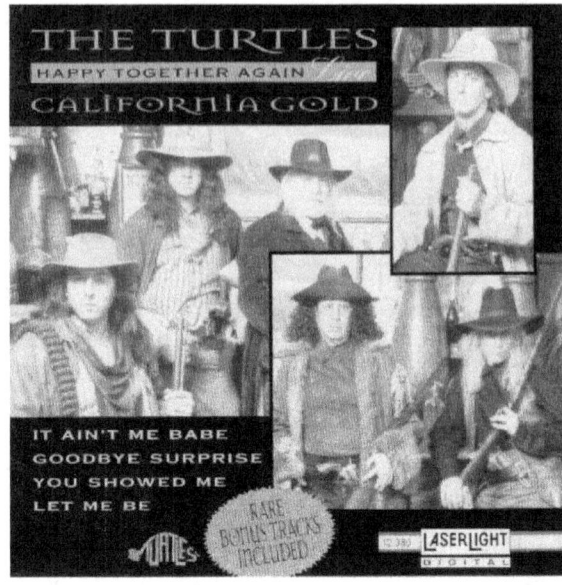

You Baby (live 1991)
It Ain't Me Babe (live 1991)
She's My Girl (live 1991)
Let Me Be (live 1991)
You Showed Me (live 1991)
Goodbye Surprise (live 1991)
Elenore (live 1991)
She'd Rather Be With Me (live 1991)
Happy Together (live 1991)
Turtles Hits Medley: It Ain't Me Babe / You Baby / Happy Together / She'd Rather Be With Me / Elenore (live 1969)
You Baby (live 1967 BBC radio)
She'd Rather Be With Me (live 1967 BBC radio)
Happy Together (live 1967 BBC radio)

These 1991 live tracks are the same ones that appeared on *The Turtles Featuring Flo & Eddie Captured Live* minus the Flo & Eddie songs, The Turtles' comedy songs and the between-song patter, giving it more of a semblance of a "serious" Turtles concert (was there one?).

Appearing on CD for the first time here was the 1969 live medley of hits and the three June 1967 live on BBC tracks for "Saturday Club" complete with Brian Matthews' introductions. Only the medley and the BBC "Happy Together" had been previously released to vinyl on *The History Of The Turtles And Flo & Eddie* from 1983. These four tracks make this collection essential.

—

CAN I GET TO KNOW YOU BETTER? (P.F. Sloan, Steve Barri) by The Turtles
Turtles involvement: Mark Volman—vocal harmony, tambourine; Howard Kaylan—lead vocals; Al Nichol—lead guitar, organ, piano, harpsichord, vocals; Jim Tucker—rhythm guitar; Chip Douglas—bass guitar; John Barbata—drums
Additional personnel: Bones Howe—producer, engineer; Armin Steiner, engineer; John Audino
Recording dates: April - September 1966 at Western Recorders, Hollywood, California
Highest chart position: #89 for single; #7 from *Golden Hits*
Original release date: October 1966 for single; October 1967 for album

Mark: I'm not a huge fan of this song, probably because of the jing-a-ling guitar every so often. It's a little too cutesy. Also, the title is kind of awkward. The only redeeming qualities are the appearance of Chip Douglas on bass and John Barbata on drums.

Charles: The Turtles hit #20 with late PF Sloan's "You Baby," one of his many charting hits. Perhaps best known for "Eve of Destruction," Sloan and Barri (Steve Barry Lipkin) co-wrote or co-produced many '60s hits. "Can I Get to Know You Better?" has the pop sensibility of so many similar songs while boasting that necessary unforgettable hook. Still, the best part may be the bridge. It sounds very much like The Grass Roots. On the *Hollywood Palace* performance of this song, Jimmy Durante introduced them as "The Toitles," while mentioning them with The Beatles. At least he didn't call them "The Toilettes."

—

CAN I GO ON (Howard Kaylan, Mark Volman) by The Turtles
Turtles involvement: Howard Kaylan—vocals, occasional percussion, organ; Mark Volman—vocals, percussion, occasional guitars; Al Nichol—vocals, guitars, keyboards, six string bass; Jim Pons—vocals, bass, occasional guitars; John Seiter—vocals, drums, occasional piano
Additional personnel: Jerry Yester—producer; Barry Keene—engineer
Recording dates: 1969 at Sunwest Recording Studios, Hollywood, California; 1970 at Crystal Sound Recording Studios, Hollywood, California
Highest chart position: #194 from *Happy Together Again!*
Original release date: November 1974

Mark: A pleasant sounding track from the aborted *Shell Shock* sessions in late 1969 and early 1970 with some nice guitar work and harmonica in there. Mark and Howard resurrected it for their first Turtles collection in 1974.

Charles: The intro conjures up a scene in a foreign art film, perhaps in an unknown part of Europe, with a fancy antique racing car driving up a deserted road to nowhere. But then it becomes a real song, with a lot of cool parts. And that road becomes the German Autobahn. The vocals are solid, and the instrumentation outstanding. Now what ever happened to that car scene?

CAN'T YOU HEAR THE COWS? aka **CAN YOU HEAR THE COWS?** (The Turtles) by The Turtles
Turtles involvement: Mark Volman—vocals, special effects; Howard Kaylan—lead vocals; Al Nichol—guitars, organ, piano, Moog synthesizer, vocals; Jim Pons—bass, vocals; John Barbata—drums, percussion, vocals
Additional personnel: The Turtles, producers
Recording dates: March - April 1968 at Sound Recorders, Hollywood, California
Highest chart position: Single did not chart; B-side of "The Story of Rock and Roll;" #194 from *Happy Together Again!*
Original release date: May 1968 for single; November 1974 for album

Charles: Not so much a song as an extended riff, this could have been the middle of a track from the Beach Boys' *Pet Sounds* (literally and figuratively). Seems unfinished but fun nonetheless. In any case, it's very moo-ving.
Mark: Charles says this sounds like something from The Beach Boys' *Pet Sounds*. I'm not so generous. It sounds like something from The Beach Boys' *Smiley Smile*, and that's not a compliment. I'm thinking "She's Goin' Bald."

CAT IN THE WINDOW aka **THE CAT IN THE WINDOW (THE BIRD IN THE SKY)** (Garry Bonner, Alan Gordon) by The Turtles
Turtles involvement: Mark Volman—harmony and backing vocals; Howard Kaylan—lead and backing vocals; Al Nichol – lead guitar, piano, backing vocals; Jim Pons—bass, backing vocals; John Barbata—drums
Additional personnel: Joe Wissert—producer; Bruce Botnick—engineer
Recording dates: 1967 at Sunset Sound Recorders, Hollywood, California
Highest chart position: #146 from *More Golden Hits*
Original release date: March 1970
Significant other versions: Petula Clark

Mark: It's a nice sweet song, but like Sloan/ Barri a couple of years earlier, there were just so many Bonner/Gordon compositions that could be released at one time, so something had to sit on the shelf. At least it got out on the higher profile *More Golden Hits* instead of *Wooden Head*. It does end a bit abruptly, however. Howard claims it needed an orchestral overdub that While Whale could not afford.

Charles: A Bonner/Gordon composition that seems simplistic at first, like a children's poem set to music. It picks up a little steam as it goes, but still remains a short (1:40) but sweet folky feline fantasy that seems to end prematurely. And you know I wanted so badly to say this recording was purr-fect!

—

CHALON ROAD (compilation) by The Turtles
Turtles involvement: See individual Turtles tracks
Additional personnel: See individual Turtles tracks
Recording dates: 1965 - 1968
Highest chart position: Did not chart
Original release date: March 1987

She's My Girl
You Know What I Mean
Sound Asleep
Can't You Hear the Cows
The Last Thing I Remember (The First Thing I Knew) (demo)
Umbassa and the Dragon

The Story of Rock and Roll
Outside Chance
Chicken Little Was Right
The Owl
To See the Sun

This oddball collection compiles various B-sides and rarities from the 1966-1968 period to make essentially a missing Turtles album. Unfortunately, since some of the B-sides are a bit eccentric, to be polite, it's not really a great album. It's like adding "You Know My Name (Look Up the Number)" to a regular Beatles album and acting like it's a major hit in its own right.

—

CHEVROLET CAMARO AD aka **CAMARO AD** (unknown) by The Turtles
Turtles involvement: Mark Volman—harmony and backing vocals; Howard Kaylan—lead and backing vocals; Al Nichol – lead guitar, piano, backing vocals; Jim Tucker—rhythm guitar, backing vocals; Chuck Portz—bass; John Barbata—drums
Additional personnel: Bones Howe—producer; unknown—girl's voice; Warren Zevon—final voice
Recording dates: 1966 at Western Recorders, Hollywood, California
Highest chart position: Did not chart from *Save The Turtles: The Turtles Greatest Hits*
Original release date: 1967 for ad; March 2, 2009 for album

Photo: Katherine McCabe

Mark: The Chevrolet Camaro first went on sale September 29, 1966, and The Turtles were right there at the beginning, advertising the 1967 model year. This undiscovered gem was first released in 2009. I'm sure no one realized it was The Turtles back then when this played on radio, much less Warren Zevon!

Charles: The Camaro will drive you absolutely mod. Not mad. Goofy, groovy, smile-invoking commercial. Sixty seconds of nostalgia. Never enough Turtles commercials.

—

CHICKEN LITTLE WAS RIGHT (The Turtles) by Fats Mallard and the Bluegrass Fireball
Turtles involvement: Mark Volman—vocals, special effects; Howard Kaylan—lead vocals; Al Nichol—guitars, organ, piano, Moog synthesizer, vocals; Jim Pons—bass, vocals; John Barbata—drums, percussion, vocals
Additional personnel: Chip Douglas—producer: Jim Hilton, Armin Steiner—engineers; anonymous—strings, woodwinds, banjo on single version
Recording dates: May - June 1968 at Gold Star Studios, Hollywood, California; Western Recorders, Hollywood, California; T.T.G./Sunset-Highland Recording Studios, Hollywood, California

Highest chart position: Single did not chart; B-side of "She's My Girl;" #128 from *The Turtles Present the Battle of the Bands*
Original release date: October 1967 for single; November 1, 1968 for album

Mark: The 7" single version is significantly different from its album counterpart, having more of a hoedown flavor with a fiddle playing and is heavy on drums, cymbals, and a twangy guitar. The Chipmunks make an uncredited cameo at the end. The album version doesn't sound like bluegrass as much and it has a much heavier sound. It is not known why they chose to re-record it, as the single version was just fine. Probably Chip Douglas' decision. There's harp and mandolin in there, but I'm not exactly sure who's playing them.

Charles: Have you ever been to a party where the DJ plays a song, and everyone in the crowd automatically knows the line-dance to it? Whether it's "The Electric Slide" or "The Chicken Dance" (no relation to this song) or some country line dance, all of a sudden the crowd turns into choreographed dance pros except for the drunk uncle, who's going backwards and screwing everyone up. Well, yee-haw, you can jump on that dance floor and do the "Cotton-Eyed Joe" dance to this song. Really! That wasn't my observation... Chicken Little told me that after he (she?) said that the sky was falling. The sky was not falling, by the way. This is a joyous, yee-haw, knee-slapper by The Turtles recording it as Fats Mallard (which guy was "Fats?") and the Bluegrass Fireball.

—

CHRISTMAS IS MY TIME OF YEAR (Howard Kaylan, Chip Douglas) by The Christmas Spirit
Turtles involvement: Howard Kaylan—vocals; John Barbata—drums
Additional personnel: Chip Douglas—producer; Gram Parsons, Gene Parson, Linda Ronstadt, Cyrus Faryar, Henry Diltz, Bessie Griffin
Recording dates: 1968 at Harmony Recorders, Hollywood, California
Highest chart position: Single did not chart: Did not chart from *Rockin' Christmas: The 60's*
Original release date: November 1968 for single; 1984 for album
Significant other versions: The Monkees

Mark: I actually am kind of surprised that this song hasn't really caught on as a Christmas perennial as it's a very catchy tune. I actually give a nod to the 1976 Monkees version as the superior version. The single's B-side "Will You Still Believe in Me" does not feature The Turtles, although Barbata may have drummed on it. It was sung by Chip Douglas and his then girlfriend, Linda Ronstadt.

Charles: "Christmas is My Time of Year" should, quite simply, be more fun and catchy. The same-titled song, with definite differences, was recorded and released by both The Turtles and The Monkees. Neither one has become a holiday staple, but then again, neither has The Beatles' "Christmas Time is Here Again." However, The Beatles' offering (to their fan club members, to be precise) actually boasts a clear and infectious hook. Ah ha! For a Christmas song to become a

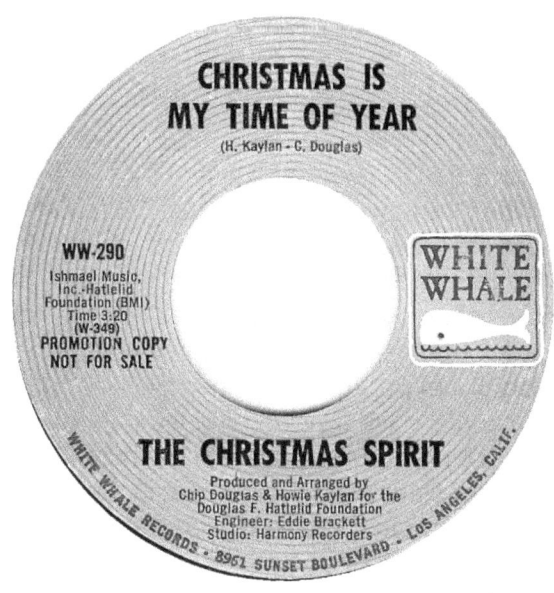

standard, it needs a catchy chorus. Some may debate that "Christmas is My Time of Year" has that catchy chorus, but they're probably the same people who feel The Turtles have the superior version. They would be wrong on both counts. Note to Mark: You're not wrong on both counts.

—

CHUNKY (Al Nichol) by The Crossfires
Turtles involvement: Mark Volman—alto sax; Howard Kaplan—tenor sax; Al Nichol—lead guitar; Dale Walton—rhythm guitar; Chuck Portz—bass; Don Murray—drums
Additional personnel: Chuck Britz—engineer
Recording dates: 1963
Highest chart position: Did not chart from *Out Of Control*
Original release date: 1981

Charles: Hey kids—what time is it? It's Chunky time! No, this isn't a commercial for Chunky chocolate candies, although it could have been. It's a surfish and mostly Dick Dale-ish instrumental... until, that is, there's a musical break to bellow "Chunky" in the most comical delivery possible. Not unlike the more familiar songs "Tequila" or "Wipe Out," this one also really rocks, and makes you want to dance the frug or the swim. It's highlighted by a mean sax, and a break with no voice so you could shout "Chunky" yourself. Just don't do it with your headphones on, or someone will either think you're nuts or maybe you're just craving a chunka' chocolate.

Mark: More influence from television: "The Lone Ranger," old monster movies, and now "Howdy Doody." Well, why not? Al and Don and the rest of The Crossfires were only teenagers and apparently obsessed with TV as much as music. The Turtles would do this sort of tune where the group plays an instrumental and then stops to shout out the tune's title to better effect with "Buzz Saw." "Chunky" is not bad, but this sort of thing has been done better by others with the tunes cited by Charles above.

—

COME BACK (Howard Kaylan) by The Turtles
Turtles involvement: Mark Volman—vocal harmony, tambourine; Howard Kaylan—lead vocals; Al Nichol—lead guitar, organ, piano, harpsichord, vocals; Jim Tucker—rhythm guitar; Chuck Portz—bass guitar; Don Murray—drums
Additional personnel: Bones Howe—producer, engineer; Armin Steiner, engineer; John Audino
Recording dates: April - September 1966 at Western Recorders, Hollywood, California
Highest chart position: Did not chart; B-side of "Grim Reaper of Love;" Did not chart from *Wooden Head*

Original release date: May 1966 for single; November 1970 for album

Mark: When it came time for the Wooden Head catch-all album in 1970, this single B-side somehow eluded inclusion on any Turtles album until this point. Admittedly, it was probably not one of Howard's best tunes. It's kind of whiny and pouty. I think Charles likes it better. Let's find out.

Charles: Not to be confused with "She'll Come Back," recorded in the same time period, this is a strong track with very solid vocals. When reviewing a tune, one tends to try to think of a similar song to compare it to, but this one is distinctive in its own right. It seems a bit short, but perhaps that's because it's so well-sung and well-produced that listeners want more of it. "Come back" with another verse and chorus.

—

COME OVER (The Turtles) by The Turtles
Turtles involvement: Mark Volman—vocals, percussion, occasional guitars; Howard Kaylan—lead vocal, occasional percussion, organ; Al Nichol—vocals, guitars, keyboards, six string bass; Jim Pons—vocals, bass, occasional guitars; John Seiter—lead vocal, drums, occasional piano
Additional personnel: Ray Davies—producer; Chuck Britz—engineer
Recording dates: April - July 1969 at United Records, Hollywood, California
Highest chart position: Single did not chart; B-side to "House on the Hill" and "You Don't Have to Walk in the Rain;" #117 from *Turtle Soup*
Original release date: May 1969 for single; October 1969 for album

Mark: A bouncy bass line with a chunky vocal kicks off *Turtle Soup* in fine style. It could have been a single track, but, by late 1969, The Turtles could no longer catch a break. They were turning out hard rocking stuff like this, but no one cared anymore. 'Tis a shame, because their late 1969-early 1970 material is some of their strongest, and is mostly self-written. There is also a demo version that was first included on 2016's *Turtle Soup* reissue that sounds about the same, but it's missing the chunky guitar and bass, so it's not as strong.

Charles: This sounds like two different songs were combined into one: the first being a fast, guitar-driven, frat-party, drinking song predating George Thorogood's best-known offerings; the other a sneaky invitation to "come over" so "we could have a ball." Both have the same goal in mind, and the result succeeds. But they never gave us the address where to go!

—

COMPLETE ORIGINAL ALBUM COLLECTION, THE (compilation) by The Turtles
Turtles involvement: See individual Turtles tracks
Additional personnel: See individual Turtles tracks
Recording dates: 1965 - 1970
Highest chart position: Did not chart
Original release date: June 22, 2016

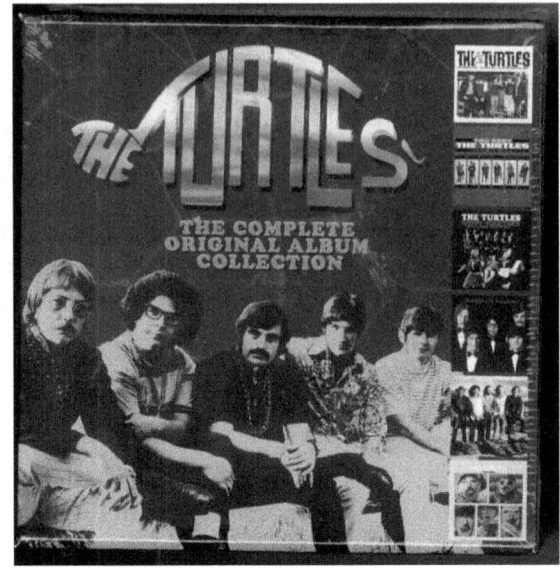

This is a box set of all six original Turtles albums with bonus tracks as released by Manifesto. It's the best set to get as it has everything and it's all remastered. It also has a nice booklet with numerous photos and commentary by the band and by Andrew Sandoval. For the true completist, get this and *All The Singles*.

—

DANCE THIS DANCE aka **DANCE THIS DANCE WITH ME** (The Turtles) by The Turtles
Turtles involvement: Mark Volman—vocals, percussion, occasional guitars; Howard Kaylan—vocals, occasional percussion, organ; Al Nichol—vocals, guitars, keyboards, six string bass; Jim Pons—lead vocal, bass, occasional guitars; John Seiter—lead vocal, drums, occasional piano
Additional personnel: Ray Davies—producer; Chuck Britz—engineer
Recording dates: April - July 1969 at United Records, Hollywood, California
Highest chart position: #117 from *Turtle Soup*
Original release date: October 1969

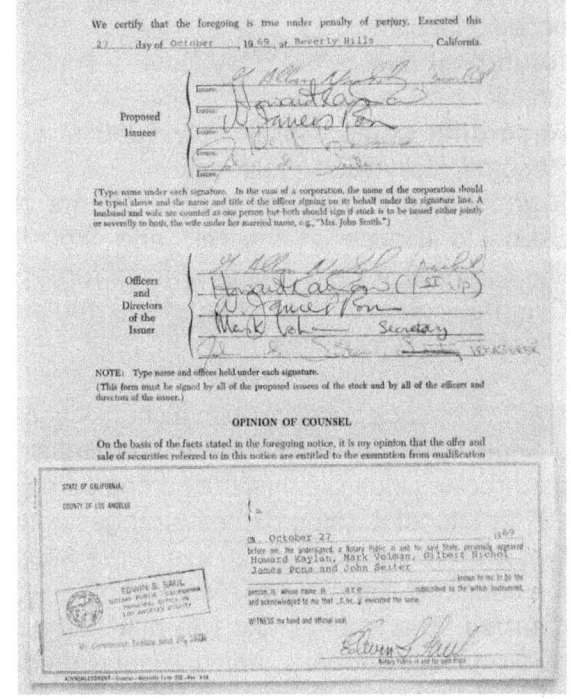

Mark: Jim Pons takes on this track. Unfortunately, it's the least effective track on the album. They probably didn't have any additional material, but this slow waltz would probably have gotten the ax if there were more songs available. Maybe I'd like it better if they had increased the tempo a notch. "Sound Asleep" never made me fall asleep. This one did. There is also a demo version that sounds about the same sans the mariachi-sounding instrumentation and sung by Howard.

Charles: Instant catchy folk vocal sounds intentionally shaky, and then a maraca brings us into the song completely. When it does, the song becomes a waltz, embellished by strings and very pretty instrumentation. That effectively shaky vocal takes us on a pretty and lovely journey which is part Western, part-Mexicana, part-fantasy. Listen to it again with these themes in mind and you'll be swept away into its imagery.

—

DOWN IN SUBURBIA (Bob Lind) by The Turtles
Turtles involvement: Mark Volman—vocal harmony, tambourine; Howard Kaylan—lead vocals; Al Nichol—vocal harmony, lead guitar, organ; Jim Tucker—rhythm guitar; Chuck Portz—bass guitar; Don Murray—drums
Additional personnel: Lee Lasseff and Ted Feigin—executive producers; Bones Howe—production, sound, engineering; Dwight Tunji Trio (Howe, Feigin & Lasseff)—percussion, special effects
Recording dates: October 1965 - January 1966 at Western Recorders, Hollywood, California
Highest chart position: Did not chart from *You Baby*
Original release date: April 1966

Imaged by Heritage Auctions, HA.com

Mark: I LOVE this song!! "All they ever smoke is to-BACC-o in suburbia!" So THERE! How many caps can I get in a line? Kind of a group chorus sing-along. Once again, it seems like a castoff from *It Ain't Me Babe* as it doesn't really get political until the song's final verse. Ay-yi-yi-yi!!! Like "Just a Room," this is another Turtles earworm song that you'll probably be singing long after you put the LP, CD, or streaming service away.

It seems like Howard's vocals are of a different take on the mono version than the stereo version, or it may just be that they are clearer on the stereo version, where you can tell that Howard is singing it kind of tongue and cheek with a chuckle in his voice.

Charles: Did you know that "nobody ever dresses sloppy in suburbia?" Bob Lind knew it, and wrote about it here, sounding nothing like his own Top 40 AM radio hit "Elusive Butterfly." And to think it was presumed Lind was a one-hit wonder. He's been recorded by more than 200 artists, and today, over 50 years into his impressive career, he's writing and singing better than ever (and he's playing his fantastic music all over the United States and Europe). By the way, Lind wrote a song titled "Eleanor," not to be confused with The Turtles' hit "Elenore." Why so much about the song's writer Bob Lind? Because I couldn't think of much to say without insulting a song that featured an obnoxious laughing scream break and a line about "Negroes, Jews, and Communists." Also because sometimes rambling can be entertaining.

—

DR. JEKYLL AND MR. HYDE (Al Nichol, Howard Kaplan) by The Crossfires
Turtles involvement: Mark Volman—alto sax; Howard Kaplan—tenor sax; Al Nichol—lead guitar; Dale Walton—rhythm guitar; Chuck Portz—bass; Don Murray—drums
Additional personnel: Chuck Britz—engineer
Recording dates: 1963
Highest chart position: Single did not chart; Did not chart from *Out of Control*
Original release date: August 1963 for single; 1981 for album

Mark: Kind of a non-descript instrumental for the first bit and then it all goes crazy. Shades of Flo & Eddie's tenure with the Mothers almost a decade early? It was kind of an inauspicious record debut for a band who would top the charts less than three and a half years later with "Happy Together." Now there's a true Jekyll and Hyde transformation! In any case, the crazy and the calm goes back and forth throughout the song, hence its two-sided title. Obviously with this and "Silver Bullet," The Crossfires were definitely influenced by what they were watching on television at the time.

Would this have become a hit for Capco Records on the national charts? Probably not. Capco didn't last very long anyway, for after releases of distinguished artists such as Cathy Wallace, Judy Proctor, The Crossfires, Cleve Herman, and The DonRays, Capco went belly-up. Someone suggested online that Capco was a label owned by the same people who owned Lute Records as they shared the same label address. Lute had a major national hit with the Hollywood Argyles' version of "Alley Oop," but by '63 they went belly-up, too. So many small Los Angeles labels crashed and burned during these years, and it probably wasn't just in L.A.

Charles: Not nearly ominous or nefarious until it shifts gear and the evil laughing begins. Then before you know it, it's back to normal. Then it's twisted and scary again. Hmmm just like Dr. Jekyll & Mr. Hyde! A novelty record that fits its theme. Gotta play this one on the coach trip during the Dracula Tour to Transylvania (www.DracTours.com) and on the Haunted GHOSTours (www.ToursOfTerror.com). Sorry, couldn't resist the plug for my spooktacular tours.

—

EARTH ANTHEM (Bill Martin) by All
Turtles involvement: Mark Volman—vocals, special effects; Howard Kaylan—lead vocals; Al Nichol—guitars, organ, piano, Moog synthesizer, vocals; Jim Pons—bass, vocals; John Barbata—drums, percussion, vocals
Additional personnel: Chip Douglas—producer: Jim Hilton, Armin Steiner—engineers
Recording dates: May - June 1968 at Gold Star Studios, Hollywood, California; Western Recorders, Hollywood, California; T.T.G./Sunset-Highland Recording Studios, Hollywood, California
Highest chart position: #128 from *The Turtles Present the Battle of the Bands*
Original release date: November 1, 1968

Mark: There is an alternate version that is essentially a different take that more or less sounds like something that could have been on *It Ain't Me Babe*. It has much less echo and reverb than the final

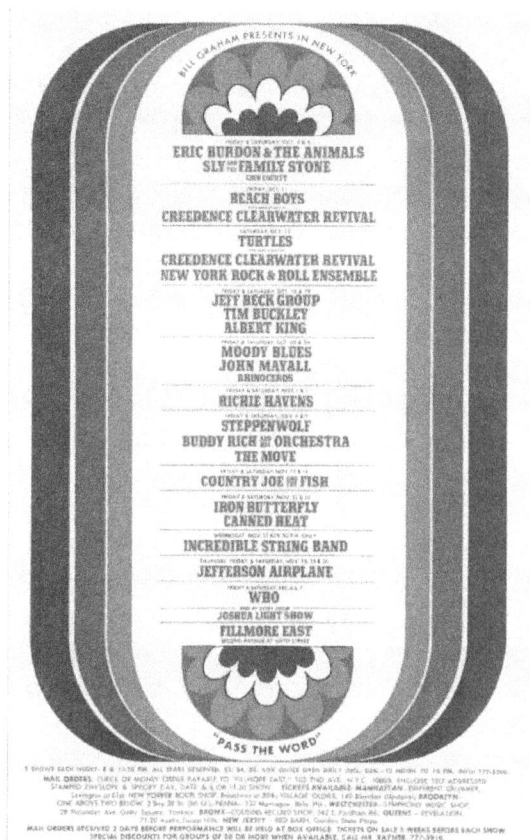

released version. It kind of reminds me somewhat of Band Aid's "Do They Know it's Christmas?" or to a lesser extent, Michael Jackson's "Earth Song." It's ages before both of those tunes or George Harrison's "Save the World" or even The Beatles' "Good Night." Someone there is blowing French horn throughout to great effect, plus some strings. I also love the album pictures for each group, the group "All" is represented by a photo of Earth. Clever and funny.

Charles: Indeed an anthem and very much earthy, this well-produced track is a sincere ecological and environmental ode to Mother Nature. Beautifully sung and played, there is a spiritual and other-worldly feel to it that somehow transcends the recording. An unappreciated classic.

—

ELENORE (Howard Kaylan, The Turtles) by Howie, Mark, Johny, Jim & Al
Turtles involvement: Mark Volman—vocals, special effects; Howard Kaylan—lead vocals; Al Nichol—guitars, organ, piano, vocals; Jim Pons—bass, vocals; John Barbata—drums, percussion, vocals
Additional personnel: Chip Douglas—producer: Jim Hilton, Armin Steiner—engineers; Paul Beaver—Moog synthesizer; Bob Jenkins—bongos
Recording dates: May - June 1968 at Gold Star Studios, Hollywood, California; Western Recorders, Hollywood, California; T.T.G./Sunset-Highland Recording Studios, Hollywood, California
Highest chart position: #6 for single; #128 from *The Turtles Present the Battle of the Bands*
Original release date: September 1968 for single; November 1, 1968 for album
Significant other versions: Flo & Eddie, Ivo Heller, Gianni Morandi, Wenzday, Me First and the Gimmie Gimmies, Dean Torrence, Las Grecas

Mark: If you watch the 1991 documentary *The Turtles: Happy Together*, you'll hear Howard Kaylan explain the situation that led to him composing "Elenore." Despite the initial credit to all of The Turtles as was the practice for them by 1968, it is really a Kaylan-only composition. The executives at White Whale Records kept pressuring Kaylan and The Turtles to come up with another "Happy Together."

Their most recent single "Sound Asleep" had little of the same chart action and the pressure was on, so, according to Kaylan, he locked himself in his hotel room and listened to and analyzed "Happy Together" to understand how it was composed. To his own admission, where "Happy Together" went up, "Elenore" went down. He purposefully wrote insipid lyrics like "pride and joy, etc." and even "fab and gear, etc." which were mercifully excised before recording.

Kaylan played his "masterpiece" to the execs at White Whale, thinking they would hate it and let The Turtles be more progressive. Instead, the exact opposite happened. Not only did they love it, they insisted it be the next Turtles single, AND it became The Turtles' final self-penned hit. Despite what Howard's intentions were, it is a great song!

Flo & Eddie sang a 1991 live version introduced by Mark that appeared on *The Turtles Featuring Flo & Eddie Captured Live*.

Charles: With the best use of the word "etcetera" since *The King And I*, "Elenore" burst onto the charts with an infectious sound that holds up and sounds fresh decades later. From the first drum beat until the epic ending, this song was the perfect single. It was moody, well-paced, and with clever lyrics, including rhyming "groovy" and "movie." One would find it surprising that it wasn't number one on the charts—until you realize that on November 2nd, 1968 two Apple releases were at the top of the charts—"Those Were the Days" by Mary Hopkin was #2 and some song by a group called The Beatles, "Hey Jude," was #1. Elenore, gee I think you're still swell!

—

ELENORE (LP): See **THE TURTLES PRESENT THE BATTLE OF THE BANDS**

—

EVE OF DESTRUCTION (P.F. Sloan) by The Turtles
Turtles involvement: Mark Volman—guitar, tambourine, vocals; Howard Kaylan—keyboards, lead vocals; Al Nichol—lead guitar, keyboards, vocals, bass guitar; Jim Tucker—rhythm guitar, vocals; Chuck Portz—bass guitar, vocals; Don Murray—drums
Additional personnel: Lee Lasseff and Ted Feigin—executive producers; Bones Howe—production, sound, engineering
Recording dates: mid-1965 at Western Recorders, Hollywood, California
Highest chart position: #100 for single; B-side of "Let Me Be" and #98 from *It Ain't Me Babe*
Original release date: September 1965 for album; June 1970 for single
Significant other versions: Barry McGuire, Jan and Dean, Paul Revere and the Raiders,

The Dickies, Dave Warner, Red Rockers, Johnny Thunders, Larry Norman, Psychic TV, Casey Abrams, Crimson Discord

For a supposed folk rock group, this is really the first truly actual protest song on the album after three general pop tracks. It almost became The Turtles' third single after "It Ain't Me Babe" and "Let Me Be," but The Turtles thought wiser as they already probably knew that they really weren't the folkies that White Whale was trying to push. After all, they were just a surfing band a month before. It was finally released as a single after The Turtles officially broke up in 1970, and amazingly charted on Billboard's Hot 100, albeit at #100.

—

FIBERGLASS JUNGLE (Howard Kaplan, Al Nichol) by The Crossfires
Turtles involvement: Mark Volman—alto sax; Howard Kaplan—tenor sax; Al Nichol—lead guitar; Dale Walton—rhythm guitar; Chuck Portz—bass; Don Murray—drums
Additional personnel: Chuck Britz—engineer
Recording dates: 1963
Highest chart position: Single did not chart; B-side of "Dr. Jekyll and Mr. Hyde;" Did not chart from *Out of Control*
Original release date: August 1963 for single; 1981 for album

Mark: A very non-descript surf song that would be the perfect type to end up on a B-side of some record... and it did! I will say in a manner of positive reinforcement, the saxophone parts as performed by Howard and Mark aren't nearly as bad as they claim. They are certainly no Charlie Parker, but they play better and more consistently than I ever could, and that's all that matters. They got a record deal. I didn't.
Charles: I get it, The Crossfires were the pre-Turtles surf instrumental band with Dick Dale guitars and drums like The Champs, fitting the mode of The Tornados and The Ventures. It doesn't have to be original; it rocks and it's fun. And you could dance to it. Points also go to the title, an obvious nod to the 1955 film, *Blackboard Jungle*.

—

FLYIN' HIGH (Al Nichol) by The Turtles
Turtles involvement: Mark Volman—vocal harmony, tambourine; Howard Kaylan—lead vocals; Al Nichol—vocal harmony, lead guitar, organ; Jim Tucker—rhythm guitar; Chuck Portz—bass guitar; Don Murray—drums
Additional personnel: Lee Lasseff and Ted Feigin—executive producers; Bones Howe—

production, sound, engineering; Dwight Tunji Trio (Howe, Feigin & Lasseff)—percussion, special effects
Recording dates: October 1965 - January 1966 at Western Recorders, Hollywood, California
Highest chart position: Did not chart from *You Baby*
Original release date: April 1966

Mark: Good harmonies accentuate this catchy, upbeat tune. Al's ability to update his sound from surf to pop seems to have succeeded nicely and this is a welcome Turtles tune that could have been a single. It was sung with gusto by Howard. I love how the harmonies sound with the separation in the stereo version over the muddled mono version.

Charles: There's a vintage clip on YouTube of The Turtles' appearance on a teen dance show hosted by Lloyd Thaxton. It features the band performing/lip-syncing this song while the teens are all dancing in the background. Thaxton admits "that it's hard to be serious around you guys." Interestingly, this is a rather serious track, and is very reminiscent of early Rolling Stones or even The Animals. Perfect harmonies and call backs embellish this period garage rocker.

—

FOLLOW THE ROCK (Tortillani) by The Crossfires
Turtles involvement: Mark Volman—alto sax, vocals; Howard Kaplan—tenor sax, lead vocals; Al Nichol—lead guitar, background vocals; Dale Walton—rhythm guitar; Chuck Portz—bass; Don Murray—drums
Additional personnel: Chuck Britz—engineer
Recording dates: 1963
Highest chart position: Did not chart from *Out of Control*
Original release date: 1981
Significant other versions: The Bay Bops

Mark: Probably not good advice for surfers, but there it is. If you want to know what Howard is singing without straining your ears, I will direct you to The Bay Bops' version. Unlike "Pull Top," the live audience here seems real. Strangely, this song is credited to someone named "Tortillani," whereas The Bay Bops record on Coral is credited to Bill Smith and Luther Dickson as writers.

Charles: Guitars attack from the first note, but then this turns into a full-fledged vocal... not all that common for The Crossfires. The guys are on fire and go full throttle here. It's tempting to say they might be Out of Control. But that would

be a too-easy nod to the title of the album. Sounds like something The Beatles might have done in Hamburg and then cleaned up for the BBC.

FOOD (The Turtles) by The Bigg Brothers
Turtles involvement: Mark Volman—vocals, special effects; Howard Kaylan—lead vocals; Al Nichol—guitars, organ, piano, Moog synthesizer, vocals; Jim Pons—bass, vocals; John Barbata—drums, percussion, vocals
Additional personnel: Chip Douglas—producer: Jim Hilton, Armin Steiner—engineers
Recording dates: May - June 1968 at Gold Star Studios, Hollywood, California; Western Recorders, Hollywood, California; T.T.G./Sunset-Highland Recording Studios, Hollywood, California
Highest chart position: #128 from *The Turtles Present The Battle Of The Bands*
Original release date: November 1, 1968

Mark: Second only to "Chief Kamanawanalaya" as one of the silliest songs on the album, this song is a really catchy lyric listing various foods, hence the name, plus a hash brownie recipe thrown in for good measure. "Why don't we go have one, hmm? I mean really!" While Zappa was calling any vegetable, The Turtles did a shout out for all of the food groups, and their waistlines showed it! There are some nice stereo popcorn and Alka-Seltzer effects added in for good measure, plus some well-timed Moog effects.

Some fun rehearsal recordings of the harmonies for this track were hidden at the end of the 2016 CD reissue of *The Turtles Present the Battle of the Bands* where they were released for the very first time. "Hyperventilate and you'll faint!"

Charles: It's a friggin' recipe turned into a song. Foreshadowing the goofiness and weirdness of Flo & Eddie, not to mention their Frank Zappa collaborations, it could work in one of two ways: If you like it, you're sure to be hungry for more; if it's not your flavor, you'll lose your appetite. In either case, it's harmless, edible fun. And then..."it's over."

45 RPM VINYL SINGLES COLLECTION (compilation) by The Turtles
Turtles involvement: See individual Turtles tracks
Additional personnel: See individual Turtles tracks
Recording dates: 1965 - 1970
Highest chart position: Did not chart
Original release date: September 22, 2014

It Ain't Me Babe b/w You Don't Have to Walk in the Rain
Let Me Be b/w Love in the City
You Baby b/w You Know What I Mean
Happy Together b/w Grim Reaper of Love
She'd Rather Be With Me b/w The Story of Rock and Roll
She's My Girl b/w Can I Get to Know You Better
Elenore b/w Outside Chance
You Showed Me b/w Sound Asleep

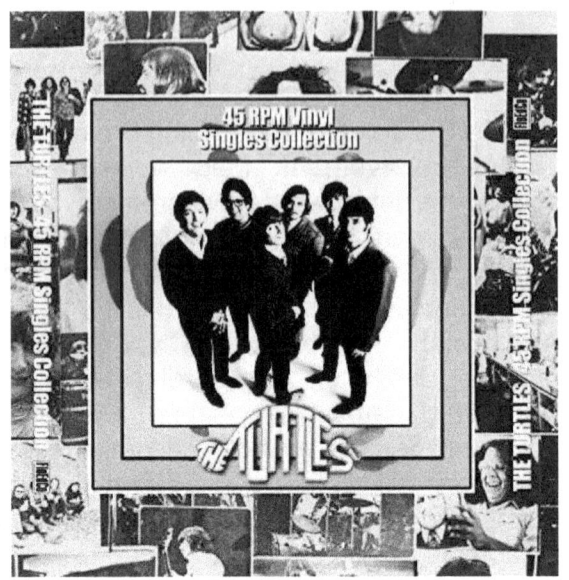

This is the second time a compilation of The Turtles' singles has been done with 45s. The first time was in 1982 with *The Turtles Greatest Hits* on eight green vinyl singles issued by Collectables Records. This time the collection of eight singles was released on black vinyl from FloEdCo through Manifesto Records.

—

GAS MONEY (Jan Berry, Arnie Ginsberg, Don Altfeld) by The Dedications
Turtles involvement: Howard Kaylan—vocals; Mark Volman—vocals, saxophone, drums; Al Nichol—trumpet; Jim Pons—lead vocals, bass; John Seiter—vocals
Additional personnel: Bobby Jimmi—producer [Note: Jerry Yester claims production credit on this track, so Bobby Jimmi may be in error.]
Recording dates: 1969 at Sunwest Recording Studios, Hollywood, California
Highest chart position: Single did not chart; #194 from *Happy Together Again!*
Original release date: November 1974
Significant other versions: Jan and Arnie

Mark: This was supposed to be the B-side to "Teardrops" by The Dedications as released in February 1970, but apparently stock copies were

never pressed during the waning days of White Whale, so it took until 1974 for this to actually see release. Jim and Howard sing lead.

Charles: The Four Seasons recorded under the pseudonym The Wonder Who, the Bee Gees gave us The Marbles, and The Turtles hit the highway as The Dedications with "Gas Money." It's pure fifties or sixties garage band giddiness in all its glory. The Dedications sounds like they would be a silky R&B band a la The Dramatics or The Delfonics, but it's closer to Freddy Cannon or The Swinging Medallions. Hard to believe the secret behind this recording (which I found out from sixties aficionado Stuart Hersh) was that all the musicians swapped instruments and played whichever ones they wanted! Reminiscent of so many other songs in chord structure and delivery, but still unique and cool. Throw on the leather jacket, jump in the Buick (everyone else is driving a Chevy) and go cruisin'. It's a gas!

—

GET AWAY (Chuck Portz, Matt Portz) by The Turtles
Turtles involvement: Mark Volman—vocal harmony, tambourine; Howard Kaylan—lead vocals; Al Nichol—lead guitar, organ, piano, harpsichord, vocals; Jim Tucker—rhythm guitar; Chuck Portz—bass guitar; Don Murray—drums
Additional personnel: Bones Howe—producer, engineer; Armin Steiner, engineer
Recording dates: April - September 1966 at Western Recorders, Hollywood, California
Highest chart position: Did not chart from *Wooden Head*
Original release date: November 1970

Charles: The first of a trio of recordings about getting away (continuing with "Getaway Back to L.A." and "Getting There"), the harmonies are amazing as always but there's not much else to what amounts to an album filler. Where's the chorus hook? The strong bridge? "I think we've said all that we can say" about "Get Away" so "say so long" and "leave me alone right now."
Mark: It really sounds like someone else other than Howard is singing lead here, perhaps Mark. Yes, I am going to agree with myself and say that Mark is singing lead here. Otherwise, I agree with what Charles said.

—

GIVE LOVE A TRIAL (Ronald Schwartz, Matt Portz) by The Turtles
Turtles involvement: Mark Volman—vocal harmony, tambourine; Howard Kaylan—lead vocals; Al Nichol—vocal harmony, lead guitar, organ; Jim Tucker—rhythm guitar; Chuck Portz—bass guitar; Don Murray—drums
Additional personnel: Lee Lasseff and Ted Feigin—executive producers; Bones Howe—production, sound, engineering; Dwight Tunji Trio (Howe, Feigin & Lasseff)—percussion, special effects
Recording dates: October 1965 - January 1966 at Western Recorders, Hollywood, California
Highest chart position: Did not chart from *You Baby*
Original release date: April 1966

Plastic EP and Charles F. Rosenay!!! interview Howard Kaylan on *The Plastic EP Show*, April 19, 2022.

Mark: Not bad, not great. Sound-wise, it reminds me of their later "Earth Anthem." I do like that it ends in a minor key. Charles will probably like it more than I do, so I'll turn it over to him...

Charles: A terrific vocal embellished by a "You've Got to Hide Your Love Away" tambourine highlights this subtle folk song. It soars when the harmonies come in, but also it ends far too soon at just over two minutes. There's a beautiful mono mix and a more dramatic stereo remaster which projects the vocal even further into the forefront.

—

GLITTER AND GOLD (Barry Mann, Cynthia Weil) by The Turtles
Turtles involvement: Mark Volman—guitar, tambourine, vocals; Howard Kaylan—keyboards, lead vocals; Al Nichol—lead guitar, keyboards, vocals, bass guitar; Jim Tucker—rhythm guitar, vocals; Chuck Portz—bass guitar, vocals; Don Murray—drums
Additional personnel: Lee Lasseff and Ted Feigin—executive producers; Bones Howe—production, sound, engineering
Recording dates: mid-1965 at Western Recorders, Hollywood, California
Highest chart position: #98 from *It Ain't Me Babe*

Original release date: September 1965 for album; June 1970 for single
Significant other versions: The Everly Brothers

Mark: It almost sounds like "Just a Room" off the second album, or should I say that "Just a Room" sounds like this song, since it came first? It's not terrible, but not that great. In recent times, I heard The Everly Brothers' version and although it was also not a hit for them, it certainly sounds more like a hit for them with better production and harmonies than The Turtles' version, which is competently done, but only an album filler.
Charles: Despite this being a Barry Mann and Cynthia Weil composition, there's a lot more glitter and not enough gold. It's not bad, it's just nothing special (kind of what Mark also said)... but in this case, it's not the fault of the artist. The Turtles do their best to add umph to what is basically a run-of-the-mill album filler indicative of the mid-sixties. We just expect more of a hook and quality from Mann/Weil.

—

GOLDEN HITS (compilation) by The Turtles
Turtles involvement: See individual Turtles tracks
Additional personnel: See individual Turtles tracks
Recording dates: 1965 - 1967
Highest chart position: #7
Original release date: October 1967

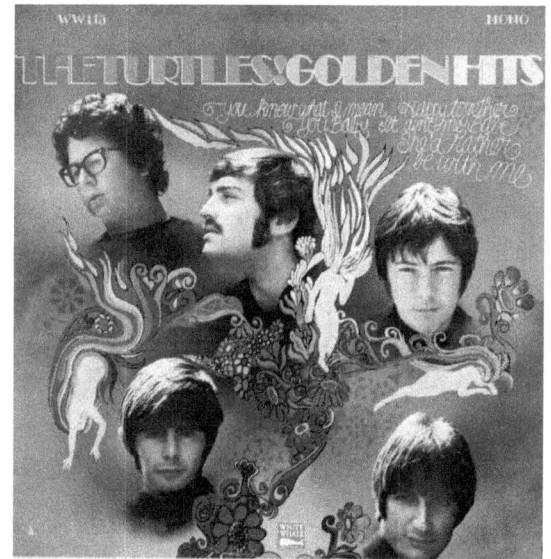

You Baby
So Goes Love
She'd Rather Be With Me
Is It Any Wonder?
Let Me Be
Grim Reaper of Love

It Ain't Me Babe
Can I Get to Know You Better
Happy Together
Outside Chance
You Know What I Mean

The best-selling album by The Turtles in their lifetime. It includes their biggest single hits from their first two years, plus a couple of unreleased tracks. It was reissued on July 31, 2020 as a 180 gram mono edition on gold vinyl from Demon Records.

—

***GOLDEN HITS* RADIO SPOT** (unknown) by The Turtles
Turtles involvement: See individual Turtles tracks
Additional personnel: unknown—announcer
Recording dates: 1965 - 1967
Highest chart position: Did not chart from *Wooden Head* (CD reissue)
Original release date: October 1967 to radio; June 22, 2016 for album

Charles: Similar to previous cool and kitsch radio promo spots, you can't help thinking that these sound like they're spoofs of commercials from that era, but they're not. You have the stereotypical (and arguably obnoxious) AM DJ delivering the hyper script with snippets of songs cut in. The snippets are the best part, but this is still a guilty pleasure.

Mark: It's a typical album radio advertisement of the time. "It Ain't Me Babe," "You Know What I Mean," "Happy Together," "She'd Rather Be With Me," and "You Baby" are all sampled, and as Charles said, it is a bit obnoxious. This radio spot and *Golden Hits* get high marks for promoting the two unreleased songs on it. Something not common at the time.

—

GOODBYE SURPRISE (Garry Bonner, Alan Gordon) by The Turtles
Turtles involvement: Howard Kaylan—vocals, occasional percussion, organ; Mark Volman—vocals, percussion, occasional guitars; Al Nichol—vocals, guitars, keyboards, six string bass; Jim Pons—vocals, bass, occasional guitars; John Seiter—vocals, drums, occasional piano
Additional personnel: Jerry Yester—producer, organ; Barry Keene—engineer
Recording dates: 1969 at Sunwest Recording Studios, Hollywood, California; 1970 at Crystal Sound Recording Studios, Hollywood, California
Highest chart position: Did not chart from *The History Of Flo & Eddie And The Turtles*
Original release date: 1983
Significant other versions: Flo & Eddie

Mark: One is to assume that had The Turtles continued, this would have been the lead-off single for the *Shell Shock* album, especially as Flo & Eddie tried to do exactly that with their debut *Phlorescent Leech and Eddie* album in 1972, where that version is decidedly stronger (see that entry in the Flo & Eddie section). This is a decent rock chunker, but I don't think it ever really had what it takes to be a strong hit single, and as such is one of the weakest songs from the Bonner-Gordon catalog. The "ooh hoo hoo hoo hoo" chorus almost saves it, but what the hell does goodbye surprise mean anyway?

Flo & Eddie sang a 1991 live version with an Olympic fanfare intro that appeared on *The Turtles Featuring Flo & Eddie Captured Live*.

Charles: What starts off as a great song unfortunately falls apart under its own weight of creativity. Too much of too much going on is packed into under three minutes. This could've been a simpler composition and subsequently a better finished product. Producer input, where art thou?

—

GRIM REAPER OF LOVE (Al Nichol, Chuck Portz) by The Turtles
Turtles involvement: Mark Volman—vocal harmony, tambourine; Howard Kaylan—lead vocals; Al Nichol—lead guitar, organ, piano, harpsichord, vocals; Jim Tucker—rhythm guitar; Chuck Portz—bass guitar; Don Murray—drums
Additional personnel: Bones Howe—producer, engineer; Armin Steiner, engineer
Recording dates: April - September 1966 at Western Recorders, Hollywood, California
Highest chart position: #81 for single; #7 from *Golden Hits*
Original release date: May 1966 for single; October 1967 for album

Mark: I didn't like this track when I first heard it, not because of the subject matter, but because of the droning sound of it. Howard says something unintelligible at about the 1:06 mark and again at 1:32. It deservedly flopped as a single, but somehow manages to make it onto most Turtles greatest hits compilations.

Charles: You would expect this to be the title of a track on a Blue Oyster Cult or Black Sabbath album, not a Turtles number, right? Fortunately the title isn't its death knell. With a continuous rhythm guitar leading the way, this is folk rock, Turtles-style, at its apex. After the first chorus, the vocals disappear into Jim Tucker's strumming, and don't return until nearly two minutes into this 2:48 recording. The ending presents a sneaky sitar-like guitar lick that leaves you yearning for more of it. Alas, the grim reaper of music engineers ended the arrangement before another much-needed chorus, or more of that sneaky but delectable sitarish guitar.

—

GUIDE FOR THE MARRIED MAN, A (film)
Turtles involvement: Theme song only. See "Guide for the Married Man" song for credits.
Additional personnel: Walter Matthau as Paul Manning; Inger Stevens as Ruth Manning; Sue Ane Langdon as Irma Johnson; Robert Morse as Ed Stander; Elaine Devry as Jocelyn; Jackie Joseph as Janet Brophy; Aline Towne as Mousey Man's Wife; Claire Kelly as Harriet Stander; Eve Brent as Joe X's Blowsy Blonde; Marvin Brody as Taxi Driver; Jackie Russell as Miss Harris, Manning's Secretary; Majel Barrett as Mrs. Fred V.; Linda Harrison as Miss Stardust. Cameo appearances: Lucille Ball as Mrs. Joe X; Jack Benny as Ollie "Sweet Lips"; Polly Bergen as Clara Brown; Joey Bishop as Charlie; Ben Blue as Shoeless; Sid Caesar as Man at Romanoff's; Art Carney as Joe X; Wally Cox as Man Married 14 Years; Ann Morgan Guilbert as Charlie's Wife; Jeffrey Hunter as Mountain Climber; Marty Ingels as Meat Eater; Sam Jaffe as Shrink; Jayne Mansfield as Girl with Harold; Hal March as Man Who Loses Coat; Louis Nye as Irving, House Buyer; Carl Reiner as Rance G.; Michael Romanoff as Romanoff's Maitre'd; Phil Silvers as Realtor; Terry-Thomas as Harold "Tiger"; Heather Young as Girl with Megaphone
Original release date: May 25, 1967

Mark: Dancer Gene Kelly actually directed this very silly movie. Its saving grace is the plethora of guest stars. Some of the vignettes like Jack Benny's are pretty funny. Some get a little tedious and the entire film comes across as an extended *Love, American Style* TV episode. Indeed, that series may have been inspired by this film.

The Turtles' involvement for this film was minimal save for singing and performing the excellent title tune.

Charles: First question: Why is the film titled *A Guide For The Married Man* but the song was titled "Guide For The Married Man?" Possibly because it didn't deserve an "A." Neither one did. The song (reviewed later) is better, though. In fairness, it's impossible to watch this film more than half a century later with the same eyes as a 1960s theater goer. If you laugh at *Borat* and the comedies of today, you won't find any humor in this movie. Just four years before it, Stanley Kramer's laugh-out-loud blockbuster, *It's A Mad Mad Mad Mad Mad World* was to comedy lovers what *Gone with the Wind* was to serious cinema. With numerous stars of its time on the big screen (plus cameos from the likes of the Three Stooges), it became the favorite of all ages. It was also nominated in five Oscar categories.

The Criterion Collection (thank you Stuart Hersh for the tip) is the ultimate package for *It's A Mad Mad Mad Mad Mad World.* But as great as that epic motion picture was, or many of the Jerry Lewis classics of the era, they simply do not hold up over time. Many of the gags are downright unwatchable, cringe-worthy, and sometimes even offensive (this refers more to Jerry's work, unfortunately, but I digress).

So when *A Guide For The Married Man* attempted the same star-filled formula, but with a slightly more risqué theme, it should have been huge. It actually was huge—a huge disappointment. Look at the amazing cast: Walter Matthau, Inger Stevens, Sue Ane Langdon, Robert Morse, Lucille Ball, Jack Benny, Polly Bergen, Joey Bishop, Ben Blue, Sid Caesar, Art Carney, Wally Cox, Jeffrey Hunter, Marty Ingels, Sam Jaffe, Jayne Mansfield, Hal March, Louis Nye, Carl Reiner, Phil Silvers, Terry-Thomas, and others (a few of whom were also in *Mad Mad...*). Sadly, a great cast does not guarantee a great film. It was a so-called bedroom comedy with more "boredom" than "bedroom." It wasn't nominated for a single Academy Award.

Back in the day, it wasn't uncommon for a hot band to be part of a film (for example, The Lovin' Spoonful in Woody Allen's *What's Up, Tiger Lily?*). The Turtles, however, were funny, charismatic, and camera-ready! They could've carried a film on their own. It may not have been *A Hard Day's Night*, but what is? It couldn't have been any worse than the Dave Clark 5 films! THERE SHOULD HAVE BEEN A TURTLES MOVIE, not an embarrassing movie with The Turtles in it.

—

GUIDE FOR THE MARRIED MAN (John Williams, Leslie Bricusse) by The Turtles
Turtles involvement: Mark Volman—harmony and backing vocals; Howard Kaylan—lead and backing vocals; Al Nichol – lead guitar, piano, backing vocals; Jim Tucker—rhythm guitar, backing vocals; Jim Pons—bass, backing vocals; John Barbata—drums
Additional personnel: Joe Wissert—producer; Bones Howe, Armin Steiner, Bruce Botnick—engineers; John Williams—conductor
Recording dates: February - March 21, 1967 at Sound Recorders, Hollywood, California
Highest chart position: Single did not chart; #25 from *Happy Together*
Original release date: April 29, 1967 for album; June 1967 for single

Mark: The theme song for the movie of the same name actually had a limited 7" single release, making it one of the more difficult Turtles 45s to come by. It's one of The Turtles' best songs and helps to make the highly abundant *Happy Together* album that much better. The stereo version has a much more prominent bassline than the mono version.

Charles: If we're being completely honest, there is no such thing as a "Guide for the Married Man," unless, perhaps, it's penned by "the married woman." Or, in the case of the film from which it came, it's a series of lessons on how a married husband can cheat on his wife. That aside, let's take a serious look at the composers, John Williams and Leslie Bricusse. The latter would go on to have hits with John Barry ("Goldfinger") and even went on to win an Academy Award for Rex Harrison's "Talk to the Animals" from 1967's *Doctor Dolittle*. Google him. You don't have to do a search for his musical partner, though. John Williams became Steven Spielberg's musical go-to, and composed orchestral soundtracks for *Star Wars*, *Raiders Of The Lost Ark*, *Jaws,* and so many others. You might say he's super, man (yes he did the soundtrack for the original Christopher

Reeves *Superman* movie in 1978). He's one of the all-time greats, who can be forgiven for such an early rock and roll foray.

Now it all makes sense since this was the film theme song for the 1967 motion picture of the same name, which boasted an all-star cast second only to *It's A Mad Mad Mad Mad Mad World*. Again, Google it.

Oh yes—the song itself…

It's good but not great, and it doesn't hold up over the years. Just like the movie.

—

HAPPY TOGETHER (Garry Bonner, Alan Gordon) by The Turtles
Turtles involvement: Mark Volman—harmony and backing vocals; Howard Kaylan—lead and backing vocals; Al Nichol – lead guitar, piano, backing vocals; Jim Tucker—rhythm guitar, backing vocals; Chip Douglas—bass, arrangements, backing vocals; John Barbata—drums
Additional personnel: Joe Wissert—producer; Bones Howe, Armin Steiner, Bruce Botnick—engineers
Recording dates: December 1966 - April 1967 at Sunset Sound Recorders, Hollywood, California
Highest chart position: #1 for three weeks for single; #25 from *Happy Together*
Original release dates: February 1967 for single; April 29, 1967 for album .
Significant other versions: Flo & Eddie, The Mothers, The Nylons, Hugo Montenegro, Tony Orlando and Dawn, T.G. Sheppard, Captain & Tennille, Mel Torme, The Piano Guys, Weezer, Petula Clark, Donny Osmond, Frank Zappa and the Mothers, Frank Alamo, Prima Vera, B.E. Taylor, Filter, Dmitri Vegas & Like Mike, Bassjackers

Mark: I like it. I think it's a great piece of work. If you don't, I'm surprised that you're actually reading this book. This song alone is enough to warrant The Turtles' inclusion in The Rock and Roll Hall of Fame. Song perfection. There is a mono and stereo version. A live version performed by Howard Kaylan and Mark Volman is included on The Mothers' *Fillmore East 1971*. It is a mainstay of virtually every Turtles greatest hits compilation and has been reissued as a single and album countless times since 1967.

Flo & Eddie sang a non-reggae 1991 live version that appeared on *The Turtles Featuring Flo & Eddie Captured Live* where he changes the lyrics to "invest three dimes" and "lose my minds" and namedrops Milli Vanilli.

It's really difficult to ruin a song like this, that's how great it is, but John Davidson and Lucie Arnaz try really hard to accomplish that feat by singing it together on the January 29, 1973 episode of "Here's Lucy."

Charles: How do you review or comment on one of the GREATEST POP ROCK SONGS OF ALL TIME? Amazing vocals? Check! Ideal instrumentation? Check! A+ arrangement? Check! Unforgettable lyrics? Check! An energy that only the most historic songs of all time possess? Check! Every other superlative imaginable? Check!

How could any act have ever passed on recording this? How could The Turtles ever live up to this immaculate concoction? It's part of the soundtrack to so many lives. It's perfect in every way.

If you're teaching a class on perfect pop rock song recordings of all time, add this to the curriculum right along with "God Only Knows," "She Loves You," "A Lover's Concerto," "Daydream Believer," "Be My Baby," "Let's Pretend," and (_____ insert your favorites here).

Thank you, Bonner. Thank you, Gordon. Thank you, Turtles.

—

HAPPY TOGETHER (LP) by The Turtles
Turtles involvement: Mark Volman—harmony and backing vocals; Howard Kaylan—lead and backing vocals; Al Nichol – lead guitar, piano, backing vocals; Jim Tucker—rhythm guitar, backing vocals; Chip Douglas—bass, arrangements, backing vocals for "Happy Together;" John Barbata—drums

Additional personnel: Joe Wissert—producer; (Bones Howe—producer, "Like the Seasons" and "Makin' My Mind Up"); Bones Howe, Armin Steiner, Bruce Botnick—engineers; Warren Zevon—guitar; Leonard Malarsky—violin; Jesse Ehrlich, Joseph Saxon—cellos; Bob Thompson—string arrangement on "Like the Seasons"; Larry Knechtel—bass; Hal Blaine—drums; John Audino, Jules Chaikin, Ray Triscari—trumpets; Bob Edmondson—trombone; Art Pepper—alto sax; Bill Perkins—tenor sax; Bill Holman—tenor sax, horn arrangement on "Makin' My Mind Up";

Lynn Blessing—vibes; Jerry Yester—horn and string arrangements on "Me About You"; Bud Brisbois, Roy Caton, Tony Terran—trumpets; Lou Blackburn, Lew McCreary—trombones; Bobby Knight—bass trombone; Ray Pohlman—horn arrangement on "She'd Rather Be With Me"

Recording dates: December 1966 - April 1967 at Sunset Sound Recorders, Hollywood, California; "Like the Seasons" and "Makin' My Mind Up" January - June 1966 at Western Recorders, Hollywood, California; "Guide for the Married Man" and overdubs for "Makin' My Mind Up" February - March 21, 1967 at Sound Recorders, Hollywood, California

Highest chart position: #25
Original release date: April 29, 1967

Makin' My Mind Up
Guide for the Married Man
Think I'll Run Away
The Walking Song
Me About You
Happy Together

She'd Rather Be With Me
So Goes Love (bonus track on Rhino reissue)

To Young to Be One
Person Without a Care
Like the Seasons
Rugs of Woods and Flowers

Bonus tracks on stereo Sundazed edition:
She's My Girl
You Know What I Mean
Is it Any Wonder?

Bonus tracks on stereo Repertoire edition:
So Goes Love
Grim Reaper of Love
Outside Chance
We'll Meet Again
Can I Get to Know You Better
You Know What I Mean
Happy Together (mono)
She'd Rather Be With Me (mono)
You Know What I Mean (mono)

Bonus tracks on mono Manifesto edition:
Entire album in stereo

As usual, the stereo version has more separation of instruments and vocals than the mono version, and "Rugs of Woods and Flowers" doesn't have the false ending on the mono version. It's really a fine album overall especially considering the piecemeal method of its construction. It doesn't seem like it was done much differently than "It Ain't Me Babe" or "You Baby," but it somehow sounds much more modern than those two albums. Probably because of layers of different instruments and sound effects that weren't really present on the earlier albums.

—

HAPPY TOGETHER AGAIN! (compilation) by The Turtles
Turtles involvement: See individual Turtles tracks
Additional personnel: See individual Turtles tracks
Recording dates: 1965 - 1970
Highest chart position: #194
Original release date: November 1974

It Ain't Me Babe
You Know What I Mean
Love in the City
Lady-O
You Baby
Grim Reaper of Love
Elenore
Let Me Be
Outside Chance

*Me Without You
Guide For the Married Man
The Story of Rock and Roll
You Don't Have to Walk in the Rain
She'd Rather Be With Me*

*She's My Girl
Can I Get to Know You Better
Somewhere Friday Night
Happy Together
Sound Asleep
You Want to Be a Woman
You Showed Me*

*The Battle of the Bands
Gas Money
Like It Or Not
Can I Go On
Can't You Hear the Cows*

*Teardrops
There You Sit Lonely
Santa and the Sidewalk Surfer*

Howard Kaylan and Mark Volman won the rights to The Turtles' songs and master recordings when White Whale Records put them up for auction in 1974 and promptly signed a deal with Sire Records to release this first post-Turtles compilation that featured a few released and unreleased rarities.

—

HAPPY TOGETHER: THE VERY BEST OF THE TURTLES (compilation) by The Turtles
Turtles involvement: See individual Turtles tracks
Additional personnel: See individual Turtles tracks
Recording dates: 1965 - 1970
Highest chart position: Did not chart
Original release date: September 28, 2004

*Happy Together
She'd Rather Be With Me
Let Me Be
You Know What I Mean
You Baby
Elenore
It Ain't Me Babe
She's My Girl
Eve of Destruction*

You Showed Me
Outside Chance
Can I Get to Know You Better
You Don't Have to Walk in the Rain
Grim Reaper of Love

Shout Factory is a label formed by some of the founders of Rhino Records who helped relaunch The Turtles back in 1977. They mainly release DVDs, but also released a few CDs over the years, of which this is one. Unfortunately, there is nothing remarkable about it, being 14 of the expected Turtles hits, where more tracks could fit.

—

HISTORY OF FLO & EDDIE AND THE TURTLES, THE (compilation) by The Crossfires, The Turtles, Flo & Eddie
Turtles involvement: See individual Crossfires, Turtles and Flo & Eddie tracks.
Additional personnel: See individual Crossfires, Turtles and Flo & Eddie tracks.
Recording dates: 1963 - 1983
Highest chart position: Did not chart
Original release date: 1983

Westchester High School Alma Mater
Silver Bullet
I Get Out of Breath
Outside Chance
Grim Reaper of Love
Battle of the Bands Album Commercial
Lady-O
Goodbye Surprise (Turtles version)
Pepsi Ad (unlisted bonus track)
Turtles Hits Medley: It Ain't Me Babe / You Baby / Happy Together / She'd Rather Be With Me / Elenore (live 1969)

Happy Together (live 1967 BBC radio)
Turtle Soup Radio Spot (unlisted bonus track)
There You Sit Lonely
We Ain't Gonna Party No More
Flo & Eddie Theme
Feel Older Now
Nikki Hoi
I've Been Born Again

Best Part of Breaking Up
Another Pop Star's Life
Just Another Town
Flo & Eddie Meet the Wolfman (excerpt) (unlisted bonus track)

Afterglow
You're a Lady
Marmendy Mill

Flo & Eddie Scandinavian Intro (unlisted bonus track)
Illegal, Immoral and Fattening
Rebecca
Let Me Make Love to You
Mama, Open Up
Keep it Warm
Flo & Eddie German Intro (unlisted bonus track)
Moving Targets

Flo & Eddie By the Fireside Radio Theme
Albert Brooks (unlisted bonus track)
The Big Showdown
Alice Cooper (unlisted bonus track)
This Could Be the Day
Keith Moon (unlisted bonus track)
(You're Nothing But a) Good Duck
David Bowie (unlisted bonus track)
Medley #1: Stop / Stop! In the Name of Love / Shadow Dancing / The Butchers Are Back / Strawberry Shortcake Theme / Mystic Martha
Marc Bolan (unlisted bonus track)
Behind the Green Door and The Resurrection of Eve Ad (unlisted bonus track)
The Flo & Eddie Show

Ringo Starr (unlisted bonus track)
Getaway (Back to L.A.)
Iggy Pop (unlisted bonus track)
Livin' in a Jungle
Harry Nilsson (unlisted bonus track)
Youth in Asia
The Move Reunion—Rick Price, Roy Wood, Bev Bevan, Jeff Lynne (unlisted bonus track)
Medley #2: Louie Louie / Eddie, Are You Kidding? / Show Me the Way to Go Ohm / Champagne / Buzz Saw / The Sanzini Brothers (spoken word)
Lou Reed (unlisted bonus track)
Closing Theme

This 3-record LP set has a bunch of goodies that have never appeared on any other release, including clips from "The Flo & Eddie Show" with Ringo Starr and the reunited Move. To this day, there are tracks here that are only available on this compilation. It also includes a decent magazine-sized history of The Turtles with many rare photos.

—

HOT LITTLE HANDS (The Turtles) by The Turtles

Turtles involvement: Mark Volman—vocals, percussion, occasional guitars; Howard Kaylan—vocals, occasional percussion, organ; Al Nichol—lead vocal, guitars, keyboards, six string bass; Jim Pons—vocals, bass, occasional guitars; John Seiter—lead vocal, drums, occasional piano

Additional personnel: Ray Davies—producer; Chuck Britz—engineer

Recording dates: April - July 1969 at United Records, Hollywood, California

Highest chart position: #117 from *Turtle Soup*

Original release date: October 1969

Mark: Probably never considered for a single release, but this one might have done quite well during the heavier Led Zeppelin/Black Sabbath days of late 1969. Even The Beatles were pulling off stuff similar to this on *Abbey Road* along with their typical melodic harmonies and ballads. John Seiter and Al Nichol harmonize lead vocals on this one.

Charles: A guitar-centric rave-up really drives what sounds like it would've been a great live song. There are some guitar riffs that sound just like Peter Townshend of The Who's work in *Tommy*. "It's too hard controlling myself when I know I don't wanna" is a male teenager's cry—here's hoping he was able to keep his "hot little hands: to himself.

—

HOUSE OF PAIN (Howard Kaylan) by The Turtles

Turtles involvement: Mark Volman—vocal harmony, tambourine; Howard Kaylan—lead vocals; Al Nichol—vocal harmony, lead guitar, organ; Jim Tucker—rhythm guitar; Chuck Portz—bass guitar; Don Murray—drums

Additional personnel: Lee Lasseff and Ted Feigin—executive producers; Bones Howe—production, sound, engineering; Dwight Tunji Trio (Howe, Feigin & Lasseff)—percussion, special effects

Recording dates: October 1965 - January 1966 at Western Recorders, Hollywood, California

Highest chart position: Did not chart from *You Baby*

Original release date: April 1966

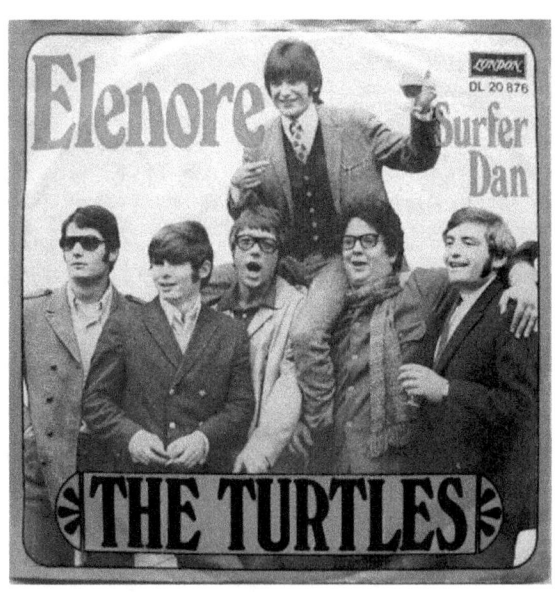

Mark: Lyric-wise, this sounds like a leftover from *It Ain't Me Babe*, and perhaps it was, or Howard was still in that frame of mind when composing this, as the group behind him was transitioning to more of a pop sound. Nevertheless, it also sounds like an Animals outtake, but as far as I can tell, no one ever covered this. It's certainly not the later song by Van Halen of the same name, although it would have been very interesting had they covered it. The highlight is the background "Ooh Ahh" "Chain Gang" chorus.

Charles: Best known for their club classic "Jump Around," House of Pain was the name of an Irish-styled American hip-hop act who released three albums in the 1990s. But a quarter century before them, The Turtles recorded this song of the same name. Both are references to H.G. Wells' fantasy novel *The Island Of Dr. Moreau*; however, this is far more influenced by "House of the Rising Sun." Howard's vocal is highly stylized, and reminiscent of Eric Burdon, and his composition is more of a short story than a song. One thing's for sure, you can't "jump around" to it.

—

HOUSE ON THE HILL (Al Nichol, John Seiter) by The Turtles

Turtles involvement: Mark Volman—lead vocal, percussion, occasional guitars; Howard Kaylan—lead vocal, occasional percussion, organ; Al Nichol—vocals, guitars, keyboards, six string bass; Jim Pons—vocals, bass, occasional guitars; John Seiter—vocals, drums, occasional piano

Additional personnel: Ray Davies—producer; Chuck Britz—engineer; Roy Caton, Manny Klein, Tony Terran—trumpets; David Duke, George Hyde, Alan Robinson—French horns; Ray Pohlman—horn arrangements

Recording dates: April - July 1969 at United Records, Hollywood, California

Highest chart position: Did not chart; #117 from *Turtle Soup*

Original release date: May 1969 for single; October 1969 for album

Mark: New drummer John Seiter wrote the lyrics and Al Nichol the tune. It's a great song with some excellent vocals and French horns and bass. It should have made Top 10 and probably would have if The Turtles actually managed to pull off the illegal maneuver and switch over to RCA Records. As such, they were still stuck with lowly White Whale Records and slowly went down with their sinking ship.

Charles: The title always reminded me of the Vincent Price film *The House On Haunted Hill*, but there's nothing spooky about this recording. Actually it's scary that this isn't a better known song. It's one of those slow boilers that build to a fiery crescendo. Nice imagery and subtle vocals at the start, followed by some rocking parts. It pulls back and then starts all over again. A truly complete song with a quasi-Beatlish harmonic vocal ending.

—

HOW YOU LOVED ME aka **HOW YOU LOVE ME** (The Turtles) by The Turtles
Turtles involvement: Mark Volman—lead vocal, percussion, occasional guitars; Howard Kaylan—vocals, occasional percussion, organ; Al Nichol—vocals, guitars, keyboards, six string bass; Jim Pons—vocals, bass, occasional guitars; John Seiter—lead vocal, drums, occasional piano
Additional personnel: The Turtles—producer for demo; Ray Davies—producer; Chuck Britz—engineer
Recording dates: March 1969 at ID Sound Studios, Hollywood, California for demo version; April - July 1969 at United Records, Hollywood, California
Highest chart position: #117 from *Turtle Soup*; Did not chart from *Solid Zinc: The Turtles Anthology* for demo
Original release date: October 1969; February 19, 2002 for demo

Mark: The demo version has Howard on lead vocals and is called "How You Love Me," but after he abruptly left the group, the leads were given to the other Turtles, and love was thrown into the past tense. The demo is very drum heavy.

When Howard came back, the other Turtles weren't willing to relinquish their lead vocal status on every song. This one really comes across as a Kinks song when drummer John Seiter sings lead on the final version, along with some good Jim Pons harmonies. Shades of Dave Davies.

Charles: Is that a cowbell we hear opening the track? This is another one that sounds like an early Raspberries cut. Does Eric Carmen realize that Howard Kaylan was doing so much of what Carmen did so well, vocally, years earlier? Does Howard realize that at times Carmen's vocals were so similar to his? Credit drummer John Seiter with solid percussion, and there are some nice breaks and changes, but it's all about the voices.

—

I CAN'T STOP (Howard Blaikley) by The Turtles
Turtles involvement: Mark Volman—vocal harmony, tambourine; Howard Kaylan—lead vocals; Al Nichol—lead guitar, organ, piano, harpsichord, vocals; Jim Tucker—rhythm guitar; Chuck Portz—bass guitar; Don Murray—drums
Additional personnel: Bones Howe—producer, engineer; Armin Steiner, engineer; John Audino, Jules Chaikin, Ray Triscari—trumpets; Bob Edmondson—trombone; Art Pepper, alto sax; Bob Perkins—tenor sax; Bill Holman—tenor sax, horn arrangement
Recording dates: April - September 1966 at Western Recorders, Hollywood, California; 3/21/67 overdubs at Sound Recorders, Hollywood, California
Highest chart position: Did not chart from *Wooden Head*
Original release date: November 1970

Charles: How could you listen to this track and not think—from the first note—that it should have been a smash single?! Everything about it screams hit single. Why didn't Paul Revere and the Raiders try this one? "I Can't Stop" (sorry, couldn't resist) singing praises of this album track. It is that good.

Mark: I agree with Charles. How could this song just remain in the vaults? It's so upbeat and is the true highlight of *Wooden Head*, and should have been a single to promote the album. Nice little organ at the end. Howard claims that there should have been a horn overdub. Maybe so, but I like it as it is just fine.

I GET OUT OF BREATH (P.F. Sloan, Steve Barri) by The Turtles
Turtles involvement: Mark Volman—vocal harmony, tambourine; Howard Kaylan—lead vocals; Al Nichol—lead guitar, organ, piano, harpsichord, vocals; Jim Tucker—rhythm guitar; Chuck Portz—bass guitar; Don Murray—drums
Additional personnel: Bones Howe—producer, engineer; Armin Steiner, engineer
Recording dates: October 1965 at Western Recorders, Hollywood, California
Highest chart position: Did not chart from *Wooden Head*
Original release date: November 1970

Mark: Wow! A Sloan-Barri composition that was actually rejected! It's not that bad, but it probably remained in the can as The Turtles and White Whale probably wanted a few more of their own

compositions on their albums to reap a bit more music publishing cash. Ultimately, it's not any better or worse than the other Sloan-Barri songs. It is performed impeccably, and as usual, has nice harmonies.

Charles: The more common phrase is "I'm Out of Breath," but "I Get Out Of Breath" is poetically acceptable here because it fits the song's lyric pattern better. The rest of the lyrics are solid, sort of like that cowboy guitar lick that highlights the song. I'm not sure why, but something about this song reminds me of a more poppy Dylan when he sang "Ah but I was so much older then, I'm younger than that now," which, despite making no sense, somehow makes sense.

—

I KNOW THAT YOU'LL BE THERE (P.F. Sloan, Steve Barri) by The Turtles
Turtles involvement: Mark Volman—vocal harmony, tambourine; Howard Kaylan—lead vocals; Al Nichol—vocal harmony, lead guitar, organ; Jim Tucker—rhythm guitar; Chuck Portz—bass guitar; Don Murray—drums
Additional personnel: Lee Lasseff and Ted Feigin—executive producers; Bones Howe—production, sound, engineering; Dwight Tunji Trio (Howe, Feigin & Lasseff)—percussion, special effects
Recording dates: January 3, 1966 at Western Recorders, Hollywood, California
Highest chart position: Did not chart from *You Baby*
Original release date: April 1966
Significant other version: Shelley Fabares

Mark: Another Sloan/Barri composition, but this one is a little more gushy and less protesty (protesty?) than their others. It's an all right track, but never rises above album filler for me. There's a nice jangly guitar break in the middle and it seems to have inspired "The Walking Song" whether intentional or not.

Charles: With a strong Jay Black-like vocal, Howard raises this above mediocre pop rock, but just barely. There's an unnecessary jangly guitar break in the middle (apologies to my co-author) that serves no purpose other than to lengthen out a song that doesn't really go anywhere. Without a strong hook, it's worthwhile mostly for the lead vocal.

—

I NEED SOMEONE (Chuck Portz, Jim Tucker) by The Turtles
Turtles involvement: Mark Volman—vocal harmony, tambourine; Howard Kaylan—lead vocals; Al Nichol—vocal harmony, lead guitar, organ; Jim Tucker—rhythm guitar; Chuck Portz—bass guitar; Don Murray—drums
Additional personnel: Lee Lasseff and Ted Feigin—executive producers; Bones Howe—production, sound, engineering; Dwight Tunji Trio (Howe, Feigin & Lasseff)—percussion, special effects
Recording dates: October 1965 - January 1966 at Western Recorders, Hollywood, California
Highest chart position: Did not chart from *You Baby*
Original release date: April 1966

Mark: A not half-bad original that truly sounds like it could have come out of The Byrds' catalog. Howard sings it earnestly which totally sells it. Lyric-wise, it's a bit trite, but hey, give Chuck and Jim credit for trying as they hadn't successfully written anything up until this point for The Turtles that was worthy of appearing on an album. It could have also been called "Love in Vain," but that's The Rolling Stones.

Charles: Definite points for it being a composition by Turtle members Chuck Portz and the late Jim Tucker, but maybe it should have been sung by one of them. Kaylan, who normally can do no wrong, seems to be uncomfortable with this one's lower register. It's far more noticeable on the stereo mix, which brings the lead vocal to the forefront. The mono version seems to actually be more melodic and enjoyable.

—

I'M CHIEF KAMANAWANALEA (WE'RE THE ROYAL MACADAMIA NUTS) (John Barbata) by Chief Kamanawanalea and His Royal Macadamia Nuts
Turtles involvement: Mark Volman—vocals, special effects; Howard Kaylan—lead vocals; Al Nichol—guitars, organ, piano, Moog synthesizer, vocals; Jim Pons—bass, vocals; John Barbata—drums, percussion, vocals
Additional personnel: Chip Douglas—producer: Jim Hilton, Armin Steiner—engineers
Recording dates: May - June 1968 at Gold Star Studios, Hollywood, California; Western Recorders, Hollywood, California; T.T.G./Sunset-Highland Recording Studios, Hollywood, California
Highest chart position: #128 from *The Turtles Present the Battle of the Bands*
Original release date: November 1, 1968

Mark: A very silly song supposedly based upon an old grade school joke, but unlike strange B-sides like "Umbassa and the Dragon," this one is actually quite catchy and actually works. This is easily one of my favorites on the album as it's so stupid, it's fun! Hoo hah, hoo hah!

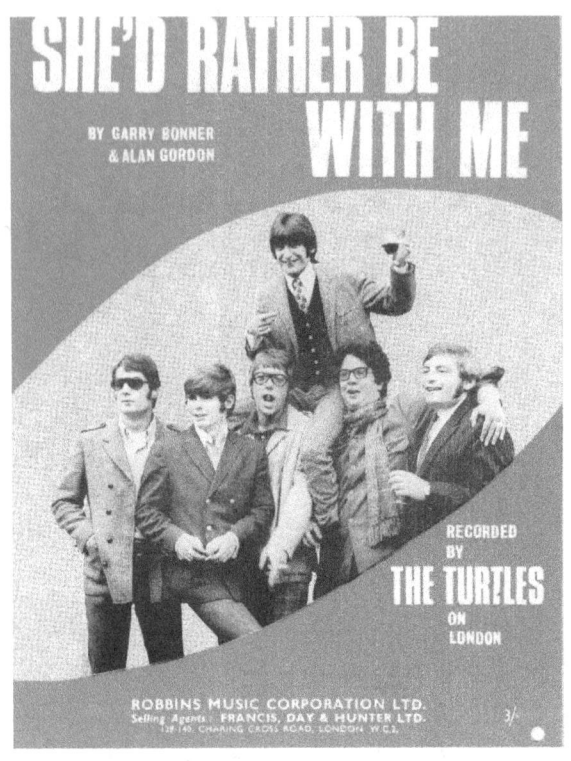

Charles: Nuts is right! These guys jumped at any excuse to sneak in (not so subtle, in this case) sexual humor, and what high-school boy wouldn't love it?! Okay, grown-ups too! If you aren't familiar with the song, just read the title out loud. "Kamanawanalea" = "Come On, I Wanna Lay Her." Not as artsy-fartsy as "In a Gadda Da Vida" being "in the Garden of Eden," but funny and obvious a la Brute Force's "The King of Fuh" on the Apple label. Shout out to Brute Force himself, Stephen Friedland.

—

IF WE ONLY HAD THE TIME (Howard Kaylan, Mark Volman) by The Turtles
Turtles involvement: Howard Kaylan—vocals, occasional percussion, organ; Mark Volman—vocals, percussion, occasional guitars; Al Nichol—vocals, guitars, keyboards, six string bass; Jim Pons—vocals, bass, occasional guitars; John Seiter—vocals, drums, occasional piano
Additional personnel: Jerry Yester—producer; Barry Keene—engineer
Recording dates: 1969 at Sunwest Recording Studios, Hollywood, California; 1970 at Crystal Sound Recording Studios, Hollywood, California
Highest chart position: Did not chart from *Turtle Soup* (CD reissue)
Original release date: June 22, 2016
Significant other versions: Flo & Eddie

Charles: Another one of those charming tempo-twist arrangements that may or may not have originally been multiple songs (bets are on that it was two or three different compositions), there's so much going on that you have to listen two or three times to absorb it all. The highlight might be the falsetto call-back vocals at the beginning after the cool intro.

Mark: The Turtles' version takes a bit too long to get going. This is one of those times where the Flo & Eddie version is better from 1973's *Flo & Eddie*. It was originally recorded during the *Shell Shock* sessions of 1969-70. Like Charles said, it's probably a combination of song fragments as The Turtles attempted to do their own *Abbey Road*-type medley. It even has the same jangly "Baby, You're a Rich Man" guitar sound, so the Beatles inspiration is not missed.

—

INFERNO (Al Nichol) by The Crossfires
Turtles involvement: Mark Volman—alto sax; Howard Kaplan—tenor sax; Al Nichol—lead guitar; Dale Walton—rhythm guitar; Chuck Portz—bass; Don Murray—drums
Additional personnel: Chuck Britz—engineer
Recording dates: 1963
Highest chart position: Did not chart from *Out of Control*
Original release date: 1981

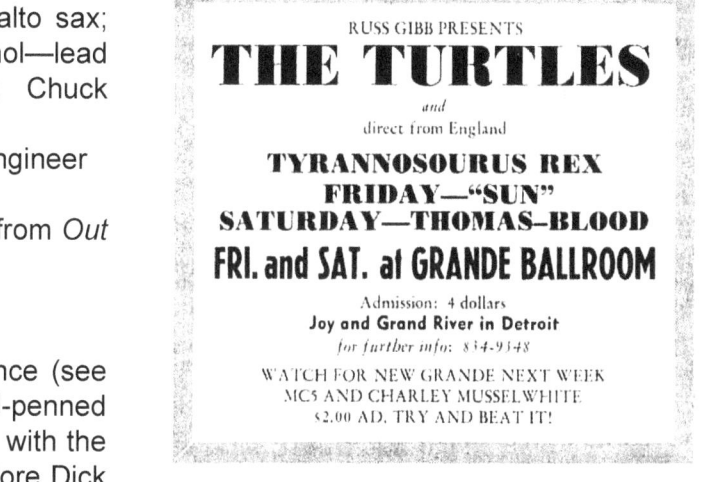

Mark: Another track with a live audience (see "Follow the Rock") and another Al Nichol-penned surf track. This one is heavy on guitars with the saxes coming in for the second half. More Dick Dale-inspired stuff.

Charles: This instrumental is blazing! C'mon it's burning the needle on my record player! I mean, it's scorching! How could anything that musically rides the surf stay this blazing? Okay, I've really gone to hell with the "Inferno" theme, but who could resist? Hottttttttt!

—

INVASION OF THE RHYTHM BUTCHERS (VOLUME 3) (compilation) by The Rhythm Butchers
Turtles involvement: Al Nichol, Jim Pons, Mark Volman—slide guitar, harmony vocals; Howard Kaylan—lead vocals, melodica
Recording dates: Summer 1967 at the Mart Inn, Chicago, Illinois
Highest chart position: Did not chart
Original release date: 1981

Honolulu Lulu
Gimme Some Lovin'
Summertime Blues
April Showers
Sentimental Journey

Hide Your Love Away
Lonely Boy
Butchers in Love
Jailhouse Rock

The Rhythm Butchers are backstage recordings done by The Turtles. To some, they are a gift of unreleased Turtles madness. To others they are just a mess of sounds recorded by the drunk or high Turtles members in their off hours while on tour.

For *Volume 3*, John Barbata and Dave Krambeck bowed out and Howard Kaylan made his Rhythm Butchers debut. Krambeck was said to have crashed out, while Barbata resigned from these after-hours recording sessions; most likely he was finding the accompaniment of a girl much more satisfying. It was unknown at this time, but Barbata's estrangement in this way eventually led to him being replaced by John Seiter.

No one signed copies of this or future Rhythm Butchers Eps, making them instantly collectible.

—

IS IT ANY WONDER? (Howard Kaylan) by The Turtles
Turtles involvement: Mark Volman—vocal harmony, tambourine; Howard Kaylan—lead vocals; Al Nichol—lead guitar, organ, piano, harpsichord, vocals; Jim Tucker—rhythm guitar; Chuck Portz—bass guitar; Don Murray—drums
Additional personnel: Bones Howe—producer, engineer; Armin Steiner, engineer; John Audino, Jules Chaikin, Ray Triscari—trumpets; Bob Edmondson—trombone; Art Pepper, alto sax; Bob Perkins—tenor sax; Bill Holman—tenor sax, horn arrangement
Recording dates: April - September 1966 at Western Recorders, Hollywood, California; March 21, 1967 overdubs at Sound Recorders, Hollywood, California
Highest chart position: Did not chart; #7 from *Golden Hits*
Original release date: October 1967 for album; April 1970 for single

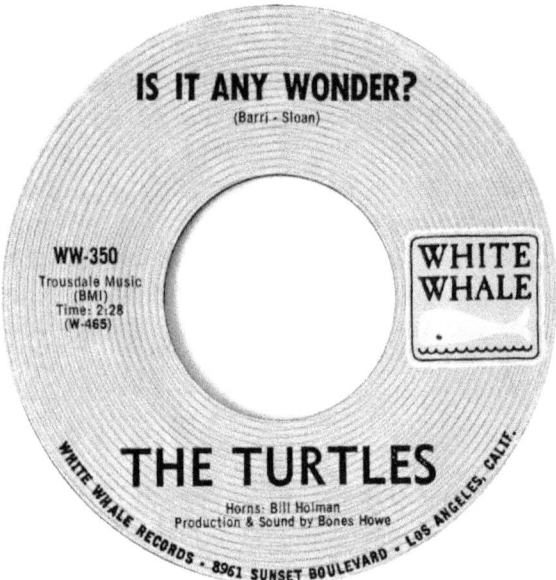

Mark: A really nice track that may have been scheduled for *Happy Together*, but probably didn't fit. The Turtles released it the next chance they got which turned out to be on *Golden Hits*.
Charles: I hear this and I think The Association, but it's pure Turtles. Written by Howard, it boasts a nice, catchy chorus hook. It sounds like it should have been a hit, perhaps it needed a better arrangement.

—

IT AIN'T ME BABE (Bob Dylan) by The Turtles
Turtles involvement: Mark Volman—guitar, tambourine, vocals; Howard Kaylan—keyboards, lead vocals; Al Nichol—lead guitar, keyboards, vocals, bass guitar; Jim Tucker—rhythm guitar, vocals; Chuck Portz—bass guitar, vocals; Don Murray—drums
Additional personnel: Lee Lasseff and Ted Feigin—executive producers; Bones Howe—production, sound, engineering
Recording dates: mid-1965 at Western Recorders, Hollywood, California
Highest chart position: #8 for single; #98 from *It Ain't Me Babe*
Original release date: July 1965 for single; September 1965 for album
Significant other versions: Bob Dylan, Johnny Cash and June Carter, Jan and Dean, Joan Baez, Sebastian Cabot, Nancy Sinatra, Flatt and Scruggs, Johnny Thunders, Silvertide, Davy Jones, Christofer Drew, New Found Glory, Bryan Ferry, Kesha, Adam Harvey and Beccy Cole, Bettye LaVette, Mellisa McClelland and Luke Doucet, Jesse Cook, Flo & Eddie.

Mark: The best part about this great song is the oft-repeated story of when The Turtles met Bob Dylan shortly after their single became a major hit and Dylan in his state suggested that The Turtles should record it, despite the fact that they already had and had a hit with it—a pretty decent one considering that this was their first song out the gate after becoming The Turtles about a week prior.

The capper to the story is from Howard's autobiography where he reveals that he met up with Bob Dylan again years later, and Bob made the exact same suggestion!

There are two stereo versions: the album version and the "(1967 Stereo Mix)" which was released on the 2017 Manifesto *Wooden Head* CD as a bonus track. A 1991 Flo & Eddie live version originally appeared on *The Turtles Featuring Flo & Eddie Captured Live*. Howard sings it in a slightly breathy way at first, but eventually sends it home. He shouts "Bob Dylan folk rock" in the middle.

Charles: The Beatles gave us "Yeah Yeah Yeah" and The Turtles gave us "No No No." Mark V. loves to joke that The Turtles missed being The Beatles by only 4 letters and some 7 billion dollars. But why discuss The Beatles when we have a Bob Dylan composition? Because this recording is good enough to be mentioned in the same breath and paragraph as The Beatles! Sure, it's Zimmerman at his best, but The Turtles improve on it! It's a perfect song in every way: sneaky unassuming British-Invasionish intro, excellent instrumentation, nice "ahhs," a killer chorus, and howzabout Howard as good as he gets. No no no? Yeah yeah yeah!

—

IT AIN'T ME BABE (LP) by The Turtles
Turtles involvement: Mark Volman—guitar, tambourine, vocals; Howard Kaylan—keyboards, lead vocals; Al Nichol—lead guitar, keyboards, vocals, bass guitar; Jim Tucker—rhythm guitar, vocals; Chuck Portz—bass guitar, vocals; Don Murray—drums

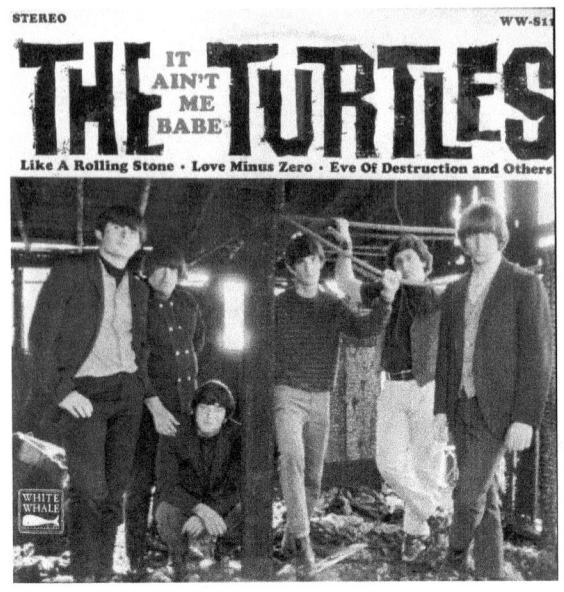

Additional personnel: Lee Lasseff and Ted Feigin—executive producers; Bones Howe—production, sound, engineering
Recording dates: mid-1965 at Western Recorders, Hollywood, California
Highest chart position: #98
Original release date: September 1965
Wanderin' Kind
It Was a Very Good Year
Your Maw Said You Cried
Eve of Destruction
Glitter and Gold
Let Me Be (removed on Sundazed edition)

Let the Cold Winds Blow
It Ain't Me Babe
A Walk in the Sun
Last Laugh
Love Minus Zero

Like a Rolling Stone

Bonus tracks on stereo Sundazed edition:
We'll Meet Again
Grim Reaper of Love
So Goes Love

Bonus tracks on mono Repertoire edition:
We'll Meet Again
Gas Money
Entire album in stereo

Bonus tracks on mono Manifesto edition:
Entire album in stereo

Not a total embarrassment and actually a pretty good effort for The Turtles' debut although there's not really that many protest songs, maybe about half the songs at best. White Whale was pretty generous as they allowed Howard to have four songs for himself, although this may have been more due to them wanting to keep as much publishing money in house and not give so much to the likes of Bob Dylan and P.F. Sloan. Also, because it was their second hit, "Let Me Be" performed double duty as a hit for both of The Turtles' first two albums. As a result, some later editions removed the track off this or off *You Baby* to avoid duplication.

There's not much difference between the mono and stereo versions except the standard way of separation at the time of putting all the vocals on the left channel and the instruments on the right. Unfortunately, some of the instruments get buried in the stereo version, and the stereo version has a lot more echo and reverb!

Amusingly, the album is known as *King Of Folk Rock* in Japan.

—

IT WAS A VERY GOOD YEAR (Ervin Drake) by The Turtles
Turtles involvement: Mark Volman—guitar, tambourine, vocals; Howard Kaylan—keyboards, lead vocals; Al Nichol—lead guitar, keyboards, vocals, bass guitar; Jim Tucker—rhythm guitar, vocals; Chuck Portz—bass guitar, vocals; Don Murray—drums
Additional personnel: Lee Lasseff and Ted Feigin—executive producers; Bones Howe—production, sound, engineering
Recording dates: mid-1965 at Western Recorders, Hollywood, California
Highest chart position: #7 in Canada; No US single release and #98 from *It Ain't Me Babe*
Original release date: September 1965
Significant other versions: Frank Sinatra, The Kingston Trio

Mark: This was always kind of a maudlin tune. At least The Turtles sped it up a bit from the dirge that Frank Sinatra sang. It improves it a little… but not much. It actually was released and performed quite decently as a single in Canada.

Charles: The Turtles do ol' blue eyes. Who woulda thunk it? This is one that The Turtles should have never touched—instead it needed to be an over-the-top, bombastic theatrical recording by Jay & The Americans a la "Some Enchanted Evening." When Sinatra sings it, you feel the pain of a middle-aged man, or a soul in his twilight years recalling better times. When Howard sings it, you just ask "Why?" I guess the answer is "because it charted in Canada." Well, then, who am I to argue? Don't EVER play this for anyone who's a true Sinatra fan. They'll never forgive you, Jack! The year it was recorded, 1965, was a very good year for most music, but clearly not all.

—

***IT'S GARRY SHANDLING'S SHOW* THEME**
(Joey Carbone) by The Turtles
Flo & Eddie involvement: Howard Kaylan—vocals; Mark Volman—vocals
Additional personnel: Garry Shandling—host
Recording dates: 1987
Original release date: February 5, 1988
Significant other versions: many, each episode

Mark: The highly-praised and hysterically funny sitcom from comedian Garry Shandling. The episode entitled "Save the Planet" harks from the series' second season featuring two treats: The Turtles (Flo & Eddie with an unnamed keyboardist and guitarist) perform the theme song to the show and, later, in a flashback bad head trip of Garry's, The Turtles perform a parody of "Elenore." The series later came out on DVD and these clips can be seen on YouTube.
Charles: You expect me to say anything bad about Garry Shandling? No way. Not a chance. The show was brilliant. The song was brilliant. This review is brilliant.

—

JOHN AND JULIE (The Turtles) by The Turtles
Turtles involvement: Mark Volman—vocals, percussion, occasional guitars; Howard Kaylan—vocals, occasional percussion, organ; Al Nichol—lead vocal, guitars, keyboards, six string bass; Jim Pons—vocals, bass, occasional guitars; John Seiter—vocals, drums, occasional piano
Additional personnel: Ray Davies—producer; Chuck Britz—engineer
Recording dates: April - July 1969 at United Records, Hollywood, California
Highest chart position: #117 from *Turtle Soup*
Original release date: October 1969

Mark: Al Nichol sings lead here. When Manifesto remastered these tracks in 2016, I noticed a distinct lisp in Nichol's voice for the first time. No wonder he rarely sang lead, but he does have a nice choir voice with vibrato if you ever wanted to know what he sounded like besides playing a

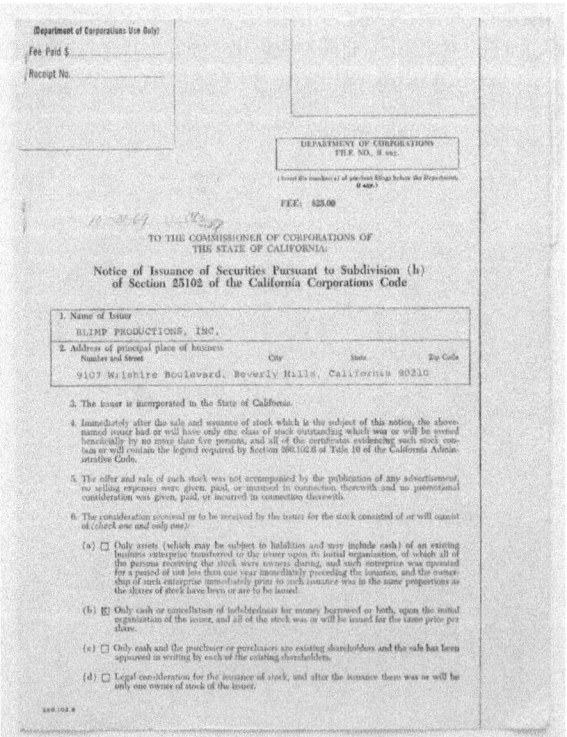

chunky type of surf guitar. As for the song itself, it gets a bit syrupy here and there with a bit too many strings.

Charles: Ray Davies was involved in this, but it sure doesn't sound like The Kinks. There's a nice string arrangement that brings to mind George Martin's symphonic contributions. My co-author points out the lisp in Al Nichol's vocal, but it's odd that it's only apparent on the word "miss"—unless it's intentionally pronounced that way as in "myth." An interesting composition that's both haunting and somber.

—

JUST A ROOM (Steve Duboff, Artie Kornfeld) by The Turtles
Turtles involvement: Mark Volman—vocal harmony, tambourine; Howard Kaylan—lead vocals; Al Nichol—vocal harmony, lead guitar, organ; Jim Tucker—rhythm guitar; Chuck Portz—bass guitar; Don Murray—drums
Additional personnel: Lee Lasseff and Ted Feigin—executive producers; Bones Howe—production, sound, engineering; Dwight Tunji Trio (Howe, Feigin & Lasseff)—percussion, special effects
Recording dates: October 1965 - January 1966 at Western Recorders, Hollywood, California
Highest chart position: Did not chart from *You Baby*
Original release date: April 1966

Mark: As I said on "Glitter and Gold," it sounds like this song. It's probably just a coincidence. In any case, it's a great earworm, and every time I hear it, I seem to be singing it to myself for days or weeks afterwards. It's kind of The Turtles' version of The Beach Boys' "In My Room" or The Beatles' "In My Life." Something like that.

Charles: To anyone else, "Just a Room" may be just a song, but it's actually a well-textured folk-pop recording. "It's everything beautiful in this world" would be an exaggeration, but the vocals build nicely, and the stereo version really accentuates the layers. One of the songwriters, Artie Kornfield, is better known as the music promoter for the historic original Woodstock Music festival held in 1969. He wrote many hits, including "Pied Piper" (which The Turtles and Flo & Eddie performed live) and one of the great pop songs of all time, The Cowsills' classic, "The Rain, the Park and Other Things."

JUSTINE (Don "Sugarcane" Harris, Dewey Terry) by The Crossfires
Turtles involvement: Mark Volman—alto sax, vocals; Howard Kaplan—tenor sax, lead vocals; Al Nichol—lead guitar, background vocals; Dale Walton—rhythm guitar; Chuck Portz—bass; Don Murrray—drums
Additional personnel: Chuck Britz—engineer
Recording dates: 1963
Highest chart position: Did not chart from *Out of Control*
Original release date: 1981
Significant other versions: The Ron Felton Four, Don and Dewey, Bob Dylan and Tom Petty

Mark: "What IS he saying?" as Augie Ben Doggie might say in *Hardware Wars*. In a hot, sweaty nightclub it probably didn't matter what Howard was singing. He could just ramble off gibberish while the rest of The Crossfires shout "WOOOHHH!!!" periodically. Of course, the lyrics aren't much anyway, as "Justine Justine Justine" is repeated mercilessly and with great vigor. Amazingly this shows that The Crossfires could COMPOSE better stuff than this right from the start, and did!

Charles: A hyper dance-fest with manic vocals, this plays along with "Chunky" and sounds like a Chuck Berry or Little Richard raver. Think "The Peppermint Twist" mixed with "Too Much Monkey Business," but on steroids!

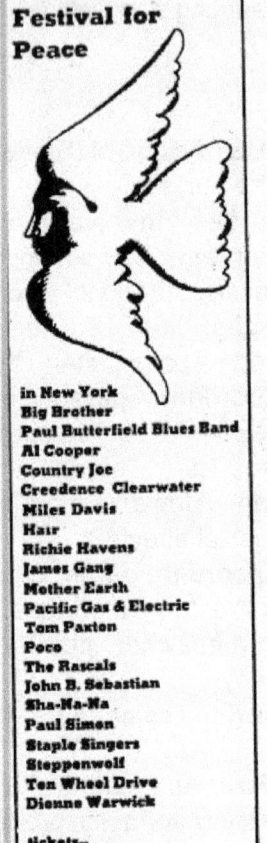

LADY-O (Judee Sill) by The Turtles
Turtles involvement: Howard Kaylan—vocals, occasional percussion, organ; Mark Volman—vocals, percussion, occasional guitars; Al Nichol—vocals, guitars, keyboards, six string bass; Jim Pons—vocals, bass, occasional guitars; John Seiter—vocals, drums, occasional piano
Additional personnel: Bob Harris, John Beck, Jim Pons—producers; Henry Lewy—engineer; Judee Sill—acoustic guitar; Bob Harris—piano, string arrangement; Bonnie Douglas, Paul Shure—violin; Allan Harsdhman—viola; Douglas Davis—cello

Recording dates: October 1969 at A&M Recording Studios, Hollywood, California
Highest chart position: #78 for single; #146 from *More Golden Hits*
Original release date: November 1969 for single; March 1970 for album
Significant other versions: Judee Sill

Mark: This is the song that Mark and Howard like to say in Turtles lore as to be their last, recorded and released as sort of an olive branch in 1969 as the lawsuits and bad blood between The Turtles and White Whale Records kept piling up. This makes for a good story, but is patently untrue as The Turtles kept plugging away at recording songs for *Shell Shock* well into 1970, and possibly may have continued had Frank Zappa not intervened. It tidies up a saga that went out with a whimper instead of a bang. Perhaps they were thinking this was truly their last as it was the last song they performed on "The Barbara McNair Show" in April 1970, their last television appearance.

As for the song itself, it's very nice and has a sweet music video of the band on horses, despite the fact that they were stoned out of their minds. I don't know if it's hit single material, but it was a nice note to go out with, even though there were more releases to come. It would have ended up on *Shell Shock*, too, had it been completed and released.

Charles: Everything about this recording begs comparisons to Eric Carmen/The Raspberries. Somebody please play this for Eric and he'll probably agree. The vocal is both sad and winsome at the same time, and even gets better with the textured vocals and harmonies, but it's not as sad as the story behind the composer. Judee Sill was described as an idiosyncratic folk singer who recorded two classic albums before "falling prey to addiction and tragedy." Influenced by Bach (especially his suites), she lyrically drew substantially from Christian themes of rapture and redemption. Sill died of a drug overdose in 1979, which makes The Turtles' rendition of her song even more poignant. There's a clip of her performing the song live at the Boston Music Hall, where she calls the composition "slow and unromantic" before sending out a shout-out to The Turtles for recording her song and "giving me some money for it."

—

LAST LAUGH (Howard Kaylan, Nita Garfield) by The Turtles
Turtles involvement: Mark Volman—guitar, tambourine, vocals; Howard Kaylan—keyboards, lead vocals; Al Nichol—lead guitar, vocals, bass guitar; Jim Tucker—rhythm guitar, vocals; Chuck Portz—bass guitar, vocals; Don Murray—drums
Additional personnel: Lee Lasseff and Ted Feigin—executive producers; Bones Howe—production, sound, engineering
Recording dates: mid-1965 at Western Recorders, Hollywood, California
Highest chart position: #98 from *It Ain't Me Babe*
Original release date: September 1965

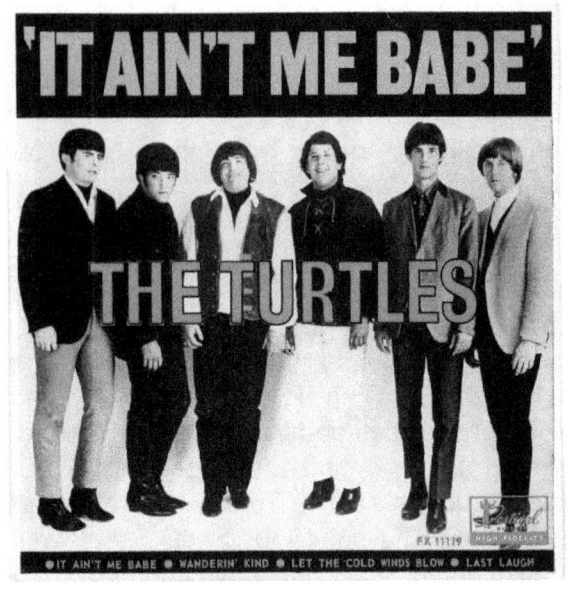

Mark: Nita Garfield was Howard Kaylan's girlfriend at the time, and co-wrote this song with him. Finally, a little bit of different instrumentation with some harpsichord from all of the other basic drums and guitar songs on the album. It almost sounds like a song that could have landed on the *Happy Together* album had it not ended up here.

It's also another song that clocks in under two minutes. "Let's get this album done quickly boys and get it into the shops!"

Charles: Nice instrumentation and a shot of rapid-fire tongue-twistin' lyrical alliteration ("he who laughs last laughs best...") make this one a stand-out. Play the stereo separation on both channels so you hear the clarity and strength of Kaylan's delivery on one side, and the nice mix of instruments on the other. Admittedly, the parts are probably better than the whole, but it's still a solid recording.

—

LAST THING I REMEMBER, THE aka THE LAST THING I REMEMBER (THE FIRST THING I KNEW) (Jim Pons) by The Atomic Enchilada
Turtles involvement: Mark Volman—vocals, special effects; Howard Kaylan—lead vocal; Al Nichol—guitars, organ, piano, Moog synthesizer, vocals; Jim Pons—bass, lead vocal; John Barbata—drums, percussion, vocals
Additional personnel: The Turtles—producers for demo; Chip Douglas—producer: various—engineers for demo; Jim Hilton, Armin Steiner—engineers
Recording dates: February 1968 at Ter-Mar Recording Studios, Chicago, Illinois; Olmsted Sound Studios, New York, New York; Sound Recorders, Hollywood, California; Mixed September 1978 by H, Lee Wolen and Jim Rayton at Ascot Recorders for demo, May - June 1968 at Gold Star Studios, Hollywood, California; Western Recorders, Hollywood, California; T.T.G./Sunset-Highland Recording Studios, Hollywood, California;
Highest chart position: #128 from *The Turtles Present the Battle of the Bands*
Original release date: November 1, 1968

Mark: The demo version has the full title of "The Last Thing I Remember (the First Thing I Knew)" and was attempted at the same time when The Turtles were recording "The Owl" and "To See the Sun" before White Whale put the kibosh on The Turtles producing their own records, and brought back Chip Douglas. I tend to prefer the demo version, but both are great *Sgt. Pepper*-inspired psychedelia with great harmonies and other little sound goodies just swirling around everywhere. The demo version just needed a few more special effects to jazz it up a little bit, not a complete re-recording, but the final version is fine, too.

Charles: Is that an actual harp opening? Just when we think it's a Beach Boys-inspired experimental recording, it becomes an all-out Lennon-ish psychedelic tour de force. This sounds like something that could have been on the *White Album* or one of the later Beatles Christmas message records (or flexis, that is), sans the Christmas motif.

—

LEGENDARY RHYTHM BUTCHERS SAMPLER, THE (compilation) by The Rhythm Butchers
Turtles involvement: Mark Volman, Howard Kaylan, Jim Pons—vocals
Recording dates: 1965 - 1973
Highest chart position: Did not chart
Original release date: 1978

The Butchers Are Back (from Volume 9)
Butchers Breakdown (from Volume 10)
Endless Sleep (from Volume 10)
Misty (from Volume 8)

Venus/Blue Moon—Medley (from Volume 3)
Exodus (from Volume 1)
The Impossible Dream (from Volume 11)
Running Scared (from Volume 6)

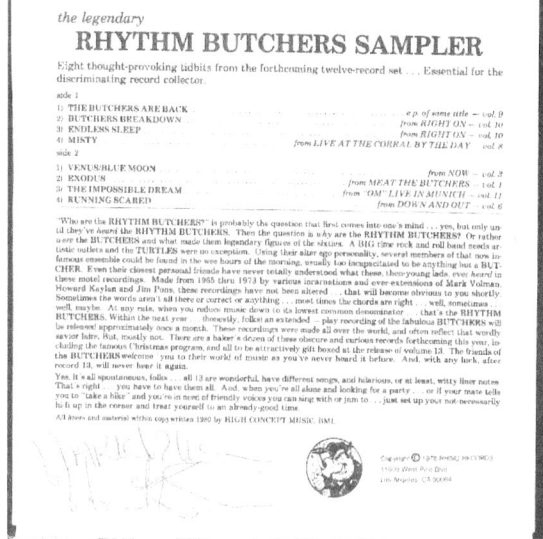

The Rhythm Butchers are backstage recordings done by The Turtles. To some, they are a gift of unreleased Turtles madness. To others they are just a mess of sounds recorded by probable intoxicated Turtles members in their off hours while on tour.

On this sampler, Mark and Howard explain that there were to be 13 EPs issued of these not in demand collections. As such, only seven (plus this sampler) have made it out to date, making this sampler essential as it has tracks that were to be from the still unreleased Volumes 8-11. If it were The Beatles, everyone would be clamoring for this stuff. I, for one, would like a proper album set compiling all of it together.

Mark and Howard also signed the sleeves of this *Sampler*, making it instantly collectible (ha!). As the sound quality, performances, and availability of these songs are marginal at best, none of the Rhythm Butchers tracks are listed individually, unless The Turtles made a proper recording of it later.

A short excerpt of "The Butchers Are Back" appears on *The History of Flo & Eddie and The Turtles* as part of "Medley #1."

—

LET ME BE (P.F. Sloan) by The Turtles
Turtles involvement: Mark Volman—guitar, tambourine, vocals; Howard Kaylan—keyboards, lead vocals; Al Nichol—lead guitar, keyboards, vocals, bass guitar; Jim Tucker—rhythm guitar, vocals; Chuck Portz—bass guitar, vocals; Don Murray—drums
Additional personnel: Lee Lasseff and Ted Feigin—executive producers; Bones Howe—production, sound, engineering
Recording dates: mid-1965 at Western Recorders, Hollywood, California
Highest chart position: #29 as single; #98 from *It Ain't Me Babe* and did not chart from *You Baby*
Original release date: September 1965
Significant other versions: Flo & Eddie

Charles: Although it wasn't written by Bob Dylan, "Let Me Be" sounds like it's the son of "It Ain't Me Babe." I usually contend that The Turtles rarely repeated themselves, and presented so many different styles, but most of the time when an act's songs sound similar, they're penned by the same songwriter(s). This P.F. Sloan composition sounds nothing like his most famous hit, "Eve of Destruction." It's pure pop-rock Turtles with a touch of folk and a nice dose of The Byrds. This should've charted higher, though it did crack the Top 30. Howard's vocals soar as always, and the chorus hooks you right in, as it's supposed to… and that's all I (it) ever can be."

Mark: I totally agree with Charles on this one. It does sound like "Son of It Ain't Me Babe," and perhaps that was the point. Howard really belts it out here and really shows off his range as a singer. It appears on both of The Turtles' first two albums. I feel cheated. There are two stereo versions: the album version and the "(1967 Stereo Mix)" which was released on the 2017 Manifesto *Wooden Head* CD as a bonus track.

Flo & Eddie sang a 1991 live version that appeared on *The Turtles Featuring Flo & Eddie Captured Live*. They kind of mangle the ending on that one.

—

LET THE COLD WINDS BLOW (Howard Kaylan) by The Turtles
Turtles involvement: Mark Volman—guitar, tambourine, vocals; Howard Kaylan—keyboards, lead vocals; Al Nichol—lead guitar, keyboards, vocals, bass guitar; Jim Tucker—rhythm guitar, vocals; Chuck Portz—bass guitar, vocals; Don Murray—drums
Additional personnel: Lee Lasseff and Ted Feigin—executive producers; Bones Howe—production, sound, engineering
Recording dates: mid-1965 at Western Recorders, Hollywood, California

Highest chart position: B-side of "It Was a Very Good Year" in Canada; #98 from *It Ain't Me Babe*
Original release date: September 1965
Significant other versions: The Crosswind Singers

Mark: Here is Howard's sole attempt to really compose something as meaty as the other protest singers featured on the album (like Dylan and Sloan), and he succeeds quite well. It's a nice upbeat number that also has bite.
Charles: This song ROCKS! Maybe the Canadians bought the "It Was a Very Good Year" single because this was the B-side! How did the DJs not flip it over and make this a hit?! It's an anti-war, protest ode disguised as a groovin' rocker. Bravo HK for your contribution to the genre, in music, vocals, and lyrics.

—

LIKE A ROLLING STONE (Bob Dylan) by The Turtles
Turtles involvement: Mark Volman—guitar, tambourine, vocals; Howard Kaylan—keyboards, lead vocals; Al Nichol—lead guitar, keyboards, vocals, bass guitar; Jim Tucker—rhythm guitar, vocals; Chuck Portz—bass guitar, vocals; Don Murray—drums
Additional personnel: Lee Lasseff and Ted Feigin—executive producers; Bones Howe—production, sound, engineering
Recording dates: mid-1965 at Western Recorders, Hollywood, California
Highest chart position: #98 from *It Ain't Me Babe*
Original release date: September 1965
Significant other versions: Bob Dylan, David Bowie (with Mick Ronson), The Four Seasons, Sixto Rodriguez, The Young Rascals, Judy Collins, Johnny Winter, Rotary Connection, Cher, Anberlin, Spirit, Michael Bolton, The Creation, David Gilmour, The Surfaris, Al Stewart, John Mellencamp, The Wailers, Green Day, DIIV, Sebastian Cabot, Bachman and Cummings, The Rolling Stones, The Jimi Hendrix Experience, Hugues Aufray, Wolfgang Ambros, BAP, Lars Winnerbäck, Articolo 31

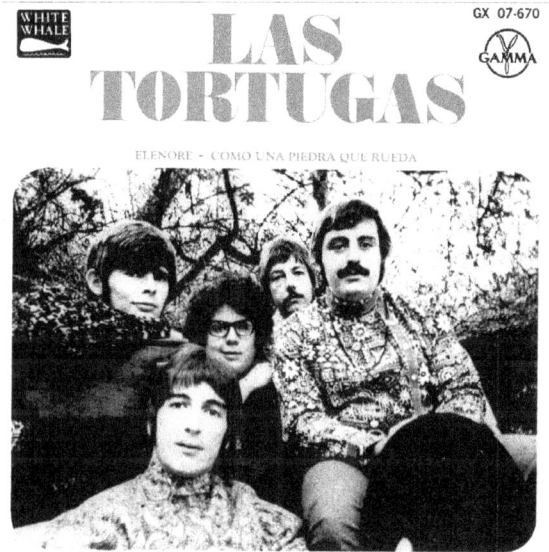

Mark: EVERYONE has done this song, including The Rolling Stones! When The Turtles did it, not as many had covered it, so it seemed much more fresh. At least Howard sang it with a little more anger than he did on "Love Minus Zero," so it comes off as a little more authentic as a protest song replete with the requisite harmonica.
Charles: Kaylan sings it better than Dylan, but then again so does everyone who ever covered this classic. Having said that, it lacks Bob's gut-wrenching pain and nuances. Sung live, you never understand Dylan's vocals (except, possibly, on David Letterman's anniversary show at Radio City Music Hall—where I was in the audience), but you still always get the feeling. And you know there's meaning and history in Dylan's version. If Dylan's original recorded rendition is the barometer to which to measure this, and if Dylan's is a 10, most others are under a 5 or 6, so

let's give this a 7 or 8 (an 8 because of the added harmonica).

—

LIKE IT OR NOT (Garry Bonner, Alan Gordon) by The Turtles
Turtles involvement: Howard Kaylan—vocals, occasional percussion, organ; Mark Volman—vocals, percussion, occasional guitars; Al Nichol—vocals, guitars, keyboards, six string bass; Jim Pons—vocals, bass, occasional guitars; John Seiter—vocals, drums, occasional piano
Additional personnel: Jerry Yester—producer; Barry Keene—engineer
Recording dates: 1969 at Sunwest Recording Studios, Hollywood, California; 1970 at Crystal Sound Recording Studios, Hollywood, California
Highest chart position: #194 from *Happy Together Again!*
Original release date: November 1974

Mark: A pretty decent song from the aborted *Shell Shock* sessions, but it does seem somewhat unfinished, and probably is. Mark and Howard apparently liked it enough to include it in the first Turtles compilation they were in control of in 1974.
Charles: Well, "like it or not," it's very musical with a decent build-up, a pleasing longer run-out, and some interesting vocals. The falsetto vocals keep it from completely sounding Beatle-ish, but the traces are there, as well as similarities to The Bee Gees and Marmalade (you don't get that comparison much, do you?).

—

LIKE THE SEASONS (Lyme aka Warren Zevon) by The Turtles
Turtles involvement: Mark Volman—harmony and backing vocals; Howard Kaylan—lead and backing vocals; Al Nichol – lead guitar, piano, backing vocals; Jim Tucker—rhythm guitar, backing vocals; Chuck Portz—bass
Additional personnel: Bones Howe—producer; Bones Howe, Armin Steiner, Bruce Botnick—engineers; Warren Zevon—guitar; Leonard Malarsky—violin; Jesse Ehrlich, Joseph Saxon—cellos; Bob Thompson—string arrangement; Hal Blaine—drums
Recording dates: January - June 1966 at Western Recorders, Hollywood, California

Highest chart position: Single did not chart; B-side of "Can I Get to Know You Better?" and "Happy Together;" #25 from *Happy Together*
Original release date: October 1966 for single; April 29, 1967 for album

Mark: Zevon wrote this under the pseudonym "Lyme." Why, I don't know, but the late Zevon always struck me as a very strange and eccentric, though also highly creative, person, as is this song.

Charles: Warren Zevon wrote this stark and poetic and way-too-short (under two minutes) love song. If you only know Zevon from "Werewolves of London," you'll delight in this lovely composition. Understated, it's another wonderful showcase of Kaylan's tender side. A pure folk rock ballad. Sad and succinct and beautiful. There's a clip of them performing it (lip-syncing) with one of the guys acting as a symphony conductor. It's on one of the episodes of the 1967 show "Shebang," hosted by Casey Kasem. Is the name "Shebang" still politically correct? Never mind, I digress.

"Shebang" was a music and dance TV show hosted by Kasem, and broadcast from Hollywood, CA. It aired on the west coast on KTLA-TV from 1965 to 1968 and was produced by (who else?) Dick Clark. Dick hired Casey, who before that was a DJ on the Top 10 AM radio station KRLA (in L.A.). It was the California version of "American Bandstand." In any case, Casey Kasem described this song as being "baroque," so what do I know?

—

LIL' BIT OF GOLD (compilation) by The Turtles
Turtles involvement: See individual Turtles tracks
Additional personnel: See individual Turtles tracks
Recording dates: 1965 - 1967
Highest chart position: Did not chart
Original release date: 1988

Happy Together
You Baby
She'd Rather Be With Me
It Ain't Me Babe

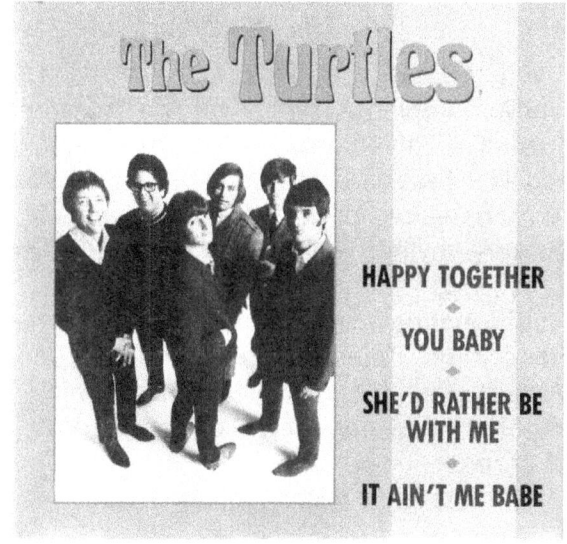

A 3" CD (remember those?). This and the *Volume 2* EP were a novelty by Rhino in the early days of compact discs. These were designed to replace the 7" vinyl single which the record labels were really anxiously wanting to discontinue by the late 1980s and succeeded by 1990. Vinyl has made somewhat of a comeback by the 2020s, but the 7" single, not so much. This covers The Turtles' biggest hits of their first two years.

—

LIL' BIT OF GOLD, VOLUME 2 (compilation) by The Turtles
Turtles involvement: See individual Turtles tracks
Additional personnel: See individual Turtles tracks
Recording dates: 1966 - 1968
Highest chart position: Did not chart
Original release date: 1988

Let Me Be
You Showed Me
She's My Girl
Elenore

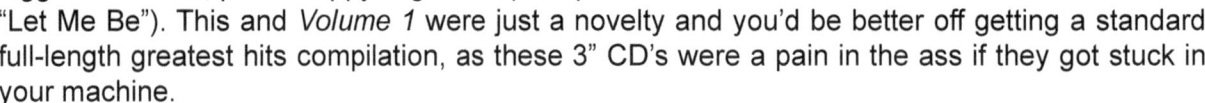

Another 3" CD. This one covers The Turtles' biggest later hits, post-"Happy Together" (except "Let Me Be"). This and *Volume 1* were just a novelty and you'd be better off getting a standard full-length greatest hits compilation, as these 3" CD's were a pain in the ass if they got stuck in your machine.

—

LIVIN' DOLL aka **SANTA'S LIVING DOLL** (Howard Kaplan, Al Nichol) by The Crossfires
Turtles involvement: Mark Volman—alto sax, vocals; Howard Kaplan—tenor sax, lead vocals; Al Nichol—lead guitar, background vocals; Tim Tucker—rhythm guitar; Chuck Portz—bass; Terry Hand—drums
Additional personnel: Chuck Britz—engineer
Recording dates: November 23, 1964 at Western Recorders, Hollywood, California
Highest chart position: Did not chart from *Out of Control*
Original release date: 1981

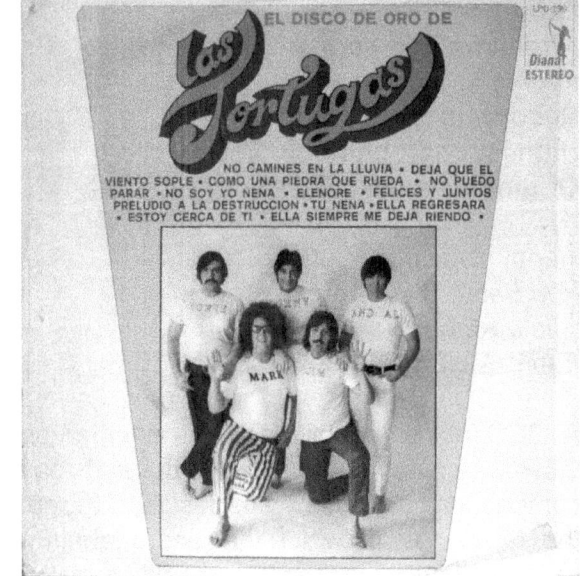

Mark: This was supposed to be a single release backed with "Santa and the Sidewalk Surfer." It's a cute little Christmas-themed song and would probably have been a hit for The Turtles. I'm wondering if this song was once again inspired by television as the Bob Cummings/Julie Newmar sitcom "My Living Doll" debuted on September 27, 1964, plenty of time for Al and Howard to be inspired to write this Christmas ditty about wishing to get their own Julie Newmar.

Charles: A cymbal-tapping intro and quick taste of "Jingle Bells" establish this as a Christmas song, even before Howard starts singing about wanting Santa to bring him a "Livin' Doll" for the holidays. Please—no jokes about a doll (living or otherwise) under the tree.

LOVE IN THE CITY (The Turtles) by The Turtles
Turtles involvement: Mark Volman—vocals, percussion, occasional guitars, congas; Howard Kaylan—lead vocal, occasional percussion, organ; Al Nichol—vocals, guitars, keyboards, six string bass; Jim Pons—vocals, bass, occasional guitars; John Seiter—vocals, drums, occasional piano
Additional personnel: Ray Davies—producer; Chuck Britz—engineer; Bud Brisbois, Roy Caton, Ollie Mitchell—trumpets; William Henshaw, Henry Sigismonti—French horns; Richard Leith, Lew McCreary, Thomas Shepard—trombones; Bobby Bruce, John DeVoogdt, Leonard Malarsky, Nick Pisani, George Poole, Paul Shure, Walter Wiemeyer, Tibor Selig—violins; Gareth Nuttycombe, Darrel Terwilliger—violas; Ray Kelley, Joseph Saxon—cellos; Ray Pohlman—horn and string arrangements

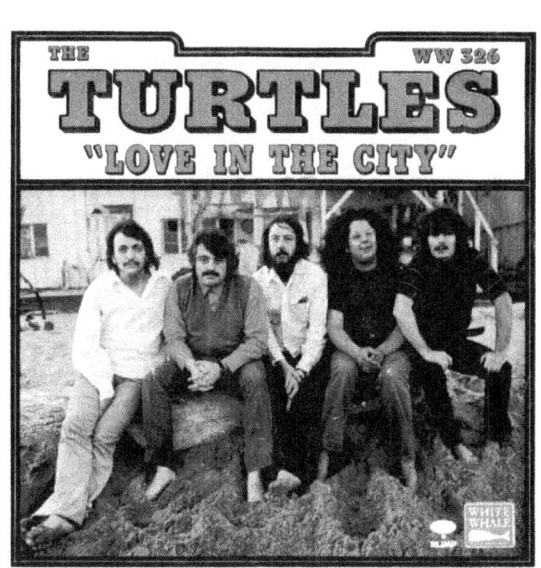

Recording dates: April - July 1969 at United Records, Hollywood, California
Highest chart position: #91 for single; #117 from *Turtle Soup*
Original release date: September 1969 for single; October 1969 for album

Mark: Like I said in my comments for "House on the Hill," this song would have made it to the Top 10 if The Turtles somehow miraculously and successfully signed with RCA Records for this album. What always impressed me and frustrated me with this track is how I was never able to sing the high notes of "in the city," even back when I was a teenager. Now, as I'm in my 50s, forget it. The Westchester High School A Capella Choir singers put their outstanding vocal chops to full three or four octave range use, and pull it off well! Jealous! As a result, I sing "in the city" about two octaves lower than they sing it, but Jim Pons I'm not, either.
Charles: Not much to write about here, except the classy "Love is Blue"-ish interlude about a minute into it. Credited to the whole band, we have no one person to blame. Not Howard's greatest vocal, and not a very cohesive arrangement. So many Turtles songs seem to be too short, but unfortunately this one goes on far too long. By the way, Mark, I can hit the high notes with ease. Sometimes I even add a higher harmony.

—

LOVE MINUS ZERO aka **LOVE MINUS ZERO/NO LIMIT** (Bob Dylan) by The Turtles
Turtles involvement: Mark Volman—guitar, tambourine, vocals; Howard Kaylan—keyboards, lead vocals; Al Nichol—lead guitar, vocals, bass guitar; Jim Tucker—rhythm guitar, vocals; Chuck Portz—bass guitar, vocals; Don Murray—drums
Additional personnel: Lee Lasseff and Ted Feigin—executive producers; Bones Howe—production, sound, engineering
Recording dates: mid-1965 at Western Recorders, Hollywood, California
Highest chart position: #98 from *It Ain't Me Babe*

Original release date: September 1965
Significant other versions: Bob Dylan, Ricky Nelson, Buck Owens, Joan Baez, Judy Collins, Fleetwood Mac, Rod Stewart, Eric Clapton, The Walker Brothers, The Leaves, Turley Richards

Mark: Since The Turtles had a hit with "It Ain't Me Babe," the logic was that they should cover more of Mr. Dylan's compositions. Unfortunately, where "It Ain't Me Babe" has the proper type of angst and anger necessary for someone to be treated seriously as a folk rock group singing protest songs, this cover comes across as protesting as a typical Beach Boys song. The lyrics are there, but the performance is all "oohs and ahhs" harmonies. It once again was a portent of things to come for this band as the folk rock bit was soon dropped in favor of a more pop rock vein.

Charles: With the success of their cover of his "It Ain't Me Babe," it's logical to have a go at another fairly commercial Dylan recording. The Turtles weren't the only ones, as this was also put on vinyl by the likes of Rod Stewart, Jackson Browne, Judy Collins, Fleetwood Mac, and Ricky Nelson, to name a few. Most versions are more polished than the songwriter's version, but The Turtles' version is fairly faithful to the original, sans the harmonica bit. It even has a Searchers or Byrds flavor. It's so beloved by so many artists, and it's been recorded so many times, so why hasn't it ever been a huge hit for anyone? What is missing, and this is simple, is a chorus/hook. There's no "No No No."

—

LOVE SONGS (compilation) by The Turtles
Turtles involvement: See individual Turtles tracks
Additional personnel: See individual Turtles tracks
Recording dates: 1965 - 1970
Highest chart position: Did not chart
Original release date: 1995

Happy Together
Elenore
So Goes Love
Me About You
Love in the City
You Showed Me
You Don't Have to Walk in the Rain
Is It Any Wonder?
Lady-O
There You Sit Lonely

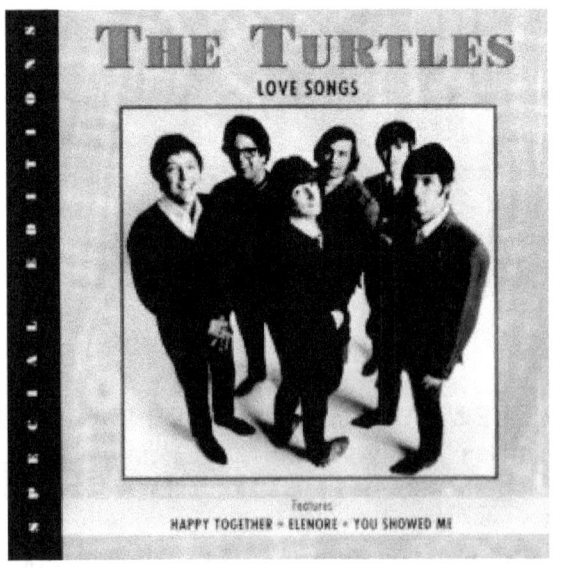

Strictly a quickie cash-in for Rhino, which is rather disappointing as the CD only has 10 tracks and could have fit about 20 more. I suppose the thought was that Capitol Records did a Beatles *Love Songs* collection in 1977, so why not do a Turtles one? The paltry results speak for themselves. Get a more robust Turtles compilation unless you are a completist.

—

MAKIN' MY MIND UP aka **MAKING MY MIND UP** (Jack Dalton, Gary Montgomery) by The Turtles
Turtles involvement: Mark Volman—harmony and backing vocals; Howard Kaylan—lead and backing vocals; Al Nichol—lead guitar, piano, backing vocals; Jim Tucker—rhythm guitar, backing vocals
Additional personnel: Bones Howe—producer; Bones Howe, Armin Steiner, Bruce Botnick—engineers; Larry Knechtel—bass; Hal Blaine—drums; John Audino, Jules Chaikin, Ray Triscari—trumpets; Bob Edmondson—trombone; Art Pepper—alto sax; Bill Perkins—tenor sax; Bill Holman—tenor sax, horn arrangement
Recording dates: January - June 1966 at Western Recorders, Hollywood, California; February - March 21, 1967 for overdubs at Sound Recorders, Hollywood, California
Highest chart position: Single did not chart; #25 from *Happy Together*
Original release date: July 1966 for single; April 29, 1967 for album

Mark: The original version sans horns was issued in 1966 as a regional single. The Turtles were annoyed that White Whale rush-released it without the horns, so White Whale pulled it back. Overdubs to correct the missing horniness occurred in 1967 and the result was released on *Happy Together*. As a result, there are actually four versions of this song: the original mono single without horns, the mono and stereo album cut with horns, and finally the "(1966 Version Stereo)" which wasn't officially released until the 2016 Manifesto CD of *Wooden Head* as a bonus track.

Do I like it? Yes, I do. Another fine Turtles production, and yes, I prefer the version with horns like it was supposed to be.

Charles: You can just picture this playing while the band is running around down Carnaby Street in London or the back streets of San Francisco. The credits don't list any horns, but it sure sounds like a brass instrument carrying this one along. Then again, there are multiple mixes, so this must be the hornier one. It's clearly a happy-go-lucky song that typifies the era.

—

MARMENDY MILL (Howard Kaylan, Mark Volman) by The Turtles
Turtles involvement: Howard Kaylan—vocals, occasional percussion, organ; Mark Volman—vocals, percussion, occasional guitars; Al Nichol—vocals, guitars, keyboards, six string bass; Jim Pons—vocals, bass, occasional guitars; John Seiter—vocals, drums, occasional piano

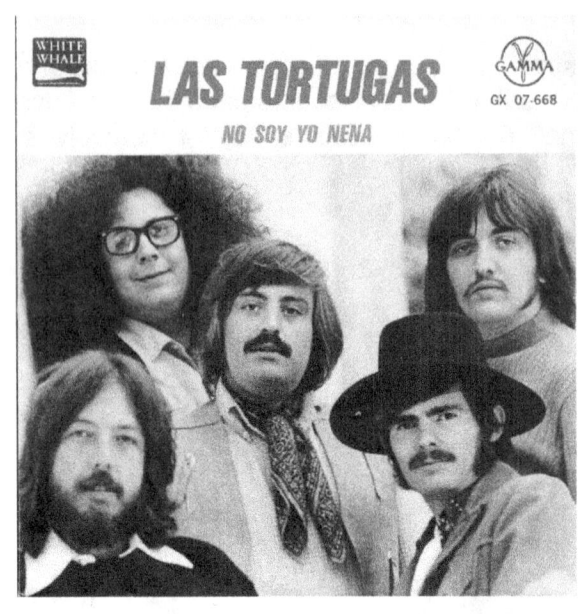

Additional personnel: Jerry Yester—producer; Barry Keene—engineer
Recording dates: 1969 at Sunwest Recording Studios, Hollywood, California
Highest chart position: Did not chart from *Solid Zinc: The Turtles Anthology*
Original release date: February 16, 2002
Significant other versions: Flo & Eddie

Mark: This is a really nice demo that finally saw the realized complete version on 1973's *Flo & Eddie* album. Had it been completed in 1970, it would have been an excellent album closer for *Shell Shock*. This demo version sat in the can until 2002. It should have been released much sooner and makes me wonder what still lurks in the vaults that we don't know about. We need Andrew Sandoval to do a Monkees-type release program. He's done very well so far, and it may be the case that there isn't much left in the vaults, but if there is, let it out! I know it's all up to Mark and Howard and they probably don't want each and every Turtles scrap out, but I can dream, can't I?

Charles: It's apparent from the longer (nearly two-minute), mature and classy—if not classical—instrumental intro that this one is going to be epic. It goes on its tangents, and manages to exude appropriate silliness both vocally and lyrically, but it reels itself in, perhaps reminiscent of The Raspberries' "I Can Remember" or The Monkees' "Shorty Blackwell," but not nearly as anthemic as Aerosmith's "Dream On" or Queen's "Bohemian Rhapsody." It's certainly adventurous and courageous, and foreshadows future Flo & Eddie recordings. Ultimately, it finds a way to come full circle with an ending that perfectly bookends the beginning.

—

ME ABOUT YOU (Garry Bonner, Alan Gordon) by The Turtles
Turtles involvement: Mark Volman—harmony and backing vocals; Howard Kaylan—lead and backing vocals; Al Nichol—lead guitar, piano, backing vocals; Jim Tucker—rhythm guitar, backing vocals; Jim Pons—bass, backing vocals; John Barbata—drums
Additional personnel: Joe Wissert—producer; Bones Howe, Armin Steiner, Bruce Botnick—engineers; Lynn Blessing—vibes; Jerry Yester—horn and string arrangements
Recording dates: December 1966 - April 1967 at Sunset Sound Recorders, Hollywood, California
Highest chart position: #105 for single; #25 from *Happy Together*
Original release date: April 29, 1967 for album; October 1970 for single

Significant other versions: The Lovin' Spoonful, The Mojo Men, Jackie DeShannon, Eric & Errol's, Garry Bonner

Mark: A much different sounding anthemic type song from Mr. Bonner and Mr. Gordon. It shows how versatile they actually were as songwriters, and very underrated, since everyone seems to remember them for "Happy Together" and the similar-sounding "She'd Rather Be with Me." I like it a lot!

Charles: How could this not have charted higher? Great vocals, strong chorus, sweet intro, driving up-front drums, and even a mellotron. What more could you want in a pop rock song? This is vintage Turtles, and ranks up there with the best of 'em. Did Natasha Bedingfield hear this somewhere in her subconscious before she came up with the hook in her hit "Pocketful of Sunshine"? Probably not, but this song is certainly more than a pocketful of musical sunshine.

—

MEAT THE RHYTHM BUTCHERS (VOLUME 1)
(compilation) by The Rhythm Butchers
Turtles involvement: Mark Volman, Jim Pons,—guitar, vocals; John Barbata—vocals
Additional personnel: Dave Krambeck—guitar, vocals
Recording dates: 1966 at the Astor Towers Hotel in Chicago, Illinois
Highest chart position: Did not chart
Original release date: 1980

Don't Ya Just Know It
Rumble
Love Me Tender
Cottonfields
Look Over Yonders Wall

Meat
Johnny B. Goode
Exodus
Good Night Irene

THE TURTLES BACKSTAGE

The Rhythm Butchers are backstage recordings done by The Turtles. To some, they are a gift of unreleased Turtles madness. To others they are just a mess of sounds recorded by the drunk or high Turtles members in their off hours while on tour.

According to the picture sleeve notes, the three Turtles recorded this nonsense with their tour manager Dave Krambeck, while Howard was trying to sleep. The whereabouts of Al are unknown, but he probably was with a girl. John Barbata sings lead on "Don't Ya Just Know It." Jim Pons sings lead on "Good Night Irene" and "Johnny B. Goode."

Mark and Howard also personally signed these sleeves as well, making them instantly non-collectible.

—

MORE GOLDEN HITS (compilation) by The Turtles
Turtles involvement: See individual Turtles tracks
Additional personnel: See individual Turtles tracks
Recording dates: 1967 - 1970
Highest chart position: #146
Original release date: March 1970

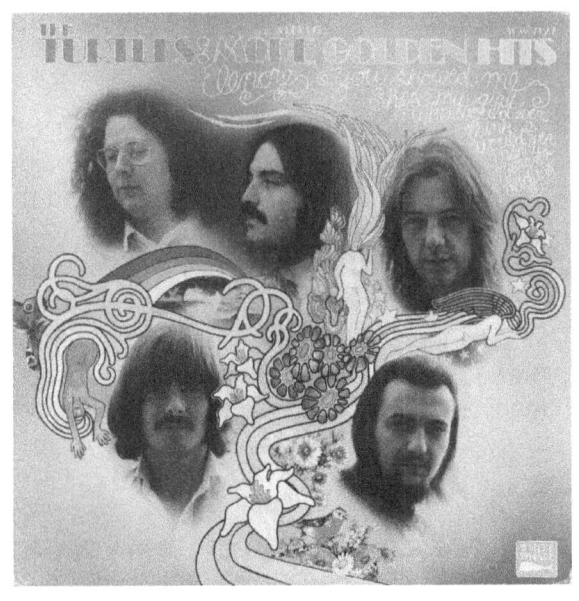

We Ain't Gonna Party No More
The Story of Rock and Roll
You Showed Me
Sound Asleep
You Don't Have to Walk in the Rain
Who Would Ever Think That I Would Marry Margaret?

She's My Girl
Elenore
Lady-O
Hot Little Hands
Love in the City
Cat in the Window

This second Turtles compilation was released shortly after their breakup. It Includes their biggest single hits from their final four years, plus a couple of unreleased tracks. It was reissued on June 3, 2020 as a 180 gram stereo edition on gold vinyl from Demon Records.

—

NEEDLES AND PINS (Jack Nitzsche, Sonny Bono) by The Turtles
Turtles involvement: Mark Volman—tambourine, vocals; Howard Kaylan—lead vocals; Al Nichol—lead guitar, vocals; Jim Tucker—rhythm guitar, vocals; Chuck Portz—bass guitar, vocals; Don Murray—drums
Recording dates: September 30, 1965
Highest chart position: Did not chart
Original release date: unreleased
Significant other versions: The Searchers, Jackie DeShannon, Ramones, Smokie, Tom Petty and the Heartbreakers with Stevie Nicks, Chris Norman, Del Shannon, Gene Clark, Crack the Sky

Mark: Live performance only. There's a version available from their appearance on "Shindig"

on September 30, 1965. Poor Jim Tucker is cut off the screen at the left. And yes, it's Sonny Bono, THAT Sonny Bono of Sonny & Cher fame who wrote this song. He talks about it in his autobiography called *The Beat Goes On* (which is an excellent read).

Charles: "And so it beginza." In a mere minute and a half, The Turtles take a pin and puncture all my preconceived notions about this song. A standard Merseybeat classic by The Searchers, I thought nothing could touch lead vocalist Mike Pinder's delivery of needles and "pinza" (which I always hoped was a tribute to the great Italian opera singer Ezio Pinza, but I'm sure it wasn't). Everything was just perfect about this British invasion pop rock masterpiece co-written by Sonny Bono. Then, in 1978, The Ramones, who could do no wrong, aced it with a faithful version that kept the intended tempo and Joey's unmistakable vocals.

To paraphrase Simon Cowell, I don't like The Turtles' version… I LOVE IT! They made this already immaculate tune their own by speeding it up, punching up the beat, and adding call-back backing vocals. It's more danceable, more energetic, and more fun. It's up to the listener if it's superior to the other versions, but it may very well be.

I can't believe I never knew Sonny Bono wrote it.

—

1968 (compilation) by The Turtles
Turtles involvement: See individual Turtles tracks
Additional personnel: See individual Turtles tracks
Recording dates: 1968
Highest chart position: Did not chart
Original release date: October 1978

To See the Sun
Surfer Dan

The Last Thing I Remember (The First Thing I Knew) (demo)
The Owl

"The Owl" b/w "To See the Sun" was supposedly going to be the follow-up single to "Sound Asleep." When "Sound Asleep" didn't make the top 40, the executives at White Whale panicked and The Turtles were no longer allowed to work on their own eccentric psychedelic compositions. Outside writers like Harry Nilsson were quickly brought in to remedy the situation. As such, these two tunes were left incomplete. Howard and Mark have said in interviews that "To See the Sun" was to have much more orchestration, but when Rhino wanted to issue a mostly-unreleased EP picture disc, these four tracks got the nod.

"The Last Thing I Remember (The First Thing I Knew)" was a demo version of what later became "The Last Thing I Remember" on *The Turtles Present the Battle of the Bands*. There were some lyric changes between demo and final product. "Surfer Dan" is from the same album and is just the standard album version, to my knowledge.

—

OH, DADDY! (The Turtles) by The L.A. Bust '66
Turtles involvement: Mark Volman—vocals, special effects; Howard Kaylan—lead vocals; Al Nichol—guitars, organ, piano, Moog synthesizer, vocals; Jim Pons—bass, vocals; John Barbata—drums, percussion, vocals
Additional personnel: Chip Douglas—producer: Jim Hilton, Armin Steiner—engineers
Recording dates: May - June 1968 at Gold Star Studios, Hollywood, California; Western Recorders, Hollywood, California; T.T.G./Sunset-Highland Recording Studios, Hollywood, California
Highest chart position: #128 from *The Turtles Present the Battle of the Bands*
Original release date: November 1, 1968

Charles: This bounces along like a Monkees song. The only thing missing is Davy Jones' lead vocals and Micky Dolenz's harmonies. The only thing added is the horn break which gives it both a Mardi-Gras feel and a carnival vibe. A jubilant party song that ends up a lil' silly.
Mark: Great bass lines highlight this somewhat silly song about prison with a Dixieland jazz break in the middle. I do agree with Charles that this would have been a great one for The Monkees' catalog. It's the same bouncy vibe of something like "Cuddly Toy."

—

ON A SUMMER'S DAY (Al Nichol) by The Turtles
Turtles involvement: Mark Volman—vocal harmony, tambourine; Howard Kaylan—lead vocals; Al Nichol—lead guitar, organ, piano, harpsichord, vocals; Jim Tucker—rhythm guitar; Chuck Portz—bass guitar; Don Murray—drums
Additional personnel: Bones Howe—producer, engineer; Armin Steiner, engineer; John Audino
Recording dates: April - September 1966 at Western Recorders, Hollywood, California
Highest chart position: Did not chart from *Wooden Head*
Original release date: November 1970

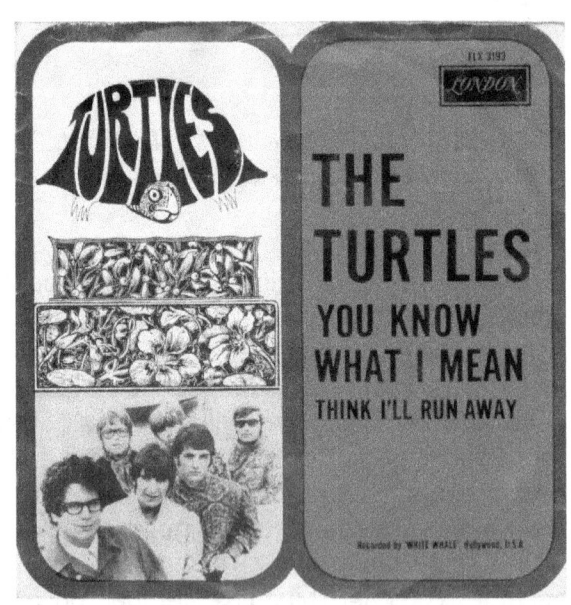

Mark: Not one of Al Nichol's better compositions. It kind of meanders around in minor keys and never really goes anywhere. It was supposed to be released as the B-side of the aborted "So Goes Love" single. "So Goes Love" did get released on *Golden Hits*, while this song deservedly remained on the shelf until 1970. 2016's *All The Singles* features the original mono mix for the first time that was supposed to be on the single.

Charles: I would prefer to disagree with my co-author whenever possible, but he's right. Actually, he's being kind by saying it meanders. This is just miserable. How could a song about a Summer's Day be so dreary? The less said about this one, the better.

—

ONE POTATO TWO POTATO (THREE POTATO FOUR POTATO) (Howard Kaplan, Al Nichol, Jim Tucker) by The Crossfires
Turtles involvement: Mark Volman—alto sax, vocals; Howard Kaplan—tenor sax, lead vocals; Al Nichol—lead guitar, background vocals; Jim Tucker—rhythm guitar; Chuck Portz—bass; Don Murrray—drums
Additional personnel: John Bradbury, Larry Johnson—producers; Chuck Britz—engineer
Recording dates: 1964
Highest chart position: Single did not chart; B-side to "That'll Be the Day;" Did not chart from *Out of Control*
Original release date: February 1965 for single; 1981 for album

Mark: It's The Crossfires' second single and the first record to feature Howard Kaylan's wonderful lead vocals. Howard sings in two distinct styles: either a sweet, spiritual-sounding operatic voice or a gruff, hard-rocking growl. This is a good example of the latter.

Apparently it charted on some local San Bernardino, California chart, so it had that going for it. It might have even made a good track for inclusion on The Turtles' debut album *It Ain't Me Babe* if the lyrics were changed to some sort of protest song. Nursery rhyme lyrics don't seem very conducive to protesting.

Charles: "Tra la la, la la la la, Tra la la, la la la la." No, it's not a TV theme song by the Banana Splits (apologies to Australian podcaster Plastic EP, the world's greatest Banana Splits fan), but maybe it inspired that bubblegum chestnut. Hey, no matter what, it's groovy! Simplistic and garage-y, there's too much tambourine and not enough horns, but that doesn't stop it from being a fun, likable Crossfires raunch-rocker.

—

OUT OF CONTROL (Al Nichol) by The Crossfires
Turtles involvement: Mark Volman—alto sax; Howard Kaplan—tenor sax; Al Nichol—lead guitar; Dale Walton—rhythm guitar; Chuck Portz—bass; Don Murray—drums
Additional personnel: Chuck Britz—engineer
Recording dates: 1963
Highest chart position: Did not chart from *Out of Control*
Original release date: 1981

Mark: The Crossfires must have LOVED performing and composing all of those surf tunes. Al was the composer for many of these and he was probably the one most saddened when the

days of surf music came to an end. This song became the namesake for the Crossfires album that Flo & Eddie eventually released in 1981, but it doesn't have "hit" written all over it. I think Flo & Eddie chose it for the album title as it was more of a statement of what The Crossfires were rather than the merits of this tune.

Charles: Another manic instrumental, this one borders on novelty with its horse-racing intro and samples (before they were called "samples") of other well-known songs and standards. "The Lone Ranger Theme" is the most obvious. Giddyup! It makes you want to jump on a horse alongside Tonto and just... play some guitars and saxophones (if you could picture that sight)! I have no doubt that this one was even more fun when performed live.

—

OUT OF CONTROL (LP) by The Crossfires
Turtles involvement: Mark Volman—alto sax, lead vocals; Howard Kaplan—tenor sax, lead vocals; Al Nichol—lead guitar, background vocals; Dale Walton—rhythm guitar; Chuck Portz—bass; Don Murray—drums
Additional personnel: Mark Volman and Howard Kaylan—compilation producers; Chuck Britz—engineer; Jim Tucker—rhythm guitar on "One Potato Two Potato," "Stay Around," and "Livin' Doll;" Tom Stanton—rhythm guitar on "That'll Be the Day," "Revelaire," and "Silver Bullet;" Terry Hand—drums on "Livin' Doll" and "Stay Around"
Recording dates: 1963, April 13 and November 23, 1964 at Western Recorders, Hollywood, California
Highest chart position: Did not chart
Original release date: 1981

Out of Control
One Potato Two Potato
Fiberglass Jungle
That'll Be the Day
Inferno
Revelaire
Justine

Silver Bullet

Follow the Rock
Dr. Jekyll and Mr. Hyde
Livin' Doll
Pull Top
Stay Around
Chunky

Bonus tracks on Sundazed edition:
Santa and the Sidewalk Surfer
Silver Bullet (alternate version)

An amazingly coherent collection of Crossfires tunes considering that it consists of a few live tracks and a few studio tracks, some with vocals, some without, recorded at a number of sessions during 1963 and 1964. Four of the songs were originally issued as two singles in 1963 and 1965, respectively, while the others mysteriously remained in the can until Flo & Eddie decided to resurrect them for disc by the urging of Rhino Records in 1981. Sundazed Records reissued Rhino's vinyl version on CD in 1995, adding "Santa and the Sidewalk Surfer" which had come out in 1974, and Take One of "Silver Bullet." A marvelous collection for those wanting to know what The Turtles sounded like pre-Turtles, or for lovers of surf music. Essential? Yes. Indispensable? No.

—

OUT OF SIGHT (film and soundtrack)
Turtles involvement: The Turtles perform "She'll Come Back"
Additional personnel: Jonathan Daly as Homer; Karen Jensen as Sandra Carter; Robert Pine as Greg; Carole Shelyne as Marvin; Deanna Lund as Tuff Bod; Wende Wagner as Scuba; Maggie Thrett as Wipeout; Rena Horten as The Girl from FLUSH; John Lawrence as Big D; Jimmie Murphy as Mousie; Billy Curtis as The Man from FLUSH; Norman Grabowski as Huh!, Forrest Lewis as Mr. Carter; Deon Douglas as Mike; Pamela Rodgers as Madge; Vicki Fee as Janet; Coby Denton as Tom; John Lodge as John Stamp; Richard Dawson as Agent; Bob Eubanks as Concert Announcer; Jamie Farr, Dobie Gray, Gary Lewis and The Playboys, The Knickerbockers, The Astronauts, Freddie and The Dreamers
Original release date: April 25, 1966

Mark: This is a silly film along the same lines as the Frankie and Annette *Beach Party* movies, but it doesn't star any of them, nor was it released by American International. It was instead released by Universal, who did have their share of B-pictures during the 1960s (Don Knotts films, anyone?). If

you want to avoid the tedium of watching the film on YouTube and only want to see The Turtles, they appear at about the 50 minute mark, sing their hit with the party crowd bopping along, and smile appreciatively when the partygoers conclude that all of the bands auditioning for them will make the cut. Mark Volman tries to do a slight bit of tambourine shtick at the beginning of their performance, but cuts it short. This is supposed to be a serious performance! The original Turtles never looked better in lush color outfits and straightened hair.

Charles: Let's discuss only the motion picture here, and we will talk about the Turtles' song "She'll Come Back" from the film later in this book when it comes up in alphabetical order. So many cool people (Richard Dawson, Deanna Lund, Jamie Farr, Bob Eubanks) and acts (the Knickerbockers, Gary Lewis, Freddie and The Dreamers) were involved in this project, it's just too bad The Turtles didn't have a better song to showcase.

Spoiler Alert: Once something is brought to your attention, you'll always cringe when you hear this track, so don't read any further if either you already like this song, or if you have never heard it before and don't want to be influenced. Never mind, just reading that, you'll play the song just to hear these annoyances with your own ears. Fast forward to the listing "She'll Come Back" (hint: the song is not SHILL COME BACK). You'll understand later...

—

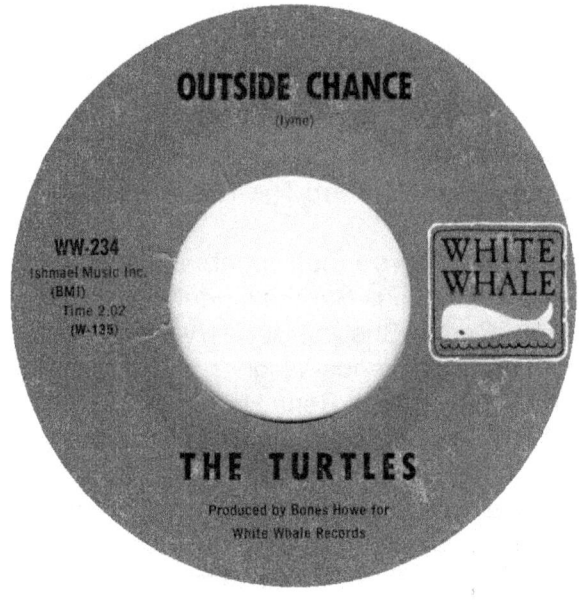

OUTSIDE CHANCE (Lyme aka Warren Zevon, Glenn Crocker) by The Turtles
Turtles involvement: Mark Volman—vocal harmony, tambourine; Howard Kaylan—lead vocals; Al Nichol—lead guitar, vocals; Jim Tucker—rhythm guitar; Chuck Portz—bass guitar; John Barbata—drums
Additional personnel: Bones Howe—producer, engineer; Armin Steiner, engineer; John Audino; Larry Knecktel—piano
Recording dates: April - September 1966 at Western Recorders, Hollywood, California
Highest chart position: Did not chart; A-side and B-side of "Making My Mind Up;" #7 from *Golden Hits*
Original release date: July 1966 for single; October 1967 for album

Mark: And now we have John Barbata on drums! Not that Don Murray was a horrible drummer by any means, it's just that Barbata was so much better! This is a great song and a great debut for him that totally showcases his skills as a hard rocking drummer and song. It should have been a bigger hit. At least it ended up on *Golden Hits* instead of oblivion.

Charles: A terrific chorus and adrenaline zips this one along. Written by Warren Zevon and clocking in at around two minutes, we are presented with a superb but subtle lead guitar, nice piano break and some pumping drums, plus solid harmonies and a "96 Tears"-ish vocal ending. Someone somewhere probably told them that they didn't stand an "outside chance" for this to be a hit, and although they were right, it should have been.

—

OWL, THE (The Turtles) by The Turtles
Turtles involvement: Mark Volman—vocals, special effects; Howard Kaylan—lead vocals; Al Nichol—guitars, organ, piano, Moog synthesizer, vocals; Jim Pons—bass, vocals; John Barbata—drums, percussion, vocals
Additional personnel: The Turtles—producers
Recording dates: February 1968 at Ter-Mar Recording Studios, Chicago, Illinois; Olmsted Sound Studios, New York, New York; Sound Recorders, Hollywood, California; Mixed September 1978 by H, Lee Wolen and Jim Rayton at Ascot Recorders
Highest chart position: Did not chart from *1968*
Original release date: October 1978

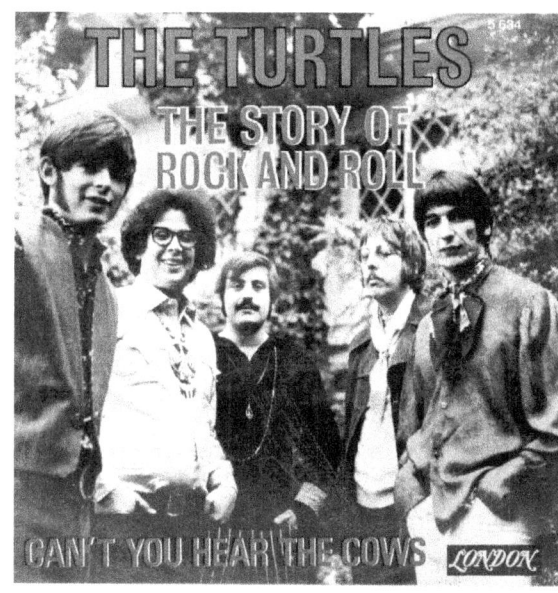

Mark: This was to be the follow up single to "Sound Asleep." When "Sound Asleep" stiffed, this went into the vaults, only to be rescued by Rhino a decade later. I don't always agree with White Whale's choices, but this time, to shelve this was the correct choice. The Turtles were getting a little out of hand with this heavy-on-the-sitar track, so it was probably a good thing to get Chip Douglas back to help reel them in a bit. Perhaps a better chorus line than "who, who, whooooo" would have helped. It seems incomplete. I feel "To See the Sun" would have been the better A-side choice.

Charles: Another psychedelic piece, at first we think we're getting "Within You, Without Out" revisited, but this is even trippier. The lyrics include "dark night drops coldly," but there may have been other things dropping (acid? pills? hallucinogens?) at the time. Only The Owl knows exactly "whoooooooooo" was doing the dropping.

—

PALL BEARING, BALL BEARING WORLD (Howard Kaylan) by The Turtles
Turtles involvement: Mark Volman—vocal harmony, tambourine; Howard Kaylan—lead vocals; Al Nichol—vocal harmony, lead guitar, organ; Jim Tucker—rhythm guitar; Chuck Portz—bass guitar; Don Murray—drums
Additional personnel: Lee Lasseff and Ted Feigin—executive producers; Bones Howe—production, sound, engineering; Dwight Tunji Trio (Howe, Feigin & Lasseff)—percussion, special effects
Recording dates: October 1965 - January 1966 at Western Recorders, Hollywood, California
Highest chart position: Did not chart from *You Baby*
Original release date: April 1966

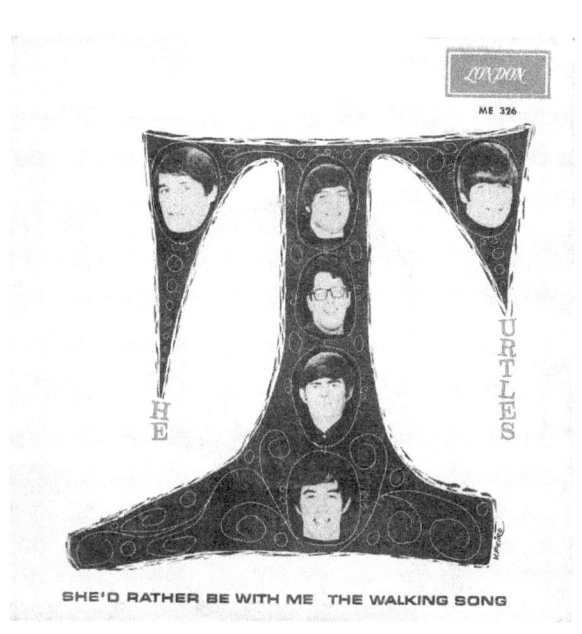

Mark: Does anybody know what a "Body by Fisher" is anymore? Fisher produced the metal bodies that General Motors used for their automobiles from 1908-1984. So now you know. Trust Howard to use that obscure reference in one of his songs in order to be hip. Now, if you don't know what a pallbearer is or a ball bearing is, *Webster's Dictionary* is sitting over there.

Charles: So who's playing the harmonica? We hear it in the beginning and then throughout the track, complimenting the lead guitar. Some Dylan-inspired phrasing (how does it "fee-yul") and a lot of vehicle references are camouflaging some sort of social consciousness message. By the way, I grabbed my Webster's and even Googled it, but I still couldn't figure out what a nasagraph or nasigraph is.

—

PEPSI AD aka **PEPSI POURS IT ON** (Anne Phillips) by The Turtles
Turtles involvement: Mark Volman—tambourine, harmony and backing vocals; Howard Kaylan—lead and backing vocals; Al Nichol—lead guitar, piano, backing vocals; Jim Tucker—rhythm guitar, backing vocals; Jim Pons—bass, backing vocals; John Barbata—drums, backing vocals
Additional personnel: Joe Wissert—producer; Bones Howe, Armin Steiner, Bruce Botnick—engineers; unknown—trumpets, trombone, saxophone
Recording dates: December 1966 - April 1967 at Sunset Sound Recorders, Hollywood, California
Highest chart position: Did not chart from *The History of Flo & Eddie and The Turtles*
Original release date: 1967 for ad; 1983 for album
Significant other versions: Linda Ronstadt and the Stone Poneys, various Pepsi commercials

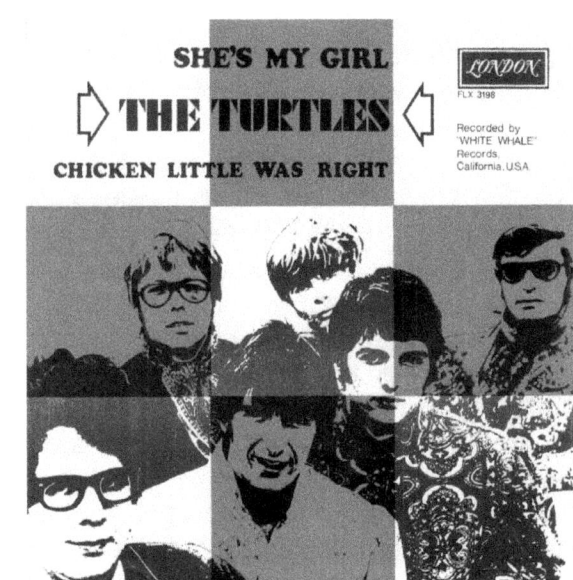

Mark: "Take six" says the producer at the top of this spot. I wonder if the other five takes still exist? A very catchy jingle with the requisite "ba ba bahs and la la las." It was used for many years in many Pepsi commercials.

Charles: I think I remember hearing this and not knowing it was The Turtles. Or maybe I just remember the jingle in general. As far as soda pop commercials go, it's very refreshing.

—

PERSON WITHOUT A CARE (Al Nichol) by The Turtles
Turtles involvement: Mark Volman—harmony and backing vocals; Howard Kaylan—lead and backing vocals; Al Nichol—lead guitar, piano, backing vocals; Jim Tucker—rhythm guitar, backing vocals; Jim Pons—bass, backing vocals; John Barbata—drums
Additional personnel: Joe Wissert—producer; Bones Howe, Armin Steiner, Bruce Botnick—engineers
Recording dates: December 1966 - April 1967 at Sunset Sound Recorders, Hollywood, California
Highest chart position: #25 from *Happy Together*

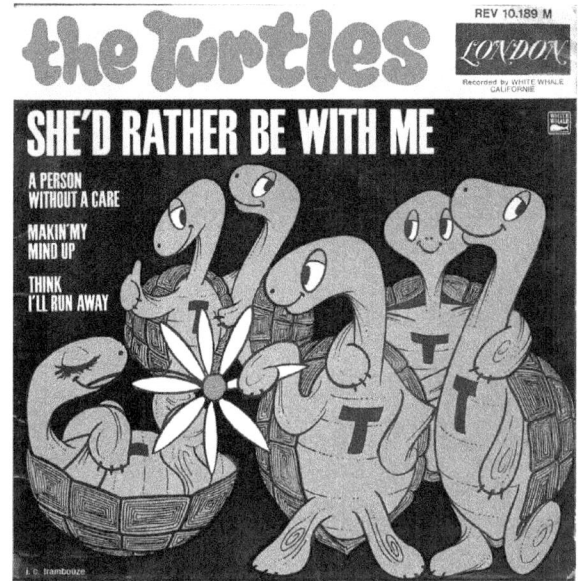

Original release date: April 29, 1967

Mark: I like the bouncy, ping-pong effect in the background. It reminds me of The Beach Boys' "Bluebirds Over the Mountain." I also love the backwards masking effects. It sounds like someone roller skating. It's highly catchy, too. Of course, there's greater separation on these effects on the stereo version than the mono version.

Charles: One of those carefree, happy-go-lucky (it even uses that phrase in the lyrics) tunes that get your shoulders shaking and feet moving. Not very sophisticated but infectious nonetheless, with some oddball sound effects popping out in the second half of the song (so who is that tinkering on the mellotron?).

—

PLAYLIST: THE VERY BEST OF THE TURTLES
(compilation) by The Turtles
Turtles involvement: See *The Turtles featuring Flo & Eddie Captured Live*.
Additional personnel: See *The Turtles featuring Flo & Eddie Captured Live*.
Recording dates: December 31, 1991
Highest chart position: Did not chart
Original release date: March 10, 2016

It Ain't Me Babe (live 1991)
Elenore (live 1991)
She's My Girl (live 1991)
Feel Older Now (live 1991)
Moving Targets (live 1991)
Goodbye Surprise (live 1991)
Keep it Warm (live 1991)
Let Me Be (live 1991)
You Showed Me (live 1991)
You Baby (live 1991)
She'd Rather Be With Me (live 1991)
Happy Together (live 1991)

The Turtles got a lot of mileage with this 1991 live performance and reissued it many times over the years. It's not bad, but it seems strange that after years and years and years of touring, this is really the only concert used to represent The Turtles live.

—

PULL TOP (Al Nichol) by The Crossfires
Turtles involvement: Mark Volman—alto sax; Howard Kaplan—tenor sax; Al Nichol—lead guitar; Dale Walton—rhythm guitar; Chuck Portz—bass; Don Murray—drums
Additional personnel: Chuck Britz—engineer
Recording dates: 1963
Highest chart position: Did not chart from *Out of Control*
Original release date: 1981
Significant other versions: The Turtles

Charles: Either this is a live track or it's got simulated live crowd noise dubbed in. Couldn't you picture this alongside "Misirlou" in the *Pulp Fiction* soundtrack album? It starts off good, and gets great when the sax literally explodes. Okay, you want to picture how this could've been even better? Add words, go back in time, and have Freddy "BoomBoom" Cannon do the vocals. Better yet, give it to The Ramones in their prime and let them Ramonize it! Now go back and play it with both those artists in mind.
Mark: The crowd sounds too large to be real for The Crossfires at this point, so it was certainly an overdub. This instrumental was first released as the backing track for "Santa and the Sidewalk Surfer" on *Happy Together Again!* in 1974. It's nice to hear without the silly Santa Claus commentary running throughout.

—

REVELAIRE (Al Nichol) by The Crossfires
Turtles involvement: Mark Volman—alto sax; Howard Kaplan—tenor sax; Al Nichol—lead guitar; Tom Stanton—rhythm guitar; Chuck Portz—bass; Don Murray—drums
Additional personnel: Chuck Britz—engineer
Recording dates: April 13 and November 23, 1964 at Western Recorders, Hollywood, California
Highest chart position: Did not chart from *Out of Control*
Original release date: 1981

Mark: An instrumental honoring the club where The Crossfires got their start. It's a little more than a passing nod to The Silhouettes' "Get a Job."
Charles: Thanks to writing for this book, my admiration and appreciation of The Turtles has filtered into a love of everything Crossfires. The speed-guitar on this one is its highlight. When we get our time machine working, I'd like to transport back to a night at the Revelaire to revel with The Crossfires.

RHYTHM BUTCHERS HATE YOU, THE (VOLUME 7) (compilation) by The Rhythm Butchers
Turtles involvement: Specifics unknown, but usually Mark Volman, Howard Kaylan, Jim Pons and Al Nichol. John Seiter is probably on this one, too.
Additional personnel: Maybe their tour manager Dave Krambeck
Recording dates: 1969?
Highest chart position: Did not chart
Original release date: 1986?

I Hate You
Quiet Village
I Hate You (Part 2)

You Never Walk Alone
I Hate the Blues
Awanawanakawah
Dropped a Cigarette

The Rhythm Butchers are backstage recordings done by The Turtles. To some, they are a gift of unreleased Turtles madness. To others they are just a mess of sounds recorded by Turtles members in their off hours, probably high, while on tour.

It is unknown as to whether this volume (or subsequent volumes) was actually released. Track listings abound online for this one, but no images of the label or the picture sleeve are accessible. If anyone actually has this record, please let us know. We'll congratulate you on your diligence in having a complete Turtles collection and maybe ask you for a scan or two.

The reason for The Rhythm Butchers series stopping at this point was almost assuredly because they weren't selling, but also because all subsequent Turtles releases treat The Turtles as a '60s act to be reckoned with (which they were) and not a novelty act (which they are that, too). The next Turtles release on 45 was a reissue of "Happy Together" b/w "There You Sit Lonely" in conjunction with a movie called *Making Mr. Right*, which was pleasant and watchable, but a big flop. This "Happy Together" single was released with a new cardboard picture sleeve promoting the film in April 1987.

—

RHYTHM BUTCHERS ON SATURN, THE (VOLUME 6) (compilation) by The Rhythm Butchers
Turtles involvement: Mark Volman—guitar, vocals; Howard Kaylan—vocals, bass; Jim Pons—lead guitar, vocals; John Barbata—table
Additional personnel: Unknown female voice on "Moonlight Bay;" Bob Buchanan—vocals on "Problems"
Recording dates: Late 1968 - Early 1969 at the Lake Shore Drive Holiday Inn, Chicago, Illinois
Highest chart position: Did not chart

THE RHYTHM BUTCHERS ON SATURN (VOL. 6)

THE TURTLES BACKSTAGE

Original release date: 1985

Boots
Miserlou
Boots (Reprise)
Moonlight Bay

Under the Boardwalk
The Space Moose Blues
Problems

Again, The Rhythm Butchers are backstage recordings done by The Turtles, either as a gift of unreleased Turtles madness, or as a mess of sounds recorded by inebriated Turtles members in their off hours while on tour.

This is the only one of The Rhythm Butchers releases that Mark actually owns. I feel honored. It features the final Rhythm Butchers appearance by John Barbata. The female voice is credited to belong to one of Al's girlfriends, but Al isn't mentioned as being on the record. Perhaps he is. Does it matter?

—

RHYTHM BUTCHERS RETURN TO THE CORRAL BY THE BAY, THE (VOLUME 2)
(compilation) by The Rhythm Butchers
Turtles involvement: Mark Volman, Jim Pons—vocals; John Barbata—drums
Additional personnel: Dave Krambeck, John Phillips (not THAT one)—vocals
Recording dates: 1967 at the Hyde Park, New York
Highest chart position: Did not chart
Original release date: 1980

Dark Moon
TV Themes
What To Do

Stardust
Pickle
26 Miles of Blue Moon

THE TURTLES BACKSTAGE

Did we mention that The Rhythm Butchers are backstage recordings done by The Turtles? To some, they are a gift of unreleased Turtles madness. To others they are just a mess of sounds recorded by the perhaps obliterated Turtles members in their off hours while on tour.

The John Phillips listed is NOT the one from The Mamas & the Papas, but instead some clown hired by road manager Krambeck who was destined to rip off The Turtles later on in their story. This time the recordings are from a hotel room in New York and not Chicago. It didn't help. "Pickle" isn't too bad, however.

Jim Pons writes the sleeve notes on this one and also signs copies, making them less than worthless.

—

RHYTHM BUTCHERS SING FOR YOUNG LOVERS, THE (VOLUME 4) (compilation) by The Rhythm Butchers
Turtles involvement: Mark Volman—slide guitar, vocals; Howard Kaylan—slide guitar, vocals; Jim Pons—guitar, lead vocals
Recording dates: 1968 at the Astor Towers, Chicago, Illinois
Highest chart position: Did not chart
Original release date: 1981

Toot Toot Tootsie
You Won't See Me
I Understand
I'll Be Me

Boss
Hello Young Lovers
Coo Coo Roo Coo Coo
Happy Birthday Baby
Hey Jude—Part II

If you don't know by now, The Rhythm Butchers are backstage recordings done by The Turtles. To some, they are a gift of unreleased Turtles madness. To others they are just a mess of sounds recorded by trashed Turtles members in their off hours while on tour.

Jim Pons takes most of the lead vocals on this one. The picture sleeve states that this is the least accessible disc in The Rhythm Butchers series. Whatever that means. Reference to Jim Tucker was made for the first time in this series on this sleeve stating that he had "flipped out" and was "never to be heard from again" after meeting The Beatles. Tucker always denied this story, by stating his reason for leaving The Turtles was touring fatigue. He was no longer available for comment as he passed away in 2020.

—

RHYTHM BUTCHERS VS. THE ZANTI MISFITS, THE (VOLUME 5) (compilation) by The Rhythm Butchers
Turtles involvement: Mark Volman—slide guitar, harmonica, vocals; Howard Kaylan—slide guitar, tabletop drums, vocals; Jim Pons—guitar, vocals; Al Nichol—guitar
Additional personnel: John Seiter
Recording dates: 1968 at the Astor Towers, Chicago, Illinois

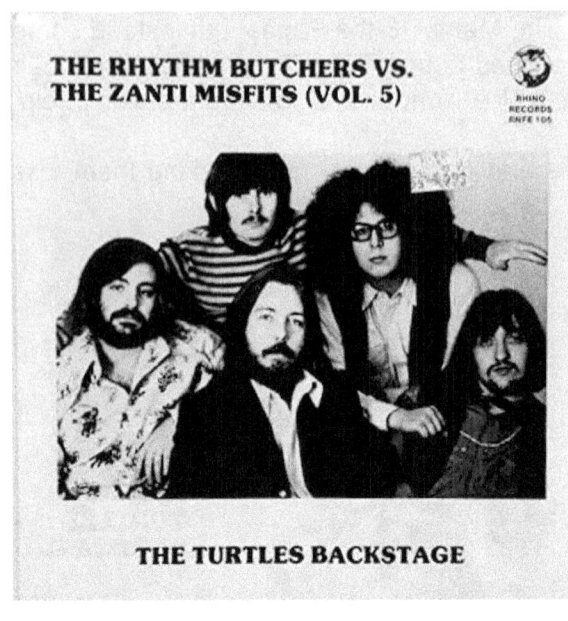

THE RHYTHM BUTCHERS VS. THE ZANTI MISFITS (VOL. 5)

THE TURTLES BACKSTAGE

Highest chart position: Did not chart
Original release date: 1983

Outer Limits
Shape of Things to Come
Zanti Misfits
Shape of Things to Come (Reprise)
Young Blood

Can't You Hear the Cows
Hacienda Del Sol
Candy Man
Cooking with the Grease

This is getting ridiculous. You should know it by heart: The Rhythm Butchers are backstage recordings done by The Turtles. To some, they are a gift of unreleased Turtles madness. To others they are just a mess of sounds recorded by barely sober Turtles members in their off hours while on tour.

This one actually has the "demo" for "Can't You Hear the Cows" which was not all that different from what was actually recorded and released as the B-side to "She's My Girl." If you can't hear The Rhythm Butchers, this track is a close approximation of what you're missing. Aren't you lucky? Future Turtles drummer John Seiter was there as part of Spanky and Our Gang and the infamous pot punch, but it wasn't clear if he's actually on these recordings.

Let's give some credit for referencing those Zanti Misfits from the 1963 episode of *The Outer Limits*.

—

RUGS OF WOODS AND FLOWERS (Howard Kaylan, Al Nichol) by The Turtles
Turtles involvement: Mark Volman—harmony and backing vocals; Howard Kaylan—lead and backing vocals; Al Nichol—lead guitar, piano, backing vocals; Jim Tucker—rhythm guitar, backing vocals; Jim Pons—bass, backing vocals; John Barbata—drums
Additional personnel: Joe Wissert—producer; Bones Howe, Armin Steiner, Bruce Botnick—engineers
Recording dates: December 1966 - April 1967 at Sunset Sound Recorders, Hollywood, California
Highest chart position: Single did not chart; B-side of "You Know What I Mean;" #25 from *Happy Together*
Original release date: April 29, 1967 for album; July 1967 for single

Charles: This is a Turtles song, not the Mothers of Invention, but it foreshadows some of Zappa's zaniness, dissonance, and peculiar vocal delivery. It's not a surprise that Flo & Eddie were a nice fit into Frank's weird but artistic musical universe. There's even a cool fake ending and musical epilogue a la "Hello Goodbye."

Mark: Interestingly, this fake ending is ONLY on the stereo version. On the mono version, it ends correctly. Sort of like The Beatles' "Helter Skelter" almost two years before they did it with their mono vs. stereo versions. Howard belts it out with a kind of operatic baritone, I guess so it sounds more important than it actually is. Nice cough there at 2:17.

—

SANTA AND THE SIDEWALK SURFER (Mark Volman, Howard Kaplan, Al Nichol) by The Crossfires
Turtles involvement: Mark Volman—alto sax, lead vocals; Howard Kaplan—tenor sax, lead vocals; Al Nichol—lead guitar; Dale Walton—rhythm guitar; Chuck Portz—bass; Don Murray—drums
Additional personnel: Chuck Britz—engineer
Recording dates: 1963; Vocals recorded November 23, 1964 at Western Recorders, Hollywood, California
Highest chart position: #194 from *Happy Together Again!*
Original release date: November 1974

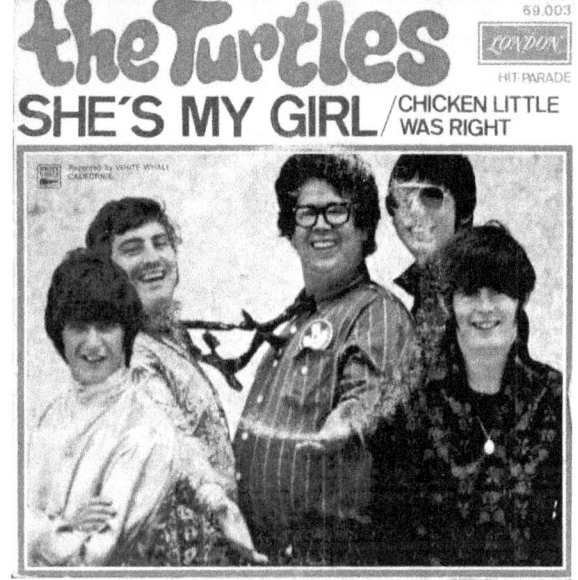

Mark: The backing track is "Pull Top." This was supposed to be a single B-side of "Santa's Living Doll" aka "Livin' Doll." Mark as Santa and Howard as a little boy exchange spoken-word lines of what he wants for Christmas. The little boy obliges with a lengthy list of what he wants in order to be a sidewalk surfer aka a skateboarder, and then some. Pretty amusing stuff.

When Sundazed Records reissued *Out of Control* on CD in 1995, this song was added as a bonus track.

Charles: Ho ho ho here we go—not to the North Pole or the waves, but to the curb for some sidewalk surfin' silliness—years before skateboards were commonplace. It's really just a Dick Dale-styled surf instrumental, with a narrative over the music, between, literally, Santa and a skateboarder. They even reference "Misirlou." No surprise that this doesn't get played on the radio with all the Christmas tunes because it's so off the reindeer radar, but it's Santastic (Santa + fantastic) nonetheless.

—

SAVE THE TURTLES: THE TURTLES GREATEST HITS (compilation) by The Turtles
Turtles involvement: See individual Turtles tracks
Additional personnel: See individual Turtles tracks
Recording dates: 1965 - 1970
Highest chart position: Did not chart

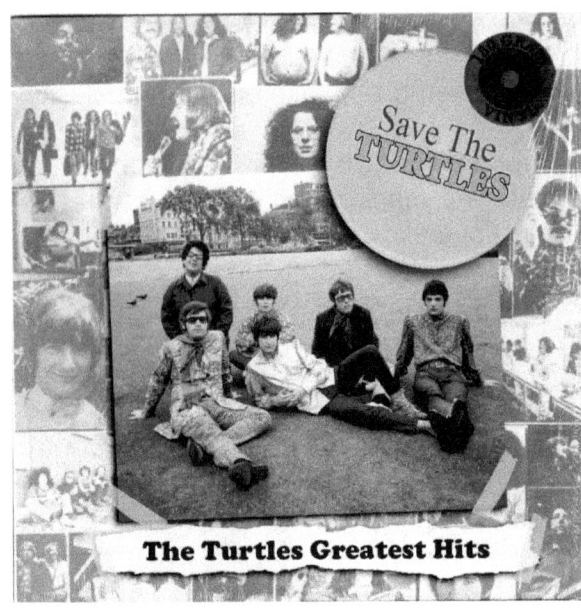

Original release date: March 2, 2009

*Happy Together
It Ain't Me Babe
She'd Rather Be With Me
You Baby
Elenore
Let Me Be
She's My Girl
Outside Chance
You Showed Me
Can I Get to Know You Better
The Story of Rock and Roll
Love in the City
Me About You
You Don't Have to Walk in the Rain
You Know What I Mean
Sound Asleep
Makin' My Mind Up
Grim Reaper of Love
Guide For the Married Man
Chevrolet Camaro Ad*

Another year, another Turtles compilation. This one is notable only for having the first appearance on CD of the "Chevrolet Camaro Ad."

—

SAY GIRL (Al Nichol, Chuck Portz, Matt Portz) by The Turtles
Turtles involvement: Mark Volman—vocal harmony, tambourine; Howard Kaylan—lead vocals; Al Nichol—lead guitar, organ, piano, harpsichord, vocals; Jim Tucker—rhythm guitar; Chuck Portz—bass guitar; Don Murray—drums
Additional personnel: Bones Howe—producer, engineer; Armin Steiner, engineer
Recording dates: April - September 1966 at Western Recorders, Hollywood, California
Highest chart position: Did not chart from *Wooden Head*
Original release date: November 1970

Mark: A cheery hand-clapping song that could have/should have been done by The Rolling Stones or a similar act. I think Mark takes the lead vocals here, but it's hard to tell sometimes as Howard and Mark sound similar at times. It gathered dust until 1970.

Charles: A frenetic guitar break beefs up this fast and furious, era-friendly number that does indeed recall early Jagger/Richards recordings, but without the attitude. Love that one extra guitar note at the very end.

—

SHE ALWAYS LEAVES ME LAUGHING (The Turtles) by The Turtles
Turtles involvement: Mark Volman—vocals, percussion, occasional guitars; Howard Kaylan—lead vocal, occasional percussion, organ; Al Nichol—lead vocal, guitars, keyboards, six string bass; Jim Pons—vocals, bass, occasional guitars; John Seiter—vocals, drums, occasional piano
Additional personnel: Ray Davies—producer; Chuck Britz—engineer
Recording dates: April - July 1969 at United Records, Hollywood, California
Highest chart position: #117 from *Turtle Soup*
Original release date: October 1969

Mark: The jangly Byrds-like guitar reminds me of something The Turtles would have done circa 1965 and 1966, and perhaps that was the point. By 1969, The Turtles didn't really have an identity as witnessed by their previous *Battle of the Bands* album. Here, they are desperately depending on The Kinks' Ray Davies to make them into a real band, something even the best producer would have difficulty with for any group, but it seemed to be especially difficult for The Turtles. The good news is, similar to The Beatles' *White Album*, there is a very eclectic choice of different sounding songs all on the same album.
Charles: These guys often leave me laughing, even when I'm singing along to their stuff (more so at their on-stage shtick through years). There's nothing funny about this track, which gives a taste of The Who's or Kinks' early years. It starts off nice enough, but as it continues, it shines with some excellent harmonies, well-placed hand claps, and even more excellent harmonies.

—

SHE'D RATHER BE WITH ME (Garry Bonner, Alan Gordon) by The Turtles
Turtles involvement: Mark Volman—harmony and backing vocals; Howard Kaylan—lead and backing vocals; Al Nichol—lead guitar, piano, backing vocals; Jim Tucker—rhythm guitar, backing vocals; Jim Pons—bass, backing vocals; John Barbata—drums
Additional personnel: Joe Wissert—producer; Bones Howe, Armin Steiner, Bruce Botnick—engineers; Bud Brisbois, Roy Caton, Tony Terran—trumpets; Lou Blackburn, Lew McCreary—trombones; Bobby Knight—bass trombone; Ray Pohlman—horn arrangement
Recording dates: December 1966 - April 1967 at Sunset Sound Recorders, Hollywood, California
Highest chart position: #3 for single; #25 from *Happy Together*
Original release date: April 1967 for single; April 29, 1967 for album
Significant other versions: Flo & Eddie

Mark: This song is every bit as good as "Happy Together." It was a hit, but didn't get the bonus of being covered by everyone. In fact, I didn't find ANY cover versions of this song. Sad, really. It is an excellent tune. The stereo version has much more prominent bass, piano, organ, brass, and cowbell ("more cowbell!") than the mono version.

The live performance from 1982 (called "She'd Rather Ending") is on *New York "Times" 1979-1994 Live at The Bottom Line* and has some silly "Honeymooners" impersonations and a segue into the *Ghostbusters* theme. Flo & Eddie also sang a 1991 live version that appeared on *The Turtles Featuring Flo & Eddie Captured Live*.

Charles: I remember kids thinking that this song was called "Some Girls" at the time! What more can you say? Every note in this one screams "hit!" So let's do this again: The vocals? Check. Background vocals? Check. The instrumentation? Check. The drumming? Check. The infectious hook? Check. The energy? Check. The danceability factor? Check. The smile-inducing factor? Check. Cowbells? Check. Lead cowbell break? Check. Use of nonsense words (ra ba ba ba)? Check.

As good as "Happy Together?" No, but not far off.

—

SHE'LL COME BACK (Howard Kaylan) by The Turtles
Turtles involvement: Mark Volman—vocal harmony, tambourine; Howard Kaylan—lead vocals; Al Nichol—lead guitar, organ, piano, harpsichord, vocals; Jim Tucker—rhythm guitar; Chuck Portz—bass guitar; Don Murray—drums
Additional personnel: Bones Howe—producer, engineer; Armin Steiner, engineer
Recording dates: April - September 1966 at Western Recorders, Hollywood, California
Highest chart position: Did not chart from *Wooden Head*
Original release date: April 25, 1966 from *Out Of Sight Soundtrack*; November 1970 on *Wooden Head*

Mark: Performed in the 1966 movie *Out Of Sight*, this song was strangely left off of the *You Baby* album released the same month. Unless there was a contractual reason, it seems like it would be a no-brainer to include the song on what was their current album or at least issue it as a single, which it wasn't. It probably would have flopped as a single anyway, as it kind of plods along with the same guitar riff being played over and over and over. Since it was released on the *Out Of Sight Soundtrack*, this marks the first time The Turtles were released on a major label, Decca.

Charles: Earlier in the book, we discussed the movie this song appeared in. I offered my spoiler alert, warning that once two things are brought to your attention, you'll always cringe when you hear this soundtrack offering. Again, don't read on if you already like this song, because I'm about to potentially ruin it for you. Similarly, if you have never heard it before, I warn you not to read further so you won't be influenced. The problem is, no matter what, you'll play the song (again or for the first time) just to hear the following annoyances for yourself. Okay, here goes...

Annoyance #1. Howard rarely gives a bland vocal performance. This is not only the exception, but for some reason he doesn't really sing "she'll" (as in "she will"). Instead, for some inexplicable reason, he sings it as "shill." And, although it's not shrill, it's downhill every time. It's even there in the outro.

Annoyance #2. That repetitive lead guitar riff that's played over and over, ad nauseam, throughout the song.

—

SHELL SHOCK (compilation) by The Turtles
Turtles involvement: See individual Turtles tracks
Additional personnel: See individual Turtles tracks
Recording dates: 1969 - 1970
Highest chart position: Did not chart
Original release date: March 1987

Goodbye Surprise
Like It or Not
There You Sit Lonely
We Ain't Gonna Party No More
Cat in the Window
Lady-O

Can I Go On
Dance This Dance With Me
You Want to Be a Woman
If We Only Had the Time
Gas Money
Teardrops
Who Would Ever Think That I Would Marry Margaret?

A creation of a might-have-been album that The Turtles were in the midst of recording at the end of 1969 and beginning of 1970 before they broke up. It does contain songs that probably wouldn't have made the final cut like "Who Would Ever Think That I Would Marry Margaret?" and missing songs that might have made the cut like "Marmendy Mill" and "Strange Girl," but it was a good attempt with what was already previously released at the time.

—

SHE'S MY GIRL (Garry Bonner, Alan Gordon) by The Turtles
Turtles involvement: Mark Volman—harmony and backing vocals; Howard Kaylan—lead and backing vocals; Al Nichol—lead 12-string guitar, piano, backing vocals; Jim Pons—bass, backing vocals; John Barbata—drums
Additional personnel: Joe Wissert—producer; Bruce Botnick—engineer; Bob Jenkins—congas
Recording dates: 1967 at Sunset Sound Recorders, Hollywood, California
Highest chart position: #14 for single; #146 from *More Golden Hits*
Original release date: November 1967 for single; March 1970 for album
Significant other versions: Flo & Eddie

Mark: One of the best Turtles tunes in their entire catalog with a great opening bass line plus excellent strings and horns throughout used to great effect. Absolute perfection! It's a shame the drug accusations (which were legit) helped this song get banned from airplay in a few places as it deserved much higher chart placement and recognition.

Flo & Eddie sang a decent live version in 1991 on *The Turtles Featuring Flo & Eddie Captured Live*, marred only by Howard's silly narration over the opening.

Charles: Ignore the lounge-lizard intro, that's over in a few seconds. From the point we hear "She's My Girl," there's no doubt that this one is the real deal. A perfect song? Not nearly. Pop purity like "You Baby" or "Happy Together"? No way. But the best parts of this recording are as solid as any from the era. Crazy as it may seem, I would have been happy with two minutes of just the "She's My Girl" chorus/refrain.

—

SILVER BULLET (Gioachino Rossini) by The Crossfires
Turtles involvement: Mark Volman—alto sax; Howard Kaplan—tenor sax; Al Nichol—lead guitar; Tom Stanton—rhythm guitar; Chuck Portz—bass; Don Murray—drums
Additional personnel: Chuck Britz—engineer
Recording dates: April 13 and November 23, 1964 at Western Recorders, Hollywood, California
Highest chart position: Did not chart from *Out of Control*
Original release date: 1981
Significant other versions: The Lone Ranger radio and TV show, Flo & Eddie

Mark: A very "honking" version as Mark and Howard might say. Doing a surf version of the classic "William Tell Overture" was decidedly ingenious, although most people in the crowd at the time probably knew it as "The Lone Ranger Theme." No matter, It was always a favorite of live performances by The Crossfires.

Take #1 was released as a previously unissued alternate version when Sundazed Records re-released *Out of Control* onto CD in 1995. Amusingly, Chuck Britz calls out "What's the name of this? Silver Boy, huh?" to which Howard irritatedly shouts back in response "Silver Bullet!" This has shades of "Daydream Believer." Other than this intro, the two versions are virtually indistinguishable.

The live performance from 1982 is on *New York "Times" 1979-1994 Live at The Bottom Line*. It achieved the same positive reception.

Charles: And they're off! From the first "William Tell Overture" notes, this one simply races. Like a trotter heading to the finish line, the drums and horns lead the pack. And we're all winners!

—

SO GOES LOVE (Gerry Goffin, Carole King) by The Turtles
Turtles involvement: Mark Volman—vocal harmony, tambourine; Howard Kaylan—lead vocals; Al Nichol—lead guitar, organ, piano, harpsichord, vocals; Jim Tucker—rhythm guitar; Chuck Portz—bass guitar; Don Murray—drums
Additional personnel: Bones Howe—producer, engineer; Armin Steiner, engineer; John Audino; Jules Chaikin, Ray Triscari—trumpets; Bob Edmondson—trombone; Art Pepper, alto sax; Bob Perkins—tenor sax; Bill Holman—tenor sax, horn arrangement
Recording dates: April - September 1966 at Western Recorders, Hollywood, California; March 21, 1967 overdubs at Sound Recorders, Hollywood, California
Highest chart position: #7 from *Golden Hits*
Original release date: October 1967
Significant other versions: The Monkees, Carole King

Mark: This was supposed to be The Turtles' fifth single after "Grim Reaper of Love" stalled. Had it been released, it would have come out in June 1966 and backed with "On a Summer's Day." As it turned out, it was quietly added to *Golden Hits* in 1967, which was a nice addition to an otherwise oldies collection. As far as the song itself, you can't go wrong with most Goffin/King material.

Charles: Did Carole King and her husband Gerry Goffin have an issue with The Turtles? Probably not, but then why didn't they give them a better song to record? Just kidding—writers don't really "give" songs to artists (usually). The song is nice enough, and there are some fine stanzas, but it's not a hit song by any measure. Perhaps it's better that it wasn't issued as a single, or it may have tanked. There's a slower, more calculated rendition by Dave Berry which somehow works better. In fact, there's an even slower version by The Monkees, which has a clear lounge vibe, but also never goes anywhere. Best option is Carole King's own demo of it.

SOLID ZINC: THE TURTLES ANTHOLOGY
(compilation) by The Turtles
Turtles involvement: See individual Turtles tracks
Additional personnel: See individual Turtles tracks
Recording dates: 1965 - 1970
Highest chart position: Did not chart
Original release date: February 19, 2002

It Ain't Me Babe
Almost There
Let Me Be
Wanderin' Kind
Your Maw Said You Cried
Glitter and Gold
It Was a Very Good Year
Let the Cold Winds Blow
Eve of Destruction
Flyin' High
You Baby
I Know That You'll Be There
Just a Room
She'll Come Back
Tie Me Down
I Can't Stop
I Get Out of Breath
So Goes Love
Grim Reaper of Love
Is It Any Wonder?
Like the Seasons
We'll Meet Again
Outside Chance
Makin' My Mind Up
Can I Get to Know You Better

Happy Together
Too Young to Be One
Me About You
She'd Rather Be With Me
Guide For the Married Man
You Know What I Mean
She's My Girl
Cat in the Window
Sound Asleep
The Last Thing I Remember (The First Thing I Knew) (demo)

The Story of Rock and Roll
The Battle of the Bands
Elenore
You Showed Me
Surfer Dan
Earth Anthem
Somewhere Friday Night
Marmendy Mill (demo)
How You Loved Me (demo)
House on the Hill
You Don't Have to Walk in the Rain
Love in the City
There You Sit Lonely
Goodbye Surprise
We Ain't Gonna Party No More
Lady-O

This is one of the better Turtles compilations to get, due to the number of tracks, the sound quality, and also the great booklet enclosed. It features the first appearance of the "Marmendy Mill" demo which didn't get a proper release as a finished song until 1973's *Flo & Eddie* album, and the first appearance of the "How You Loved Me" demo, of which the final version originally appeared on *Turtle Soup*. The only drawback to this collection now is that it is long out of print and commands a pretty hefty price tag. Grab it if you can see it cheap.

—

SOMEWHERE FRIDAY NIGHT aka **SOMEWHERE FRIDAY NITE** (The Turtles) by The Turtles
Turtles involvement: Mark Volman—vocals, percussion, occasional guitars; Howard Kaylan—lead vocal, occasional percussion, organ; Al Nichol—vocals, guitars, keyboards, six string bass; Jim Pons—vocals, bass, occasional guitars; John Seiter—vocals, drums, occasional piano
Additional personnel: The Turtles—producers; Jim Lowe—engineer
Recording dates: March 1969 at ID Sound Studios, Hollywood, California
Highest chart position: Single did not chart; B-side to "Lady-O"; #117 from *Turtle Soup*
Original release date: October 1969 for album; November 1969 for single

Mark: I sound like a broken record here, but again… if The Turtles successfully made it to RCA Records, this would have been a Top 10 hit. For God's sake, they were still promoting it on their final TV appearance on "The Barbara McNair Show" in April 1970. They knew it was a good track. Too bad no one else did. True Turtles fans know better and this one is a treasure.

Charles: There is such subtle sweetness here, it's hard to not like it. For a band that started as folk rockers, and became pop rockers before going off in so many tangents (like I do in many of my reviews here in this book), dare I say that this one has a jazz feel to it. It's also rather spacey (again, like many of my reviews here in this book).

—

SOUND ASLEEP (Howard Kaylan, Mark Volman) by The Turtles
Turtles involvement: Mark Volman—vocals, special effects; Howard Kaylan—lead vocals; Al Nichol—guitars, organ, piano, Moog synthesizer, electric sitar, vocals; Jim Pons—bass, vocals; John Barbata—drums, percussion, vocals
Additional personnel: The Turtles—producers; Eric Wangberg—engineer; Roy Caton, Freddie Hill—trumpets; Lou Blackburn, Francis Fitzpatrick, Lew McCreary—trombones; John Johnson—tuba; Sidney Miller—bassoon; Donald Peake—horn orchestration
Recording dates: January - February 1968 at Sound Recorders, Hollywood, California
Highest chart position: #57 for single; #146 from *More Golden Hits*
Original release date: February 1968 for single; March 1970 for album

Mark: Depending on which collection you listen to determines the length of this song. I believe the longer, uncut version first appeared on *Solid Zinc*. This longer version has a chorus of ducks that extends way past the original's fade-out. The stereo version has a nice speaker-spanning felled tree sound effect that was used again in Yoko Ono's "Touch Me." The mono version has fewer sound effects than the stereo version, where The Turtles really went crazy.
Charles: A sonic carousel, you couldn't fall sound asleep listening to the multiple directions this one takes. Part amusement park anthem, part sound effects experiment, part Beatles celebration (listen to that Harrison part which seems to be only missing a sitar) and part party particle (how's that for silly alliteration?), it's a musical joy ride you don't want to jump off of… sound asleep of fully awake!

—

STAY AROUND (Howard Kaplan, Al Nichol) by The Crossfires
Turtles involvement: Mark Volman—alto sax, lead vocals; Howard Kaplan—tenor sax, lead vocals; Al Nichol—lead guitar, background vocals; Jim Tucker—rhythm guitar; Chuck Portz—bass; Terry Hand—drums
Additional personnel: Chuck Britz—engineer
Recording dates: November 23, 1964 at Western Recorders, Hollywood, California
Highest chart position: Did not chart from *Out of Control*
Original release date: 1981

Mark: This song shows an early example of what would become The Turtles' signature harmonies with Howard, Mark, and Al singing together. Jim and Chuck are possibly singing along too as it's not too hard to sing "come on and stay" over and over. The song speeds up a bit as it fades out. Not their best effort, but not bad. They were still learning and growing.

Charles: Spotify shuffles this with Dick Dale, Link Wray, The Rumblers, and The Long Boards, which is interesting because The Crossfires' instrumentals land them squarely in the Ventures/Tornados territory. NRBQ could have had some fun with this one. This is basic dance-hall surf-rock stuff with perfunctory vocals and nothing really too special, but a nice ending that double-times just enough to make it worthwhile.

—

STORY OF ROCK AND ROLL, THE (Harry Nilsson) by The Turtles
Turtles involvement: Mark Volman—vocals, special effects; Howard Kaylan—lead vocals; Al Nichol—guitars, organ, piano, Moog synthesizer, vocals; Jim Pons—bass, vocals; John Barbata—drums, percussion, vocals
Additional personnel: Chip Douglas, producer; Jim Hilton—engineer; Harry Nilsson—piano; Chip Douglas—keyboards; Bob Jenkins—bongos; Jim Horn, Plas Johnson—saxophones
Recording dates: May 1968 at Gold Star Studios, Hollywood, California
Highest chart position: #48 for single; #146 from *More Golden Hits*
Original release date: May 1968 for single; March 1970 for album
Significant other versions: Harry Nilsson, The Collage

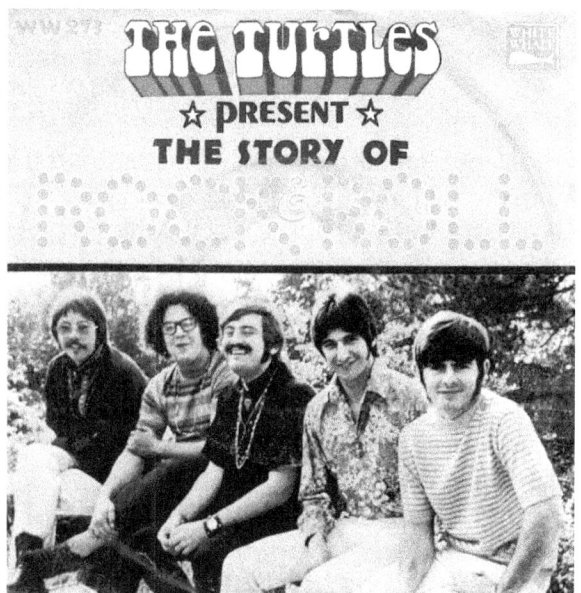

Mark: I'm a huge fan of Harry Nilsson, but this has got to be one of his lamest songs. The Turtles took the challenge, but still can't lift it above the lackluster level that it remains at. Even a key change at the end doesn't help. It should have remained in the can and definitely should not have been a single. Even the lyrics are lousy.

Charles: What a team—The Turtles and Harry Nilsson. What could go wrong? Not a lot, actually. But not a lot of greatness, either. It's all rather generic. Seems like something B.J. Thomas or Three Dog Night might have eventually recorded as an album filler.

STRANGE GIRL (Howard Kaylan) by The Turtles
Turtles involvement: Howard Kaylan—vocals, occasional percussion, organ; Mark Volman—vocals, percussion, occasional guitars; Al Nichol—vocals, guitars, keyboards, six string bass; Jim Pons—vocals, bass, occasional guitars; John Seiter—vocals, drums, occasional piano
Additional personnel: The Turtles—producer; Jim Lowe—engineer
Recording dates: March 1969 at ID Sound Studios, Hollywood, California
Highest chart position: Did not chart from *Turtle Soup* (CD reissue)
Original release date: June 22, 2016
Significant other versions: Flo & Eddie

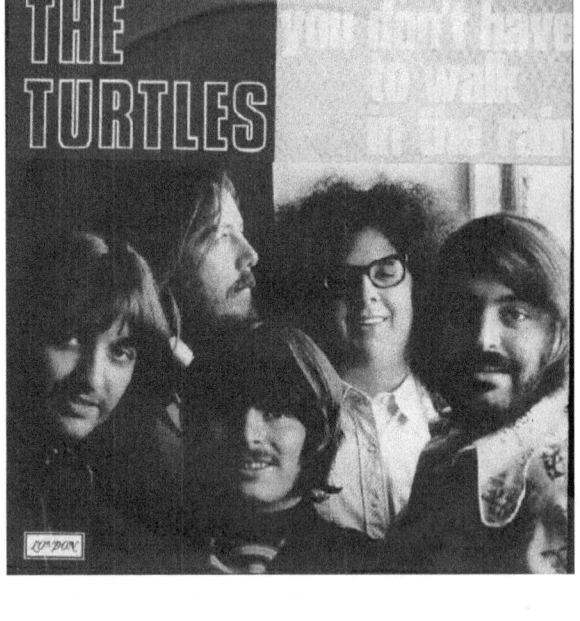

Mark: This demo was left off *Turtle Soup* and first released on the 2016 *Turtle Soup* reissue. It is unknown as to whether it was tried again for *Shell Shock*, but it was resurrected for sure for 1972's *The Phlorescent Leech and Eddie*. It's a nice, sweet song, but sounds incomplete here for obvious reasons. I think it's better than "Dance this Dance With Me," but I wasn't making the song decisions.
Charles: Mostly acoustic track written by Howard and Mark shows serious sophistication and a Micky Dolenz-esque vocal. I can picture a coven of witches prancing and dancing around a campfire while a Bohemian guitarist is plucking away at this, and two wise wizards are out in the woods purveying the scene and singing "I know your secret."

—

SURFER DAN (Al Nichol, Jim Pons, Chip Douglas) by The Cross Fires
Turtles involvement: Mark Volman—vocals, special effects; Howard Kaylan—backing vocals; Al Nichol—guitars, organ, piano, Moog synthesizer, lead vocals; Jim Pons—bass, vocals; John Barbata—drums, percussion, vocals
Additional personnel: Chip Douglas—producer: Jim Hilton, Armin Steiner—engineers
Recording dates: May - June 1968 at Gold Star Studios, Hollywood, California; Western Recorders, Hollywood, California; T.T.G./Sunset-Highland Recording Studios, Hollywood, California

Highest chart position: Single did not chart; B-side of "Elenore;" #128 from *The Turtles Present the Battle of the Bands*
Original release date: September 1968 for single; November 1, 1968 for album

Mark: Jim Pons originally composed lyrics for Al Nichol's tune. Then it was called "Flashing Man." Chip Douglas rewrote the lyrics and renamed it "Surfer Dan." Al was back in his element being able to revive The Crossfires (here named The Cross Fires) for a moment in this definitive Beach Boys/Jan and Dean homage. I love all of the coughing about 2:30 into it.
Charles: Not to be confused with "Surfer Girl," "Surfer Joe," or "Surfin' Bird," this one's a harmony-laden pop gem that sounds like it's right out of the Brian Wilson/Beach Boys/Jan and Dean songbook. It's a tribute to a song and arrangement when it manages to pay such perfect homage to the surf/beach musical style without sounding exactly like a ripoff of any one song from that genre. Grab your surfboard and boogie to the flip side of their hit "Elenore." Great line: "He's so ripped he can't see you go by."

—

TEARDROPS (Helen Stanley, Roy Calhoun, Barry Golder, Larry Brown) by The Dedications
Turtles involvement: Howard Kaylan—vocals, occasional percussion, organ; Mark Volman—lead vocals, percussion, occasional guitars; Al Nichol—vocals, guitars, keyboards, six string bass; Jim Pons—vocals, occasional guitars; John Seiter—vocals, drums, occasional piano
Additional personnel: Bobby Jimmi—producer
Recording dates: 1969 at Sunwest Recording Studios, Hollywood, California
Highest chart position: Single did not chart; #194 from *Happy Together Again!*
Original release date: February 1970 for single; November 1974 for album
Significant other versions: Lee Andrews and the Hearts

Mark: Howard says that there is no bass on this one and Mark sings lead. It's kind of difficult to determine what The Turtles were thinking at this point, by recording this and "Gas Money" as a single. It may have been just for a single, or for *Shell Shock*, and it managed to come out as a promotional single only under the moniker of The Dedications. What was happening to The Turtles after *Turtle Soup* until they broke up was definitely strange and it may never be completely revealed.
Charles: Holy moly—this is an amazing Doo-Wop song! It's got every element that has ever made a doo-wop ballad great: a sad story, solid vocal, plinking piano, chord changes, harmonies, acapella break toward the end, music return at end, and you could dance with your sweetie to it under the moonlight or make out to it in the back of your '56 Buick convertible. Somebody please play this for Kenny Vance so he can record it!

THAT'LL BE THE DAY (Jerry Allison, Buddy Holly, Norman Petty) by The Crossfires
Turtles involvement: Mark Volman—alto sax, lead vocals; Howard Kaplan—tenor sax, lead vocals; Al Nichol—lead guitar, background vocals; Tom Stanton—rhythm guitar; Chuck Portz—bass; Don Murray—drums
Additional personnel: John Bradbury, Larry Johnson—producers; Chuck Britz—engineer
Recording dates: April 13 and November 23, 1964 at Western Recorders, Hollywood, California
Highest chart position: Did not chart; Did not chart from *Out of Control*
Original release date: February 1965 for single; 1981 for album
Significant other versions: Buddy Holly and the Three Tunes, The Crickets, The Quarrymen, Linda Ronstadt, The Ravens, Pat Boone, Bobby Vee, The Everly Brothers, Skeeter Davis, Paul and Barry Ryan, The Flamin' Groovies, Foghat, Link Wray, The La's, Overboard, Modest Mouse, Stevie Nicks, Peter Asher, Chris Isaak, Boz Scaggs, Graham Nash

Mark: A nice, upbeat cover of the old Buddy Holly classic. Strangely, The Turtles' single debut (actually second and the B-side) as The Crossfires with this song was more spirited and heartfelt than The Beatles' debut as The Quarrymen. The Crossfires sound less nervous and more professional.
Charles: A rather perfunctory version of the fifties staple. It's good enough, but kind of clunks along with no real soul or spirit. We expect energy, spontaneity, and fun from The Crossfires, and this doesn't cross-fire, it mis-fires. The saving grace is the ending.

—

THERE YOU SIT LONELY (Mark Volman and Howard Kaylan) by The Turtles
Turtles involvement: Howard Kaylan—vocals, occasional percussion, organ; Mark Volman—vocals, percussion, occasional guitars; Al Nichol—vocals, guitars, keyboards, six string bass; Jim Pons—vocals, bass, occasional guitars; John Seiter—vocals, drums, occasional piano
Additional personnel: Jerry Yester—producer; Barry Keene—engineer
Recording dates: 1969 at Sunwest Recording Studios, Hollywood, California; 1970 at Crystal Sound Recording Studios, Hollywood, California
Highest chart position: #194 from *Happy Together Again!*
Original release date: November 1974
Significant other versions: Flo & Eddie

Mark: This is a nice, sweet song along the lines of "You Showed Me." It might have made for a better single release had the *Shell Shock* sessions been successful. Like "Like it or Not," Mark and

Howard felt it deserved release and they included it in their first Turtles compilation in 1974. It was remade for *The Phlorescent Leech and Eddie* in 1972, but this is the superior version. It was also the B-side of the "Happy Together" single reissue in 1987.

Charles: Like a precursor to ELO's "Can't Get it Out of My Head," or some of Harry Nilsson's more pensive piano recordings, there's a pretty, yet haunting quality which resonates during the listening of this song, and stays long after it's over. The vocals are mint, and if The Turtles ever make it into the Rock and Roll Hall of Fame, as they should, the decision should be weighted by tracks such as this one, combined with the better-known hits that dominated the airwaves in their prime. It's interesting to note that the entire band gets the writing credits for this release, but only Kaylan and Volman are credited on the Flo & Eddie version half a decade later.

—

THINK I'LL RUN AWAY (Howard Kaylan, Mark Volman) by The Turtles
Turtles involvement: Mark Volman—harmony and backing vocals; Howard Kaylan—lead and backing vocals; Al Nichol—lead guitar, piano, backing vocals; Jim Tucker—rhythm guitar, backing vocals; Jim Pons—bass, backing vocals; John Barbata—drums
Additional personnel: Joe Wissert—producer; Bones Howe, Armin Steiner, Bruce Botnick—engineers
Recording dates: December 1966 - April 1967 at Sunset Sound Recorders, Hollywood, California
Highest chart position: Did not chart; B-side of "Guide for the Married Man" and "Me About You;" #25 from *Happy Together*
Original release date: April 29, 1967 for album; June 1967 for single

Mark: Howard sings this with a dreamy voice, which suits the song. It's quite unlike anything The Turtles had done up to this point, and even afterwards, but it all somehow works. "Da da da da da da da da da da." The ending is reminiscent of a Native American drum beat. Well, you have to end a song somehow. The backing vocals are much more discernible on the stereo version than the mono version.
Charles: Are those strings that precede the percussion? No, but it's probably not Andy Cahan, who I thought was on this (Andy being "The Most Famous Musician You Never Heard Of"). Did

Jeff Lynne hear this intro and get inspired to make it an ELO sound? From that lovely intro right up until the classy vocal ending, everything about this subtle composition works, and although it's certainly not hit material, it's not intended to be.

—

30 YEARS OF ROCK 'N' ROLL (compilation) by The Turtles
Turtles involvement: See individual Turtles tracks
Additional personnel: See individual Turtles tracks
Recording dates: 1965 - 1970
Highest chart position: Did not chart
Original release date: September 26, 1995

Let Me Be:
Happy Together
Let Me Be
You Don't Have to Walk in the Rain
Lady-O
Makin' My Mind Up
Buzzsaw
Hot Little Hands
Just a Room
Who Would Ever Think That I Would Marry Margaret?
Like It Or Not
Like a Rolling Stone
Can I Go On

Eve of Destruction:
She'd Rather Be With Me
Love in the City
Grim Reaper of Love
Guide for the Married Man
Eve of Destruction
House on the Hill
It Was a Very Good Year
If We Only Had the Time
Think I'll Run Away
Almost There
We'll Meet Again
Down in Suburbia

She's My Girl:
She's My Girl
Can I Get to Know You Better
Sound Asleep
Me About You

Battle of the Bands
Out of Breath
Goodbye Surprise
Glitter and Gold
To See the Sun
I'm Chief Kamanawanalea (We're the Royal Macadamia Nuts)
To Young to Be One
You Want to Be a Woman

The Story of Rock and Roll:
It Ain't Me Babe
You Showed Me
The Story of Rock and Roll
Surfer Dan
Wanderin' Kind
How You Loved Me
Your Maw Said You Cried
Dance This Dance With Me
Can't You Hear the Cows
So Goes Love
Chicken Little Was Right
The Owl

Elenore:
Elenore
You Baby
You Know What I Mean
Outside Chance
Like the Seasons
Bachelor Mother
The Last Thing I Remember, The First Thing I Knew
Love Minus Zero
I Can't Stop
Earth Anthem
Somewhere Friday Night
We Ain't Gonna Party No More

A five-disc set sold together and also separately on the cheapie Laserlight label. The only good part is the sound quality, but many tracks are missing which could have easily fit on the CDs, and they are also placed in random order and categorized by themes. It's better to get the Manifesto box set in 2016 plus the two-disc *All the Singles*.

—

TIE ME DOWN (David Gates) by The Turtles
Turtles involvement: Mark Volman—vocal harmony, tambourine; Howard Kaylan—lead vocals; Al Nichol—lead guitar, organ, piano, harpsichord, vocals; Jim Tucker—rhythm guitar; Chuck Portz—bass guitar; Don Murray—drums
Additional personnel: Bones Howe—producer, engineer; Armin Steiner, engineer

Recording dates: April - September 1966 at Western Recorders, Hollywood, California
Highest chart position: Did not chart from *Wooden Head*
Original release date: November 1970

Mark: One of the better outtakes from the *Wooden Head* set. It's really kind of puzzling trying to figure out why some songs made the cut for release and others remained on the shelf. Again, I figure it was because The Turtles were preferring to have more originals instead of so many cover songs. The covers were probably recorded in reserve for some future time so that they could be released to fill out an album... like *Wooden Head*!

Charles: If you remember the soft-rock band Bread, you may recall their lead singer was David Gates. Gates wrote many songs for other artists, and this one is decent, albeit fairly formulaic. This is yet another track that makes me think of Eric Burdon and The Animals.

—

TO SEE THE SUN (The Turtles) by The Turtles
Turtles involvement: Mark Volman—vocals, special effects; Howard Kaylan—lead vocals; Al Nichol—guitars, organ, piano, Moog synthesizer, vocals; Jim Pons—bass, vocals; John Barbata—drums, percussion, vocals
Additional personnel: The Turtles—producers
Recording dates: February 1968 at Ter-Mar Recording Studios, Chicago, Illinois; Olmsted Sound Studios, New York, New York; Sound Recorders, Hollywood, California; Mixed September 1978 by H, Lee Wolen and Jim Rayton at Ascot Recorders
Highest chart position: Did not chart from *1968*
Original release date: October 1978

Mark: This has all the makings of a great single A-side, but it's definitely missing something. According to Howard and Mark, it's missing apparently quite a lot, as there were supposed to be many more effects and a full orchestra added to what you hear here. It would be fun if they would go back in and finish it, or hand it off to someone else like a Jeff Lynne or a Giles Martin to see what they could do with it. I'm not sure who did the child vocals at about 2:20. I'm also not sure if it was supposed to really go the full 4:28 as released in 1978, as it seems to peter out at about the three-minute mark. As with "The Owl," White Whale stopped all of this self-indulgence by The

Turtles and got them back on track with more hits and less psychedelic experimentation on the company's dime.

Charles: Lots of la-la-las and more Barbata beats highlight a pretty cool song with a nice arrangement. It takes one of those unexpected left hand turns about two minutes in, and then tricks you into thinking it's over, but it returns with a vengeance. At that point, there's no predicting where it's going, and that's just fine. We think we hear a children's choir and perhaps barn animals at the very end, but they're probably tricking us with vocal foolery. A very very very very very interesting recording, and I say "very" so many times because they do too!

—

TOO MUCH HEARTSICK FEELING (Jim Pons) by Quad City Ramblers
Turtles involvement: Mark Volman—vocals, special effects; Howard Kaylan—vocal; Al Nichol—guitars, organ, piano, Moog synthesizer, vocals; Jim Pons—bass, lead vocals; John Barbata—drums, percussion, vocals
Additional personnel: Chip Douglas—producer: Jim Hilton, Armin Steiner—engineers
Recording dates: May - June 1968 at Gold Star Studios, Hollywood, California; Western Recorders, Hollywood, California; T.T.G./Sunset-Highland Recording Studios, Hollywood, California
Highest chart position: #128 from *The Turtles Present the Battle of the Bands*
Original release date: November 1, 1968

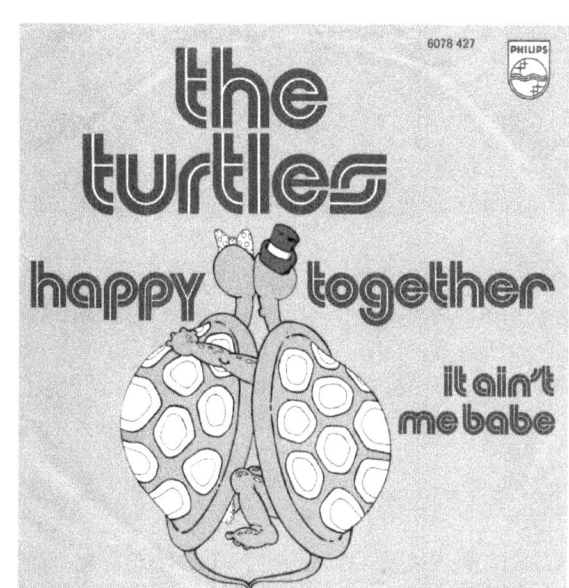

Mark: Jim Pons made many fine contributions to this *Battle of the Bands* album, and really got into making each one sound like it's from a different genre. It really worked on a different level, as folk rock groups such as The Byrds were also dabbling and then transitioning completely into Country & Western music about this time with lots of pedal steel guitar. Pons' deep voice really suits the tune well with a typically tongue-in-cheek spoken word part in the middle.

Charles: Down-home, knee-slapping, country western rambling that would make Roy Rogers proud. Throw on your overalls and jump in the hay. Hey—this sounds like the stuff that Ringo Starr was listening to when he wanted to grow up to be a cowboy—or a rock & roll drummer. Not sure why there's some drunken hysterical laughing in the background, but I stopped trying to figure out the stuff these guys threw into their recordings many pages ago. They sing, "I don't suppose you'll understand"… and they're right.

—

TOO YOUNG TO BE ONE (Eric Eisner) by The Turtles
Turtles involvement: Turtles involvement: Mark Volman—harmony and backing vocals; Howard Kaylan—lead and backing vocals; Al Nichol—lead guitar, piano, backing vocals; Jim Tucker—rhythm guitar, backing vocals; Jim Pons—bass, backing vocals; John Barbata—drums

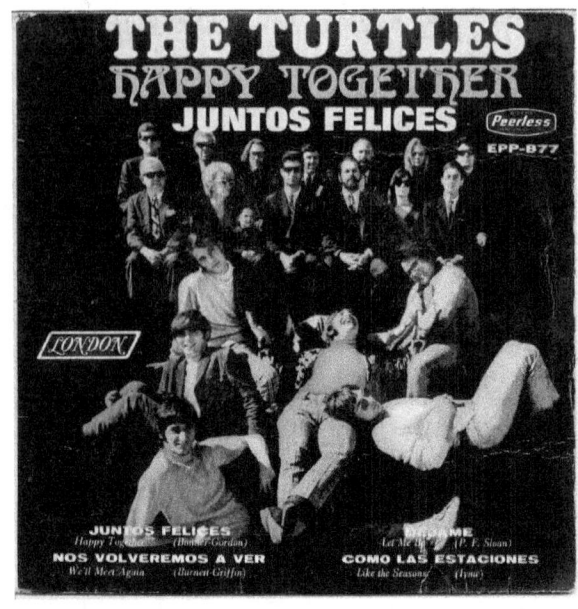

Additional personnel: Joe Wissert—producer; Bones Howe, Armin Steiner, Bruce Botnick—engineers
Recording dates: December 1966 - April 1967 at Sunset Sound Recorders, Hollywood, California
Highest chart position: #25 from *Happy Together*
Original release date: April 29, 1967
Significant other versions: Buffalo Springfield

Mark: This song is Jim Pons' debut with The Turtles on bass, shortly after Chip Douglas departed for The Monkees, thanks to Michael Nesmith. Like "Think I'll Run Away," it has the dreamy Howard singing. What's different about it is the middle section which seems like it was clipped from a modern jazz record. This alone makes the tune stand out.

Charles: This was written by Eric Eisner, a music and movie business mogul who eventually became President of the David Geffen Organization. He wrote breezy pop tunes that were recorded by The Association and Buffalo Springfield. This could easily have been a hit for The Association, actually. It is quite good. The middle section sounds far more like it was written for Chicago than any modern jazz record.

—

TORN BETWEEN TEMPTATIONS (The Turtles) by The Turtles
Turtles involvement: Mark Volman—lead vocal, percussion, occasional guitars; Howard Kaylan—vocals, occasional percussion, organ; Al Nichol—vocals, guitars, keyboards, six string bass; Jim Pons—lead vocal, bass, occasional guitars; John Seiter—vocals, drums, occasional piano
Additional personnel: Ray Davies—producer; Chuck Britz—engineer
Recording dates: April - July 1969 at United Records, Hollywood, California
Highest chart position: #117 from *Turtle Soup*
Original release date: October 1969

Mark: Mark Volman would have quite a few lead vocal lines when they became Flo & Eddie. For now, they were a bit of a rarity and he does well, with the requisite Jim Pons harmonies. Of course, he's an excellent singer and this song with the country twang comes off generally well, despite it being kind of schizophrenic. "Feels like heaven going down."

Charles: An amalgamation of styles, what we have here is mostly a country song very similar to a Mike Nesmith tune. Just another example of The Turtles' versatility, with fitting lead guitar parts, natural harmonies, and a decent hook, plus a neat heaven vs. hell lyric. Listen to the very end for some fun stuff in the fade-out.

—

TURTLE SOUP (LP) by The Turtles
Turtles involvement: Mark Volman—vocals, percussion, occasional guitars; Howard Kaylan—vocals, occasional percussion, organ; Al Nichol—vocals, guitars, keyboards, six string bass; Jim Pons—vocals, bass, occasional guitars; John Seiter—vocals, drums, occasional piano
Additional personnel: Ray Davies—producer; The Turtles—producers on "Somewhere Friday Night"; Chuck Britz—engineer; Jim Lowe—engineer on "Somewhere Friday Night;" Roy Caton, Manny Klein, Tony Terran—trumpets; David Duke, George Hyde, Alan Robinson—French horns; Ray Pohlman—horn arrangements on "House on the Hill" and "You Don't Have to Walk in the Rain;" Bud Brisbois, Roy Caton, Ollie Mitchell—trumpets; William

Henshaw, Henry Sigismonti—French horns; Richard Leith, Lew McCreary, Thomas Shepard—trombones; Bobby Bruce, John DeVoogdt, Leonard Malarsky, Nick Pisani, George Poole, Paul Shure, Walter Wiemeyer, Tibor Selig—violins; Gareth Nuttycombe, Darrel Terwilliger—violas; Ray Kelley, Joseph Saxon—cellos; Ray Pohlman—horn and string arrangements on "Love in the City"
Recording dates: March 1969 at ID Sound Studios, Hollywood, California for "Somewhere Friday Night"; April - July 1969 at United Records, Hollywood, California
Highest chart position: #117
Original release date: October 1969

Come Over
House on the Hill
She Always Leaves Me Laughing
How You Loved Me
Torn Between Temptations
Love in the City

Bachelor Mother
John and Julie
Hot Little Hands
Somewhere Friday Night
Dance This Dance With Me
You Don't Have to Walk in the Rain

Bonus tracks on Sundazed edition:

Lady-O
The Last Thing I Remember (The First Thing I Knew) (demo)
Turtle Soup Radio Spot

Bonus tracks on Repertoire edition:
Chicken Little Was Right
Lady-O
The Last Thing I Remember (The First Thing I Knew) (demo)
The Owl
To See the Sun
If We Only Had the Time
Can I Go On
Dance This Dance With Me

Bonus tracks on Manifesto edition:
Goodbye Surprise
Like It Or Not
There You Sit Lonely
Can I Go On
You Want to Be a Woman
If We Only Had the Time
Dance This Dance With Me (demo)
Come Over (demo)
How You Loved Me (demo)
Strange Girl (demo)
Marmendy Mill (demo)
Turtle Soup Radio Spot

This is kind of a schizophrenic album, but this is still The Turtles. The legend goes that after *Battle of the Bands*, The Turtles felt that they deserved to work with a top-notch producer like George Martin or someone of that ilk. Apparently, Chip Douglas and The Turtles had another falling out, or The Turtles just wanted to try a new direction. Ultimately, after whittling down their wish list, they arrived at Ray Davies, who was fresh off of producing The Kinks' *The Village Green Preservation Society*. Davies was available and they turned out a decent product, but I don't think either party was completely satisfied with the results. The Turtles wanted Davies to help make them into more of a cohesive band, while Davies was seeing orchestras and strings for The Turtles. The results vary, but it is the final album released during The Turtles' lifetime, with *Shell Shock* remaining incomplete.

—

TURTLE SOUP RADIO SPOT (unknown) by The Turtles
Turtles involvement: See individual Turtles tracks
Additional personnel: unknown—announcer
Recording dates: 1969
Highest chart position: Did not chart from *The History of Flo & Eddie and The Turtles*
Original release date: 1969 for radio; 1983 for album

Mark: The radio spot for *Turtle Soup* is much more mellow than the *Battle of the Bands* one, and was first released in 1983 on *The Best of Flo & Eddie and The Turtles* as an unlisted track. What a difference a year makes. The Turtles make the transition from AM to FM radio in one short year. The spot features audio clips from "You Don't Have to Walk in the Rain," "Bachelor Mother," "She Always Leaves Me Laughing," "Come Over," "Love in the City," and "Hot Little Hands."
Charles: "This is dynamite."

—

TURTLE TRACKS (compilation) by The Turtles
Turtles involvement: See individual Turtles tracks
Additional personnel: See individual Turtles tracks
Recording dates: 1965 - 1970
Highest chart position: Did not chart
Original release date: 2006

Happy Together
I Can't Stop
Let Me Be
Glitter and Gold
Elenore
The Story of Rock and Roll
It Ain't Me Babe
Hot Little Hands
You Baby
Makin' My Mind Up
She's My Girl
Somewhere Friday Night
You Showed Me
Almost There
She'd Rather Be With Me
Buzzsaw
Surfer Dan
Happy Together
Turtle Soup Radio Spot

This collection is yet another trip to the well, but it does contain the first appearance of the "*Turtle Soup* Radio Spot."

—

TURTLE WAX: THE BEST OF THE TURTLES, VOLUME 2 (compilation) by The Turtles
Turtles involvement: See individual Turtles tracks
Additional personnel: See individual Turtles tracks
Recording dates: 1965 - 1970
Highest chart position: Did not chart
Original release date: 1988

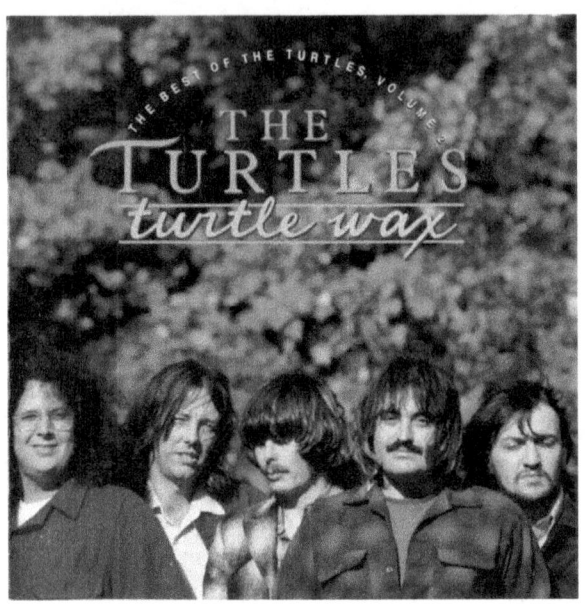

Goodbye Surprise
House on the Hill
Somewhere Friday Night
We Ain't Gonna Party No More
There You Sit Lonely
We'll Meet Again
Makin' My Mind Up
Is It Any Wonder?
Surfer Dan
The Battle of the Bands
Earth Anthem
Wanderin' Kind
Almost There
It Was a Very Good Year
Your Maw Said You Cried
Glitter and Gold
So Goes Love
I Get Out of Breath
Just a Room
Like the Seasons

What? A Turtles collection that DOESN'T have "Happy Together?" Well certainly, as this was Volume 2 from Rhino. It was very welcome at the time, as many of the tracks had not been on CD before. It has now been superseded by superior two-disc compilations like *Solid Zinc* and *All the Singles*, but it was a Godsend at the time.

—

TURTLES FEATURING FLO & EDDIE CAPTURED LIVE, THE (CD) by The Turtles
Turtles involvement: Mark Volman—vocals, guitar; Howard Kaylan—lead vocals
Additional personnel: Steve Remote, David Nelson—producers, mixers; Steve Remote—engineer; Flo & Eddie—executive producers; Joe Stefko—drums; David Nelson—lead guitar, vocals; Donnie Kisselbach—bass guitar, vocals; Chris Apostle—keyboards, vocals; Peter Zale—

keyboards; Richie Cannata—saxophones, vocals, keyboards
Recording dates: December 31, 1991
Highest chart position: Did not chart
Original release date: November 10, 1992

Feel Older Now (live 1991)
It Ain't Me Babe (live 1991)
Bruce (live1991)
Rebecca (live 1991)
Misty (live 1991)
The Night (live 1991)
Prison Song (live 1991)
She's My Girl (live 1991)
Elenore (live 1991)
Goodbye Surprise (live 1991)
Keep it Warm (live 1991)
Let Me Be (live 1991)

Doors (live 1991)
You Showed Me (live 1991)
You Baby (live 1991)
She'd Rather Be With Me (live 1991)
Happy Together (live 1991)
Moving Targets (live 1991)

This was recorded live at The Bottom Line in New York. This is the first issue of these recordings and probably the best version to get, as it is the most complete, unless you don't like the between song banter and jokey recordings such as "Prison Song," "Bruce," and "Doors." If that's the case, get *All Access*, *Playlist,* or *California Gold* instead.

—

TURTLES GREATEST HITS (compilation) by The Turtles
Turtles involvement: See individual Turtles tracks
Additional personnel: See individual Turtles tracks
Recording dates: 1965 - 1970
Highest chart position: Did not chart
Original release date: 1982

It Ain't Me Be
Let Me Be
You Baby
She's My Girl
Can I Get to Know You Better
Love in the City
Elenore

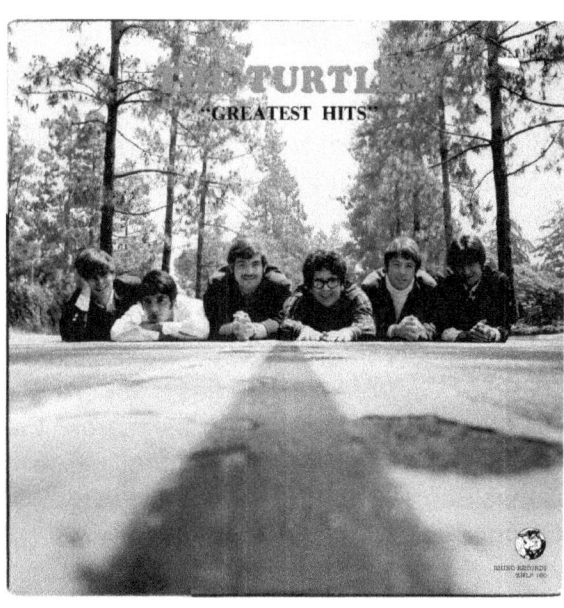

Happy Together
She'd Rather Be With Me
You Know What I Mean
Sound Asleep
You Don't Have to Walk in the Rain
You Showed Me
The Story of Rock and Roll

This very first Rhino compilation is an excellent one. Rhino proved that they were sincere in re-introducing the world to The Turtles and, back in 1982, this was the one to get. It was reissued with six more tracks on CD as (appropriately) *20 Greatest Hits*.

—

TURTLES GREATEST HITS, THE (compilation)
by The Turtles
Turtles involvement: See individual Turtles tracks
Additional personnel: See individual Turtles tracks
Recording dates: 1965 - 1970
Highest chart position: Did not chart
Original release date: 1982

Elenore b/w Is it Any Wonder?
Happy Together b/w The Walking Song
It Ain't Me Babe b/w Almost There
Let Me Be b/w Your Maw Said You Cried
She'd Rather Be With Me b/w Rugs of Woods and Flowers
She's My Girl b/w Chicken Little Was Right
You Baby b/w Wanderin' Kind
You Showed Me b/w Buzzsaw

This was the first of two times that *The Turtles Greatest Hits* was released as a compilation of 7" singles. The second time was in 2014 with the *45 RPM Vinyl Singles Collection*.

—

TURTLES: HAPPY TOGETHER, THE (film)
Turtles involvement: Howard Kaylan, Mark Volman, Don Murray, Chuck Portz, Jim Tucker, John Barbata, Jim Pons, The Turtles
Additional personnel: Ray Manzarek, Elaine "Spanky" McFarlane, Graham Nash, Stephen Stills, Garry Bonner, Alan Gordon, P.F. Sloan, Bones Howe, Allan McDougall, Robert Wood, Carlos Bernal, Henry Diltz, Bill Utley, Eddie Biscoe, Stephen Bishop, Dick Clark, Tom Smothers
Original release date: January 15, 1991

Mark: I loved this documentary so much that I literally wore out the VHS tape. It had huge white streaks through it and sound and picture dropouts. Finally, Rhino reissued it on DVD on December

19, 2000. It really needs an update again with more music performances and updated interviews.

There are also a few errors in the show that I will document here:

1. Their appearance on "Where The Action Is" is listed as November 1965, but according to IMDB, they didn't appear on that show that month of that year, but they did appear on the show seven times.
2. The "Outside Chance" performance on "The Lloyd Thaxton Show" is listed as April 1965 instead of the airdate of July 1966.
3. Their first manager Bill Utley, is misspelled as Bill Uttley.
4. Howard Kaylan exaggerates that Jim Tucker left the band due to John Lennon not acting like a Beatle, but according to Jim it was really due to touring fatigue.
5. The order in which band members left the band was presented out of order.
6. Their performance on "Kraft Music Hall" is listed as September 1968, but it actually aired in July 1968.
7. Howard Kaylan claimed that John Barbata was becoming distant to the group, but Barbata disputes this. He felt The Turtles were no longer going anywhere and that he got an opportunity to join CSNY.
8. The performance of "Somewhere Friday Night" on "The Barbara McNair Show" aired in April 1970 and not January 1970.
9. The check from The White House was more like $65 and not $7, and according to Jim Pons' book, supposedly John Sciter still has the check and the smashed metronome to this day.
10. In his book, Jim Pons disputes that their road manager ran off with his wife to Mexico with Turtles money. He claims it was fully authorized.
11. The documentary implies that "Lady O" was the last thing we heard from The Turtles. In reality, The Turtles continued recording well into 1970 for their eventually uncompleted *Shell Shock* album and some tracks were released at the time after "Lady O" on singles or *More Golden Hits*.
12. The Eagles album that Mark mentions is actually called *Desperado*, not *The Long Riders*.

In no way do these errors detract from the quality or entertainment value of the documentary.

Charles: The ultimate Turtles video. It tells their story with their own words, though often Howard doesn't give Mark equal time. We also hear from friends and contemporaries, some of whom are no longer with us. A must for new Turtles fans as well as first generation die-hards.

I must give credit to Connecticut drummer Mike "Ringo" Streeto for turning me on to this video over twenty years ago, pointing out how much The Turtles loved The Beatles.

—

TURTLES HITS MEDLEY: IT AIN'T ME BABE / YOU BABY / HAPPY TOGETHER / SHE'D RATHER BE WITH ME / ELENORE by The Turtles
Turtles involvement: Howard Kaylan—vocals; Mark Volman—vocals, tambourine; Al Nichol—vocals, guitar; Jim Pons—vocals, bass; John Seiter—vocals, drums
Additional personnel: Dean Jones—host
Recording dates: November 29, 1969
Highest chart position: Did not chart from *The History of Flo & Eddie and The Turtles*
Original release date: 1983

Mark: From *The 1969 Miss Teen USA Pageant*, introduced by Disney actor Dean Jones. On *The History of Flo & Eddie and The Turtles*, Jones is replaced by an anonymous girl who says, "Now here are The Turtles with our own Miss Teen Lovelies," probably to avoid having to pay Mr. Jones a royalty. The Turtles handle the medley quite deftly. It's kind of a shame that The Turtles had to resort to this at the end of 1969, but the hits didn't keep on comin' and by this point, they had to remind everyone who they were. No wonder Howard bailed on the group earlier in 1969 for a time.

Charles: I wish there were more medleys, live or recorded. In fact, I wish there was a "Stars On 45" type of recording that mixed all The Turtles' hits together. Sorry, I'm a DJ and I just like medleys.

—

TURTLES PRESENT THE BATTLE OF THE BANDS, THE (LP) by The Turtles
Turtles involvement: Mark Volman—vocals, special effects; Howard Kaylan—lead vocals; Al Nichol—guitars, organ, piano, Moog synthesizer, vocals; lead vocal on "Surfer Dan"; Jim Pons—bass, vocals; John Barbata—drums, percussion, vocals
Additional personnel: Chip Douglas—producer: Jim Hilton, Armin Steiner—engineers; Chip Douglas—pump organ on "You Showed Me;" Paul Beaver—Moog synthesizer on "Elenore" and "You Showed Me;" Bob Jenkins—bongos on "The Battle of the Bands" and "Elenore".
Recording dates: May - June 1968 at Gold Star Studios, Hollywood, California; Western Recorders, Hollywood, California; T.T.G./Sunset-Highland Recording Studios, Hollywood, California
Highest chart position: #128

Original release date: November 1, 1968

The Opening—The Battle of the Bands
The Last Thing I Remember
Elenore
Too Much Heartsick Feeling
Oh, Daddy!
Buzzsaw

Surfer Dan
I'm Chief Kamanawanalea (We're the Royal Macadamia Nuts)
You Showed Me
Food
Chicken Little Was Right
The Closing—Earth Anthem

Bonus tracks on Sundazed edition:
Sound Asleep
The Story of Rock and Roll

Bonus tracks on Repertoire edition:
Goodbye Surprise
She's My Girl
Sound Asleep
Umbassa and the Dragon
The Story of Rock and Roll
Can't You Hear the Cows
Elenore (mono)
You Showed Me (mono)

Bonus tracks on Manifesto edition:
She's My Girl
Chicken Little Was Right (single version)
Sound Asleep
Umbassa and the Dragon
The Story of Rock and Roll
Can't You Hear the Cows
The Last Thing I Remember (The First Thing I Knew) (demo)
The Owl
To See the Sun
Earth Anthem (alternate version)
Battle of the Bands Radio Spot
Food (rehearsal)

This is hands-down the best thing The Turtles released during their career, and certainly their best album. (We're purposefully ignoring the "Happy Together" song here.) Why the album stalled out at a paltry #128 on the *Billboard* charts is anyone's guess, but my theory is that, except for "Weird Al" Yankovic, rock and roll and comedy don't mix, especially back in 1968, when rock and roll music was taken oh-so-seriously.

The funny thing is that *Sgt. Pepper* and the *White Album* both had their silly moments, but due to the fact that The Beatles were presenting them with nary a smile on their face, they somehow got away with it. Note when The Beatles got even sillier, i.e. *Magical Mystery Tour*, the resulting reception was not so kind, not for the music, mind you, but for the film.

Of course, this is a Turtles book and as such, I should explain why this album should have done better. First of all, this album had two top 10 hits. Any other group with "You Showed Me" and "Elenore" on their album would have easily cracked the top.

The real answer, I believe, lies with White Whale. They were good at releasing and marketing hit singles, which they continued to do for The Turtles during this period, but when it came to a long player, the powers-that-be didn't know what to do. It's a telling statement that the highest charting album ever on White Whale was The Turtles' *Golden Hits,* which is just a compilation of singles.

The Turtles Present the Battle of the Bands takes the concept album to the nth level and it succeeds marvelously. Not only do The Turtles succeed in covering a wide range of genres of music, they do it on all levels with great songs and great performances, and, with a quick trip to the costume shop, carry off the charade of actually being 12 different bands.

If you're not rolling on the floor after hearing songs like "Chief Kamanawanalaya" and "Food," you don't have a sense of humor and you have no business listening to The Turtles, Frank Zappa, or Flo & Eddie.

—

TURTLES '66, THE (compilation) by The Turtles
Turtles involvement: See individual Turtles tracks
Additional personnel: See individual Turtles tracks
Recording dates: 1966
Highest chart position: Did not chart
Original release date: November 24, 2017

I Can't Stop
Outside Chance
Can I Get to Know You Better
So Goes Love
Wrong from the Start
Tie Me Down

I Get Out of Breath
Say Girl
Grim Reaper of Love
She'll Come Back
Get Away
We'll Meet Again

This was a Record Store Day release that effectively worked as what could have been The Turtles' third album between *You Baby* and *Happy Together*. As it turned out, many of the tracks were originally released on *Golden Hits* and *Wooden Head* and as singles.

TURTLESIZED (compilation) by The Turtles
Turtles involvement: See individual Turtles tracks
Additional personnel: See individual Turtles tracks
Recording dates: 1965 - 1967
Highest chart position: Did not chart
Original release date: 1982

Happy Together
Outside Chance

Eve of Destruction
She'd Rather Be With Me

A cool novelty: a green, turtle-shaped disc. It's really the only reason to have this as all of the songs are readily available elsewhere.

20 GREATEST HITS (compilation) by The Turtles
Turtles involvement: See individual Turtles tracks
Additional personnel: See individual Turtles tracks
Recording dates: 1965 - 1970
Highest chart position: Did not chart
Original release date: 1984

It Ain't Me Babe
Let Me Be
Eve of Destruction
You Baby
Grim Reaper of Love
Can I Get to Know You Better
Outside Chance
Happy Together
She'd Rather Be With Me
Me About You

Guide for the Married Man
She's My Girl
You Know What I Mean
Sound Asleep
Elenore
You Showed Me
The Story of Rock and Roll
You Don't Have to Walk in the Rain
Love in the City
Lady-O

This is really a reissue of the 1982 Rhino vinyl collection called *Turtles Greatest Hits* with six more tracks added. At the time, it was the best Turtles CD to get with every track making its CD debut. It has now been superseded by updated, remastered compilations, but it's still a marvelous set.

—

UMBASSA AND THE DRAGON aka UMBASSA THE DRAGON (The Turtles) by The Turtles
Turtles involvement: Mark Volman—vocals, special effects; Howard Kaylan—lead vocals; Al Nichol—guitars, organ, piano, Moog synthesizer, electric sitar, vocals; Jim Pons—bass, vocals; John Barbata—drums, percussion, vocals
Additional personnel: The Turtles—producers; Eric Wangberg—engineer; Roy Caton, Freddie Hill—trumpets; Lou Blackburn, Francis Fitzpatrick, Lew McCreary—trombones; John Johnson—tuba; Sidney Miller—bassoon; Donald Peake—horn orchestration
Recording dates: January - February 1968 at Sound Recorders, Hollywood, California
Highest chart position: Single did not chart; B-side of "Sound Asleep;" Did not chart from *The Rhino Brothers Present the World's Worst Records* and *Chalon Road*
Original release date: February 1968 for single; 1983 for album

Mark: Is this really one of the world's worst records? I don't know. I've heard worse. It's a pretty strange one even for Frank Zappa standards. It almost starts off as another take of "Sound Asleep." It almost could be a children's record. Almost. Portents of things to come for Flo & Eddie's career. I believe it's engineer Eric Wangberg who finally calls a halt to the proceedings after three minutes.
Charles: Knowing how much my co-author despised this recording, I sure wanted to love it. I wanted to laugh at it, or find some redeeming features. So I did. It's better than a water-torture drip (which is what the beginning of this track sounds like), it's better than being captured in a jungle by a gang of starving cannibals (which is what the middle of the song sounds like), and it's better than being trampled on your head by a mad dragon or dinosaur (which is what the end of the songs sounds like). See—it is better than other things, and that's what I liked about it.

WALKING SONG, THE (Howard Kaylan, Al Nichol) by The Turtles
Turtles involvement: Mark Volman—lead, harmony and backing vocals; Howard Kaylan—lead and backing vocals; Al Nichol—lead guitar, piano, lead and backing vocals; Jim Tucker—rhythm guitar, backing vocals; Jim Pons—bass, lead and backing vocals; John Barbata—drums
Additional personnel: Joe Wissert—producer; Bones Howe, Armin Steiner, Bruce Botnick—engineers
Recording dates: December 1966 - April 1967 at Sunset Sound Recorders, Hollywood, California
Highest chart position: Did not chart; B-side of "She'd Rather Be with Me;" #25 from *Happy Together*
Original release date: April 1967 for single; April 29, 1967 for album

Mark: It's a very oddball song and I think each Turtle actually sings a verse instead of just Howard, which makes it quite nice. Certainly Mark, Al, and Jim take leads. The "How are you? How are you? How are you?" at the end is an imitation of Arthur Godfrey. Look him up, youngsters.
Charles: It's not often that multiple Turtles get a crack at singing lead—in the same song. It sounded great when The Temptations did it, and it works here too. Fun and not the least bit boring. Listen carefully to what's going on in the background as it goes on. If you say "bah humbug" to this recording, that's only because those words are in the lyrics.

—

WALK IN THE SUN, A (Howard Kaylan) by The Turtles
Turtles involvement: Mark Volman—guitar, tambourine, vocals; Howard Kaylan—keyboards, lead vocals; Al Nichol—lead guitar, keyboards, vocals, bass guitar; Jim Tucker—rhythm guitar, vocals; Chuck Portz—bass guitar, vocals; Don Murray—drums
Additional personnel: Lee Lasseff and Ted Feigin—executive producers; Bones Howe—production, sound, engineering
Recording dates: mid-1965 at Western Recorders, Hollywood, California
Highest chart position: #98 from *It Ain't Me Babe*
Original release date: September 1965
Significant other versions: The Angry

Charles: An interesting recording which may or may not have been inspired by the 1945 Dana Andrews film *A Walk In The Sun*, the driving tempo sets this one apart from its otherwise simplistic chord changes. The background "ahhs" are very common for the period but don't really embellish the song. The lyrics offer a nice story, but am I the only one who thinks Kaylan is going to sing something else when he sings "Motherless Liar"? Imagine this track slowed down a bit and sung by Eric Burdon with his growl, and you've got a completely different animal all together.

Mark: This song is sung with great passion by Kaylan and is one of his earliest tunes. Overall, I agree with Charles' assessment that this would have made for a great Animals tune back in the day. The Angry's cover version from 1966 comes closest to showing how this version might have sounded.

—

WANDERIN' KIND (Howard Kaylan) by The Turtles

Turtles involvement: Mark Volman—guitar, tambourine, vocals; Howard Kaylan—keyboards, lead vocals; Al Nichol—lead guitar, keyboards, vocals, bass guitar; Jim Tucker—rhythm guitar, vocals; Chuck Portz—bass guitar, vocals; Don Murray—drums

Additional personnel: Lee Lasseff and Ted Feigin—executive producers; Bones Howe—production, sound, engineering

Recording dates: mid-1965 at Western Recorders, Hollywood, California

Highest chart positions: Single did not chart; B-side of "You Baby," "Is it Any Wonder?," and "Eve of Destruction;" #98 from *It Ain't Me Babe*

Original release dates: January 1966 for single; September 1965 for album

Significant other versions: The Crosswind Singers

Mark: A casual beginning for a very non-casual band! Some great guitar work. Kaylan's writing debut on record is nothing spectacular, but not an embarrassment, either. To get those royalties, the song was added as the B-side to not one, not two, but three separate singles released over the years.

It is kind of frustrating that they reissued this song so many times. It's not that the song is so bad, it's just that there were other songs that were still in the can when White Whale compiled the *Wooden Head* collection as this was already on *It Ain't Me Babe* and three single B-sides. I'm sure Howard wasn't poo-pooing the publishing money, however.

Charles: Speed this up and it's got some gumption! (But not too much faster as it clocks in at under two minutes.) As is, it comes off as a rejected take from an early Byrds album without a 12-string or a McGuinn. Even so, it's a decent Kaylan original that grows on you (but never wanders) with each successive listen.

—

WE AIN'T GONNA PARTY NO MORE (Howard Kaylan) by The Turtles
Turtles involvement: Howard Kaylan—vocals, occasional percussion, organ; Mark Volman—vocals, percussion, occasional guitars; Al Nichol—vocals, guitars, keyboards, six string bass; Jim Pons—vocals, bass, occasional guitars; John Seiter—vocals, drums, occasional piano
Additional personnel: Jerry Yester—producer, piano, string arrangement; Barry Keene—engineer
Recording dates: 1969 at Sunwest Recording Studios, Hollywood, California
Highest chart position: Single did not chart; B-side to "Who Would Ever Think That I Would Marry Margaret?;" #146 from *More Golden Hits*
Original release date: March 1970

Mark: As a compromise, The Turtles added a song more suited to them to an A-side they despised. It does show that through it all, The Turtles were protest singers all along, and it's a great tune at that. It is agreed that the A-side sucked and had this been the A-side, it might have fared better, but White Whale was going down the tubes and probably nothing would have charted well for them at this late date. It probably would have ended up on *Shell Shock*, had it been completed.

Charles: Don't judge a tune by its title. If you're thinking this is an Animal House toga-time party song, you're in for a rude awakening. If you're wondering why "we ain't gonna party no more," it's because there's a war going on in Vietnam, and nobody is happy about it. Nobody is partying over it. But artists are definitely singing about it across the land. "If it's one thing we don't need, it's your damn war." This nearly five-minute long, anti-war protest message begins with the sweetest of vocals and builds into a sophisticated anthem of its time. The instrumental epilogue brings it all home, which is all anyone wanted—to bring the troops back home. Alive. Excellence on so many levels.

—

WE'LL MEET AGAIN (Hughie Charles, Ross Parker) by The Turtles
Turtles involvement: Mark Volman—vocal harmony, tambourine; Howard Kaylan—lead vocals; Al Nichol—lead guitar, vocals; Jim Tucker—rhythm guitar; Chuck Portz—bass guitar; Joel Larson—drums
Additional personnel: Bones Howe—producer, engineer; Armin Steiner, engineer; John Audino; Larry Knechtel—piano
Recording dates: April - September 1966 at Western Recorders, Hollywood, California
Highest chart position: Did not chart; B-side of "Outside Chance;" Did not chart from *Wooden Head*
Original release date: July 1966 for single; November 1970 for album
Significant other versions: Vera Lynn, Alfie Boe and Katharine Jenkins, The Byrds, Margot Werner, Johnny Cash, The Ink Spots, Stephen Colbert, John C. Reilly

Mark: The Turtles recorded this twice. First, for the *It Ain't Me Babe* album. That version was finally released as the "We'll Meet Again (Alternate Take)" on the 2016 *Wooden Head* reissue as a bonus track. A year later, they recorded it again, as a single B-side. Not much happened with it after that, and when it was time for the *Wooden Head/Odds and Sods*-type collection, this version made the cut. The tinkly piano is a very nice touch and the entire thing is a heck of a lot more upbeat than Vera Lynn's bittersweet version. Take four was released on the 2016 Manifesto version of *Wooden Head* as a bonus track called "Alternate Take." This version is missing the tinkly piano.

Charles: A honky-town rockin' version of this classic 1939 British song made famous by singer Vera Lynn, with music and lyrics composed and written by Ross Parker and Hughie Charles. The song happens to be one of the most famous songs of the World War II era, and resonated with soldiers going off to fight with the prayer that they'd be returning before too long to meet again with their families and sweethearts. The assertion that "we'll meet again" is optimistic, as many soldiers did not survive to see their loved ones ever again. The song gave its name to the 1943 musical film "We'll Meet Again," and it was very popular in the forties and fifties. Although the music is reminiscent of Gary Lewis & The Playboys, it was a band called The Happening who more commonly turned old Americana standards into Top 40 pop hits. Here, our Turtles make a well-known war time classic their own, complete with a "jazz hands" key-change ending. There's a video clip of The Turtles performing this on "The Lloyd Thaxton Show," and he confessed that it was hard to stay serious around these guys. Appropriately enough, The Turtles often ended their live shows with "We'll Meet Again."

—

WESTCHESTER HIGH SCHOOL ALMA MATER (unknown) by The Westchester High School A Capella Choir Class of 1963
Turtles involvement: Mark Volman, Howard Kaplan, Al Nichol, Chuck Portz—vocalists
Additional personnel: Robert Wood—conductor
Recording dates: 1963
Highest chart position: Did not chart from *The History of Flo & Eddie and The Turtles*
Original release date: 1983

Mark: A traditional "Alma Mater"-type song. The only thing it has going for it is that it is the earliest known recording of The Turtles in any form, pre-Crossfires even. Think "That'll Be the Day" or "In Spite of All The Danger" by The Beatles and you'll know what I mean. There's honestly no way to distinguish the individual voices that would eventually make up The Turtles, but it "shore sounds purty"!

Charles: Great as an historic snapshot, and so cool that it was not only recorded, but kept and added to an album. To think that Mark and Howard grew up together, formed a group, and remained friends and bandmates for more than half a century speaks volumes. If someone ever said, "let's be sure to save this recording for posterity," they actually did—like a vintage teenage picture from a treasured photo album—perhaps faded or of aging quality but nonetheless valuable to completists (and to the guys themselves!)

—

WHO WOULD EVER THINK THAT I WOULD MARRY MARGARET? (Ralph Dino, John Sombello) by The Turtles
Turtles involvement: Howard Kaylan—vocals, occasional percussion, organ; Mark Volman—vocals, percussion, occasional guitars; Al Nichol—vocals, guitars, keyboards, six string bass; Jim Pons—vocals, bass, occasional guitars; John Seiter—vocals, drums, occasional piano
Additional personnel: Jerry Yester—producer, piano, string arrangement; Barry Keene—engineer
Recording dates: 1969 at Sunwest Recording Studios, Hollywood, California
Highest chart position: Single did not chart; #146 from *More Golden Hits*
Original release date: March 1970

Mark: White Whale seemingly loved this tune. Who knows what they were thinking. I guess desperate times lead to desperate measures. When Rhino made their *Shell Shock* re-creation, they included this song. I would have left it off due to how much they despised it and how more realistic that would have been, unless White Whale would have insisted or else the album couldn't be released. I feel that the poor single chart action would have negated its inclusion.

Charles: Who's Margaret, and who married her anyway? This was quite a long title for a too-short song, at barely two minutes. Thematically and musically a country folk song, it's a really good record that deserved another verse and chorus. If Ray Stevens joined the Eagles and recorded this, along with a cover of "Signs" (original version by the Canadian band Five Man Electrical Band) as the flip side, it probably would have been a bigger hit. But that could only happen in my alternate music universe, so we'll just have to enjoy this in our universe.

—

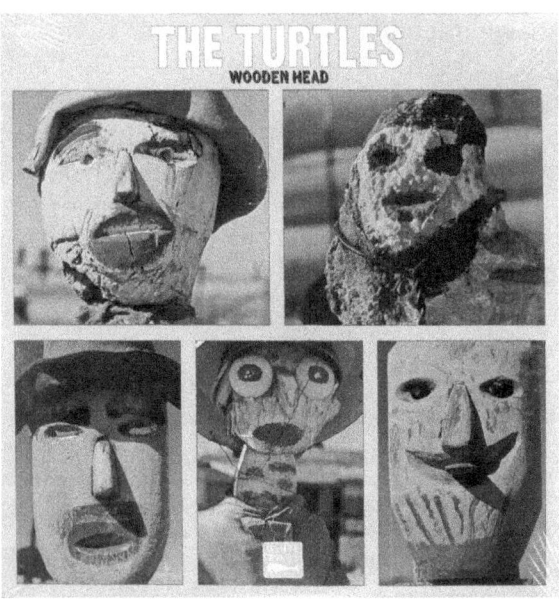

WOODEN HEAD (compilation) by The Turtles
Turtles involvement: Mark Volman—vocal harmony, tambourine; Howard Kaylan—lead vocals; Al Nichol—lead guitar, vocals; Jim Tucker—rhythm guitar; Chuck Portz—bass guitar; Joel Larson—drums
Additional personnel: Bones Howe—producer, engineer; Armin Steiner, engineer; (John Audino, Jules Chaikin, Ray Triscari—trumpets; Bob Edmondson—trombone; Art Pepper, alto sax; Bob Perkins—tenor sax; Bill Holman—tenor sax, horn arrangement on "I Can't Stop") (Joel Larson—drums; Larry Knechtel—piano for "We'll Meet Again")
Recording dates: April - September 1966 at Western Recorders, Hollywood, California; (3/21/67 overdubs at Sound Recorders, Hollywood, California on "I Can't Stop")
Highest chart position: Did not chart
Original release date: November 1970

I Can't Stop
Grim Reaper of Love (added on Rhino reissue)
She'll Come Back
Is It Any Wonder? (added to Rhino reissue)
Get Away
Wrong from the Start
I Get Out of Breath

We'll Meet Again
On a Summer's Day
Come Back
Say Girl
Tie Me Down
Wanderin' Kind (removed from Rhino reissue)

Bonus tracks on Sundazed edition:
We Ain't Gonna Party No More
Who Would Ever Think That I Would Marry Margaret?

Bonus tracks on Repertoire edition:
We Ain't Gonna Party No More
Who Would Ever Think That I Would Marry Margaret?
Is It Any Wonder?
There You Sit Lonely
Cat in the Window
Like It Or Not
You Want to Be a Woman

Bonus tracks on Manifesto edition:
You Baby (1967 stereo mix)
So Goes Love
Makin' My Mind Up (1966 stereo mix)
Is It Any Wonder?
Let Me Be (1967 stereo mix)
Grim Reaper of Love
It Ain't Me Babe (1967 stereo mix)
Can I Get to Know You Better
Outside Chance
You Know What I Mean
Cat in the Window
We'll Meet Again (alternate take)
The Turtles Golden Hits Radio Spot

This album was designed as a catch-all for everything unreleased or only previously released as single B-sides by The Turtles, pre-1967, and pre-Blimp. They mostly succeeded despite it not being authorized at all by The Turtles. Seven songs were previously unreleased, three were B-sides, and one was from a movie soundtrack. Had it been released when originally recorded, it would have come out between *You Baby* and *Happy Together*. As such, a version called *Turtles '66* was released in 2017 that approximates what this release could have been.

When Rhino reissued the album in the 1980s, they changed the cover photo from the totem pole heads to a photograph featuring The Turtles circa 1966.

The 2016 Manifesto reissue went one step further by adding the seven new tracks previously on *Golden Hits* and *More Golden Hits*, plus four previously unreleased stereo mixes, a previously unreleased alternate take of "We'll Meet Again," and a previously unreleased radio spot for *Golden Hits*.

All of these combined make this an essential release. The previous bonus tracks on earlier editions were moved to become bonus tracks on *Turtle Soup*, which makes more sense as they were originally planned for *Shell Shock*, which was supposed to be the follow-up to *Turtle Soup*.

—

WRONG FROM THE START (Gordon Waller, Peter Asher) by The Turtles
Turtles involvement: Mark Volman—vocal harmony, tambourine; Howard Kaylan—lead vocals; Al Nichol—lead guitar, organ, piano, harpsichord, vocals; Jim Tucker—rhythm guitar; Chuck Portz—bass guitar; Don Murray—drums
Additional personnel: Bones Howe—producer, engineer; Armin Steiner, engineer
Recording dates: April - September 1966 at Western Recorders, Hollywood, California
Highest chart position: Did not chart from *Wooden Head*
Original release date: November 1970
Significant other versions: Peter and Gordon

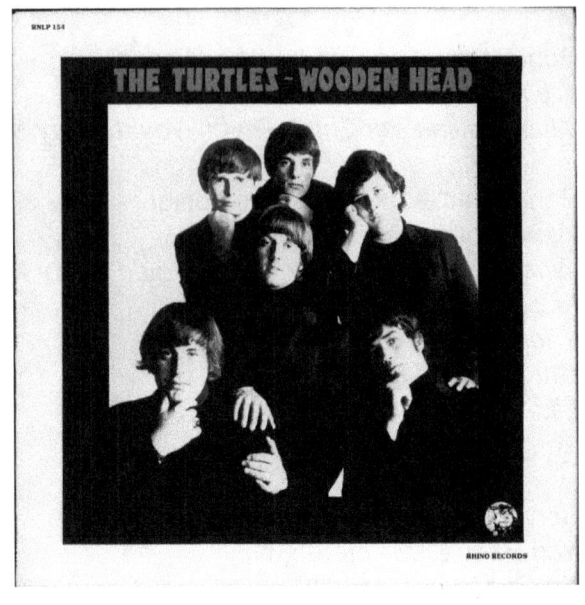

Mark: Peter and Gordon did a nice, if not superior version of this song. The Turtles' version is competent. I'm not entirely sure who's blowing harmonica here, as many of these non-hit Turtles tracks don't offer any production and performance credits.

Charles: Peter Asher and Gordon Waller were the British Invasion's greatest duo (no disrespect to Chad & Jeremy), and their hits were some of the tastiest cuts of that era. The duo was "wrong from the start" to ever have recorded this. I normally say that P & G can do no wrong, but just like Paul McCartney gifted them with "World Without Love," they would have been better off gifting this composition directly to The Turtles. It's got not only a great harmonica but also a Carl Perkins-like guitar intro and outro that echoes "Honey Don't."

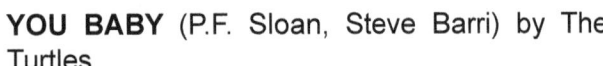

YOU BABY (P.F. Sloan, Steve Barri) by The Turtles
Turtles involvement: Mark Volman—vocal harmony, tambourine; Howard Kaylan—lead vocals; Al Nichol—vocal harmony, lead guitar, organ; Jim Tucker—rhythm guitar; Chuck Portz—bass guitar; Don Murray—drums
Additional personnel: Lee Lasseff and Ted Feigin—executive producers; Bones Howe—production, sound, engineering; Dwight Tunji Trio (Howe, Feigin & Lasseff)—percussion, special effects
Recording dates: October 1965 - January 1966 at Western Recorders, Hollywood, California
Highest chart position: #20 for single; Did not chart from *You Baby*
Original release date: January 1966 for single; April 1966 for album
Significant other versions: The Vogues, The Mamas & the Papas, Flo & Eddie

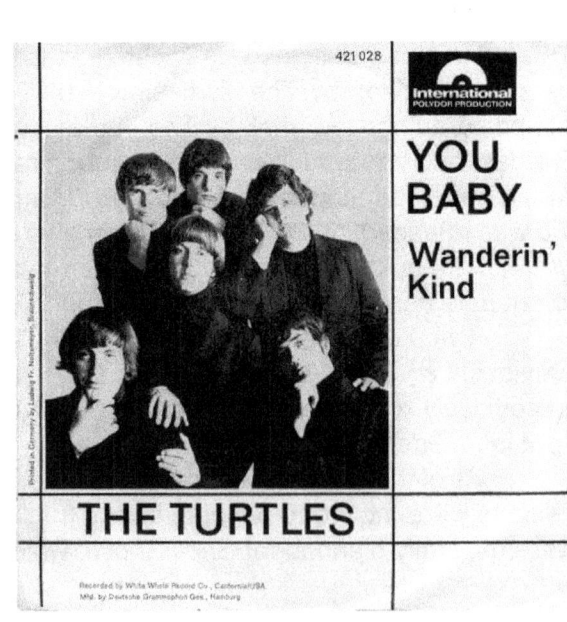

Mark: A nice, upbeat tune and a worthy follow-up to both "It Ain't Me Babe" and "Let Me Be," but perhaps it was too much of the same, so that's why it barely cracked the Top 20 this time, instead of topping the charts. It did better than "Let Me Be," however. The next single was designed to stretch them out a little more, but it probably went a little too far. It was "Grim Reaper of Love." The stereo album version adds a little echo to Howard's voice as it stands out much more prominently in the left speaker.

A different stereo version called "(1967 Stereo Mix)" cuts the amount of echo on Howard's voice and was released on the Manifesto *Wooden Head* CD in 2016.

Flo & Eddie sang a 1991 live version that appeared on *The Turtles Featuring Flo & Eddie Captured Live*.

Charles: I remember always hearing similarities between the beginning of "You Baby" and the part in Billy J. Kramer & The Dakotas' "Bad To Me," which goes "The birds in the sky would be sad and lonely if they knew I lost me one and only…" (written by Lennon and McCartney, and a UK #1 song for Billy). I don't hear it as much nowadays, but I still hear the fun and good times that come across in this song, which is clearly one of the best in The Turtles' catalog. It's yet another one of those pristine pop songs, both danceable and infectious. The breaks are perfect, and it's blessed with tremendous lead and backing vocals.

—

YOU BABY (LP) by The Turtles
Turtles involvement: Mark Volman—vocal harmony, tambourine; Howard Kaylan—lead vocals; Al Nichol—vocal harmony, lead guitar, organ; Jim Tucker—rhythm guitar; Chuck Portz—bass guitar; Don Murray—drums
Additional personnel: Lee Lasseff and Ted Feigin—executive producers; Bones Howe—production, sound, engineering; Dwight Tunji Trio (Howe, Feigin & Lasseff)—percussion, special effects
Recording dates: October 1965 - January 1966 at Western Recorders, Hollywood, California
Highest chart position: Did not chart
Original release date: April 1966

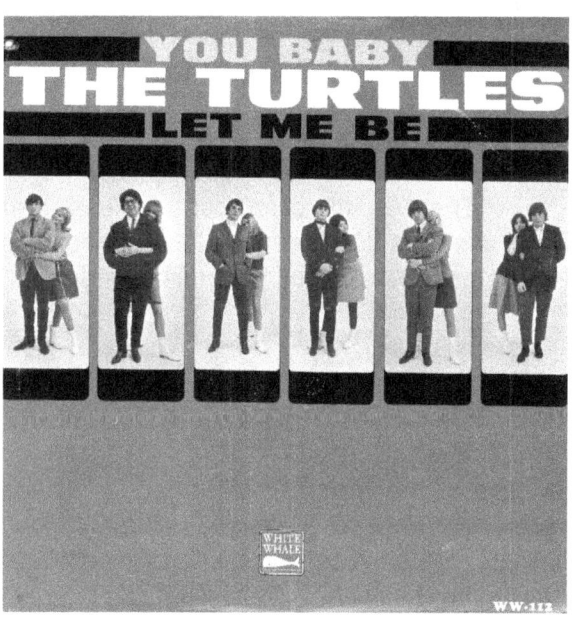

Flyin' High
I Know That You'll Be There
House of Pain
Just a Room
I Need Someone
Let Me Be (replaced by *Can I Get to Know You Better* on Rhino reissue)

Down in Suburbia
Give Love a Trial
You Baby
Pall Bearing, Ball Bearing World
All My Problems
Almost There

Bonus tracks on stereo Sundazed edition:
Outside Chance
Can I Get to Know You Better

Bonus tracks on mono Repertoire edition:
Santa and the Sidewalk Surfer
Teardrops
Entire album in stereo

Bonus tracks on mono Manifesto edition:
Entire album in stereo

The Turtles' second album sounds quite a bit like *It Ain't Me Babe, Mark II*. That's not necessarily a bad thing, but this shows off one of many of The Turtles' identity crises. Do you continue on as a folk rock protest band or transition to a pop rock band? *You Baby* comfortably straddles the line here as many of the songs sound like *It Ain't Me Babe* leftovers (and repeating "Let Me Be" for good measure), while other songs could have gone on to appear on *Happy Together* or (yuk-yuk) *Wooden Head*.

The Turtles or White Whale must have decided that, after the *You Baby* album essentially flopped, anything that sounded like it could have been on either of their first two albums be immediately shelved. This was handy when it came to compiling *Wooden Head* as there were many unreleased tracks in the can from this period. It's also worth seeking out THE *Turtles '66* from 2017 to see what could have been done had The Turtles continued down the *You Baby* path for one more album before *Happy Together*.

There is little difference between the mono and stereo versions except that Howard and harmonies are usually on the left channel while the instruments are usually on the right and there is greater separation on the stereo version.

—

YOU DON'T HAVE TO WALK IN THE RAIN
(The Turtles) by The Turtles
Turtles involvement: Mark Volman—lead vocal, percussion, occasional guitars; Howard Kaylan—lead vocal, occasional percussion, organ, keyboards; Al Nichol—vocals, guitars, keyboards, six string bass; Jim Pons—vocals, bass, occasional guitars; John Seiter—vocals, drums, occasional piano
Additional personnel: Ray Davies—producer; Chuck Britz—engineer
Recording dates: April - July 1969 at United Records, Hollywood, California
Highest chart position: #51 for single; #117 from *Turtle Soup*
Original release date: May 1969 for single; October 1969 for album

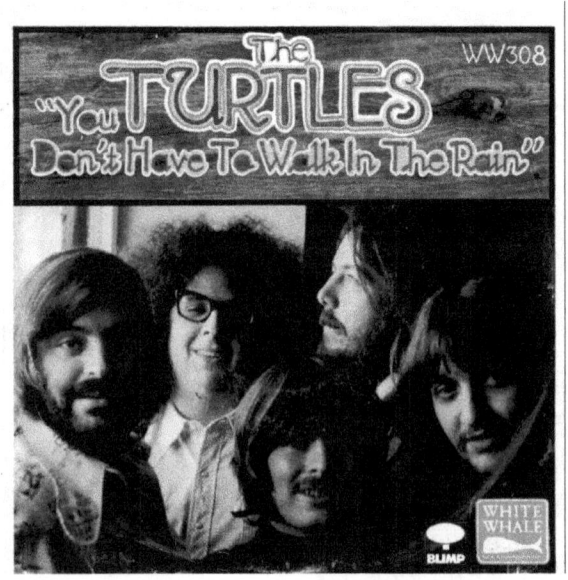

Charles: I'm always so quick to point out when a recording reminds me of another artist. This one sounds just like... THE TURTLES! It's vintage Turtles, and deserved better sales and radio play. I truly love this song.
Mark: This is and always has been a very strange and awkward sounding song to me... and not in a good way. For me, it was and is a poor choice for that all-important comeback single. It's not the worst song on the album, but certainly not the best. Charles can have it.
Charles: I will. And I got the last word on this one!

—

YOU KNOW WHAT I MEAN (Garry Bonner, Alan Gordon) by The Turtles
Turtles involvement: Mark Volman—harmony and backing vocals; Howard Kaylan—lead and backing vocals; Al Nichol—lead guitar, piano, electric sitar, backing vocals; Jim Tucker—rhythm guitar, backing vocals; Jim Pons—bass, backing vocals; John Barbata—drums
Additional personnel: Joe Wissert—producer; Bruce Botnick—engineer; Don Randi—piano; Charlie Shoemake—vibes; Bud Brisbois—trumpet; William Hinshaw, Henry Sigismonti—French horns; Lou Blackburn, Dick Hyde, Richard Leith—trombones; Tom Scott—sax; Bobby Bruce, Wilbert Nuttycombe, Isadore Roman, John Santulis—violins; Norman Botnick—viola; Irving Lipschultz—cello; Jack Nitzsche—orchestral arrangement

Recording dates: June 1967 at Sunset Sound Recorders, Hollywood, California
Highest chart position: #12 for single; B-side of "You Know What I Mean;" #7 from *Golden Hits*
Original release date: July 1967 for single; October 1967 for album

Mark: Amazingly, for such a great song, The Turtles have never performed this live, according to Howard Kaylan. I love, love, LOVE this song!!! Why it stalled at #12 can only be chalked up to me as just too many other things out at the same time like a little album called *Sgt. Pepper's Lonely Hearts Club Band*, plus *Bee Gees 1st*, The Hollies' *Evolution*, The Rolling Stones' *Flowers*, *Insight Out* by The Association, and even *The Jungle Book Soundtrack*, and *Mr. Spock's Music From Outer Space* all vying for attention at exactly the same time.
Charles: What a song! What a record! That's an important note. Sometimes you have a great song that somehow never becomes a great recording. Other times there may be an amazing recording of a mediocre song, which elevates it. This is definitely an example of both coming together and clicking on all levels... "You Know What I Mean," right?

—

YOU SHOWED ME (James McGuinn, Gene Clark) by Nature's Children
Turtles involvement: Mark Volman—vocals, special effects; Howard Kaylan—lead vocals; Al Nichol—guitars, organ, piano, Moog synthesizer, vocals; Jim Pons—bass, vocals; John Barbata—drums, percussion, vocals

Additional personnel: Chip Douglas—producer: Jim Hilton, Armin Steiner—engineers; Chip Douglas—pump organ; Paul Beaver—Moog synthesizer

Recording dates: May - June 1968 at Gold Star Studios, Hollywood, California; Western Recorders, Hollywood, California; T.T.G./Sunset-Highland Recording Studios, Hollywood, California

Highest chart position: #6 for single; #128 from *The Turtles Present the Battle of the Bands*

Original release date: November 1, 1968 for album; December 1968 for single

Significant other versions: The Byrds, The Lightning Seeds, Salt 'n' Pepa, Lutricia McNeal, The Watson Twins. Sampled by De La Soul, Kanye West, U2, Flo & Eddie

Mark: Chip Douglas came up with this then-unreleased Byrds composition as a possibility for The Turtles to record. As Chip was playing the tune on his broken pump organ, he kept apologizing for how slow he was playing it compared to the Byrds' version, but The Turtles were having none of it. They LOVED the slower tempo and in fact wanted Chip to play this same pump organ on the track. It then became The Turtles final Top 10 hit. It's a great one too!

Flo & Eddie sang a 1991 live version that appeared on *The Turtles Featuring Flo & Eddie Captured Live*. Mark Volman erroneously says that the song made #1 in 1969. Maybe it did, somewhere, but not in the U.S. Howard and Mark exchange lead vocals on this version.

Charles: As spooky as anything recorded by Classics IV, "You Showed Me" was a haunting but captivating single with as strong a bridge as the chorus. Subtle and restrained, it's a brilliant recording, and as classic as it is/was, I'm surprised it was such a hit. It's one of those tracks that, in retrospect, shouldn't have garnered as much airplay and sales as it did because it was possibly too classy and moody, but it did, and that's even better. I'm not nearly as impressed with The Byrds' more commercial version, but I'm enamored by the version by Liverpool's The Lightning Seeds, who had the phenomenal, underrated hit single "Pure."

—

YOU WANT TO BE A WOMAN (The Turtles) by The Turtles

Turtles involvement: Howard Kaylan—vocals, occasional percussion, organ; Mark Volman—vocals, percussion, occasional guitars; Al Nichol—vocals, guitars, keyboards, six string bass; Jim Pons—vocals, bass, occasional guitars; John Seiter—vocals, drums, occasional piano

Additional personnel: Jerry Yester—producer; Barry Keene—engineer

Recording dates: 1969 at Sunwest Recording Studios, Hollywood, California; 1970 at Crystal Sound Recording Studios, Hollywood, California
Highest chart position: #194 from *Happy Together Again!*
Original release date: November 1974

Mark: Not one of the stronger *Shell Shock* tracks. Had those sessions continued, this one might have been more polished up or discarded altogether. The heavier middle section saves it from being a complete miss. Again, Howard and Mark added it to their first Turtles collection in 1974.
Charles: A hodgepodge and a miss. They may be "Doin' it the way you do," but it just doesn't work. Parts of the music harken to Gary Puckett & The Union Gap instrumentation, and some vocals bring to mind Tiny Tim, both of whom do/did what they do/did much better. The song, arrangement, and sonics just don't work.

—

YOUR MAW SAID YOU CRIED (Stephen Schlaks, B. Glazer) by The Turtles
Turtles involvement: Mark Volman—guitar, tambourine, vocals; Howard Kaylan—keyboards, lead vocals; Al Nichol—lead guitar, keyboards, vocals, bass guitar; Jim Tucker—rhythm guitar, vocals; Chuck Portz—bass guitar, vocals; Don Murray—drums
Additional personnel: Lee Lasseff and Ted Feigin—executive producers; Bones Howe—production, sound, engineering;
Recording dates: mid-1965 at Western Recorders, Hollywood, California
Highest chart position: Single did not chart; B-side of "Let Me Be" and #98 from *It Ain't Me Babe*
Original release date: September 1965
Significant other versions: Kenny Dino

Mark: Here, The Turtles attempt to sound like the Dave Clark Five, especially with that rat-a-tat drum fill that happens at every opportunity. Otherwise, it's a pretty average upbeat song. Also, it's very short, clocking in at well under two minutes. Amusingly, in France, they misspelled the title to read "Your Man Said You Cried" on the picture sleeve.
Charles: Yes, this is indeed The Turtles Clark Five in pieces, "Bits and Pieces" that is. Don Murray lifts the exact atomic drumming from the DC5, and there's no hiding it. There needs to be a Dave Clark/Turtles mash-up immediately. If there's a capable DJ out there who can do such a mix, send it to us.

This raucous recording was written by Schlacks and Glazer, who were responsible for the song "Speedway" by Elvis Presley.

Alphabetically, this is the very last entry in The Turtles' song catalog, as there are no songs that start with a 'Z' (there weren't any that began with a 'K,' 'Q,' 'V,' or 'X' either—a worthless tidbit of trivia that nobody knew before now, and is a completely useless way to end this portion of the book).

A BRIEF HISTORY OF FRANK ZAPPA AND THE MOTHERS OF INVENTION
By Mark Arnold

Frank Vincent Zappa was born on December 21, 1940, in Baltimore, Maryland. He was a self-taught composer and performer, becoming an expert in numerous genres of music such as classical, jazz, doo wop, rhythm and blues, orchestral, avant-garde and, of course, good old rock and roll.

Zappa's eccentric tastes in music began at an early age when he was exposed to an equally eccentric composer by the name of Edgard Varèse. Varèse's conception of music reflected his vision of "sound as living matter" and of "musical space as open rather than bounded."

By 1956, Zappa and his family had moved to Lancaster, California, where his interest in music and his obsession with Varèse expanded further. He started off by playing drums in local bands, but eventually his interest in the guitar grew and he'd obtained his first one by 1957.

From 1957 to 1964, Zappa recorded and released a few early records and compositions, and even made an early TV appearance on *The Steve Allen Show*, where he played the bicycle. By 1965, Zappa had met most of the players in the R&B band called the Soul Giants, who eventually were renamed The Mothers when Zappa assumed the leadership role. They were soon signed to Verve Records, who insisted they adjust their name to The Mothers of Invention, and recorded and released their first album called *Freak Out!*, in 1965.

The original Mothers of Invention group cut seven albums during their heyday: *Freak Out!* (1965), *Absolutely Free* (1967), *We're Only in It For the Money* (1968), *Cruising with Ruben and the Jets* (1968), *Uncle Meat* (1969), *Burnt Weeny Sandwich* (1970), and *Weasels Ripped My Flesh* (1970), plus one authorized compilation called *Mothermania* (1969), and many unauthorized as MGM/Verve kept milking the Zappa catalog long after Zappa left for Warner/Reprise.

Zappa also recorded one solo album during this time called *Lumpy Gravy* (1967) with an orchestra consisting of members of The Wrecking Crew, who had previously worked together on The Chipmunks' record called *Alvin's Orchestra* in 1960.

By 1969, there were nine members of The Mothers of Invention and Zappa was supporting them all with publishing royalties whether they were playing or not. He eventually cut everyone loose from the payroll and also quit his contracts with Verve and MGM and joined up with Warner/Reprise where he recorded under the Bizarre label imprint.

Zappa's first album under the new arrangement was his acclaimed solo album *Hot Rats* (1970). Shortly thereafter, Zappa formed a new version of The Mothers, keeping only Ian Underwood from the previous incarnation of the group, and adding British drummer Aynsley Dunbar, jazz keyboardist George Duke, and bass and rhythm guitarist Jeff Simmons.

Zappa was also in search of a good vocalist, particularly one who also had a sense of humor. He first approached Micky Dolenz of The Monkees, as Micky's group activities were winding down by 1970. Zappa was good friends with The Monkees, even appearing on an episode of their TV series and making a cameo in their feature film, *HEAD*. Dolenz was keen, but his manager at the time said no.

Zappa next turned to another group that had also broken up in 1970—no, not The Beatles—The Turtles! The Turtles and The Mothers of Invention had bumped into each other numerous times on tour since 1965. By early May 1970, The Turtles were left out in the cold and by late May 1970, Howard Kaylan and Mark Volman were going out on tour with The Mothers. They were soon joined by a third Turtle, Jim Pons, after a short stint with a reformed Leaves with Al Nichol fizzled.

Kaylan and Volman couldn't use their own names, so they picked the names of two Zappa roadies who went by the names of Phlorescent Leech and Eddie. Originally, Kaylan was the Phlorescent Leech and Volman was Eddie, but they somehow switched roles due to their placement on the cover of the first Flo & Eddie album.

From May 1970 through December 1971, The Mothers toured at a frantic pace, but also filmed and released a major motion picture, *200 Motels*, and recorded four albums.

Chunga's Revenge was released first in October 1970 and reached #199 on the *Billboard* charts. Amazingly, singles for Zappa were released regularly during the 1970s, but rarely charted, especially at this point. Zappa really wouldn't have a charting hit until 1974 with "Don't Eat the Yellow Snow."

"Tell Me You Love Me" b/w "Will You Go All the Way for the USA?" was the single released from *Chunga's Revenge* in 1970. It stiffed of course, but it does feature vocals by Kaylan and Volman. There was also a "Radio Spots for Frank Zappa's *Chunga's Revenge*" promotional single sent out to radio stations which probably did nothing in regards to airplay.

Fillmore East – June 1971 came out next in August 1971, and rose to #38 on *Billboard*, becoming the highest-charting Zappa-related album since *We're Only in It for the Money*. The resulting single of "Tears Began to Fall" b/w "Junier Mintz Boogie," also released in 1971, also stiffed. The B-side did not appear on the album and also does not feature Flo & Eddie.

The film and the soundtrack album of *200 Motels* was released in October 1971, reaching #59 on *Billboard*. The album and the single of "Magic Fingers" b/w "Daddy, Daddy, Daddy" were both released on United Artists Records.

It all came to a crashing halt in December 1971. First, on December 4, 1971, while performing at Casino de Montreux in Switzerland, a flare was set off by an audience member and burned down the casino. The Mothers' equipment, worth $50,000, was destroyed by the fire. The event was immortalized in Deep Purple's song "Smoke on the Water."

A week later, The Mothers played at the Rainbow Theatre in London with rented gear. During the encore, a jealous audience member pushed Zappa off the stage and into the concrete-floored orchestra pit causing head trauma, injuries to his back, leg, and neck, and a crushed larynx. This final concert was eventually legitimately released in 2022 as *Live at the Rainbow Theatre*.

After the attack, Zappa needed to use a wheelchair for an extended period, making touring impossible for over half a year. Meanwhile, the Mothers were left in limbo and eventually formed the core of Flo & Eddie's band as they set out on their own, releasing their own self-titled album in September 1972.

One more album was released in the era of Zappa's Mothers. It was *Just Another Band from LA*, which reached #85 on *Billboard* in March 1972 followed by John Lennon and Yoko Ono's *Some Time in New York City*, released on June 12, 1972 on Apple. Flo & Eddie and Zappa appear on the album's second *Live Jam* disc. The album reached #48 on *Billboard*. Zappa's version of this same material eventually was released on his *Playground Psychotics* in November 1992.

Flo & Eddie remained friendly with Zappa and worked with him again, but never on a regular basis. Zappa died on December 4, 1993.

In the last years of his life, Zappa released many live performances from the 1970-1971 Flo & Eddie period for the first time. These include *You Can't Do That on Stage Anymore, Volumes 1-6* from 1988-1992, *Freaks & Mother*#@%!* on July 7, 1991, *At the Circus* on June 16, 1992, and *Swiss Cheese/Fire!* on June 16, 1992 Then the Zappa estate released various digital downloads of *Beat the Boots III* in January 2009, *Carnegie Hall* on October 31, 2011, and the four-disc set released on May 8, 2020, called *The Mothers 1970*. This set really scrapes the barrel of Flo & Eddie outtakes and is probably the last we hear of new material being released by the Zappa

Estate for this period, unless the goal of releasing EVERY concert and tape recording from that period becomes important. This was followed the next year by the eight-disc *The Mothers 1971*.

For Flo & Eddie, The Zappa years are very polarizing for fans. Some say that it contained some of Zappa's and Flo & Eddie's best material. Others claim it was a monumental waste of time for Zappa with too much dominance by Flo & Eddie. Opinions differ.

FRANK ZAPPA'S MOTHERS A-Z

AIR, THE (Frank Zappa) by The Mothers
Mothers involvement: Frank Zappa—producer, arranger, guitar, vocals; Howard Kaylan—vocals; Mark Volman—vocals, percussion; Jeff Simmons—bass, vocals; Ian Underwood—organ, keyboards, guitar; George Duke—piano, keyboards, trombone; Aynsley Dunbar—drums
Additional personnel: Roy Thomas Baker—engineer
Recording dates: June 18, 1970 at "Piknik" VPRO
Highest chart position: Did not chart from *The Mothers 1970*
Original release date: May 8, 2020
Significant other versions: Frank Zappa and the Mothers of Invention

Mark: After an amusing Zappa introduction, this is another doo-wop sounding song performed mostly straight by Flo & Eddie. The original studio version was from *Uncle Meat*.

Charles: I continue to have a problem with Mark referring to songs as doo-wop sounding, but then again he and I argue over what constitutes a disco song. With that aside, I totally agree that this is in fact a doo-wop track. In fact, it could've been at home on the *American Graffiti soundtrack* album, apart from "the hitting and beating in the car" part. Let's get Kenny Vance and The Planotones to do a multi-harmony cover of this, and then we can crash in the Nash!

—

ANY WAY THE WIND BLOWS (Frank Zappa) by The Mothers
Mothers involvement: Frank Zappa—guitar, vocals; Mark Volman—vocals; Howard Kaylan—vocals; Jim Pons—bass, vocals; Don Preston—keyboards, electronics; Ian Underwood—keyboards, alto sax; Aynsley Dunbar—drums
Recording dates: December 4, 1971 at Casino de Montreux, Switzerland
Highest chart position: Did not chart from *Swiss Cheese/Fire!*
Original release date: June 16, 1992 (bootleg version originally released after 1976)
Significant other versions: Frank Zappa and The Mothers of Invention

Mark: When Flo & Eddie performed this, they tended to slow it way down and perform it straight. It's a doo wop song that ranks right up there with the classics. It's a pretty cool song that Zappa claimed to have written during a breakup.

The performance from October 11, 1971 is on *Carnegie Hall*. The original studio version appeared on *Freak Out!* and was then re-recorded a couple of years later and released on *Cruising with Ruben and the Jets*.

Charles: I feel this is one of the more commercial cuts off The Mothers of Invention's *Freak Out!* Album. There's nothing freaky about it. It's Freddie and The Dreamers or Gerry Marsden British Invasion top 40 pop rock without the English accents. It may be the first time the title was used in a song, but not the last. "Any Way The Wind Blows" is also the name of very different songs by Brother Phelps (country), Anais Mitchell (acoustic), and on Broadway in the musical *Hadestown*. But perhaps the most famous use of the line is as the closing verse in Queen's "Bohemian Rhapsody."

—

AT THE CIRCUS (CD) by The Mothers
Mothers involvement: Frank Zappa—guitar, vocals; Mark Volman—vocals; Howard Kaylan—vocals; Jeff Simmons—bass, vocals; George Duke—keyboards; Ian Underwood—keyboards; Aynsley Dunbar—drums
Recording dates: June 18, 1970 at "Piknik" VPRO
Highest chart position: Did not chart
Original release date: June 16, 1992 (bootleg version originally released in 1978)

Side one, track six:
Mother People

Side two, track one:
Wonderful Wino

This bootleg contained many performances by later Zappa groups, but these two tracks were from the Flo & Eddie period, hence their inclusion here. These same tracks were later released on *The Mothers 1970*.

—

AÜ aka **A SMALL ETERNITY WITH YOKO ONO** (John Lennon, Yoko Ono) by John Lennon, Yoko Ono and The Mothers
Mothers involvement: Frank Zappa—producer, arranger, guitar, dialogue, vocals; Ian Underwood—woodwinds, keyboards, vocals; Aynsley Dunbar—drums; Howard Kaylan—backing vocals, dialogue; Mark Volman—backing vocals, dialogue; Jim Pons—bass, vocals, dialogue; Bob Harris—keyboards, vocals
Additional personnel: Abbey Road Studios engineers—engineers for *Some Time in New York City/Live Jam* version; Spencer Crislu—remix engineer for *Playground Psychotics* version; John Lennon—vocals, guitar; Yoko Ono—lead vocals, percussion
Recording dates: June 6, 1971 at the Fillmore East, New York, New York

Highest chart position: #48 from *Some Time in New York City/Live Jam*; Did not chart from *Playground Psychotics*
Original release date: June 12, 1972; October 27, 1992

Mark: This is the type of track, combined with the prevailing thought that Yoko Ono broke up The Beatles, is why there is STILL so much Ono hatred in the world. I actually am a Yoko fan, but am truly not a fan of this bullshit. And that's what this really is... pure bullshit. It's not avant-garde, it's just crap. It was in 1971, and over 50 years later it still is. This also appears on *Live at Fillmore East, June 1971 - 50th Anniversary* and *The Mothers 1971*.

Charles: Frank Zappa met John Lennon and Yoko Ono in 1971, and performed with them on stage. After a while Ono started screaming throughout Lennon's performance, so two of Zappa's band members put a bag over her head while she kept singing. This track eventually ended up on 1992's *Playground Psychotics*. On the anniversary of Frank Zappa's 70th birthday, Yoko reflected, "We come from more or less the same background, the classical avant-garde, though in our work we expressed ourselves quite differently. As a composer, I felt a close comradeship to him amongst more rock orientated singer/songwriters. He is one of the geniuses of our time and will always have a place there. He will go on and on and on!" Seemingly, Howard and Mark agreed.

The title of this live track recorded at New York's historic Fillmore East venue is either one of the greatest song titles ever or one of the scariest titles ever, depending on how you feel about the sound of Yoko's voice. Just imagine :a small eternity with Yoko Ono." But it's exactly what this track is, starting with a minute or two of dissonance, and then getting worse from there. To many, even a few seconds sound like an eternity. Unless, that is, you love avant-garde music and Yoko's vocals.

—

BILLY THE MOUNTAIN (Frank Zappa; Interpolates sections of "Johnny's Theme" by Paul Anka and Johnny Carson and "Suite: Judy Blue Eyes" by Stephen Stills) by The Mothers
Mothers involvement: Frank Zappa—producer, arranger, guitar, vocals, dialogue; Don Preston—keyboards; Ian Underwood—woodwinds, keyboards, vocals; Aynsley Dunbar—drums; Howard Kaylan—lead vocals, dialogue; Mark Volman—lead vocals, dialogue; Jim Pons—bass guitar, vocals, dialogue
Recording dates: August 7, 1971 at Pauley Pavilion, UCLA, Los Angeles, California
Highest chart position: #85 from *Just Another Band from L.A.*

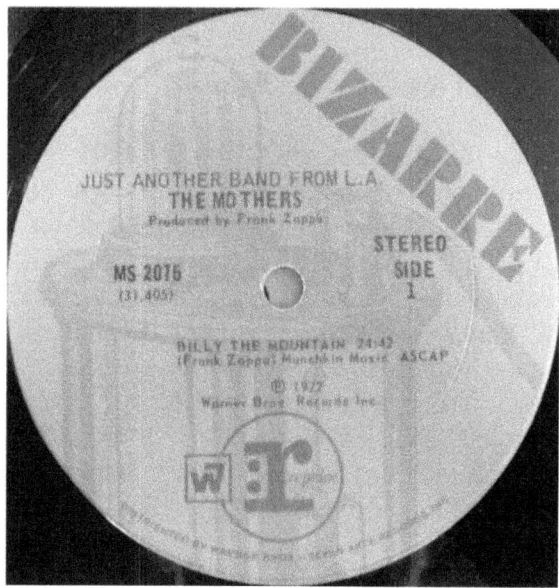

Original release date: March 26, 1972

Charles: A regular (?) picturesque Zappa composition containing all the prerequisite silliness, inside jokes, and non-sequiturs. It's definitely interesting if not puzzling. If you like and "get" Zappa, then this is a song that ascends for you. If not, at fifteen minutes in length it's just a painful climb. But it does reference Neil Sedaka, Dudley Do-Right and the *White Album*! Did Dr. Demento play any of these Mothers concoctions on his show?

Mark: If Demento did play this Mothers song, he probably avoided this one for its unwieldy length of almost a half-hour, unless he did it in his pre-syndication KMET days. This song is very polarizing for Zappa fans: Some think it's witty, charming, and funny with clever repartee by Flo & Eddie who were welcome additions to Zappa's Mothers; others feel that it's Zappa's over-indulgence and Flo & Eddie should be kicked out for ruining The Mothers of Invention. As for me, I love it, certainly more than many of the non-songs that pollute *200 Motels* and *Playground Psychotics*. The performance from October 11, 1971 is on *Carnegie Hall* and is even longer! Other versions are on *Playground Psychotics, Live at Fillmore East, June 1971 - 50th Anniversary*, and *The Mothers 1971*. A date unknown version of parts of "Billy the Mountain" called "Studebaker Hawk" and "Don't Fuck Around" appeared on the bootleg of *Randomonium*, which was eventually legitimately released as a digital download on *Beat The Boots III* in January 2009. If you're as impressed with the Tibetan Memory Trick as I am, I'm even more impressed that Flo & Eddie, et al., could remember all of this bullshit.

—

BWANA DIK (Frank Zappa) by The Mothers
Mothers involvement: Frank Zappa—producer, arranger, guitar, dialogue, vocals; Ian Underwood—woodwinds, keyboards, vocals; Aynsley Dunbar—drums; Howard Kaylan—lead vocals, dialogue; Mark Volman—lead vocals, dialogue; Jim Pons—bass, vocals, dialogue; Bob Harris—keyboards, vocals
Additional personnel: Barry Keene—engineer
Recording dates: June 5-6, 1971 at the Fillmore East, New York, New York
Highest chart position: #38 from *Fillmore East - June 1971*
Original release date: August 2, 1971

Mark. Between this and "Penis Dimension," there is enough dick material in The Turtles' catalog to last a lifetime. In this album's context, it is all part of the suite about hotels, groupies, and dicks that leads to the inevitable performance of "Happy Together" later on the album. The song recalls "I'm Chief Kamanawanalaya." The performance from September 26, 1970 is on *The Mothers 1970*. The June 5-6, 1971 versions are also on *Live at Fillmore East, June 1971 - 50th Anniversary*, and *The Mothers 1971*.

Charles: Is "Bwana Dik" a vulgar song or is it a question? It turns out to be both, and those wacky Mothers loved playing it live. If someone was to compile a collection of risqué track titles, this would follow Brute Force's "King of Fuh" (released—barely—on The Beatles' Apple label). Another hello to Stephen Friedland.

—

CALL ANY VEGETABLE aka **CHAMPAGNE LECTURE** (Frank Zappa) by The Mothers
Mothers involvement: Frank Zappa—producer, arranger, guitar, vocals, dialogue; Don Preston—keyboards; Ian Underwood—woodwinds, keyboards, vocals; Aynsley Dunbar—drums; Howard Kaylan—lead vocals, dialogue; Mark Volman—lead vocals, dialogue; Jim Pons—bass guitar, vocals, dialogue
Recording dates: August 7, 1971 at Pauley Pavilion, UCLA, Los Angeles, California
Highest chart position: #85 from *Just Another Band from L.A.*
Original release date: March 26, 1972
Significant other versions: Frank Zappa and The Mothers of Invention

Mark: The original studio version of this song was from the original Mothers of Invention album *Absolutely Free*. It is a quite amusing ode to various vegetables and prunes. The original studio version had a few funny spoken word bits that did not translate to the live versions, but then again the live versions have a different spoken word part ("Where can I go?") that wasn't on the studio version. The live performances by Flo & Eddie pack quite a punch and are quite rocking versions. The performances from June 18, August 21, and September 17, 1970 are from *The Mothers 1970*. The performance from November 13, 1970 was on *Freaks and Motherfu*#@%!* and is vastly inferior to the *Just Another Band* version mainly due to sound quality. This version includes Zappa reciting a few lines of "Do You Like My New Car?" and Flo & Eddie doing a few Nazi impersonations! The performance from December 4, 1971 was on *Swiss Cheese/Fire!* The track is called "Champagne Lecture" on *Playground Psychotics* as it is only the spoken word part in the middle.

Charles: Well, "this is a song about vegetables that keep you regular. They're real good for ya." If you like veggies and Zappa, you're already a fan of those edibles and the artist, and probably the track. If not, they're both an acquired taste.

—

CARNEGIE HALL (CD) by The Mothers
Mothers involvement: Frank Zappa—producer, arranger, guitar, vocals, band direction; Mark Volman—vocals, percussion; Howard Kaylan—vocals, percussion; Ian Underwood—keyboards, woodwinds; Don Preston—Minimoog; Jim Pons—bass, vocals; Aynsley Dunbar—drums
Additional personnel: Ron Delsener—promoter
Recording dates: October 11, 1971 at Carnegie Hall, New York, New York
Highest chart position: Did not chart
Original release date: 4-disc set released on October 31, 2011; reissued as a 3-disc set on April 3, 2020

The Persuasions:
I Just Can't Work No Longer
Working All the Live Long Day/Chain Gang
Medley #1
Pieces of a Man
Buffalo Soldier
Medley #2
Medley #3

Frank Zappa:
Hello (To FOH)/Ready?! (To the Band)
Call Any Vegetable
Any Way the Wind Blows
Magdalena
Dog Breath

Peaches En Regalia (instrumental)
Tears Began to Fall
She Painted Up Her Face/Half a Dozen Provocative Squats/Shove It Right In
King Kong (instrumental)
200 Motels Finale
Who Are the Brain Police?

Auspicious Occasion (spoken word)
Divan: Once Upon a Time
Divan: Sofa #1
Divan: Magic Pig
Divan: Stick it Out
Divan: Divan Ends Here
Pound for a Brown (instrumental)
Sleeping in a Jar (instrumental)
Wonderful Wino
Sharleena
Cruising for Burgers

Billy the Mountain, Part 1
Billy the Mountain—The Carnegie Solos
Billy the Mountain, Part 2
The $600 Mud Shark Prelude (spoken word)
The Mud Shark (spoken word)

If you want a good collection of every song Flo & Eddie sang while with Frank Zappa, and a complete concert, this is probably it. The only thing missing here is their rendition of "Happy Together." This is also the only place you can find the complete "Sofa Suite."

—

CHUNGA'S REVENGE (LP) By Frank Zappa
Mothers involvement: Frank Zappa—producer, arranger, guitar, vocals, harpsichord, drums and percussions; Ian Underwood—organ, rhythm guitar, piano, electric piano, alto saxophone, pipe organ, electric alto saxophone with wah-wah pedal, tenor saxophone, grand piano; Aynsley Dunbar—drums, tambourine; John Guerin—drums; Max Bennett—bass; Jeff Simmons—bass, vocals; George Duke—organ, electric piano, vocal sound effects, trombone; Howard Kaylan—vocals; Mark Volman—vocals, rhythm guitar; Don "Sugarcane" Harris—organ
Additional personnel: Dick Kunc, Stan Agol, Roy Thomas Baker—engineers
Recording dates: July 5, 1969 - August 29, 1970 at The Record Plant, Hollywood, California; Trident Studios, London, England; T.T.G./Sunset-Highland Recording Studios, Hollywood, California, Whitney Studios, Glendale, California
Highest chart position: #119
Original release date: October 23, 1970

Transylvania Boogie (instrumental)
Road Ladies
Twenty Small Cigars (instrumental)
The Nancy and Mary Music

Tell Me You Love Me
Would You Go All the Way?
Chunga's Revenge (instrumental)
The Clap (instrumental)
Rudy Wants To Buy Yez a Drink
Sharleena

Frank Zappa's first album after The Turtles' break-up consisted of a few leftover solo instrumental tracks and new vocal tracks featuring his two new lead singers: The Phlorescent Leech (Mark

Volman) and Eddie (Howard Kaylan). Originally, their roles were reversed, but due to a mix-up they became who they became and remained that way for the rest of their career. The story goes that White Whale Records owned not only The Turtles' name, but their own real names, hence the pseudonyms. Charles and I will only be reviewing the tracks on this album in which Flo & Eddie appear and not the instrumentals. By the way, for those non-Zappaphiles, "Chunga" is pronounced like "choonga" and roughly translates to mean "joking." Also, this album represents a shift from both the satirical political commentary of his 1960s work with The Mothers of Invention, and the jazz fusion of Frank's solo album *Hot Rats*. Overall, it kind of loosely hangs together and comes across as a somewhat cohesive work. It is a patchwork quilt of an album for sure, but more commercially accessible than something like *Uncle Meat*.

—

CONCENTRATION MOON (Frank Zappa) by The Mothers
Mothers involvement: Frank Zappa—guitar, vocals; Mark Volman—vocals; Howard Kaylan—vocals; Jeff Simmons—bass, vocals; George Duke—keyboards, trombone; Ian Underwood—keyboards; Aynsley Dunbar—drums
Recording dates: November 13, 1970 at the Fillmore East, New York, New York
Highest chart position: Did not chart from *Freaks and Motherfu*#@%!*
Original release date: July 7, 1991 (bootleg version originally released in 1983)
Significant other versions: Frank Zappa and The Mothers of Invention

Flo & Eddie sing a decent version of the original studio version which originally appeared on The Mothers of Invention's *We're Only in it for the Money*. The studio version is much, much better and is a pretty funny song. A version is on *Playground Psychotics*, which was later released on *Live at Fillmore East, June 1971 - 50th Anniversary* and *The Mothers 1971*. The performance from June 18, 1970 is on *The Mothers 1970*.

—

CRUISING FOR BURGERS aka **CRUISIN' FOR BURGERS** (Frank Zappa) by The Mothers
Mothers involvement: Frank Zappa—guitar, vocals; Mark Volman—vocals; Howard Kaylan—vocals; Jeff Simmons—bass, vocals; George Duke—keyboards, trombone; Ian Underwood—keyboards; Aynsley Dunbar—drums
Recording dates: November 13, 1970 at the Fillmore East, New York, New York
Highest chart position: Did not chart from *Freaks and Motherfu*#@%!*
Original release date: July 7, 1991 (bootleg version originally released in 1983)
Significant other versions: Frank Zappa and The Mothers of Invention

The original studio version is from *Uncle Meat* and is an amusing ode to teenage life in the '60s. The performance from October 11, 1971 is on *Carnegie Hall*. The performance from December 4, 1971 is on *Swiss Cheese/Fire!* A version is on *Playground Psychotics*. The performance from December 10, 1971 is also on *Live at the Rainbow Theatre* and *The Mothers 1971*. One wonders if this song was meant to be included on *Just Another Band from L.A.*, as the cover graphics show the band in cartoon form in a car on top of a photo of a gigantic burger, or if it was just an allusion to this song as Zappa was wont to do. Zappa continued to perform this live many years after Flo & Eddie left the band.

—

DADDY, DADDY, DADDY (Frank Zappa) by Frank Zappa
Mothers involvement: Frank Zappa—producer, orchestration, bass guitar, guitar, drums; George Duke—trombone, keyboards; Ian Underwood—keyboards, woodwinds; Big Jim Sullivan—guitar, orchestration; Martin Lickert—bass guitar; Aynsley Dunbar—drums; Ruth Underwood—percussion; Jimmy Carl Black—vocals; Howard Kaylan—vocals; Jim Pons—voices; Mark Volman—vocals, photography
Additional personnel: Bob Auger—engineer; Barry Keene—overdubs, remixing; Theodore Bikel—narrator; Royal Philharmonic Orchestra
Recording dates: January 28 - February 5, 1971 at Pinewood Studios, UK and Whitney Studios, Glendale, California

Highest chart position: Single did not chart; B-side of "Magic Fingers;" #59 from *200 Motels*
Original release date: October 4, 1971 for album; November 1971 for single

Call it what you will. This is either a tribute or a parody to fifties doo-wop. It's also pretty catchy. Much more catchier than 90% of the stuff on *200 Motels*. The performance from September 26, 1970 is on *The Mothers 1970*.

—

DIVAN ENDS HERE aka **DIVAN** (Frank Zappa) by The Mothers
Mothers involvement: Frank Zappa—producer, arranger, guitar, vocals, band direction; Mark Volman—vocals, percussion; Howard Kaylan—vocals, percussion; Ian Underwood—keyboards, woodwinds; Don Preston—Minimoog; Jim Pons—bass, vocals; Aynsley Dunbar—drums
Additional personnel: Ron Delsener—promoter
Recording dates: October 11, 1971 at Carnegie Hall, New York, New York
Highest chart position: Did not chart from *Carnegie Hall*
Original release date: October 31, 2011

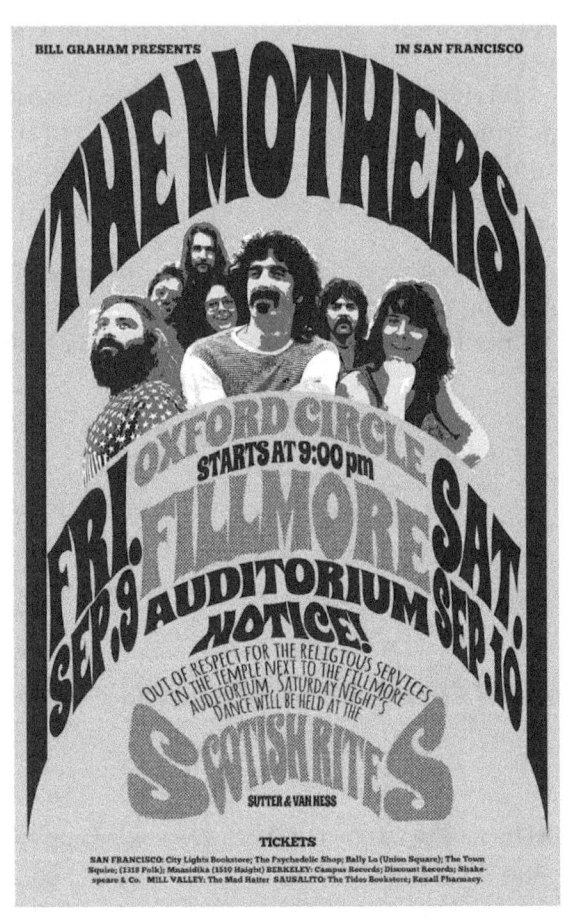

If you were wondering what a song sung by Mark Volman and Howard Kaylan would sound like in German, look no further. Zappa's typical infatuation with a single benign subject (sofas, tuna, etc.) continues here and this is part of the "Sofa Suite" with a nod to "Eddie, Are You Kidding?" at the end. A rehearsal version is on *Playground Psychotics*.

—

DO YOU LIKE MY NEW CAR? aka **THE GROUPIE ROUTINE** (Frank Zappa) by The Mothers
Mothers involvement: Frank Zappa—producer, arranger, guitar, dialogue, vocals; Ian Underwood—woodwinds, keyboards, vocals; Aynsley Dunbar—drums; Howard Kaylan—lead vocals, dialogue; Mark Volman—lead vocals, dialogue; Jim Pons—bass, vocals, dialogue; Bob Harris—keyboards, vocals
Additional personnel: Barry Keene—engineer
Recording dates: June 5-6, 1971 at the Fillmore East, New York, New York
Highest chart position: #38 from *Fillmore East - June 1971*
Original release date: August 2, 1971

"Do You LIke My New Car?" is a lengthy-spoken word section where Mark Volman plays a female groupie being seduced by rock and roll star Howard Kaylan with some additional side comments by Jim Pons and Frank Zappa. The true beginnings of Flo & Eddie start here. Previously, they just sang along to Zappa's songs. This is true Flo & Eddie material which some Zappa fans love and others really detest. Flo & Eddie continued to perform the routine live in their solo shows. This also appears on *Live at Fillmore East, June 1971 - 50th Anniversary* and *The Mothers 1971*.

—

DOG BREATH aka **DOG BREATH IN THE YEAR OF THE PLAGUE** and **THE DOG BREATH VARIATIONS** (Frank Zappa) by The Mothers
Mothers involvement: Frank Zappa—producer, arranger, guitar, vocals; Don Preston—keyboards; Ian Underwood—woodwinds, keyboards, vocals; Aynsley Dunbar—drums; Howard Kaylan—lead vocals; Mark Volman—lead vocals; Jim Pons—bass guitar, vocals
Recording dates: August 7, 1971 at UCLA's Pauley Pavilion, Los Angeles, California
Highest chart position: #85 from *Just Another Band from L.A.*
Original release date: March 26, 1972
Significant other versions: Frank Zappa and The Mothers of Invention

A pretty straightforward version was done live by Flo & Eddie. The studio version of this song originally appeared on the original Frank Zappa and the Mothers of Invention album *Uncle Meat* and was a single off that album coupled with "My Guitar Wants to Kill Your Mama." The performances from June 18, August 21 and September 17, 1970 are on *The Mothers 1970*. The performance from December 4, 1971 was on *Swiss Cheese/Fire!*

—

EASY MEAT (Frank Zappa) by The Mothers
Mothers involvement: Frank Zappa—producer, arranger, guitar, vocals; Howard Kaylan—vocals; Mark Volman—vocals, percussion; Jeff Simmons—bass, vocals; Ian Underwood—organ, keyboards, guitar; George Duke—piano, keyboards, trombone; Aynsley Dunbar—drums
Additional personnel: Roy Thomas Baker—engineer
Recording dates: 1970 from various
Highest chart position: Did not chart from *The Mothers 1970*
Original release date: May 8, 2020

Even though this song was officially released over a decade later on Frank's *Tinseltown Rebellion*, it was performed many times during the Flo & Eddie tenure of the band. The Flo & Eddie version is a slower blues jam than the rocked up and sped up later version.

—

EDDIE, ARE YOU KIDDING? (Howard Kaylan, Mark Volman, Frank Zappa, John Seiter) by The Mothers
Mothers involvement: Frank Zappa—producer, arranger, guitar, vocals; Don Preston—keyboards; Ian Underwood—woodwinds, keyboards, vocals; Aynsley Dunbar—drums; Howard Kaylan—lead vocals; Mark Volman—lead vocals; Jim Pons—bass guitar, vocals
Recording dates: August 7, 1971 at Pauley Pavilion, UCLA, Los Angeles, California
Highest chart position: #85 from *Just Another Band from L.A.*
Original release date: March 26, 1972
Significant other versions: Flo & Eddie

Mark: Although this song originated with The Mothers, it carried over for a long time into the Flo & Eddie band, which they improved upon greatly over the years. Here the group really just sings about various sizes and types of clothing for the big and tall man. The superior version on *Illegal, Immoral and Fattening* incorporates various band parody sections which was a Flo & Eddie specialty, taking this song to an entirely new level. With Zappa, it was just merely funny.

For those unfamiliar with the inspiration for this piece (which means anyone outside of L.A.), a clothier named Edward Nalbandian (1927-2006), was the owner of Zachary All Clothing, which was on Wilshire Blvd. from 1953 through 1995. Nalbandian would appear in his own TV commercials and in one of them, he said of his low prices, "My friends all ask me, 'Eddie, are you kidding?' And I tell them no, I am not kidding." Nalbandian's son took over the store in 1995, and it finally closed in 2006.

Charles: I recall a television commercial where somebody named "Eddie" promised suits to anyone on sale for fifty bucks. Frank Zappa and our boys go on a tangent asking him if he and his team of tailors can indeed come through with their wardrobe promise. Anything could be a song, and this is further proof. It's all typical (or, in the case of Frank Zappa, atypical!) zaniness and perceivably avant-garde song-making. A keen ear can hear the reference to The Crests' "Sixteen Candles" in the final bit of the composition where they sing the words "Sixty Tailors."

—

FILLMORE EAST - JUNE 1971 (LP) by The Mothers
Mothers involvement: Frank Zappa—producer, arranger, guitar, dialogue, vocals; Ian Underwood—woodwinds, keyboards, vocals; Aynsley Dunbar—drums; Howard Kaylan—lead vocals, dialogue; Mark Volman—lead vocals, dialogue; Jim Pons—bass, vocals, dialogue; Bob Harris—keyboards, vocals
Additional personnel: Barry Keene—engineer; Don Preston—mini-Moog
Recording dates: June 5-6, 1971 at the Fillmore East, New York, New York
Highest chart position: #38
Original release date: August 2, 1971

Little House I Used to Live In
The Mud Shark (spoken word)
What Kind of Girl Do You Think We Are?
Bwana Dik
Latex Solar Beef
Willie the Pimp, Part One (instrumental)

Willie the Pimp, Part Two (instrumental)
Do You Like My New Car? (spoken word)
Happy Together
Lonesome Electric Turkey (instrumental)
Peaches En Regalia (instrumental)
Tears Began to Fall

Mark and Howard's second album for Frank Zappa is their first live one. The major highlight on this record (besides the typical requisite Zappa vulgarity) is the first released live version of "Happy Together" and live Turtles singing released to record. Another highlight (lowlight) is the debut of the mud shark story and the lengthy hotel-groupie-dick suite that leads up to "Happy Together." It's an amusing and surprisingly consistent album and was the highest charting album for Zappa during the Flo & Eddie years, cracking the Top 40 Albums on Billboard.

"Willie the Pimp" is presented here in instrumental form unlike the original studio version with the Captain Beefheart vocals that premiered on Frank's *Hot Rats.* On this album, the live album was split into two parts, each one taking up part of an album side. On some CD editions, "Part Two" is mysteriously deleted. It was reinstated on later reissues.

The album cover, which was cheaply hand-written by Zappa's longtime album cover designer Cal Schenkel, was defaced by John Lennon when it came time to include a sleeve for the *Live Jam* disc of his two-disc *Some Time in New York City* collection.

In 2022, a three-disc vinyl version of the complete Fillmore East concerts was released to vinyl and CD as a *50th Anniversary Edition* and also on CD as part of *The Mothers 1971* box set.

—

FREAK JAZZ, MOVIE MADNESS AND ANOTHER MOTHERS: FRANK ZAPPA 1969-1973 (film)
Mothers involvement: Frank Zappa, Howard Kaylan, Mark Volman, The Mothers of Invention members from 1969-1973
Additional personnel: Thomas Arnold—narrator
Original release date: 2014

A direct-to-video DVD documentary covering the years of the breakup of the original Mothers of Invention group, the formation of The Mothers with Flo & Eddie, and Frank Zappa's solo projects and transition to a jazz band and some mainstream success.

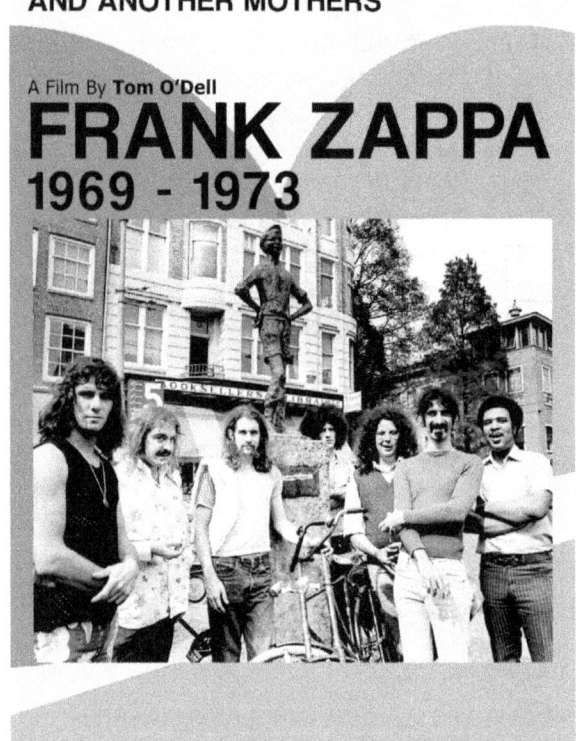

—

FREAKS AND MOTHERFU*#@%! (CD) by The Mothers
Mothers involvement: Frank Zappa—guitar, vocals; Mark Volman—vocals; Howard Kaylan—vocals; Jeff Simmons—bass, vocals; George Duke—keyboards, trombone; Ian Underwood—keyboards; Aynsley Dunbar—drums
Recording dates: November 13, 1970 at the Fillmore East, New York, New York
Highest chart position: Did not chart
Original release date: July 7, 1991 (bootleg version originally released in 1983)

Happy Together
Wino Man
Concentration Moon
Paladin's Routine
Call Any Vegetable

Little House I Used to Live In
Mudshark Variations
Holiday in Berlin
Sleeping in a Jar (instrumental)
Cruising for Burgers

One of many Frank Zappa bootlegs that Zappa appropriated and reissued as part of his *Beat The Boots* series. The original bootleg title is uncensored. The lengthy "Do You Like My New Car?" spoken-word section of this performance prior to "Happy Together" was mostly left on the cutting room floor. There are a few different songs than on *Fillmore East*, but the sound quality leaves much to be desired compared to that other collection. Listen at your own peril!

—

GRIS GRIS (Mac Rebbenack, Frank Zappa) by The Mothers
Mothers involvement: Frank Zappa—producer, arranger, guitar, vocals; Howard Kaylan—vocals; Mark Volman—vocals, percussion; Jeff Simmons—bass, vocals; Ian Underwood—organ, keyboards, guitar; George Duke—piano, keyboards, trombone; Aynsley Dunbar—drums
Additional personnel: Roy Thomas Baker—engineer
Recording dates: 1970 from various
Highest chart position: Did not chart from *The Mothers 1970*
Original release date: May 8, 2020
Significant other versions: Dr. John

Zappa, Kaylan, and Volman seemed to have an unnatural obsession with Dr. John at this time. This song cover as typical for this period devolved into a lengthy guitar instrumental that had nothing to do with the cover until it finally came back to the cover. The cover version really just consists of Flo & Eddie shouting "gris gris gumbo ya ya" over and over. Not that authentic. The original Dr. John version is from his 1968 album *Gris-Gris*.

HALF A DOZEN PROVOCATIVE SQUATS: see **SHE PAINTED UP HER FACE**

HAPPY TOGETHER (Garry Bonner, Alan Gordon) by The Mothers
Mothers involvement: Frank Zappa—producer, arranger, guitar, dialogue, vocals; Ian Underwood—woodwinds, keyboards, vocals; Aynsley Dunbar—drums; Howard Kaylan—lead vocals, dialogue; Mark Volman—lead vocals, dialogue; Jim Pons—bass, vocals, dialogue; Bob Harris—keyboards, vocals
Additional personnel: Barry Keene—engineer
Recording dates: June 5-6, 1971 at the Fillmore East, New York, New York
Highest chart position: #38 from *Fillmore East - June 1971*
Original release date: August 2, 1971
Significant other versions: The Turtles, Flo & Eddie, The Nylons, Hugo Montenegro, Tony Orlando and Dawn, T.G. Sheppard, Captain & Tennille, Mel Torme, The Piano Guys, Weezer, Petula Clark, Donny Osmond, Frank Zappa and the Mothers, Frank Alamo, Prima Vera, B.E. Taylor, Filter, Dmitri Vegas & Like Mike, Bassjackers

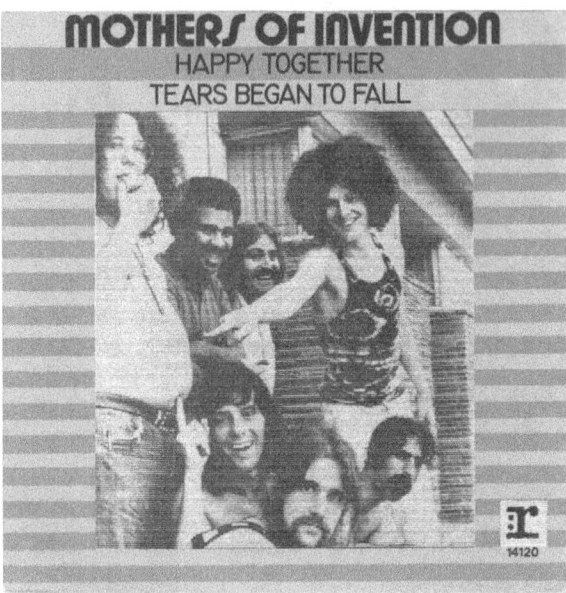

The Mothers' version with Flo & Eddie took the opportunity on stage with Frank Zappa to send up groupies by promising the groupies that they would be singing their biggest hit "with a bullet" with many sexual overtones. After this comedic lead-up, the band delivers with a surprisingly straight—but quick—version of the song. This also appears on *Live at Fillmore East, June 1971 - 50th Anniversary* and *The Mothers 1971*.

The performance from September 26, 1970 is on *The Mothers 1970*. The performance from November 13, 1970 is on *Freaks and Motherfu*#@%!* On that version, the lengthy "Do You Like My New Car?" spoken word section was mostly left on the cutting room floor.

Flo & Eddie sang a non-reggae 1991 live version that appeared on *The Turtles Featuring Flo & Eddie Captured Live* where he changes the lyrics to "invest three dimes" and "lose my minds" and namedrops Milli Vanilli.

HOLIDAY IN BERLIN (Frank Zappa) by The Mothers
Mothers involvement: Frank Zappa—guitar, vocals; Mark Volman—vocals; Howard Kaylan—vocals; Jeff Simmons—bass, vocals; George Duke—keyboards, trombone; Ian Underwood—keyboards; Aynsley Dunbar—drums
Recording dates: November 13, 1970 at the Fillmore East, New York, New York
Highest chart position: Did not chart from *Freaks and Motherfu*#@%!*
Original release date: July 7, 1991 (bootleg version originally released in 1983)
Significant other versions: Frank Zappa and The Mothers of Invention

This version includes lyrics from "Would You Like a Snack?" It's one of those unfortunately too many songs where Flo & Eddie just sing along the guitar melody line. The original version appeared on *Burnt Weeny Sandwich* and was also performed live much earlier by The Mothers of Invention.

—

I WANT TO HOLD YOUR HAND (John Lennon, Paul McCartney) by The Mothers
Mothers involvement: Frank Zappa—producer, arranger, guitar, dialogue, vocals; Ian Underwood—woodwinds, keyboards, vocals; Aynsley Dunbar—drums; Howard Kaylan—lead vocals, dialogue; Mark Volman—lead vocals, dialogue; Jim Pons—bass, vocals, dialogue; Bob Harris—keyboards, vocals
Additional personnel: Barry Keene—engineer; Don Preston—mini-Moog; Spencer Crislu—remix engineer; John Lennon—vocals, guitar; Yoko Ono—vocals, percussion
Recording dates: December 10, 1971 at the Rainbow Theatre, London, England
Highest chart position: Did not chart from *Live At The Rainbow Theatre* and *The Mothers 1971*
Original release date: January 28, 2022
Significant other versions: The Beatles, Arthur Fiedler & the Boston Pops Orchestra, Bijele Strijele, The Supremes, Al Green, Sparks, Dollar, Lakeside, Manny Manuel, Jennifer Cihi, Kurt Humel.

Mark: The Mothers ended their set and Flo & Eddie end their career with Frank Zappa with a nice cover version of "I Want to Hold Your Hand." Seconds after Zappa says his 'goodnights,' a jealous fan pushes Zappa into the orchestra pit, breaking many of his bones and almost killing him. The tragic ending is complete on this live release.
Charles: I find it to be bouncy, zippy, and fun, with a good attempt at harmonies.

—

JUST ANOTHER BAND FROM L.A. (LP) by The Mothers
Mothers involvement: Frank Zappa—producer, arranger, guitar, vocals, dialogue; Don Preston—keyboards; Ian Underwood—woodwinds, keyboards, vocals; Aynsley Dunbar—drums; Howard Kaylan—lead vocals, dialogue; Mark Volman—lead vocals, dialogue; Jim Pons—bass guitar, vocals, dialogue
Recording dates: August 7, 1971 at Pauley Pavilion, UCLA, Los Angeles, California
Highest chart position: #85
Original release date: March 26, 1972

Billy the Mountain

Call Any Vegetable
Eddie, Are You Kidding?
Magdalena
Dog Breath

Of the four original albums Flo & Eddie did with Frank Zappa during 1970-72, this one is probably the most accessible. It is also the funniest, from the side-filling "Billy the Mountain," through the amusing "Eddie, Are You Kidding?," the now dangerous "Magdalena," and a decent cover of "Dog Breath," this album is fun and funny throughout. For those who love The Turtles and possibly Flo & Eddie but can't stand Frank Zappa (Is there such a person?), this is the album for you.

—

LATEX SOLAR BEEF (Frank Zappa) by The Mothers
Mothers involvement: Frank Zappa—producer, arranger, guitar, dialogue, vocals; Ian Underwood—woodwinds, keyboards, vocals; Aynsley Dunbar—drums; Howard Kaylan—lead vocals, dialogue; Mark Volman—lead vocals, dialogue; Jim Pons—bass, vocals, dialogue; Bob Harris—keyboards, vocals
Additional personnel: Barry Keene—engineer
Recording dates: June 5-6, 1971 at the Fillmore East, New York, New York
Highest chart position: #38 from *Fillmore East - June 1971*
Original release date: August 2, 1971

Mark: Another "song" in the mudshark-groupies-dick jokes suite that's all leading to a performance of "Happy Together." These long suites seemed to be de rigueur during the Flo & Eddie years,

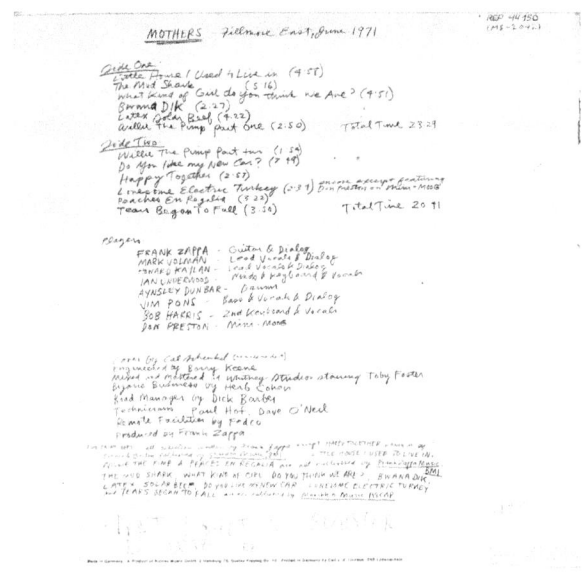

which all later culminated in the excessively long "Billy the Mountain" suite in later live shows. Of all the songs in the suite, this one is the least, mainly as it just consists of Flo & Eddie singing along the guitar melody line and occasionally shouting "mud shark" to keep the theme going. This also appears on *Live at Fillmore East, June 1971 - 50th Anniversary* and *The Mothers 1971*.

Charles: Where did Zappa come up with these titles? In an online song review by François Couture, Zappa explains the title as follows: Latex is the kind of rubber used in condoms. The sun is an ageless symbol of maleness and deity. As for the "beef" part, it refers to the organ found between the legs of a rock star, the same one that is the subject of this whole routine: "All groupies must bow down/In the sacred presence of the Latex Solar Beef." He goes on to reveal that "Latex Solar Beef" was mostly performed live during the Flo & Eddie era of the Mothers of Invention (1970-1971) as part of the "Groupie Routine," a suite of songs dealing with (sex) life on the road. It began with "What Will This Evening Bring Me This Morning," "What Kind of Girl Do You Think We Are?," and "Bwana Dik," and continued with "Daddy, Daddy, Daddy," "Do You Like My New Car?," and typically ended with a cover of the Turtles' hit "Happy Together."

All of them were meant to appear in the movie (and on the soundtrack) *200 Motels*, but some, like "Latex Solar Beef," had to be cut from the script due to a tight shooting schedule, and were salvaged on the live album *Fillmore East, June 1971*. After the pompous conclusion of "Bwana Dik" (on a Beethoven-like finale), "Latex Solar Beef" establishes a heavy rock riff similar to the one providing the backbone of "Willie the Pimp" (on *Fillmore East, June 1971*, and the band launches almost seamlessly into that song). The title must be seen in the light of the previous piece. Lyrics get confusing at times (what's the meaning of "Acetylene nirvana/ Hemorrhoids"?), but part of them ("See the screaming/Hot black steaming/Iridescent naugahyde python screaming/Steam roller") reappeared almost ten years later in the song "Stick It Out" on Zappa's album *Joe's Garage*." Thanks François, I couldn't have said it better myself, which is why I deferred to your words.

—

LITTLE HOUSE I USED TO LIVE IN (Frank Zappa) by The Mothers
Mothers involvement: Frank Zappa—producer, arranger, guitar, dialogue, vocals; Ian Underwood—woodwinds, keyboards, vocals; Aynsley Dunbar—drums; Howard Kaylan—lead vocals, dialogue; Mark Volman—lead vocals, dialogue; Jim Pons—bass, vocals, dialogue; Bob Harris—keyboards, vocals
Additional personnel: Barry Keene—engineer
Recording dates: June 5-6, 1971 at the Fillmore East, New York, New York
Highest chart position: #38 from *Fillmore East - June 1971*
Original release date: August 2, 1971
Significant other versions: Frank Zappa and the Mothers of Invention

This song was originally an 18:46 live version from *Burnt Weeny Sandwich*. The Fillmore version with Flo & Eddie is only about five minutes long, with a long piano and drum intro. It's a nice jazzy arrangement with a number of changes. Flo & Eddie mainly contribute "la la la la la" and "oink! oink!" and "mud shark," which leads into the next track. The performances from June 1971 appear on *Live at Fillmore East, June 1971 - 50th Anniversary* and *The Mothers 1971*. The performance from November 13, 1970 is on *Freaks and Motherfu*#@%!* and includes portions of "Penis Dimension." Zappa would continue to perform the song live long after the Flo & Eddie years.

—

LIVE AT THE RAINBOW THEATRE by The Mothers
Mothers involvement: Frank Zappa—producer, arranger, guitar, dialogue, vocals; Ian Underwood—woodwinds, keyboards, vocals; Aynsley Dunbar—drums; Howard Kaylan—lead vocals, dialogue; Mark Volman—lead vocals, dialogue; Jim Pons—bass, vocals, dialogue; Bob Harris—keyboards, vocals
Additional personnel: Barry Keene—engineer; Don Preston—mini-Moog; Spencer Crislu—remix engineer; John Lennon—vocals, guitar; Yoko Ono—vocals, percussion
Recording dates: December 10, 1971 at the Rainbow Theatre, London, England
Highest chart position: Did not chart
Original release date: January 28, 2022

Zanti Serenade (instrumental)
Peaches En Regalia (instrumental)
Tears Began To Fall

Shove It Right In
"Pain In The Ass" (spoken word)
Divan: Once Upon A Time
Divan: Sofa #1

Pound For A Brown—Part I (instrumental)
Super Grease (instrumental)

Pound For A Brown—Part II (instrumental)
Sleeping In A Jar (instrumental)

Wonderful Wino
Sharleena
Cruising For Burgers

"That's Your Tough Luck" (spoken word)
King Kong (instrumental)
I Want To Hold Your Hand

This concert is the final Frank Zappa and The Mothers concert to feature Flo & Eddie as a regular part of the ensemble. This was due to the fact that a jealous fan pushed Zappa off the stage right after the band performed a cover of "I Want to Hold Your Hand," which ended this phase of Zappa's career and almost his life.

—

LOLA STEPONSKY (Frank Zappa) by The Mothers
Mothers involvement: Frank Zappa—producer, arranger, guitar, vocals; Howard Kaylan—vocals; Mark Volman—vocals, percussion; Jeff Simmons—bass, vocals; Ian Underwood—organ, keyboards, guitar; George Duke—piano, keyboards, trombone; Aynsley Dunbar—drums
Additional personnel: Roy Thomas Baker—engineer
Recording dates: June 21-22, 1970 at Trident Studios, London, England
Highest chart position: Did not chart from *The Mothers 1970*
Original release date: May 8, 2020

This "lost" song was finally released in 2020. It's lyrically slight and Flo & Eddie make the best of an unrealized performance. It's easy to see why this remained in the can for so long.

—

LONESOME COWBOY BURT aka **LONESOME COWBOY NANDO** (Frank Zappa) by Frank Zappa
Mothers involvement: Frank Zappa—producer, orchestration, bass guitar, guitar, drums; George Duke—trombone, keyboards; Ian Underwood—keyboards, woodwinds; Big Jim Sullivan—guitar, orchestration; Martin Lickert—bass guitar; Aynsley Dunbar—drums; Ruth Underwood—percussion; Jimmy Carl Black—lead vocals; Howard Kaylan—vocals; Jim Pons—voices; Mark Volman—vocals, photography

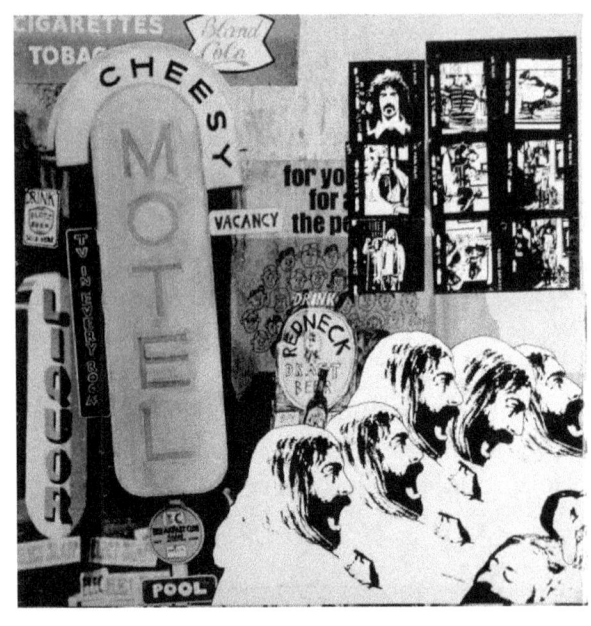

Additional personnel: Bob Auger—engineer; Barry Keene—overdubs, remixing; Theodore Bikel—narrator; Royal Philharmonic Orchestra
Recording dates: January 28 - February 5, 1971 at Pinewood Studios, UK and Whitney Studios, Glendale, California
Highest chart position: #59 from *200 Motels*
Original release date: October 4, 1971
Significant other versions: Frank Zappa and The Mothers of Invention, The Mothers

Mark: Zappa re-recorded this tune with the country twang many times over the years with such characters as Jimmy Swaggart substituting in the lyrics. This *200 Motels* version is the original and best with Jimmy Carl Black singing his heart out with Flo & Eddie backups. I love this! The performance from August 7, 1971 is on *You Can't Do That On Stage Anymore, Volume 6* with Zappa on lead vocals. "Where's my waitress?!"
Charles: As is not often the case, I love it too. Yee hah!

—

MAGDALENA (Howard Kaylan, Frank Zappa) by The Mothers
Mothers involvement: Frank Zappa—producer, arranger, guitar, vocals; Don Preston—keyboards; Ian Underwood—woodwinds, keyboards, vocals; Aynsley Dunbar—drums; Howard Kaylan—lead vocals; Mark Volman—lead vocals; Jim Pons—bass guitar, vocals
Recording dates: August 7, 1971 at Pauley Pavilion, UCLA, Los Angeles, California
Highest chart position: #85 from *Just Another Band from L.A.*
Original release date: March 26, 1972

Today, this song is now the winner of the most non-PC in our current PC and cancel culture. It's amazing to know that the main composer of this, Howard Kaylan, went on to have a prolific career with children's records a decade later. Despite its vulgar lyrics, it's actually a pretty snappy, upbeat, and singable song. Just don't be in earshot of the easily offended. The performance from December 4, 1971 was on *Swiss Cheese/Fire!*

—

MAGIC FINGERS (Frank Zappa) by Frank Zappa
Mothers involvement: Frank Zappa—producer, orchestration, bass guitar, guitar, drums; George Duke—trombone, keyboards; Ian Underwood—keyboards, woodwinds; Big Jim Sullivan—guitar, orchestration; Martin Lickert—bass guitar; Aynsley Dunbar—drums; Ruth Underwood—percussion; Jimmy Carl Black—vocals; Howard Kaylan—vocals; Jim Pons—voices; Mark Volman—vocals, photography
Additional personnel: Bob Auger—engineer; Barry Keene—overdubs, remixing; Theodore Bikel—narrator; Royal Philharmonic Orchestra
Recording dates: January 28 - February 5, 1971 at Pinewood Studios, UK and Whitney Studios, Glendale, California
Highest chart position: Did not chart; #59 from *200 Motels*
Original release date: October 4, 1971 for album; November 1971 for single

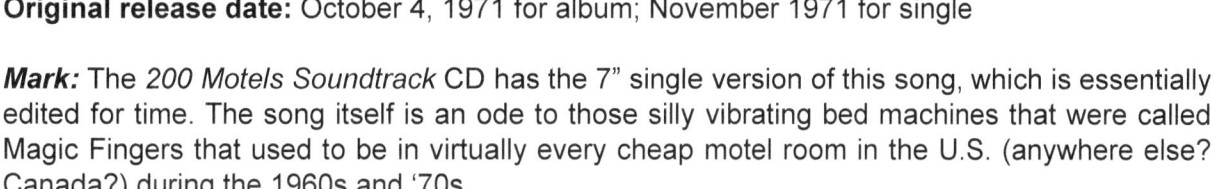

Mark: The *200 Motels Soundtrack* CD has the 7" single version of this song, which is essentially edited for time. The song itself is an ode to those silly vibrating bed machines that were called Magic Fingers that used to be in virtually every cheap motel room in the U.S. (anywhere else? Canada?) during the 1960s and '70s.

Charles: This is one of the stand-out tracks from *200 Motels* (it actually can be categorized as a song!). This can best be described as avant-garde punk funk rock. There's some outstanding guitar work by Big Jim Sullivan. It's like a musical vibrating machine from the mind of Zappa with a shout-out to the late Jeff Beck.

—

MOM & DAD (Frank Zappa) by The Mothers
Mothers involvement: Frank Zappa—producer, arranger, guitar, vocals; Howard Kaylan—vocals; Mark Volman—vocals, percussion; Jeff Simmons—bass, vocals; Ian Underwood—organ, keyboards, guitar; George Duke—piano, keyboards, trombone; Aynsley Dunbar—drums
Additional personnel: Roy Thomas Baker—engineer
Recording dates: June 18, 1970 at "Piknik" VPRO
Highest chart position: Did not chart from *The Mothers 1970*
Original release date: May 8, 2020

Flo & Eddie do a decent take of this classic Mothers of Invention song and keep it straight. There is also a version on *Playground Psychotics*. The June 1971 performances appear on *Live at*

Fillmore East, June 1971 - 50th Anniversary, and *The Mothers 1971*. The original studio version appeared on *We're Only in it for the Money*.

—

MOTHER PEOPLE (Frank Zappa) by The Mothers
Mothers involvement: Frank Zappa—guitar, vocals; Mark Volman—vocals; Howard Kaylan—vocals; Jeff Simmons—bass, vocals; George Duke—keyboards; Ian Underwood—keyboards; Aynsley Dunbar—drums
Recording dates: June 18, 1970 at "Piknik" VPRO
Highest chart position: Did not chart from *At the Circus*
Original release date: June 1992 (bootleg version originally released in 1978)
Significant other versions: Frank Zappa and The Mothers of Invention

Another straight performance by Flo & Eddie during their tenure with the band. This song kind of became the de facto theme song for The Mothers of Invention. In fact, it was the song used when Frank appeared on *The Monkees* TV show. The performances from June 18, August 21 and September 17, 1970 are on *The Mothers 1970*. The original studio version appeared on *We're Only in it for the Money*.

—

MOTHERS 1970, THE (compilation) by The Mothers
Mothers involvement: Frank Zappa—producer, arranger, guitar, vocals; Howard Kaylan—vocals; Mark Volman—vocals, percussion; Jeff Simmons—bass, vocals; Ian Underwood—organ, keyboards, guitar; George Duke—piano, keyboards, trombone; Aynsley Dunbar—drums
Additional personnel: Roy Thomas Baker—engineer
Recording dates: June 18 at "Piknik" VPRO; June 21-22 at Trident Studios, London, England; August 21 at Santa Monica, California; September 17 at Spokane, Washington; September 26, 1970 at Pepperland
Highest chart position: Did not chart
Original release date: May 8, 2020

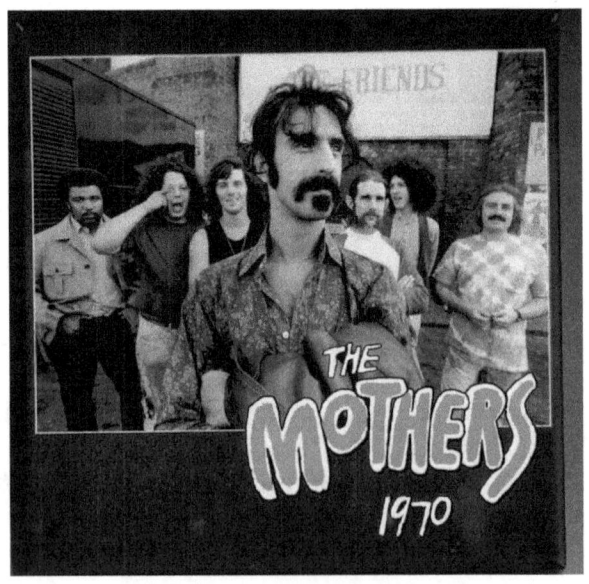

Disc 1 – Trident Studios, London, England June 21-22, 1970
Red Tubular Lighter (instrumental)
Lola Steponsky
Trident Chatter (instrumental and spoken word)
Sharleena (Roy Thomas Baker Mix)
Item 1 (instrumental)
Wonderful Wino (FZ Vocal)
"Enormous Cadenza" (instrumental and spoken word)
Envelopes (instrumental)
Red Tubular Lighter (Unedited Master) (instrumental)
Wonderful Wino (Basic Tracks, Alt. Take)
Giraffe—Take 4 (instrumental)
Wonderful Wino (FZ Vocal, Alt. Solo)

Disc 2 – Live Highlights Part 1 – "Piknik" VPRO June 18, 1970 / Pepperland September 26, 1970
Introducing…The Mothers (live on "Piknik" June 18, 1970) (spoken word)
Wonderful Wino (live on "Piknik" June 18, 1970)
Concentration Moon (live on "Piknik" June 18, 1970)
Mom & Dad (live on "Piknik" June 18, 1970)
The Air (live on "Piknik" June 18, 1970)
Dog Breath (live on "Piknik" June 18, 1970)
Mother People (live on "Piknik" June 18, 1970)
You Didn't Try To Call Me (live on "Piknik" June 18, 1970)
Agon (live on "Piknik" June 18, 1970) (instrumental)
Call Any Vegetable (live on "Piknik" June 18, 1970)
King Kong Pt. I (live on "Piknik" June 18, 1970) (instrumental)
Igor's Boogie (live on "Piknik" June 18, 1970) (instrumental)
King Kong Pt. II (live on "Piknik" June 18, 1970) (instrumental)
What Kind Of Girl Do You Think We Are? (live at Pepperland September 26, 1970)
Bwana Dik (live at Pepperland September 26, 1970)
Daddy, Daddy, Daddy (live at Pepperland September 26, 1970)
Do You Like My New Car? (live at Pepperland September 26, 1970) (spoken word)
Happy Together (live at Pepperland September 26, 1970)

Disc 3 – Live Highlights Part 2 – Hybrid Concert: Santa Monica August 21, 1970 / Spokane September 17, 1970
"Welcome To El Monte Legion Stadium!" (live) (spoken word)
Agon (live) (instrumental and spoken word)
Call Any Vegetable (live)
Pound For A Brown (live) (instrumental)
Sleeping In A Jar (live) (instrumental)
Sharleena (live)
The Air (live)
Dog Breath (live)
Mother People (live)
You Didn't Try To Call Me (live)
King Kong Pt. I (live) (instrumental)
Igor's Boogie (live) (instrumental)
King Kong Pt. II (live) (instrumental)

"Eat It Yourself…" (live) (spoken word)
Trouble Every Day (live)
"A Series Of Musical Episodes" (live) (spoken word)
Road Ladies (live)
"The Holiday Inn Motel Chain" (live) (spoken word)
What Will This Morning Bring Me This Evening? (live)
What Kind Of Girl Do You Think We Are? (live)

Disc 4 – Live Highlights Part 3 – FZ Tour Tape Recordings
"What's The Deal, Dick?" (spoken word)
Another M.O.I. Anti-Smut Loyalty Oath (live) (spoken word)
Paladin Routine #1 (live)
Portuguese Fenders (live) (instrumental)
The Sanzini Brothers (spoken word)
Guitar Build '70 (live) (instrumental)
Would You Go All The Way? (live)
Easy Meat (live)
"Who Did It?" (spoken word)
Turn It Down! (live) (instrumental)
A Chance Encounter In Cincinnati (spoken word)
Pound For A Brown (live) (instrumental)
Sleeping In A Jar (live) (instrumental)
Beloit Sword Trick (live) (spoken word)
Kong Solos Pt. I (live)
Igor's Boogie (live) (instrumental)
Kong Solos Pt. II (live)
Gris Gris (live)
Paladin Routine #2 (live)
King Kong—Outro (live) (instrumental)

This four-disc collection pretty much rounds up virtually every extant unreleased live performance by The Mothers during 1970, including a lot of general chatter by the various band members. The spoken word bits are not reviewed in this book, only the truly unique vocal performances. This type of album is truly for the completist who has to have everything Zappa as much of it is totally dispensable. Perhaps there will be a pared down single disc version in the future as four discs of this stuff is a bit much. A similar *Mothers 1971* was issued in 2022. See below. The Zappa Family Estate is only in it for the money...

—

MOTHERS 1971, THE (compilation) by The Mothers
Mothers involvement: Frank Zappa—producer, arranger, guitar, dialogue, vocals; Ian Underwood—woodwinds, keyboards, vocals; Aynsley Dunbar—drums; Howard Kaylan—lead vocals, dialogue; Mark Volman—lead vocals, dialogue; Jim Pons—bass, vocals, dialogue; Bob Harris—keyboards, vocals
Additional personnel: Barry Keene—engineer; Don Preston—mini-Moog; Spencer Crislu—remix engineer; John Lennon—vocals, guitar; Yoko Ono—vocals, percussion
Recording dates: June 1 at Watres Armory, Scranton, Pennsylvania; June 3 at State Farm Show Arena, Harrisburg, Pennsylvania; June 5-6 at Fillmore East, New York City, New York; December

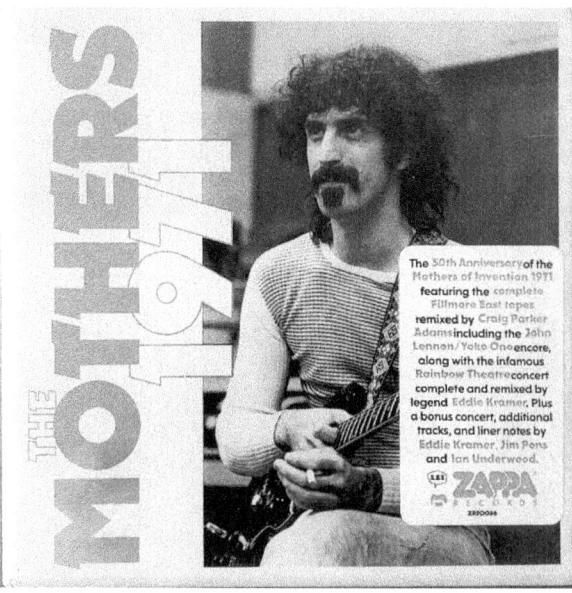

10, 1971 at the Rainbow Theatre, London, England
Highest chart position: Did not chart
Original release date: January 28, 2022

Disc 1—Fillmore East, New York City, New York, June 5, 1971—Show 1
Peaches En Regalia (instrumental)
Tears Began To Fall
Shove It Right In
Status Back Baby
Concentration Moon—Part 1
The Sanzini Brothers (Sodomy Trick) (spoken word)
Concentration Moon—Part II
Mom & Dad
Intro To Music For Low Budget Orchestra (spoken word)
Billy The Mountain
King Kong (instrumental)

Disc 2—Fillmore East, New York City, New York, June 5, 1971—Show 2
Peaches En Regalia (instrumental)
Tears Began To Fall
Shove It Right In
Intro To Music For Low Budget Orchestra (spoken word)
Billy The Mountain
Little House I Used To Live In
The Mud Shark (spoken word)
What Kind Of Girl Do You Think We Are?
Bwana Dik
Latex Solar Beef
Willie the Pimp (instrumental)

Disc 3—Fillmore East, New York City, New York, June 5, 1971—Show 2 continued
Do You Like My New Car? (spoken word)
Happy Together
"Any Chord Of Your Choice" (spoken word)
King Kong—Part I (instrumental)
Lonesome Electric Turkey (instrumental)
King Kong—Part II (instrumental)

Fillmore East, New York City, New York, June 6, 1971—Show 1
Fillmore Improvisation (instrumental)
Peaches En Regalia (instrumental)
Tears Began To Fall
Shove It Right In
Status Back Baby
Concentration Moon—Part I

The Sanzini Brothers (Sodomy Trick) (spoken word)
Concentration Moon—Part II
Mom & Dad

Disc 4—Fillmore East, New York City, New York, June 6, 1971—Show 1 continued
The Story Of Billy The Mountain (spoken word)
Intro To Music For Low Budget Orchestra (spoken word)
Billy The Mountain
Chunga's Revenge (instrumental)

Fillmore East, New York City, New York, June 6, 1971—Show 2
"Herd Of Cattle" (spoken word)
Peaches En Regalia (instrumental)
Tears Began To Fall
Shove It Right In

Disc 5—Fillmore East, New York City, New York, June 6, 1971—Show 2 continued
The Story Of Billy The Mountain (spoken word)
Intro To Music For Low Budget Orchestra (spoken word)
Billy The Mountain
"Conglomerate Assembly" (spoken word)
Little House I Used To Live In
The Mud Shark (spoken word)
What Kind Of Girl Do You Think We Are?
Bwana Dik
Latex Solar Beef
Willie the Pimp (instrumental)
Do You Like My New Car? (spoken word)
Happy Together

Disc 6—Fillmore East, New York City, New York, June 6, 1971—Show 2 continued
John and Yoko Encore Set
Well
Say Please (instrumental)
King Kong (instrumental)
Aaawk (instrumental)
Scumbag
A Small Eternity With Yoko Ono

Radio Spot, Single Version, B-Side & Outtakes
Homemade Radio Spot (spoken word)
Tears Began To Fall—Single Version
Junier Mintz Boogie—Single B-Side
Homemade Radio Spot Outtakes (spoken word)

Bonus Hybrid Concert: Harrisburg/Scranton, Pennsylvania, 1971
State Farm Show Arena, Harrisburg, Pennsylvania, June 3, 1971
Peaches En Regalia (instrumental)
Tears Began To Fall

Shove It Right In
Status Back Baby
Concentration Moon—Part I
The Sanzini Brothers (Burning Hoop Trick) (spoken word)
Concentration Moon—Part II
Mom & Dad
My Boyfriend's Back
Tiny Sick Tears

Disc 7—Bonus Hybrid Concert: Harrisburg/Scranton, Pennsylvania, 1971
State Farm Show Arena, Harrisburg, Pennsylvania, June 3, 1971 continued
Call Any Vegetable
The Story Of Billy The Mountain (spoken word)
Intro To Music For Low Budget Orchestra (spoken word)

State Farm Show Arena, Harrisburg, Pennsylvania, June 3, 1971 and Watres Armory, Scranton, Pennsylvania, June 1, 1971
Billy The Mountain

Watres Armory, Scranton, Pennsylvania, June 1, 1971
Willie the Pimp (instrumental)
King Kong (Outro) (instrumental)

Rainbow Theatre, London, England, December 10, 1971
Zanti Serenade (instrumental)
Peaches En Regalia (instrumental)
Tears Began To Fall

Disc 8—Rainbow Theatre, London, England, December 10, 1971 continued
Shove It Right In
"Pain In The Ass" (spoken word)
Divan: Once Upon A Time
Divan: Sofa #1
Pound For A Brown—Part I (instrumental)
Super Grease (instrumental)
Pound For A Brown—Part II (instrumental)
Sleeping In A Jar (instrumental)
Wonderful Wino
Sharleena
Cruising For Burgers
"That's Your Tough Luck" (spoken word)
King Kong (instrumental)
I Want To Hold Your Hand

And here it is! This eight-disc collection pretty much rounds up many live performances by The Mothers during 1971, in New York, Pennsylvania, and London. If you have *Fillmore East - June 1971, Some Time in New York City, Playground Psychotics*, and *You Can't Do That on Stage Anymore, Volume 1*, you already have most of this material, but not all of it. It is also not a complete survey of what was recorded in 1971 as it doesn't contain things like the Montreux concert and the Carnegie Hall concerts released elsewhere.

The first 5½ discs of this set were also released as a three-disc vinyl edition of *Live at Fillmore East, June 1971 - 50th Anniversary* and the last disc and a half were released as a three-disc vinyl edition called *Live at the Rainbow Theatre*. This box set is the only place where you can get the live Pennsylvanie material.

The editorial review on Amazon states: "Celebrating the 50th anniversary of the Mothers of Invention's 1971 lineup, the complete Fillmore tapes are showcased here with every note played over four shows, including the John Lennon & Yoko Ono encore. Also included is the full concert from the Rainbow Theatre in London, where Zappa was infamously pushed off the stage, newly mixed by Eddie Kramer. This Super Deluxe eight CD box set features a bonus hybrid 1971 concert from Harrisburg and Scranton, Pennsylvania, with extensive liner notes and packaging."

—

MUD SHARK aka **MUDSHARK VARIATIONS**
(Frank Zappa) by The Mothers
Mothers involvement: Frank Zappa—producer, arranger, guitar, dialogue, vocals; Ian Underwood—woodwinds, keyboards, vocals; Aynsley Dunbar—drums; Howard Kaylan—lead vocals, dialogue; Mark Volman—lead vocals, dialogue; Jim Pons—bass, vocals, dialogue; Bob Harris—keyboards, vocals
Additional personnel: Barry Keene—engineer
Recording dates: June 5-6, 1971 at the Fillmore East, New York, New York
Highest chart position: #38 from *Fillmore East - June 1971*
Original release date: August 2, 1971

Zappa was really impressed with the story of the Edgewater Inn in Seattle, Washington, where you could fish from the windows of the hotel from some of the rooms. Many infamous rock bands stayed there including The Beatles, Vanilla Fudge, The Rolling Stones, Black Sabbath, and Led Zeppelin (who were banned!). The hotel was built in 1962 and is still operating as of this writing (2022), but you can no longer fish from its windows, nor are these types of hotels allowed to be built at the edge of a pier anymore, both due to safety issues.

The song (or narration if you prefer) was played many, many times over the years. Zappa even interviewed the owner of the Inn and that is included on *Playground Psychotics*. The performance from November 13, 1970 is on *Freaks And Motherfu*#@%!* and it is very brief. The performance from October 11, 1971 is on *Carnegie Hall*. Other versions are on *Playground Psychotics* and *Live at Fillmore East, June 1971 - 50th Anniversary* and *The Mothers 1971*.

—

MY BOYFRIEND'S BACK (Bob Feldman, Jerry Goldstein, Richard Gottehrer) by The Mothers
Mothers involvement: Frank Zappa—producer, arranger, guitar, dialogue, vocals; Ian Underwood—woodwinds, keyboards, vocals; Aynsley Dunbar—drums; Howard Kaylan—lead vocals, dialogue; Mark Volman—lead vocals, dialogue; Jim Pons—bass, vocals, dialogue; Bob Harris—keyboards, vocals
Additional personnel:
Recording dates: June 3, 1971 at State Farm Show Arena, Harrisburg, Pennsylvania
Highest chart position: Did not chart from *The Mothers 1971*
Original release date: January 28, 2022
Significant other versions: The Angels, The Chiffons, Martha and the Vandellas, Melissa Manchester, Paris Bennett, Me First and the Gimme Gimmes, Bobby Comstock and the Counts, Bette Bright, Sarah Brightman, Nikka Costa, Chantoozies, Spazzy, Stacie Orrico.

Mark: Flo & Eddie poke fun at The Angels' big hit for unknown reasons. It's a serviceable cover version. Not much else.
Charles: I have a completely different read on this. When The Angels released it in 1963, it was an innocent pop song about a boyfriend coming back. Here it's a porno romp, and I wouldn't be surprised if they were singing about the boyfriend's actual "back" because they're certainly thinking about his "front." Time to take a poimenant vacation? Coitenly!

—

MYSTERY ROACH (Frank Zappa) by Frank Zappa
Mothers involvement: Frank Zappa—producer, orchestration, bass guitar, guitar, drums; George Duke—trombone, keyboards; Ian Underwood—keyboards, woodwinds; Big Jim Sullivan—guitar, orchestration; Martin Lickert—bass guitar; Aynsley Dunbar—drums; Ruth Underwood—percussion; Jimmy Carl Black—vocals; Howard Kaylan—vocals; Jim Pons—voices; Mark Volman—vocals, photography
Additional personnel: Bob Auger—engineer; Barry Keene—overdubs, remixing; Theodore Bikel—narrator; Royal Philharmonic Orchestra
Recording dates: January 28 - February 5, 1971 at Pinewood Studios, UK and Whitney Studios, Glendale, California
Highest chart position: #59 from *200 Motels*
Original release date: October 4, 1971

Mark: I think this would have been a better single off the soundtrack than "Magic Fingers" or "Daddy, Daddy, Daddy," but it probably wouldn't have mattered. Zappa didn't have any single

crack the Top 100 until 1974 with "Don't Eat the Yellow Snow." It's too bad Flo & Eddie didn't remake it as a more polished version. As it stands, it doesn't really end, it just stops.
Charles: What comes off as free-form instrumentation is in actuality well-rehearsed rock/jazz musicianship. Mark and Howard share harder-edged vocals. It's not Top 40 AM Radio fare, but it sure is FM college radio quality.

—

NANCY AND MARY MUSIC, THE (Frank Zappa) by Frank Zappa
Mothers involvement: Frank Zappa—producer, arranger, guitar; Ian Underwood—electric piano, alto saxophone; Aynsley Dunbar—drums; Jeff Simmons—bass, vocals; George Duke—electric piano, vocal sound effects; Howard Kaylan—vocals; Mark Volman—vocals
Additional personnel: Bruce Margolis- engineer
Recording dates: July 1970 at the Tyrone Guthrie Theater, Minneapolis, Minnesota
Highest chart position: #119 from *Chunga's Revenge*
Original release date: October 23, 1970

This live song is another blues track and starts off with an extended drum solo for its first two minutes. Zappa then performs one of his typically great guitar solos for the next minute or so before the drums come back and the song deteriorates into some weird native chant before the scat vocals finally begins. Flo & Eddie scream every so often and finally sing something almost unintelligible during the fade-out. It was a fine line to determine whether this is actually an instrumental or not, and I decided it was not. It's also not Flo & Eddie's or Zappa's finest moment as it's kind of a mishmash of sounds after a promising beginning, and at nine minutes, goes on way too long to not have any sort of point.

—

ONCE UPON A TIME (Frank Zappa) by Frank Zappa
Mothers involvement: Frank Zappa—producer, engineer, guitar, vocals, dialogue; Mark Volman—vocals, dialogue; Howard Kaylan—vocals, dialogue; Jim Pons—bass, lead vocals; Don Preston—keyboards, electronics; Ian Underwood—keyboards, alto sax' Aynsley Dunbar—drums
Recording dates: December 10, 1971 at the Rainbow Theatre, London, England
Highest chart position: Did not chart from *You Can't Do That on Stage Anymore, Volume 1*
Original release date: May 16, 1988

Another part of Zappa's long lost "Sofa Suite." After a lengthy spoken word introduction, Jim Pons takes the lead vocals and starts singing in German. The performance from October 11, 1971 is on *Carnegie Hall*, which also contains the entire "Sofa Suite." The performance from December 10, 1971 is also on *Live at the Rainbow Theatre* and *The Mothers 1971*.

—

PALADIN ROUTINE (Frank Zappa) by The Mothers
Mothers involvement: Frank Zappa—guitar, vocals; Mark Volman—vocals; Howard Kaylan—vocals; Jeff Simmons—bass, vocals; George Duke—keyboards, trombone; Ian Underwood—keyboards; Aynsley Dunbar—drums
Recording dates: November 13, 1970 at the Fillmore East, New York, New York
Highest chart position: Did not chart from *Freaks and Motherfu*#@%!*
Original release date: July 7, 1991 (bootleg version originally released in 1983)

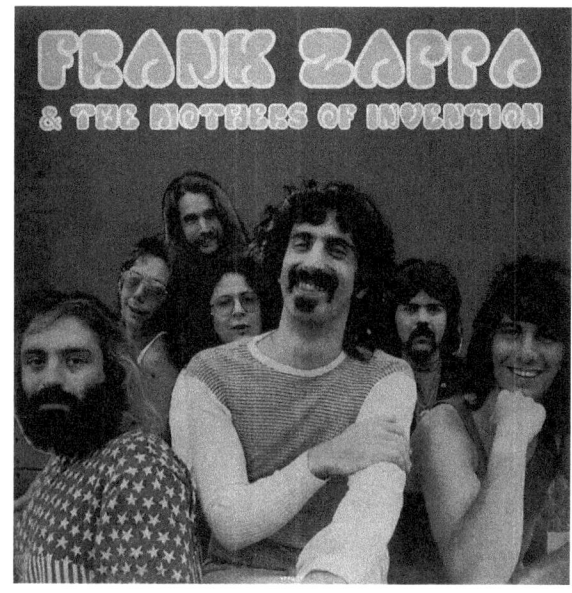

Considered obnoxiously racist today, Flo & Eddie would pull out this routine based upon the TV and radio series "Have Gun, Will Travel," emphasizing the Chinese-stereotype character named "Hey Boy." It was mainly improvised nonsense. Another version appears on *The Mothers 1970*, in which they also sing the *Have Gun, Will Travel* theme song.

—

PEACHES EN REGALIA (Frank Zappa) by The Mothers
Mothers involvement: Frank Zappa—producer, arranger, guitar, dialogue, vocals; Ian Underwood—woodwinds, keyboards, vocals; Aynsley Dunbar—drums; Howard Kaylan—lead vocals, dialogue; Mark Volman—lead vocals, dialogue; Jim Pons—bass, vocals, dialogue; Bob Harris—keyboards, vocals
Additional personnel: Barry Keene—engineer
Recording dates: June 5-6, 1971 at the Fillmore East, New York, New York
Highest chart position: #38 from *Fillmore East - June 1971*
Original release date: August 2, 1971
Significant other versions: Frank Zappa

This instrumental was originally issued in a classic studio version from Zappa's *Hot Rats*.

When Flo & Eddie joined The Mothers, they sang the "la la la's" here with such gusto that it straddles the fine line between instrumental and vocals. I treat it as a vocal song mainly because this is such an excellent Zappa tune. It was one of his songs that truly made me a Zappa convert. Even if you don't like Zappa, you should like this song. This performance also appears on *Live at Fillmore East, June 1971 - 50th Anniversary* and *The Mothers 1971*. The performance from October 11, 1971 is on *Carnegie Hall*. The performance from December 4, 1971 is on *Swiss Cheese/Fire!*

—

PENIS DIMENSION (Frank Zappa) by Frank Zappa
Mothers involvement: Frank Zappa—producer, orchestration, bass guitar, guitar, drums; George Duke—trombone, keyboards; Ian Underwood—keyboards, woodwinds; Big Jim Sullivan—guitar, orchestration; Martin Lickert—bass guitar; Aynsley Dunbar—drums; Ruth Underwood—percussion; Jimmy Carl Black—vocals; Howard Kaylan—vocals; Jim Pons—voices; Mark Volman—vocals, photography
Additional personnel: Bob Auger—engineer; Barry Keene—overdubs, remixing; Theodore Bikel—narrator; Royal Philharmonic Orchestra
Recording dates: January 28 - February 5, 1971 at Pinewood Studios, UK and Whitney Studios, Glendale, California
Highest chart position: #59 from *200 Motels*
Original release date: October 4, 1971
Significant other versions: The Mothers

Such a grandiose production over such a small thing (yuk-yuk). The second half of the song bogs down with inane Flo & Eddie commentary about the subject. The performance from November 13, 1970 is on *Freaks and Motherfu*#@%!* as part of "The House I Used to Live in." A rehearsal version is on *Playground Psychotics*.

—

PLAYGROUND PSYCHOTICS (CD) by Frank Zappa and The Mothers of Invention
Mothers involvement: Frank Zappa—producer, arranger, guitar, dialogue, vocals; Ian Underwood—woodwinds, keyboards, vocals; Aynsley Dunbar—drums; Howard Kaylan—backing vocals, dialogue; Mark Volman—backing vocals, dialogue; Jim Pons—bass, vocals, dialogue; Bob Harris—keyboards, vocals
Additional personnel: Spencer Crislu—remix engineer; John Lennon—vocals, guitar; Yoko Ono—vocals, percussion
Recording dates: September 1970 - December 10, 1971 at the Fillmore East, New York, New York; the Pauley Pavilion, UCLA, Los Angeles, California; the Rainbow Theatre, London, England; and various places on tour including Portland, Oregon and Seattle, Washington
Highest chart position: Did not chart
Original release date: October 27, 1992

A Typical Day on the Road, Part 1:
Here Comes the Gear, Lads (spoken word)
The Living Garbage Truck (spoken word)
A Typical Sound Check (spoken word)
This Is Neat (spoken word)
The Motel Lobby (spoken word)
Getting Stewed (spoken word)
The Motel Room (spoken word)
Don't Take Me Down (spoken word)
The Dressing Room (spoken word)
Learning "Penis Dimension" (spoken word)
You There, with the Hard On! (spoken word)
Zanti Serenade (instrumental)
Divan
Sleeping in a Jar (instrumental)
Don't Eat There (spoken word)
Brixton Still Life (instrumental)
Super Grease (spoken word)
Wonderful Wino
Sharleena

Cruisin' for Burgers
Diphtheria Blues (spoken word)
Well
Say Please (instrumental)
Aaawk (instrumental)
Scumbag
A Small Eternity with Yoko Ono

A Typical Day on the Road, Part 2:
Beer Shampoo (spoken word)
Champagne Lecture (spoken word part of "Call Any Vegetable")
Childish Perversions (spoken word)
Playground Psychotics (spoken word)
The Mudshark Interview (spoken word)
There's No Lust in Jazz (spoken word)
Botulism on the Hoof (spoken word)
You Got Your Armies (spoken word)
The Spew King (spoken word)
I'm Doomed (spoken word)
Status Back Baby
The London Cab Tape (spoken word)
Concentration Moon, Part One
The Sanzini Brothers (spoken word)
It's a Good Thing We Get Paid to Do This (spoken word)
Concentration Moon, Part Two
Mom & Dad
Intro to Music for Low Budget Orchestra (spoken word)
Billy the Mountain

The True Story of 200 Motels:
He's Watching Us (spoken word)
If You're Not a Professional Actor (spoken word)
He's Right (spoken word)
Going for the Money (spoken word)
Jeff Quits (spoken word)
A Bunch of Adventures (spoken word)
Martin Lickert's Story (spoken word)
A Great Guy (spoken word)
Bad Acting (spoken word)
The Worst Reviews (spoken word)
A Version of Himself (spoken word)
I Could Be a Star Now (spoken word)

Most of the tracks on this two-disc set are spoken word recordings from The Mothers' tours of 1970-1971. Rather than list every single spoken word title throughout this book, the overall titles are the only ones listed, unless it really is a known song. The highlight of the set is Zappa's take on the John Lennon and Yoko Ono *Some Time in New York City/Live Jam* material at the end of the first disc, which features Flo & Eddie much more prominently in the mix. Zappa also retitled and recredited these tracks.

Many of the tracks on disc two describe how Jeff Simmons quit The Mothers and was replaced by Ringo's chauffeur Martin Lickert, who also happened to play the bass, from the film *200 Motels*.

—

RADIO SPOTS FOR FRANK ZAPPA'S *CHUNGA'S REVENGE* (Frank Zappa) by Frank Zappa
Mothers involvement: See individual Frank Zappa tracks
Additional personnel: Dick Kunc, Stan Agol, Roy Thomas Baker—engineers
Recording dates: July 5, 1969 - August 29, 1970 at The Record Plant, Hollywood, California; Trident Studios, London, England; T.T.G./Sunset-Highland Recording Studios, Hollywood, California, Whitney Studios, Glendale, California
Highest chart position: Did not chart
Original release date: 1970 for radio

This record was a 7" promotional only release. It consists of two 60-second spots in mono that were repeated on both sides. It's a pretty rare recording and not available to listen to on YouTube or anywhere. They don't come up for sale very often, and the one that did sold for over $100. I assume that it's a standard promotion using sound clips from various songs, specifically "Tell Me You Love Me" and "Would You Go All the Way?," but maybe not. It's Zappa. Does anyone have a copy to share with us?

ROAD LADIES (Frank Zappa) by Frank Zappa
Mothers involvement: Frank Zappa—producer, arranger, guitar, vocals; Ian Underwood—rhythm guitar; Aynsley Dunbar—drums; Jeff Simmons—bass, vocals; George Duke—organ; Howard Kaylan—vocals; Mark Volman—vocals
Additional personnel: Dick Kunc, Stan Agol, Roy Thomas Baker—engineers
Recording dates: Summer 1970 - August 29, 1970 at The Record Plant, Hollywood, California; Trident Studios, London, England; T.T.G./Sunset-Highland Recording Studios, Hollywood, California, Whitney Studios, Glendale, California
Highest chart position: #119 from *Chunga's Revenge*
Original release date: October 23, 1970

Flo & Eddie's debut with Frank Zappa starts off like a gospel recording in a church. Zappa actually sings lead on the first verse of this heavy blues track with Flo & Eddie singing backups and on the choruses only until the second verse where Howard really lets loose his vocal chops and rips out a roaring vocal. If you're looking for The Turtles here, forget it, brother. They ain't never done anything like this, man!

A live version appears on *The Mothers 1970* recorded on either August 21 or September 17, 1970.

RUDY WANTS TO BUY YEZ A DRINK (Frank Zappa) by Frank Zappa
Mothers involvement: Frank Zappa—producer, arranger, guitar, vocals; Ian Underwood—electric piano; Aynsley Dunbar—drums, tambourine; Jeff Simmons—bass, vocals; George Duke—trombone; Howard Kaylan—vocals; Mark Volman—vocals, rhythm guitar
Additional personnel: Dick Kunc, Stan Agol, Roy Thomas Baker—engineers
Recording dates: Summer 1970 - August 29, 1970 at The Record Plant, Hollywood, California; Trident Studios, London, England; T.T.G./Sunset-Highland Recording Studios, Hollywood, California, Whitney Studios, Glendale, California
Highest chart position: #119 from *Chunga's Revenge*
Original release date: October 23, 1970

After a couple of interesting instrumentals on the album, Flo & Eddie come back to sing this Dixieland-sounding comedy song with Howard singing it with gusto. "Hi and Howdy Doody!" with a nice barf to round it out at the end. Zappa continued to play it live in concert on occasion after Flo & Eddie's departure.

—

SCUMBAG (John Lennon, Yoko Ono, Howard Kaylan, Frank Zappa) by John Lennon, Yoko Ono and The Mothers
Mothers involvement: Frank Zappa—producer, arranger, guitar, dialogue, vocals; Ian Underwood—woodwinds, keyboards, vocals; Aynsley Dunbar—drums; Howard Kaylan—vocals, dialogue; Mark Volman—vocals, dialogue; Jim Pons—bass, vocals, dialogue; Bob Harris—keyboards, vocals
Additional personnel: Abbey Road Studios engineers—engineers for *Some Time in New York City/Live Jam* version; Spencer Crislu—remix engineer for *Playground Psychotics* version; John Lennon—vocals, guitar; Yoko Ono—vocals, percussion
Recording dates: June 6, 1971 at the Fillmore East, New York, New York
Highest chart position: #48 from *Some Time in New York City/Live Jam*; Did not chart from *Playground Psychotics*
Original release date: June 12, 1972; October 27, 1992

On Lennon's version released on *Some Time in New York City/Live Jam*, Lennon mixed out Flo & Eddie's vocals, completely! On Zappa's version on *Playground Psychotics*, they just as mysteriously return! Regardless, the song is fairly senseless. Flo & Eddie's vocals actually help make it into something, but still not much. Without them, it's just Lennon singing "scumbag" over and over and over. Strangely, Lennon did leave Zappa's announcement to the audience to sing along. It makes me wonder what Lennon really did think of The Turtles and of Flo & Eddie over all those years and encounters. Probably not much? This also appears on *Live at Fillmore East, June 1971 - 50th Anniversary* and *The Mothers 1971*.

—

SEALED TUNA BOLERO, THE: see THIS TOWN IS A SEALED TUNA SANDWICH

SHARLEENA (Frank Zappa) by Frank Zappa
Mothers involvement: Frank Zappa—producer, arranger, guitar, vocals; Ian Underwood—tenor saxophone, grand piano; Aynsley Dunbar—drums; Jeff Simmons—bass, vocals; George Duke—organ; Howard Kaylan—vocals; Mark Volman—vocals
Additional personnel: Dick Kunc, Stan Agol, Roy Thomas Baker—engineers

Recording dates: Summer 1970 - August 29, 1970 at The Record Plant, Hollywood, California; Trident Studios, London, England; T.T.G./Sunset-Highland Recording Studios, Hollywood, California, Whitney Studios, Glendale, California
Highest chart position: #119 from *Chunga's Revenge*
Original release date: October 23, 1970

Mark: This sounds like one of those doo wop songs that pre-date The Mothers of Invention. It would have fit in well on *Cruising with Ruben and the Jets*. It was performed live by Zappa a lot, even long after Flo & Eddie left The Mothers. The performances from July 21-22, August 21, and September 17, 1970 are on *The Mothers 1970*. The performance from October 11, 1971 is on *Carnegie Hall*. The performance from December 4, 1971 is on *Swiss Cheese/Fire!* A version is on *Playground Psychotics*. The performance from December 10, 1971 is also on *Live at the Rainbow Theatre* and *The Mothers 1971*.
Charles: I like the name 'Charleena' but dispute that it's anything near a 'doo wop' song. More like a slow, boring 'doo-doo' song with some nice instrumentation and grunts.

SHE PAINTED UP HER FACE / HALF A DOZEN PROVOCATIVE SQUATS / SHOVE IT RIGHT IN (Frank Zappa) by Frank Zappa
Mothers involvement: Frank Zappa—producer, orchestration, bass guitar, guitar, drums; George Duke—trombone, keyboards; Ian Underwood—keyboards, woodwinds; Big Jim Sullivan guitar, orchestration; Martin Lickert—bass guitar; Aynsley Dunbar—drums; Ruth Underwood—percussion; Jimmy Carl Black—vocals; Howard Kaylan—vocals; Jim Pons—voices; Mark Volman—vocals, photography
Additional personnel: Bob Auger—engineer; Barry Keene—overdubs, remixing; Theodore Bikel—narrator; Royal Philharmonic Orchestra
Recording dates: January 28 - February 5, 1971 at Pinewood Studios, UK and Whitney Studios, Glendale, California
Highest chart position: #59 from *200 Motels*
Original release date: October 4, 1971
Significant other versions: The Mothers

Mark: Funny songs (finally) on this soundtrack. Well "Lonesome Cowboy Burt" is funny, too. What does "practicing, practice, practicing" mean anyway? Not a bad song as far as these *200*

Motels non-songs go. It's too bad that the better song ideas aren't developed any further than a couple lines and a chorus. It would have been better if "She Painted Up Her Face," "Half a Dozen Provocative Squats," and "Shove it Right In" were joined together to make an actual song. Hey, they DID do that when they played this live! The performance from June 5-6, 1971 is on *You Can't Do That on Stage Anymore, Volume 6*, *Live at Fillmore East, June 1971 - 50th Anniversary* and *The Mothers 1971*. The performance from October 11, 1971 is on *Carnegie Hall*. The performance from December 4, 1971 is on *Swiss Cheese/Fire!* The performance from December 10, 1971 is on *Live at The Rainbow Theatre*.

Charles: Who counted the half-a-dozen provocative squats? Who really knows for sure? Is it 25 or 6 or 4? And what makes those particular squats so provocative? The answer, of course, is Frank Zappa, who could make any non-sequitur title or couplet of lyrics provocative, or anything else he desired. From the *200 Motels* project, this is more of his lunacy with Flo & Eddie onboard in one form or another.

—

SHOVE IT RIGHT IN: See **SHE PAINTED UP HER FACE**

—

STATUS BACK BABY (Frank Zappa) by Frank Zappa and The Mothers of Invention
Mothers involvement: Frank Zappa—producer, arranger, guitar, vocals; Ian Underwood—woodwinds, keyboards, vocals; Aynsley Dunbar—drums; Howard Kaylan—vocals; Mark Volman—vocals; Jim Pons—bass, vocals; Bob Harris—keyboards, vocals
Additional personnel: Barry Keene—engineer; Spencer Crislu—remix engineer
Recording dates: June 5-6, 1971 at the Fillmore East, New York, New York
Highest chart position: Did not chart from *Playground Psychotics*
Original release date: October 27, 1992

According to the liner notes of *Playground Psychotics*, this was a leftover track from *Fillmore East - June 1971*. Instead of adding it as a CD bonus track there, Zappa included it here. It's a pretty straightforward version of a song that originally appeared in a studio version on *Absolutely Free*. It later appeared on *Live at Fillmore East, June 1971 - 50th Anniversary*, *Live at the Rainbow Theatre*, and *The Mothers 1971*.

—

SLEEPING IN A JAR (Frank Zappa) by The Mothers
Mothers involvement: Frank Zappa—guitar, vocals; Mark Volman—vocals; Howard Kaylan—vocals; Jeff Simmons—bass, vocals; George Duke—keyboards, trombone; Ian Underwood—keyboards; Aynsley Dunbar—drums
Recording dates: November 13, 1970 at the Fillmore East, New York, New York
Highest chart position: Did not chart from *Freaks and Motherfu*#@%!*
Original release date: July 7, 1991 (bootleg version originally released in 1983)
Significant other versions: Frank Zappa and The Mothers of Invention

This version morphs into the instrumental melodies from "Inca Roads" and "Easy Meat," as the original songs as sung by Flo & Eddie were only about a minute long. Another version appears on *The Mothers 1970*. The performance from October 11, 1971 is on *Carnegie Hall*. The performance from December 10, 1971 is on *Live at the Rainbow Theatre* and *The Mothers 1971*. A rehearsal version is on *Playground Psychotics*. The original studio version with lyrics appeared on *Uncle Meat*.

—

SOFA #1 (Frank Zappa) by Frank Zappa
Mothers involvement: Frank Zappa—producer, engineer, guitar, vocal; Mark Volman—vocal; Howard Kaylan—vocal; Jim Pons—bass, vocal; Don Preston—keyboards, electronics; Ian Underwood—keyboards, alto sax' Aynsley Dunbar—drums
Recording dates: December 10, 1971 at the Rainbow Theatre, London, England
Highest chart position: Did not chart from *You Can't Do That on Stage Anymore, Volume 1*
Original release date: May 16, 1988

Mark: More German singing by Flo & Eddie. The performance from October 11, 1971 is on *Carnegie Hall*, which also contains the entire "Sofa Suite." This song appeared later on Frank's *One Size Fits All*, which has a painting of a sofa on its cover, in both instrumental and vocal versions. I prefer the instrumental version. The performance from December 10, 1971 is also on *Live at the Rainbow Theatre* and *The Mothers 1971*.

Charles: At this point of the book, I re-read everything up to now and commented "sofa, so good."

—

SOMETIME IN NEW YORK CITY/LIVE JAM
(LP) by John Lennon, Yoko Ono and The Mothers
Mothers involvement: Frank Zappa—producer, arranger, guitar, dialogue, vocals; Ian Underwood—woodwinds, keyboards, vocals; Aynsley Dunbar—drums; Howard Kaylan—backing vocals, dialogue; Mark Volman—backing vocals, dialogue; Jim Pons—bass, vocals, dialogue; Bob Harris—keyboards, vocals
Additional personnel: Abbey Road Studios engineers—engineers; John Lennon—lead vocal, guitar; Yoko Ono—vocals, percussion
Recording dates: June 6, 1971 at the Fillmore East, New York, New York
Highest chart position: #48
Original release date: June 12, 1972

Woman is the Nigger of the World
Sisters, O Sisters
Attica State
Born in a Prison
New York City

Sunday Bloody Sunday
The Luck of the Irish
John Sinclair
Angela
We're All Water

Cold Turkey
Don't Worry, Kyoko

Well (Baby, Please Don't Go)
Jamrag (instrumental)
Scumbag
Aü

Some Time in New York City was and is John Lennon's most controversial music album released in his lifetime, mostly for the opening track. I say "music" because the cover to *Unfinished Music No. 1 Two Virgins* is arguably more controversial, and there is no music on THAT album. Lennon offered a second disc of various live performance titles called *Live Jam* to somewhat offset the retail price increase of albums in 1972. Admittedly, this second disc is mostly garbage highlighted only by an okay live version of Lennon's "Cold Turkey" and a decent cover of "Well (Baby Please Don't Go)." The rest of the tracks on this second disc are dispensable.

The performance of John and Yoko with Frank Zappa and the Mothers was the version that everyone heard for 20 years. Zappa finally released his version of these same tracks in 1992 as part of his *Playground Psychotics* collection. There, you can finally hear Flo & Eddie sing as they were completely mixed out on the *Some Time in New York City/Live Jam* version!

—

STICK IT OUT (Frank Zappa) by The Mothers
Mothers involvement: Frank Zappa—producer, arranger, guitar, vocals, band direction; Mark Volman—vocals, percussion; Howard Kaylan—vocals, percussion; Ian Underwood—keyboards, woodwinds; Don Preston—Minimoog; Jim Pons—bass, vocals; Aynsley Dunbar—drums
Additional personnel: Ron Delsener—promoter
Recording dates: October 11, 1971 at Carnegie Hall, New York, New York
Highest chart position: Did not chart from *Carnegie Hall*
Original release date: October 31, 2011
Significant other versions: Frank Zappa

Yet even more of that ridiculous "Sofa Suite" sung in German. Zappa would put this song to much better use on his later *Joe's Garage*. Of all the songs in the "Sofa Suite," this one is the most amusing and also the most vulgar.

—

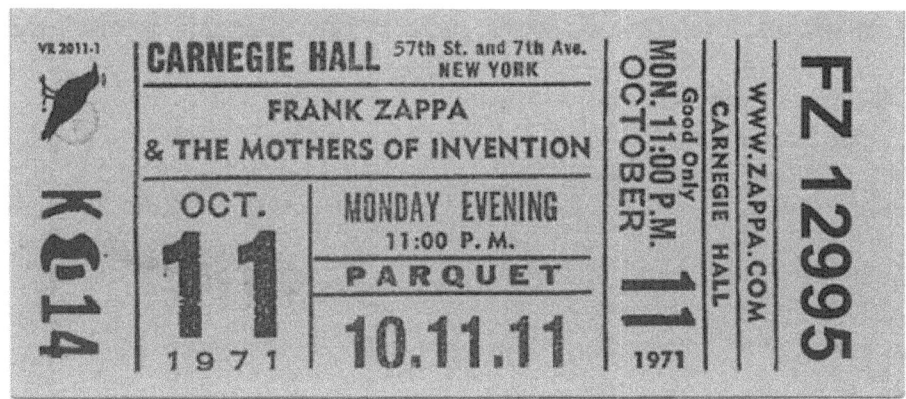

STRICTLY GENTEEL (THE FINALE) aka *200 MOTELS* **FINALE** (Frank Zappa) by Frank Zappa
Mothers involvement: Frank Zappa—producer, orchestration, bass guitar, guitar, drums; George Duke—trombone, keyboards; Ian Underwood—keyboards, woodwinds; Big Jim Sullivan—guitar, orchestration; Martin Lickert—bass guitar; Aynsley Dunbar—drums; Ruth Underwood—percussion; Jimmy Carl Black—vocals; Howard Kaylan—vocals; Jim Pons—voices; Mark Volman—vocals, photography
Additional personnel: Bob Auger—engineer; Barry Keene—overdubs, remixing; Theodore Bikel—narrator; Royal Philharmonic Orchestra
Recording dates: January 28 - February 5, 1971 at Pinewood Studios, UK and Whitney Studios, Glendale, California
Highest chart position: #59 from *200 Motels*
Original release date: October 4, 1971

Mark: This is the only section we've decided to review that has some of that opera stuff that is far too prevalent in *200 Motels* and its soundtrack. I have no problem with opera. It's just that it really has no place within a book that's supposed to be about The Turtles. Fortunately, about halfway through this 11-minute piece Flo & Eddie take over from the opera singers and bring this track to a rousing finish.

The performance from August 7, 1971 is on *You Can't Do That on Stage Anymore, Volume 6*. The performance from October 11, 1971 is on *Carnegie Hall*.

Charles: I met one of the actors in *200 Motels*, the respected thespian, Theodore Bikel. He confided to me that he had no idea what he was getting himself into, and he couldn't be more uncomfortable in this film's finale. He's even nauseous and crying. Mark and Howard are featured prominently in this grand finale, vocally and also visually in the scene—where we also see Ringo Starr, musicians and an array of dancers. It's more fun to listen to this track while watching the movie's scenes, where we get to see Mark really looking like a rock star, Howard looking like a messiah, and our poor, unfortunate, schlemiel Bikel looking like he felt his career was over. It wasn't. Happy Zappadan.

—

SWISS CHEESE/FIRE! (CD) by The Mothers
Mothers involvement: Frank Zappa—guitar, vocals; Mark Volman—vocals; Howard Kaylan—vocals; Jim Pons—bass, vocals; Don Preston—keyboards, electronics; Ian Underwood—keyboards, alto sax; Aynsley Dunbar—drums
Recording dates: December 4, 1971 at Casino de Montreux, Switzerland
Highest chart position: Did not chart
Original release date: June 16, 1992 (bootleg version originally released after 1976)

Intro (instrumental)
Peaches En Regalia (instrumental)
Tears Began to Fall/She Painted Up Her Face/Half a Dozen Provocative Squats
Call Any Vegetable
Any Way the Winds Blow

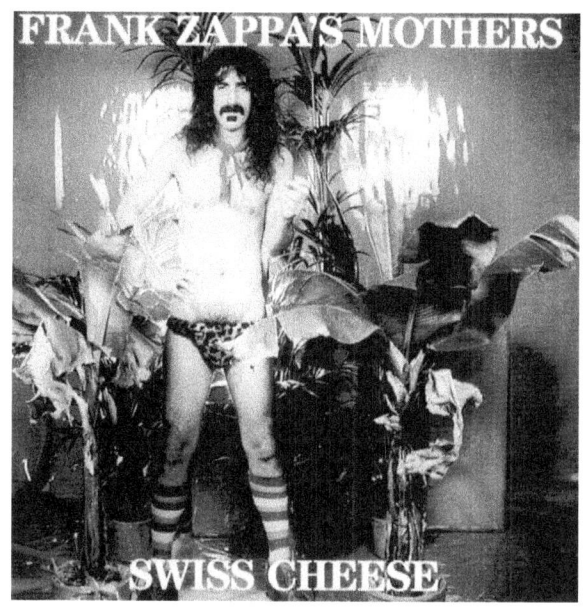

Magdalena/Dog Breath
Sofa
A Pound for a Brown (On the Bus) (instrumental)
Wonderful Wino/Sharleena/Crusin' for Burgers
King Kong (instrumental)
Fire! (spoken word)

Yet another Zappa bootleg that was later appropriated by Zappa and re-released without any fidelity changes himself. This one is of much historical significance and this contains the complete Mothers concert that ends when some idiot shot a flare gun into the concert hall's ceiling, setting fire to the place, and burning all of the group's instruments. We actually hear that moment on this disc while the band was playing "King Kong" when alarms go off and Howard loudly quips "Fire! Arthur Brown in person!" and everyone is told to calmly evacuate. Fortunately, none of the band was hurt. (That would happen at the next concert when Zappa was pushed from the stage.) This concert served as the inspiration for Deep Purple's "Smoke on the Water."

—

TEARS BEGAN TO FALL (Frank Zappa) by The Mothers
Mothers involvement: Frank Zappa—producer, arranger, guitar, dialogue, vocals; Ian Underwood—woodwinds, keyboards, vocals; Aynsley Dunbar—drums; Howard Kaylan—lead vocals, dialogue; Mark Volman—lead vocals, dialogue; Jim Pons—bass, vocals, dialogue; Bob Harris—keyboards, vocals
Additional personnel: Barry Keene—engineer
Recording dates: June 5-6, 1971 at the Fillmore East, New York, New York
Highest chart position: #38 from *Fillmore East - June 1971*
Original release date: July 21, 1971 for single; August 2, 1971 for album

Mark: This sounds like a song that could have been done for the doo wop *Cruising with Ruben and the Jets* album, and as such, is probably why it was selected for yet another non-charting Zappa single. The live version of "Happy Together" might have made for a more commercial choice for a single from *Fillmore East*, but I'm sure it was vetoed from all sides. It also appears on *Live at Fillmore East, June 1971 - 50th Anniversary*. The performance from October 11, 1971 is on *Carnegie Hall*. The performance from December 4, 1971 is on *Swiss Cheese/Fire!* The performance from December 10, 1971 is on *Live at the Rainbow Theatre* and *The Mothers 1971*.

The B-side of the single is "Junier Mintz Boogie," which is a very rare Zappa instrumental as it hasn't appeared officially on an album until *The Mothers 1971* box set in 2022. It doesn't feature Flo & Eddie, (even though Jim Pons is on bass) so it doesn't rate a separate listing in this book. It turns out that it is the excerpted guitar solo from "Latex Solar Beef" from the May 25, 1971 Zappa concert.

Both sides of this single finally appeared on *Live at Fillmore East - 50th Anniversary Edition* and *The Mothers 1971*.

Charles: Again, I don't agree that this is in any way, shape, or form a doo-wop song, but instead see it as a bubblegum track. It could've been an interesting release with an arrangement by the teams that recorded the 1910 Fruitgum Company, the Ohio Express, or the Lemon Pipers. It actually has a memorable hook and gets great at about the 2:20 mark.

—

TELL ME YOU LOVE ME (Frank Zappa) by Frank Zappa
Mothers involvement: Frank Zappa—producer, arranger, guitar, Condor; Ian Underwood—rhythm guitar, pipe organ; Aynsley Dunbar—drums; Jeff Simmons—bass; George Duke—electric piano; Howard Kaylan—vocals; Mark Volman—vocals
Additional personnel: Dick Kunc, Stan Agol, Roy Thomas Baker—engineers
Recording dates: Summer 1970 - August 29, 1970 at The Record Plant, Hollywood, California; Trident Studios, London, England; T.T.G./Sunset-Highland Recording Studios, Hollywood, California, Whitney Studios, Glendale, California
Highest chart position: did not chart; #119 from *Chunga's Revenge*
Original release date: October 23, 1970 for album; November 1970 for single

The first song by Flo & Eddie with Zappa that has any semblance to anything The Turtles had done before. It almost could have made it on to their *Shell Shock* album, but the lyrics are a little dirtier than usual for a Turtles song. Overall, it's a great driving, harder-rocking song that was even released as a single. Of course, it didn't chart. This is Frank Zappa, for goodness sake. What were YOU thinking? Zappa continued to play it live long after Flo & Eddie left the group.

—

THIS TOWN IS A SEALED TUNA FISH SANDWICH (PROLOGUE) / TUNA FISH PROMENADE / THIS TOWN IS A SEALED TUNA FISH SANDWICH (REPRISE) / THE SEALED TUNA BOLERO (Frank Zappa) by Frank Zappa

Mothers involvement: Frank Zappa—producer, orchestration, bass guitar, guitar, drums; George Duke—trombone, keyboards; Ian Underwood—keyboards, woodwinds; Big Jim Sullivan—guitar, orchestration; Martin Lickert—bass guitar; Aynsley Dunbar—drums; Ruth Underwood—percussion; Jimmy Carl Black—vocals; Howard Kaylan—vocals; Jim Pons—voices; Mark Volman—vocals, photography
Additional personnel: Bob Auger—engineer; Barry Keene—overdubs, remixing; Theodore Bikel—narrator; Royal Philharmonic Orchestra
Recording dates: January 28 - February 5, 1971 at Pinewood Studios, UK and Whitney Studios, Glendale, California
Highest chart position: #59 from *200 Motels*
Original release date: October 4, 1971

Mark: There're too many songs on this soundtrack where Flo & Eddie just follow the melody line of the other instruments i.e. no melody at all. Zappa seemed to like this sort of thing and did it repeatedly throughout his work. Here they do it with a much-too-long ode to tuna fish sandwiches.
Charles: This guy was obsessed with sealed tuna sandwiches, which may or may not have been a metaphor for something else entirely. We'll leave that up to the Zappaphiles to decipher. We just listen to the songs; we're not privy to the brilliance or madness of the creative team or individual responsible. It's still just a rancid little snack however you cut it.
    Part of the multi-track tuna suite, it makes you realize you can indeed tuna piano but you can also tuna fish.
    Almost an actual song, but more of a march with vocal silliness, it's another piece of the puzzle that is *200 Motels*. Like I said, it's just a rancid little snack. Not the track, that's a line from the song.

—

TINY SICK TEARS aka 96 TEARS (Rudy Martinez) by The Mothers
Mothers involvement: Frank Zappa—producer, arranger, guitar, dialogue, vocals; Ian Underwood—woodwinds, keyboards, vocals; Aynsley Dunbar—drums; Howard Kaylan—lead vocals, dialogue; Mark Volman—lead vocals, dialogue; Jim Pons—bass, vocals, dialogue; Bob Harris—keyboards, vocals
Additional personnel:
Recording dates: June 3, 1971 at State Farm Show Arena, Harrisburg, Pennsylvania
Highest chart position: Did not chart from *The Mothers 1971*
Original release date: January 28, 2022
Significant other versions: Question Mark and the Mysterians, Big Maybelle, Aretha Franklin, The Thunderboys, Jimmy Ruffin, Shane Martin, The Music Explosion, The Residents, Thelma

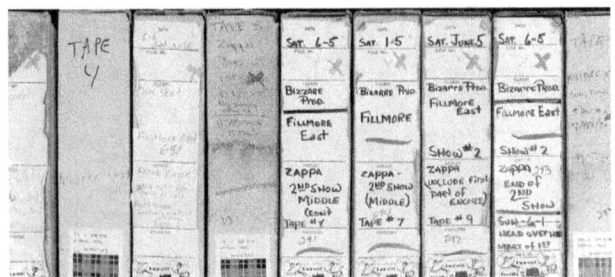

Houston, The Modern Lovers, Garland Jeffreys, Inspiral Carpets, The Stranglers, Eddie and the Hot Rods, Primal Scream, Suicide, The Bonne Villes, The Fuzztones, Satan's Pilgrims, Bob Rivers.

Mark: Flo & Eddie poke fun at Question Mark and the Mysterians' big hit, "96 Tears," with middling results. They think it's funny. It's actually more annoying. Fortunately, it only lasts about a minute in length.
Charles: I just wish they did a parody of the original hit.

—

TRUE STORY OF 200 MOTELS, THE (film)
Mothers involvement: Frank Zappa; Howard Kaylan, Mark Volman; Jimmy Carl Black; George Duke; Aynsley Dunbar; Don Preston; Euclid James 'Motorhead' Sherwood; Ian Underwood
Additional personnel: Theodore Bikel; Janet Ferguson; Martin Lickert; Lucy Offerall; Ringo Starr; Sarina-Marie Volman
Original release date: 1988

This is a documentary on the making of *200 Motels*, which is perhaps just as strange as the final film. It was released direct-to-video many years later, in 1988. For completists only.

—

200 MOTELS (film)

Mothers involvement: Frank Zappa as himself; Howard Kaylan as himself; Mark Volman as himself; Jim Pons as himself; Ian Underwood as himself; Ruth Underwood as herself; Don Preston as himself; Jimmy Carl Black as Lonesome Cowboy Burt; Euclid James 'Motorhead' Sherwood as himself; Aynsley Dunbar as himself; George Duke as himself

Additional personnel: Theodore Bikel as Rance Muhammitz, the narrator/Master of Ceremonies; Ringo Starr as Larry the Dwarf, dressed as Frank Zappa; Keith Moon as the hot nun; Pamela Des Barres as the interviewer; Martin Lickert as Jeff; Janet Neville-Ferguson as Groupie #1; Lucy Offerall as Groupie #2; Dick Barber as Chunga—The Vacuum Cleaner; Judy Gridley as the chorus leader; London Philharmonic Orchestra as the bewildered orchestra

Original release date: October 29, 1971

Imaged by Heritage Auctions, HA.com

As a film, this is an even bigger mess than *Magical Mystery Tour*, but it is a chance to see a few fine set pieces including an animated dream sequence, but as typical for many Zappa video projects, it can be a bit disturbing. It is a chance to see Kaylan, Volman, and Pons post-Turtles and pre-Flo & Eddie since precious little video was shot otherwise during their tenure with The Mothers. It's also fun to see the various cameos by Bikel, Moon, Starr, and the bewildered orchestra.

—

200 MOTELS (LP) by Frank Zappa
Mothers involvement: Frank Zappa—producer, orchestration, bass guitar, guitar, drums; George Duke—trombone, keyboards; Ian Underwood—keyboards, woodwinds; Big Jim Sullivan—guitar, orchestration; Martin Lickert—bass guitar; Aynsley Dunbar—drums; Ruth Underwood—percussion; Jimmy Carl Black—vocals; Howard Kaylan—vocals; Jim Pons—voices; Mark Volman—vocals, photography

Additional personnel: Bob Auger—engineer; Barry Keene—overdubs, remixing; Theodore Bikel—narrator; Royal Philharmonic Orchestra
Recording dates: January 28 - February 5, 1971 at Pinewood Studios, UK and Whitney Studios, Glendale, California
Highest chart position: #59
Original release date: October 4, 1971

Semi-Fraudulent/Direct-from-Hollywood Overture (instrumental with spoken word)
Mystery Roach
Dance of the Rock and Roll Interviewers (instrumental)
This Town is a Sealed Tuna Fish Sandwich (Prologue)

Tuna Fish Promenade
Dance of the Just Plain Folks (instrumental)
This Town is a Sealed Tuna Fish Sandwich (Reprise)
The Sealed Tuna Bolero
Lonesome Cowboy Burt

Touring Can Make You Crazy (instrumental)
Would You Like a Snack?
Redneck Eats (instrumental with spoken word)
Centerville (instrumental with spoken word)
She Painted Up Her Face
Janet's Big Dance Number (instrumental)
Half a Dozen Provocative Squats
Mysterioso (instrumental)
Shove It Right In
Lucy's Seduction of a Bored Violinist and Postlude (instrumental)

I'm Stealing the Towels (instrumental with spoken word)
Dental Hygiene Dilemma (instrumental with spoken word)
Does This Kind of Life Look Interesting to You? (instrumental with spoken word)
Daddy, Daddy, Daddy
Penis Dimension
What Will This Evening Bring Me This Morning

A Nun Suit Painted on Some Old Boxes (opera)
Magic Fingers
Motorhead's Midnight Ranch (instrumental)
Dew on the Newts We Got (opera)
The Lad Searches the Night for His Newts (instrumental)
The Girl Wants to Fix Him Some Broth (opera)
The Girl's Dream (instrumental)
Little Green Scratchy Sweaters and Corduroy Ponce (opera)
Strictly Genteel (The Finale)

CD bonus tracks:
Coming Soon! (radio spot)
The Wide Screen (radio spot)
Coming Soon! (radio spot)
Frank Zappa's 200 Motels (radio spot)
Magic Fingers (single edit)
Original Theatrical Trailer (video spot)

Mark: Since this is a Turtles book and not a Frank Zappa book, separate listings for the operatic singing and instrumental songs performed by The Royal Philharmonic Orchestra and instrumentals with spoken dialogue will not be getting separate listings and reviews. *200 Motels* is a very challenging album, even for this Zappa and Turtles fan. There are flashes of brilliance from this incarnation of The Mothers. It just doesn't appear too often on this album as there are too many operatic and instrumental and spoken word parts, and many songs are broken up in pieces. A 50th Anniversary Edition was released on CD and vinyl on September 24, 2021.

Charles: I had the pleasure of meeting thespian/screen-star/singer/musician Theodore Bikel (1924-2015), who was one of the actors in the Frank Zappa film *200 Motels*. I knew I'd have the opportunity to say hello, so I brought along a promotional theater one-sheet from the *200 Motels* movie in the hopes Bikel would autograph it. I asked politely, and Mr. Bikel made a pained face, half-kiddingly (but mostly not) saying, "Ugh. Couldn't you find something else for me to sign?!" He was very nice about it, but wasn't proud to be part of that particular project. Having previously seen the film, I walked away knowing exactly what he meant—I wasn't a fan either. Listening to this short—just over a minute—choir-like musical bit, it's hard to be a fan.

Operatic orchestral piece from the soundtrack of *200 Motels*. Who's doing the singing on this? Howard is versatile but not this operatic! One thing's for sure, it's not Theodore Bikel, who probably wouldn't even want to be mentioned here if he were still alive.

—

200 MOTELS FINALE: see **STRICTLY GENTEEL (THE FINALE)**

—

WELL (BABY, PLEASE DON'T GO) aka **WELL** (Walter Ward) by John Lennon, Yoko Ono and The Mothers
Mothers involvement: Frank Zappa—producer, arranger, guitar, dialogue, vocals; Ian Underwood—woodwinds, keyboards, vocals; Aynsley Dunbar—drums; Howard Kaylan—backing vocals, dialogue; Mark Volman—backing vocals, dialogue; Jim Pons—bass, vocals, dialogue; Bob Harris—keyboards, vocals
Additional personnel: Abbey Road Studios engineers—engineers for *Some Time in New York City/Live Jam* version; Spencer Crislu—remix engineer for *Playground Psychotics* version; John Lennon—lead vocal, guitar; Yoko Ono—vocals, percussion
Recording dates: June 6, 1971 at the Fillmore East, New York, New York
Highest chart position: #48 from *Some Time in New York City/Live Jam*; Did not chart from *Playground Psychotics*
Original release date: June 12, 1972; October 27, 1992
Significant other versions: The Olympics

Sometime in New York City '72.

John Lennon and Yoko Ono joined Frank Zappa and The Mothers on stage to sing five songs, of which this cover of The Olympics is the only acceptable one. Although I am a fan of Yoko Ono, I am still not a fan of songs featuring her intrusive screaming. In the Lennon-released version of this on *Some Time in New York City/Live Jam*, Ono's "vocals" were mostly mixed out or low. On

Zappa's version on *Playground Psychotics*, Ono's shrieks are there at full volume. Perhaps, even enhanced! This also appears on *Live at Fillmore East, June 1971 - 50th Anniversary* and *The Mothers 1971*.

—

WHAT KIND OF GIRL DO YOU THINK WE ARE? (Frank Zappa) by The Mothers
Mothers involvement: Frank Zappa—producer, arranger, guitar, dialogue, vocals; Ian Underwood—woodwinds, keyboards, vocals; Aynsley Dunbar—drums; Howard Kaylan—lead vocals, dialogue; Mark Volman—lead vocals, dialogue; Jim Pons—bass, vocals, dialogue; Bob Harris—keyboards, vocals
Additional personnel: Barry Keene—engineer
Recording dates: June 5-6, 1971 at the Fillmore East, New York, New York
Highest chart position: #38 from *Fillmore East - June 1971*
Original release date: August 2, 1971

This slow blues jam about rock and roll groupies is half-spoken, half-sung by Flo & Eddie, along with Jim Pons and Frank Zappa. It's all a big monumental build up on the album to get them all to play "Happy Together" a few tracks later. The performances from August 21, September 17 and 26, 1970 are also on *The Mothers 1970*. The June 5-6, 1971 performances are also on *Live at Fillmore East, June 1971 - 50th Anniversary* and *The Mothers 1971*.

—

WHAT WILL THIS EVENING BRING ME THIS MORNING (Frank Zappa) by Frank Zappa
Mothers involvement: Frank Zappa—producer, orchestration, bass guitar, guitar, drums; George Duke—trombone, keyboards; Ian Underwood—keyboards, woodwinds; Big Jim Sullivan—guitar, orchestration; Martin Lickert—bass guitar; Aynsley Dunbar—drums; Ruth Underwood—percussion; Jimmy Carl Black—vocals; Howard Kaylan—vocals; Jim Pons—voices; Mark Volman—vocals, photography
Additional personnel: Bob Auger—engineer; Barry Keene—overdubs, remixing; Theodore Bikel—narrator; Royal Philharmonic Orchestra
Recording dates: January 28 - February 5, 1971 at Pinewood Studios, UK and Whitney Studios, Glendale, California
Highest chart position: single did not chart; #59 from *200 Motels*
Original release date: October 4, 1971

Another Zappa song where if you know the title, you know the lyrics. It's not badly sung by Flo & Eddie and could have fit nicely on one of their albums. It was released as a single in some countries like the Netherlands and France.

—

WHO ARE THE BRAIN POLICE? (Frank Zappa) by The Mothers
Mothers involvement: Frank Zappa—producer, arranger, guitar, vocals, band direction; Mark Volman—vocals, percussion; Howard Kaylan—vocals, percussion; Ian Underwood—keyboards, woodwinds; Don Preston—Minimoog; Jim Pons—bass, vocals; Aynsley Dunbar—drums
Additional personnel: Ron Delsener—promoter
Recording dates: October 11, 1971 at Carnegie Hall, New York, New York
Highest chart position: Did not chart from *Carnegie Hall*
Original release date: October 31, 2011
Significant other versions: Frank Zappa and The Mothers of Invention

Flo & Eddie do a very light and upbeat version of this song that came out as a slow dirge in its original form. The original studio version appeared on *Freak Out!* and on a single.

—

WONDERFUL WINO aka **WINO MAN WITH DR. JOHN ROUTINE** (Frank Zappa, Jeff Simmons) by The Mothers
Mothers involvement: Frank Zappa—guitar, vocals; Mark Volman—vocals; Howard Kaylan—vocals; Jeff Simmons—bass, vocals; George Duke—keyboards, trombone; Ian Underwood—keyboards; Aynsley Dunbar—drums
Recording dates: November 13, 1970 at the Fillmore East, New York, New York
Highest chart position: Did not chart from *Freaks and Motherfu*#@%!*
Original release date: July 7, 1991 (bootleg version originally released in 1983)

For this bootleg version, Flo & Eddie kick it off with a rousing version of "Bringing in the Sheaths," then it transitions into a hard-rocking groove. Howard really belts it out here! For inexplicable reasons, Frank suggests that they should sing the song like Dr. John (later best known for his hit "Right Place, Wrong Time"), which the band complies with by singing "Gris Gris." The performance from June 18, 1970 is on *At The Circus* and *The Mothers 1970*. The performances from June 21-22, 1970 are from *The Mothers 1970*. The performance from October 11, 1971 is on *Carnegie Hall*. The performance from December 4, 1971 is on *Swiss Cheese/Fire!* A version is on *Playground Psychotics*. The performance from December 10, 1971 is also on *Live at the Rainbow Theatre* and THE MOTHERS 1971.

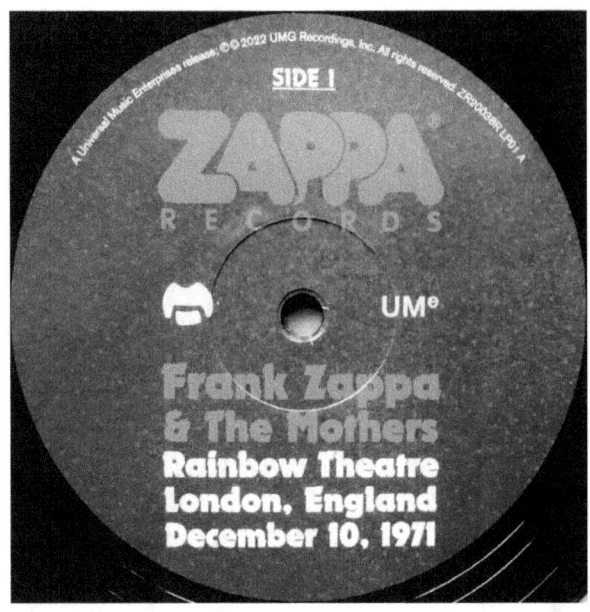

The title "Wonderful Wino" comes from an old George Carlin comedy routine that he used to perform in the 1960s and early 1970s. The song itself originally appeared on Jeff Simmons solo album called *Lucille Has Messed My Mind Up*. Zappa himself later recorded a studio version on his *Zoot Allures* album.

—

WOULD YOU GO ALL THE WAY? aka **WOULD YOU GO ALL THE WAY FOR THE USA?** (Frank Zappa) by Frank Zappa
Mothers involvement: Frank Zappa—producer, arranger, guitar, vocals; Ian Underwood—electric piano; Aynsley Dunbar—drums; Jeff Simmons—bass; George Duke—trombone; Howard Kaylan—vocals; Mark Volman—vocals
Additional personnel: Dick Kunc, Stan Agol, Roy Thomas Baker—engineers
Recording dates: Summer 1970 - August 29, 1970 at The Record Plant, Hollywood, California; Trident Studios, London, England; T.T.G./Sunset-Highland Recording Studios, Hollywood, California, Whitney Studios, Glendale, California
Highest chart position: Single did not chart; B-side to "Tell Me You Love Me;" #119 from *Chunga's Revenge*
Original release date: October 23, 1970 for album; November 1970 for single

This is the most commercial track on *Chunga's Revenge* next to "Tell Me You Love Me" and, hence, it became its B-side. The song is pretty funny, but in today's political climate where people can and do literally "go all the way for the USA," it can get pretty scary. What was once gentle sarcasm about the extent of one's beliefs has now become stone cold reality. A live version appears on *The Mothers 1970*. It was also played live at a lot of post-Flo & Eddie concerts, during the 1976 U.S. Bicentennial year.

—

WOULD YOU LIKE A SNACK? (Frank Zappa) by Frank Zappa
Mothers involvement: Frank Zappa—producer, orchestration, bass guitar, guitar, drums; George Duke—trombone, keyboards; Ian Underwood—keyboards, woodwinds; Big Jim Sullivan—guitar, orchestration; Martin Lickert—bass guitar; Aynsley Dunbar—drums; Ruth Underwood—percussion; Jimmy Carl Black—vocals; Howard Kaylan—vocals; Jim Pons—voices; Mark Volman—vocals, photography
Additional personnel: Bob Auger—engineer; Barry Keene—overdubs, remixing; Theodore Bikel—narrator; Royal Philharmonic Orchestra
Recording dates: January 28 - February 5, 1971 at Pinewood Studios, UK and Whitney Studios, Glendale, California
Highest chart position: #59 from *200 Motels*
Original release date: October 4, 1971
Significant other versions: The Mothers

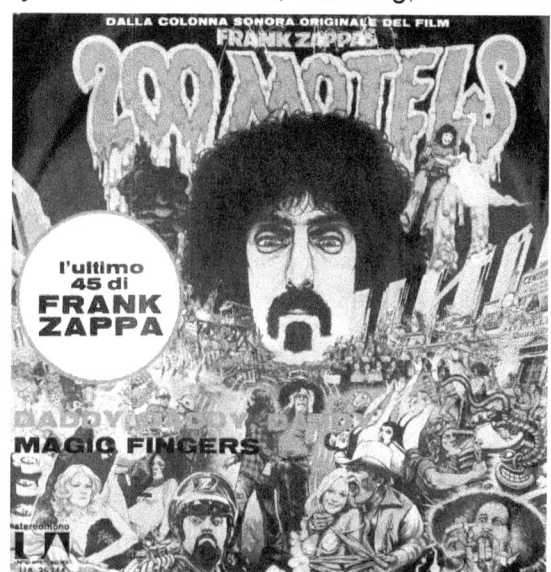

How high can Flo & Eddie sing... or get? The performance from November 13, 1970 was on *Freaks and Motherfu*#@%!* as an uncredited part of "Holiday in Berlin."

—

YOU CAN'T DO THAT ON STAGE ANYMORE, VOLUME 1 (CD) by Frank Zappa
Mothers involvement: Frank Zappa—producer, arranger, guitar, vocals, dialogue, Mark Volman—vocals, dialogue; Howard Kaylan—vocals, dialogue; Jim Pons—bass, vocals, dialogue; Don Preston—keyboards, electronics; Ian Underwood—keyboards, alto sax' Aynsley Dunbar—drums
Recording dates: 1969 - 1984
Highest chart position: Did not chart
Original release date: May 16, 1988

Turtles-related tracks:
Disc 1, tracks 1-3:
The Florida Airport Tape (spoken word)
Once Upon a Time
Sofa #1

Disc 1, track 9:
The Groupie Routine (spoken word)

Mark: Scraps from various Zappa concerts over the decades. It's not one of the best *You Can't*

Do That collections, where Volume 2 is the best. "The Groupie Routine" is also known as "Do You Like My New Car?" Both "Once Upon a Time" and "Sofa #1" are part of the "Sofa Suite," which was released in complete form on *Carnegie Hall*. "The Florida Airport Tape" is more of Zappa recording conversations.

Charles: You can't do a lot of all this on the stage anymore.

—

YOU CAN'T DO THAT ON STAGE ANYMORE, VOLUME 3 (CD) by Frank Zappa
Mothers involvement: Frank Zappa—producer, arranger, guitar, vocals, dialogue; Mark Volman—vocals, dialogue; Howard Kaylan—vocals, dialogue; Jim Pons—bass, vocals, dialogue; Don Preston—keyboards, electronics; Ian Underwood—keyboards, alto sax' Aynsley Dunbar—drums
Recording dates: December 10, 1971 - December 23, 1984
Highest chart position: Did not chart
Original release date: November 13, 1989

Turtles-related tracks:
Disc 2, tracks 10:
King Kong (instrumental)

This disc is only mentioned here because Flo & Eddie vocalize with grunts and screams on stage during the performance of this 24-minute instrumental track. Inessential.

—

YOU CAN'T DO THAT ON STAGE ANYMORE, VOLUME 6 (CD) by Frank Zappa
Mothers involvement: Frank Zappa—producer, arranger, guitar, vocals, dialogue, band direction; Mark Volman—vocals, dialogue, percussion; Howard Kaylan—vocals, dialogue, percussion; Ian Underwood—keyboards, woodwinds; Don Preston—Minimoog; Jim Pons—bass, vocals, dialogue; Aynsley Dunbar—drums
Recording dates: 1970 - 1988
Highest chart position: Did not chart
Original release date: July 10, 1992

Turtles-related tracks:
Disc 1, track 1:
The M.O.I. Anti-Smut Loyalty Oath (spoken word)

Disc 1, track 13:
Shove It Right In (comprising "She Painted Up Her Face," "Half a Dozen Provocative Squats," and "Shove It Right In")

Disc 2, tracks 13-14:
Lonesome Cowboy Nando
200 Motels Finale

More random live versions of various Mothers tracks done elsewhere, mostly from *200 Motels*. "Lonesome Cowboy Nando" was originally "Lonesome Cowboy Burt." Here, Zappa takes on the lead vocals and changes some of the lyrics, although it sure sounds like Jimmy Carl Black is also singing on this version, albeit uncredited.

—

YOU DIDN'T TRY TO CALL ME (Frank Zappa) by The Mothers
Mothers involvement: Frank Zappa—producer, arranger, guitar, vocals; Howard Kaylan—vocals; Mark Volman—vocals, percussion; Jeff Simmons—bass, vocals; Ian Underwood—organ, keyboards, guitar; George Duke—piano, keyboards, trombone; Aynsley Dunbar—drums
Additional personnel: Roy Thomas Baker—engineer
Recording dates: June 18, 1970 at "Piknik" VPRO
Highest chart position: Did not chart from *The Mothers 1970*
Original release date: May 8, 2020
Significant other versions: Frank Zappa and the Mothers of Invention

Mark: Yet another doo-wop sounding song here done straight by Flo & Eddie. The fidelity on this version isn't the greatest and they do some strange vocal effects during the end. The original studio version is from *Freak Out!* in 1966 and redone for *Cruising with Ruben and the Jets*.

Charles: I must gripe yet again—not about the song—but about it being called doo-wop. Charles, a DJ who knows his doo-wop, puts his foot down here. This definitely isn't doo-wop. Add some horns and it could've been an interesting release by a band like Ides of March, Lighthouse, or Blood, Sweat & Tears.

—

ZAPPA (film)
Mothers involvement: Frank Zappa, Howard Kaylan, Mark Volman, Jimmy Carl Black, Ian Underwood, Don Preston, Euclid James 'Motorhead' Sherwood, Ray White, Roy Estrada, Ray Collins, Bunk Gardner, Buzz Gardner
Additional personnel: David Bowie, Arsenio Hall, Kathie Lee Gifford, Ringo Starr, Mick

Jagger, Paul McCartney, Alice Cooper, Timothy Carey, George Harrison, Regis Philbin, John Lennon, Larry King, Steve Vai, Charles Manson, Joni Mitchell, Jimi Hendrix, Brian Jones, Pamela Des Barres, Bill Wyman, Don Van Vliet, Ted Koppel, Gail Zappa, Václav Havel, Arthur Brown, Ruth Underwood, Murray Roman, Bruce Bickford, Edgard Varèse, Lonnie Lardner, Mike Keneally, David Harrington, Johnny "Guitar" Watson, Carl Zappa, Patrice Zappa, Tom Wilson, Cal Schenkel, Arthur Dyer Tripp III, Billy Mundi, Miss Mercy, John Lofton, Scott Thunes, The GTOs
Original release date: November 27, 2020

This is an excellent documentary from Alex Winter, best known as Bill from the Bill and Ted film series. Of course, it covers the 1965-1970 version of The Mothers of Invention the most, despite Zappa's misgivings about that period. There is some rare footage from the Flo & Eddie period. Overall, it's an excellent overview of the man that is especially designed for the uninitiated. I found more complaints raised by Zappa completists that have already seen or heard practically everything the man ever recorded. If you are a new or casual fan or just curious, this is a great documentary!

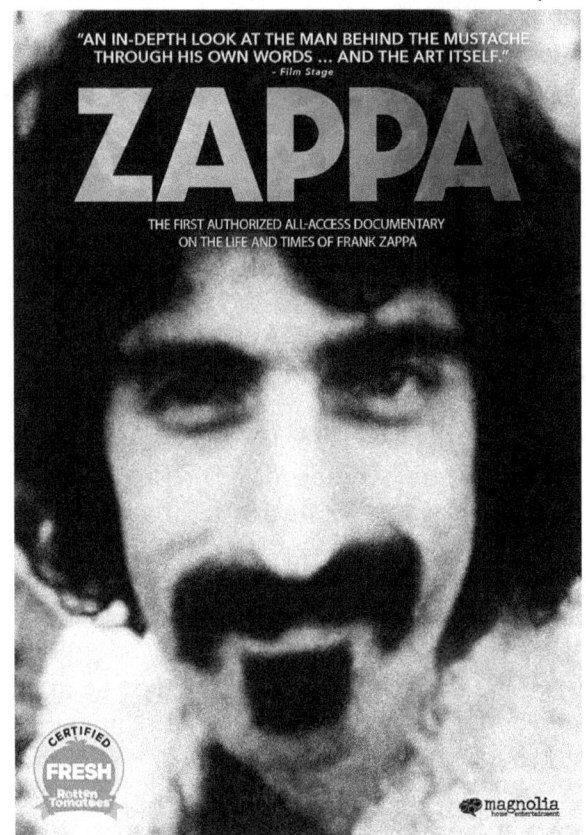

A BRIEF HISTORY OF FLO & EDDIE
by Mark Arnold

When Frank Zappa got injured in December 1971, the rest of The Mothers did not know what to do. Howard Kaylan and Mark Volman took it upon themselves to tour the U.S. during 1972 and also record and release their first solo album with the other Mothers under the name of *The Phlorescent Leech and Eddie*. It was released in September 1972 and became their only charting album at #211 on *Billboard*.

Many of the songs on the album were re-recordings of those that were originally recorded for The Turtles' unreleased *Shell Shock* album from 1969-1970. There was a discussion as to whether this new album should be released as a Turtles album or a Flo & Eddie album. Reprise Records decided that Flo & Eddie was now a more valuable commodity as they had just come straight from a Frank Zappa tour where the four albums Flo & Eddie recorded with him charted better than the majority of The Turtles albums.

Strangely, even though they were still not allowed to use their real names, Reprise issued two promo singles for the album billed as by "Mark Volman and Howard Kaylan." "Radio Spot for *The Phlorescent Leech and Eddie*" b/w "Goodbye Surprise" was issued first and then "Goodbye Surprise" b/w "Nikki Hoi." Stock copies exist of this second single from the Netherlands, but any copies are very rare as no Flo & Eddie singles ever charted.

Flo & Eddie then went on tour from September through December in support of the album, opening for such acts as The Doors, Cheech and Chong, Ten Years After, and Mott the Hoople. They also hit some European dates in November.

"Afterglow" b/w "The Original Sound Track from 'Carlos and De Bull'" became the first single off of their second album, released in January 1973.

Their second album was titled simply *Flo & Eddie* and featured a defaced Norman Rockwell painting, giving the girl character thick black glasses and frizzy black hair, and a beard and long hair on the boy character. Their second album featured a few more Turtles castoffs and more cover songs and comedic songs than their first album. It was released in 1973, but some sources say 1974.

"Flo & Eddie Meet the Wolfman Part 1" b/w "Flo & Eddie Meet the Wolfman Part II" was a February 1973 promo only release featuring Wolfman Jack and clips from some songs from the Flo & Eddie album.

With two albums under their belt, Flo & Eddie went out on a U.S. tour in support of Alice Cooper. The tour lasted from March 23-June 3.

A second single of "You're a Lady" b/w "If We Only Had the Time" was released in June 1973 and also did not chart.

Flo & Eddie went on tour again, this time as headliners: The Flo & Eddie radio show on KROQ and Flo & Eddie by the Fireside on KMET. Their shows were usually three hours of zaniness where they would play bits of old records, sometimes mere seconds' worth, and also had many live guests. They then moved from KROQ to KMET with Shadoe Stevens, who had created their show in the first place.

Their radio show featured all sorts of craziness with guests like Ringo Starr who took phone calls from listeners and uttered the F-bomb dozens of times on air as well as Keith Moon, Harry Nilsson, and many, many others. A highlight was when they got the members of The Move together in a reunion live on air with Jeff Lynne and Roy Wood having no prior knowledge about it. The radio show lasted through 1974 and resumed in the 1980s.

Touring resumed in September 1974, the same month their new label Columbia issued their first single. "Let Me Make Love to You" b/w "Come to My Rescue Webelos" was released in

September 1974, then reissued September 1975. The more-deserving single did not chart either time. The B-side is unique to this single and is now quite a rare track.

Touring continued throughout 1975, and in July, Flo & Eddie toured Australia. They also did a few shows during this year billed as The Turtles, but the billing was to be short-lived as although Flo & Eddie had the rights to The Turtles recordings which they had purchased in 1974, they still didn't have the rights to The Turtles' name.

Their third album and the first for Columbia was a mostly live album with a couple of studio tracks called *Illegal, Immoral and Fattening*, released in 1975. A second single off the album "Rebecca" b/w "Illegal, Immoral and Fattening" was released in December 1975.

After another U.S. tour in 1976, they toured Australia again during the summer.

Moving Targets was the name of Flo & Eddie's second and final Columbia album in 1976 and fourth album overall. This was a completely made-in-the-studio creation with some new songs, some covers, and a remake of "Elenore," which became the album's first single: "Elenore" b/w "The Love You Gave Away," released in October 1976. The inclusion of "Elenore" was a suggestion of Columbia's, thinking it would help bring Flo & Eddie into the mainstream. It didn't.

A second single of "Keep it Warm" b/w "Hot" followed in December 1976, and became the final Flo & Eddie single to date.

Touring continued into 1977 and then resumed again from 1979-1983. By this point, their live show was typically titled The Two and a Half Man Show. They toured along with keyboardist Andy Cahan and performed such wild things as "The Fence," a parody of Pink Floyd's *The Wall*.

Flo & Eddie no longer took recording seriously enough to try making a hit album. Instead, they issued sporadic albums during the 1980s as pet projects with certain themes.

Rock Steady with Flo & Eddie came out in 1981. It was reissued as *Prince Flo and Jah Edward I* in 1987 by Rhino Records and was supposed to be the record's original title. It is a reggae album with actual Jamaican reggae musicians. A highlight is a reggae version of "Happy Together." No singles were released.

Another pet project was called *Checkpoint Charlie*, released in 1982 by Rhino. It's Flo & Eddie's parody of German music artists like Kraftwerk. The crazy thing is that the resulting EP plays from the center of the record out.

At this point, Flo & Eddie got the rights to The Turtles' name. In 1983, they issued via Rhino Records a massive three-disc LP set covering every aspect of their careers called *The History of Flo & Eddie and The Turtles*. Rhino also started reissuing a number of other Turtles-related albums, plus a limited edition seven tape set called *The Winds of Flo & Eddie*, where they narrate their career life story.

In 1984, Flo & Eddie carried on as The Turtles featuring Flo & Eddie and started their ongoing Happy Together Tour with David Fishof. Later, Fishof went on to produce The Monkees' reunion tour, but the Happy Together Tour continues to this day.

Flo & Eddie closed off their Reprise and Columbia years with a Rhino compilation of their best material from 1972-1976 called appropriately enough *The Best of Flo & Eddie*, released in 1987.

Flo & Eddie also hosted a new radio show for about two years in the late '80s and early '90s called *The Flo & Eddie Show* at K-Rock in New York City.

Years of touring again as The Turtles caused Flo & Eddie to release a live album of Turtles hits and Flo & Eddie songs as *The Turtles featuring Flo & Eddie Captured Live!* It was a 1991 concert recorded live at New York's Bottom End and released in 1992 by Rhino Records. Many of the songs were reissued over the years on live Turtles compilations.

Mark Volman went back to school in the 1990s and got a degree in business, while Howard Kaylan compiled his only solo CD called *Dust Bunnies*, recorded and released in 2006. It was recorded in actor Billy Bob Thornton's basement studio and he features on one of the cuts. The tracks are songs that Kaylan has liked over the years including two by The Left Banke. Kaylan hinted at a follow-up in his autobiography, but nothing has been released to date, and probably won't be since Kaylan retired in 2018.

Flo & Eddie's last gasp on disc to date was the two CD *New York "Times"* release in 2009 featuring highlights from various concerts over the years 1979-1994, again played at New York's Bottom Line.

Flo & Eddie also did a number of children's albums and that will be the subject of our next chapter.

FLO & EDDIE A-Z (including CHECKPOINT CHARLIE)

AFTERGLOW aka **AFTERGLOW OF YOUR LOVE** (Steve Marriott, Ronnie Lane) by Flo & Eddie
Flo & Eddie involvement: Howard Kaylan—vocals; Mark Volman—vocals and guitar; Gary Rowles—lead guitar; John Herron—keyboards; Jim Pons—bass; Aynsley Dunbar—drums
Additional personnel: Bob Ezrin—producer, piano; Jack Douglas, Shelly Yokus—engineers; Steve Hunter—guitar
Recording dates: 1973 at Sunset Sound, Paramount, Los Angeles, California; and The Record Plant, New York, New York
Highest chart position: Did not chart; B-side to "You're a Lady;" Did not chart from *Flo & Eddie*
Original release date: June 1973
Significant other versions: Small Faces, Daryl Braithewaite, Quiet Riot, Great White

Mark: Not the Ed Sheeran song. Kaylan belts this out with an intensity and some loud screams. The original Small Faces version starts off quietly and builds, whereas every other version seems to take on Flo & Eddie's more intense version. Too bad none of these Flo & Eddie songs charted or got much, if any, airplay, as many of them were equal or better than any of the glam rock or power pop songs littering the airwaves back in 1973.

This probably would have been a hit had the likes of Mott the Hoople or Big Star or T. Rex released it at the time. Great White made it into a greater epic anthem. The Quiet Riot version sounds almost exactly like Flo & Eddie's. Australian singer Daryl Braithewaite also does a version that sounds like Flo & Eddie's.

Charles: Strong track with solid drumming and a tasty lead guitar, matched by great vocals. This one sounds as if it could have fit perfectly on Tommy James' *Crimson and Clover* album.

—

AGITA (Nick Apollo Forte) by Flo & Eddie
Flo & Eddie involvement: Howard Kaylan—executive producer, vocals, saxophone; Mark Volman—executive producer, vocals, guitar; Joe Stefko—producer, drums; Russ Shirley—guitar, background vocals; Mike Reed—keyboards, background vocals; Mike Visceglia—bass, background vocals
Additional personnel: Denny McNerney—recording, assembling, mastering
Recording dates: December 1984 at the Bottom Line, New York, New York
Highest chart position: Did not chart from *New York "Times" 1979-1994 Live at The Bottom Line*

Photo courtesy of Emily Wells

Original release date: October 20, 2009
Significant other versions: Nick Apollo Forte

Mark: After a lead-in of "It's Kama Sutra Time," this almost sounds like the "Who Stole the Kishka" polka! There is a version on YouTube with Mark and Howard singing it live on video from 2010 that's very fun. It's originally from Woody Allen's *Broadway Danny Rose*.
Charles: Turtle-Italiano! Nick Apollo Forte (1938-2020) was a New Haven, CT club singer who garnered national attention when cast by Woody Allen for his 1984 black & white comedy, *Broadway Danny Rose*. This track is everything an Italian party song should be—lively, danceable, and with lots of food references. If you know what "agita" means, and your life is filled with it, play this and your agita will fade—for two minutes anyway. With Howard credited as contributing sax and Mark adding guitar, try not smiling when you listen to this. Marrrrrone!

—

AMERICAN BANDSTAND aka **BANDSTAND BOOGIE** (Charles Albertine, Barry Manilow, Bruce Sussman) by Flo & Eddie
Flo & Eddie involvement: Howard Kaylan—executive producer, vocals, saxophone; Mark Volman—executive producer, vocals, guitar; Joe Stefko—producer, drums; Russ Shirley—guitar, background vocals; Mike Reed—keyboards, background vocals; Mike Visceglia—bass, background vocals
Additional personnel: Denny McNerney—recording, assembling, mastering
Recording dates: December 1984 at the Bottom Line, New York, New York
Highest chart position: Did not chart from *New York "Times" 1979-1994 Live at The Bottom Line*
Original release date: October 20, 2009
Significant other versions: "American Bandstand," Barry Manilow

Photo courtesy of Emily Wells

Mark: A quickie snippet of the original "American Bandstand" theme sans lyrics is played as everyone exits the theater.
Charles: I'll take Barry Manilow's vocal version.

—

ANOTHER BRICK IN THE WALL (Roger Waters) by Pink Floyd & Eddie
Flo & Eddie involvement: Mark Volman—puppets; Howard Kaylan—puppets; Andy Cahan—puppets; Pink Floyd—sped up vocals
Recording dates: 1980
Highest chart position: Did not chart
Original release date: unreleased

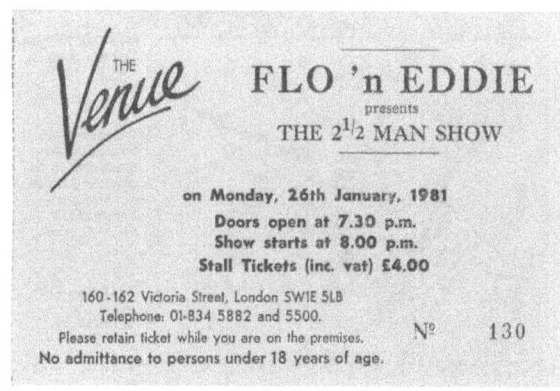

Significant other versions: Pink Floyd, Roger Waters, Korn

Mark: Live performance only. Mark and Howard and Andy Cahan satirized Pink Floyd's *The Wall* from 1979, by speeding up their vocals to Chipmunks levels and rolling out the fence. Next, they all proceeded to toss around a number of puppets and plush toys singing the chorus for about a minute and a half of their "Two and a Half Man Show" during their 1980 European Tour. It remains unreleased due to copyright issues, but is hysterically funny if you watch it on YouTube.
Charles: Anything that sounds like The Chipmunks is gold to me. I grew up feeling *The Chipmunks Sing The Beatles Hits* (Liberty label, 1964) was part of The Beatles' actual library. I might still think so.

—

ANOTHER POP STAR'S LIFE (Mark Volman, Howard Kaylan) by Flo & Eddie
Flo & Eddie involvement: Howard Kaylan—vocals; Mark Volman—vocals and guitar; Gary Rowles—lead guitar; John Herron—keyboards; Jim Pons—bass; Aynsley Dunbar—drums
Additional personnel: Bob Ezrin—producer; Jack Douglas, Shelly Yokus—engineers; Steve Hunter—guitar
Recording dates: 1973 at Sunset Sound, Paramount, Los Angeles, California; and The Record Plant, New York, New York
Highest chart position: Did not chart from *Flo & Eddie*
Original release date: June 1973

Charles: Beyond the Eric Carmen shriek at the beginning, this rocker screams (yes, actually screams) hair bands of the eighties, even though it came out in the early seventies. To be more precise, it sounds more like one of Alice Cooper *Killer*-era rockers. Was it written about any one specific pop star? Hmmmm.
Mark: Funny you mention Alice Cooper, Charles, as they were on tour opening for him at the time of this song's and this album's release. It's a very hard rocking ode to the typical excesses of rock and roll life, and certainly by 1973 we had already had our shares of real casualties from Jimi to Janis to Jim (all 27 and all starting with J!) and career casualties, too. "Look in his eyes!" "Look at the charts!"

—

AULD LANG SYNE (public domain) by Howard Kaylan and Cast
Flo & Eddie involvement: Howard Kaylan—lead vocals
Additional personnel: Sparks—arrangers
Recording dates: 1983
Highest chart position: Did not chart from *Get Crazy Soundtrack*
Original release date: August 5, 1983
Significant other versions: Guy Lombardo, Charles Samuel Myers and Alfred Cort Hadden, Frank C. Stanley

Photo: JoAnn Kassoff

Mark: It's Howard's first solo-credited performance where he sings a very straight version of the New Year's Eve/Day classic to ring in New Year's 1983. Though Flo & Eddie contributed two other tracks to the *Get Crazy* movie soundtrack, this was the only one on the official *Soundtrack* album.
Charles: Why would I ever play Guy Lombardo again on December 31st after 11:59pm?!

—

BALD MOUNTAIN aka **NIGHT ON BALD MOUNTAIN** (Modest Mussorgsky) by Flo & Eddie
Flo & Eddie involvement: Howard Kaylan—executive producer, vocals, saxophone; Mark Volman—executive producer, vocals, guitar; Joe Stefko—producer, drums; David Nelson—guitar, background vocals; Chris Apostle—keyboards, background vocals; Donnie Kisselbach—bass, vocals; Richie Cannata—sax, clarinet, background vocals
Additional personnel: Denny McNerney—recording, assembling, mastering
Recording dates: December 28, 1988 at the Bottom Line, New York, New York
Highest chart position: Did not chart from *New York "Times" 1979-1994 Live at The Bottom Line*
Original release date: October 20, 2009

Mark: This is kind of a disco version of Mussorgsky's "Night on Bald Mountain" as heard in more traditional form in Walt Disney's *Fantasia*. It's a competently played instrumental.
Charles: Well said, Mark.

—

BANG A GONG (GET IT ON): See **GET IT ON (BANG A GONG)**

—

BEST FRIENDS (THEME FROM THE UNSOLD TV PILOT) (Mark Volman, Howard Kaylan) by Flo & Eddie
Flo & Eddie involvement: Howard Kaylan—producer, vocals; Mark Volman—producer, vocals, guitars; Phil Reed—lead guitar; Andy Cahan—keyboards; Erik Scott—bass; Craig Krampf—drums
Additional personnel: Ron Nevison—producer, recorder, mixer; Skip Taylor—producer; Alan MacMillan—strings and horns arranger; Rick Smith, Eric Schilling, Cathy Callan—assistants
Recording dates: 1976 at the Record Plant, Sausalito and Los Angeles, California
Highest chart position: Did not chart from *Moving Targets*
Original release date: October 1976

Photo: Daniel Coston

Mark: This really was what it said it was, a theme song for an unsold pilot called "Best Friends." It's not bad and could have and should have been retooled for use later. *Friends*, anyone? In any case, it is a very catchy tune not unlike Elton John's "Theme from a Non-Existent TV Series" from his 1976 *Blue Moves* album. Like "The Love You Gave Away," there's a real Chicago vibe here.
Charles: The first of three songs with "best" in the title, none of which ever made it to a "best of" compilation, this deserves to be on one. Many TV intro themes were ingrained in the public's aural consciousness, like John Sebastian's "Welcome Back, Kotter" or Harry Nilsson's "Courtship Of Eddie's Father," to name a few, but those were actual network hit shows. If this pilot sold, and was a success, the theme song may very well have been a hit. Play it and deny it sounds like Chicago at their bounciest.

—

BEST OF FLO & EDDIE, THE (compilation) by Flo & Eddie
Flo & Eddie involvement: See individual Flo & Eddie tracks
Additional personnel: See individual Flo & Eddie tracks
Recording dates: 1972 - 1978
Highest chart position: Did not chart
Original release date: 1987

Goodbye Surprise
Feel Older Now
Nikki Hoi
Another Pop Star's Life

Just Another Town
Afterglow
You're a Lady

Marmendy Mill (CD only)
Illegal, Immoral and Fattening (CD only)
Rebecca
Let Me Make Love to You
Mama, Open Up
Keep it Warm
Moving Targets
This Could Be the Day (CD only)
Getaway (Back to L.A.) (CD only)

This is really a marvelous collection although it should have had more unreleased rarities at the end. Confusingly, nothing from *Rock Steady with Flo & Eddie* or *Checkpoint Charlie* were included, nor were any of Flo & Eddie's rare B-sides or promotional records. Will there be a *Volume 2*?

—

BEST PART OF BREAKING UP (Phil Spector, Vince Poncia, Peter Andreoli) by Flo & Eddie
Flo & Eddie involvement: Howard Kaylan—vocals; Mark Volman—vocals and guitar; Gary Rowles—lead guitar; John Herron—keyboards; Jim Pons—bass; Aynsley Dunbar—drums
Additional personnel: Bob Ezrin—producer; Jack Douglas, Shelly Yokus—engineers; John Sebastian—vocals
Recording dates: 1973 at Sunset Sound, Paramount, Los Angeles, California; and The Record Plant, New York, New York
Highest chart position: Did not chart from *Flo & Eddie*
Original release date: June 1973
Significant other versions: The Ronettes, Shana, Roni Griffith, The Devil Dogs, The Dixie Cups

Mark: I suppose Mark and Howard did a decent version of this old Ronettes hit, but I kinda wish they had stuck with more originals and perhaps redone more unreleased Turtles material. It's not bad; it's just that I'm not a huge fan of remakes, especially when there is nothing new or remarkable brought to the table.
Charles: This starts with a Gary Glitter-ish intro, but before we know it we're in wall-of-sound doo wop heaven. Finally a track that could be listed

under the "doo wop" category, and Mark doesn't even mention it. The original was a Top 40 hit written by Phil Spector for The Ronettes. It was a classic then, and Flo & Eddie's version holds its own with a barrelful of energy, great vocals and a nice arrangement... proving once again that the best part of breaking up is, indeed, making up.

—

BEST POSSIBLE ME (Mark Volman, Howard Kaylan) by Flo & Eddie
Flo & Eddie involvement: Howard Kaylan—producer, vocals; Mark Volman—producer, vocals, guitars; Phil Reed—lead guitar; Andy Cahan—keyboards; Erik Scott—bass; Craig Krampf—drums
Additional personnel: Ron Nevison—producer, recorder, mixer; Skip Taylor—producer; Alan MacMillan—strings and horns arranger; Rick Smith, Eric Schilling, Cathy Callan—assistants
Recording dates: 1976 at the Record Plant, Sausalito and Los Angeles, California
Highest chart position: Did not chart from *Moving Targets*
Original release date: October 1976

Mark: Flo & Eddie's attempt to do some mid-'70s big stadium rock. This one is reminiscent of ELO or The Moody Blues. For once, this is a positive autobiographical song, probably composed because things like "Mama, Open Up" were too jaded. Unfortunately, it didn't help.
Charles: Imagine what Freddie Mercury could have done with this! After a gala piano intro, this explodes into an epic composition that is so interesting and musical, it could have gone on for another four or five minutes. It's the best possible flow and ebb(bie).

—

BIG SHOWDOWN, THE (Mark Volman, Howard Kaylan) by Flo & Eddie
Flo & Eddie involvement: Howard Kaylan—producer, vocals; Mark Volman—producer, vocals, guitar; Billy Steele—guitar; Andy Cahan—keyboards; Erik Scott—bass; Craig Krampf—drums, bells
Additional personnel: Howard Wolen—engineer
Recording dates: 1977 at Studio Sound Recorders, Los Angeles, California

Photo: Daniel Coston

Highest chart position: Did not chart from *The History of Flo & Eddie and The Turtles*
Original release date: 1978 for film *Texas Detour*; 1983 for album

Mark: This has an assuredly intentional Bruce Springsteen feel to it complete with shades of "Born to Run," but this is so much better (not a BS fan).
Charles: Not sure there are many Springsteen fans who would agree that this is much better, but it is very well done.

—

BOOGIE (Howard Kaylan, Mark Volman) by Flo & Eddie
Flo & Eddie involvement: Howard Kaylan—executive producer, vocals, saxophone; Mark Volman—executive producer, vocals, guitar; Joe Stefko—producer, drums; David Nelson—guitar, background vocals; Dave Lebolt—keyboards; Andy Cahan—piano, Casio; Steve Buslowe—bass, background vocals
Additional personnel: Denny McNerney—recording, assembling, mastering
Recording dates: December 1979 at the Bottom Line, New York, New York
Highest chart position: Did not chart from *New York "Times" 1979-1994 Live at The Bottom Line*
Original release date: October 20, 2009
Significant other versions: *Down And Dirty Duck*

Mark: To date, Flo & Eddie have not commercially released the studio version of this song, so we'll have to settle for this live version which includes a snippet of "Boogie Oogie Oogie." Basically, if you know the title, you know the lyrics. "You wanna boogie?" The audio for this live performance was taken from a WLIR radio broadcast.
Charles: Get Down, Boogie Oogie Oogie! More proof that Howard and Mark could play any style, any format, any genre. Wish there was an all-disco album in their catalog.

—

BRUCE (Mark Volman, Howard Kaylan) by Flo & Eddie
Flo & Eddie involvement: Mark Volman—executive producer, lead vocals, guitar; Howard Kaylan—executive producer, lead vocals; ; Joe Stefko—drums; David Nelson—lead guitar, vocals; Donnie Kisselbach—bass guitar, vocals; Chris Apostle—keyboards, vocals; Peter Zale—keyboards; Richie Cannata—saxophones, vocals, keyboards
Additional personnel: Steve Remote, David Nelson—producers, mixers; Steve Remote—engineer

Recording dates: December 31, 1991 at the Bottom Line, New York, New York
Highest chart position: Did not chart from *The Turtles Featuring Flo & Eddie Captured Live*
Original release date: November 10, 1992

Mark: This is a Bruce Springsteen parody done in Flo & Eddie's typical mocking fashion with "tacky New Jersey piano music." I'm not the hugest Springsteen fan, and I especially wasn't back then, so when they decided to mock him, I was totally into it. "Bruce... Bruce!!!" Howard says that Bruce will show up if only you believe. No one did, so they got Mark Volman instead aka "This asshole!" The best part is where they both sing the *Car 54, Where Are You?* theme song in the style of Springsteen.

Charles: We noted it before, but as a reminder, Flo & Eddie sang back-up on Bruce Springsteen's hit "Hungry Heart."

—

BURN THE HOUSE (Mark Volman) by Flo & Eddie
Flo & Eddie involvement: Howard Kaylan—producer, vocals; Mark Volman—producer, vocals and guitar; Gary Rowles—lead guitar; Don Preston—keyboards; Jim Pons—bass; Aynsley Dunbar—drums
Additional personnel: Barry Keene—engineer
Recording dates: 1972 at Ike Turner's Bolic Sound, Inglewood, California
Highest chart position: #211 from *The Phlorescent Leech and Eddie*
Original release date: September 1972

Mark: Mark and Howard share lead vocals on this ode to indecision about what to do today. As usual, their sweet harmonies cover up some of the more sinister messages being sung about.

Charles: The opposite of Talking Heads' "Burning Down the House," this is a subversive pyromaniac's anthem disguised as a slower, folk rock song with some solid harmonies. But burning down the house isn't the only option, as "all they want to do is you." Even though it's a laid-back tempo, it's very melodic and memorable.

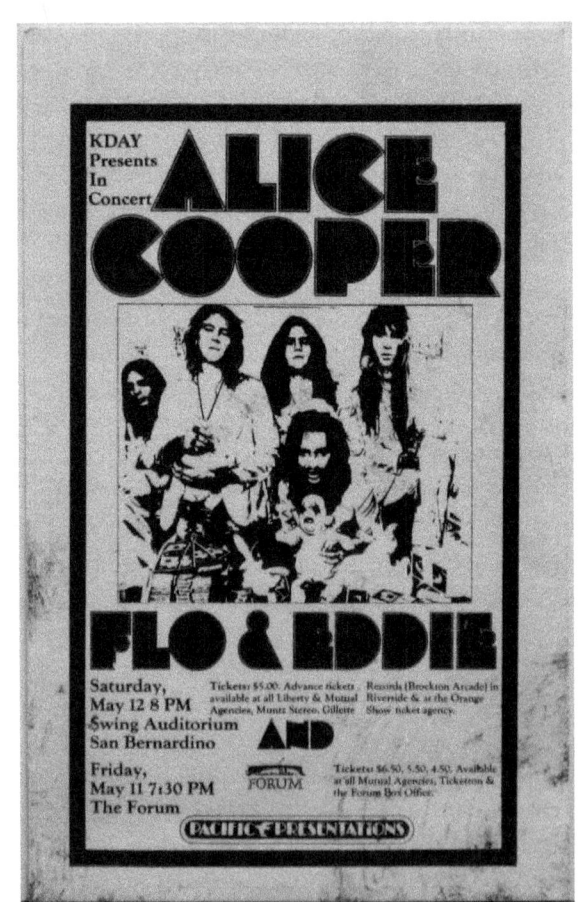

—

CALIFORNIA DREAMING (film and soundtrack)
Flo & Eddie involvement: Howard Kaylan—vocals; Mark Volman—vocals, guitars; Phil Reed—lead guitar; Andy Cahan—keyboards; Erik Scott—bass; Craig Krampf—drums
Additional personnel: Glynnis O'Connor as Corky; Seymour Cassel as Duke; Dennis Christopher as T.T.; Dorothy Tristan as Faye; Tanya Roberts as Stephanie; John Calvin as Rick; Todd Susman as Jordy; Alice Playten as Corrine
Original release date: March 16, 1979

A cheap sex comedy when cheap sex comedies were all the rage in Hollywood. Flo & Eddie contributed "Pass You By," which also appeared on the *California Dreaming Soundtrack*.

—

CARLOS AND DE BULL aka **THE ORIGINAL SOUNDTRACK TO "CARLOS AND DE BULL"**
(Howard Kaylan, Mark Volman, Barnaby Conrad) by Flo & Eddie
Flo & Eddie involvement: Howard Kaylan—vocals; Mark Volman—vocals and guitar; Gary Rowles—lead guitar; John Herron—keyboards; Jim Pons—bass; Aynsley Dunbar—drums
Additional personnel: Bob Ezrin—producer; Jack Douglas, Shelly Yokus—engineers
Recording dates: 1973 at Sunset Sound, Paramount, Los Angeles, California, and The Record Plant, New York, New York
Highest chart position: Single did not chart; B-side to "Afterglow;" Did not chart from *Flo & Eddie*
Original release date: January 1973 for single; June 1973 for album

Mark: This is more Turtles-like silliness in the vein of "Umbassa and the Dragon," with a large spoken dialogue section telling some nonsensical story about bullfighting. "What do they want?" It's an okay track, but I sometimes find myself skipping over this one.
Charles: Olé! Is there any style these guys can't handle? In what sounds like a theme song for an animated toreador short film (wait—is it just that), we're taken on a matador's adventure in authentic accents, instrumentation, and sincerity.

—

CHAMPAGNE (Mark Volman, Howard Kaylan) by Flo & Eddie
Flo & Eddie involvement: Howard Kaylan—producer, vocals; Mark Volman—producer, vocals, guitar; Billy Steele—guitar; Andy Cahan—keyboards; Erik Scott—bass; Craig Krampf—drums, bells
Additional personnel: Howard Wolen—engineer
Recording dates: 1977 at Studio Sound Recorders, Los Angeles, California
Highest chart position: Did not chart from *The History of Flo & Eddie and The Turtles*
Original release date: 1978 for film *Texas Detour*; 1983 for album

FLO and EDDIE

Mark: This sounds a bit like *The Love Boat Theme*. Not much more. A brief snippet of this appears as part of "Medley #2" on *The History of Flo & Eddie and The Turtles*.
Charles: Not enough to get drunk on. Pour another glass of bubbly and we'll discuss it further.

—

CHARLIE DOES SURF (Salz-Pfeffer) by Checkpoint Charlie
Flo & Eddie involvement: Howard Kaylan and Mark Volman as M. Salz and H. Pfeffer—producers, vocals
Additional personnel: Andy Cahan—keyboards; Johann Moier, Peter Jebsen
Recording dates: 1982 at Herb Cohen's studio complex
Highest chart position: Did not chart from *Checkpoint Charlie*
Original release date: 1982

Mark: Are you a fan of George Harrison's *Electronic Sound*? Do you like to smoke pot until you get catatonic? If not, this Checkpoint Charlie stuff may not be for you. Basically, it's Flo & Eddie's over-indulgence with Andy Cahan in the studio.
Charles: Does Charlie surf? Is Charlie supposed to be Charles Manson? Perhaps it's Charlie Sheen. Or is Charlie a racial slur aimed at the Viet Cong? It seems to be the famous line from the film *Apocalypse Now* but there are conflicting reports. So many theories. So many conspiracies. The Clash insists "Charlie Don't Surf" but according to the Pretty Girls "Charlie Does Surf." In any case, you either surf or fight—or debate over the title. The mystery remains.

—

CHEAP (Mark Volman, Howard Kaylan) by Flo & Eddie
Flo & Eddie involvement: Howard Kaylan—lead vocals; Mark Volman—vocals, guitar; Phil Reed—lead guitar; Erik Scott—bass; Andy Cahan—keyboards; Craig Krampf—drums
Additional personnel: Joe Wissert—producer; Alex Kazanegras—engineer; Tom Perry—Mixing Engineer, Hollywood Sound
Recording dates: 1975 at the Roxy Theatre by the Haji Mobile Facility and the Crossroads of the World, Hollywood, California
Highest chart position: Did not chart from *Illegal, Immoral and Fattening*
Original release date: December 1975

Mark: There is also a studio version of this from *Down And Dirty Duck*, but so far it remains unreleased to an album. As for this released version, Flo & Eddie used it for many years as their concert opener to reflect the low or no budget performance that everyone was about to see. This feature added to their humor.
Charles: Oh yeah! How can you not love lyrics that call session musicians "schmucks in the street." It's what Flo & Eddie always did best: rock & roll + comedy/parody = entertainment. No eardrum abuse. Not a cheap sham. This one clicks on all cylinders. Oh yeah Oh yeah!

—

CHECKPOINT CHARLIE (EP) by Checkpoint Charlie
Flo & Eddie involvement: Howard Kaylan and Mark Volman as M. Salz and H. Pfeffer—producers, vocals
Additional personnel: Andy Cahan—keyboards; Johann Moier, Peter Jebsen
Recording dates: 1982 at Herb Cohen's studio complex
Highest chart position: Did not chart
Original release date: 1982

Das Watusi
Show Me the Way to Go Ohm

Helmut (Row the Boat Ashore)
Charlie Does Surf

WARNING: THIS RECORD PLAYS INSIDE OUT!

This crazy EP plays from the center out! It was Flo & Eddie's recorded tribute to many Kraut-rock bands like Kraftwerk, apparently borne out of a night of heavy pot smoking. Does it show?

COME TO MY RESCUE WEBELOS (Howard Kaylan, Mark Volman) by Flo & Eddie
Flo & Eddie involvement: Howard Kaylan—lead vocals; Mark Volman—lead vocals, guitar; Danny Kortchmar—guitar; Leland Sklar—bass; Ian Underwood—keyboards; Aynsley Dunbar—drums **Additional personnel:** Joe Wissert—producer; Dee Robb—engineer
Recording dates: 1974 at Cherokee Studios, Los Angeles, California
Highest chart position: Did not chart; B-side to "Let Me Make Love to You"
Original release date: September 1974; reissued September 1975

Mark: This song is quite rare as it has never been on an album. It has a mid-'70s funky soul vibe and deserves much more exposure than it got. It's too bad nobody remembered it when *Illegal, Immoral and Fattening* was released to CD and added it as a bonus track. For those who don't know, Webelos is the highest-ranking Cub Scout one can become before becoming a Boy Scout. It's short for WE'll BE LOyal Scouts.

Charles: One of the most iconic radio stations in Southern Connecticut is WEBE 108. In the '80s and '90s, they were the radio sponsors of my NY/New England Beatles Conventions. Because this is one of the few tracks I didn't get a chance to review, I thought I'd plug Danny Lyons and my friends at WEBE(los).

—

DANCING MOOD (Delroy Wilson) by Flo & Eddie
Flo & Eddie involvement: Mark Volman, Howard Kaylan—vocals; Earl "Chinna" Smith—lead guitar, rhythm guitar; Dean Fraser, Enroy "Tenor" Grant—saxophones; Walt Fowler—trombone; Augustus Pablo—organ, piano; Leslie "Professor" Butler—piano, organ; Phil Ramocon—Fender Rhodes; Aston "Family Man" Barrett—bass; Carlton "Santa" Davis—drums; Uziah "Sticky" Thompson—percussion; The Brackenridge Brothers—trumpets; Nambo—trombone
Additional personnel: Earl "Chinna" Smith—producer; Errol Brown—producer, recorder, mixer; Warren Smith, Michael "Eppy" Epstein—executive producers; "Sticko" Warren Weinberg, Richard Kaplan—engineers; Albert Wing—sax

Photo: Daniel Coston

Recording dates: 1981 at Tuff Gong Studios, Kingston, Jamaica and Indigo Ranch, Malibu, California
Highest chart position: Did not chart from *Rock Steady with Flo & Eddie*
Original release date: 1981
Significant other versions: Delroy Wilson, Jo Jo Zep and the Falcons, Billy T

Mark: I actually heard Flo & Eddie perform this when they actually were billed as The Turtles. It is a nice reggae tune that is truly conducive to dancing, and at a live concert, people did.
Charles: I remember the first time I Googled this track, I was auto-corrected to "Dancing Nude." They must have known Flo & Eddie! This tropical good-timin' island nugget could've been done by The Wailers if they had Clarence Clemons to supply the great sax. I don't like Reggae—I love it.

—

DARLIN' (Brian Wilson, Mike Love) by David Cassidy with Flo & Eddie
Turtles involvement: David Cassidy—lead vocals; Mark Volman—vocals; Howard Kaylan—vocals
Additional personnel: Bruce Johnston—producer
Recording dates: 1975 for album version; December 16, 1977 for live TV version
Highest chart position: Did not chart from *The Higher They Climb, The Harder They Fall*
Original release date: July 1975
Significant other versions: The Beach Boys, Paper Dolls, Herb Alpert and the Tijuana Brass,

American Spring, Paul Davis, Triumvirat, Tatsuro Yamashita, The Records, Darlin', BMX Bandits

Mark: Flo & Eddie guested on many, many records basically incognito during the 1970s, which aren't all listed separately in this book (they are listed at the end). What they didn't always do was perform with the artist when they appeared on various shows to promote the record, which is exactly what Flo & Eddie did when they backed Cassidy on December 16, 1977 in an amusing live version that appeared on Canadian television's *90 Minutes Live*, complete with dance moves. The fun appears on YouTube.
Charles: Do the musical math: Flo + Eddie + David Cassidy + Bruce Johnston production = a total delight.

—

DAS WATUSI aka **EL WATUSI** (Ray Barretto) by Checkpoint Charlie
Flo & Eddie involvement: Howard Kaylan and Mark Volman as M. Salz and H. Pfeffer—producer, vocals
Additional personnel: Andy Cahan—keyboards; Johann Moier, Peter Jebsen
Recording dates: 1982 at Herb Cohen's studio complex
Highest chart position: Did not chart from *Checkpoint Charlie*
Original release date: 1982
Significant other versions: Ray Barretto y su Charanga Moderna, The Vibrations, The Orlons

FLO & EDDIE

Mark: If you love all the other Checkpoint Charlie tunes or if you're a fan of The Rhythm Butchers, you'll love this. Otherwise, beware.
Charles: El Watusi was a Latin boogaloo song originally written and recorded by Ray Barretto. Stick to the original or search out the completely different Watusi song by The Orlons.

—

DAYS (Ray Davies) by Flo & Eddie
Flo & Eddie involvement: Howard Kaylan—vocals; Mark Volman—vocals and guitar; Gary Rowles—lead guitar; John Herron—keyboards; Jim Pons—bass; Aynsley Dunbar—drums
Additional personnel: Bob Ezrin—producer; Jack Douglas, Shelly Yokus—engineers
Recording dates: 1973 at Sunset Sound, Paramount, Los Angeles, California; and The Record Plant, New York, New York
Highest chart position: Did not chart from *Flo & Eddie*
Original release date: June 1973
Significant other versions: The Kinks, Kirsty MacColl, Petula Clark, James Last, Luke Kelly, Elvis Costello, Claire Tourneur, Ray Davies and Mumford & Sons, Colin Meloy, Tanya Donelly

FLO and EDDIE

Mark: Obviously, Mark and Howard were already devoted Kinks fans, especially since they got Ray Davies' to produce The Turtles' *Turtle Soup* album, back in 1969. They adored *The Kinks are The Village Green Preservation Society*, of which this was originally a track on the European version of the album. In the U.S. and UK, "Days" was a single track released about the same time, and there was talk to issue it on a companion album called *Four More Respected Gentlemen*, but this was scrapped. Nowadays, with CD bonus tracks, "Days" is typically included on most *Village Green* reissues. Flo & Eddie's version is competent, but nothing spectacular.
Charles: I was ready to compare this to a Kinks song, when I realized it was one! Written by Ray Davies, with additional vocals by John (Lovin' Spoonful) Sebastian, Flo & Eddie get their Brit on

with this song also covered by the likes of Petula Clark and Elvis Costello. Nothing kinky about it (unlike other Flo & Eddie works). The song "really got me" "all day and all of the night."

—

DEBARKATION, THE (John Carpenter) by Flo & Eddie
Flo & Eddie involvement: Howard Kaylan—executive producer, vocals, saxophone; Mark Volman—executive producer, vocals, guitar; Joe Stefko—producer, drums; Russ Shirley—guitar, background vocals; Mike Reed—keyboards, background vocals; Mike Visceglia—bass, background vocals
Additional personnel: Denny McNerney—recording, assembling, mastering
Recording dates: December 1984 at the Bottom Line, New York, New York
Highest chart position: Did not chart from *New York "Times" 1979-1994 Live at The Bottom Line*
Original release date: October 20, 2009
Significant other versions: *Escape from New York Soundtrack*

Photo: Daniel Coston

Mark: This track contains actual dialogue from John Carpenter's *Escape from New York* narrated by Jamie Lee Curtis, which leads to an instrumental version of that movie's theme song from the soundtrack. Again, another instrumental. Are Flo & Eddie here yet?
Charles: If you read any of my other previous comments you know what a John Carpenter/*Halloween*/*Escape from New York* fan I am. The fact that I could connect any portion of this book with my other favorite topic is music to my ears.

—

DOORS (Mark Volman, Howard Kaylan) by Flo & Eddie
Flo & Eddie involvement: Mark Volman—executive producer, vocals, guitar; Howard Kaylan—executive producer, lead vocals; Joe Stefko—drums; David Nelson—lead guitar, vocals; Donnie Kisselbach—bass guitar, vocals; Chris Apostle—keyboards, vocals; Peter Zale—keyboards; Richie Cannata—saxophones, vocals, keyboards
Additional personnel: Steve Remote, David Nelson—producers, mixers; Steve Remote—engineer
Recording dates: December 31, 1991 at the Bottom Line, New York, New York
Highest chart position: Did not chart from *The Turtles Featuring Flo & Eddie Captured Live*
Original release date: November 10, 1992

Mark: A parody of The Doors with Chris Apostle doing ersatz "Riders on the Storm" keyboards as Mark takes the Jim Morrison lead part. All he wants to do is show everyone his Lizard King. Then, it really does transition into "Spill the Wine" as written by War and performed by War with Eric Burdon.
Charles: Not being a fan of The Doors (yes, I'm the one and only), I expected this to be as dark and moody, and as boring. It wasn't as dark or as moody or as boring.

—

DOWN AND DIRTY DUCK (film)
Flo & Eddie involvement: Howard Kaylan—Willard Isenbaum / Negro Lady / Side Hack Rider; Mark Volman—Duck / Side Hack Rider
Additional personnel: Robert Ridgely; Car Salesman / Man at Bus Stop / Negro Gentleman / Big Fag / Police Officer / Tank; Walker Edmiston; Bus Driver / Jail Orator / Small Fag / Prospector / Mexican Official / President / Man in Elevator; Lurene Tuttle; Duck's Mother; Aynsley Dunbar; Additional Voices; Cynthia Adler; Lady In Car / Boss Lady / Small Dyke / Lady In Elevator; Joëlle Le Quément; Land Lady / Lady at Bus Stop / Madam / Big Dyke; Jerry D. Good; Transvestite
Original release date: July 8, 1974

Due to the success of such adult animated films as *Fritz The Cat* (1972) and *Heavy Traffic* (1973), the Murakami-Wolf studio tried their hand with an adult cartoon that is not based upon the Bobby London comic strip that appeared in *National Lampoon* and *Playboy*. The film was a middling success and had much greater success when it appeared on home video. Unlike most of their other projects with Murakami-Wolf, this time Howard and Mary voice the characters.

Flo & Eddie contributed "Livin' in a Jungle," "Mystic Martha," "This Could Be the Day," and "(You're Nothing But a) Good Duck" to the film, all of which appeared on *The History Of Flo & Eddie and The Turtles*. "This Could Be the Day" also appears on *The Best of Flo & Eddie* (CD version only). The studio versions of "Boogie" and "Cheap" that appear in this film have not been commercially released to record.

—

DUKE, THE (John Carpenter) by Flo & Eddie
Flo & Eddie involvement: Howard Kaylan—executive producer, vocals, saxophone; Mark Volman—producer, vocals, guitar; Joe Stefko—producer, drums; Russ Shirley—guitar, background vocals; Mike Reed—keyboards, background vocals; Mike Visceglia—bass, background vocals
Additional personnel: Denny McNerney—recording, assembling, mastering
Recording dates: December 1984 at the Bottom Line, New York, New York

Photo: Daniel Coston

Highest chart position: Did not chart from *New York "Times" 1979-1994 Live at The Bottom Line*
Original release date: October 20, 2009
Significant other versions: *Escape from New York Soundtrack*

Mark: Even more instrumental from John Carpenter's *Escape from New York*. Gee, I didn't know when I came to see a Flo & Eddie show that I would be hearing an entire performance of a movie soundtrack. Where the $@#& are Flo & Eddie?
Charles: See previous comment.

—

DUST BUNNIES (CD) by Howard Kaylan
Flo & Eddie involvement: Howard Kaylan—producer, vocals; Rick Howard—guitar; Robert "Cricket" Cohen—bass; David Forman—drums; Andy Cahan—producer, engineer, programming, keyboards, background vocals
Additional personnel: Jim Mitchell, Randy Mitchell—engineers; Billy Bob Thornton—vocals on "Music"
Recording dates: 2005 at the Dungeon in Billy Bob Thornton's House, Beverly Hills, California; Threshold Sound, Santa Monica, California; Footprint Audio Services, Brooklyn, New York; Andy's House, Van Nuys, California
Highest chart position: Did not chart
Original release date: March 21, 2006

Snowblind
Easy Street
Eloise
Love Songs in the Night
What's That Got to Do With Me
A Young Girl
Have I the Right
Two By Two
Pleasant Street
Music

If memory serves, the only reason this album exists is that Mark Volman was no longer living in the vicinity of Los Angeles where this was recorded in actor Billy Bob Thornton's home studio. Volman now makes Nashville his home and only joined up with Kaylan for their Happy Together tours. Kaylan retired from stage performing in 2018 and was replaced by Ron Dante of Archies fame. Volman was the co-writer of the track "Easy Street."

As for the album itself, it is mostly excellent except for the inferior singing on "Have I the Right" and Billy Bob Thorton's narration on "Music".

—

EASY STREET (Mark Volman, Howard Kaylan) by Howard Kaylan
Flo & Eddie involvement: Howard Kaylan—producer, vocals; Rick Howard—guitar; Robert "Cricket" Cohen—bass; David Forman—drums; Andy Cahan—producer, engineer, programming, keyboards, background vocals
Additional personnel: Jim Mitchell, Randy Mitchell—engineers
Recording dates: 2005 at the Dungeon in Billy Bob Thornton's House, Beverly Hills, California; Threshold Sound, Santa Monica, California; Footprint Audio Services, Brooklyn, New York; Andy's House, Van Nuys, California
Highest chart position: Did not chart from *Dust Bunnies*
Original release date: March 21, 2006

Photo: Daniel Coston

Mark: Another autobiographical song from Mark and Howard. Even though Howard was trying to sing only covers of songs that he felt that The Turtles and Flo & Eddie ignored, he probably felt obligated to give his longtime buddy a nod and a few bucks while doing his first completely solo project. It IS a good tune, and since Flo & Eddie were probably not going to get around to doing another studio album anytime soon, this was probably as good a place to do this, and Howard gives it his all.
Charles: "Easy Street" showed up on "The Walking Dead," but that was a completely different song with the same title. This one is a great example of a Kaylan-written and Kaylan-sung pop-rocker, which should've been a hit. Really!

—

EDDIE, ARE YOU KIDDING? (Mark Volman, Howard Kaylan, Frank Zappa, John Seiter) by Flo & Eddie
Flo & Eddie involvement: Howard Kaylan—lead vocals; Mark Volman—vocals, guitar; Phil Reed—lead guitar; Erik Scott—bass; Andy Cahan—keyboards; Craig Krampf—drums
Additional personnel: Joe Wissert—producer; Alex Kazanegras—engineer; Tom Perry—Mixing Engineer, Hollywood Sound
Recording dates: 1975 at the Roxy Theatre by the Haji Mobile Facility and the Crossroads of the World, Hollywood, California
Highest chart position: Did not chart from *Illegal, Immoral and Fattening*

Original release date: December 1975
Significant other versions: The Mothers

Mark: Of the two released versions of this song, this one is the superior one due to years of playing it since the Zappa days have allowed it to improve it to this present state of multiple song and artist parodies, so much so that the copyright vultures came out and insisted that items like "My Sweet Lord" needed their own track listing by the time the CD version of this album came out. I'm sure George Harrison wouldn't care and, in fact, was probably amused by the ribbing of his voice from his then-recent *Dark Horse* tour. At least I think he was. The Beatles and The Turtles always seemed to have this weird relationship, except maybe Ringo who seemed to get along with everyone. A brief snippet of this appears as part of "Medley #2" on *The History of Flo & Eddie and The Turtles.*

Charles: Apparently, there was a television commercial where somebody named "Eddie" promised suits to anyone on sale for fifty bucks. Frank Zappa and our boys go on a tangent asking him if he and his team of tailors can indeed come through with their wardrobe promise. Anything could be a song, and this is further proof. It's all typical (or, in the case of Frank Zappa, atypical!) zaniness and perceivably avant-garde song-making. A keen ear can hear the reference to The Crests' "Sixteen Candles" in the final bit of the composition where they sing the words "Sixty Tailors."

—

ELENORE (Howard Kaylan, The Turtles) by Flo & Eddie
Flo & Eddie involvement: Howard Kaylan—producer, vocals; Mark Volman—producer, vocals, guitars; Phil Reed—lead guitar; Andy Cahan—keyboards; Erik Scott—bass; Craig Krampf—drums
Additional personnel: Ron Nevison—producer, recorder, mixer; Skip Taylor—producer; Alan MacMillan—strings and horns arranger; Rick Smith, Eric Schilling, Cathy Callan—assistants
Recording dates: 1976 at the Record Plant, Sausalito and Los Angeles, California
Highest chart position: Did not chart; Did not chart from *Moving Targets*
Original release date: October 1976 for album; November 1976 for single
Significant other versions: The Turtles, Ivo Heller, Gianni Morandi, Wenzday, Me First and the Gimme Gimmes, Dean Torrence, Las Grecas

Mark: Regarding the Flo & Eddie version, I suppose Flo & Eddie felt that lightning might strike twice if they just re-recorded one of The Turtles' biggest hits. Again, they were wrong about this song and it duly flopped just like all of the other Flo & Eddie singles from 1972-1976. It's too bad, but it also isn't that remarkably different from The Turtles' version, so it was kind of an exercise in futility to re-record it. According to producer Ron Nevison, it was Columbia Records that insisted on the remake in order to make Flo & Eddie more "user friendly." Personally, I think it was a mistake to have them redo such a well-known hit. They should have tackled a lesser-known song or not bothered. It also seems much too fast this time out.

Flo & Eddie sang a 1991 live version introduced by Mark that appeared on *The Turtles Featuring Flo & Eddie Captured Live.*

Charles: With the best use of the word "etcetera" since *The King and I*, "Elenore" burst onto the charts with an infectious sound that holds up and sounds fresh decades later. From the first drum beat until the epic ending, this song was the perfect single. It was moody, well-paced, and with clever lyrics, including rhyming "groovy" and "movie." One would find it surprising that it wasn't number one on the charts—until you realize that on November 2nd, 1968 two Apple releases were at the top of the charts—"Those Were the Days" by Mary Hopkin was #2 and some song by a group called The Beatles, "Hey Jude," was #1. "Elenore" gee I think you're still swell!

—

ELOISE (Paul Ryan) by Howard Kaylan
Flo & Eddie involvement: Howard Kaylan—producer, vocals; Rick Howard—guitar; Robert "Cricket" Cohen—bass; David Forman—drums; Andy Cahan—producer, engineer, programming, keyboards, background vocals
Additional personnel: Jim Mitchell, Randy Mitchell—engineers
Recording dates: 2005 at the Dungeon in Billy Bob Thornton's House, Beverly Hills, California; Threshold Sound, Santa Monica, California; Footprint Audio Services, Brooklyn, New York; Andy's House, Van Nuys, California
Highest chart position: Did not chart from *Dust Bunnies*
Original release date: March 21, 2006
Significant other versions: Barry Ryan, The Damned

Photo: Daniel Coston

Mark: Kaylan's version of "Eloise" packs a punch, is one of the best songs on *Dust Bunnies*, and really shows his range as a singer. The Damned's version is still better as it is sung with much more gruffness, so if they knocked it out of the park, Howard at least rounded the bases from an RBI. The instrumentation is great, too! I especially love the dreamy middle section and the Beach Boys throwback. If singles were still being made, this would have been a great one!

Charles: Love the piano and vocal intro. Actually, I love everything about this song—for the first two minutes or so. It wanders off, but elegantly, and gets back on track at three and a half minutes. "My Eloise-a, I'd love to please her" is just brilliant and pure Turtles. If anyone you know questions the talent behind The Turtles, play them this song.

—

ESCAPE FROM NEW YORK (John Carpenter) by Flo & Eddie
Flo & Eddie involvement: Howard Kaylan—executive producer, vocals, saxophone; Mark Volman—executive producer, vocals, guitar; Joe Stefko—producer, drums; David Nelson—guitar, background vocals; Chris Apostle—keyboards, background vocals; Donnie Kisselbach—bass, vocals; Richie Cannata—sax, clarinet, background vocals

Photo: Daniel Coston

Additional personnel: Denny McNerney—recording, assembling, mastering
Recording dates: December 1984 at the Bottom Line, New York, New York
Highest chart position: Did not chart from *New York "Times" 1979-1994 Live at The Bottom Line*
Original release date: October 20, 2009
Significant other versions: *Escape from New York Soundtrack*

Mark: This is the theme song of John Carpenter's *Escape from New York* played by the band this time instead of a prerecorded track playing over the loudspeakers. I'm sure this played better visually and was one of those "had to be there" moments.
Charles: Unabashed plug: Fans of John (*Halloween*) Carpenter please check out the book www.BookOfTop10HorrorLists.com.

—

EVERYONE'S COMING TO NEW YORK (Nick Castle) by Flo & Eddie
Flo & Eddie involvement: Howard Kaylan—executive producer, vocals, saxophone; Mark Volman—executive producer, vocals, guitar; Joe Stefko—producer, drums; David Nelson—guitar, background vocals; Chris Apostle—keyboards, background vocals; Donnie Kisselbach—bass, vocals; Richie Cannata—sax, clarinet, background vocals
Recording dates: December 1984 at the Bottom Line, New York, New York
Additional personnel: Denny McNerney—recording, assembling, mastering
Highest chart position: Did not chart from *New York "Times" 1979-1994 Live at The Bottom Line*
Original release date: October 20, 2009
Significant other versions: *Escape from New York Soundtrack*

Photo: Roger Dilernia

Mark: Flo & Eddie cover the song the prisoners sing from John Carpenter's *Escape from New York*. I'm going to have to watch this film again. I didn't remember it being so fun, but leave it to Flo & Eddie to find the humor in anything grim.
Charles: Sounding like a Broadway spoof of "Everything's Coming Up Roses," this belongs in a musical version of the John Carpenter classic film.

—

FAST CAR (Tracy Chapman) by Flo & Eddie
Flo & Eddie involvement: Howard Kaylan—executive producer, vocals, saxophone; Mark Volman—executive producer, vocals, guitar; Joe Stefko—producer, drums; David Nelson—guitar, background vocals; Chris Apostle—keyboards, background vocals; Donnie Kisselbach—bass, vocals; Richie Cannata—sax, clarinet, background vocals
Additional personnel: Denny McNerney—recording, assembling, mastering
Recording dates: December 28, 1988 at the Bottom Line, New York, New York
Highest chart position: Did not chart from *New York "Times" 1979-1994 Live at the Bottom Line*
Original release date: October 20, 2009
Significant other versions: Tracy Chapman

Photo: Roger Dilernia

Mark: Howard rambles on as the band plays the backing instrumental to Tracy Chapman's "Fast Car." They finally start singing it after he shuts up, but here it's reworked as "Fast Career." Funny!
Charles: Is there any band that gave us so many different musical styles? Oh yes, The Beatles. But is there any other band besides The Turtles who gave us so many musical styles and so much to laugh or, at least, smile about? I don't think so.

—

FEEL OLDER NOW (Howard Kaylan) by Flo & Eddie
Flo & Eddie involvement: Howard Kaylan—producer, vocals; Mark Volman—producer, vocals and guitar; Gary Rowles—lead guitar; Don Preston—keyboards; Jim Pons—bass; Aynsley Dunbar—drums
Additional personnel: Barry Keene—engineer
Recording dates: 1972 at Ike Turner's Bolic Sound, Inglewood, California
Highest chart position: Did not chart; #211 from *The Phlorescent Leech and Eddie*
Original release date: September 1972

Charles: A decent rocker with some unnecessary high-pitched vocal shrills thrown in. Nice drumming and some theatrical bits, but tough to listen to because of those shrill fills.
Mark: Read what I said about Mark and "Really Love" as this is the type of song more suited to Howard and how he likes to sing—a nice, hard rocker. What a contrast and what a great voice. You can tell the ex-Mothers preferred this type of song to play as well. I agree with Charles that the vocal screams weren't really necessary to "sell" this song. The instrumentation should have. Flo & Eddie sang this live for that 1991 Turtles

recording that has been reissued so many times, but originally on *The Turtles Featuring Flo & Eddie Captured Live*. This live version has a lot more sax.

—

FLO & EDDIE (LP) by Flo & Eddie
Flo & Eddie involvement: Howard Kaylan—vocals; Mark Volman—vocals and guitar; Gary Rowles—lead guitar; John Herron—keyboards; Jim Pons—bass; Aynsley Dunbar—drums
Additional personnel: Bob Ezrin—producer, piano on "Afterglow" and "Marmendy Mill"; Jack Douglas, Shelly Yokus—engineers; John Sebastian—vocals on "The Best Part of Breaking Up;" Steve Hunter—guitar on "If We Only Had the Time," "Afterglow" and "Another Pop Star's Life," Dick Wagner—guitar on "Marmendy Mill;" Steve Madaio—trumpet on "You're a Lady"
Recording dates: 1973 at Sunset Sound, Paramount, Los Angeles, California; and The Record Plant, New York, New York
Highest chart position: Did not chart
Original release date: June 1973

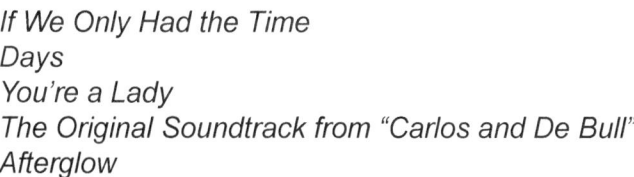

If We Only Had the Time
Days
You're a Lady
The Original Soundtrack from "Carlos and De Bull"
Afterglow

The Best Part of Breaking Up
The Sanzini Brothers (spoken word)
Another Pop Star's Life
Just Another Town
Marmendy Mill

Flo & Eddie's second solo go 'round was a little looser than the first with much more humor, and as such, is a very uneven affair. Unreleased Turtles leftovers "If We Only Had the Time" and "Marmendy Mill" from the aborted *Shell Shock* album make their formal debuts here. There is also a cover of The Kinks' "Days" thrown in for good measure. When it finally was released to CD, it was paired up with 1972's *The Phlorescent Leech and Eddie*. Somewhere between these two albums, a truly excellent album exists.

—

***FLO & EDDIE BY THE FIRESIDE* RADIO THEME** and **CLOSING THEME** (Mark Volman, Howard Kaylan) by Flo & Eddie
Flo & Eddie involvement: Howard Kaylan—vocals; Mark Volman—vocals, guitar
Additional personnel: Shadoe Stevens—vocals, engineer
Recording dates: 1973
Highest chart position: Did not chart from *The History of Flo & Eddie and The Turtles*
Original release date: 1973 for radio; 1983 for album

A nice sounding theme that seems to borrow a little from "Cheap" tune wise, not lyric wise, tune wise. This was used on one of their many radio series.

—

FLO & EDDIE MEET THE WOLFMAN (Wolfman Jack, Mark Volman, Howard Kaylan) by Flo & Eddie
Flo & Eddie involvement: Howard Kaylan—dialogue; Mark Volman—dialogue; Wolfman Jack—interviewer
Additional personnel: Bob Ezrin—producer
Recording dates: 1973
Highest chart position: Did not chart
Original release date: February 1973

Mark: This is a two-sided promotional only release. On Side A, DJ Wolfman Jack (1938-1995, real name: Robert Weston Smith) is introduced by his own theme as are Flo & Eddie by their theme. The Wolfman interviews Mark and Howard where they reveal that they met in 1962 and go through their history in a semi-comical fashion. They sing "It Ain't Me, Babe,"

"You Baby," and "Let Me Be" a capella. There's a lot of giggling going on. Side B features "Carlos and De Bull" and "Afterglow" and a little more of the interviews. A brief excerpt of the interview appears on *The History of Flo & Eddie and The Turtles* in 1983.
Charles: Folks who didn't know Wolfman Jack certainly were exposed to him in the movie *American Graffiti*. He was as big as any DJ at the time, and "Clap for the Wolfman" by the Guess Who came out at about the same time. Written by Burton Cummings, Bill Wallace, and Kurt Winter in 1973-74 and released in 1974, it hit #8 on the Billboard charts, but Flo & Eddie's Wolfman Jack project was an odd promo-only release, never intended as anything beyond that. A great novelty collectible for completists nonetheless.

FLO & EDDIE SHOW, THE (Marc Bolan, Mark Volman, Howard Kaylan) by Flo & Eddie
Flo & Eddie involvement: Howard Kaylan and Mark Volman—vocals
Additional personnel: Marc Bolan—vocals, guitar
Recording dates: 1973
Highest chart position: Did not chart from *The History of Flo & Eddie and The Turtles*
Original release date: 1973 for radio; 1983 for album

Photo: Daniel Coston

Mark: T. Rex's Marc Bolan drops by the radio show to sing his version of "The Flo & Eddie Show Theme."
Charles: Why not? Howard and Mark V sang on Marc B, and he returned the favor.

—

FLO & EDDIE THEME (Mark Volman and Howard Kaylan) by Flo & Eddie
Flo & Eddie involvement: Howard Kaylan—producer, vocals; Mark Volman—producer, vocals and guitar; Gary Rowles—lead guitar; Don Preston—keyboards; Jim Pons —bass; Aynsley Dunbar—drums
Additional personnel: Barry Keene—engineer
Recording dates: 1972 at Ike Turner's Bolic Sound, Inglewood, California
Highest chart position: #211 from *The Phlorescent Leech and Eddie*
Original release date: September 1972

Mark: According to the liner notes of *The Phlorescent Leech and Eddie* CD version, Mark and Howard wanted to release this as a new Turtles album. Reprise Records said no, stating that their recent Zappa status was more important and current. I probably would have opted for The Turtles, but hindsight is always 20/20. In any case, if the album was released as a Turtles album, it probably would have had a different title and it definitely wouldn't have had this song on it.

As for the song itself, after a cough and someone saying "Pete Townshend," Mark introduces Howard and then Howard in turn introduces Mark. Simple. Then, a chorus of thousands "hope you're ready for Flo & Eddie." Are we?

Charles: We're always ready for Flo and Eddie! This is more of a jingle than a song, and it would have served well for the lead-in to a TV show starring Flo and Eddie. Why didn't they have a network television musical comedy variety show a la Sonny & Cher or The Hudson Brothers? I would've watched it!

—

FLO & EDDY INTERVIEW WITH BARRY MANN
(LP) by Flo & Eddie
Flo & Eddie involvement: Howard Kaylan, Mark Volman
Additional personnel: Barry Mann
Recording dates: 1975
Highest chart position: Did not chart
Original release date: June 9, 1975

This is a promotional only interview album. Eddie has been misspelled as "Eddy." The music track listing has been omitted as there are no Turtles-related tracks on the records, just songs by Mann and other songs by The Crystals, Paul Petersen, Gene Pitney, The Vogues, The Animals, The Righteous Brothers, Tony Orlando, and other artists.

—

GERSHWIN (George Gershwin) by Flo & Eddie
Flo & Eddie involvement: Howard Kaylan—executive producer, vocals, saxophone; Mark Volman—executive producer, vocals, guitar; Joe Stefko—producer, drums, Vanna White; David Nelson—guitar, background vocals; Peter Zale—keyboards, background vocals; Mike Visceglia—bass, background vocals; Richie Cannata—sax, clarinet, background vocals
Additional personnel: Denny McNerney—recording, assembling, mastering
Recording dates: December 1986 at the Bottom Line, New York, New York
Highest chart position: Did not chart from *New York "Times" 1979-1994 Live at The Bottom Line*
Original release date: October 20, 2009

Photo: Roger Dilernia

Mark: After a "Rhapsody in Blue" introduction, Howard does his best Dashiel Hammett or some other narrative writer impersonation with commentary about New York that starts again and again with multiple "Chapter Ones." "Strike Up the Band" sneaks in there, too. It's not particularly funny, but the piano playing is nice. "Drugs" gets a big cheer multiple times too, so we know where this audience is at.

Charles: I just want to do a shout-out to musician Richie Cannata, who is on this track. He is a fine keyboardist, but he's most notable for being a saxophonist, which he was in Billy Joel's band along with drummer Liberty DeVitto. Liberty and Richie still tour together in a great band called The Lords of 42nd Street.

—

GET CRAZY (film and soundtrack)
Flo & Eddie involvement: Howard Kaylan—vocals; Mark Volman—vocals, guitars; Phil Reed—lead guitar; Andy Cahan—keyboards; Erik Scott—bass; Craig Krampf—drums
Additional personnel: Malcolm McDowell as Reggie Wanker; Allen Garfield as Max Wolfe (credited as Allen Goorwitz); Daniel Stern as Neil Allen; Gail Edwards as Willy Loman; Miles Chapin as Sammy Fox; Ed Begley Jr. as Colin Beverly; Stacey Nelkin as Susie Allen; Bill Henderson as King Blues; Lou Reed as Auden; Howard Kaylan as Captain Cloud; Lori Eastside as Nada; Lee Ving as Piggy; John Densmore as Toad; Anna Bjorn as Countess Chantamina; Robert Picardo as Connell O'Connell; Bobby Sherman as Mark; Fabian Forte as Marv; Franklyn Ajaye as Cool; Paul Bartel as Dr. Carver; Dan Frischman as Joey; Mary Woronov as Violetta; Clint Howard as the Head Usher; Denise Galik as Nurse Gwen; Linnea Quigley as Groupie; Jackie Joseph as Susie's Mom; Dick Miller as Susie's Dad; Chuck Hanson as Savage Beast; Susan Saiger as Buffy; Barry Diamond as Stagehand
Original release date: August 5, 1983

Photo: Roger Dilernia

Yet another sex, drugs, and rock and roll comedy, this one starred Howard Kaylan along with a few other aging rock and pop stars such as Lou Reed, John Densmore, Bobby Sherman, and Fabian Forte. It's not a very good film but Howard does sing "Auld Lang Syne" to ring in 1983. "Auld Lang Syne," "Metal Guru," and "Walking in the Clouds" appear in the film, but only "Auld Lang Syne" appears on the *Get Crazy Soundtrack*.

—

GET IT ON (BANG A GONG) aka **BANG A GONG (GET IT ON)** (Marc Bolan) by Flo & Eddie
Flo & Eddie involvement: Howard Kaylan—lead vocals; Mark Volman—vocals, guitar; Phil Reed—lead guitar; Erik Scott—bass; Andy Cahan—keyboards; Craig Krampf—drums
Additional personnel: Joe Wissert—producer; Alex Kazanegras—engineer; Tom Perry—Mixing Engineer, Hollywood Sound

Recording dates: 1975 at the Roxy Theatre by the Haji Mobile Facility and the Crossroads of the World, Hollywood, California
Highest chart position: Did not chart from *Illegal, Immoral and Fattening*
Original release date: December 1975
Significant other versions: T. Rex, Power Station, Blondie, U2 with Elton John, Witch Queen, Michael Des Barres, Bus Stop

Mark: Mark and Howard actually sang backup vocals on the original "Get it On" by T. Rex, so it's only natural that they would send it up whenever they performed in concert, and they did in the interlude of "Kama Sutra Time."

Charles: Marc Bolan, not to be confused with Mark Volman, and his T. Rex, were mega-stars everywhere except the U.S. "Bang a Gong/Get it On" was a monster hit here and worldwide, and few realized our boys sang back-up vocals. This is their take on the rock classic.

—

GETAWAY (BACK TO L.A.) (Mark Volman, Howard Kaylan) by Flo & Eddie
Flo & Eddie involvement: Howard Kaylan—producer, vocals; Mark Volman—producer, vocals, guitar; Billy Steele—guitar; Andy Cahan—keyboards; Erik Scott—bass; Craig Krampf—drums, bells
Additional personnel: Howard Wolen—engineer
Recording dates: 1977 at Studio Sound Recorders, Los Angeles, California
Highest chart position: Did not chart from *The History of Flo & Eddie and The Turtles*
Original release date: 1978 for film *Texas Detour*; 1983 for album

Photo: Roger Dilernia

Mark: A nice, bouncy song definitely inspired by the likes of The Beach Boys and Bruce Springsteen. It has kind of a "Born to Run" vibe to it. This was a solid Flo & Eddie tune that would be considered totally lost if Rhino hadn't seen fit to include it on a couple of Flo & Eddie compilations.

Charles: Fun is in, it's no sin, it's that time again. How can I breakaway from... Sorry about that—it's only the intro that is reminiscent of those Beach Boys. The rest is a guitar-driven, drum-pounding ode to hitting the road. Breaking down ceilings, smashing down the walls, and doing whatever necessary not to just get away as they did in the mid-1960s (see previous song), but to get away to L.A. That's Los Angeles, not Lower Ansonia (CT).

—

GIRLS, GIRLS, GIRLS (Jerry Leiber, Mike Stoller) **/ ROCK-A-HULA BABY** (Ben Weisman, Fred Wise, Dolores Fuller) **/ GO EAST YOUNG MAN** (Bernie Baum, Bill Giant, Florence Kaye) **/ HARUM HOLIDAY** (Peter Andreoli, Vince Poncia) **/ GIRLS REPRISE** (Jerry Leiber, Mike Stoller) by Flo & Eddie

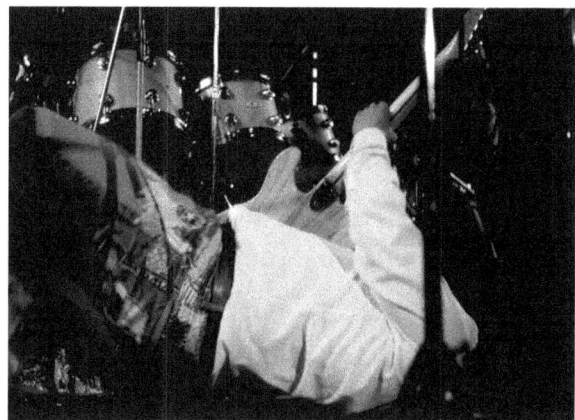

Photo: Roger Dilernia

Flo & Eddie involvement: Howard Kaylan—executive producer, vocals, saxophone; Mark Volman—executive producer, vocals, guitar; Joe Stefko—producer, drums; David Nelson—guitar, background vocals; Peter Zale—keyboards, background vocals; Mike Visceglia—bass, background vocals; Andrew Craig—lead vocals; Caroline Dow—background vocals; Lisa Miller—background vocals

Additional personnel: Denny McNerney—recording, assembling, mastering
Recording dates: December 28-29, 1985 at the Bottom Line, New York, New York
Highest chart position: Did not chart from *New York "Times" 1979-1994 Live at The Bottom Line*
Original release date: October 20, 2009
Significant other versions: Elvis Presley

Mark: Flo & Eddie's tribute to Elvis done between choruses of "Nikki Hoi" by singing favorites from some of his movies. Leave it to them to sing some of the more campy songs in Elvis' oeuvre, but it wouldn't be Flo & Eddie if they did the Elvis standards. I'm surprised they didn't even dig deeper and sing things like "Clambake" or "Yoga is as Yoga Does" or even "There's No Room to Rumba in a Sports Car."

"Go East Young Man" was sung by drummer Joe Stefko as Mark stepped behind the drums.

Charles: We know how much The Turtles loved and respected The Beatles, and you could hear The Beach Boys' influence through the years. It's no secret that many of their songs have the imprint of The Beatles Boys stamped right on them. They certainly honored and were influenced by their heroes. Here is a case where they get to pay tribute to the King. What's commendable is that they don't bother with any of the expected hits (though it would've been a hoot to hear them do "Heartbreak Hotel," "Are You Lonesome Tonight?" or, especially, "Promised Land"). Instead, it's a bevy of B-movie bounty from the Elvis Presley filmography, where often the songs were worth the price of admission and a small bucket of popcorn. Thank you... thank you very much.

—

GOODBYE SURPRISE (Garry Bonner, Alan Gordon) by Flo & Eddie
Flo & Eddie involvement: Howard Kaylan—producer, vocals; Mark Volman—producer, vocals and guitar; Gary Rowles—lead guitar; Don Preston—keyboards; Jim Pons—bass; Aynsley Dunbar—drums
Additional personnel: Barry Keene—engineer
Recording dates: 1972 at Ike Turner's Bolic Sound, Inglewood, California
Highest chart position: Did not chart; B-side to "Radio Spot for The Phlorescent Leech and Eddie;" #211 from *The Phlorescent Leech and Eddie*
Original release date: September 1972
Significant other versions: The Turtles

Charles: The Turtles' version is a great song which somehow doesn't put it all together The right way. It's like a soup (not turtle) with all the tasty ingredients, but when you pour it in your bowl it just doesn't taste as good as it should. Granted it's good, but it should be great.

Flo & Eddie's version, only three years later, is a lot better, but still missing something. They should've recorded a new version every three years. By now, they would've come up with a definitive, well-produced, recording of "Goodbye Surprise" and it probably wouldn't have been a hit anyway.

Mark: I agree with Charles 100%. The Turtles and Flo & Eddie tried this twice and there is STILL something missing. It may be that this is not a great tune! The version on the B-side of the "Radio Spot" seems to be a different mix than what was actually released. This may be the problem. Too much tinkering. Flo & Eddie did perform it live later on and this seems to be the more definitive version. The Turtles' version would have been on their aborted *Shell Shock*.

Flo & Eddie sang a 1991 live version with an Olympic fanfare intro that appeared on *The Turtles Featuring Flo & Eddie Captured Live*.

—

GUNS (Jim Pons, Mark Volman, Howard Kaylan) by Flo & Eddie
Flo & Eddie involvement: Howard Kaylan—producer, vocals; Mark Volman—producer, vocals, guitars; Phil Reed—lead guitar; Andy Cahan—keyboards; Erik Scott—bass; Craig Krampf—drums
Additional personnel: Ron Nevison—producer, recorder, mixer; Skip Taylor—producer; Alan MacMillan—strings and horns arranger; Rick Smith, Eric Schilling, Cathy Callan—assistants; Graeme "Shirley" Strachan—chorus vocals
Recording dates: 1976 at the Record Plant, Sausalito and Los Angeles, California
Highest chart position: Did not chart from *Moving Targets*
Original release date: October 1976

Mark: Hey, it's a happy-go-lucky song about guns. Something you could easily do in the 1970s, not so easily in the 2020s. This appears to be the final song to be composed by three-fifths of the original Turtles. Pons does not appear on this record as he was well-situated by this time, working for the New York Jets. Howard holds a very long note at the end to great effect.

Charles: After a quick Lou Christie-esque falsetto intro, this one quickly comes out like guns ablazin' with jumpy instrumentation and matching bouncy vocals. There's a funky guitar that "shoots" in at times, and the piano playing is top-notch, with a hint of a "Let's Spend the Night Together" riff. Whether you are in favor of gun control or not, it's hard not to be in favor of Flo & Eddie's "Guns." Rat-tat-tat.

—

***HALLOWEEN* INTRO/*HALLOWEEN* THEME**
(Cody Carpenter, Daniel Davies, John Carpenter) by Flo & Eddie
Flo & Eddie involvement: Howard Kaylan—executive producer, vocals, saxophone; Mark Volman—executive producer, vocals, guitar; Joe Stefko—producer, drums; David Nelson—guitar, background vocals; Peter Zale—keyboards, background vocals; Mike Visceglia—bass, background vocals; Andrew Craig—Monster vocals; Caroline Dow—background vocals; Lisa Miller—background vocals
Additional personnel: Denny McNerney—recording, assembling, mastering
Recording dates: December 28-29, 1985 at the Bottom Line, New York, New York
Highest chart position: Did not chart from *New York "Times" 1979-1994 Live at The Bottom Line*
Original release date: October 20, 2009
Significant other versions: *Halloween*

Photo: Roger Dilernia

Mark: Like disc one's *Escape From New York* tracks, this disc starts off with sound bites from John Carpenter's original *Halloween* from 1978. This leads directly into the theme. It's all a ploy to delay Flo & Eddie's entrance.
Charles: Any excuse to bring up the Halloween theme makes me happy, so it's time for more personal plugs. If you're even in Connecticut for Halloween, check out www.TheHauntedTrolley.com. If you want to take a vampire vacation to Transylvania (really!) and spend Halloween in Dracula's Castle, visit www.DracTours.com. My prior books fit the genre, so check out www.BookOfTop10HorrorLists.com and for *True Ghost Stories Of Connecticut* visit www.ParanormalConnecticut.com. Thank you, Mark, for letting me go on that terror tangent. Okay, back to The Turtles…

HAPPY TOGETHER (Garry Bonner, Alan Gordon) by Flo & Eddie
Flo & Eddie involvement: Mark Volman, Howard Kaylan—vocals; Earl "Chinna" Smith—lead guitar, rhythm guitar; Dean Fraser, Enroy "Tenor" Grant—saxophones; Walt Fowler—trombone; Augustus Pablo—organ, piano; Leslie "Professor" Butler—piano, organ; Phil Ramocon—Fender Rhodes; Aston "Family Man" Barrett—bass; Carlton "Santa" Davis—drums; Uziah "Sticky" Thompson—percussion; The Brackenridge Brothers—trumpets; Nambo—trombone

Photo: Roger Dilernia

Additional personnel: Earl "Chinna" Smith—producer; Errol Brown—producer, recorder, mixer; Warren Smith, Michael "Eppy" Epstein—executive producers; "Sticko" Warren Weinberg, Richard Kaplan—engineers
Recording dates: 1981 at Tuff Gong Studios, Kingston, Jamaica and Indigo Ranch, Malibu, California
Highest chart position: Did not chart from *Rock Steady with Flo & Eddie*
Original release date: 1981
Significant other versions: The Turtles, The Mothers, The Nylons, Hugo Montenegro, Tony Orlando and Dawn, T.G. Sheppard, Captain & Tennille, Mel Torme, The Piano Guys, Weezer, Petula Clark, Donny Osmond, Frank Zappa and the Mothers, Frank Alamo, Prima Vera, B.E. Taylor, Filter, Dmitri Vegas & Like Mike, Bassjackers

Mark: The Flo & Eddie version is a reggae version of The Turtles' biggest hit. They do an amazing job with it, as while it is an obvious choice for a reggae version, it isn't necessarily a song that would actually lend itself to a reggae version. Astonishingly, it succeeds quite well and is a highlight of the album.

Flo & Eddie sang a non-reggae 1991 live version that appeared on *The Turtles Featuring Flo & Eddie Captured Live* where he changes the lyrics to "invest three dimes" and "lose my minds" and namedrops Milli Vanilli.

Charles: Cyndi Lauper did a similar reggae take on her biggest hit "Girls Just Want to Have Fun," which isn't the classic the original is, but it's damn good and fun in its own right. Same with this version.

—

HARVEY SCHIFFLER (Mark Volman, Howard Kaylan) by Flo & Eddie
Flo & Eddie involvement: Howard Kaylan—executive producer, vocals, saxophone; Mark Volman—executive producer, vocals, guitar; Joe Stefko—producer, drums; Gus Weiland—guitar, background vocals; Peter Zale—keyboards, background vocals; Mike Visceglia—bass, background vocals; Andrew Craig—Harvey Schiffler, AM-FM guy
Additional personnel: Denny McNerney—recording, assembling, mastering
Recording dates: December 1982 at the Bottom Line, New York, New York
Highest chart position: Did not chart from *New York "Times" 1979-1994 Live at The Bottom Line*

Photo: Roger Dilernia

Original release date: October 20, 2009

Mark: Andrew Craig as DJ Harvey Schiffler introduces The Crossfires at the Westchester High Sock Hop and they lead into a live rendition of "Silver Bullet." Very nostalgic for those who weren't there.
Charles: This makes me want to produce a Crossfires convention!

—

HAVE I THE RIGHT (Ken Howard, Alan Blaikley) by Howard Kaylan
Flo & Eddie involvement: Howard Kaylan—producer, vocals; Rick Howard—guitar; Robert "Cricket" Cohen—bass; David Forman—drums; Andy Cahan—producer, engineer, programming, keyboards, background vocals
Additional personnel: Jim Mitchell, Randy Mitchell—engineers
Recording dates: 2005 at the Dungeon in Billy Bob Thornton's House, Beverly Hills, California; Threshold Sound, Santa Monica, California; Footprint Audio Services, Brooklyn, New York; Andy's House, Van Nuys, California
Highest chart position: Did not chart from *Dust Bunnies*
Original release date: March 21, 2006
Significant other versions: The Honeycombs, Dead End Kids

Photo: Daniel Coston

Mark: One of the weaker songs on the album only because Howard sings it in such a breathy way at times that he sounds like he has emphysema, and he sounds like he's straining his voice in other parts. Once he stops doing this, the song begins to cook. Perhaps he should have chosen to sing it in a lower key? P.S. I always thought that this song was called "Come Right Back." Silly me.
Charles: "Have I The Right" by The Honeycombs is one of those one-hit wonders that I forget about when I play the one-hit wonder game. It's such a cool tune and Howard doesn't give up the "cool" even by slowing it down. The chorus is powerful, and he sings it great. Nice instrumental break too.

—

HELMUT (ROW THE BOAT ASHORE) (Salz-Pfeffer) by Checkpoint Charlie
Flo & Eddie involvement: Howard Kaylan and Mark Volman as M. Salz and H. Pfeffer—producer, vocals
Additional personnel: Andy Cahan—keyboards; Johann Moier, Peter Jebsen
Recording dates: 1982 at Herb Cohen's studio complex
Highest chart position: Did not chart from *Checkpoint Charlie*
Original release date: 1982

Photo: Roger Dilernia

Mark: Yet another of those "great" Checkpoint Charlie tracks. At least there's only four.
Charles: Warning: This Record Plays Inside Out. I would give it some points if it were Checkpoint Charles instead of Checkpoint Charlie.

—

HISTORY OF FLO & EDDIE AND THE TURTLES, THE (compilation) by The Crossfires, The Turtles, Flo & Eddie
Flo & Eddie involvement: See individual Crossfires, Turtles and Flo & Eddie tracks.
Additional personnel: See individual Crossfires, Turtles and Flo & Eddie tracks.
Recording dates: 1963 - 1983
Highest chart position: Did not chart
Original release date: 1983

Westchester High School Alma Mater
Silver Bullet
I Get Out of Breath
Outside Chance
Grim Reaper of Love
Battle of the Bands Album Commercial
Lady-O
Goodbye Surprise (Turtles version)
Pepsi Ad (unlisted bonus track)
Turtles Hits Medley: It Ain't Me Babe / You Baby / Happy Together / She'd Rather Be With Me / Elenore (live 1969)

Happy Together (live 1967 BBC radio)
Turtle Soup Radio Spot (unlisted bonus track)
There You Sit Lonely
We Ain't Gonna Party No More
Flo & Eddie Theme

Feel Older Now
Nikki Hoi
I've Been Born Again

Best Part of Breaking Up
Another Pop Star's Life
Just Another Town
Flo & Eddie Meet the Wolfman (excerpt) (unlisted bonus track)
Afterglow
You're a Lady
Marmendy Mill

Flo & Eddie Scandinavian Intro (unlisted bonus track)
Illegal, Immoral and Fattening
Rebecca
Let Me Make Love to You
Mama, Open Up
Keep it Warm
Flo & Eddie German Intro (unlisted bonus track)
Moving Targets

Flo & Eddie By the Fireside Radio Theme
Albert Brooks (unlisted bonus track)
The Big Showdown
Alice Cooper (unlisted bonus track)
This Could Be the Day
Keith Moon (unlisted bonus track)
(You're Nothing But a) Good Duck
David Bowie (unlisted bonus track)
Medley #1: Stop / Stop! In the Name of Love / Shadow Dancing / The Butchers Are Back / Strawberry Shortcake Theme / Mystic Martha
Marc Bolan (unlisted bonus track)
Behind the Green Door and The Resurrection of Eve Ad (unlisted bonus track)
The Flo & Eddie Show

Ringo Starr (unlisted bonus track)
Getaway (Back to L.A.)
Iggy Pop (unlisted bonus track)
Livin' in a Jungle
Harry Nilsson (unlisted bonus track)
Youth in Asia
The Move Reunion—Rick Price, Roy Wood, Bev Bevan, Jeff Lynne (unlisted bonus track)
Medley #2: Louie Louie / Eddie, Are You Kidding? / Show Me the Way to Go Ohm / Champagne / Buzz Saw / The Sanzini Brothers (spoken word)
Lou Reed (unlisted bonus track)
Closing Theme

This 3-record LP set has a bunch of goodies that have never appeared on any other release, including clips from "The Flo & Eddie Show" with Ringo Starr and the reunited Move. It also has a decent comic book-sized history of The Turtles included with many rare photos.

—

HORROR MOVIE (Greg Macainsh) by Flo & Eddie
Flo & Eddie involvement: Howard Kaylan—executive producer, vocals, saxophone; Mark Volman—executive producer, vocals, guitar; Joe Stefko—producer, drums; David Nelson—guitar, background vocals; Peter Zale—keyboards, background vocals; Mike Visceglia—bass, background vocals; Andrew Craig—Monster vocals; Caroline Dow—background vocals; Lisa Miller—background vocals' Graeme "Shirley" Strachan—vocals
Additional personnel: Denny McNerney—recording, assembling, mastering
Recording dates: December 28-29, 1985 at the Bottom Line, New York, New York
Highest chart position: Did not chart from *New York "Times" 1979-1994 Live at The Bottom Line*
Original release date: October 20, 2009
Significant other versions: Skyhooks

Mark: A decent cover of the Skyhooks' song, albeit very short. I wish it were longer.
Charles: Horror movie??? Okay, I'll control myself. I had never heard the Skyhooks' version before but looked more into the Australian glam rock band from the '80s. I guess Howard and Mark liked some stuff (like Marc Bolan) that was lesser-known in the U.S., and sometimes did versions of them. This is a bit of a throw-away, but fairly faithful to the original.

—

HOT (Mark Volman, Howard Kaylan) by Flo & Eddie
Flo & Eddie involvement: Howard Kaylan—producer, vocals; Mark Volman—producer, vocals, guitars; Phil Reed—lead guitar; Andy Cahan—keyboards; Erik Scott—bass; Craig Krampf—drums
Additional personnel: Ron Nevison—producer, recorder, mixer; Skip Taylor—producer; Alan MacMillan—strings and horns arranger; Rick Smith, Eric Schilling, Cathy Callan—assistants; Donnie Dacus, Jeff Baxter—slide guitars
Recording dates: 1976 at the Record Plant, Sausalito and Los Angeles, California
Highest chart position: Did not chart; B-side to "Keep it Warm"; Did not chart from *Moving Targets*
Original release date: December 1976

Mark: This almost sounds like something The Who would have recorded at this time. Howard sings it with his usual gusto to bring it all home, and you can hear Mark harmonize well this time.
Charles: Don't even think of playing this in a set with their recording "Fire" with Frank Zappa (get it—"fire" and "hot?" Never mind, we'll have it edited out). Just a truly blazing and perfectly constructed pop/rock track with all the elements of a hit single. Play this one loud in the car with the windows rolled down. Then play it again. Why weren't more of their songs hits? Was it the label? Was it that they weren't interested in hits? Was there an anti-Turtle conspiracy? That's the book that needs to be written.

—

I BEEN BORN AGAIN aka **I'VE BEEN BORN AGAIN** (Mark Volman and Howard Kaylan) by Flo & Eddie
Flo & Eddie involvement: Howard Kaylan—producer, vocals; Mark Volman—producer, vocals and guitar; Gary Rowles—lead guitar; Don Preston—keyboards; Jim Pons—bass; Aynsley Dunbar—drums
Additional personnel: Barry Keene—engineer
Recording dates: 1972 at Ike Turner's Bolic Sound, Inglewood, California
Highest chart position: #211 from *The Phlorescent Leech and Eddie*
Original release date: September 1972

Mark: This is another autobiographical song by Mark and Howard as they comment on being "born again" by this thing called rock and roll. Being with Frank Zappa for two years permanently changed both their outlook and their style of music, making it much more complex than the Beatlesque type melodies they were used to turning out during their Turtles days. Basically, it's The Turtles all growed up. A snippet of this song was used on the "Radio Spot for *The Phlorescent Leech and Eddie*." It could have made a good single as it's very catchy. Crazy organ in the middle of the track.
Charles: "I Been Born Again" ain't exactly good grammar (thus the AKA), but who cares?! It's a musician's showcase, not a bubblegum single. Before you know it, Don Preston goes on a loony keyboard solo resurrection, in line with the title, followed by a similar lead guitar tangent by Gary Rowles. Sometimes you just gotta get it out of your system.

I HAPPEN TO LIKE NEW YORK (Cole Porter) by Flo & Eddie
Flo & Eddie involvement: Howard Kaylan—executive producer, vocals, saxophone; Mark Volman—executive producer, vocals, guitar; Joe Stefko—producer, drums; Tristan Avakian—guitar, background vocals; Donnie Kisselbach—bass, background vocals
Additional personnel: Denny McNerney—recording, assembling, mastering
Recording dates: December 1994 at the Bottom Line, New York, New York
Highest chart position: Did not chart from *New York "Times" 1979-1994 Live at The Bottom Line*
Original release date: October 20, 2009
Significant other versions: Bobby Short, Judy Garland, Caterina Valente, Liza Minelli

Mark: After a lengthy humorous introduction, Flo & Eddie sing this classic Cole Porter tune originally written for the play called *The New Yorkers*. Well, with a few lyrical changes about New York.

Charles: Mark and Howard sing Cole Porter. Yes they take some liberties with it (not Statue of Liberty's) but it's actually sweet. I happen to like it… and I would have loved a whole album of them having fun with standards.

—

I LOST MY HEART AT THE DRIVE-IN MOVIE (Jack Brooks, David Raksin) by Flo & Eddie
Flo & Eddie involvement: Howard Kaylan—executive producer, vocals, saxophone; Mark Volman—executive producer, vocals, guitar; Joe Stefko—producer, drums; Gus Weiland—guitar, background vocals; Peter Zale—keyboards, background vocals; Mike Visceglia—bass, background vocals; Andrew Craig—Harvey Schiffler, AM-FM guy
Additional personnel: Denny McNerney—recording, assembling, mastering
Recording dates: December 1982 at the Bottom Line, New York, New York
Highest chart position: Did not chart from *New York "Times" 1979-1994 Live at The Bottom Line*
Original release date: October 20, 2009
Significant other versions: Jerry Lewis

Mark: Comedic film star Jerry Lewis (1926-2017) originally sang this song in his 1964 film *The Patsy*.

Howard and Mark are fans of the comedy legend and loved to sneak in goofy songs like this into the mix in their Bottom Line shows.

Charles: Jerry Lewis as Stanley Belt doesn't exactly belt this one out, but you must see him mug the lip-sync in the film clip. We're here to not only review and comment, but also to educate, so let's tell you about another drive-in song you never heard of, and should: "When The Second Feature Starts" by a band called Blotto. Find it, then play the rest of the songs by Blotto, and tell me you're not a huge fan. They were another band, like our Turtles, who combined comedy with rock & roll. The problem was that they were simply too clever, and perhaps Mark is right that people just don't like mixing their rockin' music with laughs.

—

IF WE ONLY HAD THE TIME (Howard Kaylan, Mark Volman) by Flo & Eddie
Flo & Eddie involvement: Howard Kaylan—vocals; Mark Volman—vocals and guitar; Gary Rowles—lead guitar; John Herron—keyboards; Jim Pons—bass; Aynsley Dunbar—drums
Additional personnel: Bob Ezrin—producer; Jack Douglas, Shelly Yokus—engineers; Steve Hunter—guitar; Steve Madaio—trumpet
Recording dates: 1973 at Sunset Sound, Paramount, Los Angeles, California; and The Record Plant, New York, New York
Highest chart position: Single did not chart; B-side to "You're a Lady;" Did not chart from *Flo & Eddie*
Original release date: June 1973
Significant other versions: The Turtles

Mark: As I said over in The Turtles section, this Flo & Eddie version is the more superior version and it seems to be their attempt to make an *Abbey Road*-type medley. As Howard and Mark say in the CD reissue liner notes, they "actually spent money to make this one." This was originally planned for *Shell Shock*.

Charles: Another one of those charming tempo-twist arrangements that may or may not have originally been multiple songs (bets are on that it was two or three different compositions), there's so much going on that you have to listen two or three times to absorb it all. The highlight might be the falsetto call-back vocals at the beginning after the cool intro.

—

ILLEGAL, IMMORAL AND FATTENING (Howard Kaylan, Mark Volman) by Flo & Eddie
Flo & Eddie involvement: Howard Kaylan—lead vocals; Mark Volman—vocals, guitar; Phil Reed—lead guitar; Erik Scott—bass; Andy Cahan—keyboards; Craig Krampf—drums
Additional personnel: Joe Wissert—producer; Alex Kazanegras—engineer; Tom Perry—Mixing Engineer, Hollywood Sound
Recording dates: 1975 at the Roxy Theatre by the Haji Mobile Facility and the Crossroads of the World, Hollywood, California

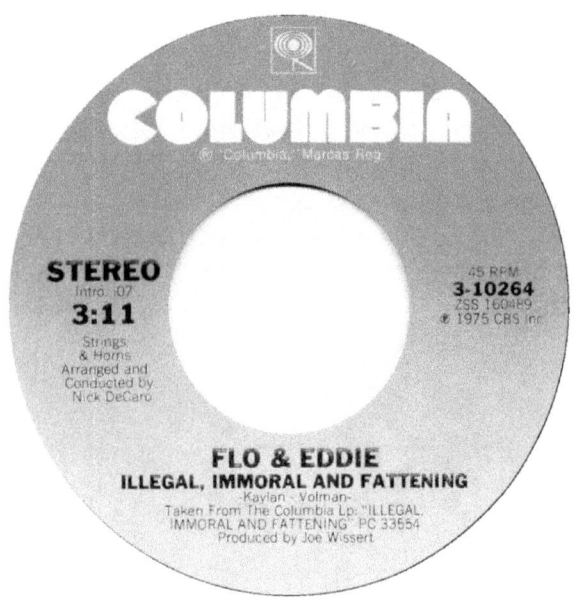

Highest chart position: Single did not chart; B-side to "Rebecca;" Did not chart from *Illegal, Immoral and Fattening*
Original release date: December 1975

Mark: This is a very hard-rocking sounding studio song that could have easily been covered by KISS or some similar big hair group of the '70s and '80s. If one of those groups had covered it, it probably would have had a darker and more sinister and serious tone. As it is, along with the goofy cover photo shoot of a topless Flo & Eddie adorning a celebrity scandal mag, it comes across as tongue in cheek.

Charles: The title of this rocker may have been autobiographical (wouldn't be the first time) but it shows Flo & Eddie at their mid-1970s' heavier extravagance. It's not heavy metal—the guys never really quite cross that bridge—but it's unquestionably hard rock that's equal to their peers at the time. Sometimes you just want to do a needle drop and let music aficionados guess the artist. Unless they know, they'd never guess it's "those guys from The Turtles."

—

ILLEGAL, IMMORAL AND FATTENING (LP) by Flo & Eddie
Flo & Eddie involvement: Howard Kaylan—lead vocals; Mark Volman—vocals, guitar; Phil Reed—lead guitar; Erik Scott—bass; Andy Cahan—keyboards; Craig Krampf—drums
Additional personnel: Joe Wissert—producer; Alex Kazanegras—engineer; Tom Perry—Mixing Engineer, Hollywood Sound; Dee Robb—engineer; Danny Kortchmar—guitar; Leland Sklar—bass; Ian Underwood—keyboards; Aynsley Dunbar—drums on "Let Me Make Love To You"
Recording dates: 1974 at Cherokee Studios, Los Angeles, California for "Let Me Make Love To You;" and 1975 at the Roxy Theatre by the Haji Mobile Facility and the Crossroads of the World, Hollywood, California
Highest chart position: Did not chart
Original release date: December 1975

Illegal, Immoral and Fattening
Rebecca
Kama Sutra Time (with *Bang a Gong (Get It On)*)

The Sanzini Brothers Return (with the Tibetan Memory Trick) (spoken word)
Livin' in the Jungle

Cheap
The Kung Fu Killer
Eddie, Are You Kidding?
The Pop Star Massage Unit (with *Jumpin' Jack Flash* and *My Sweet Lord*)
Let Me Make Love To You
There's No Business Like Show Business

Flo & Eddie's third album and first for Columbia Records. This album is mostly live, save for two studio songs that were released as singles: "Let Me Make Love to You" and "Rebecca," plus the title track and a studio cover of "There's No Business Like Show Business." This is my favorite of Flo & Eddie's albums due to the incredible ability of their band to just switch gears at the drop of a hat and start performing a spot on performance of someone famous in rock and roll be it George Harrison or Mick Jagger, and then just twist the knife just ever so slightly to make it even funnier.

—

IT NEVER HAPPENED (Mark Volman) by Flo & Eddie
Flo & Eddie involvement: Howard Kaylan—producer, vocals; Mark Volman—producer, vocals and guitar; Gary Rowles—lead guitar; Don Preston—keyboards; Jim Pons—bass; Aynsley Dunbar—drums
Additional personnel: Barry Keene—engineer
Recording dates: 1972 at Ike Turner's Bolic Sound, Inglewood, California
Highest chart position: #211 from *The Phlorescent Leech and Eddie*
Original release date: September 1972

Mark: Mark takes the lead on his own credited composition. Preston excels on the keyboards on this one with a nice honky-tonk sound. I like the pauses between verses. Very effective. Short and sweet.
Charles: Written and sung by Mark. Love when it breaks and comes back a-rockin! Reminds me of another song but for the first time in this book I can't think of what it reminds me of.

—

JUMPIN' JACK FLASH (Mick Jagger, Keith Richards) by Flo & Eddie
Flo & Eddie involvement: Howard Kaylan—lead vocals; Mark Volman—vocals, guitar; Phil Reed—lead guitar; Erik Scott—bass; Andy Cahan—keyboards; Craig Krampf—drums
Additional personnel: Joe Wissert—producer; Alex Kazanegras—engineer; Tom Perry—Mixing Engineer, Hollywood Sound

Recording dates: 1975 at the Roxy Theatre by the Haji Mobile Facility and the Crossroads of the World, Hollywood, California
Highest chart position: Did not chart from *Illegal, Immoral and Fattening*
Original release date: December 1975
Significant other versions: The Rolling Stones, Aretha Franklin, Thelma Houston, Alex Harvey, Ananda Shankar, Leon Russell, Peter Frampton, Johnny Winter, Dr. John, Ace Frehley, and Lita Ford

Mark: Two lines of the song are imitated and performed by Flo & Eddie in the midst of "The Pop Star Massage Unit,, which in itself is within "Eddie, Are You Kidding?" Confused? Most of us are, but that is the nature of a Flo & Eddie concert with many asides and quick one-off parodies and imitations.
Charles: ... it's a gas gas gas.

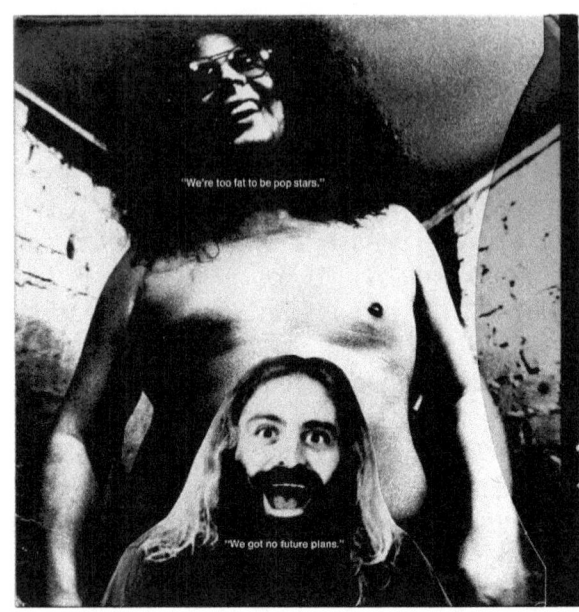

JUST ANOTHER TOWN (Howard Kaylan, Mark Volman) by Flo & Eddie
Flo & Eddie involvement: Howard Kaylan—vocals; Mark Volman—vocals and guitar; Gary Rowles—lead guitar; John Herron—keyboards; Jim Pons—bass; Aynsley Dunbar—drums
Additional personnel: Bob Ezrin—producer; Jack Douglas, Shelly Yokus—engineers
Recording dates: 1973 at Sunset Sound, Paramount, Los Angeles, California; and The Record Plant, New York, New York
Highest chart position: Did not chart from *Flo & Eddie*
Original release date: June 1973

Mark: The harshness of "Another Pop Star's Life" segues nicely into this much sweeter ode to touring, making it a double-shot medley of life on the road, sung very authentically by Mark Volman. Both songs are bittersweet and both pack a solid punch in the gut.

Charles: Mostly acoustic, the first third of the song is all guitars. When the vocals kick in, it's like a classic straight out of the band America's catalog. It may be just another town, but we visit there in what is a beautiful but sad reminder of the touring life of an artist.

JUST LIKE A RIVER (J. Gibson, S. Cole) by Flo & Eddie
Flo & Eddie involvement: Mark Volman, Howard Kaylan—vocals; Earl "Chinna" Smith—lead guitar, rhythm guitar; Dean Fraser, Enroy "Tenor" Grant—saxophones; Walt Fowler—trombone; Augustus Pablo—organ, piano; Leslie "Professor" Butler—piano, organ; Phil Ramocon—Fender Rhodes; Aston "Family Man" Barrett—bass; Carlton "Santa" Davis—drums; Uziah "Sticky" Thompson—percussion; The Brackenridge Brothers—trumpets; Nambo—trombone
Additional personnel: Earl "Chinna" Smith—producer; Errol Brown—producer, recorder, mixer; Warren Smith, Michael "Eppy" Epstein—executive producers; "Sticko" Warren Weinberg, Richard Kaplan—engineers
Recording dates: 1981 at Tuff Gong Studios, Kingston, Jamaica and Indigo Ranch, Malibu, California
Highest chart position: Did not chart from *Rock Steady with Flo & Eddie*
Original release date: 1981
Significant other versions: Stranger Cole and Gladdy, The Mighty Diamonds and Ranking Joe

Mark: After a couple of reggae stinkers on the *Rock Steady* album, this one has a little more life to it.
Charles: It may start like a Jimmy Buffett buffet, but before you know it, the groove proves to be a reggae splash/smash that would sound right at home on an album by Jimmy Cliff, Bob Marley, or Johnny Wakelin. In fact, Johnny Nash should have had a hit with this one. Put it on the setlist right before Inner Circle's "Sweat" (A La La La La La Long). All right!

—

KAMA SUTRA TIME (Howard Kaylan, Mark Volman, Jim Pons) by Flo & Eddie
Flo & Eddie involvement: Howard Kaylan—lead vocals; Mark Volman—vocals, guitar; Phil Reed—lead guitar; Erik Scott—bass; Andy Cahan—keyboards; Craig Krampf—drums
Additional personnel: Joe Wissert—producer; Alex Kazanegras—engineer; Tom Perry—Mixing Engineer, Hollywood Sound
Recording dates: 1975 at the Roxy Theatre by the Haji Mobile Facility and the Crossroads of the World, Hollywood, California
Highest chart position: Did not chart from *Illegal, Immoral and Fattening*
Original release date: December 1975

Mark: The live section of the album begins here and this is definitely played for laughs, replete with a few non-PC items to show how swinging the '70s really were. Since this has Jim

"Witty, tuneful, spiky and intelligent. This is an excellent album."
— OBSERVER

"I assumed it'd (the album) be interesting. Wrong again. I couldn't really find anything much interesting."
— S.P.

"I'd suggest putting out every tune on the album as a single if I were working over there at Warner/Reprise. There are definitely plenty of top 10-ers in here. If you like good music that you can dance to, fall in love to, and break up to, get The Phlorescent Leach and Eddie."
— By Mark Leviton, UCLA Summer Bruin

"Maybe they're better live."
— S.P.

"One of the most unique sessions of music unleashed this year — the album qualifies as something between beautiful and bizarre. There are even times when you suspect that the whole thing is a put-on. But if it is a put-on, it is the most imaginative put-on of all time."
— By Jack Lloyd, PHILADELPHIA INQUIRER

"I kind of expected more, somehow, but I'm glad to have this. Just don't expect it to scare anybody."
Volman – "It's just an album ya'know."
"Somewhere between 'The Lonely Surfer' and 'Return of the Son of Monster Magnet,' there's something on this album for everybody who doesn't mind listening."
— By Nigey Lennon, PHONOGRAPH RECORD

"It's hard to imagine them having any particular appeal."
— M.M. C.W.

"The only problem is that once you hear it, you can't get that moronic Flo and Eddie theme out of your head."
— By Rob Houghton, ROLLING STONE

Pons' input, it seems like it would have been played live while all were in The Mothers, but no live version by Zappa and/or The Mothers has been released. Mott the Hoople, Woodstock, Marc Bolan, Joni Mitchell, Yoko Ono, and Elton John get name dropped during the proceedings. During a break in the proceedings the band jumps into a rendition of "Bang a Gong (Get it On)," and why not since Flo & Eddie actually did backing vocals on the original recording with Marc Bolan and T. Rex.

Strangely, Joni's "Help Me" doesn't get a separate credit as "Bang a Gong" did. Maybe because Flo & Eddie didn't play enough of it to warrant it or her copyright owners didn't care as much. "It's a fine line between Joni and Yoko."

Nor was there a separate credit for Elton John's "Benny and the Jets," or *The Howdy Doody Show* theme, probably because THAT one is really the now public domain "Ta Ra Ra Boom De Ay."

Charles: If you don't already know what the Kama Sutra is, put down this book right now, read up on the positions, and try them all immediately (just not by yourself, and not without consent). Any song with the words "Kama Sutra" in the title has the potential to be a winner... unless it's "Kama Sutra" by Tiffany off her *Dust Off and Dance* album. Armed with an instantly lovable intro and laden with Flo & Eddie's typical chord changes and tempo twists (wait—if tempo twists are twists, they can't be typical, right? Right. Except when it comes to F&E, nobody should be surprised by Flo & Eddie's unique tempo twists, therefore they're atypical in any other context, but typical of F&E's creativeness. Got it?), the six-plus-minutes consists of humor, sexual references, and fun foolery. Who else could get away with rhyming "leather jocks" and "Nova Scotia lox," sneak in a whole slew of P. Incorrectness (which was probably more acceptable at the time), and even slip in a comparison of Joni Mitchell with Yoko Ono. Right in the middle, they break into a near-perfect T. Rex imitation of "Bang a Gong," so maybe "banging" a gong was a Kama Sutra position nobody else knew about.

—

KEEP IT WARM (Mark Volman, Howard Kaylan) by Flo & Eddie
Flo & Eddie involvement: Howard Kaylan—producer, vocals; Mark Volman—producer, vocals, guitars; Phil Reed—lead guitar; Andy Cahan—keyboards; Erik Scott—bass; Craig Krampf—drums
Additional personnel: Ron Nevison—producer, recorder, mixer; Skip Taylor—producer; Alan MacMillan—strings and horns arranger; Rick Smith, Eric Schilling, Cathy Callan—assistants
Recording dates: 1976 at the Record Plant, Sausalito and Los Angeles, California

Highest chart position: Did not chart; Did not chart from *Moving Targets*
Original release date: October 1976 for album; December 1976 for single

Charles: This political protest statement ("another jerk in the White House"), disguised as a Beach Boys tribute, actually sounds like something that really could have come out of the genius mind of Brian Wilson. It sneaks up on you at first, just hinting at it being a Carl Wilson or Mike Love-sung Beach Boys-influenced song, and then it goes all Beach Boys ballistic with Wilson harmonies and arrangement at the 1:45 mark. "Good Vibrations" and "All You Need is Love" phrases are thrown in for good measure, but the message is also up front and center, and it's more positive than negative by the end. Keep it warm, but don't burn out or belabor the point—keep it positive. And we'll have "fun fun fun" while we surf the social-political spectrum.
Mark: A belated protest song from the belated Turtles. I agree with Charles as there are many Beach Boys and Beatles references throughout and, to drive the point all of the way home, Howard and Mark do some of their best harmonic singing on record. Blah blah blah... it should have been a hit... blah blah blah... maybe Flo & Eddie wasn't such a marketable name after all. This was their final single.

Flo & Eddie sang a 1991 live version that appeared on *The Turtles Featuring Flo & Eddie Captured Live*.

—

KUNG FU KILLER, THE (Mark Volman, Howard Kaylan) by Flo & Eddie
Flo & Eddie involvement: Howard Kaylan—lead vocals; Mark Volman—vocals, guitar; Phil Reed—lead guitar; Erik Scott—bass; Andy Cahan—keyboards; Craig Krampf—drums
Additional personnel: Joe Wissert—producer; Alex Kazanegras—engineer; Tom Perry—Mixing Engineer, Hollywood Sound
Recording dates: 1975 at the Roxy Theatre by the Haji Mobile Facility and the Crossroads of the World, Hollywood, California
Highest chart position: Did not chart from *Illegal, Immoral and Fattening*
Original release date: December 1975

Photo: Daniel Coston

Charles: What do you get when you have a "You Showed Me" musical background playing throughout, and only tease at playing the song "Kung Fu Fighting," but instead make fun of it—as well as anyone who bought the song? You get a comedy skit more than an actual song! Some may contend that it's a little hypocritical that a band with such comedy "chops" (pun intended) and love for novelty-songs of their own would "kick" (yes, another pun) another song in the groin. Hey—at a time when everybody was kung-fu fighting, it was all in good fun.
Mark: "Who the fuck bought it? Oriental negroes, that's who. Watch out for them [sic]." Once again, the loosey-goosey '70s with free language you can't say anymore without getting massacred. BTW, I did buy "Kung Fu Fighting" when there was a Record Store Day reissue in 2016, admittedly because of this song.
Charles: Just for the record, I'm far too politically correct to approve of the language, as well as Mr. Mark Arnold reprinting it here. Great! We just lost our PG rating.

LADY BLUE (Howard Kaylan) by Flo & Eddie
Flo & Eddie involvement: Howard Kaylan—producer, vocals; Mark Volman—producer, vocals and guitar; Gary Rowles—lead guitar; Don Preston—keyboards; Jim Pons—bass; Aynsley Dunbar—drums
Additional personnel: Barry Keene—engineer
Recording dates: 1972 at Ike Turner's Bolic Sound, Inglewood, California
Highest chart position: #211 from *The Phlorescent Leech and Eddie*
Original release date: September 1972

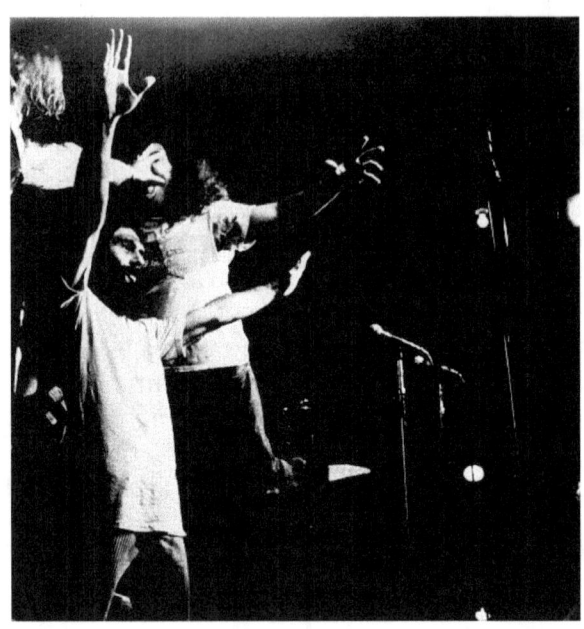

Mark: This song wanders around in various minor keys, but still comes out sounding good. It's a little bit more acoustic than some of the harder rocking material on this album and that's a good thing. The second half rocks it up a bit more, but it is a bit reserved, and then it all builds to a rousing crescendo, before returning to a small acoustic finish. Nicely done.

Charles: "I guess I got what I deserved." Oh no, sorry, that's "Baby Blue," which sounds nothing like this slower, bluer composition, highlighted by pretty harmonies and a nice change after about two minutes before it settles back before the three-minute mark. So I guess we did get what we deserved.

LET ME MAKE LOVE TO YOU (Howard Kaylan, Mark Volman) by Flo & Eddie
Flo & Eddie involvement: Howard Kaylan—lead vocals; Mark Volman—vocals, guitar; Danny Kortchmar—guitar; Leland Sklar—bass; Ian Underwood—keyboards; Aynsley Dunbar—drums **Additional personnel:** Joe Wissert—producer, Dee Robb—engineer
Recording dates: 1974 at Cherokee Studios, Los Angeles, California
Highest chart position: Did not chart; Did not chart from *Illegal, Immoral and Fattening*
Original release date: September 1974; reissued September 1975 for single; December 1975 for album

Mark: Once again with Flo & Eddie, this coulda/shoulda/woulda been a studio hit. It's as good

as anything The Turtles ever did. Columbia liked it so much, they issued it twice! It undeservedly flopped both times!!
Charles: Smile-inducing love song that should have been a chart-topper. Who wouldn't let them make love to you, when they ask so nicely? Admittedly, it could use a strong bridge, but no need for perfectionism when there's such a joyous sentiment.

—

LETTERMAN **THEME** (Paul Shaffer) by Flo & Eddie
Flo & Eddie involvement: Howard Kaylan—executive producer, vocals, saxophone; Mark Volman—executive producer, vocals, guitar; Joe Stefko—producer, drums; Russ Shirley—guitar, background vocals; Mike Reed—keyboards, background vocals; Mike Visceglia—bass, background vocals
Additional personnel: Denny McNerney—recording, assembling, mastering
Recording dates: December 1984 at the Bottom Line, New York, New York
Highest chart position: Did not chart from *New York "Times" 1979-1994 Live at The Bottom Line*
Original release date: October 20, 2009
Significant other versions: *Late Night with David Letterman*

Mark: A straight rendition of the *Late Night with David Letterman* theme is performed with a Howard narration introducing The Turtles and their band, plus Dr. Ruth Westheimer and Stupid Human Tricks.
Charles: I miss *Late Night with David Letterman*, and I could give you a Top 10 list why, but that would take up too much space.

—

LIVIN' IN A JUNGLE (Howard Kaylan, Mark Volman) by Flo & Eddie
Flo & Eddie involvement: Howard Kaylan—producer, vocals; Mark Volman—producer, vocals; Jim Pons—bass; Gary Rowles—guitar; John Herron—piano; Aynsley Dunbar—drums; Bruce Robb aka Robert Donaldson—organ
Additional personnel: Dee Robb aka David Donaldson—engineer
Recording dates: 1974 at Cherokee Studios, Los Angeles, California
Highest chart position: Did not chart from *The History of Flo & Eddie and The Turtles*
Original release date: 1974 for *Down and Dirty Duck* film; 1983 for album

Mark: This is the studio version of the more familiar live version as listed directly below, minus all of the onstage banter. Without that, it seems strange that Flo & Eddie couldn't have had a hit with it a la Average White Band. It's just that good. I guess the "death to whitey, burn the honky" chorus didn't sit too well.
Charles: Uh oh—electronic effects. Uh oh—they think they're black. Could be offensive.

—

LIVIN' IN THE JUNGLE (Howard Kaylan, Mark Volman) by Flo & Eddie
Flo & Eddie involvement: Howard Kaylan—lead vocals; Mark Volman—vocals, guitar; Phil Reed—lead guitar; Erik Scott—bass; Andy Cahan—keyboards; Craig Krampf—drums
Additional personnel: Joe Wissert—producer; Alex Kazanegras—engineer; Tom Perry—Mixing Engineer, Hollywood Sound
Recording dates: 1975 at the Roxy Theatre by the Haji Mobile Facility and the Crossroads of the World, Hollywood, California
Highest chart position: Did not chart from *Illegal, Immoral and Fattening*
Original release date: December 1975

Photo: Daniel Coston

Mark: "This is our negro song," Howard explains, once again showing how different the language was in the 1970s. You couldn't get away with that now. Nor could you sing "stabbing whites, shooting whites, gunning down whites..." and "death to whitey, burn the honky." It is a time capsule of its time. War, Malo, Santana, Earth Wind & Fire, Osibisa, and Helen Reddy are all namedropped.
Charles: Again, could be offensive.

—

LOUIE LOUIE (Richard Berry) by Flo & Eddie
Flo & Eddie involvement: Howard Kaylan—producer, vocals; Mark Volman—producer, vocals, guitar; Billy Steele—guitar; Andy Cahan—keyboards; Erik Scott—bass; Jimmy Hunter—drums, bells
Additional personnel: Howard Wolen—engineer
Recording dates: 1977 at Studio Sound Recorders, Los Angeles, California
Highest chart position: Did not chart from *The History of Flo & Eddie and The Turtles*
Original release date: 1983
Significant other versions: Too many to list but The Kingsmen have the original hit version.

FLO & EDDIE ON VINYL. *Flo & Eddie* produced by Bob Ezrin (Alice's own) in Los Angeles and New York.

Mark: This apparently was a rehearsal track for something else and ended up being released in part as part of "Medley #2" on *The History of Flo & Eddie and The Turtles*. It's a classic, but Flo & Eddie's version is just okay.
Charles: I love that in the "significant other versions" notes, our comment is "too many to list but The Kingsmen have the original hit version." Flo & Eddie are just another of the many.

—

LOVE SONGS IN THE NIGHT (Michael Brown) by Howard Kaylan
Flo & Eddie involvement: Howard Kaylan—producer, vocals; Rick Howard—guitar; Robert "Cricket" Cohen—bass; David Forman—drums; Andy Cahan—producer, engineer, programming, keyboards, background vocals
Additional personnel: Jim Mitchell, Randy Mitchell—engineers
Recording dates: 2005 at the Dungeon in Billy Bob Thornton's House, Beverly Hills, California; Threshold Sound, Santa Monica, California; Footprint Audio Services, Brooklyn, New York; Andy's House, Van Nuys, California
Highest chart position: Did not chart from *Dust Bunnies*

Photo: Daniel Coston

Original release date: March 21, 2006
Significant other versions: The Left Banke

Mark: One of two great Left Banke songs given justice by Howard's powerful vocals on this album. Some great guitar work and piano highlight this excellent cover.
Charles: I never heard the original by Left Banke (of "Walk Away Renee" fame), but it's not the love song ballad you would expect. I don't know why, but I felt this was something Eddie Money should've recorded. It's good but nothing special.

—

LOVE YOU GAVE AWAY, THE (Mark Volman, Howard Kaylan) by Flo & Eddie
Flo & Eddie involvement: Howard Kaylan—producer, vocals; Mark Volman—producer, vocals, guitars; Phil Reed—lead guitar; Andy Cahan—keyboards; Erik Scott—bass; Craig Krampf—drums
Additional personnel: Ron Nevison—producer, recorder, mixer; Skip Taylor—producer; Alan MacMillan—strings and horns arranger; Rick Smith, Eric Schilling, Cathy Callan—assistants
Recording dates: 1976 at the Record Plant, Sausalito and Los Angeles, California
Highest chart position: Single did not chart; B-side to "Elenore" by Flo & Eddie; Did not chart from *Moving Targets*
Original release date: October 1976

Mark: This sounds totally like something Chicago would have done during this vintage with all that brass. I suppose that might have been the point, or maybe not. You can never tell with Flo & Eddie, but I like to think it was the point.
Charles: Good call, Mark. Very reminiscent of what Chicago was recording at the time. Well-produced, but perhaps a hair sluggish.

—

MADE IT TO THE TOP (Graham Gouldman) by Flo & Eddie
Flo & Eddie involvement: Howard Kaylan—executive producer, vocals, saxophone; Mark Volman—executive producer, vocals, guitar; Joe Stefko—producer, drums; Russ Shirley—guitar, background vocals; Mike Reed—keyboards, background vocals; Mike Visceglia—bass, background vocals
Additional personnel: Denny McNerney—recording, assembling, mastering

Photo: Daniel Coston

Recording dates: December 1984 at the Bottom Line, New York, New York
Highest chart position: Did not chart from *New York "Times" 1979-1994 Live at The Bottom Line*
Original release date: October 20, 2009
Significant other versions: *"Animalympics" Soundtrack,* Graham Gouldman with 10cc

Mark: A strange cover that originated from the animated TV special called "Animalympics." Even though it was written by 10cc's Graham Gouldman, it seemed well suited for Flo & Eddie and The Turtles, so they did it. The minor key changes are what make it work. The song deserves much better exposure.
Charles: Graham Goulding is not a household name, but so many of his songs deserve to be classics. I can think of three great ones from 10cc, and now I can add this to that list.

—

MAMA, OPEN UP (Mark Volman, Howard Kaylan) by Flo & Eddie
Flo & Eddie involvement: Howard Kaylan—producer, vocals; Mark Volman—producer, vocals, guitars; Phil Reed—lead guitar; Andy Cahan—keyboards; Erik Scott—bass; Craig Krampf—drums
Additional personnel: Ron Nevison—producer, recorder, mixer; Skip Taylor—producer; Alan MacMillan—strings and horns arranger; Rick Smith, Eric Schilling, Cathy Callan—assistants
Recording dates: 1976 at the Record Plant, Sausalito and Los Angeles, California
Highest chart position: Did not chart; Did not chart from *Moving Targets*
Original release date: October 1976

Mark: Yet another autobiographical song that tells the bittersweet lives of Howard and Mark. It's so overwhelming to them, they literally want to climb back into their mother's womb. Amusing and poignant, it's one of the best songs in the Flo & Eddie oeuvre and sung with tremendous passion by Howard along with some great electric guitar work by Phil Reed.
Charles: With a subtle build-up and a beautifully fragile vocal before it becomes a rocker, this one has a split personality, and both sides work congruently. "From the Filmore to the White House" is just one of the autobiographical lyrics that highlight "Mama, Open Up." Somewhere in the world there's a mad mash-up of this and the refrain of "Take me home oh muddah faddah" from Allan Sherman's comedy recording "Hello Muddah, Hello Faddah."

—

MARMENDY MILL (Howard Kaylan, Mark Volman, Bob Ezrin, Dick Wagner) by Flo & Eddie
Flo & Eddie involvement: Howard Kaylan—vocals; Mark Volman—vocals and guitar; Gary Rowles—lead guitar; John Herron—keyboards; Jim Pons—bass; Aynsley Dunbar—drums
Additional personnel: Bob Ezrin—producer, piano; Jack Douglas, Shelly Yokus—engineers; Dick Wagner—guitar

Photo: Daniel Coston

Recording dates: 1973 at Sunset Sound, Paramount, Los Angeles, California; and The Record Plant, New York, New York
Highest chart position: Did not chart from *Flo & Eddie*
Original release date: June 1973
Significant other versions: The Turtles

Mark: This is the fully realized version that was originally attempted by The Turtles for their *Shell Shock* set. Here, the full orchestration is added to complete the full majesty of this epic song, an excellent way to end an otherwise uneven album. Sod Queen's "Bohemian Rhapsody," THIS is the operatic masterpiece that SHOULD have gotten the same recognition as Queen's signature work and also should have been a single. The performance from December 28-29, 1985 is on *New York "Times" 1979-1994 Live at The Bottom Line* to a rousing response.

Charles: It's apparent from the longer (nearly two more minutes), mature, and classy—if not classical—instrumental intro that this one is going to be epic. It goes on its tangents, and manages to exude appropriate silliness both vocally and lyrically, but it reels itself in, perhaps reminiscent of The Raspberries' "I Can Remember" or The Monkees' "Shorty Blackwell," but not as anthemic as Aerosmith's "Dream On" or Queen's "Bohemian Rhapsody." It's certainly adventurous and courageous, and foreshadows future Flo & Eddie recordings. Ultimately, it finds a way to come full circle with an ending that perfectly bookends the beginning.

—

METAL GURU (Marc Bolan) by Flo & Eddie
Flo & Eddie involvement: Howard Kaylan—vocals; Mark Volman—vocals, guitars; Phil Reed—lead guitar; Andy Cahan—keyboards; Erik Scott—bass; Craig Krampf—drums
Additional personnel: Sparks—arrangers
Recording dates: 1983
Highest chart position: Did not chart from *Get Crazy* film
Original release date: August 5, 1983
Significant other versions: T. Rex

Photo: Daniel Coston

Mark: Flo & Eddie sang backing vocals on T. Rex's version and then re-recorded it themselves for the *Get Crazy soundtrack*, but it's not on the *Soundtrack*. If you like T. Rex, you'll like it. If you don't, what's wrong with you?

Charles: Another case of the guys being the back-up singers on a Marc Bolan track that isn't well known in the States, and then doing their version of it. With contributions by Sparks!

—

MISTY (Erroll Garner, Johnny Burke) by The Turtles

Flo & Eddie involvement: Mark Volman—executive producer, vocals, guitar; Howard Kaylan—executive producer, lead vocals; ; Joe Stefko—drums; David Nelson—lead guitar, vocals; Donnie Kisselbach—bass guitar, vocals; Chris Apostle—keyboards, vocals; Peter Zale—keyboards; Richie Cannata—saxophones, vocals, keyboards

Additional personnel: Steve Remote, David Nelson—producers, mixers; Steve Remote—engineer

Photo: Daniel Coston

Recording dates: December 31, 1991 at the Bottom Line, New York, New York

Highest chart position: Did not chart from *The Turtles Featuring Flo & Eddie Captured Live*

Original release date: November 10, 1992

Significant other versions: Johnny Mathis, Ray Stevens, Ella Fitzgerald, Frank Sinatra, Count Basie, Hank Crawford, Bing Crosby, Lloyd Price, Aretha Franklin, Larry Corryel, Mitch Miller, Lesley Gore, Richard "Groove" Holmes, Ahmad Jamal, Dave Koz, Carmen McRae, Donna Hightower, Wes Montgomery, Johnny Smith, Steve Turre, Sarah Vaghan

Mark: A nice jazz interlude that was captured live. Here it is done as the Erroll Garner instrumental instead of the vocals most famously sung by Johnny Mathis.

Charles: Don't try google-ing this one—you'll only get "Misty The Turtle." I'm beseeching the powers-that-be to release an album of standards by The Turtles/Flo & Eddie. I'd call up my station and say "Play Misty For Me."

—

MOVING AWAY (Copyright Control) by Flo & Eddie

Flo & Eddie involvement: Mark Volman, Howard Kaylan—vocals; Earl "Chinna" Smith—lead guitar, rhythm guitar; Dean Fraser, Enroy "Tenor" Grant—saxophones; Walt Fowler—trombone; Augustus Pablo—organ, piano; Leslie "Professor" Butler—piano, organ; Phil Ramocon—Fender Rhodes; Aston "Family Man" Barrett—bass; Carlton "Santa" Davis—drums; Uziah "Sticky" Thompson—percussion; The Brackenridge Brothers—trumpets; Nambo—trombone

Photo: Daniel Coston

Additional personnel: Earl "Chinna" Smith—producer; Errol Brown—producer, recorder, mixer; Warren Smith, Michael "Eppy" Epstein—executive producers; "Sticko" Warren Weinberg, Richard Kaplan—engineers

Recording dates: 1981 at Tuff Gong Studios, Kingston, Jamaica and Indigo Ranch, Malibu, California

Highest chart position: Did not chart from *Rock Steady with Flo & Eddie*

Original release date: 1981

Mark: This reggae song was competently done, but it is truly one of the lesser songs from the entire *Rock Steady* project. Basically, album filler with no excitement. It sounds like a reggae version of "He Ain't Heavy, He's My Brother."

Charles: I love all the guys' island-flavored tracks. This is a slower reggae jam which is nice, and that's good enough. By the way, there is nothing about it that sounds anything like The Hollies' "He Ain't Heavy, He's My Brother." Unless my co-author was looking at a photo of Flo & Eddie and was picturing what Howard might've been thinking about Mark at the time.

—

MOVING TARGETS (Mark Volman, Howard Kaylan) by Flo & Eddie
Flo & Eddie involvement: Howard Kaylan—producer, vocals; Mark Volman—producer, vocals, guitars; Phil Reed—lead guitar; Andy Cahan—keyboards; Erik Scott—bass; Craig Krampf—drums
Additional personnel: Ron Nevison—producer, recorder, mixer; Skip Taylor—producer; Alan MacMillan—strings and horns arranger; Rick Smith, Eric Schilling, Cathy Callan—assistants; Ian Underwood—saxophone on "Moving Targets"
Recording dates: 1976 at the Record Plant, Sausalito and Los Angeles, California
Highest chart position: Did not chart from *Moving Targets*
Original release date: October 1976

Photo: JoAnn Kassoff

Mark: "Is this record all that you could have hoped for? Don't you wish you could get your money back?" What I loved about Flo & Eddie was the self-deprecation. Unfortunately, I think I was in the minority here as maybe all the cynicism of this title track and the other songs on this album detracted from sales.

Flo & Eddie sang a 1991 live version that appeared on *The Turtles Featuring Flo & Eddie Captured Live*. The crowd wants more!

Charles: This guitar-driven rocker could've been a hit from any of a number of 1970s bands like Blue Oyster Cult, Uriah Heep, or Mountain, but it might be a little more melodic and better sung when delivered by Flo & Eddie. The addition of the cowbell rounds it out, and the chorus continues until it's fully engrained. A band named "Moving Targets" was around in the early 1980s, and never had a song this good.

—

MOVING TARGETS (LP) by Flo & Eddie
Flo & Eddie involvement: Howard Kaylan—producer, vocals; Mark Volman—producer, vocals, guitars; Phil Reed—lead guitar; Andy Cahan—keyboards; Erik Scott—bass; Craig Krampf—drums
Additional personnel: Ron Nevison—producer, recorder, mixer; Skip Taylor—producer; Alan MacMillan—strings and horns arranger; Rick Smith, Eric Schilling, Cathy Callan—assistants; Donnie Dacus—slide guitar on "Hot;" Jeff Baxter—slide guitar on "Hot;" Graeme "Shirley"

Strachan—chorus vocals on "Guns;" Ian Underwood—saxophone on "Moving Targets"
Recording dates: 1976 at the Record Plant, Sausalito and Los Angeles, California
Highest chart position: Did not chart
Original release date: October 1976

Mama, Open Up
The Love You Gave Away
Hot
Best Friends (Theme from the Unsold T.V. Pilot)
Best Possible Me

Keep it Warm
Guns
Elenore
Sway When You Walk
Moving Targets

A mighty fine album. This might as well have been called *Flo & Eddie Present the Battle of the Bands* as every song tries to imitate other bands from Chicago to The Who. It's a great album. It's too bad no one else thought it was in 1976. It was really the final straw for Flo & Eddie as they only made very specialized albums after this. This was the final album where they really tried to make a hit record, and somehow failed.

—

MTM (Sonny Curtis) by Flo & Eddie
Flo & Eddie involvement: Howard Kaylan—executive producer, vocals, saxophone; Mark Volman—executive producer, vocals, guitar; Joe Stefko—producer, drums; Russ Shirley—guitar, background vocals; Mike Reed—keyboards, background vocals; Mike Visceglia—bass, background vocals
Additional personnel: Denny McNerney—recording, assembling, mastering
Recording dates: December 1984 at the Bottom Line, New York, New York
Highest chart position: Did not chart from *New York "Times" 1979-1994 Live at The Bottom Line*
Original release date: October 20, 2009
Significant other versions: Sonny Curtis, Sammy Davis Jr., Ray Conniff, Frank Chacksfield and his Orchestra, Hüsker Dü, Christie Front Drive, Joan Jett and the Blackhearts

Photo: Daniel Coston

Charles: MTM are the initials of Mary Tyler Moore. Flo and Eddie can take a nothing day (and sometimes a nothing song), and suddenly make it all seem worthwhile!
Mark: Flo & Eddie played almost anything on stage. Howard pledges his love for Mary Tyler Moore and Mary Richards and he sings the theme song to her classic TV series called "Love is All

Around" in her honor. This leads into "It's Kama Sutra Time," which does not appear on this album and jumps straight to "Agita."

—

MUSIC (John Miles) by Howard Kaylan
Flo & Eddie involvement: Howard Kaylan—producer, vocals; Rick Howard—guitar; Robert "Cricket" Cohen—bass; David Forman—drums; Andy Cahan—producer, engineer, programming, keyboards, background vocals
Additional personnel: Jim Mitchell, Randy Mitchell—engineers; Billy Bob Thornton—vocals
Recording dates: 2005 at the Dungeon in Billy Bob Thornton's House, Beverly Hills, California; Threshold Sound, Santa Monica, California; Footprint Audio Services, Brooklyn, New York; Andy's House, Van Nuys, California
Highest chart position: Did not chart from *Dust Bunnies*
Original release date: March 21, 2006
Significant other versions: John Miles

Photo: Daniel Coston

Mark: Easily the worst song on the album if only for Billy Bob Thornton's narration. I know this was recorded in his home studio and he probably felt the need to be on the album somewhere, but sorry Billy Bob, this wasn't your moment. Howard's singing saves it and one wonders if there is a version sans Billy Bob.
Charles: Lovely piano intro in a song that begins so melodically it could have been the offspring that may have come from a Barry Manilow meets Paul McCartney session. Omit the rest of it and skip to 4:48 and it's just beautiful. Can someone please do an edit for me?

—

MY SWEET LORD (George Harrison) by Flo & Eddie
Flo & Eddie involvement: Howard Kaylan—lead vocals; Mark Volman—vocals, guitar; Phil Reed—lead guitar; Erik Scott—bass; Andy Cahan—keyboards; Craig Krampf—drums
Additional personnel: Joe Wissert—producer; Alex Kazanegras—engineer; Tom Perry—Mixing Engineer, Hollywood Sound
Recording dates: 1975 at the Roxy Theatre by the Haji Mobile Facility and the Crossroads of the World, Hollywood, California
Highest chart position: Did not chart from *Illegal, Immoral and Fattening*
Original release date: December 1975

Photo: Daniel Coston

Significant other versions: George Harrison, Billy Preston, Andy Williams, Peggy Lee, Edwin Starr, Johnny Mathis, Nina Simone, Julio Iglesias, Richie Havens, Megadeth, Boy George, Elton John, Jim James, Bonnie Bramlett, and Elliott Smith

Mark: A nice, hoarse-voiced George Harrison imitation of his ill-fated 1974 *Dark Horse* tour within "The Pop Star Massage Unit," which is itself within "Eddie, Are You Kidding?" "Take it, Billy!" goes into a brief snippet of "Nothin' From Nothin,'" which doesn't get separate credit as "My Sweet Lord" does. Probably because enough of it wasn't played.
Charles: Merely a snippet. Wonder if there's a potential "He's So Fine" copyright infringement?

—

MYSTIC MARTHA (Mark Volman, Howard Kaylan) by Flo & Eddie
Flo & Eddie involvement: Howard Kaylan—producer, vocals; Mark Volman—producer, vocals; Jim Pons—bass; Gary Rowles—guitar; John Herron—piano; Aynsley Dunbar—drums; Bruce Robb aka Robert Donaldson—organ
Additional personnel: Dee Robb aka David Donaldson—engineer
Recording dates: 1974 at Cherokee Studios, Los Angeles, California
Highest chart position: Did not chart from *The History of Flo & Eddie and The Turtles*
Original release date: 1974 for *Down and Dirty Duck* film; 1983 for album

Photo: Daniel Coston

Mark: A brief bit of this was released as part of "Medley #1" on *The History of Flo & Eddie and The Turtles*. Nothing special.
Charles: Sometimes there just isn't anything to say. There are actually mystics named Martha, though.

—

NEW YORK "TIMES" 1979-1994 LIVE AT THE BOTTOM LINE (CD) by Flo & Eddie
Flo & Eddie involvement: Howard Kaylan—executive producer, vocals, saxophone; Mark Volman—executive producer, vocals, guitar; Joe Stefko—producer, drums, lead vocals on "Go East Young Man", Vanna White, Batman, Dracula; David Nelson—guitar, background vocals; Dave Lebolt—keyboards; Andy Cahan—piano, Casio, background vocals; Steve Buslowe—bass, background vocals; Gus Weiland—guitar, background vocals; Mike Visceglia—bass, background vocals; Peter Zale—keyboards, background vocals; Andrew

Craig—Harvey Schiffler, AM-FM guy, monster vocals; Russ Shirley—guitar, background vocals; Mike Reed—keyboards, background vocals; Chris Apostle—sax, keyboards, background vocals; Caroline Dow—background vocals, harem girl; Lisa Miller—background vocals, grapes; Richie Cannata—sax, clarinet, background vocals; Donnie Kisselbach—bass, vocals; Tristan Avakian—guitar, background vocals

Additional personnel: Denny McNerney—recording, assembling, mastering
Recording dates: December 1979 - December 1994 at the Bottom Line, New York, New York
Highest chart position: Did not chart
Original release date: October 20, 2009

Wheel of Fortune
I Happen to Like New York
Gershwin
Bald Mountain
Tidy Bowl
The Debarkation
Escape from New York
The Duke
Pied Piper
Everyone's Coming to New York
She'd Rather Ending
MTM
Agita
Tibetan Memory Trick
Letterman Theme
Harvey Schiffler
Silver Bullet
Prison Song
Fast Car
I Lost My Heart at the Drive-In Movie
Who Outro

Halloween Intro
Halloween Theme
Horror Movie
Marmendy Mill
Steven
Steven Attacks
Nikki Hoi
Girls, Girls, Girls
Rock-a-Hula Baby
Go East Young Man
Harum Holiday
Girls Reprise
Nikki Hoi Recapitulation
Who Needs the Peace Corps?
Concentration Moon
The Ugliest Part of Your Body
Absolutely Free

Peaches En Regalia (instrumental)
Magic Fingers
Saturday in the Park
Made it to the Top
American Bandstand
Boogie

Random songs and clips from many many many Flo & Eddie New Year's shows over a 15-year period at New York's Bottom Line Club. Some segments are more effective than others, but if you are looking here for some classic unreleased Turtles or Flo & Eddie songs, look further.

—

NIGHT, THE (Mark Volman, Howard Kaylan) by Flo & Eddie
Flo & Eddie involvement: Mark Volman—executive producer, vocals, guitar; Howard Kaylan—executive producer, lead vocals; ; Joe Stefko—drums; David Nelson—lead guitar, vocals; Donnie Kisselbach—bass guitar, vocals; Chris Apostle—keyboards, vocals; Peter Zale—keyboards; Richie Cannata—saxophones, vocals, keyboards
Additional personnel: Steve Remote, David Nelson—producers, mixers; Steve Remote—engineer
Recording dates: December 31, 1991 at the Bottom Line, New York, New York
Highest chart position: Did not chart from *The Turtles Featuring Flo & Eddie Captured Live*
Original release date: November 10, 1992

Photo: Daniel Coston

Flo & Eddie claim that they wrote this for Michelob to use in their ads. I don't think I ever heard it used there, so like "Best Friends," it's another rejected song. It's pretty good, however.

—

NIKKI HOI (Mark Volman, Howard Kaylan, Jeff Simmons) by Flo & Eddie
Flo & Eddie involvement: Howard Kaylan—producer, vocals; Mark Volman—producer, vocals and guitar; Gary Rowles—lead guitar; Don Preston—keyboards; Jim Pons—bass; Aynsley Dunbar—drums
Additional personnel: Barry Keene—engineer, narrator
Recording dates: 1972 at Ike Turner's Bolic Sound, Inglewood, California

Highest chart position: Single did not chart; B-side to "Goodbye Surprise;" #211 from *The Phlorescent Leech and Eddie*
Original release date: September 1972

Mark: This light-hearted and fun track was the only Flo & Eddie track that achieved any sort of significant airplay, therefore cementing Flo & Eddie into a novelty act. Too bad, as there is much more to Flo & Eddie than just their comedy, but once you show you have good comedy chops and don't take your music 100% seriously, you get shunned by the press and are ignored by the various Hall of Fames no matter how deserving you are. Dr. Demento used to play this a lot. The performance from December 28-29 1985 is on *New York "Times" 1979-1994 Live at The Bottom Line*. It segues into Starship's then hit "We Built This City" and it is all a wraparound to their Elvis Medley.
Charles: Nikki Oy! If you have any doubt about Flo & Eddie's versatility, say aloha (hello, that is, not goodbye) to this Hawaiian ode to diving for pearls and diving for love. Would have been a treat to hear them playing this in an outdoor island hut in Maui or at one of the defunct New England Hu Ke Lau restaurants. Add this to your music playlist along with some pirate music, Don Ho's "Tiny Bubbles" and the Davy Jones/Monkees Christmas song "Mele Kalikimaka."

—

PARTY TIME (Leroy Sibbles) by Flo & Eddie
Flo & Eddie involvement: Mark Volman, Howard Kaylan—vocals; Earl "Chinna" Smith—lead guitar, rhythm guitar; Dean Fraser, Enroy "Tenor" Grant—saxophones; Walt Fowler—trombone; Augustus Pablo—organ, piano; Leslie "Professor" Butler—piano, organ; Phil Ramocon—Fender Rhodes; Aston "Family Man" Barrett—bass; Carlton "Santa" Davis—drums; Uziah "Sticky" Thompson—percussion; The Brackenridge Brothers—trumpets; Nambo—trombone
Additional personnel: Earl "Chinna" Smith—producer; Errol Brown—producer, recorder, mixer; Warren Smith, Michael "Eppy" Epstein—executive producers; "Sticko" Warren Weinberg, Richard Kaplan—engineers

Photo: Daniel Coston

Recording dates: 1981 at Tuff Gong Studios, Kingston, Jamaica and Indigo Ranch, Malibu, California
Highest chart position: Did not chart from *Rock Steady with Flo & Eddie*
Original release date: 1981
Significant other versions: Leroy Sibbles, The Upsetters, The Heptones

Mark: Yet another cover version that's a pretty standard reggae song. This one has a bit of a slower beat.
Charles: Granted, one would think that a song with this title might be more up-tempo and kickin', but the chill groove would fit perfectly on a Marley album, and then it would be considered a classic. Yah mahn!

PASS YOU BY (Fred Carlin, Rob Royer) by Flo & Eddie
Flo & Eddie involvement: Howard Kaylan—vocals; Mark Volman—vocals, guitars; Phil Reed—lead guitar; Andy Cahan—keyboards; Erik Scott—bass; Craig Krampf—drums
Additional personnel: Vincent Albana—producer
Recording dates: 1978 at Studio 55, Los Angeles, California
Highest chart position: Did not chart from the *California Dreaming Soundtrack*
Original release date: March 16, 1979

Photo: Daniel Coston

Mark: A pretty and also pretty rare track from a raunchy late 1970s American International film called *California Dreaming*.
Charles: When I was playing this, my kids (who are musically astute) asked why I was playing such "meh" (which they translate to "eh" or "blah") songs. I told them I was reviewing recordings for a book. They asked if this track was a hit. I told them "no." They weren't surprised. Agreed.

—

PEARL (Copyright Control) by Flo & Eddie
Flo & Eddie involvement: Mark Volman, Howard Kaylan—vocals; Earl "Chinna" Smith—lead guitar, rhythm guitar; Dean Fraser, Enroy "Tenor" Grant—saxophones; Walt Fowler—trombone; Augustus Pablo—organ, piano; Leslie "Professor" Butler—piano, organ; Phil Ramocon—Fender Rhodes; Aston "Family Man" Barrett—bass; Carlton "Santa" Davis—drums; Uziah "Sticky" Thompson—percussion; The Brackenridge Brothers—trumpets; Nambo—trombone

Photo: Daniel Coston

Additional personnel: Earl "Chinna" Smith—producer; Errol Brown—producer, recorder, mixer; Warren Smith, Michael "Eppy" Epstein—executive producers; "Sticko" Warren Weinberg, Richard Kaplan—engineers
Recording dates: 1981 at Tuff Gong Studios, Kingston, Jamaica and Indigo Ranch, Malibu, California
Highest chart position: Did not chart from *Rock Steady with Flo & Eddie*
Original release date: 1981

Mark: Yet another bouncy reggae track with basically the refrain "Pearl, I love you so." Not terrible, but not terrific.

Charles: You either love their reggae recordings, or you don't. I do. My co-author Mark not so much. This one is particularly infectious with its chorus and "ooo ooo's." I wish it was included in the Mia Goth film, *Pearl*.

—

PHLORESCENT LEECH AND EDDIE, THE
(LP) by Flo & Eddie
Flo & Eddie involvement: Howard Kaylan—producer, vocals; Mark Volman—producer, vocals and guitar; Gary Rowles—lead guitar; Don Preston—keyboards; Jim Pons—bass; Aynsley Dunbar—drums
Additional personnel: Barry Keene—engineer, narrator on "Nikki Hoi"
Recording dates: 1972 at Ike Turner's Bolic Sound, Inglewood, California
Highest chart position: #211
Original release date: September 1972

Flo & Eddie Theme
Thoughts Have Turned
It Never Happened
Burn The House
Lady Blue
Strange Girl
Who But I

I Been Born Again
Goodbye Surprise
Nikki Hoi
Really Love
Feel Older Now
There You Sit Lonely

The booklet for the CD release states that there was discussion whether this should be released as a Turtles album. Warner Bros. stated that The Turtles was old news by 1972 and that Mark and Howard should tie their album in with Frank Zappa. One wonders if it would have charted better as a Turtles album considering that *Battle of the Bands* and *Turtle Soup* didn't chart that well, but they now were on a major label. It is one-third Turtles anyway as three-fifths of the final Turtles group are here and three of the tracks were planned for *Shell Shock* and re-recorded here ("Strange Girl," "Goodbye Surprise," and "There You Sit Lonely").

Of Flo & Eddie's studio albums, this one is probably their best, but all are good in their own way. When it finally was released to CD, it was paired with their 1973 follow-up *Flo & Eddie*, and as such makes for a marvelous double album that could have been pared down to an absolutely fantastic single one!

—

PIED PIPER (Steve Duboff, Artie Kornfeld) by Flo & Eddie
Flo & Eddie involvement: Howard Kaylan—executive producer, vocals, saxophone; Mark Volman—executive producer, vocals, guitar; Joe Stefko—producer, drums; Russ Shirley—guitar, background vocals; Mike Reed—keyboards, background vocals; Mike Visceglia—bass, background vocals
Additional personnel: Denny McNerney—recording, assembling, mastering
Recording dates: December 1984 at the Bottom Line, New York, New York
Highest chart position: Did not chart from *New York "Times" 1979-1994 Live at The Bottom Line*
Original release date: October 20, 2009
Significant other versions: The Changing Times, Crispin St. Peters

Photo: Daniel Coston

Mark: Finally, after a lengthy *Escape from New York* opening, Flo & Eddie sing this 1960s classic, co-written by Artie Kornfeld, one of the co-founders of the Woodstock Festival in 1969. It's a very well done cover and one wishes they had cut a studio version as well. At least we have this. The singing inevitably segues into the theme song for "Car 54, Where Are You?" but then comes back.
Charles: Herman Munster's call of "Car 54, Where Are You" was one of the few highlights in the Rob Zombie *Munsters* movie, and it's welcome in any form (the original TV show starred original Herman Munster, Fred Gwynne). As for the track, I think a studio recording could've been a hit, possibly surpassing the 1966 one-hit-wonder by Crispian Sr. Peters.

—

PLEASANT STREET (Tim Buckley) by Howard Kaylan
Flo & Eddie involvement: Howard Kaylan—producer, vocals; Rick Howard—guitar; Robert "Cricket" Cohen—bass; David Forman—drums; Andy Cahan—producer, engineer, programming, keyboards, background vocals
Additional personnel: Jim Mitchell, Randy Mitchell—engineers
Recording dates: 2005 at the Dungeon in Billy Bob Thornton's House, Beverly Hills, California; Threshold Sound, Santa Monica, California; Footprint Audio Services, Brooklyn, New York; Andy's House, Van Nuys, California
Highest chart position: Did not chart from *Dust Bunnies*
Original release date: March 21, 2006
Significant other versions: Tim Buckley

Photo: Daniel Coston

Mark: This starts off with some nice acoustic guitar work and as usual, Howard sings well on this Tim Buckley cover.

Charles: Take a drive down the throughway past "Easy Street," and sit for a while on "Pleasant Street," where the guitar-playing is tasty, the vocals are excellent, and there are no wrong turns.

—

POP STAR MASSAGE UNIT, THE (Howard Kaylan, Mark Volman) by Flo & Eddie
Flo & Eddie involvement: Howard Kaylan—lead vocals; Mark Volman—vocals, guitar; Phil Reed—lead guitar; Erik Scott—bass; Andy Cahan—keyboards; Craig Krampf—drums
Additional personnel: Joe Wissert—producer; Alex Kazanegras—engineer; Tom Perry—Mixing Engineer, Hollywood Sound
Recording dates: 1975 at the Roxy Theatre by the Haji Mobile Facility and the Crossroads of the World, Hollywood, California
Highest chart position: Did not chart from *Illegal, Immoral and Fattening*
Original release date: December 1975

Photo: Daniel Coston

Mark: Essentially the spoken word part of "Eddie, Are You Kidding?," about a dildo invented by Howard as Eddie that can be programmed to be the exact dimensions of your favorite rock stars' schlong. John Denver ("How do YOU know?"), Jimi Hendrix, Alan Douglas, Mick Jagger, and George Harrison are name dropped as possible dildo variations. "Jumpin' Jack Flash" and "My Sweet Lord" are given separate track names on the CD version.
Charles: Bang a dong. Get it on. This is just too huge for me to grasp.

—

PRINCE FLO AND JAH EDWARD 1: See **ROCK STEADY WITH FLO & EDDIE**

—

PRISON SONG (Mark Volman, Howard Kaylan) by Flo & Eddie
Flo & Eddie involvement: Mark Volman—executive producer, vocals, guitar; Howard Kaylan—executive producer, lead vocals; ; Joe Stefko—drums; David Nelson—lead guitar, vocals; Donnie Kisselbach—bass guitar, vocals; Chris Apostle—keyboards, vocals; Peter Zale—keyboards; Richie Cannata—saxophones, vocals, keyboards
Additional personnel: Steve Remote, David Nelson—producers, mixers; Steve Remote—engineer
Recording dates: December 31, 1991 at the Bottom Line, New York, New York

Photo: Daniel Coston

Highest chart position: Did not chart from *The Turtles Featuring Flo & Eddie Captured Live*
Original release date: November 10, 1992

Mark: Mark claims this song was made for a new Turtles album. It's a really silly joke song and I won't spoil it here. The live performance from 1982 is on *New York "Times" 1979-1994 Live at The Bottom Line*.
Charles: Oh mannn, you set me up to do the spoiler, but I'll resist.

—

PRISONER OF LOVE (Russ Columbo, Clarence Gaskill, Leo Robin) by Flo & Eddie
Flo & Eddie involvement: Mark Volman, Howard Kaylan—vocals; Earl "Chinna" Smith—lead guitar, rhythm guitar; Dean Fraser, Enroy "Tenor" Grant—saxophones; Walt Fowler—trombone; Augustus Pablo—organ, piano; Leslie "Professor" Butler—piano, organ; Phil Ramocon—Fender Rhodes; Aston "Family Man" Barrett—bass; Carlton "Santa" Davis—drums; Uziah "Sticky" Thompson—percussion; The Brackenridge Brothers—trumpets; Nambo—trombone
Additional personnel: Earl "Chinna" Smith—producer; Errol Brown—producer, recorder, mixer; Warren Smith, Michael "Eppy" Epstein—executive producers; "Sticko" Warren Weinberg, Richard Kaplan—engineers; Jimmy "Senya" Haynes—bass; Phil Ramocon—Fender Rhodes

Recording dates: 1981 at Tuff Gong Studios, Kingston, Jamaica and Indigo Ranch, Malibu, California
Highest chart position: Did not chart from *Rock Steady with Flo & Eddie*
Original release date: 1981
Significant other versions: Russ Columbo, Billy Eckstine, Perry Como, The Ink Spots, James Brown, Roy Fox, Mildred Bailey, Teddy Wilson and Lena Horne, Bing Crosby, Les Paul and Mary Ford, Coleman Hawkins and Ben Webster with Oscar Peterson, Jerry Vale, Matt Munro, The Platters, Connie Francis, Frank Sinatra, Keely Smith, Pat Boone, The Vogues

Mark: Your tolerance for all of these songs really depends upon your tolerance of ska or reggae. All of the songs Howard and Mark tackled for this project are at least mostly well-known covers of classic reggae songs.
Charles: With the tinkling of the ivories at the start, it's clear that this is not another run-of-the-mill reggae chill pill. This is Howard crooning at his best! The tropical instrumentation is secondary to the song, which is one of those Sinatra-esque classics. Quick—tell Michael Bublé to listen to this version and record his rendition of it immediately.

—

PUFF, THE MAGIC DRAGON aka **PUFF** (Peter Yarrow, Leonard Lipton) by Flo & Eddie with Martin Mull
Flo & Eddie involvement: Mark Volman—lead vocals; Howard Kaylan—lead vocals; Martin Mull—lead vocals; Andy Cahan—keyboards
Recording dates: 1978
Highest chart position: Did not chart
Original release date: unreleased
Significant other versions: Peter, Paul and Mary, Jason Rebello, Trobar de Morte

Photo: Daniel Coston

Mark: Live performance only. Singer and comedian Martin Mull joined Flo & Eddie onstage for a memorable performance on TV's "The Midnight Special" impersonating folk artists Peter, Paul and Mary. Mull portrayed Peter, Howard was Paul, and Mark in drag played Mary.

Charles: This was from a time when Martin Mull was the next big thing, except he never was. However, he was wise enough to include Flo & Eddie (the best example of this being the 4/24/76 "Soundstage" show). Find the visuals on YouTube.

—

RADIO SPOT FOR *THE PHLORESCENT LEECH AND EDDIE* (Howard Kaylan, Mark Volman) by Flo & Eddie
Flo & Eddie involvement: See individual Turtles, Frank Zappa, and Flo & Eddie tracks
Additional personnel: Barry Keene—engineer
Recording dates: 1972 at Ike Turner's Bolic Sound, Inglewood, California
Highest chart position: Did not chart
Original release date: 1972 for radio

Mark: This record was a 7" promotional only release. Side one features a 60 second radio spot where Mark and Howard argue about what songs to play to promote themselves. They play clips from "Happy Together," "Call Any Vegetable (live version)," "Bang a Gong (Get it On)," and "I Been Born Again." Between each track there is an audible scratch and the entire thing sounds like something Cheech & Chong would do. The ad appears twice on the side.

The B-side is a slightly different mix of "Goodbye Surprise."

Charles: Did The Turtles/Flo & Eddie cut more promo-only releases than any other artist? Aside from anything else, they may very well have been the kings of radio spots.

—

REALLY LOVE (Mark Volman) by Flo & Eddie
Flo & Eddie involvement: Howard Kaylan—producer, vocals; Mark Volman—producer, vocals and guitar; Gary Rowles—lead guitar; Don Preston—keyboards; Jim Pons—bass; Aynsley Dunbar—drums
Additional personnel: Barry Keene—engineer
Recording dates: 1972 at Ike Turner's Bolic Sound, Inglewood, California
Highest chart position: #211 from *The Phlorescent Leech and Eddie*
Original release date: September 1972

Photo: Daniel Coston

Mark: A nice sweet melody sung sweetly by Mark and some decent guitar playing by him, too. Some nice harmonies, too. It was always nice when Howard let Mark sing lead, as Mark was seemingly better on these ballad-type songs. Howard could also sing a decent ballad, but you could always tell that he was chomping at the bit to let loose, vocally, and not stay in a sweet operatic voice.

Charles: With an intro that hints at the Everly Brothers, it's only a tease when you think about the harmonies that could have run through the entire song. It quickly sounds more Grateful Dead than Everlys. There are nice vocal arrangements and directions. It's chill! More of a jam song than most—it only needed to go on for another fifteen minutes.

—

REBECCA (Albert Hammond, Michael Hazelwood) by Flo & Eddie
Flo & Eddie involvement: Howard Kaylan—lead vocals; Mark Volman—vocals, guitar; Phil Reed—lead guitar; Erik Scott—bass; Andy Cahan—keyboards; Craig Krampf—drums
Additional personnel: Joe Wissert—producer; Alex Kazanegras—engineer; Tom Perry—Mixing Engineer, Hollywood Sound
Recording dates: 1975 at the Roxy Theatre by the Haji Mobile Facility and the Crossroads of the World, Hollywood, California
Highest chart position: Single did not chart; Did not chart from *Illegal, Immoral and Fattening*
Original release date: December 1975

Mark: Another studio track from the *Illegal* album. It has "hit" written all over it, but alas it was not. By this point, Flo & Eddie could have/should have changed their name, but they were stuck in a rut. At least it was released as a single. With the strings, the song comes off as ersatz ELO. In 1991, they did a great live version that can be found on *The Turtles Featuring Flo & Eddie Captured Live*.

Charles: How could this not have been a hit? From the soft and tender beginning into the build, and onward, "Rebecca" has everything a single needs. There is a strong chorus, decent lyrics, extraordinary musicianship, some nice changes, and a classy ending. Maybe "Rebecca" was too normal and AM radio was waiting for the odder "Elenore" to arrive.

—

ROCK STEADY WITH FLO & EDDIE (LP) by Flo & Eddie

Flo & Eddie involvement: Mark Volman, Howard Kaylan—vocals; Earl "Chinna" Smith—lead guitar, rhythm guitar; Dean Fraser, Enroy "Tenor" Grant—saxophones; Walt Fowler—trombone; Augustus Pablo—organ, piano; Leslie "Professor" Butler—piano, organ; Phil Ramocon—Fender Rhodes; Aston "Family Man" Barrett—bass; Carlton "Santa" Davis—drums; Uziah "Sticky" Thompson—percussion; The Brackenridge Brothers—trumpets; Nambo—trombone

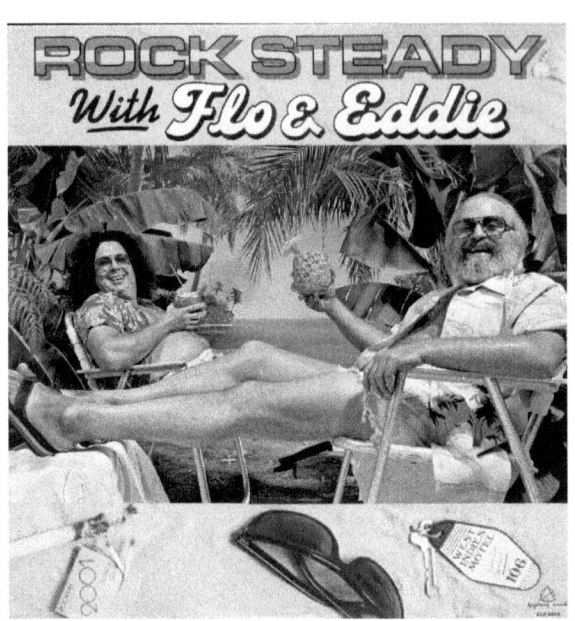

Additional personnel: Earl "Chinna" Smith—producer; Errol Brown—producer, recorder, mixer; Warren Smith, Michael "Eppy" Epstein—executive producers; "Sticko" Warren Weinberg, Richard Kaplan—engineers; Albert Wing—sax on "Dancing Mood"; Andy Cahan—organ solo on "Those Guys," Jimmy "Senya" Haynes—bass and Phil Ramocon—Fender Rhodes on "Prisoner of Love"

Recording dates: 1981 at Tuff Gong Studios, Kingston, Jamaica and Indigo Ranch, Malibu, California
Highest chart position: Did not chart
Original release date: 1981

Prisoner of Love
Swing and Dine
Stop
Moving Away
Pearl
Dancing Mood

Party Time
Sitting in the Park
Rock With Me
Those Guys
Just Like a River
Happy Together

And so a new phase starts with this album for Flo & Eddie, who seem to be now resigned to the fact that they will no longer have any hit records, so they decided to only do records they wanted to do like this reggae one and the children's albums in subsequent years. This was reissued in 1987 by Rhino with the originally planned title of *Prince Flo and Jah Edward 1*. As for this album, a little reggae goes a long way. The overall sameness of the sounds and the rhythms kind of kill any great excitement for the entire album.

—

ROCK WITH ME BABY (Johnny Clarke) by Flo & Eddie
Flo & Eddie involvement: Mark Volman, Howard Kaylan—vocals; Earl "Chinna" Smith—lead guitar, rhythm guitar; Dean Fraser, Enroy "Tenor" Grant—saxophones; Walt Fowler—trombone; Augustus Pablo—organ, piano; Leslie "Professor" Butler—piano, organ; Phil Ramocon—Fender Rhodes; Aston "Family Man" Barrett—bass; Carlton "Santa" Davis—drums; Uziah "Sticky" Thompson—percussion; The Brackenridge Brothers—trumpets; Nambo—trombone

Photo: Daniel Coston

Additional personnel: Earl "Chinna" Smith—producer; Errol Brown—producer, recorder, mixer; Warren Smith, Michael "Eppy" Epstein—executive producers; "Sticko" Warren Weinberg, Richard Kaplan—engineers
Recording dates: 1981 at Tuff Gong Studios, Kingston, Jamaica and Indigo Ranch, Malibu, California
Highest chart position: Did not chart from *Rock Steady with Flo & Eddie*
Original release date: 1981
Significant other versions: Johnny Clarke

Mark: Another reggae snoozefest as the overall sameness of the *Rock Steady* album is now reaching its zenith here.
Charles: My only issue with these reggae cuts is that the songwriters used the word "rock" so loosely. It's just as light and enjoyable as the rest, but don't expect anything about it to rock.

—

SANZINI BROTHERS, THE (Howard Kaylan, Mark Volman, Ian Underwood) by Flo & Eddie
Flo & Eddie involvement: Howard Kaylan—vocals; Mark Volman—vocals and guitar; Gary Rowles—lead guitar; John Herron—keyboards; Jim Pons—bass; Aynsley Dunbar—drums
Additional personnel: Bob Ezrin—producer; Jack Douglas, Shelly Yokus—engineers
Recording dates: 1973 at Sunset Sound, Paramount, Los Angeles, California; and The Record Plant, New York, New York
Highest chart position: Did not chart from *Flo & Eddie*
Original release date: June 1973
Significant other versions: The Mothers

Photo: Daniel Coston

Mark: Like "Carlos and De Bull," it's more spoken-word nonsense by the boys. Astonishingly, this studio version is the best version of this "song," and also twice as long since it adds a lengthy musical orgasm. Charles and I didn't even bother to review The Mothers' versions of this. A live version is on *Playground Psychotics*. Other live versions appear on *The Mothers 1970, Live at Fillmore East, June 1971 - 50th Anniversary* and *The Mothers 1971*. A brief bit appears as part of "Medley #2" on *The History of Flo & Eddie and The Turtles*.

Charles: First we get an intro to The Sanzini Brothers' horror "sodomy trick" illusion which we probably should be thankful that we could only hear and not see. Don't even try to visualize it. But then, all of a sudden, at almost a minute and a half into it, it transforms into a Plastic Ono Band-inspired primal scream fest for another orgasmic minute.

—

SANZINI BROTHERS RETURN, THE (WITH THE TIBETAN MEMORY TRICK) aka THE ANNOUNCER'S TEST (Howard Kaylan, Mark Volman, Ian Underwood) by Flo & Eddie
Flo & Eddie involvement: Howard Kaylan—lead vocals; Mark Volman—vocals, guitar; Phil Reed—lead guitar; Erik Scott—bass; Andy Cahan—keyboards; Craig Krampf—drums
Additional personnel: Joe Wissert—producer; Alex Kazanegras—engineer; Tom Perry—Mixing Engineer, Hollywood Sound
Recording dates: 1975 at the Roxy Theatre by the Haji Mobile Facility and the Crossroads of the World, Hollywood, California
Highest chart position: Did not chart from *Illegal, Immoral and Fattening*
Original release date: December 1975
Significant other versions: Del Moore, Jerry Lewis, Danny Kaye, Frank Zappa, The Mothers, Dick Summer

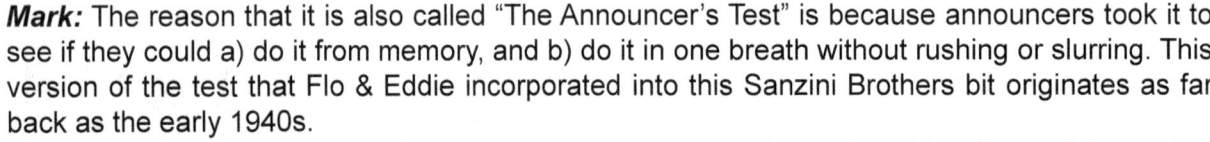
Photo: Daniel Coston

Mark: The reason that it is also called "The Announcer's Test" is because announcers took it to see if they could a) do it from memory, and b) do it in one breath without rushing or slurring. This version of the test that Flo & Eddie incorporated into this Sanzini Brothers bit originates as far back as the early 1940s.

The performance from 1984 of "Tibetan Memory Trick" is on *New York "Times" 1979-1994 Live at The Bottom Line*. It was also performed as part of "Billy the Mountain" on Frank Zappa's *Carnegie Hall*.

Charles: A live circus act starring brothers Adolph, Rudolph, Gustof, Ripoff, and Jackoff. They even beg us to take it off the record. Actually, the recitation is very impressive. Who would have the time to memorize this?

—

SATURDAY IN THE PARK (Robert Lamm) by Flo & Eddie
Flo & Eddie involvement: Howard Kaylan—executive producer, vocals, saxophone; Mark Volman—executive producer, vocals, guitar; Joe Stefko—producer, drums; Gus Weiland—guitar, background vocals; Peter Zale—keyboards, background vocals; Mike Visceglia—bass, background vocals
Additional personnel: Denny McNerney—recording, assembling, mastering
Recording dates: December 1983 at the Bottom Line, New York, New York
Highest chart position: Did not chart from *New York "Times" 1979-1994 Live at The Bottom Line*
Original release date: October 20, 2009
Significant other versions: Chicago

Photo: Daniel Coston

Mark: A cover of Chicago's classic hit from 1972 with everyone in the audience playing their holiday noisemakers. Very silly. "A man selling cocaine…"
Charles: I wish I was in the audience. So many of these would've been so much fun in their place in time.

—

SHADOW DANCING (Mark Volman, Howard Kaylan) by Flo & Eddie
Flo & Eddie involvement: Howard Kaylan—vocals; Mark Volman—vocals; John Hoier—bass; Albert Wing—sax
Recording dates: 1983
Highest chart position: Did not chart from *The History of Flo & Eddie and The Turtles*
Original release date: 1983

Mark: An excerpt of this appeared as part of "Medley #1" on *The History of Flo & Eddie and The Turtles*. It seems to be inspired by their reggae album or an outtake.
Charles: Andy Gibb should have recorded this one.

Photo: Daniel Coston

—

SHELL SHOCKED (Howard Kaylan) by Howard Kaylan
Flo & Eddie involvement: Howard Kaylan—narrator
Additional personnel: Penn Gillette—narrator, Foreword
Recording dates: 2013
Highest chart position: Did not chart
Original release date: 2013

Audio book only available from Audible. Howard Kaylan gives a very animated and spirited performance reading his autobiography. Comedic magician Penn Gillette reads his own Foreword.

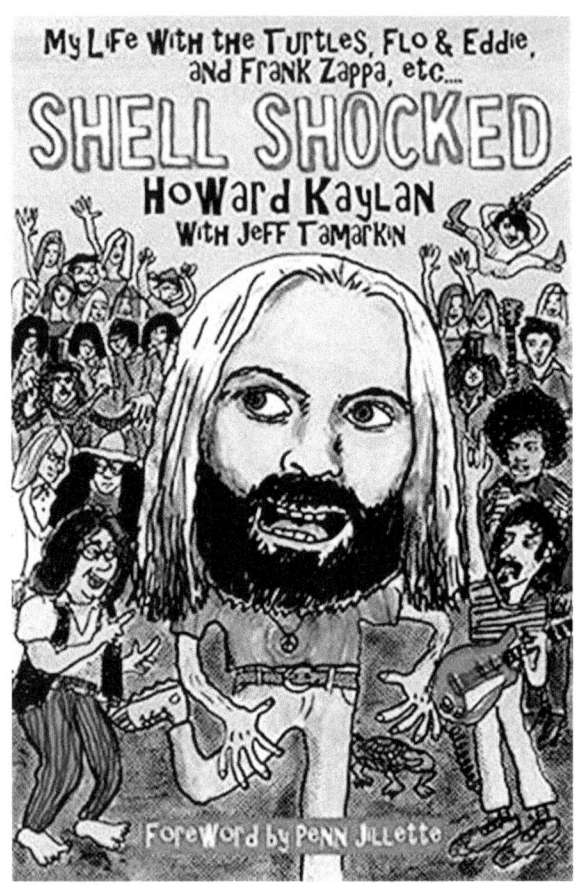

SHOW ME THE WAY TO GO OHM (Salz-Pfeffer) by Checkpoint Charlie
Flo & Eddie involvement: Howard Kaylan and Mark Volman as M. Salz and H. Pfeffer—producers, vocals
Additional personnel: Andy Cahan—keyboards; Johann Moier, Peter Jebsen
Recording dates: 1982 at Herb Cohen's studio complex
Highest chart position: Did not chart from *Checkpoint Charlie*
Original release date: 1982

Mark: Yet another of the Checkpoint Charlie tunes, dignified by also being part of "Medley #2" on The History of Flo & Eddie and The Turtles. The punny title is better than the song.
Charles: Speed up this instrumental and it could've been the background music for an early computer game.

SITTING IN THE PARK (Billy Stewart) by Flo & Eddie
Flo & Eddie involvement: Mark Volman, Howard Kaylan—vocals; Earl "Chinna" Smith—lead guitar, rhythm guitar; Dean Fraser, Enroy "Tenor" Grant—saxophones; Walt Fowler—trombone; Augustus Pablo—organ, piano; Leslie "Professor" Butler—piano, organ; Phil Ramocon—Fender Rhodes; Aston "Family Man" Barrett—bass; Carlton "Santa" Davis—drums; Uziah "Sticky" Thompson—percussion; The Brackenridge Brothers—trumpets; Nambo—trombone

Photo: Daniel Coston

Additional personnel: Earl "Chinna" Smith—producer; Errol Brown—producer, recorder, mixer; Warren Smith, Michael "Eppy" Epstein—executive producers; "Sticko" Warren Weinberg, Richard Kaplan—engineers
Recording dates: 1981 at Tuff Gong Studios, Kingston, Jamaica and Indigo Ranch, Malibu, California
Highest chart position: Did not chart from *Rock Steady with Flo & Eddie*
Original release date: 1981
Significant other versions: Billy Stewart, Georgie Fame, Owen Gray and Maximum Breed, Keith Hampshire, Slim Smith, Mike Patto, Winston Francis, Dr. Alimantado, Bobby Thurston, GQ, Bobby McClure, Steve Beresford, John Zorn, Tonie Marshall, David Toop, NRBQ, The Zombies, Quix*o*tic, Alton Ellis. Sampled versions: Hi-C, Slick Rick, Tomppabeats, Lily Allen

Mark: A soul classic that seemingly everyone has done, so why not Flo & Eddie in a reggae version?
Charles: Now here's a track that fits its title. Have the bartender pour you a glass of sex on the beach, pull up a wicker chair, put your feet up, and just do some sitting in the park with this song, and the whole album.

—

SNOWBLIND (Judy Henske, Jerry Yester, Zal Yanovsky) by Howard Kaylan
Flo & Eddie involvement: Howard Kaylan—producer, vocals; Rick Howard—guitar; Robert "Cricket" Cohen—bass; David Forman—drums; Andy Cahan—producer, engineer, programming, keyboards, background vocals
Additional personnel: Jim Mitchell, Randy Mitchell—engineers
Recording dates: 2005 at the Dungeon in Billy Bob Thornton's House, Beverly Hills, California;

Photo: Daniel Coston

Threshold Sound, Santa Monica, California; Footprint Audio Services, Brooklyn, New York; Andy's House, Van Nuys, California
Highest chart position: Did not chart from *Dust Bunnies*
Original release date: March 21, 2006
Significant other versions: Judy Henske and Jerry Yester

Mark: A chunky guitar starts this off and gets *Dust Bunnies* off to a rollicking start. Howard belts his heart out to bring this rocker home. I love it! I let co-composer Jerry Yester know that Howard had covered it in the interview contained later in this book.
Charles: This gives me a George Thoroughgood meets Slade vibe. I love it too.

—

SOUND OF THE SURF (film)
Flo & Eddie involvement: Mark Volman—interview; Howard Kaylan—interview
Additional personnel: Robert Berryhill, Eddie Bertrand, Jello Biafra, John Blair, Dick Dale, Robert J. Dalley, Richard Delvy, Jim Fuller, Paul Johnson, Kathy Kohner, David Marks, Kathy Marshall, Bill Medley, Tom Morey, Art Munson, Randy Nauert, Nick O'Malley, Steve Pezman, Domenic Priore, Bob Spickard, Lloyd Thaxton, Terry Tracy
Original release date: filmed in 2015; released June 30, 2021

A documentary about the history of surfing and surf music. Flo & Eddie are interviewed because of their previous incarnation as surfing band The Crossfires.

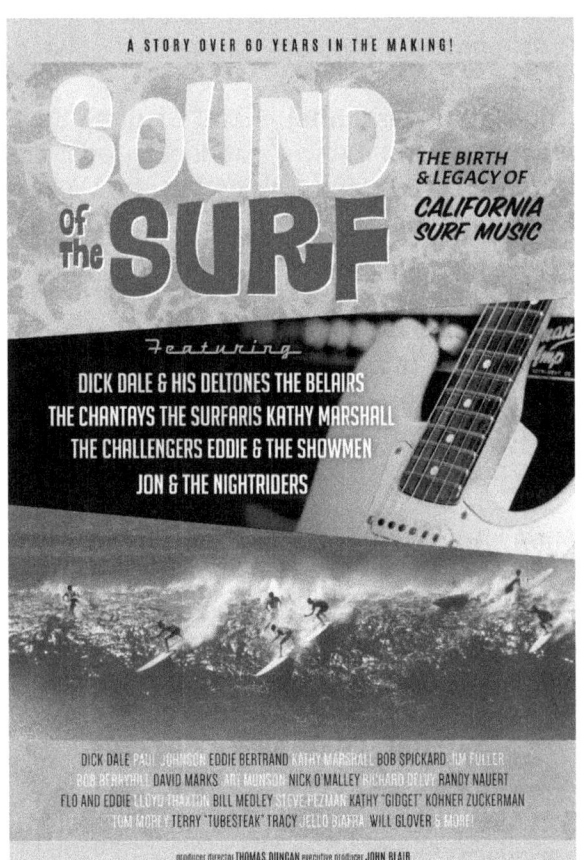

—

SOUNDSTAGE (film)
Flo & Eddie involvement: Mark Volman—lead vocals; Howard Kaylan—lead vocals
Additional personnel: Martin Mull and his Fabulous Furniture
Original release date: April, 24, 1976

A PBS special starring singer and comedian Martin Mull. Flo & Eddie appear and sing "Cheap," "Elenore," "Nikki Hoi," "Help Me," "Whole Lotta Love," "My Sweet Lord," and appear in a couple of comedy sketches.

—

STEVEN/STEVEN ATTACKS (Alice Cooper, Bob Ezrin) by Flo & Eddie
Flo & Eddie involvement: Howard Kaylan—executive producer, vocals, saxophone; Mark Volman—executive producer, vocals, guitar; Joe Stefko—producer, drums; David Nelson—guitar, background vocals; Peter Zale—keyboards, background vocals; Mike Visceglia—bass, background vocals; Andrew Craig—Monster vocals; Caroline Dow—background vocals; Lisa Miller—background vocals
Additional personnel: Denny McNerney—recording, assembling, mastering
Recording dates: December 28-29, 1985 at the Bottom Line, New York, New York
Highest chart position: Did not chart from New York "Times" 1979-1994 Live at The Bottom Line
Original release date: October 20, 2009
Significant other versions: Alice Cooper

Photo: Daniel Coston

Mark: Here is more scary music, this time a cover from Alice Cooper's *Welcome to my Nightmare* album. Andrew Craig takes the lead vocals with Flo & Eddie backups, first as the monster and then as Shecky.
Charles: I would've rather heard Mr. Kaylan attack the vocals, but anything connected with Alice Cooper is a win.

—

STOP (T. Chin) by Flo & Eddie
Flo & Eddie involvement: Mark Volman, Howard Kaylan—vocals; Earl "Chinna" Smith—lead guitar, rhythm guitar; Dean Fraser, Enroy "Tenor" Grant—saxophones; Walt Fowler—trombone; Augustus Pablo—organ, piano; Leslie "Professor" Butler—piano, organ; Phil Ramocon—Fender Rhodes; Aston "Family Man" Barrett—bass; Carlton "Santa" Davis—drums; Uziah "Sticky" Thompson—percussion; The Brackenridge Brothers—trumpets; Nambo—trombone
Additional personnel: Earl "Chinna" Smith—producer; Errol Brown—producer, recorder, mixer; Warren Smith, Michael "Eppy" Epstein—executive producers; "Sticko" Warren Weinberg, Richard Kaplan—engineers
Recording dates: 1981 at Tuff Gong Studios, Kingston, Jamaica and Indigo Ranch, Malibu, California
Highest chart position: Did not chart from *Rock Steady with Flo & Eddie*
Original release date: 1981

Mark: A real reggae classic done very well by Howard and Mark. As Flo & Eddie, Mark and Howard had now given up on singles, although they should have still given the nod to this one. It could have been a surprise hit for them. A brief snippet of this was also a part of "Medley #2" from *The History of Flo & Eddie And The Turtles*.
Charles: Yes Mr. Arnold. It's righteous reggae done great—like so many of the others!

—

STOP! IN THE NAME OF LOVE (Brian Holland, Lamont Dozier, Eddie Holland) by Flo & Eddie
Flo & Eddie involvement: Howard Kaylan—producer, vocals; Mark Volman—producer, vocals, guitar; Billy Steele—guitar; Andy Cahan—keyboards; Erik Scott—bass; Craig Krampf—drums, bells
Additional personnel: Howard Wolen—engineer
Recording dates: 1977 at Studio Sound Recorders, Los Angeles, California
Highest chart position: Did not chart from *The History of Flo & Eddie and The Turtles*
Original release date: 1983 for album
Significant other versions: The Supremes, The Hollies, La Toya Jackson

Photo: Daniel Coston

This cover was a brief snippet as part of "Medley #2" on *The History of Flo & Eddie and The Turtles*.

—

STRANGE GIRL (Howard Kaylan) by Flo & Eddie
Flo & Eddie involvement: Howard Kaylan—producer, vocals; Mark Volman—producer, vocals and guitar; Gary Rowles—lead guitar; Don Preston—keyboards; Jim Pons—bass; Aynsley Dunbar—drums
Additional personnel: Barry Keene—engineer
Recording dates: 1972 at Ike Turner's Bolic Sound, Inglewood, California
Highest chart position: #211 from *The Phlorescent Leech and Eddie*
Original release date: September 1972
Significant other versions: The Turtles

Mark: This version of this song is superior to The Turtles one, for no other reason that The Turtles one was only a demo and was only discovered and released recently. As it is, this final Flo & Eddie version is more commanding and demanding, probably the way The Turtles' version would have been if it had been completed for *Shell Shock*.
Charles: A Flo and Eddie track that actually charted! I hear early Alice Cooper? I'm not fond of the breaks, but it somehow works. Nice drumwork too.

—

SWAY WHEN YOU WALK (Mark Volman, Howard Kaylan) by Flo & Eddie
Flo & Eddie involvement: Howard Kaylan—producer, vocals; Mark Volman—producer, vocals, guitars; Phil Reed—lead guitar; Andy Cahan—keyboards; Erik Scott—bass; Craig Krampf—drums
Additional personnel: Ron Nevison—producer, recorder, mixer; Skip Taylor—producer; Alan MacMillan—strings and horns arranger; Rick Smith, Eric Schilling, Cathy Callan—assistants
Recording dates: 1976 at the Record Plant, Sausalito and Los Angeles, California
Highest chart position: Did not chart from *Moving Targets*
Original release date: October 1976

Photo: Daniel Coston

Mark: This sounds like another song. It may come to me later, but regardless, it's done well and Mark and Howard do some nice harmonies. I think Mark kind of pushes through and takes the lead at times.

Charles: It reminds me of the band America, and the song actually "sways." It's hard not to like the textures, and I really love the ending. "Every note that you sing will be... fine."

—

SWING AND DINE (Brent Dowe, Tony Brevette, Trevor McNaughton) by Flo & Eddie
Flo & Eddie involvement: Mark Volman, Howard Kaylan—vocals; Earl "Chinna" Smith—lead guitar, rhythm guitar; Dean Fraser, Enroy "Tenor" Grant—saxophones; Walt Fowler—trombone; Augustus Pablo—organ, piano; Leslie "Professor" Butler—piano, organ; Phil Ramocon—Fender Rhodes; Aston "Family Man" Barrett—bass; Carlton "Santa" Davis—drums; Uziah "Sticky" Thompson—percussion; The Brackenridge Brothers—trumpets; Nambo—trombone

Photo: Daniel Coston

Additional personnel: Earl "Chinna" Smith—producer; Errol Brown—producer, recorder, mixer; Warren Smith, Michael "Eppy" Epstein—executive producers; "Sticko" Warren Weinberg, Richard Kaplan—engineers
Recording dates: 1981 at Tuff Gong Studios, Kingston, Jamaica and Indigo Ranch, Malibu, California
Highest chart position: Did not chart from *Rock Steady with Flo & Eddie*
Original release date: 1981
Significant other versions: The Melodians

Mark: Though not nearly as well known as "Prisoner of Love," this song has a charm all its own in the classic reggae style.
Charles: Faithful adaptation of the original by The Melodians and just as sweet.

—

TEXAS DETOUR (film and soundtrack)
Flo & Eddie involvement: Howard Kaylan—vocals; Mark Volman—vocals, guitars; Phil Reed—lead guitar; Andy Cahan—keyboards; Erik Scott—bass; Craig Krampf—drums
Additional personnel: Patrick Wayne as Clay McCarthy; Mitch Vogel as Dale McCarthy; Lindsay Bloom as Sugar McCarthy; R.G. Armstrong as Sheriff Burt; Priscilla Barnes as Claudia Hunter; Anthony James as Beau Hunter; Michael Mullins as Billy Forest; Cameron Mitchell as John Hunter; Kathy O'Dare as Karen; Jeri Blender as Singer; Gary Davis as Cooper; Alan Sands as Carl; Michael Alan Honaker as Butch; Beau Gibson as Convict #1; Dee Cooper as Chet; Paul Nuckles as Deputy Norm; Larry Dunn as Convict #2; Denver Mattson as Convict #3; Pam Harvey as Bar Fly; George Harvey as Bar Customer; Marlene Schmidt as Lady Bartender
Original release date: June 1978

Three California teenagers have their van stolen and seek revenge is the basic plot for this low-budget B-picture. Flo & Eddie contributed "Champagne," "Getaway (Back to L.A.)," and "The Big Showdown" to the film, all of which appeared on *The History of Flo & Eddie and The Turtles*. "Getaway (Back to L.A.)" also appears on The Best of Flo & Eddie (CD version only).

—

THERE YOU SIT LONELY (Mark Volman and Howard Kaylan) by Flo & Eddie
Flo & Eddie involvement: Howard Kaylan—producer, vocals; Mark Volman—producer, vocals and guitar; Gary Rowles—lead guitar; Don Preston—keyboards; Jim Pons—bass; Aynsley Dunbar—drums
Additional personnel: Barry Keene—engineer
Recording dates: 1972 at Ike Turner's Bolic Sound, Inglewood, California
Highest chart position: #211 from *The Phlorescent Leech and Eddie*
Original release date: September 1972
Significant other versions: The Turtles

Photo: Daniel Coston

Mark: Many times I prefer the Flo & Eddie version of some of these *Shell Shock* songs, but this isn't one of them. The Turtles' version is vastly superior. This time it seems they overdid it like they were trying to prove something with all of the extra instrumentation. It would have been much better if they had held back this time.

Charles: "Here I sit, broken hearted, tried to… but only…" is a bathroom stall quote that has no place in this book nor in any context with this song, aside that the title makes it come to a warped mind. Speaking of things that are warped, this one flows along like a warped record. The instrumentation is certainly of a high level, but that seems to be the problem of the song—everyone sounds like they're high. The Turtles' released their original version of this Howard & Mark composition in 1969, roughly five years before this mess, and it makes you wonder why they ventured to record a new rendition. The original is highly preferable.

—

THERE'S NO BUSINESS LIKE SHOW BUSINESS (Irving Berlin) by Flo & Eddie
Flo & Eddie involvement: Howard Kaylan—lead vocals; Mark Volman—vocals, guitar; Phil Reed—lead guitar; Erik Scott—bass; Andy Cahan—keyboards; Craig Krampf—drums
Additional personnel: Joe Wissert—producer; Alex Kazanegras—engineer; Tom Perry—Mixing Engineer, Hollywood Sound
Recording dates: 1975 at the Roxy Theatre by the Haji Mobile Facility and the Crossroads of the World, Hollywood, California
Highest chart position: Did not chart from *Illegal, Immoral and Fattening*
Original release date: December 1975
Significant other versions: Ethel Merman, Judy Garland, The Andrews Sisters with Bing Crosby and Dick Haymes, Frank Sinatra, Harry Connick, Jr., Susannah McCorkle, Mary Hopkin, Bernadette Peters, Sonny Rollins, Allan Sherman, Liza Minelli

Mark: Everyone seems to love this song. Even John Lennon sang it a capella in *Magical Mystery Tour*. Howard refers to the group as Flo & Eddie's Turtles and he gives a shout out to keyboardist Andy Cahan. The live introduction leads into a studio version of the song.

Charles: You know how when there's a horrible version of a song, they say so-and-so (the original singer or writer) "would be turning over in their grave"? Just the opposite here! Irving Berlin would be kvelling in his, and Ethel Merman would be high-fiving the boys. They intro it as if they're going to break into a Chick Corea or modern jazz bit but instead they tease at a *Some Girls* tour de force before executing a faithful rendition of the venerable classic "There's No Business Like Show Business." In the 1960s, The Happenings could have had a hit with this version, but here, Flo & Eddie own it. "Let's go on with the show!"

—

THIS COULD BE THE DAY (Mark Volman, Howard Kaylan) by Flo & Eddie
Flo & Eddie involvement: Howard Kaylan—producer, vocals; Mark Volman—producer, vocals; Jim Pons—bass; Gary Rowles—guitar; John Herron—piano; Aynsley Dunbar—drums; Bruce Robb aka Robert Donaldson—organ
Additional personnel: Dee Robb aka David Donaldson—engineer
Recording dates: 1974 at Cherokee Studios, Los Angeles, California
Highest chart position: Did not chart from *The History of Flo & Eddie and The Turtles*
Original release date: 1974 for *Down and Dirty Duck* film; 1983 for album

Mark: This is a nice, refreshing song for Flo & Eddie considering some of their more dour output. It proves that they could write a nice, sunshiny pop tune if they so desired.
Charles: Again, their versatility and pop sensibility can't be repressed. My first inclination was to ask why this wasn't a Partridge Family hit, but in all fairness, couldn't this have been a perfect song for The Cowsills? It still could—they should perform it together when they all appear on a Happy Together tour. Susan, are you listening?

—

THOSE GUYS (Bryan, Harris) by Flo & Eddie
Flo & Eddie involvement: Mark Volman, Howard Kaylan—vocals; Earl "Chinna" Smith—lead guitar, rhythm guitar; Dean Fraser, Enroy "Tenor" Grant—saxophones; Walt Fowler—trombone; Augustus Pablo—organ, piano; Leslie "Professor" Butler—piano, organ; Phil Ramocon—Fender Rhodes; Aston "Family Man" Barrett—bass; Carlton "Santa" Davis—drums; Uziah "Sticky" Thompson—percussion; The Brackenridge Brothers—trumpets; Nambo—trombone
Additional personnel: Earl "Chinna" Smith—producer; Errol Brown—producer, recorder, mixer; Warren Smith, Michael "Eppy" Epstein—executive producers; "Sticko" Warren Weinberg, Richard Kaplan—engineers
Recording dates: 1981 at Tuff Gong Studios, Kingston, Jamaica and Indigo Ranch, Malibu, California
Highest chart position: Did not chart from *Rock Steady with Flo & Eddie*
Original release date: 1981

Photo: Daniel Coston

Mark: Please make it stop! I'm sorry, I love reggae music, but at this point on the *Rock Steady* album, it seems like after 10 tracks, the entire project has really run out of gas. Some strangely interspersed organ music almost saves this track. Almost.

Charles: He's lying. He doesn't love reggae music. If he did, he would enjoy this track, it's as good as the rest. This one is closer to UB40 than Toots and the Maytals, and a DJ could mix it in or out of "Red Red Wine."

—

THOUGHTS HAVE TURNED (Mark Volman and Howard Kaylan) by Flo & Eddie
Flo & Eddie involvement: Howard Kaylan—producer, vocals; Mark Volman—producer, vocals and guitar; Gary Rowles—lead guitar; Don Preston—keyboards; Jim Pons—bass; Aynsley Dunbar—drums
Additional personnel: Barry Keene—engineer
Recording dates: 1972 at Ike Turner's Bolic Sound, Inglewood, California
Highest chart position: #211 from *The Phlorescent Leech and Eddie*
Original release date: September 1972

Photo: Daniel Coston

Mark: This starts off with an early-1970s Who vibe. There are some very nice harmonies and very high singing. The new Turtles kick it off in grand style. This would have been a snazzy single despite it being yet another song about groupies and sex.
Charles: It really does sound like an early Who track, but definitely pre-1970s. I could play this for miles and miles and miles.

—

TIBETAN MEMORY TRICK: See **THE SANZINI BROTHERS RETURN (WITH THE TIBETAN MEMORY TRICK)**

—

TIDY BOWL (Howard Kaylan, Mark Volman) by Flo & Eddie
Flo & Eddie involvement: Howard Kaylan—executive producer, vocals, saxophone; Mark Volman—executive producer, vocals, guitar; Joe Stefko—producer, drums; David Nelson—guitar, background vocals; Chris Apostle—keyboards, background vocals; Donnie Kisselbach—bass, vocals; Richie Cannata—sax, clarinet, background vocals
Additional personnel: Denny McNerney—recording, assembling, mastering
Recording dates: December 28, 1988 at the Bottom Line, New York, New York
Highest chart position: Did not chart from *New York "Times" 1979-1994 Live at The Bottom Line*

Photo: Daniel Coston

Original release date: October 20, 2009

Mark: A 30-second instrumental interlude that kind of sounds like the "Hill Street Blues" theme song or some other theme song. Very theme song-ish. By this point on the album, what happened to Flo & Eddie?
Charles: Was this written as a commercial for Tidy Bowl? If so, it would be far too easy to review it as something to flush in the toilet.

—

TURTLES FEATURING FLO & EDDIE CAPTURED LIVE, THE (CD) by The Turtles
Flo & Eddie involvement: Mark Volman—executive producer, vocals, guitar; Howard Kaylan—executive producer, lead vocals; ; Joe Stefko—drums; David Nelson—lead guitar, vocals; Donnie Kisselbach—bass guitar, vocals; Chris Apostle—keyboards, vocals; Peter Zale—keyboards; Richie Cannata—saxophones, vocals, keyboards
Additional personnel: Steve Remote, David Nelson—producers, mixers; Steve Remote—engineer
Recording dates: December 31, 1991 at the Bottom Line, New York, New York
Highest chart position: Did not chart
Original release date: November 10, 1992

Photo: Daniel Coston

Feel Older Now (live 1991)
It Ain't Me Babe (live 1991)
Bruce (live 1991)
Rebecca (live 1991)
Misty (live 1991)
The Night (live 1991)
Prison Song (live 1991)
She's My Girl (live 1991)
Elenore (live 1991)
Goodbye Surprise (live 1991)
Keep it Warm (live 1991)
Let Me Be (live 1991)
Doors (live 1991)
You Showed Me (live 1991)
You Baby (live 1991)
She'd Rather Be With Me (live 1991)
Happy Together (live 1991)
Moving Targets (live 1991)

This was recorded live at The Bottom Line in New York. Flo & Eddie add their trademark humor through relatively straight versions of Turtles and Flo & Eddie classics.

TWO BY TWO (Michael Brown) by Howard Kaylan
Flo & Eddie involvement: Howard Kaylan—producer, vocals; Rick Howard—guitar; Robert "Cricket" Cohen—bass; David Forman—drums; Andy Cahan—producer, engineer, programming, keyboards, background vocals
Additional personnel: Jim Mitchell, Randy Mitchell—engineers
Recording dates: 2005 at the Dungeon in Billy Bob Thornton's House, Beverly Hills, California; Threshold Sound, Santa Monica, California; Footprint Audio Services, Brooklyn, New York; Andy's House, Van Nuys, California
Highest chart position: Did not chart from *Dust Bunnies*
Original release date: March 21, 2006
Significant other versions: The Left Banke

Photo: Daniel Coston

Mark: The second and final Left Banke cover from this album and what a recording. It's such a great song and Howard sings it with great gusto! Of course, Andy Cahan's piano pounds out the great melody background.
Charles: I must look into the Left Banke's musical catalog! A quick intro grabs you and the rest of the recording is solid but not memorable. For some reason I'm not crazy about Howard's vocals, which is rare. It reminds me of something that could've been a Three Dog Night album.

WALKING IN THE CLOUDS (Mark Volman, Howard Kaylan) by Flo & Eddie
Flo & Eddie involvement: Howard Kaylan—vocals; Mark Volman—vocals, guitars; Phil Reed—lead guitar; Andy Cahan—keyboards; Erik Scott—bass; Craig Krampf—drums
Additional personnel: Sparks—arrangers
Recording dates: 1983
Highest chart position: Did not chart from *Get Crazy* film
Original release date: August 5, 1983

Another track recorded for *Get Crazy*, but not included on the *Soundtrack* album.

WHAT'S THAT GOT TO DO WITH ME (Jim Glover) by Howard Kaylan
Flo & Eddie involvement: Howard Kaylan—producer, vocals; Rick Howard—guitar; Robert "Cricket" Cohen—bass; David Forman—drums; Andy Cahan—producer, engineer, programming, keyboards, background vocals
Additional personnel: Jim Mitchell, Randy Mitchell—engineers
Recording dates: 2005 at the Dungeon in Billy Bob Thornton's House, Beverly Hills, California; Threshold Sound, Santa Monica, California; Footprint Audio Services, Brooklyn, New York; Andy's House, Van Nuys, California
Highest chart position: Did not chart from *Dust Bunnies*
Original release date: March 21, 2006
Significant other versions: Jim and Jean, Sly and the Family Stone

Photo: Daniel Coston

Mark: Andy Cahan's pounding piano gives this cover version the proper punch. Maybe too much echo on the fadeout, but that's a mild criticism to another great cover by Howard.

Charles: Howard K covers an old Jim Glover non-hit from 1967 (released originally by Glover's duo, Jim & Jean, on the Verve label, with alternating male/female vocals, it actually cracked the Top 100) and he makes it his own haunting love song with some nice changes. Sporting a Bacharach-esque chorus that Dionne Warwick could've had a huge hit with, it's hard to believe that Sly & The Family Stone also did a take on this and funk'd it up. Three distinct versions of the same relatively obscure song, with the original being the worst, Sly's coming in second, and Kaylan presenting the best of the bunch.

—

WHEEL OF FORTUNE (Mark Volman, Howard Kaylan) by Flo & Eddie
Flo & Eddie involvement: Howard Kaylan—executive producer, vocals, saxophone; Mark Volman—executive producer, vocals, guitar; Joe Stefko—producer, drums, Vanna White; David Nelson—guitar, background vocals; Peter Zale—keyboards, background vocals; Mike Visceglia—bass, background vocals; Richie Cannata—sax, clarinet, background vocals
Additional personnel: Denny McNerney—recording, assembling, mastering
Recording dates: December 1986 at the Bottom Line, New York, New York
Highest chart position: Did not chart from *New York "Times" 1979-1994 Live at The Bottom Line*
Original release date: October 20, 2009

Photo: Daniel Coston

Mark: Mainly a spoken word sketch with Mark as Vanna and Howard as Pat. Other band members buy vowels. To spoil all their fun, they are trying to spell "The Turtles," or is it "Ike and Tina Turner."

Charles: Knowing their minds, Flo & Eddie must have always wondered why the only thing Vanna White revealed was letters. Rim shot.

—

WHO BUT I (Mark Volman and Howard Kaylan) by Flo & Eddie
Flo & Eddie involvement: Howard Kaylan—producer, vocals; Mark Volman—producer, vocals and guitar; Gary Rowles—lead guitar; Don Preston—keyboards; Jim Pons—bass; Aynsley Dunbar—drums
Additional personnel: Barry Keene—engineer
Recording dates: 1972 at Ike Turner's Bolic Sound, Inglewood, California
Highest chart position: #211 from *The Phlorescent Leech and Eddie*
Original release date: September 1972

Photo: Daniel Coston

Mark: This mellow rocker is very sparse instrumentally with some piano and a lot of drums and then some groovy guitar fills. A slightly underwhelming track, but it fills out the album nicely.
Charles: "Who But I" is not as commercial as many other Flo & Eddie cuts, but is unquestionably well-sung and played, with lush vocal and musical layers. It swerves in interesting directions structurally, and definitely keeps your attention throughout. Perhaps there's a little overplaying by drummer Aynsley Dunbar, but that's indicative of the era, and his style.

—

WHO NEEDS THE PEACE CORPS? / CONCENTRATION MOON / THE UGLIEST PART OF YOUR BODY / ABSOLUTELY FREE / PEACHES EN REGALIA / MAGIC FINGERS (Frank Zappa) by Flo & Eddie
Flo & Eddie involvement: Howard Kaylan—executive producer, vocals, saxophone; Mark Volman—executive producer, vocals, guitar; Joe Stefko -producer, drums; Tristan Avakian—guitar, background vocals; Chris Apostle—keyboards, background vocals; Donnie Kisselbach—bass, background vocals
Additional personnel: Denny McNerney—recording, assembling, mastering
Recording dates: December 1993 at the Bottom Line, New York, New York
Highest chart position: Did not chart from *New York "Times" 1979-1994 Live at The Bottom Line*
Original release date: October 20, 2009
Significant other versions: Frank Zappa and The Mothers of Invention

Photo: Daniel Coston

Mark: Shortly after Frank Zappa's passing in 1993, Flo & Eddie did this live medley of the songs they mostly did with Frank back in the day. It was only natural that they would perform these songs. Mark gives a heartfelt introduction before their performance.
Charles: A magical lyrical tour poking fun at phony hippies, with obligatory drug mentions, a zippy Zappa rant, a dirty word or two, and never any sign of trying to be commercial nor any attempt to please the masses.

—

WHO OUTRO (Pete Townshend) by Flo & Eddie
Flo & Eddie involvement: Howard Kaylan—executive producer, vocals, saxophone; Mark Volman—executive producer, vocals, guitar; Joe Stefko—producer, drums; Gus Weiland—guitar, background vocals; Peter Zale—keyboards, background vocals; Mike Visceglia—bass, background vocals; Andrew Craig—Harvey Schiffler, AM-FM guy
Additional personnel: Denny McNerney—recording, assembling, mastering
Recording dates: December 1982 at the Bottom Line, New York, New York
Highest chart position: Did not chart from *New York "Times" 1979-1994 Live at The Bottom Line*
Original release date: October 20, 2009
Significant other versions: The Who

Photo: Daniel Coston

Mark: Flo & Eddie do a decent rendition of The Who's "See Me, Feel Me"/"Listening to You" from *Tommy* to close their show.
Charles: We know how much The Turtles admired The Beatles, and it's clear they loved The Who as well. They cover some of their songs, while writing their own in the style of their influencers. Who knew there were influencers before social media!?!

—

WINDS OF FLO & EDDIE, THE (seven-tape set) by Flo & Eddie
Flo & Eddie involvement: Howard Kaylan and Mark Volman—writers, producers, performers
Recording dates: 1983
Original release date: 1983

This was a seven-cassette tape set of Howard Kaylan and Mark Volman telling stories for nine hours. It was sold as "Dialogues: An Intimate Audiobiography of Flo & Eddie" at the then-insane price of $32.98! It was a limited edition

of 100 that was signed, numbered, and not available in stores. It really needs a reissue. C'mon, guys!!

—

YOU'RE A LADY (Peter Sarstedt) by Flo & Eddie
Flo & Eddie involvement: Howard Kaylan—vocals; Mark Volman—vocals and guitar; Gary Rowles—lead guitar; John Herron—keyboards; Jim Pons—bass; Aynsley Dunbar—drums
Additional personnel: Bob Ezrin—producer; Jack Douglas, Shelly Yokus—engineers; Steve Madaio—trumpet
Recording dates: 1973 at Sunset Sound, Paramount, Los Angeles, California; and The Record Plant, New York, New York
Highest chart position: Did not chart from *Flo & Eddie*
Original release date: June 1973
Significant other versions: Peter Sarstedt

Mark: An early excursion into reggae-sounding material by Flo & Eddie and quite a nice cover. Peter Sarstedt's (1941-2017) original single version dates from 1971, and is from his album *Every Word You Say is Written Down*, but Flo & Eddie's is a slightly superior punched up version.
Charles: Down in the boondocks with a *Double Fantasy/Milk and Honey* Lennon-ish reverb vocal. I really liked every element of this song. And I just noticed it was engineered by Jack Douglas, who produced John Lennon's *DF* and *M&H* sessions. Do I have good ears, or what?!

—

(YOU'RE NOTHING BUT A) GOOD DUCK (Mark Volman, Howard Kaylan) by Flo & Eddie
Flo & Eddie involvement: Howard Kaylan—producer, vocals; Mark Volman—producer, vocals; Jim Pons—bass; Gary Rowles—guitar; John Herron—piano; Aynsley Dunbar—drums; Bruce Robb aka Robert Donaldson—organ
Additional personnel: Dee Robb aka David Donaldson—engineer
Recording dates: 1974 at Cherokee Studios, Los Angeles, California
Highest chart position: Did not chart from *The History of Flo & Eddie and The Turtles*
Original release date: 1974 for *Down and Dirty Duck* film; 1983 for album

Mark: Typically starting off with a "Happy Together" beat, this upbeat tune goes in a slightly different direction. Basically it was the theme song for the animated feature that Mark and Howard voiced for. It's pretty good.

Charles: This might be their most Monkee-ish song. Davy could have sung the verse with Micky coming in for the chorus, or Davy could've handled both. Peter or Mike would've been right there for the fade out. Anyone who says this sounds like "Happy Together" is a quack (duck reference).

—

YOUNG GIRL, A (Charles Aznavour, Oscar Brown, Jr., Robert Chavigny) by Howard Kaylan
Flo & Eddie involvement: Howard Kaylan—producer, vocals; Rick Howard—guitar; Robert "Cricket" Cohen—bass; David Forman—drums; Andy Cahan—producer, engineer, programming, keyboards, background vocals
Additional personnel: Jim Mitchell, Randy Mitchell—engineers
Recording dates: 2005 at the Dungeon in Billy Bob Thornton's House, Beverly Hills, California; Threshold Sound, Santa Monica, California; Footprint Audio Services, Brooklyn, New York; Andy's House, Van Nuys, California
Highest chart position: Did not chart from *Dust Bunnies*
Original release date: March 21, 2006
Significant other versions: Oscar Brown, Jr., Edith Piaf, Noel Harrison

Photo: Daniel Coston

Mark: I love the whiny guitar work on this song and the tinkly piano. Kind of an odd choice for Kaylan to tackle, but he makes this his own with a certain ferocity to his voice. It has a little bit of a Hawaiian sound at the start.

Charles: When Paul Simon was scoring solo hit singles with different musical styles in such songs as "Me and Julio Down By The Schoolyard" and "50 Ways to Leave Your Lover" (before stalling with his epic Broadway foray "The Capeman" in 1998), he was in one of those career zones, where every single was different, and each managed to be a hit—and deservedly so. After The Turtles, Flo & Eddie and, more specifically, Kaylan, never settled into that "career roll," where hits came easily. Had there ever been such a period for Flo & Eddie, "A Young Girl" would have (should have) been a radio staple.

—

YOUTH IN ASIA (Mark Volman, Howard Kaylan) by Flo & Eddie
Flo & Eddie involvement: Howard Kaylan—vocals; Mark Volman—vocals, guitars; Phil Reed—lead guitar; Andy Cahan—keyboards; Erik Scott—bass; Craig Krampf—drums; Tim Weisberg—flutes; Lynn Blessing—vibes
Additional personnel: Alex Kastenegras—engineer
Recording dates: 1975 at the Haji Mobile Facility
Highest chart position: Did not chart from *The History of Flo & Eddie and The Turtles*
Original release date: 1983

Photo: Daniel Coston

Mark: This is a nice sweet lullaby-sounding song with the same tinkly "Riders on the Storm" keyboards used throughout.

Charles: Clever use of words ("Youth in Asia" is much safer than euthanasia) brought to mind the film *Isle Of Dogs* ("I love dogs).

A BRIEF HISTORY OF MARK AND HOWARD'S CHILDREN'S ALBUMS
by Mark Arnold

Our story begins a few steps backwards. An animator by the name of Fred Wolf worked for years in the animation industry during the 1950s and '60s. In the 1960s, Wolf set up a studio with animator Jimmy Murakami and they called their studio Murakami-Wolf. In 1978, animator Charles Swenson became a partner and the studio became Murakami-Wolf-Swenson. Eventually, both Murakami and Swenson left the company, and in 1992 it became Fred Wolf Films.

The studio began by producing short films and commercials, including one of their most memorable, the Tootsie Pop's "How Many Licks" commercial in 1970. The success and notoriety of this commercial led to two ambitious early projects for the studio: Harry Nilsson's *The Point*, which was the first fully animated made-for-TV movie of the week in 1971, segments of Marlo Thomas' "Free to Be, You and Me" special from 1972, and the animated segments from Frank Zappa's *200 Motels* feature film from 1971.

Murakami-Wolf remembered Kaylan and Volman and decided to use them on a few projects over the years for composing, singing, and performing. The first was for the decidedly not-for-children film called *Down and Dirty Duck*.

Kaylan and Volman met with Swenson about the project on June 7, 1973. The project originally had the working title of *Cheap!* The film was released on July 8, 1974, and has nothing to do with Bobby London's *Dirty Duck* cartoon from *National Lampoon* and *Playboy*. There was no soundtrack album released, but Flo & Eddie did release a few of the songs on various compilations.

Flash forward a few years and Swenson contacted Kaylan and Volman again to produce some new songs for a new character called Strawberry Shortcake from American Greetings in 1980. They ended up working on Strawberry Shortcake's first three TV specials that were also released as LPs from Kid Stuff Records.

The World of Strawberry Shortcake was the first special, which originally aired on March 28, 1980, with the soundtrack album released shortly after.

This was followed by *Strawberry Shortcake in Big Apple City*, which aired on April 10, 1981, and another soundtrack album was released shortly after.

Next was *Strawberry Shortcake: Pets on Parade*, which aired on April 9, 1982. The follow-up album was called *Strawberry Shortcake presents Pets on Parade*, and was also released in 1982.

Strangely, only the first and third specials were animated by Murakami-Wolf-Swenson, while the second was animated by Perpetual Motion Pictures in New York. Later specials were animated by Nelvana and featured music by John Sebastian as Kaylan and Volman had moved on to other projects.

Kaylan and Volman did provide the songs and the performance on two more Strawberry Shortcake albums that did not have TV specials to accompany them. The first was *Let's Dance*, released in 1982 and the second was *Splash Dance Party*, released in 1984.

Kaylan and Volman also did the music for *Peter and the Magic Egg*, an animated TV special by Murakami-Wolf-Swenson that aired in syndication in 1983. There was no accompanying soundtrack album issued.

Around this same time, Kaylan and Volman got involved with another American Greetings creation, The Care Bears. This time, they were only involved with the record albums and not any animation. When animation was done later in 1985, it was handled by Nelvana.

Like the latter two Strawberry Shortcake discs, the Care Bears albums were heavy on songs and light on story. Five albums were produced, again released by Kid Stuff Records.

The first was (naturally) *Introducing the Care Bears*, first issued as a picture disc in 1982, and reissued on standard black vinyl in 1984.

The second album was *The Care Bears Care for You*, released in 1983, followed by *The Care Bears Adventures in Care-a-Lot*, also from 1983. This album is significant as it features a pre-*Married With Children* Christina Applegate among the album's cast.

Kaylan and Volman next took a cue from The Chipmunks and did a Christmas album in 1983 called *A Care Bears Christmas*, and followed it with their fifth and final Care Bears album called *The Care Bears Off to See the World*, released in 1984.

Also in 1984, Kaylan and Volman were involved with their final Kid Stuff record, this one involving the then-popular animated cartoon character G.I. Joe. The guys wrote and performed the story album called *Castle of the Doomed*. This one plays like an old-time radio show and is quite different from the other albums that they had done for Kid Stuff.

Kaylan and Volman were involved with Murakami-Wolf-Swenson one last time in 1986, when they did the music for the animated theatrical feature called *The Adventures of the American Rabbit*. The film was released on January 17, and there was an accompanying soundtrack album issued by Rhino Records as *The American Rabbit Original Soundtrack*.

Kaylan and Volman's final dabbling with children's records was with a 1989 album issued by Buena Vista Records and Disney called *Gumby*. Many artists contributed to this, including Jonathan Richman, Frank Sinatra, Jr., and both Dweezil and Moon Unit Zappa. Flo & Eddie's contribution was singing the song "We Are All Gumby," which sounds quite a lot like The Beatles' "I Am the Walrus." The *Gumby* album cover looks like The Beatles' *White Album*, except it's green, so we all know what the inspiration was.

Over the years, Kaylan and Volman have shown their range from Zappa's "Magdalena" to the sugar-coated Strawberry Shortcake and Care Bears and all points between. They are a force to continue to be reckoned with.

Note: for this section, we will only be reviewing the various albums in total rather than the individual songs as many of these albums are basically soundtrack material to animated shows and movies.

But first, a letter from Howard:

The Bubblegum Achievement Awards were held at the Magic Castle in Hollywood, California on January 18, 2003. The program was organized by Kim Cooper (Bubblegum Music is the *Naked Truth* co-editor) and Kelly Kuvo (The Bubblegum Queen). Honorees were Artie Ripp, Mark Volman and Howard Kaylan, Toni Wine, and Ritchie Cordell.
This originally appeared in *SCRAM* magazine #17:

Absent Bubblegum Achievement Awards honoree Howard Kaylan said it for all of us with his touching statement, which Mark Volman read on his behalf:

On behalf of my partner and myself, I would like to thank whoever the hell is responsible for this amazing Bubblegum Music Award.
In the past, the term "bubblegum" has represented, to some, a lightweight frivolous form of pre-adolescent pap. But take it from a man who uses "Pap," as a middle name, Bubblegum is much more than that.
During the most heinous war of our baby boomer lifetimes, bubblegum music got us through, brought the troops home, and took some of the pressure off a society that sang "Eve of Destruction" as their anthem. "Eve of Destruction" was basically a bubblegum song anyway, written by Steve Barri and P.F. Sloan who had written our bubblegum hit, "You Baby" and countless others. So there. Gum for the people.
When Mark and I wrote the music for the Strawberry Shortcake television shows and later the albums that would find a home anywhere a child lived in the 1980s, we didn't treat those projects as "children's music". We never "talked down" to anybody and we never excluded any age group in our lyrics. We made happy music for happy people... the same way that we wrote songs for The Turtles.
In fact, many of the songs written for Strawberry Shortcake and the Care Bears could have been hits for The Turtles, had the band been around that long.
Or for someone else. Hell, they still sound good to me. Make us an offer. Yes, they are predictable. They are easy to learn and fun to sing. They make you feel good when you hear them.
They embody a more perfect state of being and conjure up images of a more innocent time.
They send out positive vibes, if you will. Hey, anything wrong with that?
"What's so bad about peace, love and understanding?" Elvis once said. Costello, not the other one.
It is a great honor for me to accept this award in the hopes that maybe someone out there actually grew up listening to the positive music that we made, and that we changed his or her life—or at least their musical tastes—just a little and for the better.
If so, and you appreciate what we and so many others here tonight have done, pass the music and the attitude on to your children and their children, so that we may keep that innocence alive and so that we, too, can remain forever young.
Long Live Bubblegum Music!

Howard Kaylan
Seattle, WA
January 14, 2003

CHILDREN'S ALBUMS A-Z

ADVENTURES OF THE AMERICAN RABBIT, THE (film)
Flo & Eddie involvement: Howard Kaylan and Mark Volman—vocals, writers, producers
Additional personnel: John Hoier—co-producer; Barry Gordon as American Rabbit/Rob/Punk Jackal; Laurie O'Brien as Bunny O'Hare; Bob Arbogast as Teddy/Penguin 2; Ken Mars as Walt/Vultor the Buzzard; Pat Fraley as Tini Meeny; Russi Taylor as Rob's Mother/Lamb; Bob Holt as Rotten Rodney, Jackal Biker Leader/Penguin 3; Norm Lenzer as Brutal Bruno, Assistant Head Jackal; Lorenzo Music as Ping Pong; Hal Smith as Mentor/Mad Marvin, Sergeant-At-Arms Jackal/Too Loose; John Mayer as Horrible Hugo, Road Captain Jackal/Penguin 1; Lew Horn as Dip/Additional Voices; Maitzi Morgan as Lady Pig; Fred Wolf as Fred Red
Original release date: January 17, 1986

A Murakami-Wolf-Swenson feature length animated film with voices and songs by Flo & Eddie. The soundtrack is very difficult to find so if one wants to hear the songs, just check out this film.

—

AMERICAN RABBIT—THE ORIGINAL SOUNDTRACK (LP) by Howard Kaylan and Mark Volman
Flo & Eddie involvement: Howard Kaylan and Mark Volman—vocals, writers, producers
Additional personnel: John Hoier—co-producer
Recording dates: 1985 at Studio City Sound Recorders, Studio City, California
Highest chart position: Did not chart
Original release date: January 17, 1986

Main Title Theme from Adventures of the American Rabbit
School Band
Father and Sun March
The Legacy / Flying
As Long As You Can Rock and Roll

The Threatening Jackals
Meet Ping Pong
The Kidnapping
In Vultor's Cave
Problem's For Our Hero

Introducing Chocolate Mousse / The City
The Corporation
Torch It!
Getting There
The Moose, The Statue, The Hero and The Villain
American Cities in Peril
Panic in the Streets
New Hope
Vultor's Flight and Fall
The Grand Finale

This is the hard-to-find soundtrack for the feature length animated film from Murakami-Wolf-Swenson called *The Adventures Of The American Rabbit* or simply *The American Rabbit* in the UK. Rhino issued it on vinyl and cassette way back when and it went out of print shortly after. The film itself is somewhat easier to find having been released on VHS and DVD, if you want to hear the songs.

—

CARE BEARS ADVENTURES IN CARE-A-LOT, THE (LP) by The Care Bears
Flo & Eddie involvement: Howard Kaylan and Mark Volman—writers, producers, performers
Additional personnel: John Hoier—co-producer; Anita Ferry, Monica Lauren, Christina Applegate—voices; Andy Cahan—Casio and Ensoniq Performance Sampler; Bunk Gardner—flute; Stanley Behrens—harmonica; Buzz Gardner—trumpet; Dusty Wakeman—bass; Brian Madey—drums
Recording dates: 1983 at Sunswept Studios, Studio City, California
Highest chart position: Did not chart
Original release date: 1983

We're the Care Bears
Care-a-Lot
Hall of Hearts
I Feel So Alone

Make a Wish
The Birthday Song
We Can Count on Each Others

We're the Care Bears (Reprise)

This is the third Care Bears album with more of the same format as album two. The big highlight for this album is a young, pre-*Married With Children* Christina Applegate.

—

CARE BEARS CARE FOR YOU, THE (LP) by The Care Bears
Flo & Eddie involvement: Howard Kaylan and Mark Volman—writers, producers, performers
Additional personnel: John Hoier—co-producer; Anita Ferry, Monica Lauren—voices; Andy Cahan—Casio and Ensoniq Performance Sampler; Bunk Gardner—flute; Stanley Behrens—harmonica; Buzz Gardner—trumpet; Dusty Wakeman—bass; Brian Madey—drums
Recording dates: 1983 at Sunswept Studios, Studio City, California
Highest chart position: Did not chart
Original release date: 1983

Fun and Loving Bears
Smile From Inside Out
Someone Cares For You
A Sunny Thought (A Funshine Kind of Day)
Ten Cozy Bears

Fuzzy and Furry
A Care Bear Lullaby
Things Are Getting Better All the Time
Be a Bear!
One Good Hug Deserves Another

This is the second Care Bears album. After the first album basically introduced all of the characters in song, this album encourages various happy and fun things to do.

—

CARE BEARS CHRISTMAS, A (LP) by The Care Bears
Flo & Eddie involvement: Howard Kaylan and Mark Volman—writers, producers, performers
Additional personnel: John Hoier—co-producer; Anita Ferry, Monica Lauren—voices; Andy Cahan—Casio and Ensoniq Performance Sampler; Bunk Gardner—flute; Stanley Behrens—harmonica; Buzz Gardner—trumpet; Dusty Wakeman—bass; Brian Madey—drums
Recording dates: 1983 at Sunswept Studios, Studio City, California
Highest chart position: Did not chart
Original release date: 1983

Care Bear Theme
A Care Bear Christmas
Here Comes Christmas
(Fafalala) Happy Christmas Time
Christmas Time Care-a-Lot

Christmas Theme
Christmas Without Santa
The Ten Bears of Christmas
The Greatest Gift of All
Christmas is All Year
We Wish You a Merry Christmas (traditional)
Christmas Theme (reprise)

This is the fourth Care Bears album. A loose story is intertwined between each song about the meaning of Christmas. The songs on these Care Bears albums are actually pretty good. The only issue I have is that the voices of Kaylan and Volman are sped up to a kind of an annoying level.

Some of the tunes are good enough that if Flo & Eddie or The Turtles decided to do a straight Christmas album, these could be polished off and re-recorded to get rid of the Care Bears references.

—

CASTLE OF THE DOOMED (LP) by G.I. Joe
Flo & Eddie involvement: Howard Kaylan and Mark Volman—writer, producer, performer
Additional personnel: John Hoier—voice actor; Joe Bacal, Ford Kinder, Spence Michlin—words and music
Recording dates: 1984
Highest chart position: Did not chart
Original release date: 1984

Castle of the Doomed, Part 1

Castle of the Doomed, Part 2

Mark: This G.I. Joe album is the only one with Flo & Eddie involvement. It's more of a radio show than a song album, but it seems like they're having lots of fun. It's a difficult album to find now as it has never been reissued, plus the fact that there are many G.I. Joe fans who want it, and not for The Turtles connection.
Charles: www.3DJoes.com tells us the following: "*Castle of the Doomed* was released in 1984 by Kid Stuff Records & Tapes under license from Hasbro. *Castle of the Doomed* was the only Kid Stuff story to not feature an accompanying book. *Castle of the Doomed* was written, produced

and performed by Mark Volman and Howard Kaylan with John Hoier. The G.I. Joe theme words were written by Ford Kinder, Spence Michlin and Joe Bacal. The G.I. Joe theme music was written by Ford Kinder and Spence Michlin. All material was published by Gabrielle Amanda Music, Inc. (BMI)."

Hopefully Mark and Howard had fun with the music and voicing of this, because it's a project not even G.I. Joe or a superhero could rescue. The theme song is banal, childish, amateur, and sounds like it's been discarded from the fifties or early sixties (not 1984). If that's actually what they were going for… it still fails.

—

GUMBY (CD) by Flo & Eddie and various artists
Flo & Eddie involvement: Mark Volman, Howard Kaylan
Recording dates: 1989
Highest chart position: Did not chart
Original release date: 1989

(In Love) With You Gumby
Concrete and Clay
Zydeco Gumby Ya Ya
Bend Me, Shape Me
Gumby, We Love You
I Like Gumby
Pokey's Polka
The Ballad of Gumby
We All Are Gumby (Michael Silversher, Jeff Borgeson) by Flo & Eddie
The Gumby Heart Song

Mark: Disney decided to issue a Gumby tribute album complete with a green cover done a la The Beatles' *White Album*. The tracks from the various artists, including Dweezil Zappa and Frank Sinatra, Jr., go all over the map as far as musical styles, with only Flo & Eddie's contribution of "We All Are Gumby" keeping with the spirit of The Beatles like the CD cover. What all this has to do with Gumby is befuddling, but it makes for an eccentric but fulfilling listening experience.
Charles: Despite the intro, this is not "Strawberry Fields Forever," but it may be "I Am the Walrus." On second thought, it's both! As Beatle-ish as anything The Rutles did. Listen to that beginning and Howard's spot-on Lennon sound! Raise your hand if you love John, Paul, George, and Ringo. C'mon. We're waiting. Raise it. Okay that's better. Now raise your hand if you love this affectionate tribute to the Fab Four. How could you not? While the world was singing "Give Peace a Chance," Flo & Eddie were singing "Give Gumby a Chance." Did Eddie Murphy ever hear this? They're talking about Gumby, dammit. From the unmistakable opening "SFF" chords to the live crowd roar drop-in to the horn parts to the fake-fade-and-return and then to the "I Am the Walrus"-esque "Everybody Is Gumby" repeat outro, this is pure brilliance. A fab gear classic.

—

INTRODUCING THE CARE BEARS (LP) by The Care Bears
Flo & Eddie involvement: Howard Kaylan and Mark Volman—writers, producers, performers
Additional personnel: John Hoier—co-producer; Anita Ferry, Monica Lauren—voices; Andy Cahan—Casio and Ensoniq Performance Sampler; Bunk Gardner—flute; Stanley Behrens—harmonica; Buzz Gardner—trumpet; Dusty Wakeman—bass; Brian Madey—drums
Recording dates: 1983 at Sunswept Studios, Studio City, California
Highest chart position: Did not chart
Original release date: 1983

Good Luck Bear
Cheer Bear
Tenderheart Bear
Grumpy Bear
Wish Bear

Funshine Bear
Birthday Bear
Love-a-Lot Bear
Friend Bear
Bedtime Bear

This is the first Care Bears album. After the surprising success with Flo & Eddie on the Strawberry Shortcake albums, American Greetings approached them to produce record albums based upon these colorful bear characters. Each song introduces each bear and their individual traits. The album came in a picture disc version as well as a standard black vinyl version.

—

LET'S DANCE (LP) by Strawberry Shortcake
Flo & Eddie involvement: Howard Kaylan and Mark Volman—writers, producers, performers
Additional personnel: John Hoier—co-producer; Russi Taylor—voice; Andy Cahan—Casio and Ensoniq Performance Sampler; Bunk Gardner—flute; Stanley Behrens—harmonica; Buzz Gardner—trumpet; Dusty Wakeman—bass; Brian Madey—drums
Recording dates: 1983 at Sunswept Studios, Studio City, California
Highest chart position: Did not chart
Original release date: 1983

Let's Dance

The Strawberry Twist
One, Two, Cha-Cha-Cha
The Berry Silly Hat Dance
Strawberry Square Dance Tonight

The Limbo Dance
Do the Strawberry Stomp
The Strawberry Waltz
Huckleberry's Polka
I Was Born to Disco

This is the third Strawberry Shortcake album with Flo & Eddie involvement. The album steals its title from David Bowie's hit album of that year. Songs are of various musical genres and it seems like everyone is having fun.

—

OFF TO SEE THE WORLD (LP) by The Care Bears
Flo & Eddie involvement: Howard Kaylan and Mark Volman—writers, producers, performers
Additional personnel: John Hoier—co-producer; Anita Ferry—voice; Andy Cahan—Casio and Ensoniq Performance Sampler; Bunk Gardner—flute; Stanley Behrens—harmonica; Buzz Gardner—trumpet; Dusty Wakeman—bass; Brian Madey—drums
Recording dates: 1983 at Sunswept Studios, Studio City, California
Highest chart position: Did not chart
Original release date: 1983

Off to See the World
Happy Switzerland
Floating in Hawaii
Here in Russia (Not in Prussia)
Somos Los Care Bears

Oui, Ooh La La, The Care Bears
Ahh, Japan
Arm in Arm with Greece
Sunny Africa
A Care Bear Can Be Cared For in Scotland
Off to See the World (reprise)

This is the fifth and final Care Bears album with Flo & Eddie involvement. This is most certainly inspired from *The Chipmunks Go Around the World* album from 1960 with songs focused on various countries around the world, hence the title.

PETER AND THE MAGIC EGG (film)
Flo & Eddie involvement: Howard Kaylan and Mark Volman—writers, producers, performers
Additional personnel: Andy Cahan—Keyboards; Romeo Muller—writer, lyrics
Recording dates: 1983
Highest chart position: Did not chart
Original release date: 1983

Strangely, there was no soundtrack album released of this Murakami-Wolf-Swenson TV special starring Ray Bolger, so the only way to hear the songs is to get the VHS or DVD of the special itself. The songs are similar in vein to what Flo & Eddie were already doing for Strawberry Shortcake and The Care Bears. The show was a tie-in to the PAAS Easter egg dye kits.

SPLASH DANCE PARTY (LP) by Strawberry Shortcake
Flo & Eddie involvement: Howard Kaylan and Mark Volman—writers, producers, performers
Additional personnel: John Hoier—co-producer; Russi Taylor—voice; Andy Cahan—Casio and Ensoniq Performance Sampler; Bunk Gardner—flute; Stanley Behrens—harmonica; Buzz Gardner—trumpet; Dusty Wakeman—bass; Brian Madey—drums
Recording dates: 1983 at Sunswept Studios, Studio City, California
Highest chart position: Did not chart
Original release date: 1984

Splash Dance Celebration
The Strawberry Splashdance
Warming Up
Reach for the Sky

Simple Balance
Splash Dance Celebration (Reprise)

Dance Mad
Standing and Bending
Walking on the Ceiling
The Stand Up and Sit Down Dance
Relaxing
Dance Mad (Reprise)

This is the fifth and final Strawberry Shortcake album with Flo & Eddie involvement. Like *Let's Dance*, the album title is inspired by the title of the popular film *Flashdance*, and features songs of various musical genres.

—

STRAWBERRY SHORTCAKE IN BIG APPLE CITY (LP) by Strawberry Shortcake
Flo & Eddie involvement: Howard Kaylan and Mark Volman—writers, producers, performers
Additional personnel: Andy Cahan—Keyboards; Romeo Muller—writer, lyrics
Recording dates: 1981
Highest chart position: Did not chart
Original release date: 1981

Strawberry Shortcake in Big Apple City, Part One

Strawberry Shortcake in Big Apple City, Part Two

Soundtrack includes songs:
What a Day
Big Apple City
New Friends
Bake Off
Strawberry Land

This is the second Strawberry Shortcake album with Flo & Eddie involvement. It's basically the soundtrack to the TV special of the same name by Murakami-Wolf-Swenson.

—

STRAWBERRY SHORTCAKE PRESENTS PETS ON PARADE (LP) by Strawberry Shortcake
Flo & Eddie involvement: Howard Kaylan and Mark Volman—writers, producers, performers
Additional personnel: Romeo Muller—writer, lyrics
Recording dates: 1982
Highest chart position: Did not chart
Original release date: 1982

Strawberry Shortcake Presents Pets on Parade, Part One

Strawberry Shortcake Presents Pets on Parade, Part Two

Soundtrack includes songs:
Perfect Place to Be
Lower Than You
Kids Best Friend
March Back to Town

This is the fourth Strawberry Shortcake album with Flo & Eddie involvement. It's basically the soundtrack to the TV special of the same name by Murakami-Wolf-Swenson, and the last to have Flo & Eddie involved. The album is focused on the story, but there are four songs interspersed throughout.

—

STRAWBERRY SHORTCAKE THEME (Mark Volman, Howard Kaylan, Romeo Muller) by Strawberry Shortcake
Flo & Eddie involvement: Howard Kaylan and Mark Volman—writers, producers, performers
Additional personnel: John Hoier—co-producer; Andy Cahan—Casio and Ensoniq Performance Sampler; Bunk Gardner—flute; Stanley Behrens—harmonica; Buzz Gardner—trumpet; Dusty Wakeman—bass; Brian Madey—drums
Recording dates: 1983 at Sunswept Studios, Studio City, California
Highest chart position: Did not chart from *The History of Flo & Eddie and The Turtles*
Original release date: 1983

Strangely, the actual "Strawberry Shortcake Theme" seemed to avoid inclusion as a separate track on the various Strawberry Shortcake albums, but it was featured as part of "Medley #1" on *The History of Flo & Eddie and The Turtles*. The song was covered by others on later albums.

—

WORLD OF STRAWBERRY SHORTCAKE, THE (LP) by Strawberry Shortcake
Flo & Eddie involvement: Howard Kaylan and Mark Volman—writers, producers, performers
Additional personnel: Andy Cahan—Keyboards; Romeo Muller—writer, lyrics
Recording dates: 1980
Highest chart position: Did not chart
Original release date: 1980

The World of Strawberry Shortcake

The World of Strawberry Shortcake (continued)

This is the first Strawberry Shortcake album with Flo & Eddie involvement. It's basically the soundtrack to the TV special of the same name by Murakami-Wolf-Swenson.

THE TURTLES REUNION 2003
by Mark Arnold

In the 1990s, I emailed The Turtles' website and asked if there was ever a chance that the original Turtles would ever reunite for a concert and/or tour. Mark Volman actually responded with the very flippant and dismissive, "Why would we want to tour with those guys?"

I really didn't know the background of their recent relationships at the time as they always seemed so close in younger years and that their break-up in 1970 had more to do with lawsuits and White Whale Records running out of money than any genuine animosity between group members. I didn't reckon the eventual purchase of The Turtles masters by Kaylan and Volman might have caused a rift within the group, but apparently it did.

As stated earlier in the book, the closest the original Turtles came to fully reuniting was at a fundraiser for The David Center on September 6, 2003, in Hempstead New York. John Seiter, Howard Kaylan, Jim Pons, and Mark Volman performed. The only missing member was Al Nichol.

Photographer Al Pereira was there that night and graciously allowed us to publish what may be the only photos taken of the almost fully reformed 1969-1970 version of The Turtles.

He said of the event, "This was on Long Island, a reunion to benefit the David Center, which Pons and his wife, Dr. Pat Elvira (?), created to help their son. At the time, Jim and John Seiter worked at the NY Jets as did I (as the team photographer). They got the two big boys involved, and off it went. It was a festive night, they played all the hits, ending of course on "Happy Together." They also gave an award to Center Kevin Mawae of the Jets for helping the charity. Mawae is in the hall of fame now."

Photos: Al Pereira

Photos: Al Pereira

INTERVIEWS WITH THE TURTLES AND FRIENDS
by Mark Arnold (MA) and Charles F. Rosenay!!! (CR)

Andy Cahan—February 9, 2021

MA: Andy Cahan is a new friend who played keyboards and Mellotron on a lot of Turtles records and a number of other records that we'll probably talk about.

AC: I'm very honored to be here, my friends. This is fun. You guys are a lot of fun I can tell already. Let me just start off by saying I never played Mellotron with The Turtles.

CR: So many of the credits list you as that?

AC: Do you mind me asking what album or what record that says that?

MA: We'll have to look again.

CR: I can shoot you copies, because I can't look while I'm doing a recording.

MA: I know. We'll have to do it afterwards. We'll keep it on keyboards, okay?

AC: Basically, I played grand piano, Hammond B-3, and the Arp String Ensemble was the name of the synthesizer that I used back in 1975. So those were the three instruments that I had on stage and also a Casio. A little Casio with one octave. I used that for comedic effect.

MA: I think on this album *New York Times*, you got credited as Casio keyboardist.

AC: Yes, and there's another album called *Checkpoint Charlie*...

MA: I was going to ask you about that. I don't have it, but I know it plays from the center out. It's the only thing I know about it.

AC: Yes, it's Mark Volman, Howard Kaylan, and Andy Cahan sitting in the office of Flo & Eddie at the Herbie Cohen Complex, which had Frank Zappa, George Duke, Tom Waits, and Flo & Eddie. Mark Volman would roll these gigantic joints with four papers like a cigar. Each one of us had a Casio—a little Casio keyboard—and we would jam and smoke and sing. We added on to a project that Flo & Eddie did with The Turtles backstage and in hotel rooms. It was called The Rhythm Butchers. There's a whole bunch of EPs that Rhino Records put out called The Rhythm Butchers. In any event, Checkpoint Charlie is an extension of The Rhythm Butchers, with us stoned out of our brains, sitting in the office and playing the Casio keyboards. On that particular album, I'm on a song called "Show Me the Way to Go Ohm." You know, instead of "home," "ohm."

CR: Right. Thank you for telling us about Checkpoint Charlie because that was one of our questions. Before we go any further, we want listeners to know that you have written one of the coolest books of all time. It's called *The Most Famous Musician You've Never Heard Of: A Rock and Roll Scrapbook*. It's got Hendrix and Ringo and Nilsson and Little Richard. It goes on and on and on. Ray Bolger, Grace Slick. I know our readers will want to pick up a copy of that to start with. A big part of your musical scrapbook is being the most famous musician that people have never heard of, which is changing quickly with all of these great interviews you are doing. When did you get started? How did you meet Howard and Mark and how did you get started with The Turtles?

AC: I was with Jimmy Carl Black, the Indian of the group with Frank Zappa. Jimmy and I started a band called Geronimo Black, and Bunk Gardner and Tom Leavey, Tjay Contrelli, and there were a lot of other musicians that we had in the band as well. We had Oz Bach from Spanky and Our Gang. Jimmy Carl Black was asked by Frank Zappa to be in *200 Motels*. Jimmy and I got into my VW bus and we drove down La Cienega Blvd. to the rehearsal studio where Flo & Eddie were with Zappa and all the crew from *200 Motels* and the musicians. They were rehearsing the material for *200 Motels*. You know, "Lonesome Cowboy Burt." (sings) "My name is Bertram, I am a redneck..." At that rehearsal, Frank didn't allow anyone to smoke pot, but anyway, Mark Volman and I went out to the parking lot and smoked a joint. We started talking and he said, "Wow, you play keyboards with Jimmy!" I said, "Yeah, I play keyboards and I play drums, guitar and all that." So, eventually, Mark asked me to join the band when we were at Cherokee Studios. It was a four-track studio in Box Canyon in Topanga. I was doing Little Richard organ overdubs for a movie called *Let the Good Times Roll* and Flo & Eddie were there doing overdubs on a cartoon that they did called *Dirty Duck*. It was also called *Cheap*, which is one of the songs on *Illegal, Immoral and Fattening*. Bruce Robb is one of the owners of Cherokee Studios and he was the keyboard player for Flo & Eddie's first two albums. Whatever the case may be, he couldn't go out on the road as he was also an engineer so Mark Volman just said, "Hey Andy, would you be interested in going out on the road?" and that's what happened in 1973. I joined The Turtles.

CR: So '73 is when you started?

AC: Yes, it was like mid-year. It was the touring season. We were doing a lot of concerts. Lots of concerts.

CR: You came on as both a session guy and a touring guy and you were a member of the band, officially?

AC: Officially, yes, and I was the clown. Everybody liked to pick on me, but I enjoyed the attention. It was always fun to be the guy.

MA: So, you weren't in *200 Motels*, you were just around it?

AC: Yeah, it actually helped our band, Geronimo Black, get a record deal because since Jimmy was a star of the movie, with "Lonesome Cowboy Burt" and everything, the record company was very impressed and signed us to a record deal in 1972. That was Russ Regan and he was with Universal Records—UNI Records.

MA: Yeah, UNI became MCA, I believe.

AC: We had so much fun on the road. There are some great stories. One time we went to Australia. I don't know if I spoke about this earlier, but I will state it again. It really sticks out as a really wonderful story. We're on a Pan American 747, flying to Australia and the stewardess knew that we were from The Turtles. She went to the captain and said, "You've got some celebrities on board. You have The Turtles." So the captain—this is 1975—so there was no 9/11 or anything and the pilot's door was wide open. He invited us up to the cockpit, and Mark Volman and I sat in these little chairs that were in the cockpit and the pilot turned around and said, "Do you guys play Backgammon?" and I said, "Sure. Yeah." So, here we are sitting in this 747 that's on auto pilot and playing Backgammon. I'm looking out at the ratio and I'm looking on top of the windshield and there's a whole series of numbers at the top. I asked the captain, "What are those numbers? What do they do? What is this?" He said, "Go ahead. Put your finger on that little wheel there and turn the wheel." and so I start moving the numbers and the airplane starts to bank to the right. I was driving this plane with my index finger with 350 souls aboard. Their lives were in my hands. With my little index finger, I flew a 747. To me, that was very exciting.

CR: I guess that wasn't the only time you were "flying" with The Turtles.

AC: I tell you, we were doing some heavy duty flying. We had a special way of hiding marijuana in the band so nobody knew we had it.

CR: You wanna tell us your secret?

AC: Yeah, you buy empty capsules. Capsules for medicine. You'd buy them empty, with nothing in it. You'd open them up and then you ground up the marijuana and you put it in the capsules. Then, you put the capsules in your vitamin jar and then you put them in your suitcase and nobody knew the difference.

CR: Now they do!

MA: You should have told Paul McCartney!

AC: Oh, I know, we should have told Paul McCartney when he got busted in Japan!

MA: You never got busted?

AC: Our drummer did. Our drummer had a joint in his fanny pack at the place where they check you for guns and shit. The TSA? Whatever.

CR: Right. Security.

AC: Yeah, he had a joint in his fanny pack and the German Shepherd dog went running up to him and shoved his nose right in his fanny pack. They busted him for possession of a joint and he had to pay $125 and that was it.

CR: You toured everywhere? You went around the world with The Turtles?

AC: Well basically, we went to Europe as *The Two and a Half Man Show*, which was just Mark and Howard and myself. We did Australia two times and New Zealand. That's about it that I did with The Turtles. We did a lot of great television.

MA: We'll jump right into Flo & Eddie now. The first album you worked on was *Illegal, Immoral and Fattening*. Did you work on just the live tracks or on the studio tracks, too?

AC: There's one studio track that I played on that's on that album and that's "Rebecca."

CR: Great song!

AC: The album was recorded live on a 24-track truck that was parked in the alley next to the Roxy. If you know what a 24-track machine looks like, those reels only last 15 minutes, but they needed hours of music so they used extra large 24-track reels that lasted a half hour each or close to it. So, we recorded two nights of us performing live at the Roxy. Grace Slick and Alice Cooper and Bernie Taupin and Commander Cody would come down. It was a really big deal. Later on, we did some other tracks in the studio. That was all recorded live at the Roxy. It was wonderful.

MA: Was there a lot of stuff that didn't make the album or was that pretty much the entire concert?

AC: It's the whole concert with a couple of extra added studio tracks like "Rebecca." "Let Me Make Love to You" was a song they did with Aynsley Dunbar and some other guys like Don Preston and Gary Rowles, I think.

MA: Yeah, it was from 1974, a year before, I think.

AC: Right.

MA: And I think they released it twice if I read it correctly. They released it as a single and then when the album came out, they released it again and it was still a flop which was unfortunate, because it was a great song.

AC: Oh yeah, I love that material. That album was so much fun to record because of all the satire with the Pop Star Dildo and all these really funny skits by Mark and Howard. Howard got a lot of his humor from George Carlin. Howard idolized George Carlin, you know, his amazing intelligent humor.

MA: I love Carlin, too. I know that The Turtles got the rights to their master tapes. Was there ever a conversation at the time to just bill themselves as The Turtles or was the Flo & Eddie thing carrying on during the 1970s?

AC: When The Turtles broke up, their management screwed Mark and Howard and they were forced not to use the name Turtles because of contracts. They had to change their name to Flo & Eddie. Do you know the history of how they got that name?

MA: I believe they're named after two ex-roadies or something like that, if I remember correctly.

AC: Yes, Frank Zappa had two roadies named the Phlorescent Leech and Eddie, and Flo & Eddie adopted those names and they changed it to Flo & Eddie instead of Phlorescent Leech, although you can see on that one album that it says "Phlorescent Leech and Eddie."

MA: Yes, that's their first one. Did they ever consider touring at that time as The Turtles because eventually they did get the rights to the name?

AC: They couldn't go out as The Turtles so they had to go out as Flo & Eddie. Eventually, for $80,000 they purchased the masters of "Happy Together" and all the White Whale masters for 80 grand and now they are officially Turtles again, so they were able to tour as The Turtles. But they kept Flo & Eddie because that was their new thing, so they would book as Flo & Eddie and The Turtles. They called the band The Turtles and they would be Flo & Eddie. That's how that came about.

MA: Okay. I was just wondering if after they purchased it they had reservations about using it, but it sounds like they used both, eventually. So, their next album was *Moving Targets*. This was mainly a studio album and my question on this: Was there a concern about not making #1 hits like they did as The Turtles or [was it] we're just going to have some fun and screw it if we have a hit or not?

AC: Actually, there are two or three songs on that album that we were trying to make into a hit. As a matter of fact, there's a song on that album that's called "Keep it Warm…"

CR: Another great song!

MA: There are great songs on it, but they weren't charting hits.

AC: It was a wonderful song, but every time we performed on stage, as soon as I started that piano part intro, the audience would cheer. They loved that song and it's really unfortunate that it didn't become a hit. There was another song on that album that I'm very proud of. It's called "Best Possible Me." The string arrangements and the horn arrangements by Allan MacMillan were all based upon my piano part. It made me feel really good. The whole arrangement of the strings and horns were all based upon the way I played my piano part on that album.

MA: How did they accept your input? I know you didn't get major writing credit, but did you say, "Can I play the keyboards this way?" ever on any track, or were you told how to play?

AC: Well, their stuff is so easy and simple and you just have to be tasty. You can't overplay. You have to play basic rock and roll simple. You can't be complicated. Both Mark and Howard guided me on how they wanted me to play this song. It was really easy so there was really nothing wrong. If I did something stupid, they would tell me.

CR: There's some overplaying on the drumming on some parts. "Moving Targets" is definitely more of a rocker. I think the ones you mentioned are certainly standouts, but you wouldn't put that on and say, "This is a Turtles album."

AC: Right, right.

MA: Except for maybe a remake of "Elenore."

AC: Yeah, that remake of "Elenore," that's when I used that Arc String Ensemble for the chorus.

CR: Why the remake?

AC: The Turtles owned the song "Elenore," and Howard Kaylan wrote the song because "Happy Together" was #1. The record company said, "We want another 'Happy Together' tomorrow, so Howard was on the road and he went into his hotel room and on a napkin, he wrote the lyrics to "Elenore." He really did take the same formula as "Happy Together." The vocals on "Happy Together" were designed after The Zombies "Tell Her No." The verses are very silky and soft. (sings) "And if she should tell you…" like (sings) "Imagine me and you, I do…" You know, really soft. Then the chorus was (sings) "Tell her no no no nono nono no…" That's why Howard went (sings) "I can't see…" really strong. That was the formula for "Happy Together" and the rhythm was straight four. You know bomp bomp bomp bomp. So what he did with "Elenore" was (sings) "You've got a thing about you…" You know, very soft and airy and silky and then (sings) "Elenore, gee I think you're swell…" That was the big, loud chorus and it became #1. Howard brought the napkin to rehearsal and John Barbata, Jim Pons, Al Nichol, and Mark Volman all arranged "Elenore" with Howard, so they all got writer's credit on that song, so The Turtles own the publishing and the writing for "Elenore," and that's the reason that they released it on this reissue.

MA: True. They owned it by now, so yeah.

CR: The way you described both those songs also applies to "It Ain't Me Babe." It's a Dylan song where it's that silky sweet verse and then it's then it's (sings) "No no no…" It just rocks!

AC: That is the formula of The Turtles, yes. That is the formula.

MA: You figured it out!

AC: Literally, Howard Kaylan did that because… who's the lead singer on The Zombies?

CR: Colin Blunstone.

AC: Yes, that's the reason. That's the reason that Howard used that formula: a silky verse and strong chorus.

CR: You can't compare the two because Kaylan's vocal and strong choruses would blow away anything The Zombies did or most of the other bands around.

AC: Can I just say something and I'm being honest from the bottom of my heart? Howard Kayland is the best vocalist I have ever run into in my life. He's right there with Little Richard. He's right there with Paul McCartney. He's right there with every amazing vocalist. Howard never sings out of tune ever. Ever, ever, ever, ever. He never sings out of tune and he can sing any note you give him.

MA: Yes, he has an excellent range. The song I always know which I know you didn't record, was "Love in the City." It goes way up there. I can't hit those notes. Even when I was young, I couldn't hit those notes.

AC: And then, Mark Volman has an extremely high range on the harmonies. You know "Bang a Gong (Get it On)," that's Mark totally singing on the top of their range. (sings) "Bang a gong…"

MA: I guess after you did those two albums, you kept touring around during the late '70s because the next album wasn't until 1981. Were you constantly on tour with them during the late '70s and early '80s?

AC: Absolutely. We were touring all the time. We did a couple of TV shows. We did *Lloyd Thaxton* and we did *Dinah Shore* and we did a pilot with The Unknown Comic called *Sunset Strip*. We did just a bunch of stuff. We did *The Garry Shandling Show* in 1980.

MA: I remember that. Actually the first time I had heard of Flo & Eddie, I didn't know the Turtles' connection because I was a kid. I was a big fan of Martin Mull from *Fernwood 2night* and he had Flo & Eddie on there.

AC: Oh yeah.

MA: They did Bun 'n' Run commercials and other really weird stuff. Were you part of that?

AC: Well, yeah. Martin Mull was sitting next to me at the piano. We did "Midnight Special" with Flo & Eddie. Flo & Eddie and Martin Mull and an accordion player by the name of Murray Sheaths, they did some funny skits. Flo & Eddie and The Turtles went on and did a cover tune. I forget which. Martin Mull did a skit with Flo & Eddie. It's on YouTube because I posted it where they are playing Peter, Paul and Mary and they do "Puff, the Magic Dragon." Martin Mull is Peter, Howard is Paul, and Mark is Mary.

CR: Mark, you're going to have to add that to this book!

MA: Yeah, I guess so! I saw a photo of that. I've never seen the footage.

AC: It's on my YouTube channel. I've got it posted. I can send you the link or whatever, but it's hilarious.

CR: You mentioned hilarious. That goes hand in hand with these guys: humor and music. It's such an asset. Most of the videos we see Mark goofing around. The question is if he played instruments and he played horns and he's credited on the records, how come he's not doing it on the videos and in the live spots we see on TV? How come he's just throwing a tambourine or just being silly? If he's such a good musician, why didn't we see that in the visuals?

AC: A lot of saxophone stuff was with The Crossfires. You know, when they were in that surf band way before The Turtles. Mark and Howard both played sax. They weren't really great saxophone players. They were just average. You know, one note shit. Mark is a good guitar player, but he plays rhythm and there's some really funny stuff that he did with the guitar, too, of course, but he is the clown. He's the one that makes everybody laugh and Howard is the straight man. That's how they've always been. You look at their early videos and Howard's trying to be a serious guy singing and Mark is all over him trying to make him laugh. Mark Volman is the manager. He's the businessman of The Turtles. He created the West Coast band and the East Coast band for financial purposes with airplanes and hotel rooms and all that. It's much easier to have an East Coast band and a West Coast band so you don't have to pay for all that extra expense. In any event, Flo & Eddie are completely.... Their resume is so extensive, you will be mind blown, if you ever Google all of the stuff they've been on from Blondie to Bruce Springsteen to Marc Bolan to Todd Rundgren. It's just on and on. Every celebrity loves Flo & Eddie. They're the best.

MA: The next album you did, I didn't even know you were credited on it, *Rock Steady with Flo & Eddie*, the reggae album. Did you appear on this? All of the reggae artists are listed, but I didn't see any keyboardists listed, but then it's mentioned on your website.

AC: Absolutely! I play an organ solo on one song. It's my only appearance on that album.

MA: Oh, so you weren't on the entire album.

AC: On the vinyl, it lists my name Andy Cahan—Keyboards on that specific song title.

MA: Let me look. "Those Guys?"

AC: "Those Guys!" I play the organ solo on that particular item. They went to Tuff Gong Studios in Jamaica and they used all of Bob Marley's musicians on this album, so "Happy Together" was reggae. That photograph on the front of the album was taken in the alleyway behind Herb Cohen's office. I was there when they shot that picture.

MA: So, not technically in Jamaica?

AC: That was the same day as the Checkpoint Charlie—smoking the joint—Casio stuff. It was the same era, because that's all we did was listen to Bob Marley. That's all we did was smoke joints and listen to Bob Marley.

MA: So you're listening to Bob Marley and then you do Checkpoint Charlie like Kraftwerk and then you start doing children's albums like The Care Bears and Strawberry Shortcake. How does that all mesh together?

AC: Financially, Mark and Howard were really not doing too good. They had to find work and Murakami-Wolf-Swenson, the same people who did Jolly Green Giant and all this, had hired Mark and Howard to do the music for Strawberry Shortcake and G.I. Joe and The Care Bears. So they hired me to hire all the musicians, but basically it was the Casio, that same Casio keyboard. So we did all these Strawberry Shortcake albums and G.I. Joe and Care Bears and it was all hilarious doing kids records.

MA: Now who else worked on it because nobody got credit? Flo & Eddie barely got credit, so who's on it? I didn't even know you were on it.

AC: Well, there's an incredible harmonica player by the name of Stanley Barenz who played with everyone in the world. This guy is used by everybody. Buzz Garner, the trumpet player from The Mothers of Invention, played on this album. Dusty Wakeman, the owner of Mad Dog Studios who owns a microphone company and who was the bass player? I think my friend Tom Leavey was the bass player. Anyhow, I contracted all these guys.

MA: Now did all of these albums just run their course? They did more albums without them, so why did they do only so many? Did they just get tired of doing them?

AC: That was what the contract was. They did x amount of recordings and Strawberry Shortcake split them up to a dozen different albums with G.I. Joe and Care Bears, but it's all the same stuff.

MA: Was it all done in just a few sessions?

AC: I did most of the work on the Casio. Then we got the drummer to come in and then the guitar player and the horn player and the harmonica player, but it was all really simple simple stuff. I mean really simple stuff.

MA: I have one of the albums and I have heard some of it on YouTube. Did they speed up their voices? It sounds like they did a little bit.

AC: Absolutely. Absolutely. Yes, that was a whole strange era. Their office was in Miss America. The same office where Miss America was, Flo & Eddie got an office there. So they were in the same office as Miss America. It was hilarious.

MA: One thing I read, I think it was one of the Strawberry Shortcake ones or The Care Bears, but one of them had Christina Applegate before she was on *Married: with Children* as doing one of the voices. Were you present when they were doing the voices?

AC: No, the only character I met was the girl who played Strawberry Shortcake. We went to her house, but a lot of celebrities did the voiceovers on all that, so yeah, it's true.

MA: Moving on, *The Turtles Featuring Flo & Eddie Captured Live*. Did you work on that one?

AC: It all depends on the songs and where the venue was. Where does it say?

MA: It says, "Recorded at the Bottom Line in New York City," and I know it's a 1991 concert.

AC: Oh, there was a time when I was not with The Turtles. I was fired from the band.

MA: What?

AC: My wife and I were getting a divorce. I was very depressed and my musical chops on the keyboards were down. I wasn't up to par. We were going to go out on the road with two keyboard players and it was too expensive to hire an extra guy on the stage, so they wanted me to learn all the synthesizer strings and play the piano and the organ and the Wurlitzer so I have to play all these string parts and horn parts plus rhythm, which I wasn't in any condition to do. Mark Volman loaned me a synthesizer so I could practice doing all of this stuff and I failed the audition.

MA: Wow!

AC: The same week that Mark and Howard said, "Andy, we're going to have to get a guy who can play all of this stuff. We love you, but we can't use you." That was the same week my wife said, "I'm taking the kids and I'm moving to Phoenix!" So, in that one week, I was fired from The Turtles and I was divorced and my wife took my kids to Arizona. I was completely blown off the planet Earth. Later on, I did the demo doctor which I had Harry Nilsson and Ringo Starr and Jimmy Webb and a lot of celebrities, including Eric Carmen, record in my living room. That brought me back to The Turtles again. Mark Volman called me up six years later and said, "We want you back in the West Coast band. You're going to run the West Coast band." That was in 1993 or whatever.

MA: Okay, that was after this. The two listed are Chris Apostle and Peter Zael. I don't know if you know them.

AC: Yeah. Peter Zael and Chris Apostle, yes. Those were the guys who took my place. That's when they did a whole bunch of Bottom Line recordings. I'm on one of them from the '80s. On *New York Times*, I'm on one song or something. I was doing a lot of stuff with Mark and Howard in the studio during those six years. You know, the Strawberry Shortcake and all that stuff. We did *The Garry Shandling Show*. We did a couple of other things. I did a thing at Universal City Studios where I met Harry Nilsson. I met everybody—Elvira and Micky Dolenz. I already knew Micky from the road. Eric Burdon, Dean Torrance, Richard Lewis, Kevin Meaney, so yeah, I was doing a lot of stuff when I was fired from the band like studio stuff and I would still get high with them and hang out in the office and stuff. There were no bad feelings, but my chops got really good being a demo doctor. I got all my chops back and I was able to play everything perfectly. Now, I'm okay.

MA: That's great. I think also on your website, there were a couple of non-Turtles albums I want to talk about. One is, The Monkees' *Pool It!* What did you do for *Pool It!*?

AC: Yeah, I was hired by their producer at Rhino Records, Harold Bronson, who called up Louis Natkin, I think that's his name. He said, "Andy, we want you to play some keyboards on the *Pool It!* album." There was a Davy Jones song called "I'll Love You Forever." That's the one I'm on the keyboards. There was a really really funny story. When we toured, when I rejoined the band, in 1993 or whenever it was, they would introduce me as the guy who played this keyboard part, and I would go (plays "Daydream Believer") and everyone in the audience thought I was the guy who wrote that part. It was apocryphal. Mark Volman treats it as theater. He'll tell you that the drummer was with Santana washing his car and the guitar player was with Stevie Ray Vaughan and the bass player played with The Four Tops and they said that I was with The Monkees. It's all a lie. It's all theater. That's how Mark Volman explains it.

MA: So you only played on that one song on that album? You didn't tour with them ever?

AC: Nope, never did, but we did tour WITH The Monkees a lot.

MA: So you did tour with them, but as part of The Turtles?

AC: Yes. There was one really wonderful concert with The Animals, The Monkees, and The Turtles. I say to myself, "How cool is that?"

CR: Just for Mark's edification, it was for Dolenz, Jones, Boyce, and Hart at that time.

AC: Yeah!

CR: And The Animals and The Turtles!

MA: Oh, it was back in the '70s. I thought it might have been in the '80s.

AC: Yeah, I think that was in the '70s, yeah. There was a Happy Together tour, but in between that we would do some Monkees concerts.

MA: I'm sure with all those Happy Together tours, you're always bumping into people. You're bumping into Micky. You're bumping into Ron Dante. You're bumping into over the years David Cassidy and Bobby Sherman, when they joined forces, right?

AC: I've met every idol that I grew up listening to like Tommy Roe and all these guys. What's that other guy (sings)?

CR: Billy J. Kramer.

AC: Yeah! I met him. I met all these amazing people, all the different bands on the Happy Together Tour and all the different acts. I got to meet so many amazing people because of my relationship with Flo & Eddie that I'm very grateful for, which made it really easy to write the book.

CR: Andy, during your tenure with The Turtles, were you always a hired gun? Were you ever on salary? Was it pay by play? What was your financial scenario with them?

AC: Yeah, it was pay by play. You got a gig, you get paid. You got a recording session, you get paid. It wasn't a salary.

CR: Gotcha. And that was the same except for the two bosses, right?

AC: Right. They owned everything and they ran the ship, but they treated everybody fantastically. Everybody who's been in their band has always been completely happy because Mark and Howard are great entertainers and very professional and it's a complete wonderment to play with The Turtles.

MA: I don't know if they do this now, and not since Howard's been out of commission for a while, but they used to have a contract on The Turtles' website that you could print out, and it basically had a list of all their demands that they needed to have a show. If you paid the fee and had all the things they needed—like water or certain treats or a limo or whatever—I forgot all those things, but if you met all of those qualifications, they'd play at your wedding, they'd play at your Bar Mitzvah, they'd play anywhere. Did you ever do anything like that?

AC: We did several of those. These wealthy, wealthy, wealthy people hired The Turtles for their private party. There was one party we played when we ended the night, we did "Happy Together" and everybody loved it. Then the owner of the place, the guy who the party was for, said, "I'll give you guy's extra money. Will you please play "Happy Together" again?" All the equipment was torn down. There was no more equipment on stage, so the guitar player picked up an acoustic guitar and Howard sang "Happy Together" with the guitar player. We've done amazing small party stuff. Yeah, that is a very true thing.

MA: Wow! Yeah. I was even tempted as a fan saying, "Hmmm," because it wasn't a lot of money, it was a decent amount, but if you got a few friends together, you could put it on. It was only a few thousand dollars.

AC: I know. I actually did all of the advance work. I was the road manager for the West Coast band, so they paid me a little extra to do all the advance work with the hotels, the airplanes, the backstage food, you know, all the stuff that we wanted, taken care of. I would do that, too.

MA: I basically have one more question, but it might take a while to answer. I have Howard Kaylan's one and only solo album, *Dust Bunnies*, and I love this album. How did that come about and why wasn't Mark involved? Was he busy or he just didn't want to do it? What were the circumstances behind it?

AC: We were on an airplane flying to Belgium to play a concert with The Monkees, Procol Harum, The Troggs, and like Slade, or something. We were on the airplane and I was sitting next to Davy Jones and all we did was talk about horses, because I love horses and he loves horses. Then, I got up out of my seat, and I sat next to Howard. I said, "Howard, I'll tell you what..." I was doing all these demos with Harry Nilsson and Ringo Starr and Eric Carmen and I said, "Let's do a Howard Kaylan album. Pick out 10 songs that you always wanted to sing and I'll sequence and program them in my living room on my synthesizer and we'll put out an album." That's how it came about. Howard would send me all these songs, 10 songs that are on the album, and I would duplicate them with my synthesizer—the bass, the drums, the guitar, all the instruments, and then Howard would sing it in my living room. So we made this album and then all of a sudden, a guy named David Spiro, who was good friends with Ringo and good friends with Billy Bob and he was running the Rock and Roll Hall of Fame called up Howard and said, "Hey listen, Billy Bob Thornton is offering his studio to you to finish your album that you're doing with Andy." So, we went over to Billy Bob Thornton's house. Now, I gotta tell you about this. This is the most amazing story that you're ever going to hear. Billy Bob Thornton lives on Roxbury in Beverly Hills. The house he lives in used to belong to Cecil B. DeMille. During Prohibition, Cecil would hold alcohol parties in his basement. The basement had a tunnel going from Roxbury Drive to La Cienega Blvd. in Beverly Hills.

MA: Wow!

AC: There was a funny storefront on La Cienega Blvd. and all these movie stars would take their limos, go into this phony storefront, go down the elevator to the tunnel, and take the tunnel to Cecil B. DeMille's house for the party. This is the house that Billy Bob still lives in. Cecil B. sold the house to Roger Corman. Roger Corman sold the house to Roman Polanski. Polanski sold the house to

Slash of Guns 'n' Roses. Slash is the one who built the studio in the basement. So when Billy Bob Thornton bought that house, it came with the studio in the basement. It's a complete studio and he would get all these people to come over and get Holly Williams, Hank Williams Jr.'s daughter. She would go there. Moon Zappa would go there. Don Was, the producer. He and I were in the studio playing guitars and we were jamming on a song by Major Lance called "Monkey Time." Recording in that studio was completely amazing and Billy Bob Thornton did a cameo performance on a song called "Music." I produced the whole thing on Pro Tools. I had to transfer my demos from my living room into the studio so we could finish it there. Howard actually had some musicians in New York play drums and bass and guitar, but they used a reel-to-reel tape recorder and they should have used Pro Tools because when we got the recordings from them, we tried to sync it up with my recording and it got out of sync because it was a reel-to-reel machine that changed speed. So it was a pain in the ass, but we got a good album out of it. It's a good album.

MA: Yeah, I like this album. Two of the tracks are by The Left Banke, so apparently he was a big fan of them.

AC: Oh, totally. Totally. Billy Bob has in his living room hallway, a gigantic wall like a blackboard, and all these celebrities and these movie stars would sign it to him. So when Howard Kaylan came over, he asked Howard to sign it, so Howard signed it. Then Billy Bob got down on his knees and he prayed to Howard with his hands up and down like he's praying and he said, "You're the best in the world. I love you. You're great!" So, Billy Bob knew every single word to all of the Frank Zappa and Flo & Eddie songs, and he knew every word to every Turtles song. Billy Bob was a gigantic fan of Howard Kaylan and Mark Volman.

MA: Now was there any thought of bringing Mark in on this project? Or was it, "Let's just do it with Howard?"

AC: It was just designed as a Howard solo album. When I sat next to him on that airplane in 1993 or whenever it was, I said, "Howard, let's do an album. Just pick out 10 songs that you want to do and we'll do it."

MA: Although you did get Mark on there from the standpoint that he did co-write "Easy Street," so I guess that was his nod to him.

AC: Yeah, he co-wrote "Easy Street." The demos that we made for that one. I've done so many demos with them, it's incredible.

CR: How come you didn't do a solo Mark Volman album?

AC: I should have. I wanted to. In fact, I spoke to Mark the other day. Are you guys familiar with the Two and a Half Man Show I did with Flo & Eddie? It was a Vaudeville comedy act. We had a slide projector and showed movies and had stuffed animals and all these props on the stage. It was called the Two and Half Man Show and we toured Europe. So Mark Volman was on the phone with me and he said, "Let's go on the road and do the One and a Half Man Show." Of course, Howard is unable to go on the road anymore. His health prevents him. As a matter of fact, Ron Dante is the current lead singer of The Turtles. What they did was, every concert tour, they would sell a CD of all the groups on the Happy Together Tour. They wanted to put out "Happy Together," but they didn't want Ron Dante to sing it, they wanted Howard Kaylan to sing it. So, they had me record Howard singing in my living room, "Happy Together" for this live track of the band on stage. It was the very final definitive version that I recorded with Howard.

CR: Ron is a great guy and so talented beyond The Archies and everything else. Why was he selected as the vocalist? What was the criteria for selecting him to take Howard's place?

AC: Mark Volman made the decision because Mark Volman had toured with Ron Dante and Ron has a good voice.

CR: He's got a great voice, yeah! We love him!

AC: So Mark decided to have Ron and he enjoys it because Ron is very uppity and very happy and very positive. He stands on the edge of the stage and he watches the whole show and he's always very very enthusiastic. He's a really cool guy. He produced Barry Manilow. Did you know he produced Barry Manilow?

CR: Yes. He also produced Broadway shows. It's beyond what we know. Ron Dante's credits are amazing.

AC: Yeah, he's just a really sweet guy. Very nice.

CR: He's a real mensch. One of the nicest guys in show business, no doubt.

AC: Oh yeah, he's really terrific. We both have friends back in New York, Dave Espinoza, the guitar player. He played on Archies stuff. We know the same people from way back.

MA: So, what are the plans now?

AC: I'm not a member of the touring band anymore. Mark Volman has a guy named Godfrey Townsend, who is a guitar player and he put together a band: the drummer, the bass player and the keyboards for The Turtles with Mark and Howard, so they're sticking with Godfrey and his crew for their touring on the Happy Together Tour. I'm very grateful I was with them for 46 years.

CR: I don't know if you knew this, but for a while The Turtles keyboardist was Greg Hawkes from The Cars. How did that come about?

AC: Well, Mark knew him. Mark and Howard know everybody. They needed another touring group for the East Coast band. So, either Joe Stefko or Tristan Karvekian recommended him, or maybe Mark just decided to hire Greg. He did play in the East Coast band.

CR: Another great guy.

AC: Yeah, there's a lot of musicians that have played with Flo & Eddie. A lot.

MA: I've seen The Turtles and they have this ability to imitate Bruce Springsteen or on the one you did, *Illegal, Immoral and Fattening*, you suddenly go into "Bang a Gong," then you do "Jumpin' Jack Flash," and then you do "My Sweet Lord" with what seems like no effort. Is it hard to take those cues to do a song like that?

AC: That was what our rehearsal was. The Comedy. We already knew how to play the hit records. It was just working out the comedy routines. They did that with Zappa. They took a Zappa show and put it into their own show with Flo & Eddie and all the funny stuff with the costumes. It was really funny stuff. Really funny.

MA: I love that album. Like the song "Cheap," just the way it's done, makes it sound cheap. Of course, that's the whole point. They sing "cheap" off key.

AC: The greatest part of that song is (sings) "this whole concert is a great big pile of shit!" At the Crater Bowl, we opened up for Fleetwood Mac, and the News in Hawaii recorded Flo & Eddie doing "Cheap." You can hear Flo & Eddie sing it and it was on the News! "That is so funny!" It was great working with Fleetwood Mac and I used to hang out with Stevie Nicks on the beach there and oh my God, what a beautiful woman.

Dinky Dawson—February 20, 2021

CR: What's your Turtles story?

DD: Carlos Bernal was a roadie for The Byrds and he also played bass. One day, a man came to my house named Al Hirsch. At that time, we called him "Al, the Kiddies Pal," because he had a shop that sold clothes and pot. He introduced me to other characters like Spanky and Our Gang. It was mainly Spanky and her family more than anything that was coming out to Topanga. We were going to Topanga to the Corral to see them play and stuff.

The next thing I know Howard and Mark from The Turtles come over. I had no idea who these characters were. I knew of them, but we've got a new kid in town, so let's see what's going on here. And they were fun. They came in here and we smoked a lot of weed and bongs. It was really just a get together to have fun and meet people.

After that, I started my own sound company in 1972. Some years later, in 1982, I got a call and heard this on the phone, "Will you come down to New York and help us?" I said, "What do you need?" He said, "We're reforming The Mamas & the Papas."

I went down to New Jersey in the Cadillac Eldorado I had. We did rehearsals and all kinds of shows. We did *Entertainment Tonight* and we did this, that and the other. It was great to see Spanky and she was singing her ass off in The Mamas & the Papas. They were just fantastic.

Meanwhile, Al introduced me to David Fishof. Why I bring David Fishof in is because he's the key to everything. David was a sports agent and a lawyer, but more of an agent than anything. He was just getting into the music stuff. He was getting us out there and putting us into Grossinger's in New York. Then he got us into the Sands in Las Vegas.

This is where the Howard and Mark story starts. The first night we played, it was a Tuesday night and we were doing three shows a night. We were playing until 3am and the group was really playing well. After the show, I get a call from Al who says, "Don't come into the dressing room," because Frank Sinatra was there.

Sinatra said, "You've got to get all these '60s acts into Vegas."

Al jumped in and said, "I'll get them. No problem."

Next day, he calls Fishof and then he starts chanting off all these acts, "I want The Turtles. I want The Association, Gary Puckett, and anyone else you can find."

Frank came back the next day and found out that he was getting Gary Puckett, The Association, and The Turtles. The next thing we know, he's got these opening acts. It was a nice sixties thing and it was packed every night. We had no problem packing the place. This started 11 January 1983.

The next big event is what happened next with The Turtles. On March 16, 1983, we were doing a TV show in Salt Lake City. They asked me because I was with The Mamas & the Papas and because we were the first ones in there, if I would stay and work with The Association and The Turtles. So, Howard and Mark come in and—oh man—they're wonderful to work with because they're so professional. We had fun just going back and forth, emotional-wise. It was just like we'd always been together. It was like we were always friends but this was the first time we had ever worked with them.

Now, on May 10, 1983, they come to Boston and I get a call that The Mamas & Papas were in South Shore. They're performing at Jonathan Swift's in Cambridge. It's a funky little place. During the performance, Mark jumps up and puts his shoulder out. The next thing they're taking him to the emergency room to put his shoulder back and all he wanted to do was go back on stage. That's typical Mark. These guys just want to perform. They're just so wonderful and really do perform well.

At that time, big hair was just starting to come in and they had a band with their guitarists and they'd just let it rip. They'd sing their high parts and it was like watching Zappa in a lot of ways. Their shows were fantastic.

Fishof kept calling them and calling them saying, "We've got to put a package together and we're going to call it Happy Together," and that's what it's been for the last 30+ odd years. It's Happy Together and you'll see The Association and Gary still going at it. Howard and Mark loved it. They could do Happy Together in the summer and then in the winter, go to Hawaii and smoke ganja. They had a good thing going for years.

John Barbata—February 20, 2021

MA: We are thrilled and excited today to have one of the actual Turtles, John Barbata.

CR: Not just one of the Turtles, but one of the great rock and roll drummers of all time, ever. You watch him and you want to be a drummer. You want to twirl. You want to go crazy on the drums. There's not a lot like him. Johny, how'd you get your style?

MA: How'd you start twirling them sticks?

JB: I was in high school in San Luis Obispo and I was in a group called The Sentinals. I was a sophomore. We had a #1 hit all the way up and down the California coast called "Latinia" and I started spinning my sticks way back when, from the beginning, from day one. They had a marching band thing going that I did with the sticks that I invented that no one else does.

CR: Were you classically trained?

JB: No, I trained myself.

CR: Were you originally one of The Crossfires?

JB: No, I came later. I was always the second drummer. I was the second drummer in The Turtles. Second in CSNY. Starship, I was the first drummer and I was the third drummer in the Airplane.

Photo taken at Rock Con: Weekend of 100 Rock Stars in the Meadowlands, NJ July 31, 2010. From the www.RockFanFest.com collection.

CR: That alone is like playing in the major leagues and playing for the best teams in baseball. It was Crosby, Stills, and Nash who stole you from The Turtles. Is that correct?

JB: Yeah. I did albums with those guys collectively and individually. I did two albums with Graham Nash and one with Stephen. One with Neil Young; the *Time Fades Away* album. What else? I did a Crosby-Nash album and I did the *Four Way Street* album. I did seven or eight albums with those guys.

CR: *Four Way Street*—One of the great albums of all time! So tell us how you hooked up with The Turtles.

JB: Lee Michaels found out that The Turtles were looking for a drummer. They loaded my drums in the back of this van and we went out down there. I did an audition and Bones Howe, who produced The Mamas & the Papas and other people said, "Get that drummer!" and he did. The rest is history. The first song I played on was "Happy Together," which was a #1 hit single. They had four hits in a row by Bonner and Gordon. Then we had two more hits after that. There were seven, eight or nine hits of The Turtles, but they had their first #1 hit when they had "Happy Together." When I left, they never had another hit.

MA: It's all you!

CR: That's amazing!

JB: Well, not totally. The writers, Bonner and Gordon, wrote some really great hits.

CR: You mentioned Lee Michaels. Is that "Do You Know What I Mean?" The same guy?

JB: Yes, absolutely. He was one of my best friends. He played with The Sentinals. I played with him when he had his own band. Lee, he's a trip. He's down in Venice.

MA: John, I've heard that Gene Clark of The Byrds introduced you to The Turtles. Is that correct?

JB: He did as well, but it was Lee Michaels who took me down there. That's how I got the gig. Gene was a good friend as well.

CR: It was pretty much a straight drum introduction to recording, or did you go on the road? What was first?

JB: I sat in there and jammed with them and that's when Howe said, "Get that drummer," and I was with Howard after that and was with the band. That was the first thing and we started recording.

MA: You also did the "music videos"—as you would call them now—for "Happy Together" and for "She's My Girl" at the time. There weren't too many that they did. What was it like to film those little promotional films back then?

JB: We did two *Smothers Brothers*, two *Hollywood Palaces* and um…

MA: *Ed Sullivan*…

JB: Yeah, we did *Ed Sullivan!*

MA: Howard Kaylan talks about *Ed Sullivan* and says that he was a bundle of nerves when he went on there. How were you before you did *Ed Sullivan*?

JB: No problem, man, no problem.

CR: Johny's a rock and roll gangster. C'mon! You think *Ed Sullivan*'s going to faze him?

JB: On the show, Mark Volman hands him a flower and Ed Sullivan didn't know what to do, so he went to a commercial. Ed's all "What is the flower?" Mark said, "Ed, it's flower power." We had just followed The Stones. They had semen all over the toilets, beer cans and shit. They were like crazy wild.

MA: Sometimes Howard says things that are apparently exaggerated, so I have to ask: Were you trying to get The Turtles to wear matching suits on stage?

JB: I tried to get them to dress better because they dressed terribly. They had no class. They grew up from The Crossfires and they knew nothing about wearing clothes. They just didn't know. They were sloppy. In The Sentinals, we all wore Nehru suits. We had all that stuff going for us. We did the Vegas thing and had all that stuff going for us. I will say this about The Turtles, they never gave me anything. They were kind of jealous of me. When I left the group, they say I left because of personal reasons, but I left because they weren't going anywhere. They were writing their own songs and they weren't very good. I decided to leave and go on to bigger and better things, which I did.

CR: They gave you credit later on. They said that you were their superior drummer, but the guy who came in after you [John Seiter], he was just a friend. He was just a buddy, but they said that no way did he have the chops that you did. That's on record.

JB: That pissed me off, too, because I was just as much of a buddy as he was. In all the different interviews, they never mention me. They were jealous of me, man. When The Turtles would play, the girls would punch through and come up on stage. They wouldn't look at Mark and Howard because they were heavy. They looked at the drummer. End of story. That was the way it was. They were always jealous of me. The show was really Mark shaking his tambourine and me twirling my sticks. Howard had a great voice and THAT WAS The Turtles. When you saw The Turtles live, it sounded just like the records which was important because a lot of groups don't sound like their records and we did.

CR: Well, a lot of groups didn't play their own music. It was recorded by The Wrecking Crew or whatever and then they'd come out and play. You were a real band!

JB: Yeah, people used to ask if that was Hal Blaine, "Did you play on "Happy Together?" He'd say, "No, that's John Barbata." "Wow, it sounded like you!" I knew Hal Blaine. He was a great guy.

MA: How were the executives at White Whale? Did you deal with them directly? I've heard stories that they were notoriously cheap.

JB: They were weird. They didn't want me to play what I was playing on "She'd Rather Be With Me" and "Happy Together." They wanted me to play something different. The producer—what the hell is his name?—he said, "Man, you're crazy. That's great stuff!" Actually, "She'd Rather Be With Me" stylized me as a drummer. In fact, it got me #7 of the best songs of the '60s as a drummer. Ginger Baker got #1. All he did was play on the one and the three. He didn't do any fills or anything. The fill I did, no one could even do that fill.

MA: Were you referring to Chip Douglas as producer?

JB: Yeah. He was on "Happy Together." He produced *The Battle of the Bands* album. He left to produce The Monkees and also produced Linda Ronstadt, which I played on, but never got credit for that, either. He produced "Happy Together" and then he moved to a plantation. He's over there now.

CR: Were you credited on all The Turtles tracks that you played on?

JB: Oh yeah, of course. As far as I know.

CR: Okay, so that was legit. Johny, we're sensing that there's bitterness after all of these years. Do you not keep in touch? They're not friends?

JB: I'll be honest with you for truth that's never been told, Howard's a great guy. Nobody likes Mark. Mark's an asshole. He tries to play the leader and all that stuff. He was a saxophone player. That was his whole thing with The Crossfires. Mark and Howard are like a comedy team. Flo & Eddie didn't make it. That pissed them off because they had to go back to being The Turtles. Everybody wants to hear their hits. It's reality. It's just the way it is. That's all.

CR: Your drumming on their hits is unbelievable and it definitely stands out, along with Howard with his phenomenal voice.

JB: Yes, he was a crooner. I don't think anybody in CSNY could sing as well as he could as far as crooning goes. Grace Slick and Marty Balin, Marty Balin especially, were crooners. Mark, he really wasn't a crooner. They had great chemistry, but Howard, he was the crooner.

CR: You and probably the other guys in the band were the teen idols. The girls would probably salivate over you, and the guys in the audience would probably listen to the two front people sing, and the grown-ups would enjoy the humor of it.

JB: The Turtles were an act. You didn't just see just a group that would sing and then leave. Mark would throw his tambourine up one side of his arm then go down his other side. I always did a drum solo and that really brought me out to the forefront so to speak.

CR: Tell us what you did with The Turtles that you're most proud of.

JB: Well, I co-wrote "Elenore." I wrote some words in that song. "Happy Together"—that badumpump badumpump. That's stylized musical drumming. On "She'd Rather Be With Me," I totally turned the beat around and the bridge, I did a fill that was coming out of that.

MA: Did you play on "Guide for the Married Man," because that was kind of a different situation?

JB: The only song that I played where they used a click track. I did the click track on that song.

CR: Was that by the songwriter's choice? That was John Williams that wrote that, the famous composer that went on to do orchestration.

JB: Right.

CR: Was click track your choice?

JB: No, that wasn't my choice. They just wanted to do that. And I've done over 100 albums.

CR: Over 100 albums as a studio drummer? Whoa!

JB: Yeah, Dr. John, Booker T, Leon Russell, Dave Mason, Linda Ronstadt, Everly Brothers, a lot of people.

CR: Who was the very first?

JB: Besides all the groups I was in? Maybe it was Linda Ronstadt. I'm not sure. That's a good question. I don't know if my memory can go back that far.

CR: Was that with Peter Asher as the producer?

JB: No, Chip Douglas produced it. He produced The Turtles and then produced Linda Ronstadt and got me to play drums on that. She had a voice! She really had the best voice of everybody.

MA: I'm going to have to ask a bunch of stuff if you're telling it like it is. Now, the story that has differing outcomes is the one about Jim Tucker when you guys went to England. Now the way Howard tells it is that Jim Tucker got all pissed off at John Lennon and quit the band, and Jim Tucker before he passed away said that no, that wasn't true at all. I just got tired of playing or something like that. What do you feel is the real story?

JB: Everything was bullshit. He said it like everything it was. He never talked to John Lennon about that, it was all bullshit. That was the thing about John and Ringo. They were stoned on acid. We were drunk off bottles of French red wine. I didn't know what to say. I froze and our roadie came along and tripped and spilled a whole pitcher of beer on John Lennon's lap. He was smoking a cigarette and he kept smoking like it never happened. He was stoned on acid and I leaned over and said, "I'm sorry about that," and he said, "Oh, don't worry about it. It's no big deal. If it wasn't for you guys, we wouldn't be here." I said, "What do you mean by that? It's all Beatles-Turtles and all that." He said, "Everything we've got, we stole from Chuck Berry."

CR: He said that?

JB: Yeah, he said that to me.

CR: Oh, wow! In his LSD mind, he still gave Chuck Berry credit.

JB: Oh yeah. I mean, The Stones did, too. Keith Richards, probably the best rhythm guitar player in the world.

CR: What was it like touring England, because Mark and Howard always say that that was their goal was to have a hit in England and show The Beatles. What was that like for you, personally?

JB: Well, when we went to the Speakeasy, it was packed with every rock musician you can imagine with all of these French and English models. As soon as we came through the doors, they all turned their heads. We came in with our entourage of seven or eight people. We went in and sat in the back. I'm looking at the bar and there's Paul McCartney having a drink and Rod Stewart was there. They were all there. Brian Jones was there with a blonde and I look over next to us and there's John and Ringo. I knew their road manager. I had met him in L.A. So, our manager asked if we could go over to him and he said, "Sure, come on over." So, I'm sitting between them and that's when the whole thing happened. The Speakeasy was a small place. We ended up playing there the next night and it was packed. Hendrix and Clapton were there. He was just coming up the ladder and everybody was there. That little guy I can't stand was there, Eric Burdon from The Animals.

CR: Here you are in England, and you're at the top of your game and everyone came to see you. Did anyone sit in? Did anyone jam? Did anyone jump on stage?

JB: We opened up at The Speakeasy in front of everybody. Brian Jones was like 10 feet in front of me. We opened up and we were all nervous. We opened up with "It Ain't Me Babe" by Bob Dylan, the first hit that The Turtles had. We got a standing ovation and then we were comfortable. Everybody loved us.

CR: Did you do vocals, too, on those shows?

JB: Yeah, I sang on some stuff. Yeah, I did. They didn't really need me, but I did sing later on.

MA: Did you perform anything back then that didn't make it onto an album that you performed live on tour?

JB: Mmmm, I don't think so.

MA: … because I discovered a *Shindig* performance, but I think it's before you joined, where they performed "Needles and Pins" and I go, "Wow, that's not on a record anywhere," so I thought maybe you performed other things that weren't on albums anywhere.

JB: "Outside Chance" was really the first thing we recorded, and that was a bomb. It didn't really go anywhere. Then we recorded "Happy Together" next and that was it, a #1 hit single. Boom!

CR: You were there for the best of The Turtles, from "Happy Together" through "Elenore" and "You Showed Me." Pretty much, that was it.

JB: Yeah, "She'd Rather Be With Me," "You Know What I Mean," "She's My Girl." They were all big hits.

MA: If you're going to be in a certain span of time, that was the best time to be in the group.

JB: No doubt about it.

MA: One thing nobody's probably asked you. You did a couple of commercials. One for Pepsi and one for Camaro. What were those situations like?

JB: It was just another recording session. We went into the studio. It was no big deal.

MA: Well, was it attached to a regular recording session? Was it something special? How did that work?

JB: I think one was in New York. The other one was in L.A. It was just like anything else. We ran the song down and then we recorded it. It was all pretty fast.

CR: Any deep tracks or B-sides that you're proud of that a typical Turtles fan wouldn't know?

JB: I'd have to look at the albums, but there is some good stuff on there. There's a bunch of weird stuff on there, too, but there's some good stuff.

CR: Nothing hits you right off the bat and [you] go, "I love my own drumming. I love the fills on this one. I can't believe it wasn't a hit. I wish people knew this one a little more"?

JB: Well, *The Battle of the Bands* album's "Chief Kamanawanalaya." That was fun.

MA: If you get that album, the center spread has you all in these crazy costumes. What was that like setting up those costumes for the album?

JB: We went out to Warner Bros. They kept bringing out this stuff that we kept setting up. We went to the beach to do the "Surfer Dan" thing. That was fun. It was cool. That was something. The Beatles had *Sgt. Pepper*. We wanted to do something that was really different. A concept album. So we did that album. The Stones never did a concept album. The Beatles did. *Sgt. Pepper* was their concept album. That was our album. That album had two hits on it: "Elenore" and "You Showed Me." It's hard to get two hits on one album.

CR: John, I think The Stones would say their *On Her Satanic Majesties Request* was their *Sgt. Pepper*-ish album. Maybe they wouldn't admit it, but it came out at the same time with all the weird covers, but you outdid The Beatles because I think you were all naked in one of the pictures. I don't think they had the balls to do that.

JB: That's true. Mark was holding my fig leaf. I wasn't even holding it on the album. I had my arms folded.

MA: That's right. You're not holding it.

JB: The Turtles were a trip. They were a funny group. They were not your normal rock and roll group. That's for sure.

CR: Aside from the after-effect, you enjoyed your time with them? Was it a happy time?

JB: Absolutely, yeah. Great times. Why wouldn't it be? I got to do a drum solo all the time. Nobody ever upstaged me. The only time we did a gig with The Rascals. I was good friends with Dino Danelli. He and I were probably the only stick-rolling drummers in the sixties. I love The Rascals. They're more of an R&B band. It was the kind of stuff I really liked. The Turtles were more of a pop band.

CR: Drummers who love the '60s will put you and Dino at the top of every list.

JB: Yeah, absolutely. We were the stick-rolling drummers. I don't know if Dino ever did a drum solo. I never saw him do a drum solo. I always did. I'm sure he was capable of it. He called me from Paris about four or five years ago. He said he was really depressed. He's a really moody guy. I wasn't really around him all that much to really know. I don't know what it is that drummers are always the best looking guys in the band. Michael Clarke was good looking in The Byrds. Dave Clark was pretty good looking. Micky Dolenz is pretty good looking.

MA: Ringo?

CR: Pete Best with The Beatles.

JB: McCartney probably had Ringo beat.

CR: Did you ever get to hang out with Ringo?

JB: Yeah. Twice. The time I sat next to him in the Speakeasy, he never said a word to me, but I'm at the club called the Rainbow in Hollywood. I'm in there and it's packed. There's a bar and a restaurant downstairs and anyway, I'm standing there up at the top and there's this little loft with a few seats. I see Buddy Miles up there and he sees me and he signals me to come up there. We go up there and there's Ringo. He introduces me to Ringo. He goes, "Hey Ringo, this is John Barbata!" Ringo goes, "You're John Barbata!" Ringo almost flipped out and Buddy was pissed.

CR: Did you also play some bass?

JB: No. Just drums and percussion.

MA: When you said you wrote a few lyrics for "Elenore," did you also contribute to the writing or how to drum on a particular song especially on *The Battle of the Bands* because you're trying to be other bands. Did you give any input or did you just do your thing?

JB: I wrote three words. "Elenore, love me" were the three words I wrote for "Elenore." I always came up with my own ideas and arrangements with the songs. I came up with a lot of that. Some things I didn't get credit for.

MA: Well, yeah. That's why we're asking because we don't know. It always seems like the Mark and Howard show. One of the things I wanted to ask about are about some of the weirder songs that you did with The Turtles. Were you a fan of doing those like "Sound Asleep?"

JB: Yeah, that was kind of a weird one. They had a lot of strange songs.

MA: Did you prefer doing the silly, weird ones, or did you prefer doing the straight stuff?

JB: It didn't matter. I was a Turtle and I did whatever they put in front of me no matter what they did. I didn't like that song that much, but we just did what we did. We recorded it and put 'em out there.

MA: You're part of those recordings that they did in the hotel room which came out later as The Rhythm Butchers. What were those like? Was that any sophisticated thing at all or just goofing around?

JB: I don't remember too much about The Rhythm Butchers. It may have been after me, I don't know. They might have been demos, but it was nothing that we ever did that was ever put out.

MA: These came out late in the '80s or something. It was supposed to be some undiscovered Turtles stuff.

CR: We were trying to discover if this was stuff you were on that was released later.

JB: What were the titles of the songs?

MA: Um, I'll have to look them up. Well, ones that were like that ended up as B-sides like "Umbassa and the Dragon" and "Can't You Hear the Cows?"

JB: Yeah right.

MA: Silly stuff like that. You said you were always game for stuff like that so it didn't matter.

JB: Yep. Those were the days.

MA: We always hear about Mark and Howard, but talk about the other guys like Al Nichol. What was he like?

JB: Al was kind of a quiet guy. They really didn't give him much credit either. He had the third voice and he wasn't a lead guitar player. The Turtles never had one song where a guy played a lead solo on eight bars in a song. It never happened. He was a signature style guitar player. Badump ba da-da, badump ba da-da. Jim Tucker was in the background. He didn't do much. He was just kind of in the background. Jim Pons was really a great guy. A great character. He was a good bass player. A field bass player. He had a good voice. Chip Douglas may have been a more professional bass player, but he didn't last long. He only played on one album. One song, and produced us and left. He did some Monkees and now lives on a plantation in Hawaii. I speak to him every now and then. He still plays over there in Hilo with steel guitars. The Turtles were all different, but Al was cool. Al, Tucker, and I lived together in Stanley Hills in a three bedroom apartment. It was a house, I guess you could say. We were all together all of the time. Al was good. He wrote some good songs. He was a good vocalist. Pons was a good bass player and had a good voice. He was kind of a downstream kind of guy. Kind of quiet. Laid back.

MA: There were a couple tracks that were unreleased that I believed you played on because they were recorded in 1968. They weren't released until later, but they were never truly finished. It was on Rhino Records. One's called "To See the Sun" and the other's called "The Owl." Were those made for any particular purpose or were they leftover tracks from *Battle of the Bands*? Do you remember them?

JB: I don't know. They may have been leftover tracks that just were never released. I think so, yeah. It rings a bell.

MA: You were in the *Happy Together* documentary that Rhino made a while back. It was Mark and Howard talking about a bunch of financial problems with the managers. Were you immune to all that or were you exposed to all that like everybody else? How did you work through all that at the time?

JB: Well, when I came home, I had given $1000 to my manager. I was going to sell these cars that Stefanie Powers had that looked like a Ferrari. It was going to bring in like $400K or $500K. They never existed. I bought a house in Malibu that I was going to get for like 50 grand. It was like a $200K house. It was bigger than that. That never existed. Then we were told that the managers took all of our money. I went to… bed and cried for a minute. Then I woke up and it was like the movie *Gone with the Wind*. Well, there's always tomorrow because we can go back out and make money. So we got it back together and went out there and did it. My best friend ended up managing them, Rick Soderlind, for a while.

CR: Was Bill Cosby a manager for a while, too?

JB: Bill Cosby, the…? No. I recorded him one time when they were filming *Combat!* next door. No, he had nothing to do with producing The Turtles. He had nothing to do with The Turtles at all. Nothing.

MA: I'm curious about rumors. It might have been when you were with CSNY or Jefferson Starship, I read that you were considered to drum for the Eagles and you had to turn it down because you liked the gig that you were doing.

JB: That's exactly what happened. David Geffen was the top guy. They were all William Morris dropouts and Elliot Roberts had Neil Young, Joni Mitchell, The Cars, Tom Petty, DEVO, John Hartman and America, all in the same building. So, I go in there and David and Elliot look at me and they say that they got this new band and they wanted me to be the drummer. They're going to be a really big thing and they want you. "Well, David, who are they?" He said, "The Eagles." I said, "Eagles? Never heard of them. I'm getting ready to work on some albums. I can't get any bigger than Neil Young." He says they were a political group. I would rather be in a political group than an Eagles kind of group. Same thing with Aynsley Dunbar, who followed me in Starship. He was asked to be the drummer in Led Zeppelin and he turned that down. Who knows? Then maybe Don Henley would have been a guitar player. I don't know.

CR: So what do you do now?

JB: I've got a lot of drum clinics that I do in New York.

JB: You asked me about Joe Wissert. He produced one of The Turtles' albums. When he got me, Joe Wissert and the new writers, and a new bass player in Jim Pons, Chip Douglas changed their whole sound. The rhythm section was totally different. Of course, the bass player and the writer. Chip produced it. He changed the whole thing. Joe Wissert was a great guy. He ended up producing Earth, Wind & Fire.

CR: Big difference.

JB: Yeah, he's really good. When he came to California, we had this pot called Ice Bag. He smoked some of that shit and it just made him a vegetable. He couldn't do nothin.'

MA: Now, you've probably been asked this more than any of these other questions, but I was just curious how you got into… Jefferson Starship. Was CSNY winding down? What was going on then?

JB: They kind of were winding down and Crosby says the Airplane needs a new drummer and I was recommended to them. That's how I got the gig. I went up to them and it was the same way I got the gig with CSNY. I was at Leo Makota's house in La Honda, Santa Cruz, and Neil Young and David Crosby came walking in and they said they were kind of down because they fired Alex Taylor because Neil didn't like him. He wanted to be an equal part of the group and he was pissed off because Neil was in there. He said, "Fuck this guy. Either he goes or I go." So he went and I came. I talked to Fuzzy Samuels about a week ago. He's in Ohio. He's not doing much anymore, but he was a great bass player. That's how I got into the Airplane. Crosby got me into the Airplane. It was the same thing. We rehearsed and I came in and jammed with those guys and they loved it and I got the gig right on the spot. That led to Paul Kantner saying, "What do you think about the name Starship?" He looked at me and said, "You know, star ship." I said, "I'd love to be in a group about a starship."

CR: Yeah, it was a natural progression from an airplane to a starship. It was brilliant.

JB: Exactly.

MA: I have to kind of touch on a delicate subject, but it seems like you were doing fine with Jefferson Starship, and you had a car accident, correct, and that's what ended your association with the group?

JB: Oh yeah, it really did. It broke my neck and my jaw and broke my arm, but I came back. In six months, I came back. I did a tour with Rita Coolidge and tried to put a band together called California with one guy from Spirit. Geffen loved it, but they wanted to put a Michael McDonald type guy on keyboards. Geffen's notorious for trying to break groups up and put other people together.

CR: You sluff off this accident. I mean, dude, you came back in six months. That's unbelievable. Some people may never come back.

JB: The reason is because I'm organic. Everything I eat is organic. I'm 75 years old. I've got all my hair. My hair's a little bit gray. Most of my friends are already dead and gone. All I ever did was smoke pot and drink a little red wine.

Ron Dante—March 6, 2021

MA: Were you on the same Caravan of Stars with The Turtles? They had Tom Jones and Chad & Jeremy, and Herman's Hermits.

RD: I think we missed The Turtles that year. They were on earlier in the year or later in the year. This was 1965. A long time ago. We missed them then, but I've been in contact with them in subsequent years. The years I got to open for them once or twice which was great. We did a Monterey Car Show together. I actually used their band to back me up.

MA: How did you get into The Cufflinks?

RD: It was Paul Vance. He called me up and he said we're doing a demo on this song. Could you come in and do the lead vocal and then make up a background? I came in. I listened to it. I said, "Oh, I like the name—Tracy. There's not many songs named Tracy, ever." I worked on the lead vocal. Paul and his writing partner, Lee Pockriss. Lee did the arrangement. It was really a cute arrangement on "Tracy." Really nice horns and strings. Very nice. I did about 20 voices on "Tracy." I wanted it to sound like The Turtles! I did. I loved their sound! I love the way they multi-tracked backgrounds and how they had answers to things and a lot of ba-pa-pas. If you listen to "Tracy," you'll hear (sings) ba-pa pa-pa-pa-pa all through it. I was really imitating Howard and Mark.

MA: Very cool. You said earlier that you used to open for The Turtles and I was just curious what The Turtles were like on stage in those days? You see the TV performances on Ed Sullivan seem to be structured as one song and then off. Were they crazy and madcap like they were later on as Flo & Eddie?

RD: I didn't work with them in their early years. It was more the mid-years like the 1990s.

MA: By that point they were doing the Flo & Eddie type stuff.

RD: Yeah, they were doing their madcap stuff. They were wild men onstage. I just loved their comedy, and Howard is the loosest guy I have ever seen onstage, and Mark with his tambourines flinging up in the air, telling jokes and dressing up. You've seen their act. We honestly talked about that, Mark and I, should I do this when I became lead singer of The Turtles group on the Happy Together Tour. Should I dress up in something? Should we wear wigs? I don't know. He said, "No no. We're going to pay attention to the music this time. Pay attention to the great songs we recorded and reproduce them exactly the way they were done—same arrangements, same keys and nothing unusual. I really actually copied Howard's phrasing and tone when I was doing the lead.

CR: When I go and see a show, and I used to see Flo & Eddie and The Turtles as much as possible, I would go there with the mindset that I was getting as much comedy as I was getting music. There's certain acts like that. Bette Midler, her show has her talking a lot of shtick, and if you go back to Jay Black of Jay and the Americans, half the time he's on stage, he's insulting Frankie Valli. That was part of it and if you knew the show and you were up for it, you were going in there and you were loving the comedy as much as the music.

RD: Yes.

CR: I know there were many people who never saw The Turtles before who went to see the show where you guys were "just playing the music!" So is it going to be a culture shock for those expecting some comedy? You're always going to get that balance of people who know the show and love what they're getting and the ones that aren't familiar with it. I guess you've done it for a little while, and hopefully you will continue to be going out more with The Turtles, so are there people now who go, "Where's the slapstick? Where's the silliness?" Or, are there more now that are happy that it's pure Turtles?

RD: I've done The Turtles show two summers in a row. We toured like 50-60 cities. There was not one comment that they wanted more comedy. People were very very happy to hear Happy Together pure. They were very pleased to hear "She'd Rather Be With Me" and the hits, because this is what's ingrained in their minds. We didn't feel that pressure at all. It's nice to know that we can rely on the strength of those great songs. Those songs will last forever. "Happy Together" is going to be in the vernacular forever and ever. That song will be used in commercials. We didn't get any static, whatsoever, and the promoters were very happy about that.

CR: Is the set shorter now? Because half the stuff was goofing around so if you did five songs so that's 20 minutes of songs, there was probably 15 minutes of silly stuff. So, is there more stuff in the set, or is it just tighter. What songs are in the set, and how is it different than when Mark and Howard were a comedy duo?

RD: We added one or two songs. Mark does his own comedy, though, in between songs, just not as long. He tells stories. He plays around. It's still fun and laughter. It's very different from the other acts that precede us. We do about seven songs, mainly because there's a time limit on the entire show. There's like two and a half hours, a 15 minute break, three acts in the beginning, three acts in the second half. The casinos are very strict about that. "It's 11 o'clock. You'd better be off the stage or we'll pull the plug!" We're limited that way, but we still do get everything in. Mark gets his comedy in and sings with me. We have a great time, but the purity of the songs comes through and I must say, I'm very happy about that. Maybe next year we'll add one more song that hasn't been in the catalog.

MA: Do you do the exact same set every night or do you switch a few in and out during the tour?

RD: We don't switch anything in and out. We do the whole set every night, same as before. It's all programmed in. The band has their little computers in front of them with what's coming next. If we throw them a curve, it'll be five minutes before we get the band going again.

MA: So, how were you selected for this? I know Howard has had some health problems and things like that. Were you the first choice or how did it come about that you got on the tour?

RD: In 2017, I was the opening act. I opened for the whole show. I'm doing my Cufflinks, my Archies, and some of my commercials. I was a commercial singer. You guys both know I sang for Pepsi, Coke, and everything under the sun. Every job I could get, I got. So, after that first season, probably when we were off during the year about January, I got a call. The call was "We're interested in you being the lead singer of The Turtles. What do you think about that?" I almost dropped the phone. I said, "You want me to sing their set? What an honor! That's great stuff! I love that catalog of stuff. I can sing every one of them in the same key that the record was in. I watched Howard every night when I was on the tour with them as The Archies, so immediately I said yes. I said count me in. I'm going to learn every nuance of those songs right now, so I was ready. That was it. They saw me live every night, Mark and Howard, so they understood my range, my sound and my discipline of showing up and doing a job every night. We did like five shows a week out of seven days. That's a lot of traveling and singing. I was prepared for it and I was very happy to get that call. I don't know if I was the first call, but I was the one that took it.

MA: Very cool. Now, do you stay in touch with Howard? Is there any chance that he may come back? Or, is he pretty much out of commission at this point?

RD: I can't speak for Howard, but what I get is that he cannot do the road work. He's not physically up for the road. It took a lot out of him. He busted his butt. He injured his foot, I think, one tour and he had to perform in a wheelchair. I think he's kind of retired in a way, but you never know. He may come back. I was booked for this year. That would have been the third year I would have been on it. He didn't want to do it, and they're talking about putting me on for next year.

MA: Is this the only touring you do, or do you also do Archies shows in addition?

RD: Yeah, I do. I'll take other gigs. My Archies/Cufflinks/Commercials shows are a lot of fun to do and people get a kick out of it. I always like that, and when I need a band, I have a band out here on the West Coast and I have a band on the East Coast. All I need is a band in Chicago and I'm set.

CR: I know you didn't get involved with Mark and Howard until the 1990s and all that, but did you work with any of the other members of The Turtles? Did you know any of the other guys in the band aside from the two leads?

RD: No, I just knew Howard and Mark.

CR: If you had to describe Howard in a few words, what would come to mind?

RD: The first thing out of my mouth would be, what a great singer. What a great sound! He sang every night when I was on tour with him. He brought it, vocally, every night. Of course, all the hit records, if you listen to all those vocals, it's magic. No Auto-tune, no computer, just pure, they caught the vocal. That's what you get and he sold those songs. He just sold all those records that they made all through the years. So, that's the first thing I would say is a great voice and a serious person. I spent many a night listening to him tell me stories about his early beginnings and about his times with different people and acts, of course. He's had a wonderful life and he's not only serious, he cares about things. So that's what I would say about Howard. He cares about artists and that's why he and Mark promoted the idea that artists should get more money when they're getting their records played on YouTube or Sirius radio. They had a whole legal thing with Sirius radio that ended up getting all the other artists money, but they were booted from Sirius for a couple of years because Sirius was upset with them. That's what I would say about him. He's a smart guy and not the wild and crazy guy you see on stage. That's part of what he does and he does it well.

CR: And if we ask the same thing about Mark?

RD: Mark is just a hoot. First of all, he's an avid baseball fan. He follows the Dodgers. He follows his teams. He listens on the radio. He's a very warm guy. He can play instruments. He can sing. He can write. He can produce. He's got all those things going for himself. What you see on stage is just basically who he is. He cares and he's telling funny things, but in his private moments, he's also serious about his life. I really enjoyed my time with both of them.

CR: Ron, I admire your versatility when you sing. You can do anyone. You can imitate. You can sound like yourself. You can sound like others which is proven in the Turtles' shows. I always felt that way about Howard. Yes, he had his own distinct voice, but if he was doing a Beatles tribute or a Beach Boys tribute, or if he was doing a reggae song, he could pull it off. There's so much to be said about both of you, but we're focusing on The Turtles. Do you think they're happy with their lot in life? Do you think they're content with the way the rock community perceives them? Do they feel they should be in the Rock and Roll Hall of Fame, or they weren't respected enough? Mind you, that was a band that went out as a band. It wasn't just the two lead singers and then they'd pick up whoever they went with. They were a real set unit at a time where The Wrecking Crew was playing behind everybody. A lot of the greatest bands of all had other bands doing their recordings, but they did their own. So, it's a long question, but probably a short answer. Do you think they're happy with their lot in life as it is now?

RD: I can't say what they're feeling. I never got the indication that they were resentful of the notoriety that they had. They might have been upset about the amount of money that was taken from them, by the money they were not receiving when their records were being played all the time, and when they were used in commercials and nobody paid them. That's why they had to sue. As I said, they're serious musicians. I don't know what they feel and they never confided in me about the Rock and Roll Hall of Fame or anything like that. For my money, and I've been in the business all of my life, nobody deserves to be more in the Rock and Roll Hall of Fame than The Turtles! They should be in the Rock and Roll Hall of Fame. They had 10-20 hits. They were influences. They influenced other groups, other artists, all through their careers. That's my personal take on it. I can't speak for them personally on that subject because, like I said, they're serious guys. They took their life and their music seriously and they had a lot of fun with it. That was their act to have the most fun in the world and be wild and raucous, but they took the songs seriously. Those records were beautifully made. Those records will last forever. No doubt.

MA: The only thing that Howard ever said in his autobiography was "politics." That was the only thing he said about the whole Rock and Roll Hall of Fame. It always seemed kind of weird. Like with The Monkees, they always say, "They didn't write their own stuff and they didn't play their own instruments," which isn't true. Or "they were formed inorganically," but The Turtles don't have any of that. They formed naturally. They started in high school and went from there. It's so weird.

RD: It is kind of weird. They were the genuine articles and I have to say that The Monkees were the genuine articles, also. Look at the impact they had on musical culture. You can't deny that they had a huge impact. It lasts till today. There are millions of fans out there that still love The Monkees and deservedly so. However groups evolve, whether it's one guy leading the group or two guys who sing in duets, this is music, and the music lasts. Longevity is the key here and they both have it. The Turtles of course, they are going to get into the Rock and Roll Hall of Fame. When the leadership changes, they'll be put into the Rock and Roll Hall of Fame. There's no doubt about it. It's the leadership. They have their own set of priorities of who they want to put in and how hip they want to be and authentic they want to be, which they're not. Let's face it, all of their choices are not so great, but it's a combination of a whole bunch of people voting for the top things. Things change. Change is the only thing that you can expect will happen. Really. It will happen.

Elaine "Spanky" McFarlane—March 6, 2021

MA: Charles and I are working on a Turtles project and I know you were in the *Happy Together* documentary years ago talking about being in a love pile. Did you encounter them a lot back in the day?

SM: Playing in Chicago, The Turtles were playing in one of the set rooms in a nightclub and we were doing a concert and they were running late and they invited me onstage and I'm not sure if other members of my band went up there, too, but I know I got up there and sang "Happy Together." All of a sudden we started hugging each other and we got into a dogpile on the stage and we couldn't stop laughing. You had to kind of be there. It was crazy. There is no one who could sing like Howard Kaylan except maybe Denny Doherty of The Mamas & the Papas. Those two voices. Those two men had golden throats as I call them. I mean, they could do no wrong. They just had a beautiful tone, beautiful pitch, beautiful voices.

CR: Did you stay in touch with Howard or any of the guys over the years?

SM: I do hear from The Turtles every once in a while. I hear from Mark Volman. I guess Howard is not touring anymore. I'm sorry to hear that. We go way back. My husband was their road manager for a while, so you know, it was all really complex.

CR: What years was your husband the road manager for The Turtles?

SM: I believe it was '67, '68, '69, around that time. Somewhere in there.

MA: What was his name?

SM: Charly Galvin. That was my husband and there was Carlos Bernal and then Jimmy Seiter, who was my drummer's brother.

CR: So six degrees of separation going on all around?

SM: Yeah. That's right.

CR: Can I ask you about the Happy Together Tour? Did you only do that once or did you do that multiple times?

SM: I did it multiple times. It was basically Spanky using Gary Puckett's band and then The Mamas & the Papas, when I went back in with them, we got on the Happy Together Tour. I'd say that I probably did it for at least three years. It was a summer thing. It didn't go on all year long.

CR: It's still going on. Interestingly enough, because Howard isn't touring with The Turtles, Ron Dante is doing the leads with Mark as The Turtles.

SM: How do they sound?

CR: We haven't heard it yet. I think it's supposed to be great. Last year it didn't tour for the first time because of Covid, unfortunately.

SM: Oh yeah. I forget that there's Covid until I step outside and then it's, "Where is everybody?" It's nice to know that there's someone still around that still loves the music.

[Editor's Note: We've seen the show since the interview. It sounds great!]

Photo: Kelley Adinolfi Mullon

Rick "Squid" Guidotti—April 7, 2021

MA: Rick "Squid" Guidotti, you were a guitarist for The Turtles and for Flo & Eddie for about 30 years. How did you get involved with them? Obviously, you weren't in the original Turtles in the sixties, so when did you encounter Mark and Howard?

RG: It was around 1986. I had a very popular cover band in Los Angeles and we were doing a British Invasion show. We started in 1981 and we used to dress up with white shirts and pants and little pin ties and we used to play songs—not the ones you hear all the time—stuff from their first two albums and also The Hollies, The Kinks, The Dave Clark Five, The Animals, The Rolling Stones, all those bands. We had four good singers and we could harmonize really well, and we became extremely popular. People would line up at the club all night long. So, word got around and a guy came into the club who knew Flo & Eddie, and he happened to know that The Turtles were coming to Disneyland and they were going to do a show. He thought why should they fly their band from New York to Los Angeles when there's a band here already that knows all their songs and can play them perfectly. So he told Flo & Eddie about us and they heard us. I don't know how. I know they didn't come into the club, but we met with them at Disneyland. They really liked us and we became the West Coast back-up band for The Turtles. At that point in time, they had a New York band and a West Coast band. We did all of the shows on this side of the Rockies and that continued for quite a while. There were some alcohol problems with some of the members and we had to lose a few extra guitar players that we didn't need. In the end, I was the one who stayed with them for 30 years because I behaved myself.

MA: Now did you play with Andy Cahan? We also interviewed him.

RG: Oh yeah. I was going to suggest you call him. Andy and I are best buddies. We would travel together all the time. In fact, in any of the shows we had here in California, it turned out it was way more fun to rent a car and drive than fly to Frisco or to Vegas. We didn't have to deal with all the security and the parking at the airport and all that, so Andy and I had quite a few adventures together.

MA: Howard Kaylan wrote in his autobiography that in the latter years of the original Turtles, they preferred being on buses instead of airplanes and everything else after a time because it was just more fun and they could do whatever they wanted.

RG: Yeah, exactly.

MA: Now, Andy participated in a lot of their recordings as well. Even some of their children's albums like Strawberry Shortcake. Did you participate in any of those projects as well or did you only go on tour?

RG: No. I was just their back up guitar player. I didn't do any recording with them at all.

MA: When it's East Coast and West Coast, does it ever overlap? Like if you said, "Hey, Mark and Howard, can I come with you to the Bottom Line in New York when you do one of your Halloween shows or New Year's shows or whatever?

RG: No, absolutely not. Although I was on good terms and if our bass player couldn't make it, they would fly the New York bass player out and at certain times they flew the drummer out to work with us, but that was about it.

MA: Because you and everyone knew all the songs, backwards and forwards as it were, did it take a lot of time to rehearse or did you just kind of just do it? Did you have a set of like 10 songs and you only did those 10 songs?

RG: Any rehearsal we did was usually at the sound check right before the set. These are all seasoned musicians and if you say, "Born to Be Wild," they know how to play it.

MA: That's what I kind of figured.

RG: In the early days they used to use me to pad out the hour because they didn't have enough hit songs to take up the whole show and although Mark would take some time to talk about the history of the show and make a lot of jokes, they would say, "Our guitarist is a human jukebox," and they would let people call out oldies from the audience and try to stump me. So it would be "In-A-Gadda-Da-Vida" and boom, I would go into the lick and blah blah blah. Some of the songs became part of the act. For example—Andy probably told you that he worked with The Monkees—and I taught the band how to play "Daydream Believer," and boom, that was one of the hits that they would play just for fun sometimes in the middle of the show. They'd say, "You guys like oldies? How about this one? Our keyboard player did this one," and we'd do "Daydream Believer." "Our drummer washed Santana's car," and we'd do "Black Magic Woman." "Our bass player can sing like Robert Plant," and we'd do "Whole Lotta Love," and just add a lot of fun into the show.

MA: Was it pretty much on those types of things that it was totally ad libbed or was it pre-scripted at all?

RG: It was pretty much up to Mark. Whatever he felt like hearing, he'd yell out, and we'd do it. If it worked really well, it would become part of the show.

MA: So a little of both. So, on the West Coast, did you literally tour everywhere on the West Coast, or say west of the Mississippi, which was the cut-off, probably?

RG: Yeah, more or less. When it started off, they were doing like 60 shows a year. Roughly, 30 for New York and 30 for the West Coast. Then things changed over the years. In fact, that's what happened in about 2015, I guess. They were tired of doing these one-nighters. We would never go on the road with them. What we would do was fly to Phoenix, play a concert, fly back to L.A. Then in a few weeks, fly to Seattle, do a concert, fly back. They were all one-nighters. Eventually, they decided that they did want to go back on the road and sadly that was the end of them using either of the bands from either coast because then they were traveling with Micky Dolenz and The Grass Roots and all of these guys know how to play "Happy Together," and so they saved a lot of money by using whatever band that was in the bus with them at the time.

MA: So you were officially in a Turtles featuring Flo & Eddie band vs. The Happy Together tour? You weren't on that. Is that correct?

RG: Exactly.

MA: I probably saw you and didn't know it because I know I saw The Turtles a couple of times at the Santa Cruz Beach Boardwalk. They did free summer concerts probably 10-15 years ago, so you were probably there.

RG: Yeah.

MA: Are there any particular venues or concerts that you found particularly memorable or anything that stands out over the years? Either a great concert or just a funny thing that happened on the road?

RG: Boy, I wish I was good at those kinds of stories, but I'm not. After 30 years, it's all kind of a two hotel LSD trip of blurry memories. I know I really had a lot of fun when we played Hawaii. It was one of the smaller islands like Maui, I can't even remember. We got to spend a day driving around and seeing the sights and going into a lava tube and all kinds of stuff like that. Stuff like that I really enjoyed. Here's one that I'll never forget. Right after 9/11, things changed of course. The airport security got really tough and a few weeks after that horrible experience, we had a show in Texas and I talked them into opening the show with "The Star Spangled Banner."

MA: Aw.

RG: And I did it sort of Jimi Hendrix-like. I left out the bombs and the machine guns and just more or less played it straight and loud and to have thousands of Texans in front of me taking their hats off and standing at attention, that was heartwarming.

MA: You said that you all flew in separately for a gig, so other than performing, did you spend that much time together? How did that work? What would be your schedule for you?

RG: We had a schedule and this never varied. After the show, splash some water on your face and grab a little snack if you can and go to Howard's room and puff until three in the morning. It was great. That means that all those stories that you might have read in Andy's book, or—I don't know if you saw the movie *My Dinner With Jimi*—all of those stories I heard straight from Howard's stoned mouth. We just smoked with him until three in the morning and just let him talk and talk and talk. It was actually Andy and my suggestion that he put those stories into the book which he did. The night he told us the story about going out with Jimi Hendrix and getting so blitzed that he threw up, I said, "Man, that should be made into a movie," and it was.

MA: Right.

RG: A lot of good times with Howard. Now Mark rarely participated in any event. He would go to his room, call his wife and go to bed. He was very very business-oriented and, in fact, when we first met him, he was taking pride in the fact that he didn't do drugs anymore. Over the years, there were some occasions where he broke that rule. He was a lot more fun when he was high.

MA: You probably know that he went back to school for a few years. Were you touring with him during those times?

RG: Yeah, he became a Professor at Marymount College here in Los Angeles. Then, of course, he moved to Tennessee. He worked at the school there. He was doing both at the same time. Like I said, we weren't really touring. We'd just go out on a weekend. We'd be back by Sunday and he would go to school from Monday to Friday.

MA: After it was over, I assume you got a little time to sleep afterwards, but then you just had to fly back home, so it was just zipping around quickly like that? What did you do between gigs? Did you have other gigs, or do Beatlemania-type things?

RG: Yeah, that had its ups and its downs. Back in the '80s and into the '90s, my cover band was extremely popular. In fact, there was one point where we would work six shows at Disneyland in the hot sun and then go play in a bar from 9 till 1:30 in the morning. I'm telling you, I got very sick of that. I was so burnt out. Working with The Turtles was never that grueling. Here at home I kept the band working up until somewhere in the 2000s, I started losing my voice, the band fell apart and we changed some members. We went from being the most popular band to working at these hotels when there was nobody in there. It was no longer fun anymore. I did a variety of silly jobs. I worked as a background extra in movies and one of my friends got me a job driving on a feature film, and I was actually Halle Berry's driver before she was famous in one of her first movies, and she liked me!

MA: Cool!

RG: Like a fool, I was very business-like and never flirted and I blew it! Then when things got really slow, I ended up in a delivery job with a big printing company. That was hell on earth.

MA: Now, during those years were you still touring with The Turtles?

RG: No. During those years, the gigs slowed down to about two per year. I did have another band here in Los Angeles. Once again it was an oldies band, but it was a surf instrumental band. We were still playing Beatles, Moody Blues, stuff from movies like *The Good, the Bad and the Ugly* and *Goldfinger*, James Bond, all this instrumental stuff because in the '90s, I lost my voice and I could no longer sing. I had a surf band, but they weren't working a lot. Only a few times per year.

MA: I don't know if you mentioned it, but what was the name of your earlier cover band?

RG: The name of that band was "Rave Up."

MA: Apart from The Turtles, were there any other big groups that you worked in or with?

RG: I didn't get to work with any big names, but working with The Turtles I got to work alongside other groups and people like Peter Noone; I got to work alongside him with Herman's Hermits. We did a lot of shows with Paul Revere and the Raiders and a lot of shows with The Grass Roots. I got to know them as buddies, but only one time I got to go onstage with The Beach Boys. We played "Barbara Ann" and I got to do a solo and I played it in the wrong key! No one told me and I was so excited to be playing with them that I didn't check their fingers! It was awful!

MA: People's voices change over time. Did you have to change keys in songs over the years?

RG: Not really. Howard has a great voice. Mark's voice got a little weak later in life, but then we'd have our bass player cover for him and double his part to make it sound good.

MA: When I saw them at the Boardwalk, it was pretty much a straightforward show with just music, but I know from various recordings, and I have one here that you're not on called *The Turtles Featuring Flo & Eddie*, that at concerts they sold variations of that one. There's like a few jokey tracks in the middle. Did they try to keep those to a minimum? There was one called "The Prison Song" that's just a few bars of (sings) DAH DAH DAH. Mark says, "That was a song I wrote in prison. I was in for a very short time." Things like that. Did you do little shtick like that or did you pretty much just do the hits?

RG: No, we did a lot of shtick. It was all up to Mark. Whatever his mood was. In fact, there were times when I was standing on stage thinking, "Mark, you're talking too much. Let's play a song!" He could go on and on and on. Most of the time he was really funny and the crowd loved what he was up to. We'd do a lot of bits. When they'd give a little bit of the history of Strawberry Shortcake and we'd play a couple of bars of the Strawberry Shortcake theme. Then they said, "We worked for the Care Bears," and we'd play the exact same music and change the words a little. There was lots of humor, but I've got to say I always had a great time and I would laugh on stage and it was always genuine. Mark could be really funny when he was on point.

MA: What about Howard? I know he has a sense of humor, but did he instigate anything or was he, "I'm the singer and I'm going to be the singer here." How does he operate?

RG: He does, in general, play the role of a straight man. It's like Abbott & Costello. Mark is a clown, Howard is a straight man. Mark would mess with Howard. Howard would feign annoyance. It was just part of the show.

MA: I know they've been friends since childhood, but did they seem to get along after all the years together? Or, was it all an act? It seemed like they genuinely loved each other and still do.

RG: They did. They did. Once or twice there might have been a little friction there, but in general, they had gone way beyond holding grudges or disagreements. They realized they had a good thing and the smart thing was to keep it going.

MA: For their concerts, were you always just on call at the ready, or were there some times where you could just not make a gig, like "I got a wedding to go to," or something else you had to do or I'm sick or whatever?

RG: I never in 30 years missed a show. They were never at the last minute. They always called us weeks, if not more, in advance and let us know what was going on. Only one time, I missed a flight, and lo and behold, Mark, who was living in Los Angeles at the time, had missed it also. It was both of us, so he couldn't get mad at me for doing the same thing he did. We both got on another flight and made the gig. One time I was supposed to be in Seattle and all my equipment was supposed to be in Seattle and it went to Hawaii. They somehow got it back in time and after that I stopped bringing in my own guitar and said, "Just have two Strats on stage for me." The first time I brought my Strat, the damn airline people smashed my new case that my girlfriend had bought for me, to pieces! I said, "I'm not bringing my guitar anymore. A Strat is a Strat."

MA: I used to see on The Turtles website years ago when you were doing these tours, that there was this agreement that anybody could actually fill out, but you had to fulfill all of the obligations. It said stuff like that, you had to have a certain amount of guitars, a certain amount of water, you have to have this type of food, all these different qualifications, and then the amount was like $5000. I don't remember. It was some blanket amount. If you do all this, we'll fly out anywhere. We'll do your birthday. We'll do anything, just as long as you fulfill the contract. Have you ever seen those agreements? Did you add anything to that to get the guitar on stage?

RG: Yeah, in the beginning, we had what is called a rider. It was just what you're talking about. It was a list of demands. The bass player wants a big tall amp hanging up and the guitar player wants two Fender twins in case one of them crapped out or whatever, and so yeah, all that was all written out, but later on a lot of the sound people we worked with on a regular basis and they kind of knew what we wanted. They got the stuff ready for us.

MA: Was there ever a show that you signed up for and then found out that it wasn't worth it and you just walked away and didn't do it, or did you fulfill any obligation that you agreed to do?

RG: Oh my God. Twice. The first we were playing at a swimming pool in the middle of nowhere in Arizona. Finally, somebody, the promoter, I use the term loosely, didn't promote a damn thing and nobody knew The Turtles were playing at this pool, and nobody was going to drive into the middle of nowhere where they didn't know where to go and see it. We arrived there and there were about five overweight ladies floating in inner tubes with their kids. That was the whole crowd. We stood at the edge of the pool and we did the show just as if it was a real show and that was it. The other time we set up in this big auditorium and the only person was a little five-year-old kid standing in the middle of this hall by himself. We were actually performing for the sound crew and the caterers. Nobody came to the show. I don't know why, but we still played as if there was a roomful of people. We still got paid. By the way, Mark and Howard were jilted early in their career and that was a set of rules that you didn't break. You gave them the money before they hit the stage.

MA: I think I read about that in Howard's autobiography, because they were stiffed a few times. Pay up and then we'll play. So, when things were kind of winding down for you with Mark and

Howard, I know you said you did some other gigs and stuff like that, but did it just get to the point where you just said the heck with it and you did that other job for a while and you don't perform anymore? Or, do you still perform?

RG: I still have my band here in Los Angeles and we're dying to get out and to start working again. I was never one to walk away from a situation like that, but our drummer did. He eventually got a fear of flying and didn't want to fly anymore, and he quit the band. Our bass player also got to the point where when we were working only once every couple of months, he said, "This isn't worth it for me," and so from that point on, they would fly the New York band out.

MA: I'm familiar with the New York guys. Besides yourself and Andy and Mark and Howard, who were the ones pretty consistent with the band for the 30 years?

RG: The New York bassist, he had been with them the same amount of time I had, so he was very consistent. A great player and a great guy to hang around with.

MA: Is it Donnie?

RG: Yes, Donnie Kisselbach.

MA: You mentioned drummers, so was it Joe Stefko who came out occasionally?

RG: Joe was the New York drummer and occasionally did a few shows out here. Our first drummer from our band Rave Up was Bob, and Bob got the acclaimed airplane phobia thing, and then we got another guy named Rick Croucier and he joined and stayed.

MA: Okay. Do you stay in contact with him or anybody else?

RG: Just via Facebook. On birthdays and holidays we say hi to each other. Andy and I still stay in touch and we would party except that he lives in Palm Springs. I live in L.A. I don't want to drive 90 miles to see him. I'm sorry. In the summertime, he's got a boat in the harbor in Oxnard and sometimes I'll go and visit him there. Of all the guys, Andy and I used to hang out the most.

MA: Did you know him prior?

RG: No. I met him in The Turtles. Our keyboard player got a chance to join The Beach Boys. He considered that a step up. They hired Andy and then he was fired for a while, and then they hired him back.

MA: Do you ever contact Mark or Howard at this point?

RG: No, I don't. However, there's one exception. I got a couple of phone calls a few weeks back and I didn't know who it was and they said, "Rick, call me." I said, "Who the hell is that?" It might be Mark Volman. It might be. Maybe they're going to do a concert. So I called Mark and lo and behold, he was sick in a hospital and he sounded so bad, I could hardly understand what he was saying. I kind of left it at that. He was not doing well. I know a few years back Howard had heart surgery and had back surgery and didn't want to perform anymore and so I haven't spoken to him since.

Artie Kornfeld—April 12, 2021

CR: Thank you for coming on with us, Artie. It means a lot. You are a legend in the music business with Woodstock. How many total songs have you been involved with?

AK: I've written around 300.

MA: We're working on a Turtles book and you wrote a song that was on their second album called "Just a Room." Did you write that song intentionally for The Turtles or was it just among a number of demos that they were going through and they just chose one?

AK: In a certain community, Steve Duboff and I became popular writers. It was sort of in the middle of that that it was sort of a business to me and we're always trying to make change with what we're doing.

CR: Do you remember that specific song?

AK: Yes, of course I do. It was one of those times where I sat down with Steven. We might have been aiming for a "Happy Together" type of feeling, but we were very good writers. We really learned how to write, you know? That's how you do it.

CR: Were you pleased with the way it came out? Sometimes you write a song one way and an artist performs it a different way.

AK: Yeah. It's a different part of my world with the other stuff that I do.

CR: What was your relationship with Howard and Mark? Were you friends with any of The Turtles?

AK: Steve and I were writers for changing times and sold folk rock, and that's what was happening then. I loved "Happy Together" because two friends of mine produced it and it was through a company where I did A&R. These artists and their repertoire or whatever.

CR: Were you involved with White Whale, their record label, at all?

AK: No. I knew what was going on. I didn't particularly like it.

CR: Any stories about Mark and Howard? What do you remember about them as performers or individuals?

AK: They were great to be around. They were very close friends with my writing partner, Steve Duboff. It was fun to go over and work with the guys in the rehearsal halls, even when I was teaching them "Just a Room." The way that we did it is that we played it the way we did it. As a producer, I had some sort of arrangement.

CR: Any other memories of The Turtles?

AK: Yeah. Bowling, eating at the kosher restaurant by the bowling alley. Bowling on Sunday with Duboff. Stuff like that. We were friends, but Steve was a lot closer than I was.

Bob Lind—April 29, 2021

CR: In doing the research for this book, I'm seeing all of these people that I never knew wrote songs that The Turtles covered and sure enough, The Turtles had you as a songwriter. We'll go right to that one. Was it only one song?

BL: Yeah. The first thing that I can tell you is that my memory is not sharp for the past, but I cannot say enough good things about The Turtles. Mark and Howard are just incredible guys. Here's something of note. They were the absolute first band and first artists to cover one of my songs. This was months before "Elusive Butterfly" was even released, and so they had no idea who I was. They just came in and mentioned that they were looking for material and I had this song called "Nobody Smokes Marijuana in Suburbia." I walked into the publishers. I had no idea which, if any, of my songs were going to get covered and Lenny Waronker said "The Turtles are going to do one of your songs." I said, "Which one?" and he said, "Nobody Smokes Marijuana in Suburbia." I said, "You're kidding!" These guys were doing "It Ain't Me Babe" and they were megastars then. I don't remember how I met them, but they were so incredibly generous with their time and their counsel. They came over to my place and I was in the studio when they recorded. Of course, White Whale, who was scared shitless, made them change the title.

CR: Right.

BL: So now it was called "Down in Suburbia." They couldn't even say the word. All it said was "Nobody smokes tobacco down in suburbia." "Nobody smokes marijuana" fits the meter perfectly so they had to squeeze it in, in order to make it work. I just think from a personal standpoint, how helpful they have been over the years. We toured together. It was a big massive tour all over and throughout Oregon and Washington and Los Angeles. There's all kinds of people. I don't know who else was on the bill and they were just so helpful to me so anything good I can say about them, I want it on the record.

CR: Had you not toured with them, would you not have met them? Was it common to have a songwriter meet the artist?

BL: I don't know how common it is. I had over 200 covers and I know very few of them, personally. They either hear them on my records or hear them in person. They'll come to a gig or something. Now, it's YouTube. You can get just anything you want on YouTube now.

CR: Yes.

BL: I had known them way before. I had known them because Lenny Markin, who was the head of Metric Music, my publishing company then, must have introduced us. I have no idea, but I remember they were over at my little shabby apartment making $50 a week from my publishing company. There was just a little retainer against royalties. They would give me $50 a month so I had this little shabby studio apartment.

CR: It wasn't the Brill Building.

BL: No, I'm talking about where I lived, but they came over and then I remember being at the session. It was very un-star-like. As a matter of fact, they were so down to earth, I just thought they were just fakes, just like me. I thought they were just stoners with no awareness of music. I didn't realize for a long time how astute they were, how sharp they were about music and the music business. They know everything. I don't know if it was because they got ripped off at one point, but boy if you ever want to know how to handle yourself in the business, they're the guys to talk to.

CR: Have you stayed in touch with them throughout the years?

BL: Sporadically, I've stayed in touch with them. The last contact I had with them was when I was just starting back into the music business. I took a long vacation which is a story for another interview. To keep this on point, I don't know what else I can say about them or "Down in Suburbia," but they didn't like White Whale even then. Even then there was some animosity brewing. I don't know what "It Ain't Me Babe" did, but it must have been in the top five and they were surprised that they had not actually heard from Bob Dylan about that song. Dylan wasn't commonly covered back then, unless you count The Byrds and "Mr. Tambourine Man," but at that point, they were helping him a lot. Anyway, that's the way it goes.

CR: I think years later, he saw them live and he said to them, "You guys should cover that song!" Cluelessly.

BL: Who said that?

CR: Dylan. That's the rumor. I don't know if it's true.

BL: Ah. Well, I don't know what else to tell you about The Turtles.

CR: The song itself ("Down in Suburbia"), with lyrics like "everyone has a list of negroes, Jews, and communists and checks it off before their daughter marries..." These are strong lines for the time. It's amazing that such a mainstream band would record it.

BL: I know! And they wanted to go with the original title and the original line because they could see that things were changing. Anyone who spent any time on the streets around that time knew that things were about to burst wide open. All this oppressive shit was about to get thrown over. I never knew it was that good of a song. It was some sort of cheap satire of American society at the time. I do admire them covering it.

CR: Absolutely. When they did it live, did they do the correct lyrics and the correct title?

BL: I don't think I ever saw them do it live. I think it was only in the studio.

CR: Yeah. Do you have your recording of the song that's out there?

BL: No. That song would be so far down the list of songs that I would want to re-record. I like what they did with it, but a lot of my older stuff really makes me cringe.

CR: Any other Turtles stories?

BL: I'll just say that their looseness as it were, their goofy, flakey facade blinds people to the fact that these guys know more about the business than most any artist. I can't think of any more people that have been so helpful with their advice and their counsel.

Ron Nevison—May 1, 2021

MA: How did you get involved with Flo & Eddie in the first place?

RN: I had just got hired as the Chief Engineer for the Record Plant in Los Angeles. They also had a studio in Sausalito, so I was kind of the Chief Engineer for all of the five studios. This is somewhere in early 1976 and this is the second album project that I did when I was there. I had other duties as the engineer other than just doing sessions. This was brought to me and Skip Taylor who was the manager, and in fact, he's still the manager of Canned Heat. Skip brought this to me and we kind of co-produced it in Los Angeles at the Record Plant. We also went up to the Sausalito Record Plant for a week or two, I remember, to do the vocals, which was a lot of fun having Mark and Howard do vocals together because they're like a comedy team. One would start talking and the other would finish the thought. It was a hilarious time. A great time, in fact. The band was really good. I brought in an arranger. For me, one of the most significant things was that I brought in an arranger named Alan MacMillan. Since I was actually new in town after spending five years in London doing The Who and Led Zeppelin and bands like that, to come and do a Flo & Eddie, they wanted some horns that were kind of like Chicago horns. I ended up producing Chicago about 10 years later. They wanted horns like Chicago and I asked around and this fellow Alan MacMillan had done a lot of work for Alice Cooper in Canada for Bob Ezra, I think. He was highly recommended and I brought him in from Toronto to write the charts and that's a lot of the part of the orchestrations on *Moving Targets* are directly from Alan.

MA: I think he gets credited as "Strings and horns arranged and conducted by Alan MacMillan."

RN: Yep! I went on to use him on The Babys, Dave Mason, and on lots of different bands, so he was a guy I used to fly in on a regular basis.

MA: For this project, was there any sort of direction? What I mean by this is that this was Flo & Eddie's fourth solo album and the first two were kind of Turtles leftovers, but that had some silly stuff too like "The Sanzini Brothers." The third album, Illegal, Immoral and Fattening, was mostly live with a couple studio tracks and it really showed the comedy. Was there a mandate to make this one more straight, or what was the direction at [that] point?

RN: When I took on this project, I didn't really know about Flo & Eddie. I knew about The Turtles. I had been in England the whole of the 1970s. I hadn't heard much about Flo & Eddie as a breakout of The Turtles. I was familiar with "Elenore." I was familiar with "Happy Together." I wasn't really up on their other solo projects. I don't remember. It's like fifty years ago I don't exactly remember the discussions that we had. I wasn't the only producer. I was the producer-engineer and I trusted those guys who were all pretty seasoned. I loved all those guys. Skip Taylor was great. The band was terrific. I remember having a great time doing the record.

MA: Did Mark and Howard come in with finished tracks, or demos you created with them?

RN: No, they were pretty finished. I just colored them in. Like the song "Keep in Warm" had a lot of verses, so we just had to come in with different things on each verse with instrumentations, and sounds like a sitar and different kinds of things like that. That was one of my favorite tracks on the record.

MA: Yes, that's a very good one. Another one I like is the opening track "Mama, Open Up."

RN: Yeah. I did it in a Bad Company style with the big guitars and a very funny serious rock track.

MA: The album does have a remake of "Elenore." Whose choice was that?

RN: You know, it was one of my favorite tunes. I don't know if they did it because of me. We wanted to do a Turtles tune in there and so it ended up being "Elenore." I can't quite remember. They approved of it and said, "Well okay, let's do it."

MA: Looking at the album, it looks like there was a lot of slide guitar on a track called "Hot." Was that an intentional thing to get a little different sound? The credits read "Donnie Dacus and Jeff Baxter came in to do slide guitar…"

RN: Ah! Jeff "Skunk" Baxter. That makes sense. Baxter, that was his thing, so maybe he was a friend of Skip's. These were all L.A. guys and I was a bit of an outcast at that point. Not outcast, but I didn't have my "go to" guys like I did in England.

MA: Another person listed on the back is Graham "Shirley" Strachan as backing vocals on "Guns." "Guns" is an interesting track. I don't know if you have any particular memories. If not, that's fine.

RN: You know, I don't. I remember "Sway When You Walk." I remember "Mama Open Up" and "Best Friends" was like a soundtrack kind of thing, and "Keep it Warm." I haven't listened to this in 40 years.

MA: Well, you're doing pretty good on remembering some of the titles. And then the title track of "Moving Targets" was a good track itself, I thought.

RN: Right.

MA: Did you do anything else on the project like select the cover image?

RN: That's a good question because I have the original artwork of that!

MA: Oooh! Credits here say the illustration is by Dave McMacken. Did you know him?

RN: I guess I ended up with it. In those days, they made the artwork and we weren't ready for CDs then. I'm not sure if it's the original. It's been so long that maybe they gave each of us a copy of the artwork. I'll send you a copy of it.

MA: We did interview Andy Cahan and he had some memories of playing keyboards on the album. Did you remember working with him?

RN: No, but one of my fondest memories of working with Howard and Mark and Skip was that we had a tank of nitrous oxide and we were at the Record Plant house listening to Vanilla Fudge and getting high on nitrous oxide. I do remember that. I had a lot of fun with those guys. They were great people. The other thing is later on I lived in Bel Air and lived right opposite UCLA, and I got a call from Mark. He was teaching a class at UCLA. I came over as a guest to talk about music production. That was in the early nineties and I haven't really talked to anybody since. I have talked to Skip Taylor in the last 10 years who is in Tucson, but I don't know where those guys are. Overall, it was just a great experience.

MA: The album had 10 tracks. Was there anything left on the proverbial "cutting room floor" or was that pretty much it?

RN: No friggin' idea. I have no idea. A lot of times we'll cut more than one extra track just to see how things develop if a dark horse comes along, but I don't think we did it on that.

MA: Flo & Eddie were in Zappa's band and now they're putting out every little scrap. There's this album called *The Mothers 1970*, and it has them talking in the car and stuff like that.

RN: Yeah. I did a bunch of sessions with Zappa and he told me once, "Hey Ron, I've got this great concept." I said, "What's that?" He said, "Ok, picture this. This guy and his son are watching television, sitting watching television in the living room and they have these plastic bags over their hands and over their face. While they're watching TV with these plastic bags on their hands and face, they're stuffing popcorn through the bags, eating it. Then, the son asks the dad, "Dad, how come we have these plastic bags over our hands and face while watching TV like this?" And the dad goes, "It's because we're ugly as fuck." That was Frank Zappa.

MA: Now, which albums did you work on with him?

RN: I did editing for him. He used to come in since I was the Chief Engineer at the Record Plant, I would do a lot of individual sessions, not albums. I also did album work, but I don't remember. It was something he was putting together and I would just edit, edit, edit and he'd say, "Cut this and do that." Whatever.

MA: What years are we talking about? Late '70s? Early '80s?

RN: Early, mid-'70s. Around the time of *Moving Targets*, I guess, within '75, '76, '77. What's *Moving Targets*, '76?

MA: '76, yes. I was curious because Flo & Eddie were with Zappa for about a year and a half from 1970-71, and then Zappa had the fall off the stage and that pretty much ended that, and they went on solo as it were and Zappa went on to do more jazzy stuff.

RN: Yeah, like what he was doing with The Mothers. Right. That was really his thing.

MA: Any last stories about Mark and Howard that you care to share?

RN: No last stories about Mark and Howard. Like I said, the last time I saw Mark was at UCLA. They were just great people to work with. I had a wonderful time with that record.

Gary Puckett—June 6, 2021

MA: How did you get involved with the Happy Together Tour?

GP: I started to get calls from people who said, "You know we've got radio stations out here that are starting to play the music of the 1960s, and they're wondering where you are and what you're doing." All that kind of stuff. So, there came a point where somebody said, "I can put together some dates out here in the Midwest and let's see what happens." So they did and it was a little bit disastrous. At the same time, it kind of showed me that people were willing and wanting to have me be back on stage again and come and see me and all that kind of stuff. I continued to work at it until we got back East and we were working at a concert at the Meadowlands. I can't remember what all the acts were. So a guy came backstage and said, "My boss would like to talk with you."

I said, "Really? Who's your boss?" He said, "His name is David Fishof and he works in the city." So, I said, "All right. let's make an appointment." He said, "Well, come in tomorrow morning." I went in and met with David and with Howard Silverman, who is now one of the owners of the agency I have been with for a number of years, and they said, "We're working with The Turtles and we're working with The Association, and "we'd like to work with you."

I said, "That sounds like a good idea." I went back to California and I suggested to David that he put us all out on tour. I don't know if they'll remember this exactly, but in his office he decided that it was a good idea, and they wanted to add a fourth group to that which became The Happy Together Tour with Spanky and Our Gang, Gary Puckett and the Union Gap, The Association, and The Turtles. That's what really got rolling again, because we went out that year in 1984 and I think we worked a good eight months together. We were all responsible for getting ourselves around from gig to gig and back home. Nobody really knew how to do it, so they said, "We're going to book the gigs and you're going to show up."

We did it. It was highly successful and they put out another Happy Together in 1985, and then you know the rest of that story. In 1986, it became The Monkees' 20 year reunion tour. It worked because for two years straight when we were doing The Happy Together Tour, they were playing The Monkees 24/7 on MTV.

CR: We had a nice conversation with Spanky not too long ago.

GP: Good. I'm glad. I've tried to talk with her on several occasions, but we just never connected. I've always loved Spanky and she's such a great lady.

MA: These groups that you worked with on The Happy Together Tour, did you work with them in the sixties or did you cross paths with them back then?

GP: Yeah, I worked with The Association in the '60s. I'm pretty sure that I worked with The Grass Roots back then. I'm pretty sure I worked with The Buckinghams. Spanky and Our Gang, I don't think so. She and Our Gang, they were hipper than we were. They were along the lines of The Mamas & The Papas, who I didn't work with until later because they were considered drug bands.

MA: Sonny and Cher didn't take drugs, either, but they had that "hippie" image.

GP: That's right. Howard Kaylan would say on stage on these Happy Together tours, "We were a drug band back then, and we're a drug band now," and they'd bring up Lipitor and the drugs they have to take because of their health.

MA: Did you work with The Turtles or encounter them back then?

GP: No, I don't think so, because they were definitely a different genre. They were more hip. They would work with (sings) "Going up the country…"

MA: Canned Heat?

GP: Yeah, yeah. That kind of thing. The Turtles, they were, once again, hipper than we were. That sort of clean cut, not hip type. It's funny, I still feel that I don't sort of fit it, but there was a time way back when, that Chicago opened for us. Creedence Clearwater opened for us. People of that nature opened for us. Things changed and that's how life goes. I'm fortunate that I have a gazillion fans out there that love the songs.

MA: I always equate just because of how you looked with the dress and the garb with Paul Revere and the Raiders. The music's different, but the fact that you had the uniforms on kind of became some sort of genre in itself.

GP: You're probably right. I did that for a reason. I felt that having an arresting look whether it was arresting or not, it made people stop and go, "What's that?" I figured that if I could make them stop and look at it, maybe they'd stop and listen to it, and that's what happened.

MA: On the later Happy Together tours, any fun stories on the road?

GP: There's probably worse or better things I could tell you about The Beach Boys. The Turtles to me were always friendly, always arms open to me as a performer. When I started running across them, they would say, "Gary, hello, how are you?" but I wasn't really privy to the inside stuff until we started traveling together a little bit more, but even on The Happy Together 1984, they traveled in their own vehicle, I traveled in my own vehicle. The fact that they may have worn something around their neck containing something that they could sniff, I don't know if that's the kind of stuff we want to talk about. I don't want to blow anything and I don't want to be saying things out of school here.

CR: Is the word "blow" the operative word in that sentence?

GP: The funny thing about blow is that you "sniff blow."

MA: It's not too much of a secret. Howard put out his autobiography. He didn't really hold back. He talked about the various orgies and the various drugs and the various everything he went through in his life. I don't think any little hints of drug taking along the way would be inappropriate. We are more curious about fun times on the road, not necessarily drug related.

GP: I've always loved both those guys. I just think they really have been really iconic and I know that they were playing a part throughout. Howard's part in life is who Howard is. If that makes sense to you, it makes sense to me because Howard was always fairly acerbic. He was unwilling to be the nice guy, usually. He wanted to get the autographs over and take the picture and get the you know what out of here. That's how Howard was. I think that went along with his persona for The Turtles. So many great, great songs and what a great performer he was. I'm sad that he cannot do these tours now, but I know his health is paramount to a happy life. I haven't talked to Howard in a long time or to Mark in a long time and he's usually my connection to Howard's well-being.

    I witnessed a few things that were kind of cool. We used to stand back behind Joey Stefko on stage and Joey would have joints hanging out of his mouth. He'd be getting stoned during the concert. I would just be standing behind him and say, "Man, this guy is a drummer." He had it in his hands. He was one of those guys that you talk about being a great musician. I would just stand behind him where no one could see me and just go "Wow! This is incredible!" Of course, I suppose Howard would run back and grab a little taste and then run back, but what a great performer. I will always love Mark because he always took care of his guys. What a great band they had later on. I didn't know any of the original Turtles, so I can't really give you much there.

CR: When the talk always comes out about the great bands that are not in the Rock and Roll Hall of Fame, The Turtles, The Monkees, and Gary Puckett's name comes up. What's your read about you and these guys not being in it?

GP: Well, it's funny. My feelings about awards are different from most people's feelings about awards. People love to be awarded things. They love to have Oscars. They love to have Emmys. They love to have gold records. I've got a number of gold records and they are an indication of success and I'm pleased with them. I'm proud of them, but if they were put into storage tomorrow, I wouldn't miss them, if you know what I mean. My take on the Hall of Fame is it seems to change a little bit as time goes on. I have a good friend, whose name is Eddie DeBartolo. Eddie and his wife, Candy, are iconic people in the football business. He used to own the 49ers. He took them to five Super Bowls and has five rings. Being from Cleveland, he's tuned in to the Hall of Fame. He used to donate lots and lots of money. One day he said to me, "I stopped giving them money. Every time I would say to them, 'Hey, what about Puckett?'" They would just pass and he stopped giving them money. I don't know how true that is, but he is a very wealthy man, and is capable of doing that sort of thing. I would like to see a lot of people in the Hall of Fame. I wish that politics weren't what they are. You know, you do this for me, I do that for you. That's just a given in the world of politics no matter what business you're in. Things have changed over the years. I don't know. I suppose one day that they might consider putting me in the Hall of Fame, but if they never do it, it's not something that I'm going to complain about. I think that the proof is in the pudding. When I see a Turtles song in a movie, I go, "There ya go! That deserves the Hall of Fame!" The other day we were watching *The Assassination of Gianni Versace*, and there's a Turtles song in there, and I went, "Yeah! Hall of Fame, you guys! What's taking you so long? What are you doing?" So, I don't know. I don't really care about awards. A lot of people should be in the Hall of Fame that aren't.

MA: Howard said the same thing in his autobiography. Just one word: "politics." That seems to be the recurring theme.

GP: Sure.

CR: We can't mention Happy Together today without mentioning Ron Dante.

GP: That's true. Ron is a great, great talent. I have to say that if I could get the money together, I would have Ron produce an album for me because of all the great producing he did with Barry Manilow. It's just that we don't have it in the budget to spend that kind of money and I don't have a studio of my own If I found the right people. I still have a great voice.

Jerry Yester—July 23, 2021

MA: A one-time member of The Lovin' Spoonful and one-time producer for The Turtles. Here he is, Jerry Yester.

JY: After the Modern Folk Quartet broke up, Chip Douglas joined The Turtles as the bass player and he did the arrangement of the horns and vocals and guided the basic track of "Happy Together." He came up to my house on Laurel Canyon one afternoon and he said, "Hey, I want you to listen to something. Let me see what you think." I put it on and it was "Happy Together." I said, "Are you kidding? That's a number one record!" He said, "Do you really think so?" I said, "Yeah!"

MA: It's funny that he had doubts.

JY: It was just undeniable. Bonner and Gordon were the writers. The guys that when we got the folk rock thing going, was really happening by the autumn of 1965. In November, we started a three month tour in a Clark Cortez which was the first motor home you could drive on the inside instead of towing. There were five in the group and Cyrus' wife and all in this thing and three months across country and back. During that time, Henry Diltz got his first camera as we were going east. Eight months later, he was making his living with it. He'd be laying out in the middle of a field. We'd stop and take a leak or something and we'd be, "Jesus, where's Henry?" and he'd be way out there, lying on the ground, taking pictures. "Come on, for Christ's sake, Henry!" At the end of that tour, we had a party and everyone had pictures, and when we got to Henry's, we all went, "Woah!" That's what he was doing out in the field. It was obvious from the very beginning how amazing he was as a photographer and it just really took off. Anyway, back to Chip, he stayed with The Turtles for a while and then ended up producing The Monkees. He had two big hits with them and a big album, *Headquarters*.

MA: Right.

JY: Eddie Hoh played on some stuff for that. He played on "Daydream Believer." I don't think that was on that album.

MA: No, it's on *The Birds, The Bees and The Monkees*. It was a single before that.

JY: Right. I played bass on "Shades of Gray," and sang background on a few things. It's funny, I did a cruise with Peter Tork, may he rest in peace, and I told some other people about that I played bass on "Shades of Gray" and Eddie Hoh played drums on blah blah blah, and Peter said, "Hey man, we played on all that stuff," and I said, "Well, not quite." It's like Clapton playing on some stuff for The Beatles, it was not a big thing. It was like a guest thing. That album was important to them because it wasn't The Wrecking Crew. It was basically them and Micky became a drummer for the TV show. He wasn't really a full-fledged drummer.

MA: Sure.

JY: So, he didn't mind if Eddie played and I played on a couple of things. Right about that time, I did a session. Jack Nitzsche called me and he said, "Listen, I've got a gig with The Turtles and I don't have time to take on both of them. Can you take on one of the arrangements?" I said, "Sure." Jack was a really good friend. It helped me get started as an arranger. This was a full-fledged one between Jack and me, and he did "She'd Rather Be With Me," which turned out big, and I did "Me About You." I loved the way that came out and Joe Wissert was the producer. Right after that, I got a call from John Sebastian who said that Zally (Zal Yanovsky) was leaving the group (The Lovin' Spoonful) and would I replace him. I said, "Jesus, John, let me think about it. I'll call you back." I called him back about five minutes later and said, "Yeah, I'll do it."

[After venturing into the history of The Lovin' Spoonful and of The Yester Brothers, Jerry mentions his first manager, Herb Cohen.]

JY: Herbie came back from being a mercenary soldier. Herbie was kind of a wild man when he came back, but he calmed down and became our manager and The In Group's manager.

MA: Frank Zappa's manager.

JY: Yes, Zappa, Tom Waits, Tim Buckley, Linda Ronstadt…

MA: And Flo & Eddie way later.

JY: Well, Howard Kaylan is Herbie's cousin. Herbie set them up in an office in his office building when they were on their own as Flo & Eddie and got them with Frank Zappa in the beginning.

MA: But they knew Zappa already when they were in The Turtles as they went around with The Mothers in the early days. Everybody seemed to play the same clubs. You're probably part of that, too.

JY: Yeah. It's funny, when The Modern Folk Quartet was working together at The Action, Frank was very new to the scene. I had no idea who he was and neither did a whole lot of people. He came up on one of those 10 minute breaks and he said, "Hey Man, do you mind if I sit in on guitar?" It was a night that we were really cooking, so I said, "I'm sorry, man, but I've got to have this one." I didn't know who he was. I didn't know if he could play or not and I wanted that set, so I turned him down. It didn't really sour him on me, I guess. Shortly after that, he was my neighbor on Kirkwood in Laurel Canyon, just like three houses down. We'd visit him and we became good friends. I was walking up Kirkwood when they had come back from their first gig, I think it was. The Mothers. The band was just standing outside of his house all pissed off.
    I said, "What's wrong?" They said, "Can you believe that guy? He won't let us smoke pot!" I said, "Really? How about that?" They said, "We're going to show him!" But they didn't show him. He said, "If you want a job, great. If you don't, smoke away."

MA: So, obviously you're friends with The Turtles already in the '60s. Had you already done production because you had production credit for Pat Boone? Was that at that time?

JY: Basically, at the time, we went into Pat Boone's studio. He owned Sunwest at the time out at the far end of Sunset at one of those streets where Sunset wants to end. There was a huge roller rink across the street. It was actually one of the first studios I ever recorded in like [at age] 16. I was in a garage band with some local friends of mine in Burbank.

Years later, I went in to record *Farewell Aldebaran*. I called Zally to see if he wanted to be partners in the production, so we formed Hair Shirt Productions and started working on *Farewell Aldebaran*. The manager of the studio really liked what we were doing and he said, "Listen, Pat wants to make an album, and would you be interested in producing it?"

We said, "Sure." He said, "We need to start it right away." I said, "Well, I'll put *Aldebaran* on hold for the time that we do Pat." His album was called *Departure*. It turned out really well. We got to pick the tunes and the people, and Pat sang his ass off. He really came through. We finished that album and then we finished *Farewell Aldebaran*, and did a few others like Tim Buckley's third album, *Happy Sad*. Then Zally and I ended our partnership. He went off and became part of the thing that the founding members of "Saturday Night Live" were doing on Broadway or off-Broadway with Chevy Chase and those guys.

MA: Oh, you mean *Lemmings* with *National Lampoon*?

JY: Yeah! There were a lot of Canadian people and Zally was Canadian. Then, I started producing other people and I got a call from The Turtles.
[Editors' Note: *Lemmings* was in 1972. *Shell Shock* by The Turtles was 1969 and 1970.]

MA: I can tell you the chronology. They had Chip Douglas doing *The Battle of the Bands*. That was in 1968. Then, in 1969, they did *Turtle Soup* with Ray Davies from The Kinks.

JY: Right.

MA: Then, they started working on what you were working on, which was going to be an album called *Shell Shock*, but this is where the story gets kind of muddy. They never really talk about you much, because if you see that Turtles documentary, you're not mentioned at all, and they act like "After *Shell Shock*, we produced 'Lady-O' and then broke up." It's like, wait a minute, you [Turtles] were still doing stuff well into 1970 with you, Jerry, and that's kind of the whole reason for us contacting you because I want to know that part of the story.

JY: Well, I produced like nine things for them. What ended it was the label (White Whale) going out of business. Then, they bought the masters of all their stuff—Howard and Mark did—and they never paid me. Which has a lot to do with them not talking about it, and they never paid Chip, either, for his production.

MA: Ooohhh!

JY: In fact, they told Chip to get a lawyer and go after them. He was on the phone with Howard and Mark and they said, "Yeah, go for it. We've got Mutt Cohen here in this office. Yeah, go for it!" It would have meant spending a lot of money on a really good lawyer and Chip just said, "Screw it!" I never went after them, either. It's just surprising because I don't think they paid the band, either.

MA: They were going through a lot of turmoil. They were being sued by their managers...

JY: I don't think Mark and Howard were going through a lot of turmoil. They had Mutt Cohen's office behind them handling any legal problems. I just don't think so.

MA: So, obviously, you were friends before this, but why did they call you to produce?

JY: Maybe because John Seiter was in the group. I don't know.

MA: Did he recommend that you produce the group?

JY: Could be. I really don't know.

MA: Back to the recording sessions, do you have memories of specific tracks? If I mentioned a track title, would that spark a memory of what you produced? Some of them came out and some of them didn't.

JY: I saw an album called *Shell Shock* that had those things on it.

MA: Yeah, but a lot of them weren't released at the time, in 1969. A few of them were released in 1974 when Flo & Eddie got the rights to everything. A few were released later and then some were released after that *Shell Shock* album. It's kind of surprising that they still find things. I guess I will go through track by track. If you say that you don't have any memory of it, that's fine. One was called "Can I Go On?" That spring a memory?

JY: Not exactly. No.

MA: The next one seemed designed to become a hit because later Flo & Eddie re-recorded it on their solo album, "Goodbye Surprise," a Bonner-Gordon one.

JY: Yeah, that was an absolutely dynamite record, the way we did it. This guy named Barry Keene was the engineer at Sunwest and he put the basses out of phase on the left and right, which sounded great in stereo. When you put it into mono, the bass disappears. There's ways of doing that now these days, but something happened. It also came right about the time that White Whale went belly up. There was no promotion because there was no label, but it was a really good record. Howard sang really great.

MA: Next one is "If We Only Had the Time."

JY: Yeah, that sounds familiar.

MA: Okay, another called "Like It Or Not."

JY: Yeah. That's another Bonner and Gordon, I think.

MA: Okay. Now, when you were producing these, did you have any input?

JY: Oh yeah. When I produce, I don't like to get in the way of the band. I like bringing out the band. Not like Phil Spector. God knows. The band has nothing to do with Phil, but if I had an idea, I'd run it past them. I certainly wouldn't insist on it, but I would run it past them. It was a good relationship. We had a good time doing it.

MA: Were they pretty much still considered together at that time, or were they already kind of drifting apart?

JY: No, they were very together.

MA: Okay. I've heard differing accounts that they were a pretty tight group until they broke up, and then after that, well…

JY: Yeah. It was after that that they broke up, so yeah they were very tight and really enthusiastic. "Gas Money" was one of the ones that they had a great time with.

MA: Now, did you produce that? It didn't say that you produced that.

JY: Yeah.

MA: And "Teardrops" was the other one?

JY: I'd have to hear it to make sure.

MA: They're both like doo wop sounding ones. If you're saying "Gas Money," it's similar to that. It was Mark singing "Teardrops" and I think it was Jim Pons singing "Gas Money," if I remember correctly.

JY: I don't think it was Pons. Howard and Mark did all of the leads.

MA: How did that one come about to be in a doo wop style instead of standard rock and roll?

JY: They came in with it and said, "We want to do this song that we knew way back when." They played it and I said, "Great! Let's do it!" and I think we did it in one afternoon. It was very loose, but that was the way those things were in the old days. That came out really good, that and "Who Would Ever Think That I Would Marry Margaret?" was another one. I believe that was the B-side of "Goodbye Surprise."

MA: It was the A-side with "We Ain't Gonna Party No More."

JY: Right. Right. Right.

MA: Actually, "Goodbye Surprise" never got released back in the day. It wasn't until Flo & Eddie did it.

JY: Like I say, it happened right when White Whale went belly up.

MA: Now, Flo & Eddie or Howard and Mark always insisted that they never wanted to record "Who Would Ever Think That I Would Marry Margaret?" Were they really that adamant about it?

JY: No. Nope. They wanted to do it. They brought it in. Unless they were putting on a big face for me. They brought it in, they wanted to do it, and we did it.

MA: Okay. They acted like, and this is the part of the story that I've heard, is that White Whale insisted that they had to record this, and they didn't want to. They hated it, but then they said, "Fine. We'll do it," just so they could keep recording.

JY: I've never heard that part of the story. It didn't seem to me that they were against it.

MA: You can't hear it on the recording. It sounds like they're having fun. Another one that didn't come out and they later redid again as Flo & Eddie was "Marmendy Mill." It was kind of this epic thing.

JY: That I don't remember.

MA: Okay another one. "There You Sit Lonely."

JY: Yeah. That we did. I didn't do anything when they were Flo & Eddie.

MA: No, I don't mean then. Maybe they just demoed it and they never did a final recording. Some of these have come out in recent times and they're listed as "demo," not as a final recording.

JY: Yeah. Somewhere I have tapes of rough mixes of the stuff we did. I'll have to go through those some day.

MA: A couple more. "You Want to Be a Woman"? That sound familiar?

JY: Yeah.

MA: Okay. I know I'm straining your brain after over 50 years on this stuff!

JY: It was a while ago, yeah.

MA: The last one was also re-recorded by Flo & Eddie. I think this was only a demo, and you may not have helped on it. "Strange Girl?" Does that sound familiar?

JY: Naah. I'm not sure about that one.

MA: And then, this is a really obscure thing. Apparently, before White Whale closed, they copyrighted a bunch of song titles. Now this doesn't mean that they were actually real titles, but I'll just rattle them off if anything sounds familiar. None of these have been officially released, at least with these names. One was called "John's Medley." One was called "I've Been Gone Too Long." One called "Kathleen's Brain." "Let's Pack and Beat It." "On the Inside…"

JY: Now that almost sounds familiar "Let's Pack and Beat It."

MA: If you don't remember those, I don't blame you. I just mention all these things because you were kind of there at the end and maybe you knew something about it and if you didn't, that's fine. I'm straining your brain here on some of these things.

JY: Yeah. The only time I saw them after that, after they stopped being The Turtles, was when Howard and his wife split up, and my wife Judy and I had split up and I started dating his ex-wife. She was really a sweetheart. I really liked her a lot. I wasn't really crazy about the way Howard treated her, but I liked her a lot, and she ended up doing well, having a nice life.

MA: How did it stop for you? Did they stop coming to sessions or what?

JY: The record company ceased to be so there were no more sessions.

MA: Did they call you and say, "Stop. There are no more sessions."

JY: Pretty much. Yeah. They said, "White Whale doesn't exist anymore, so we're going to see what we can do." That was it for me and them as far as recording went.

MA: Wow. Now they did release a compilation later in the year that had earlier songs called *Wooden Head*. That was in late 1970. That was after your involvement. I guess the label still existed as a label, but not for recording new songs.

JY: Yeah, I'm not aware of that.

MA: Mark and Howard act like it was eons before they got the call to go into Zappa's band, but upon looking things up, it looks as if it was less than two weeks. Maybe two weeks seems like a long time back in the day when you don't know what's coming next.

JY: It's like what I was saying about my time with Tom Driscoll and the Tomcats. Things that seemed like a year were actually like a month. Time was stretched out so much more at that age.

MA: During the time you were recording them, everything went pretty smoothly? You didn't have any bickering or fighting?

JY: No, it was a lot of fun.

MA: That's cool. They always acted like it was all falling apart, but everyone's emotions were different. If you were not actively involved with the group and just producing them, it was probably just fun every time.

JY: Yeah, and there were some social get-togethers. We went to dinner at Howard's house one time. It was a very social thing and there weren't any rough edges in that whole time that I recall. There may have been because Howard and Mark were close since they were very young. Before The Turtles. So, they were like an entity inside an entity. So, they may have had some planning for the future that didn't include the band. It's very likely, but I wasn't aware of any of that.

MA: Did you ever work with any of them again either on stage or in the studio?

JY: Johnny. John Seiter.

MA: Oh yeah, Seiter, but not with Mark or Howard later on?

JY: No.

MA: Not even those reunion tours? The Happy Together Tours?

JY: No, but my brother, Jim, has done a ton of them.

MA: That's true. Yes, The Association is usually part of those.

JY: They've got one coming up and I was not aware that Howard had been gone from it for three or four years.

MA: So, I have one last question. Around 2006, Howard Kaylan did a solo album called *Dust Bunnies* and they did cover a song which I believe you wrote called "Snowblind." I don't know if you knew about that or had anything to do with it. Can you talk about the song for a moment?

JY: It's a song that Judy and I and Zally wrote and no, I wasn't aware of that.

MA: He does a decent job with it. He really belts it out.

JY: Well, good! Howard is a fine singer. He really is!

MA: What was that song originally for?

JY: It was from *Farewell Aldebaran*. It was the opening song for *Farewell Aldebaran*. It came together one night in the studio and Larry Beckett was staying with us for a while and it was Beckett and Judy and I and Zally. It was the four of us in one house. Judy had just finished the lyrics. I guess we were waiting for Gary Brandt to say something, but we just started messing with it and it just started taking hold. It just started working. Within an hour it was done with Zally playing bass, Beckett playing drums, because he was the drummer in The Tim Buckley Band when they were in high school. It was like in two takes. Gary recorded it live with the vocals and everything going, except for a lead guitar solo and then Zally put on a lead guitar, and that was it.

MA: Now the way Howard performs it, it has a really thumping beat, and then he sings "Snnnnooooowwwblllliiinnddd!" He really grinds it out like that.

JY: Well yeah. Judy sang it and she sang her ass off. She was really quite good.

MA: So the genesis of that [Howard solo] album that I found out from Andy Cahan, the keyboard player, is that he said, "Let's record something. Why don't you do songs that you always wanted to do?" and that was one he chose.

JY: Wow! Omnivore re-released that album in 2016. We went out to California and performed at the Grammy Museum and then at McCabe's, and just had a great time. All five of my kids sang background. It was wonderful. We had a great time.

Godfrey Townsend—October 18, 2021

MA: Tell me about what happened when you were touring with John Entwistle.

GT: One of the tours that he was asked to go on was a thing called "A Walk Down Abbey Road." It was a specialty package tour that they were putting together with John Entwistle, Ann Wilson from Heart, Todd Rundgren, and Alan Parsons. It was a tribute to The Beatles. Each artist would do a few of their own hit songs and then a few Beatles covers or renditions. I went on that tour with John, basically to sing his Who stuff with him, but I became the musical director for it because every few minutes at rehearsals, someone like Todd would be coming over and say, "Hey, what's that chord on 'Lady Madonna,'" or whatever and I knew them all, so they made me the musical director. That same tour company is the same production company that did Hippie Fest where The Turtles started and then that became the Happy Together tour which I've been on for the last 10 years as the musical director. It's a stepping stone that leads to a circuit of things like a network of gigs.

MA: I think I did see that "Abbey Road" tour.

GT: Yes. After "A Walk Down Abbey Road," we did the Hippie Fest, and it was my band of musicians, the guys I put together for the Alan Parsons Live Project. That was the same band for the Hippie Fest tour and for the Happy Together tours. Some of them would bring their band for the first tour, and then they would hear us backing up someone else and they'd go, "Damn! These guys sound good. I'm not bringing my band next time and [will] let them back me up!" The idea of it was to save money, first of all. That's always the prime directive of touring for the producers. It also takes away that changeover time between acts. Even if you have everything all set up already, you've got to make sure this is working, that's working. There's none of that. They're just there and the two singers come out and they sing their six songs and then they run off and then the next minute, there's another guy coming out, so you can do six acts in two hours or something like that.

MA: So how long do you play since you're supporting every act on the bill?

GT: Every act gets 20 minutes, so like on Happy Together, there are six acts. It used to be five, then they figured they'd stick another one in. Six acts for 20 minutes is two hours with a 20 minute intermission.

MA: It just seemed like when you have so many acts, you're going to be playing for like six hours.

GT: No, and you see what I mean. There's literally no change-over time. It's "Thank you, everybody, have a great rest of the show!" and as they're going off the stage, the next guys are coming out and we have a pre-recorded introduction done by Shadoe Stevens. As those guys are walking off, he's already going, "Our next artist is blah, blah, blah, and has 10 gold records."

MA: Now, were you with the Happy Together tour from the beginning or did you come in somewhere along the way?

GT: I was there from the beginning because it was a concept that came out of the Hippie Fest tour, so I was already in place with my band as the backup band for everybody that needs one, right? Then, Happy Together was "Now, we're going to just have whoever wants to come on the tour and they just come themselves and you're the backup band for everybody no matter what. One was Mark Lindsay from Paul Revere and The Raiders. Micky Dolenz from The Monkees, of course Mark and Howard, and I forget who else…

MA: The Grass Roots, Gary Puckett, The Buckinghams, The Association…

GT: That's right. Yes. Yes. We were basically the guys, you know. Grass Roots was Rob Grill, just the singer, and we just backed him up. He may have brought his guitar player, as well. [Editors' note: Dusty Hanvey has been the guitarist for the Grass Roots since 1984]

MA: If they're normally instrumentalists and you're doing all the backing, the people just do the vocals then and that's about it?

GT: Yeah. Mark and Howard would come out and they'd just sing and we'd back them up and, like I said, with four lead singers backing them up. We're covering all the vocals.

MA: So, it was just the situation after Hippie Fest that "these were the guys" then?

GT: Yeah. Mark and Howard had a band who weren't The Turtles, but they were guys that they had been playing with for a long time. As a matter of fact, I auditioned for them back in 1982 or something like that. Back then, I had met their drummer, a guy named Joe Stefko. He played with Meat Loaf and with Mick Ronson and people like that. Another guy named Chris Apostle was their keyboard player and he worked at The China Club where I did a pro jam. Somehow or other, the word got around that, "Hey, you know our guitar player is leaving, and we need another guitar player. Would you like to audition for the band?" and I went, "Sure! That would be great!" I knew them more as Flo & Eddie when they sang with Frank Zappa and The Mothers. We used to listen to that stuff in high school every night.

Joe gave me a cassette with four songs to learn and I took it home and learned it. I went down to a rehearsal space in Manhattan. Mark and Howard weren't there. It was just the band guys. We played through it. I sang some vocals with them and they said, "Sounds good to me! You're in. Mark and Howard will definitely approve, so you're in." A couple of days later, I got a phone call. I was in bed and the message came in. I was just listening to it on my answering machine. It was Joe, going, "Hey man, I'm really sorry to have to tell you, but our guitar player decided that he doesn't want to leave the band. So, you got the audition, but you didn't get it." I just remember laying there thinking, "I'm not getting out of bed today." I was really depressed.

MA: You're talking about The Turtles' Flo & Eddie band, not the Happy Together band?

GT: Yeah, yeah. This was way, way before that. They were doing like a week at The Bottom Line between Christmas and New Years that they used to do. My consolation prize was a pair of tickets to see the gig at The Bottom Line. I remember being really depressed at that time about that, but we don't recognize things when they happen to us. We only realize years later why that was meant to happen like that. Chances are, had I gotten the audition and had been in that band, I wouldn't have done the other things that I would have that took me really nice places and then round full circle back to them again.

MA: It is interesting that they had their separate band. Very rarely did they cross over because they had they're East Coast band for which you were trying out and then they had their West Coast band, and then there's the Happy Together band. There's like three separate things going on. I think nowadays they only do the Happy Together tour.

GT: What happened then was that different guys came and went. They had Joe Stefko on drums, Donnie Kisselbach on bass, Benjy King was the keyboard player and he played in one of my cover bands years before and even then we had Greg Hawkes on keys.

MA: From The Cars.

GT: At one point, the original guy who was going to leave, that I was going to take his gig, but he finally left again. His name is Tristan Avakian. He's a great guitar player. He plays in a Queen thing. It's really, really good. Marc Martel is the singer. He did the singing for the *Bohemian Rhapsody* movie. Tristan is an amazing player and he's got the Brian May thing down, so he left to do that. Another guy named Joel Hoekstra came in and was playing guitar for them. He was on Hippie Fest with them and then he left and they asked me to join. So, I was the guy on Hippie Fest and Happy Together and I was in The Turtles when they played gigs on the side. We did a couple of years like that as well. It was me, Greg Hawkes, Donnie Kisselbach, and Joe Stefko backing up Howard and Mark. I was an actual member of The Turtles as well for a while, or whatever you want to call it.

MA: I've interviewed a lot of the players, but mostly the West Coast band. You're the first one I've interviewed from the East Coast band. How did you interact with Mark and Howard? Did you work with them offstage or just professionally onstage? What did you do?

GT: When it was time to rehearse for the tours like when we did the Happy Together tour and stuff like that, we would rehearse, just maybe for a day or two, and we would have to rehearse all of the acts in two or three days' time. We'd do a day of rehearsal where we'd do The Buckinghams in the morning, The Grass Roots in the afternoon, and tomorrow we'll do The Turtles in the morning, and then Chuck Negron in the afternoon. We would do it like that and in two or three days of rehearsing with these guys, we'd go out on a major tour of 50 shows. That was mostly what it was. I don't remember rehearsing a lot with The Turtles. I had to learn their whole show, so they basically gave me a live CD of them playing the Bear's Den up in upstate New York, or somewhere like that, and I had to learn that. It's a live version. That's the arrangement. That's the key. Learn that. I really learned The Turtles' songs through the eyes and ears of another guitar player whose place I had taken. My real thing is with my band when we'd do "Happy Together," I'd tell my guys, "Yeah, we're going to get some live versions from these artists and get their arrangements and maybe the keys are different, but before you hear that or listen to that, you go back and listen to the records."

MA: The originals.

GT: The original records with the friggin' Wrecking Crew guys that played on those records, and they were singles and they were hits because of what was on those records. You learn that first. Then you can translate that into what they want us to do. So many of these artists are so grateful for that, because they don't know what they're getting into until they go do some fly dates with some pick up band. They're going to rehearse for a half hour at sound check with these guys. It doesn't matter what it sounds like. They've gotta go and do the show. "Okay, we'll get through this. Whatever," and wing it. With us, Mark Lindsey said it in an interview on a tour bus. We heard him talking to a guy. He said, "This is such an amazing experience for me. It feels like I'm coming out on stage and singing with my master recordings playing behind me."

MA: That's a pretty good compliment.

GT: Like I said, we learned those records, so pretty much every part is covered. We've got a keyboard player who can play piano and organ and strings and horns and sing harmony. He's got it all down.

MA: Do you play the same set year after year after year?

GT: Pretty much, unless something is really not working. Then, maybe we want to try another thing. Usually, we have pretty much rounded it out to your three, four, five biggest hits because that's what the tour is about. It's about us playing the hit songs that people know you for and playing them like the record. Not your Christmas version or your shuffle version or your reggae version. No one wants to hear that. They don't want to hear that. They want to come to the show and when they're walking out the door at the end, they go, "Ooh, he sounded just like his records!" That's what you want, and that's been the success of it.

MA: I've seen The Turtles, but never the Happy Together tour. It seemed like they had a little more opportunity to goof around than compared to Happy Together, where it seems like you just have time to play the hits, and not too much between song cut-up stuff.

GT: They kind of stretch it out. Mark Volman is always the one who's telling the other acts to "keep it short" and "we're running late" and "keep it under 20 minutes." "Keep the talking to a minimum" and then once he gets out there, he's just like walking around on the stage saying, "I don't know where I am anymore!" He's doing this whole shtick, and when Howard was doing it with us, Howard was kind of like the straight man, and Mark was the crazy clown fool. Whatever. Howard hasn't been out with us for a couple of years.

MA: Right. We also interviewed Ron Dante. In fact, Ron said what you just said about the songs. Ron already knew certain songs like "Happy Together," and probably sang them in his solo show for years anyway, but he said that Mark Volman said, "Go back to the original record and sing it like that."

GT: That's as close as you're going to get. It sounded like the real deal, you know what I mean? Two different voices. Howard's voice is very powerful. I never realized that until I worked with them for years and just went "Wow! He is just slammin' it!" Ron's got a great voice and he's a great musician and he produced Barry Manilow's records, so it's a no-brainer for him to just go, "Just learn these songs." The hardest part about it all is just remembering all the words. We're getting by because we have a good lead singer.

MA: You worked with Howard all those years and he's now having these health problems. Is there ever a chance for him to come back, or is he basically retired and done?

GT: I've been doing this for 25 years. People like Mark and Howard have been doing it for over 50 years, so there's no real monetary incentive for them to do it. It's just the love of going on stage. As for me, the Happy Together tour features songs that I grew up with. Those songs are like embedded in your DNA. To get up on stage and play those songs behind the guy, and you go, "That's the guy, right there!" It's a feeling of a sense of accomplishment. We'll do 50 to 60 songs and every night it's the same songs and the same shtick and you have to stand there and listen to it. "He's going to do his little punchline… BOOM!... There it is!" So we look at the audience. Tonight they were really kind of active, or tonight they were kind of like a painting. That's how we rate the shows, how the audience reacts to it. We're putting out, but the more they put out, the more we put out. It's only a natural reaction.

MA: Do you mingle with these guys off stage?

GT: Oh yeah. I'll tell you some funny stuff. Mark Volman and I have a relationship that we're usually the first ones up on the tour bus in the morning. Usually it's me, and then he'll come out. I'll come out and make the coffee. I'll be sitting there drinking my coffee and he'll come out and he'll plop down next to me and he just looks over at me with that look and I go, "Wanna cup of coffee?" And he says, "I would love a cup of coffee."

MA: I thought you'd never ask!

GT: And I make him a cup of coffee with a little bit of Splenda and I give it to him and we're rolling down the highway. He sits down and manages to take the first sip and goes, "Ahhh! Great! Great!" It's quiet in the morning. We're both kind of sitting there, taking in the day, looking out the window. It's a moment of coolness hanging out. We'll talk to each other on the phone the rest of the year and he'll just call and go, "Hey!! I was just thinking about you. I'm thinking about what it's going to be like having that morning coffee. I'm so looking forward to that morning coffee on that bus!!" Certain situations, I have relationships like that.

MA: When you go on tour, do you lug your own equipment or do you have handlers and you send them the guitars and they send them from city to city?

GT: For a simple tour like the Happy Together tour, I just need to bring two instruments. I have a double gig bag with two guitars and I put them on my shoulders. I don't like shipping guitars or putting guitars in with the cargo like luggage or suitcases because you're not guaranteed that that's going to get to the other side. You're not guaranteed that you'll get to the other side, let alone something you're watching go out into the distance. I've gone to gigs where my luggage didn't show up, but I know if I'm able to take the guitar on the plane with me, if I'm getting there, my guitar is getting there. Of course, all of the other equipment like the amps and stuff, that's all back line rental that we rent for the whole summer. It travels on a trailer on the back of one of the tour buses.

Chip Douglas—December 3, 2021

CD: When I was in the Gene Clark Group, that impressed the members of The Turtles and they said, "We've got to get this guy!" and Gene Clark dismissed me. I wasn't doing anything, so Mark Volman came along and said, "Hey, we need a new guy to play bass for us." I said, "Uh, I'm not doing anything, so let's go." That's what happened there.

CR: Whose place did you take on bass?

CD: Chuck Portz was his name, and the way that Mark described it was "Portz is getting crazy on us!" I never really hung out with Portz too much. I saw him and met him a few times when he was still in the group, but anytime someone would act weird in The Turtles when I was with them, Howard and Mark would look at each other and their eyes would get big and they'd go, "Portz!" It was a running joke for someone who was getting a little nutty. I'll have to talk to Mark about it someday and ask him, "Well, what was it exactly?" or you can have him on the show and ask him, "What was it about Portz?"

MA: Well, they were all high school buddies. There was probably some chemistry there since they were together in choir. How far back do you go with them as far as knowing them because you said you knew of them prior to you joining The Turtles?

CD: I didn't really know them until I got into the group. We had seen each other on the road and passing by at Western Recording Studios while they were doing a session and Modern Folk Quartet were doing a session, we'd go, "Hey, how are you doing?" We knew who each other was. They knew us and we knew them, but we never got to be really close until we went on the road together and started working out "Happy Together" which was one of the main things about that record why it turned out as well as it did. We worked it on the road for about two and a half months or at least a month or two. We'd practice things and change things and had it pretty well down pat when we went into the studio, and then we did it in two or three takes and it was done. There was no fiddling around in the studio with "Okay, let's change this and let's change that." No, it all worked out and went right down, which I never had a chance to do ever again except for MFQ stuff which we did live. Even then, we were always working it out in the studio. There's something to be said about doing it on the road for a little while and getting it really good.

MA: Was that the only song you did that with or did you do that frequently with Turtles songs?

CD: I didn't record too many things with them. I really only recorded that and something else called "Can't You Hear the Cows?" and one or two things preceding the "Happy Together" session, but once "Happy Together" was done, I don't remember recording anything subsequently. We did *The Smothers Brothers Show* and then a live performance at the Whisky a Go Go and Michael Nesmith came along and I left The Turtles.

MA: Now, is this you on the *Happy Together* album cover?

CD: Um, no. Jim Pons is resting his head on Howard's thigh, I think it is. There are just a few pictures. There's about two pictures of me with them and one of them I'm kind of sitting in the front middle of all of them and I have a string tie on, and the other one is around a water fountain and we're all happy together. Everybody's smiling a big smile.

CR: You know which picture he's talking about, Mark?

MA: Yeah, I know which one he's talking about because I've seen it before, but I don't have it here. The other book I have has even later pictures in this *Shindig* magazine.

CD: Jim Pons, as far as The Turtles go, everyone comes up to me and says, "Oh, I saw your picture and I saw the TV show you did," and I go, "No, that's not me. That's the guy who replaced me." You have to look at *The Smothers Brothers Show* with all the chairs on it. We did a couple of others. We did *The Mike Douglas Show* and *The Hollywood Palace*. I'm in the upper right as you face the stage in that show in kind of a brown jacket. That's a good show. We were all really happy there.

MA: I've seen a lot of clips like The Smothers Brothers.

CR: That was great!

MA: That one made it into the *Happy Together* documentary that was made quite a while back.

CD: Yes, it did. It did.

MA: What influence did Michael Nesmith have to get you to quit The Turtles?

CD: Well basically, I guess the big selling point was… I told him, "I don't know about this Mike. I'm having an awfully good time with these guys and we got a hit record and is this really going to work out? You already have got a guy that's running the show and you're sure that you're on the level about this?" He said, "I assure you that you'll be making six figures in six months!" and I said, "Well, all right. I'll give it a shot." I had my doubts all the way until I met them and started working with them. I then met Kirshner and thought, "Wow, I'm really doing this now!" That was the selling point. One of them. I knew him and he was sincere about it, so it was okay.

CR: Was it a drastic change going from a band that played all of their own instruments to a band that could play their instruments, but were being supplemented by The Wrecking Crew and by other musicians? Was that a very big change of worlds?

CD: For them, it was. For instance, Micky never really played the drums. He was just beginning on the drums and he played left-handed and he was not the steadiest drummer in the world, but I learned how to edit tape. We're getting off the subject of The Turtles, but we can come back to that.

CR: What I meant was The Turtles, they could go out live, that was a set group. This was another world for you because you were coming in not as the bass player, not as a musician, but now as a producer.

CD: I decided to play bass just so that we could have a four part combo, besides the fact that I like to play.

MA: Is bass the only thing you play or did you play other things?

CD: No, bass is basically it.

MA: So, flash forward, you did *Headquarters*, you did *Pisces, Aquarius, Capricorn and Jones, Ltd.* and "Daydream Believer" and then suddenly you went back to The Turtles. How did that happen?

CD: Well, The Monkees wanted to do their own thing and there was no room for me anymore because they were doing their own sides. I was basically out of a job and then The Turtles came along. Actually, I think it was Herb Cohen. I don't know if Herb was managing them at the time, but they wanted to do an album called *The Battle of the Bands* and I had written a tune with Harry Nilsson. I didn't do all that much in the way of writing it. That song was born, incidentally. The title song—"Battle of the Bands." When Harry Nilsson visited me at my place in Laurel Canyon, one evening. We sat around and I got my rhythm guitar and I started playing a D7 rhythm chord. He was sitting at my harmonium. I had bought this pump organ years ago before with the MFQ, and he was playing it, but he turned away from the harmonium and started to clap his hands and ad-lib this song. I happen to have my tape cassette recorder going and so he ad-libbed that song word for word, just like you see it on the album. One time through.

CR: Wow!

CD: Somewhere I have that tape, too. I have to look for it and hopefully it's not covered in mold. (sings) "Two bucks a ticket, got to get with it on the night they have the Battle of the Bands." One time through. I happened to make a chord change at one point and he went on to do a different thing. All I was doing was playing rhythm guitar, but really the song belongs all to him. I did change the chord at one point and offered a new place to go with the melody and stuff like that. That was amazing. I couldn't believe that he did that. He was a genius, Harry. I loved him. He was so fun to hang out with, with that smile and I loved that voice. I knew him before he came in with songs for The Monkees.

CR: Harry Diltz is really alongside you with Modern Folk Quartet, with Turtles and with Monkees. You're producing; he's doing photo shoots, and playing, too, right? You guys were close from the beginning and still are, is that right?

CD: Still are. I talk to him once or twice a week if I can, mostly when he's driving from Laguna to L.A. and vice-versa, because that's his lifestyle. He leaves Tuesday night and drives down to L.A. and spends Wednesday and Thursday there, and then drives back to Laguna on Friday to be at another place with his lady friend. I talk to him during those times when he has nothing to do because otherwise he says, "I've got to sign 50 photos right now," because that's what he does when he's back in L.A., he's signing photos, 40 or 50 each time he's there because that's what he does. That's for the gallery.

MA: So back to The Turtles, you had the song "The Battle of the Bands," but was that the natural thing for you to come up with that as the theme for that album where each song was done in a completely different style, or did that just evolve?

CD: I guess Mark and Howard kind of came up with that idea along with their road manager at the time, Rick Soderling, I think that was his name. He put together all of the pictures for that album and got the costumes rented and all of that stuff. Somewhere along the line, it became *Battle of the Bands*. Great. We'll do an album and we'll take a picture as a different band on every song, so every song would supposedly be played by a different group. The Bluegrass Fireball was one for some song that had a banjo in it ("Chicken Little Was Right").

MA: There was one with enchilada as part of the name of the group.

CD: Yeah, The Atomic Enchilada, yeah. That was for a psychedelic song that we did. That sort of thing with "the voices of light"... ("The Last Thing I Remember").

MA: I've always wanted to know this and I don't have the album in front of me, but some of the pictures of the groups have five members, and some of the pictures have six, but the face was obscured. Were you that sixth member or is it somebody else in those pictures?

CD: The only picture that I'm in, I'm wearing a coonskin cap, and that's that Bluegrass Fireball group.

MA: Yes. A few of the photos feature six members, so I always wondered if you were the sixth member not officially playing, but just for the photo shoot.

CD: I didn't really play anything on that album except the B3 Hammond Organ and kicking off the "You Showed Me" tune. That was me getting the thing started on that. I believe it's the only song I play on the album because Jim Pons was the bass player, so I wasn't playing bass. I was just coaching him a little bit saying, "Put this part in and bomp bomp omb om..." You know, the little accents and stuff like that, but "You Showed Me" was the one thing that I played on with them.

MA: So tell me the story on that. I've heard it before, but I'd rather hear it from you as to why "You Showed Me" came out like it did, with the tempo it did.

CD: I guess that was the way I kind of liked it and I showed it to them that way on my harmonium that Harry had clapped his hands and sung "The Battle of the Bands" earlier. They had come up to my place and I played it the best I could on the harmonium. It's the kind of an instrument that you have to pump your feet and you can't play too much uptempo stuff, so I just played it that way and their eyes just lit up and they said, "This is great! This is for us!" Mark and Howard's eyes would get big whenever they liked an idea. Anyway, that was the approach we took. McGuinn and Crosby and Clark, they sat around at the Troubadour on Monday nights and played that song among others before they became The Byrds, and that's where I heard it. It was (sings quickly) "You showed me how to do, exactly what you do…" It was more Beatle-like, the way they did it. I had my own approach to it, I guess.

MA: The story I've heard and this is what I was trying to get from you, but that's okay. If it's different, I'd like to hear the truth. I heard it was an upbeat song when The Byrds played it (or whatever their name was then), and then when you played it on your organ, it wasn't quite working correctly, so you couldn't play it fast even if you wanted to, and that's why they said, "Let's keep it this way." That's the story I've heard. I don't know if that's correct.

CD: That's probably correct. I think I kind of played it that way, is my recollection, because I liked it in that little slower tempo, and yeah, I didn't play it on the guitar. If I did play it on the guitar, I might have played it like Crosby and all of them with the 'Beatle' approach. But yeah, you're probably right.

MA: Now how did you happen to remember it because it wasn't released by The Byrds at that point, correct?

CD: I guess I must have just sat around and played it or something because I knew it. I talked to Roger McGuinn at some point and asked him, "What's the rest of those words?" I heard it so many times at The Troubadour that it was just drummed into my head. That's basically where I heard it. There was a tape floating around that had them playing that song just like that and I think I have it. As a matter of fact, it's an old tape of Gene Clark's that I wound up hanging on to for some reason. It's them playing it like The Beatles with The Beatle approach. It might exist on an album somewhere. I'm not sure.

MA: I think it came out on this album called *Preflyte*, that came out a long time later where they put early Byrds tracks. They put it out because, "Hey, The Turtles did this song!" It was already a hit by that point.

CD: Yeah, I think you're right.

MA: Now, did you play it when you were in The Gene Clark Group?

CD: You know, I don't remember. I don't think we worked that one up.

MA: The next thing that you did was with The Turtles in a certain way and with The Monkees in a certain way, was your song "Christmas is My Time of Year." How did that come about?

CD: That's funny, I just told these stories to The Cowsills yesterday. These very same questions. I'll explain it better here. Howard Kaylan had come up to my house one day and we were sitting around, smoking a doobie or whatever. We got to talking about Christmas or something. It was right around that time of year, I guess, and Howard, he looked at me with those eyes again, and looking down and looking up and sang, "That's what brings good love and good cheer…" We might have tried to write a few verses, but those words never stuck to the verses. Later, I did a version with Mark and maybe Howard, too, and called it "Christmas Spirit" and had the Holy Pearls in the background. It was a forerunner of the version that I later did with The Monkees, but it had different words. They weren't as good, I didn't think. It bothered me a year or two later. These words and the verses, they're not good. So, I rewrote it a bit and then got a hold of Eddie Hoh, who was in a halfway house at that point. I dragged him out to play drums at Annex Studios and I called up Peter Tork. I called Mike Nesmith, too, but he was too busy and did not want to do anything.

MA: Of course.

CD: And that's how The Monkees' track was done, and then I called Micky and Davy and said, "Hey, I've got this track. Do you want to come in and maybe we'll put it together?" I still love it because it's Micky and Davy sharing the lead vocal. Too bad we didn't have a little better idea for the chorus. I don't know. I don't want to analyze my own stuff. Howard's chorus would have been better if we had done, "Christmas is that wonderful time of year" instead of "my time of year." I don't know.

CR: Can I ask which version you like better, The Monkees' or The Turtles' version?

CD: Oh, The Monkees' version. The Turtles' version, it wasn't really The Turtles. It was just Mark and Howard and I put together a track. I don't know who played on that, Joel Larson or somebody? I haven't heard it in so long and what were The Gospel Pearls doing in there in the background? We were just into those kinds of voices in those days. We'd call them the incredi-voices. We tried to sound like gospel singers, you know, a black gospel choir. Mark was always singing those high parts in a high falsetto. We wanted to do that. I hadn't heard it in a while, but I like The Monkees' version. That was the version I settled on, so to speak.

MA: I do have two questions about it, though. Why wasn't the original one released by The Turtles, because John Barbata played drums on it, so it had three-fifths of The Turtles?

CD: I guess you're right, he did play drums on it.

MA: Yeah, he told us in an interview we did.

CD: Okay. Whoever was running the record company wasn't interested or something. I'm sure I played it for them, Lee Lasseff and Ted Feigin.

MA: It seems like it would have sold better. Is Linda Ronstadt on that one, too, or is she only on the B-side?

CD: I believe she is on that one, too. It turned out to be something called "The Christmas Spirit." Linda and I were going together at the time and so I was involving her in everything I did. I would have done 10,000 more things if I had known what value they would have had in the future.

MA: After *Battle of the Bands* and "Christmas Spirit," did you do anything more with The Turtles? Did they want you for *Turtle Soup*?

CD: No, that was it with The Turtles. We had a big disagreement one day. I didn't look at it as anything to disagree over, but they were sitting around and they were really hitting the bong in those days, so to speak. I came over to have a meeting with them and I said, "Well, *The Battle of the Bands* came out and it did okay, but it didn't really go to the top of the charts. I think what we need to do is to feature Howard's voice more on the songs with Mark singing that marvelous high harmony to them, and I'll just never forget. They said, "Noooo, Chip," was the unanimous reply. It's almost as if they all said it together. "Noooo, Chip, we're a family here. We all share in everything equally." They regret that now, as "Elenore" has five writers on it, and Howard wrote it, but everybody else got credit despite the fact. John Barbata wrote "Elenore, love me." He wrote that, and I came up with the line to replace "and you really ring the bell" to "and you really do me well." I changed that line. "And you really ring the bell" doesn't quite cut it, does it? How about "and you really do me well"? They said, "Okay, okay," and so they did that. Actually, I got a great compliment from Larry Knechtel one time, a studio musician I rubbed shoulders with. He was going one way and I was going another and he said, "Hey, I like that 'Elenore.' I like that line 'you really do me well.'"

I said, "Oh, thank you very much!" He's not with us anymore, but he was a beautiful guy and I wished I had used him more on sessions because he was the man that would play the piano and everything, but I was producing groups that played their own instruments, so that's how it went.

MA: It's interesting that they had such a group camaraderie, when only a year or two later they became Flo & Eddie and remained that way for the rest of their career and they didn't really participate with the rest of the guys anymore.

CD: I know. I totally disagreed with them becoming Flo & Eddie. You guys are The Turtles. You have four or five hits to your credit. Why don't you just keep going and make more Turtle hits? They were in awe of Zappa, I guess, and perhaps Herb Cohen was Zappa's manager at the time and he may have had a little bit of influence in talking them into coming with Zappa. So yeah, they are known as Flo & Eddie and The Turtles now or whatever. I just thought they had this great track record with all these songs and you come out with another one with that voice of Howard Kaylan singing it, and whatever you guys can do in the background, you're bound to keep going. But no, and so all things must pass, as George Harrison said.

MA: Which group was more fun to work with, The Turtles or The Monkees?

CD: We had more disagreements in The Monkees from time to time, but mostly during the *Headquarters* album, it was just a blast. It was a real labor of love, that album. Later, we weren't all together then.

MA: Do you keep in touch with any of The Turtles?

CD: No, I haven't. I called Mark just to see how Howard was doing. I had heard that he had health problems so I called Mark and that's the last time I talked to him and he said, "Well, I'm not sure if he's going to join us on the Happy Together tour or not. Then, I talked to The Cowsills and I didn't realize that they share the bill with The Turtles on that Happy Together tour which I would like to see sometime if I get to California.

MA: Ron Dante is filling in for Howard now from The Archies.

CD: I see. Yeah, yeah. I never met him.

CR: It's all full circle with "Sugar, Sugar." One [of the] things interviewers like to do is to say a name and ask you to say the first thing that comes to your mind, so if I say "John Barbata," what's the first thing that comes to your mind?

CD: John Barbata—he had this little thing that he always did when he was feeling slightly devilish. He would go [makes weird sounds] with his nose. I don't know if it was a reaction to something someone would say, but he was all [makes weird sounds], but I remember going to his place sometimes and he was always working out, lifting weights and stuff. Fun guy. We had a lot of fun. He was good fun on the road.

CR: And a great drummer, right?

CD: Yeah. A great drummer and a great drum solo. One of the best. He'd come off the stage and play all the drums and do a little dance at the end of it and a bow. He's quite something.

CR: What about Jerry Yester? What comes to mind?

CD: Jerry Yester. Beautiful, beautiful voice. Just a wonderful ballad voice. He can sing those tender love song ballads, and he's still got that voice, too. That's the thing about him. Definitely.

MA: And he helped produce the unreleased final Turtles album which was going to be called *Shell Shock*, but it never got released.

CD: Oh really? I didn't realize that.

MA: He claims he never got paid.

CD: Oh, probably not. None of us have. Nobody sees anything from Turtles. I'm afraid that we… I don't know. I don't really want to go there. When you own the masters of something, I think you're obliged to—once you get your money back from purchasing them—then you're supposed to pay the boys, hopefully. Some would disagree.

CR: What about Mark Volman? A memory of Mark? What comes to mind?

CD: Mark is just the clown to the max. He was just always, always having fun. What a performer, though. Tossing the tambourine 50 feet in the air and catching it with his big toe, or whatever he did. Great voice. He had a great, high falsetto. Just wonderful. I just love the two of those voices together. I always had a burning desire to do more things with Howard singing lead and Mark doing the high harmony, like Micky Dolenz and Michael Nesmith did on "Pleasant Valley Sunday," and then Davy and Micky would do that. That's the kind of harmony that I really like, in spite of the fact that I come from a four part harmony, Four Freshman-like group. I love the country approach to music where one guy sings the lead and then in the chorus, his buddy sings the high harmony on top of him. I've fronted a country band from time to time, not too regularly, but while I've been here on the Big Island. I went and learned country music and played in clubs all the time. I never could find a guy to do those harmony parts.

CR: I just wanted to finish with Mark, as a musician. We know he sang, and played the tambourine and did all of that goofy stuff, but he also played some instruments, correct?

CD: Yes, he probably plays keyboards. I never actually saw him play keyboards all that much, but I know he plays Telecaster guitar [from] when he lived down the street from me and I lived in Laurel Canyon. I could hear him practicing during the day, and I'd wander down and talk stories a little bit. He plays the rhythm guitar a little bit. He never did in the days when I was with The Turtles. It was later that he played guitar, I think. Maybe he didn't know how then. If I know Mark, maybe he didn't want to. He could move more when he's with the tambourine and get all over the stage and all over the place. With a guitar, that would probably be with a cord because there weren't wireless guitars in those days. It probably would hang him up a little bit more, so maybe that's why.

MA: Al Nichol.

CD: Al Nichol. Slightly serious about things, but he had ideas now that I'm thinking about him. He would have these little melody ideas that Howard and Mark would kind of pick up on and he sang them very softly when he'd play the guitar and sing. You could barely hear him and then Mark and Howard would get on it and write some words. They had a couple of things. One of them was called "Dance This Dance With Me" and another one was called "Happy to Remember," which I really liked. I thought "Happy to Remember" could be really good, and we never did cut it. I thought that could really be the next single for you and it never came together. They let me go and they didn't want to do that and they did something else.

MA: "Dance This Dance" did make it onto *Turtle Soup*, eventually, though.

CD: Did it? Okay.

MA: I don't recognize that other song, unless they changed the title.

CD: (sings) "Once I wished that I could be a king. Now I find that I have everything…"

MA: Ooh, that sounds familiar. I think that's on *Turtle Soup*, also.

CD: (sings) "If I ever lose it all somehow, I'll be happy to remember…" It wasn't quite arranged like that.

MA: Okay, they changed the title, it's called "How You Loved Me."

CD: "How You Loved Me," yeah!

MA: Jim Tucker. He was in the band for a while with you.

CD: Jim Tucker, he was kind of a good old guy. Just a regular guy.

MA: Now, were you there when he left or were you already gone?

CD: No, I was already gone.

MA: And of course, Howard…

CD: Howard Kaylan, I just mostly remember that little laugh. He always sat on the floor when we had meetings. Howard would sit on the floor and every once in a while would go "a hoo-hoo-hoo." This little laugh would come out. He had this little falsetto laugh. It was as cute as can be. He was very descriptive whenever he would talk about things. He'd go, "Well, I think…." His way of talking was very descriptive and it would suck you right in, too. You listened, because he was very smart and knew what he was talking about. They all were More things about Howard. That lead vocal on "You Baby" blows my mind every time I hear it. I think, "Geez!" He is actually my all time favorite pop singer. I love his voice and I would have loved to have worked with him and made 25 more records, just because of that voice. It's just a beautiful, beautiful voice. It's such a gift when you've got a voice like that.

CR: You worked with two of the greatest pop vocalists ever with Micky Dolenz and with Howard! Forget the impact both bands have made. Both bands should be in the Rock and Roll Hall of Fame for the vocals alone. The two of them are from a different stratosphere.

CD: It would have been great to do some sort of album with the two of them. You still could, I guess. Maybe I will just send them some tracks and say, "Hey Micky, do you mind putting some harmony parts on Howard's little lead here?" I'll have to think of something.

MA: They should do a cover of "No More Tears (Enough is Enough)."

CR: No, they should do a vocal over dueling stratospheres or whatever that dueling extra-terrestrial song. You take that music and you give them a vocal over that and have them do dueling vocals and wow!

CD: I have and I'll have to get over to my studio and pull it out and transfer it to digital, but I did and I haven't even heard it since I did it. I went to Gold Star one time and I did a recording of a guitar part that I had made up at one point, and I made words to this little song. It was kind of an anti-smoking commercial and it went (sings), "Every day when you wake. Every day when you rise up and shine in the morning, be sure that you put on a small pot of tea. It's a wonderful way to start off the day. When you find that you've been up all night till three and if you feel like having a smoke, just have some more tea. You'll feel much better all day long. You'll be strong. You'll live long." It went like that. They came in and sang it and did these harmony parts. It's called "Cup of Tea." I've got to resurrect that and put it into some form that's listenable. The tapes are there, but I've got to be careful running them through the tape machine because they get moldy over time. I don't have a perfect environment to source stuff. Maybe I'll do that tomorrow. I'll try to get that down and see what it sounds like after all these years.

CR: Cool! I hope we were the inspiration for that.

CD: Yes, you have been. Thank you. There's a lot of unreleased things in my library that need to be gone through and pulled and digitized and see what they're worth. My archives are somewhat extensive. There's more things by Davy Jones in there and Micky and some goofy stuff.

Greg Hawkes—December 4, 2021

GH: Speaking of a small world, in a funny coincidence, when I moved up to Boston, the first concert that I went to was at the Boston Tea Party, and it was The Mothers of Invention with Mark and Howard with Frank Zappa. Jeff Simmons was in the band playing bass. He's the same guy who would sing "Lucille." There was Ainsley Dunsbar on drums and I'm pretty sure George Duke on electric piano.

MA: That sounds like the line-up then from like 1970 to 1972, something like that.

GH: Yeah, yeah, yeah.

CR: Never knowing that you would actually be a Turtle!

GH: Yeah, yeah, yeah.

MA: I do my research and it's not going to be all Cars, Cars, Cars, but you were in Martin Mull and his Fabulous Furniture in the 1970s?

GH: Yes, I was. It would have been just previous to The Cars. In 1975, I got an offer from Rich Adelman who plays drums with Martin Mull to go down as Martin wanted to augment his band for a show in Central Park in an outdoor concert. He hired me and another guy. I played mainly saxophone, but also clarinet, a little flute, I played harmonica on one song, a little glockenspiel, sort of novelty instruments, but it turned into working for him for like a year. It was the first time I was ever paid a salary for being a musician which was like a big deal for me. Then, after that year, Martin was getting a divorce. He disbanded his band, moved to Los Angeles to pursue his acting career. Within a year, he had gotten a job on *Mary Hartman, Mary Hartman*, which later spun off

[into] *Fernwood 2 Night*. This directly ties in with Mark and Howard because with Martin we did a show for PBS in Chicago called *SoundStage*. Martin basically wrote the show, and so the name of the show was "60 Minutes to Kill." He wrote these little commercial parodies and stuff and invited Flo & Eddie to be the guests.

MA: I saw that at the time. I had no idea that you were in the band.

GH: Yeah, I'm playing saxophone and I'm in the band and that's when I met Mark and Howard. It's funny. I'm trying to think of more, because like I said, by the end of the year, Martin had let the band go, but that's when Ric and Ben got in touch and they were starting a new band called The Cars. The Cars played early on in Los Angeles. It was either at the Whisky or the Roxy. One of those two clubs on Sunset Blvd. I think, and Mark and Howard both came to the show and came back and chatted.

    Then, it seemed like whenever The Cars would go out and play in L.A., they would come see the show. I remember them coming for the *Candy-O* tour. I remember going out to dinner for Mexican food at La Via Taxco with them and they ordered these peach margaritas and a very good time was had by all. Mark, in particular, just made a point of staying in touch and I'd get a call from him every once in a while with "Hi. How are you doing?" If they were in town I'd go see them and vice versa.

    Quite a while after The Cars broke up and I hadn't been performing for a long time, it was Mark who called me up and said, "What are you doing?" I said, "Hanging around." He said, "Well, our keyboard player is leaving and we need someone." So I'm like, "Uh, okay!"

    So then before my first show I was, "What do I need to do? How am I going to rehearse and stuff?" Basically he just sent me the list of songs and said, "We'll go over them at soundcheck."

    So, yikes! That was like the trial by fire for me, plus it was the first time I used rental equipment and didn't have my own synthesizers and stuff on hand. It was like "We'll rent you a couple of things," and you're lucky if it's actually what you requested. I did it for a number of years for quite a while. At that point, they actually had two different bands working. I was in the East Coast version of the band. For economy's sake, when they did the West Coast shows, they had a core group of musicians that they used out there. It saves on transportation and flights and things like that. One thing about Mark and Howard is that they are practical about stuff like that. They know the business because they've gotten the business as they explain on that video where they go through that list of managers and how each one had sued them and vice versa. The way that they've navigated their career I have always admired. Just going from The Turtles to The Mothers of Invention is pretty much of a sharp left-hand turn. Then, having their own radio show and being TV writers. I've got a lot of respect for the two of them.

MA: When you saw them way back when, did you know that they were the same guys from The Turtles, or did it dawn on you later?

GH: Yeah, I knew that from the first time I heard the *Fillmore* album from Frank Zappa from 1971, and at the end they did "their hit with a bullet," which was "Happy Together." Bless their hearts, but there's no mistake when you see them.

CR: Yeah, Mark isn't your typical rock star guy. What would fascinate me was the comedy aspect of the show. Was there anyone else in the East Coast touring Turtles band that you knew? Was it a regular ensemble?

GH: Yeah, the drummer was always Joe Stefko, who has played with them for a long time, forever, years before me. Before them, I think he was in Meat Loaf's band. Then there was Donnie Kisselbach on bass. He was always the bass player, too. He played with Rick Derringer, but also was with Mark and Howard for years. Maybe as long as Joe Stefko. For a long time anyway, years before I entered the picture.

MA: Did you play any of those Bottom Line shows that they did for New Year's?

GH: No. No. I was after that period. We did a lot of the package shows with other '60s acts like Mark Lindsay, sometimes with Paul Revere, sometimes with Peter Noone, and then they would also do their own shows in small theaters, like a 90-minute show and go through the whole history. Of course, they would do comedy bits in between and the hits. We would play a couple of Frank Zappa songs. We'd play snippets of "Peaches En Regalia." We'd play "Magic Fingers" (sings) "Open up your pocket book, get another quarter out…"

MA: Were you a big fan of Zappa's *200 Motels* and everything?

GH: Yeah. I was a fan of The Mothers of Invention, previously. He was a big influence on me. At that time, probably second to The Beatles. The whole orchestrated era of *Hot Rats, Burnt Weenie Sandwich, Uncle Meat, Lumpy Gravy…* Those albums in particular, were the classical music combined with little snippets of doo wop music and weird psychedelic jams and then bizarre music concrete, so to speak.

MA: Were you a fan of The Turtles back in the day?

GH: I liked them, but I grew to appreciate them more as time passed on, and then, once I really went back and studied their repertoire, when I knew I was going to be learning a lot of their songs, then I really grew to appreciate things like *The Battle of the Bands* album and the early stuff, too. They should be in the Rock and Roll Hall of Fame.

MA: We talk about that a lot.

CR: I always say the three, The Monkees, The Turtles and The Raiders. The Turtles and The Raiders, they played on all of their own material. They toured with their own groups. Who knows? Maybe, someday.

GH: I especially like Paul Revere and The Monkees. They were the first TV bands. The Monkees were put together for the show, but Paul Revere and The Raiders were so recognizable from the Dick Clark show.

CR: *Where The Action Is*.

GH: Yeah, *Where The Action Is*.

MA: When did you join up with The Turtles, was it in the 1990s?

GH: No, later than that, like 2004-2005.

MA: Okay. I have an end date. It says that you ended around 2010. Was that your choice or was that their choice? Or were The Cars coming back at that point?

GH: The Cars might have been coming back at that point to do the *Move Like This* record. That came out in 2011 and we were recording it in 2010, so that makes sense. Also, The Turtles started getting to the point where they only really did the Happy Together tour during the summer and I was never in the band for any of those Happy Together shows. I just did the shows when they had their own shows. One of the reasons why was if you were in the band, the Happy Together tours had a core band that basically backed up all the other acts. I was never asked to do one of those tours, but I'm not sure I would have done it.

MA: I interviewed Godfrey Townsend, and he was on the Happy Together tours and he didn't do the individual Flo & Eddie/Turtles concerts like you did, and he said that he would play in the core band and back all the bands that night.

GH: Yeah. I think he was the musical director of the band. That's one thing with The Turtles when I was working with them. I mentioned Joe Stefko and Donnie Kisselbach on bass. The guitar players; we had a couple different ones. They would mix and match. There was a guy named Tristan (Avakian), a Canadian guy, for a while and then Godfrey did a few of those. He did some fill-ins for some of the other guitar players and then later on, he was more or less the regular guitar player. That's when they pretty much exclusively did the Happy Together tours.

CR: Do you have a favorite Turtles song?

GH: I love "Happy Together." I love "Elenore," "She'd Rather Be With Me," "You Baby," "You Showed Me," they're great!

CR: Were there any of those songs that you dreaded playing?

GH: No, I always liked theirs. None that I dreaded. I can't think of any. They were fun shows to do. I told you before, for rehearsal, Mark always said that we'll have a sound check, so that's the rehearsal, but even at sound check, you'd make sure that all the instruments were working. Then, you'd go into a song and it would be (sings) "imagine me and you, I do, I think about you day and night…" and then Howard would go, "Okay, okay, we don't want to over-rehearse." He'll do like a couple lines of a song and then say, "Okay, that's it. You got it. We're not going to do the whole song." He'd even talk about how he didn't like to be over-rehearsed. He liked having a little bit of an edge to the show, where it's not where you would necessarily expect the same thing every night. I can appreciate that.

MA: Charles and I interviewed Andy Cahan, who played keyboards in the West Coast version and he was saying that he had to have a big repertoire in his mind in case they said, "Hey, let's talk about The Monkees," and suddenly they would go into "Daydream Believer." Or, they'd mention Bruce Springsteen and suddenly they would go into "Hungry Heart" or something. Did you have that ability to just change with the flow whenever they asked?

GH: Not to that degree.

MA: So, it was more straightforward on your shows. You just played the hits and maybe there would be some spoken comedy between the songs.

GH: Yeah. I'm trying to think of an example.

MA: Well, I know you said they did "Peaches En Regalia," and maybe some other Zappa ones. I know, back in the day they would do parodies of "Jumpin' Jack Flash" and "My Sweet Lord" and "Bang a Gong (Get it On)."

GH: Yeah, yeah. The one that we would do sometimes was "Nicki Hoi," the Hawaiian song. (sings) "You think we're diving for gold; we know we're diving for pearls. You think we're diving for pearls; we know we're diving for love…" During the course of that song, they'd go into an entire shtick or talk and they would parody little bits of Joni Mitchell and Bruce Springsteen.

MA: They had their own repertoire. I've heard that they did that way back even before Zappa days, where they would just segue into something arbitrarily. Even in the sixties The Turtles did that.

GH: Yeah. Another cross-pollination of my influence is that they did the backing vocals on the Psychedelic Furs album that has "Love My Way" on it, which Todd Rundgren produced.

MA: No backing vocals on any Cars albums?

GH: No.

CR: You didn't do any recordings with Flo & Eddie? There's no released stuff that you're on?

GH: No.

MA: It was all live stuff then, huh?

GH: Yeah.

Henry Diltz—April 18, 2022

MA: When did you first encounter The Turtles?

HD: I lived in Laurel Canyon, and in 1968, I moved into a house on Lookout Mountain Avenue. Mark Volman lived across the street and three houses down. Over the years we got to be good friends. My wife Elizabeth and I would go play board games with Mark and his wife. What was her name again?

CR: Mrs. Volman!

HD: Yeah, Mrs. Volman! Oh, it was Pat… Pat Volman! So we were friends. I'd go down there once in a while and he'd come up once in a while. We were both musicians. Musicians belong to a club, kind of. If you were a musician, you were automatically in the club and I got to be friends with all kinds of musicians. We got to be really really good friends, and then I know Chip Douglas started playing with them and producing them, so that was another connection, and then I finally went on the road with them. I'll have to look at the slides to see what year that was. I went on a weekend tour somewhere in Wisconsin and there's a picture of them standing next to a sign on a telephone pole and the sign says, "Vegetables." They had to put another piece of wood to finish putting the name down. You want me to tell you this story about me being on the road with them?

MA and CR: Yes!!

HD: Okay. It goes with that picture. We were in Wisconsin and we were in a rented station wagon or maybe two of them with all the equipment in the back. We were going to some school in Wisconsin. We were plenty early and we saw these signs that said "Cheese" with an arrow. As all musicians were and usually are, we were a little stoned. You know, when you're on the road, you smoke a little bit of God's herb because it can be deadly boring riding for hours in a freakin' van or a bus or whatever it is. So you have a little tiny toke of God's herb and it makes things kind of come alive and makes things a little more interesting. So we saw these signs that said "Cheese" and we all thought, "Oh shit, let's follow that! What does that mean?" We followed a couple of these Cheese signs with the arrows and we came to a place called the Bass Lake Cheese Factory. B-A-S-S Bass Lake Cheese Factory. So we went in and went on the tour and then they gave us cheese on a stick. We were back in the car driving and we drove a little ways and I saw that sign that said "Veg-e-ta-bles" and when I do my slide show, I tell the story that when I was in high school, I went with this girl whose father was a paratrooper who would say, "That's PPP," or poor prior planning, and I said, "Look at that sign. It took three pieces of wood to paint "Vegetables" and I said, "Well, that's PPP." I said, "I've got to stop and take a picture of that." So, I did and then they all got out of the car and posed with it. It looks like they're eating popsicles, but it's really pieces of cheese on a stick.

So, that was our fun adventure. For years after that, Mark and I would always get a catalog from the Bass Lake Cheese Factory delivered up to Laurel Canyon.

CR: So your first memories of The Turtles is not musical, it's not in the studio, it's vegetables and cheese.

HD: Yeah, that was our fun adventure we had. I think I met Mark more as a neighbor in Laurel Canyon where of course all musicians lived anyway in the '60s and '70s.

MA: Those photos date from 1969 because one of them was used for *Turtle Soup*. Didn't they use one of your photos or a similar one?

HD: *Turtle Soup*? Yeah, I did *Turtle Soup*! I did some for *Battle of the Bands*.

ayMA; Ok, so that's 1968 and *Turtle Soup*, that's 1969. I just wanted to get your memory of what year it was since you said earlier that it was in the 1970s.

HD: Okay, I was just guesstimating! You say 1969, then so be it. Yeah!

MA: When you hung out with them, did you talk about anything in particular or was it just going from one location to another? Were you their official photographer? What was your role with them?

HD: No, I wasn't their official photographer with them. I photographed all the bands, really. I can check in my journal. I kept a journal. I didn't give a whole lot of details especially when I was out on the road with a group. I would just say the date and "On the road with The Turtles." I can look and see if there are any other little interesting tidbits. I'm not sure how I happened to be on the road with them in Wisconsin. Somebody asked me to. I guess the record company.

MA: Were you between gigs yourself?

HD: No, no. My gigs were usually one day. I would mostly shoot pictures in L.A. One afternoon with CSNY. One afternoon with Steppenwolf. You just never knew. The phone would ring and I would be ready to shoot anything. And I had a partner named Gary Burden. Gary Burden was a graphic artist and we ended up doing about 100 album covers together. At one point, I know The Turtles asked us to do their *Turtle Soup* album cover and Gary lived out there in Malibu. He thought the ocean would be great at Leo Carrillo Beach. We spent an afternoon out there taking pictures. I don't remember a whole lot of details, and certainly not conversations. Driving around with them in Wisconsin, oh yeah, spirited conversations. Mark and Howard were funny as hell. I probably wrote down some of the stuff they said. It was my habit to write down interesting phrases, probably from smoking a little bit of pot. It kind of tunes your ears. Sort of found poetry. Somebody would say a line that was so funny and you knew you were going to forget it, so you wrote it down. I did that. That'll probably take me years to uncover all that stuff.

CR: Henry, what were your impressions of the guys as individuals? What comes to mind when you think of Howard or Mark or Al or any of the guys?

HD: Mainly, the two guys on stage were funny as hell and so talented. Howard with the voice and Mark with the tambourine twirling it around and they were so fun and so fun-loving. Chip did an interview with Coast to Coast AM and he talked all about The Turtles and The Monkees. Mostly the Turtles and he said, "Yeah, they were the most fun-loving group of all." He said he just loved touring with them because they were just so much fun. That was their main thing to have fun. I do remember that about them, they were just really fun-loving, particularly Mark and Howard. The other guys were just great musicians and a little quieter, maybe, than the two lead guys. Most of my conversations were with Mark and Howard.

MA: Did you continue the friendship when they became Flo & Eddie with Zappa and everything?

HD: Oh yeah, definitely, and I took photos with them with Zappa, when they were Flo & Eddie. I took photos of a rehearsal one day. There were photos of a group shot of all of them together with Zappa sitting up front and them sitting with their heads sitting all around him. That would be a good group shot of Zappa and Flo & Eddie and the others. I saw occasional concerts, but mostly it was my personal friendship with Mark. I wasn't really close to those guys. I saw them play more than a half a dozen times. I saw them at the Hollywood Bowl. I was certainly on the road with them to various colleges and high schools. I was never there when they recorded.

CR: That was going to be my question. Were you ever at any recording sessions?

HD: I was at many, many recording sessions, but really, the late '60s and early '70s, I was really busy. I was always shooting something or somebody. It's not like I had a whole lot of time to hang out. They were the hang-out days. It was just hanging out, but taking pictures at the same time. With Chip, my buddy in the MFQ, I went to lots of Monkees recordings, and even played the tambourine and sang background and different things like that, but not with The Turtles for some reason, when Chip was producing them. I sure did love "Elenore" and of course, "Happy Together" was great. I know Chip had a lot to do with arranging that, and then "Elenore," I just thought, was a great song. I know you've got that story. They needed a follow up to "Happy Together," so they wrote "Elenore" kind of tongue-in-cheek, right? Let's write something that sounds like a hit. (sings) "My pride and joy, etc." That was so funny. They were really a great band just busting out of the gate. They were just full of pep, vim and vigor, lots of energy on stage and a lot of fun to watch. They were very involving.

MA: Did you take those photos that they used on *Battle of the Bands*?

HD: *Battle of the Bands*, I took pictures of them as Chief Kamanawanalea, the Hawaiian band.

MA: You also took those shots, the ones in the centerfold that have them as different groups?

HD: Right! Right! Not all of them. The ones with their shirts off. They were Chief Kamanawanalea, and then there was another one. I think I took pictures of them at the beach as surfers for that album. I have to look at it again to see if I took any others. I think those were the two.

MA: They did this one where they're wearing these giant fig leaves. Did you take that one?

HD: Giant fig leaves, wasn't that "Kamanawanalea?"

MA: No, that was "You Showed Me."

HD: You mean this is another shot on the inside of that cover?

MA: Yeah.

HD: I'm not sure. I'd have to look.

MA: The surfer one was for a song called "Surfer Dan," so yeah, they're all representing a song.

HD: I'm in Laguna right now, not up in my L.A. studio where I would have that album to look at. I've got to look at them to see if I did any others. I do remember taking more pictures of them out on that same tour in Wisconsin. Pictures of them out in a cornfield and then pictures of them kind of laying in the bushes. There were autumn leaves kind of around them. We were out in the countryside and we just pulled over a couple of times and just took pictures of them wherever they were in 1969.

MA: Rhino used a lot of those later on for various greatest hits compilations. That's where I've seen them.

HD: That's true. They did. Even though the only album cover I did as an album cover was *Turtle Soup*, which was them with the big waves crashing behind them. Some of them, like you say, got used later for reissues and compilations and stuff.

MA: How did that work? Did Rhino just call you up and say, "Hey, we know you have Turtles photos. We need one for a new greatest hits collection"?

HD: Yup. Usually, the art director calls and says, "Have you got anything?" Yeah.

CR: Did you decide shots or what it was going to be? Or, did Mark or someone say, "Hey, let's pull over and take a picture here?" Or, was it a combination of everything?

HD: It was usually just kind of a bubbly moment where we would say, "Hey, let's stop near that cornfield!" I don't know who would say that and then we would jump out. None of it was ever planned. We did plan the *Turtle Soup* thing at the beach, but we didn't plan what it would look like. We just said, "Let's go to the beach and we'll find a good place." Then, when we were traveling around, it was all spur of the moment. "Oh wow, look at that great sign! Let's jump out!" It was just spontaneous.

MA: I know you've probably taken thousands and thousands of pictures. Do you know how many you might have taken of The Turtles?

HD: Oh God, no. A thousand? I don't know. Probably. I have boxes of slides. They hold about 400 slides a box. There's got to be a couple for The Turtles and then there's all kinds of proof sheets. There's 36 on the proof sheet. There's got to be somewhere around a thousand… 1500… Quite a few, I think. I know there's a great shot of Mark and Howard sitting in Mark's garage that we took for The Phlorescent Leech and Eddie. Was there ever a *Phlorescent Leech and Eddie* album?

MA: It was their first one and yes, they're sitting in the garage. I think they're both drinking beer. That was the back cover photo.

HD: Yeah, I took that. I went down to Mark's house, down the street from me.

MA: Did you take the front cover photo? The front cover is just them standing next to each other, not smiling.

HD: I think I did. Yeah, yeah, yeah. I think they had cowboy shirts on. Mark was wearing a yellow shirt or something. Yeah, I did that album.

Jimmy Hunter—April 25, 2022

MA: Today we have Flo & Eddie of The Turtles' drummer Jimmy Hunter. How did you meet Flo & Eddie?

JH: We had these two great roadies and they became Flo & Eddie's roadies—Chuck Churella and Bub Brown. Do you have those in your archives?

MA: Those names sound familiar. Yes.

JH: They were awesome. They weren't their roadies. They were our roadies. They weren't Flo & Eddie's roadies. We had them and when we were looking for a new gig, they found a gig before we did and sure enough, Chuck called us up and said, "Hey, Flo & Eddie's doing the '77 tour and we've got to leave in two days. Can you get down here and try out real quick? You really don't have to try out. Just come on out and start practicing with these guys." So, I went down and learned the whole Flo & Eddie show in two days. Mick Manspare was on guitar. Bob Bolan was on keyboards. The famous Turtle of all time, Andy Cahan, was on keys as well. Erik Scott, who passed away last year or the year before, was a great bass player. That was pretty much the band. Mark Volman did a little guitar and we did "The Mud Shark" for a few months.
    I can remember fondly playing The Bottom Line with them. Morristown, New Jersey, was a fond memory because I had some girlfriends in that town and those guys were very impressed that I knew girls that I could bring to the gig and they were just very impressed with that. They were impressed with my girls.

MA: I know later on Flo & Eddie had a West Coast band and an East Coast band. Did you play in both versions of the band if you're talking about East Coast gigs?

JH; I'm the West Coast guy and I only did one recording with them. It's on an album. It's on *The History of Flo & Eddie and The Turtles* record. Do you have that record? It's on the Rhino label. It's a compilation of some sort of outtakes like The Beatles do those outtakes records. We went into the studio and recorded "Louie Louie." I tried my best to give it The Kingsman spirit with all the cliches I could pull out and did a nice version of "Louie Louie" and that's on that album. I'm so proud to be on a recording with them. A little bit of rock and roll history, "Louie Louie."

MA: So how many years did you spend with them then?

JH: The 1977 Tour. Well, first of all, I love one of the original drummers, Ainsley Dunbar. My number one white boy drummer. I loved him a lot. I like my funky stuff, too, but I really love Ainsley. I loved his foot. I copied it. The other drummer that I copied as much or more than Ainsley would be the drummer from White Trash. Bobby Ramirez passed away. He got killed in a Chicago bar brawl.

MA: I didn't know that.

JH: You know about that drummer? It was a really sad day for me. So, those two guys were my main man for kick-ass drumming. They had great feet, fancy stuff between their hands and feet and I copied as much of that stuff as I possibly could and used it to my advantage and then personalized it and put my own thing on it. I got a style from just copying the guys that I thought were just off the chain. Between those two and whatever was coming up underneath my own childhood pain and misery, it became what was propelling me. So, Ainsley had the gig way before me and then a guy named Johnny Brado (John Barbata). Had we discussed him before?

MA: When we talked briefly on the phone, yes.

JH: I was in Detroit at the time. I think I was washing my car and I was listening to the radio and Flo & Eddie were doing a radio interview out in California, and they're talking about Johnny Brado. I looked up Johnny Brado because really, I coveted his gig. I'll be damned that I didn't get it when Chuck and Bub took over the roadie gig. Now before me was Craig Krampf, a great blond-headed drummer that moved to Nashville. He didn't have anything to do with me getting this gig, but he had to do with me getting more gigs after he found out that I was the guy who replaced him in Flo & Eddie. So what happened was Chuck and Bub got me in. I did the '77 tour and that kind of petered out for Mark and Howard. By the end of the summer, they weren't working so I didn't have any job and then I went with Nick Gilder. Craig went with Nick Gilder and then when [he] left, he got me that job. Probably Cher and Flo & Eddie are the two top people that I ever rehearsed with. They made everything feel like fun. They made their errors feel like fun. It was great and like a party and everybody tried hard because they treated you so nice. I want to say that about Mark and Howard while we're primarily discussing them. I worked with Ray Manzarek and that lasted for two to three years before I joined the Flo & Eddie band.

MA: I'm going to ask you a couple more questions about Flo & Eddie. When you did that one tour in '77, did you tour all over the place or were you stuck in a certain spot like Vegas?

JH: We flew out there and then we took the bus to different places. The gigs I do remember really well were the really successful night at The Bottom Line and there was My Father's Place on Long Island, which was a big concert bar. Billy Joel's played there and everything. Everybody's played there, and then down to Morristown. I remember those three gigs. I remember on the West Coast,

The Golden Bear was a fantastic gig. We did a thing at the Shrine Auditorium with John Sebastian and Tiny Tim! I think that was right before those guys started doing those oldies shows. That gig right there spawned that tendency of them getting together with The Lovin' Spoonful and that kind of thing. That was the gig that did that and I left the band shortly after that.

MA: Now, when you were performing, were you doing mainly Turtles songs or mainly Flo & Eddie or a little of everything?

JH: They did some of the Zappa stuff and all the hits: "Elenore," "Happy Together." You could probably rattle the titles off and we probably did them. I tried to be true to the record but still tried to bring in my own style and enthusiasm to it and they appreciated it. I remember them introducing me at The Golden Bear. I took my 10-speed down in my pick-up truck because I wanted to ride down on that beach on the 10-speed and they said, "And now our drummer, the Metamucil King!" That was their nickname for me that week. I love those guys. I loved them before I knew them and I loved them after I met them. My dad loved them. My dad talked about them before he died, a lot. That was part of his California experience when he came out to visit me. Those are some golden years. Golden days and diamond nights.

MA: Did you do the typical comedy shtick between songs?

JH: Yep, yep, and I'm a good show drummer and so I threw in all the razzamatazz and the sound effects and all that. It's like circus drumming, man.

MA: They'd always jump around and say something like, "What do you think this is, a Bruce Springsteen concert?" And then they'd jump into it.

JH: Yep. They did "Turn the Page" by Bob Segar, too.

MA: Were you able to just shift on a dime like that?

JH: Oh yeah, it's easy, man!

MA: I always ask, because when we interviewed Andy Cahan, he said, "Yeah, we had to be ready. If they introduced me as The Monkees, I would have to do a little 'Daydream Believer.'"

JH: He was awesome at that stuff! He's really good. You just go with the flow and I think they respected me knowing that I was a quick study and I'm a heads-up kind of guy. My cymbals, I used to set them up here and hang them from the top so I could see everything going around. There weren't any music stands getting in my way. I could see a complete circumference. It was really the way I liked it. It was heads up, a lot of eye contact and a lot of good interplay and plenty of feeling and mojo, you know. I hit 'em hard and if we didn't get a good sound check, we're still going to sound good because I'm going to hit 'em hard and it's going to be tight..

MA: You mentioned this, but it kind of just ended, right?

JH: Yeah, there didn't seem to be much happening after that Tiny Tim gig. It just kinda sort of dissolved and by the time and then they got that East Coast/West Coast thing going on. I think Howard already stopped wanting to be on the bus and if they had a chance to have a band over here, they could bus them down on this side and we could fly and bus the band. It worked out better and a lot of artists do that.

. . . .

MA: Right, and then they started the Happy Together tours which were all totally packaged with a central band that played for everybody.

JH: Yeah. I think they were starting to sniff that coming with John Sebastian and Tiny Tim being there at that gig at the Shrine Auditorium. That was a good gig.

MA: Apart from working with them, have you stayed friends over the years?

JH: I talked to Howard on the phone, but before that I saw Mark because he has a daughter that sings and he knew that I had a little studio, so he brought his daughter over to sing at my studio. We did a few recordings. I don't know if they were karaokes or what, but I have them here somewhere. It was probably in the 1990s. A couple years ago I talked to Howard and mostly I was calling and I sought him out because I was concerned about his health and I wanted to talk to him. I got a hold of him and he was kind of complaining about it now, so what I'm hearing from you makes me feel uplifted.
[Editors' Note: We explained what Howard said about touring from [a] previous interview in this book]

JH: It's a difficult situation because they may not be getting the gigs where they get flown and get in first class. Any kind of budget situation has got to be fatiguing on an old fart like me. I was thinking while you were talking to me, Ray Manzarek and The Turtles had the same accountant. You spawned a memory. Bernstein-Fox in Century City on Avenue of the Stars. I used to pick up my little puny paycheck from Ray every week when I first got here, and then I got to go pick up for Flo & Eddie from the same place and the secretary—her name was Maggie—became my girlfriend. It didn't last that long. It wasn't long before I figured out HOWARD'S GOING WITH MAGGIE NOW!! We have an old girlfriend in common.

MA: We interviewed Greg Hawkes of The Cars who was also in Flo & Eddie's band for a time and he saw Flo & Eddie the first time going to a Zappa concert, so did you see Flo & Eddie pre-playing with them?

JH: I saw them with Zappa at Cobo Hall. I also toured with Greg when I was with Nick Gilder. We were one of the warm-up bands on the *Candy-O* tour. I know all those guys!

MA: It's all intertwined! Another intertwining, I don't know if you've ever seen The Turtles' documentary in the 1990s. They actually interviewed Ray Manzarek and he said, "The Turtles came out with matching suits, and us (the future Doors) as Rick and the Ravens, we came out with matching suits, too!" They all got their start in these small L.A. clubs.

JH: Sunset Blvd. was flourishing during the Summer of Love!

MA: So they all knew each other, just like you seem to know everyone.

JH: Behind me is the actual bass drum head that was used on tour with Flo & Eddie and you said that you know the artist.

MA: I know the artist because it's listed on their *Moving Targets* album. That image is printed on the inner sleeve of the LP. I'm pretty sure they gave him artist credit, but I can't remember who it is off the top of my head.
[Editors' Note: Mick Haggerty.]

JH: It was a great experience working with Mark and Howard.

Steve Boone—June 22, 2022

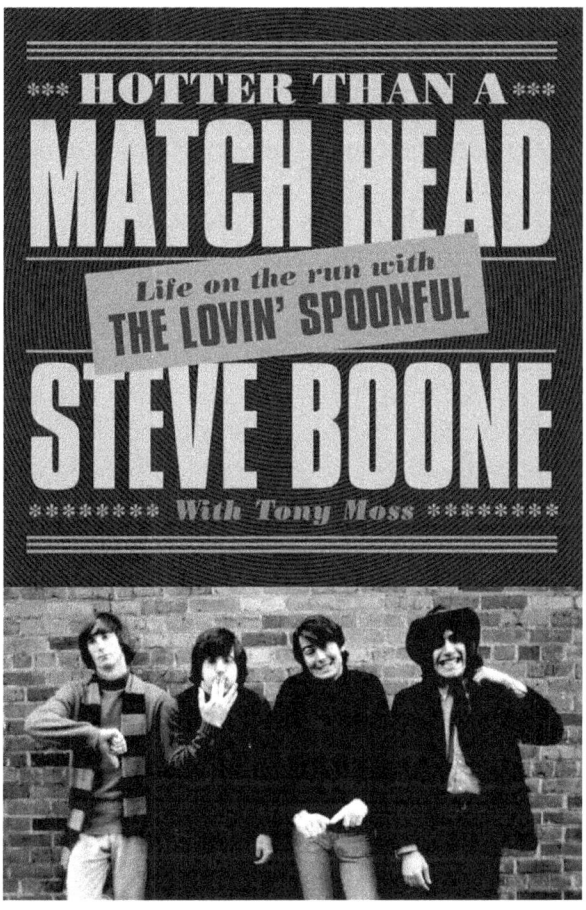

MA: We're writing a book about The Turtles and my co-author Charles Rosenay!!! said you had some interesting anecdotes about working with The Turtles.

SB: I wouldn't say they were anecdotes as much as we enjoyed their music and their style was very similar to The Lovin' Spoonful style. Their producer became the producer on our last album. The album we did was called *Everything Playing*. Joe Wissert was the producer. He made his money on producing hits for what they call the "Philadelphia Sound" in the early 1960s. When Eric Jacobsen got fired for producing The Lovin' Spoonful because he wiped out a vocal track that was one of John Sebastian's favorite vocal tracks, he got a ticket to go home. Then, Joe Wissert came in and he had a tremendous recommendation. He was one of those producers that really had the magic touch. We fit in really well with him and he was really able to handle us during the dawn of the recording era because we were the first rock band to record on a 16-track tape recorder. Joe Wissert was able to master it with Jerry Yester's help because it was technically too hard for people to grasp that 16 tracks [thing]. Eight tracks seemed to be it. We were very lucky that Joe Wissert was able to navigate that type of technology and make the 16 tracks available to us on that album.

 Wissart had some great hits on his own, The Turtles being one of them. You can see where Joe Wissert fits into the whole scene of pop music of late 1968. That's where he came to life for The Lovin' Spoonful. The Turtles took off just before that. We were not only very friendly with them, but we were similar stylewise from our music. It was sort of a kind of relationship that was good because it was something that we all felt comfortable with while listening to them. The Turtles turned out to be really a hot record-producing act that had that knack for producing hit records. As a result, they really did fabulously when it came to the Top 10.

MA: Back in the day, did you ever tour with The Turtles?

SB: I think we did a couple of stand-alones, but it wasn't a tour. The only tours we ever did that was with other groups was The Beach Boys and The Association. It was the dawning of the era of groups touring under a producer. It worked out very well for us.

MA: Did you ever sit in on any Turtles sessions or play on any of their records?

SB: No. That was not something we did. The only person we ever sat in on a recording was Bob Dylan's *Bringing it All Back Home* album. I played bass on four of the cuts on that album. I'm very proud of that. There was some controversy as to whether I actually played, but they found some old pay stubs, so that settled that.

MA: Did you hang out with Howard and Mark and the others, back in the day?

SB: Hanging out was something you did with your girlfriend. By the time we got started doing tour dates, we barely had time to brush our teeth, go to bed and get up and do the next one. It never let up from March 1, 1965 to a year later when we had our first hit. We were doing non-stop rehearsals, gigs, new songs, new instruments being played... It was very obvious that we had hooked on to a new style of music and it was sort of our style and the public liked it. It was very obvious from the beginning, that this band [The Lovin' Spoonful] was going to do well.

    In the early days, it was kind of like a club. It was a group of guys that all became successful and they went around the circuit playing in these nightclubs out in Los Angeles and San Francisco. The Grateful Dead saw us perform a gig at the Cow Palace. I think The Turtles might have been there for that gig, too. That was when The Grateful Dead decided to become a folk band.

[Editors' Note: According to Concerts Wiki, The Lovin' Spoonful played with The Turtles on three occasions: August 7, 1965, at the Rose Bowl in Pasadena, California; May 6, 1967, at Upbeat WEWS-TV Show in Cleveland, Ohio; and June 17, 1967, at Municipal Auditorium in Birmingham, Alabama. The Turtles played at the Cow Palace on April 4-5, 1966, not with The Lovin' Spoonful. The Lovin' Spoonful played the Cow Palace with The Beach Boys on June 24, 1966.]

MA: Now you may or may not know this, but Jerry Yester went on to produce The Turtles' final album which was never released. It was going to be called *Shell Shock*.

SB: Just to put another wrench in the story, Jerry Yester is my father-in-law, so we're very close.

Mitch Weissman—January 11, 2023

MA: When did you meet up with The Turtles?

MW: We had met up a bunch of times in New York and I had friends who played with them in the band, like Chris Apostle on keyboards. I knew everybody in the band, so I'd see them if we ran into each other at clubs and stuff. I actually went to see them at the Bottom Line once in the late '80s or something like that. I saw them perform a few times. The next time I saw them before I did the tour in 2012, they were doing Hippiefest with Mountain. They were The Turtles, but they also MC'd everything. All of the acts. The same thing that they did on the Happy Together Tour. They were funny and it was the first time I ever thought about taking drugs, but now we take Lipitor and other stuff instead of every drug then, and now it's this. They were very cordial. I saw them at the Gibson Amphitheater. We've always had a love of each other whenever we would all get together at airports or something.

    The Happy Together Tour was how I got to work with them finally. Godfrey Townsend was the musical director and my friend. He credits me with giving him his start to go to the big leagues. He had gotten out of New York and came with me to Laughlin, Nevada in 1995 to do a sit-down show that had stars coming in and out. Everyone from Tiny Tim, Dennis Yost, Pat Upton (sings "I love you more today than yesterday"). All of these different artists came through. Mitch Ryder, who did his song so fast, I don't know how anybody else could ever sing them, but we had to. Joey Molland from Badfinger. It was a revolving cavalcade and then we got the call from the Entwistle camp to do that band that he left, so he and I saw them, I think, at Atlantic City, before that. They were doing a David Fishof show where they had The Turtles. They had The Byrds—one of the versions of The Byrds with some of the real guys in it. I don't know who else. Fishof said to me, "I can't use you. You're not a real guy."

MA: You're not a real guy!

MW: Yeah, I didn't take it as an insult. I knew what it was. I knew him from back when I had made a name for myself. In 2012. Godfrey called me and said a tour is going on. He said, "You're a great bass player and you could probably do this. You have to play bass for Micky Dolenz, you have to play bass for Gary Puckett, you have to play bass for The Turtles..." I'm missing one. They had The Grass Roots, but Mark Dawson was that guy. The other act was The Buckinghams. So I did that one tour. There was some production stuff that was a pain and they didn't ask me back. I was fine on stage and when they introduced the band, Mark and Howard had the greatest intro for me. I would play a little bit of "Day Tripper" or something like that. I think he called me the "Portly Paul." Something like that. It was pretty funny. They were great. They were very fantastic and always very supportive and down-to-earth. Human. I'm glad I did that tour with Howard, because obviously he's not touring now and you've got Ron Dante. Every once in a while, I send Howard a message and he messages me back. This interview will probably prompt me to do it, so it's fun!

MA: It was just one year, basically?

MW: For me, it was one year. We still talked after that and kept in touch, but for whatever reason, I didn't do the subsequent ones. I almost didn't do that one, but John Montagna, who was usually the bass player on these configurations and played with Godfrey on The Alan Parsons Project and all this other stuff, was selling his house or something that summer, so he had to be home for the whole thing. He and I were friends, so I think he recommended me as well and Godfrey said "no brainer" and it worked out fine. I think he came back after that.

MA: What were the performances like? The big hits with some comedy shtick in between?

MW: Yeah, always the shtick between songs and it was the hits. I remember they did "Peaches En Regalia" as a big instrumental piece leading into "Happy Together," I think it was. I wished they had done "Elenore," but they didn't do "Elenore" at that time.

MA: Really?

MW: But it was the hits. I can't remember the list now.

MA: "She'd Rather Be With Me"?

MW: Yeah, "She'd Rather Be With Me," "You Showed Me." What am I forgetting?

MA: "It Ain't Me Babe"?

MW: Actually no. They did "You Baby," but I don't think we did "It Ain't Me Babe." They had enough hits.

MA: That's true. They have about 10-15 hits depending on what you count. I guess over time since they have toured forever, they get tired of certain ones and drop them out of the set list for a time.

MW: Yeah. Exactly.

MA: But you always have to have "Happy Together."

MW: Always have to have it. Exactly.

MA: Did you sing as well or play any other instruments?

MW: I only played bass on this tour. Godfrey played guitar. You had Manny Focarazzo on the keyboards. He was great. Steve Murphy on drums. We basically could play anything. Wayne Avers came in to play guitar. We had him and Godfrey on guitar for The Monkees stuff—Micky's stuff. Gary Puckett—there was just the four piece band backing him up. Manny's an amazing keyboard guy who could play multiple keyboards and all the orchestral parts and stuff like that. Steve's vocal prowess was amazing. He could sing almost anything, all the harmonies. We had everything covered for all this sort of stuff. It was great. It was a pretty easy gig now that I think about it. I only played with three of the five acts and got paid the same amount of money, so how bad was that?

Jim Pons interview with Joel Miller on *Party Like a Rockstar Podcast*— August 26, 2022 (Used with permission from Joel Miller)

JM: *The Ed Sullivan Show* with The Turtles. What was that day like?

JP: The day—it was a long day, actually. We started rehearsing in the morning with the stage crew and the sound technicians. We did it to a pre-recorded music track and Mark and Howard sang the lead live. It was all very exciting. We didn't see Ed until the minute before the show went on the air live. I remember, it was remarkable. He had red hair. I had never seen him on a color television. It was a thrill. One of the great moments of my musical career—"The Ed Sullivan Show."

JM: So, how did you get into The Turtles? The bass player left, right, and then you jumped in, immediately?
JP: Yeah, he quit to produce The Monkees. He became the record producer for The Monkees. I had known Mark and Howard and we played together up and down the Sunset Strip. They sent John Barbata, the drummer, to my house and he told me they needed a bass player and they wanted it to be me, so they knew I was able to. I didn't have to audition. I just had to start rehearsing with them.
    It was a time when The Leaves were starting to fail. We were just college kids acting like rock guys and we just didn't have what it takes to last, so I was ready to do something else and it happened at a good time.

JM: What drove you to play the bass?

JP: The Beatles! When I saw them on *The Ed Sullivan Show* that day, I thought. I was in college. I didn't know what I wanted to be. It's where you go after you get out of high school.

JM: What were you studying in college?

JP: Art, but I wasn't an art major. I was only two years in, so I wasn't serious about anything. I was in a fraternity and I was just having a good time. Then The Beatles came out and I realized what it is I wanted to do with my life. I said, "I want to be an entertainer and I want to be in a rock and roll band." I wanted to be Paul McCartney and I started a band in my fraternity, and none of us knew music.

JM: How did The Mothers of Invention start with you? What was the process of you joining that band?

JP: That's the same thing. I knew Frank. He and I had dinner occasionally. He played on Sunset Strip in those days and we got to be friends and then when The Turtles died and Flo & Eddie wasn't formed yet, I got the word that Mark and Howard were playing in the new Mothers of Invention creation by Frank Zappa. I thought that was a pretty remarkable combination of things. Then one day Mark called me and said Frank's bass player quit and he needed a bass player. So, it was the same kind of thing and he wanted me to be the guy. That's what it was. That's all it took.

JM: So, you were at the Montreux show with the flare?

JP: They said it was a flare gun. I'm not sure it was. It was like a sparkler to me, but there was a fire up in the balcony, yeah. A small fire. Then it fell down to the floor and the crowd went crazy and stormed the stage and we had to run. It was an old wooden-built theater, so it caught fire very quickly.

JM: And you guys just sat outside and watched it burn?

JP: We didn't get outside at first. We thought we were going to be trapped downstairs in the kitchen and our bus driver broke a glass wall with his arm. We crawled through the hole in the glass and then we got outside to the loading dock and stood there with the Swiss fire department and watched it burn down to the ground.

JM: So, you lost all your instruments, back line, everything?

JP: Yes, instruments, lights, amps, sound equipment, all of Frank's guitars, everything. Everything, but a cowbell. We found a cowbell the next day. A burned-up cowbell.

JM: And then, what about the show when he was pushed off the stage?

JP: That was the next show we did. We had to have two weeks to rent new equipment and rehearse with it, so the very first show we played was back in London. I forgot the place and it was in the middle of our encore, just like the fire. Somebody pushed past me on the stage and ran over to Frank and pushed him into the orchestra pit.

JM: You felt the guy come by you?

JP: Yeah. He bumped me as he ran by me. I turned around to look where he came from and the next thing I knew everybody was standing by the edge of the stage looking down into the orchestra pit. That's where Frank had landed. It turns out the guy thought his girlfriend was having a relationship with Frank and he was mad about that and he came on stage. That was the end of our career with Frank Zappa. We were told that he wasn't going to be able to play again and we went back home and we never saw him again. Well, I did see him in the hospital before we left London and that was it.

JM: Heavy. After that, did you quickly jump into the football stuff?

JP: No. Mark and Howard had an offer to go on the road with Alice Cooper. We still had Frank's band. We couldn't be The Turtles because White Whale Records owned the name and we were in a lawsuit with them, so they took the name from our two road managers whom we called The Fluorescent Leech and Eddie. We went back on the road with the Zappa band and toured with Alice Cooper. That was the beginning of Flo & Eddie.

JM: No way! I didn't know that part.

JP: Yeah. That was the *Billion Dollar Babies* Tour in 1973.

JM: Do you have any stand-out performances that you can remember at odd places or special evenings?

JP: A couple, I think. The White House was one of them.

JM: I was going to bring that one up.

JP: That one was with The Turtles. We were Tricia Nixon's, the daughter of Richard Nixon, The Turtles were her favorite band, so she invited us to play at her Sweet 16 birthday party, and what made that fun was that the Secret Service guys took all of our equipment apart on the East Wing steps and they heard a ticking sound. First of all, they were already suspicious of us. Long-haired hippies from Hollywood, California, during the war years. We had a new drummer [John Seiter] and he needed a metronome to tell him the pace and the sounds. It had turned on during the flight and they broke it apart and they thought it might have been a bomb or something. So, they returned the broken metronome and they gave him a check for 75 bucks, I think. He still has the White House check.

JM: That's a good one.

JP: We played with The Temptations and the United States Marine Corps Band.

JM: That's incredible!

JP: She loved us and sent us a nice letter afterwards. So, that was remarkable! I played on the roof of a gas station in Anchorage, Alaska, with Procol Harum. They were awesome. It snowed the night before and we were all on this roof and it was not very substantial and I almost fell in. One of my feet went through the roof of the building and it had to be pulled out. That was something I remember.

JM: Is this why you went into football?

JP: Football was worse!

JM: Why did you leave music, though?

JP: I got tired of it. We weren't having any hit records anymore and it became a job and not any fun.

JM: But you were a football fan, too?

JP: Yeah, I was a football fan. I took the job because—I write about it in the book—I met someone that I wanted to spend time with in New York, and I moved there. Just as I moved there, my friend, who was in The Leaves with me when we started, offered me a job as an office boy for the New York Jets football club, which he had taken for the summer and now he's leaving and he wanted me to fill in for him.

JM: You were living in L.A. at the time, right?

JP: Right, but I got to New York and I said I'd do the job for a month and it turned out to be 27 years. It turned into assistant equipment manager and then film coordinator and cameraman. It's a long story, but it's detailed in the book.

JM: When did you feel famous? In other words, when would be a moment in your career that switched things up or pushed your career into the next level? What do you believe would be that moment?

JP: I guess it would be when we [The Leaves] got our first gig in Hollywood at Ciro's nightclub. That's where all the new breed of hippies were hanging out everywhere every night. We were just San Fernando Valley kids trying to act like musicians. We actually auditioned for the job at Ciro's when The Byrds went on the road and we got the gig. We really were playing for those people that we were enamored with on Sunset Blvd. That's when I realized this is taking off. This is more than just a fraternity combo. This was more than just a hobby. This could be big. Then, Pat Boone signed us to a record contract. So, I guess it was then at the beginning for me.

JM: If you had one more tour, which band would you pick? Who would you choose to work with? You could do a lineup of any of the groups you played with. Who would be in the lineup?

JP: I enjoyed touring with Alice. I liked him a lot. We had a lot of fun. We did 90 one-nighters in 102 days. We played poker on the airplane. The back of the airplane was turned into a casino. We played there every time we were in the air. I lost a lot of money.

THE TURTLES' DOUBLE YUMMY BLOW YOUR MIND: STRAWBERRY SHORTCAKE RECIPE REVEALED
Interview with Mark Volman
by Kelly Kuvo from *SCRAM* magazine
(Used with permission from Kim Cooper and Kelly Kuvo Richardson)

Many moons ago I found the courage to go public with my Strawberry Shortcake & Friends record collection and knick-knack fetish. Once I was out, flocks of secret Strawberry fans came out of their own closets to share rare specks of information about the series. I was thrilled to learn that Flo & Eddie (AKA Mark Volman and Howard Kaylan, late of the Turtles) were responsible for my favorite Strawberry Shortcake albums.

It was an honor to get the chance to speak with Mark Volman about his experiences producing the Strawberry Shortcake & Friends records between 1980-83, and how he and Howard got involved in writing music for children.

SCRAM: Hello Mr. Volman. Thanks for talking with me! Just a few questions for you, if you don't mind? Who started Kid Stuff Records? How did you and Howard get involved with them to make music for Strawberry Shortcake & Friends records? And where are the Kid Stuff record people now?

MV: The animators for the Frank Zappa film *200 Motels* that we were involved with were doing the animation for the television shows *The World of Strawberry Shortcake* and *Strawberry Shortcake in Big Apple City*. They asked us to audition for the job of creating the soundtrack music via the company creating the Strawberry Shortcake cartoons, which was American Greetings. A production company out of Florida called Those Characters From Cleveland was producing records on the Kid Stuff Records label at the time. We pitched our ideas and they bought them. We have no idea what is up with the label now. You know, you should make a good CD copy of all of those Strawberry Shortcake vinyl records you have, because who knows where the master tapes are?! We don't own any of that stuff.

SCRAM: Your Strawberry Shortcake records are far superior to the other Strawberry Shortcake record productions. I want to know... why?

MV: Howard and I took on the Strawberry Shortcake & Friends job because our career has never been about inroads or about just one project, but about a series of various accomplishments. We wanted to go deeper than with just "Happy Together," and that's why we used our real names on the credits of each Strawberry Shortcake record we made. Back then, children's records weren't really a respected medium and companies weren't used to paying people for producing something slick for kids. We wanted to do something different with children's records and provide positive messages. At the same time, we didn't try to save money on our TV show soundtrack recordings. We brought in the original voice of Strawberry Shortcake from the TV show and tried to keep all the other actors, and we charged Kid Stuff a lot of money to do that. Strawberry Shortcake was so popular in 1980-81 that a huge balloon of her led the Macy's Thanksgiving Day Parade, and they used our song on the float, the Strawberry Shortcake theme song from the TV show that goes "Who sleeps all night in a cake made of strawberry?" all the way down 5th Avenue! Making those records wasn't easy; it was a challenge. We were confined by what the TV shows had to give us. However, it opened up other opportunities. We sold five or six million copies of those Strawberry Shortcake records, and at a time when children's music wasn't fashionable! We wanted to try to make songs that kids would recognize, rhythms that would be familiar to kids even listening to them for the first time. We wanted to make songs that also just plain stood alone as good songs, regardless of if they were for kids or not—songs that a Turtles fan would love, yet always dealing with the age group we were creating for. Oh, and everyone has got to understand that nothing would have gotten accomplished on those Strawberry Shortcake records without John Hoier. He was our partner that owned Sun Swept Studios in Studio City, CA. That was the studio where we made all of our Strawberry Shortcake records. Everything was written, played, and sung by John, Howard and myself on those records.

SCRAM: I'm interested in your involvement with the cartoon TV show *Strawberry Shortcake in Big Apple City*. Did you guys write the soundtrack and the script for that?

MV: We had nothing to do with the scripts. They were all pre-written and we wrote songs to accompany the story. Howard acted as the voice of the Purple Pie Man on the records, but not on the TV show. We all acted as the Care Bears characters on the Care Bears records we produced, too.

SCRAM: Do you remember a particularly favorite song from any of the Strawberry Shortcake recordings? I really love the heavy Pink Floyd-ish "Big Apple City" song when Strawberry Shortcake is flying on the butterfly from Strawberryland to the city for the first time!

MV: All of the songs and records were fun to do, but I would have to say that "I Was Born To Disco" on *Let's Dance with Strawberry Shortcake* is one of my favorites. Howard sang on that as the Purple Pie Man. That was a fun novelty disco record to do.

SCRAM: I thought the theremin you all used as the sound effect for the butterfly on *The World of Strawberry Shortcake* soundtrack record was very innovative and cool! Was there a Strawberryland character that you took a shine to? The Southern belle Lemon Meringue? The little cat friend, Custard?

MV: Lemon Meringue, now, she was a cutie. But I really appreciated Strawberry Shortcake's leadership skills. She is a real Pollyanna who sees the best through the worst of things. She's like John Lennon. Strawberry Shortcake saw goodness in the Purple Pie Man. She's a religious figure who understands the importance of Love Thy Neighbor. You either love that kind of person, or you hate them. Like John Denver. It's all about positivity. Strawberryland couldn't have existed without her. She was the center of the universe, a very enduring person to write music for. The Purple Pie Man was a real cad. Not bad, just unloved. He was misunderstood and raised badly. Strawberry Shortcake and The Purple Pie Man are the yin/yang of their universe. Strawberry Shortcake music is very Rubber Soul for kids.

SCRAM: Okay, so what is your favorite flavor anyway? If you lived in Strawberryland, what flavor would you be? How about Howard?

MV: Anything having to do with lemons, that would be me. I'm "lemon flavored." Howard is the Purple Pie Man. That's who he is. The flavor of Purple Pie Man. You should know that we also made a G.I. Joe album for Kid Stuff. On that we wrote the story and script and came up with the characters. Deep war stories. The *Sgt. Pepper* of the genre out of all those Kid Stuff records was the G.I. Joe album. They were all full feature story-type records, not song based. John, Howard and I played all the characters.

SCRAM: Oh, man, I'm gonna comb the thrifts for GI Joe stuff now! Thanks for the tip. And thanks for your time. Good-bye!

Photos: Cathy Lynch

Howard Kaylan—April 19, 2022

[Editors' Note: This interview was conducted by Charles F Rosenay!!! on the Plastic EP podcast show. PE is Plastic EP.]

PE: How are you Howard?

HK: Never better, sir. Feeling very well, thank you. You too, I hope.

CR: You look great, my friend.

HK: Compared to what, sir? You know, when you've looked like this since you were 20, it's easy to keep looking great.

CR: And the voice, still in shape, if you needed to belt it, you could do it right now, right?

HK: If I had to sing "Stratospheric Parts" for Marc Bolan, it would be a simple thing to do.

CR: (Laughs)

HK: But I don't have to do that, so it's easy to speculate.

PE: Howard, I've seen your documentary. It's the greatest documentary where you explain about your managers and how you used to sign in at the hotels under Gerry and the Pacemakers and how you met The Beatles, could you go through that story for all the great fans out there?

HK: You're talking about seven years of my life in that sentence. I don't think I can encapsulate all that so quickly for you guys, but there were a whole bunch of events there that were kind of separate from each other. Let me address them one at a time if I can.

Okay, we were just a bunch of punks. We're still punks. We're just older punks. We were really punks once as young "snively" kids in high school, and we just didn't know anything better. So, we were a surf band. The Crossfires was our name and that's all we did was play surf music. That's all we knew was music by Johnny and the Hurricanes and The Ventures and The Dakotas even. We stretched our fingers across the long ocean at that time to find surf music from everywhere, but that's all we knew. We did a couple of necessary R&B songs in our teenage set because everyone wanted to hear "Money" and "What'd I Say?," and the songs that they could boogie to as 15-year-old kids on a slippery linoleum dance floor. Then we just graduated. When The Beatles came along, we put down our saxophones, my friend and I, and we decided we were singers. So, we sang. That was all there was to it. We did whatever was required of us and did the hits of the day because the kids would leave if you didn't play Peter and Gordon's new song or something. We had to do all that stuff and then there were times when we were in Los Angeles in the suburbs, there were big rock acts that were actually coming through our vicinity and needed back-up bands, so we backed up everybody in America as they came through, and that was our education. It was also our primitive way of networking because we were able to meet people who would come into our lives later like Sonny and Cher. When they needed a backup band, we were their guys. We came in with them to Hollywood and we played a few shows at this little dinky mob club on Sunset Blvd. called The Red Velvet. You know that's trouble. Then, we actually worked with them at the Hollywood Bowl and a couple of other places early in our Turtle career as soon as we changed our name from the fascist-sounding Crossfires to the deceivingly dorky and dumb sounding Turtles. A name, I think, that has plagued us forever.

CR: Aww!

HK: I don't know about that. If we were called Air Supply or something, our longevity would have carried us a little bit farther. C'mon now, you have to admit, of all the animal names that you can think of, that's certainly one of them.

CR: I have a question. You mentioned going to California, but before that, you recorded stuff as kids in Coney Island. Whatever happened to those songs? Are you ever going to release those?

HK: Are you kidding? I was four years old. No, I'm never going to release those. That would be insane. I believe they still exist, but I don't believe anybody needs to hear my version of some of those great Broadway tunes that my parents instilled into my very young, supple idiot mind.

CR: Fans demand that stuff.

HK: No. Nonsense. They don't. I don't believe there's a fan in the world that would like a four-year-old's recording of anything.

CR: Yeah, well, if McCartney had a four-year-old voice doing Broadway and Howard Kaylan had that and we put together an album of that, I think that would be a top seller.

HK: If Paul produced it and put his name on it, it might be.

CR: It's amazing how you guys loved The Beatles and reached that level of, maybe not universal greatness, but hit after hit after hit, and your voice being right up there with the best of the rock and roll voices of all time. I don't think that [there] is enough credit for all that.

HK: You know, what you just said there is certainly more credit than what I'm due. You just sing the songs. They bring you the songs and you listen to them, and in my case you have to go, "Yeah, I like that one. I'll sing it," or "No, you're out of your mind. Give that to Gary Lewis or something." Everybody was coming up in Hollywood at the same time. We were just another one of those bands and we were lucky enough to have a record label such as it was. It was mostly just a warehouse, but they had a pressing plant and they printed labels, so it was good enough for me. They were able to get the stuff out there which was the only thing we really cared about. We didn't know anything about promotion. We didn't aspire to be anything bigger than what we certainly turned into. There's a certain level of peaceful mediocrity I believe that you can achieve. The problem in my vision is that everybody wants to be number one and I think that's ridiculous. I've always held the contention that it's a lot safer to shoot for number six, because nobody gives a shit. Nobody ever tries to shoot down number six. That's the safest thing in the world. It's still enough. You're a Top Ten guy and you have a hit record. Nobody's going to recognize you when you walk into a Wimpy bar or something, but that's wonderful. You don't need that in your life, anyway, right? And, if you can kind of crawl along, cashing those six figure checks instead of the seven figure checks, yeah, you're not running with Beyonce, but by the same token, you don't have to put up with Jay-Z.

CR: Plastic, he's being very modest, right?

PE: I've got to say, every time I've seen Howard on the TV in these documentaries, he has a sense of humor and the guy is intelligent. When Chip Douglas left to be the producer of The Monkees, can you tell me how you felt when he left and what you thought of The Monkees?

HK: I love those guys. Everybody loved those guys. They were universally-liked because they were all nice people. It wasn't that they were luckier than anybody else, although they were. There were very few people who resented those guys unless you were turned down by their producers. If you were Stephen Stills, you had something to resent I suppose. I just looked at them as if they were trying really hard to be America's little Beatles on a television level and they more than succeeded. I think they surprised even their producers with how popular they became, even aside from the show. I saw them perform when all four of them were on the stage and they were good. They were a really good band. You can't fault them. You can't fault their material. It was the greatest. They had the best writers in the world from Goffin and King to Neil Diamond. How can you go wrong? The production was flawless, always flawless, and Chip brought a great thing to them because he knew they were a band and he recorded them as a band. They didn't want to use extra players and professional musicians because that ruined everything. When The Wrecking Crew was playing on The Beach Boys records at the same time they were playing on The Monkees records and The Mamas & Papas records, nobody maybe would have noticed it, but the players did. The real musicians out there did. You could put on a record and you could hear a Hal Blaine drum fill at the start of a song and know right away what you were getting yourself into. It was a guaranteed good rock track and you also knew that there wasn't anybody from the band playing on that session. It was a problem that I believe was just endemic to the rock and roll scene on the West Coast, certainly. As it was, with a different set of players, in the East. When you heard a Rascals record start, nobody fooled themselves into thinking that it was Dino Dinelli. In person, that guy could twirl sticks and he was a mother. On the records, they couldn't take that chance. You were talking about Atlantic Records funding them. Big time! It wasn't like Turtles. The Turtles went into the studio and it was just six guys and an engineer. We crossed our fingers and hoped it would work. With everybody else, it was a big-time record business. We were small potatoes at this garage band stuff. When you had Columbia Pictures' money invested in a project like The Monkees, it had to pay off.

CR: I always mention The Monkees and The Turtles in the same breath whenever I talk about The Rock and Roll Hall of Fame and the two most glaring omissions, but I don't want to get you started on that because you might feel the same way and I don't want to put this in that kind of a mode.

HK: I have certain reservations about the entire building in Cleveland.

CR: Say no more. A specific question. "To See the Sun" and "The Owl." Recorded but unreleased in 1968, was that supposed to be part of a whole album or concept or just a single? Do you remember that part?

HK: I remember everything about it and quite frankly, we didn't know what the hell it was. We didn't know what it was when we recorded it. We didn't know after the fact, either. The record company certainly didn't have a clue. It was so psychedelic and we were so psychedelic that we were lucky to have crawled out of Chess Studios in Chicago with anything.

PE: You probably don't know how big you were in Australia. Did you ever come to Australia?

HK: Yes, sir. We went to Oz twice, but not as Turtles, certainly. That would have been terrific. I would have loved that, but that was again something that was purview of the record company. At our company, we were lucky enough to get a leased Mercedes out of the deal every month, so they were in no position to put us on a Qantas plane to anyplace and we didn't have enough support from a label in Australia at all. There was nothing there. It was just White Whale Records because our record company in America, they made their deals over breakfast at some coffee shop on Hollywood Blvd. called Aldo's. I watched it happen a couple of times. There was a handshake and then something went down and somebody opened the trunk of a car and then there was some nonsense in the parking lot, but it wasn't anything that I could control. It wasn't good. It wasn't healthy. It wasn't until we went down to Australia, in fact, as Flo & Eddie, that we had any contact at all with the good people of your country, which was really ridiculous. I mean, it's a big world and you would think that if you were having any modicum of success in any of the areas that you could get to by plane, then you would do it and say hello to everybody and hope that maybe you could sell another record or two the next time around. These guys didn't really have the insight to see that coming.

CR: Too bad.

HK: So, we never made it down there and the first time we did come down to Australia—let me see, what was the record that was involved? It was, I think, *Moving Targets*, or it could have been the one before it [*Illegal, Immoral and Fattening*]. At the time, Columbia Records, which is a giant record label in America, one of the mega labels. I believe they had an office in Australia that had a guy at a desk and a secretary and if I'm not mistaken, a macaw. I don't believe the macaw was answering phones, but it was a small operation. There wasn't anybody there. So when we went down there expecting, "Oh, this is going to be great! All the Columbia people are going to be there!" Well, a lady and a macaw, that's not enough, and so, it sort of fell apart and our tour fell apart. We were under the auspices of a guy who I don't believe actually had a phone number.

CR: No!

HK: It was pretty rough. The gentleman meant really well. He was a really good guy, but I gotta say, we should have known from the very first that our Australian tour was destined for trouble because the first place we played was Toowoomba.

PE: I've got a very good photographer friend of mine in Sydney and he was at the concert in 1976. He's taken a lot of photos from that concert and I'll get him to email you and he can send you photos.

HK: Oh, that would be wonderful, sir. I think by 1976 we were kind of remembering everything and knew where we were, so that's good.

PE: He was also at the Sydney Town Hall and your back up band was Jo Jo Zep and the Falcons.

HK: Oh, I remember those guys. I do remember that. I remember the backstage area. I kind of remember the food. That's the stuff you recall. I remember the tea service. I remember the food. I kind of remember the lady who was serving the food and her daughter. You always remember the daughter!

PE: I've got the poster here! I don't know if you can see the poster, but there's the poster from the show.

HK: Oh yes, I do see it. Flo & Eddie over Australia. I remember that. The guy—I shouldn't say his name—couldn't handle it and he ended up dropping the financial ball at the time. A wonderful thing happened. The partnership of Evans and Gadinski got involved with us right at that moment. We were stranded in Australia—literally stranded. The tour, such as it was, was limping towards its conclusion. The promoter of the tour was on a fast train to Perth. We didn't know what we were going to do and then these wonderful gentlemen stepped in and said, "We like your record. Tell you what we are going to do. We'll finish the tour for you," and we talked to the macaw and they're going to let you out of your Columbia contract in fact, if you want to come along with us and sign with Mushroom." Well, hell yeah. Let's do that, and that really was wonderful. They saved both of those albums and they were great with us on tour, and the group finished and they were wonderful, wonderful guys, so my memories of Australia turned out to be wonderfully pleasant. They made everything first class. At the time, Skyhooks was their big band.

PE: That's right!

HK: I loved those guys. I loved Shirley. I loved the whole band, the sound, the voice, the sound of that rhythm section. What a wonderful organization. They were great kids and had great records. I mean, "Ego is not a Dirty Word." They just did wonderful, classic rock songs. The fact that they weren't as big as Rush or something in the States, I really couldn't believe it. Back in the 1970s, they should have been gigantic in America. They really should have been. I love those guys.

CR: Howard, is there ever a chance that *The History of Flo & Eddie and The Turtles* or *The Winds of Flo & Eddie* or *The Rhythm Butchers* will ever be released on CD?

HK: The Rhythm Butchers going digital is the equivalent of—how should I say it?—polishing a turd. You can't repackage that stuff. The fact that it was released at all just shows that there was an abundance of vinyl and cardboard in America and people with time on their hands and disposable money because those things probably should not have been issued by anybody, let alone more than one volume, let alone how many that came out, like nine or something. Nine of those Rhythm Butchers records and really, the balls of the people who kept buying those things and understood what they were. I wish I had a list because they would be on the "no fly" zone in Palm Springs, California. I would make sure those guys would never get into an L.A. airport.

CR: Okay. "Lady-O," which I love, is always mentioned as the final Turtles recording, but Turtles recordings continued with *Shell Shock* into the early 1970s, right?

HK: That wasn't our fault. We didn't want that to happen, but when we left the label, there was just a bunch of stuff that had not come out. The entire project that we did with Jerry Yester had not been released yet and White Whale had a bunch of other stuff that they sort of liked but they weren't sure and some of the things were unfinished, some of the things we intended to put orchestration to, like "So Goes Love," and some of those ballad pieces. You listen to them now and the way they just shoved them out. They shoved out the demo releases. They didn't care much about it. As demos, they still hold up okay, but they would have been so great had we had the chance to go in there and do what we wanted to do. The difference between our version of "Happy Together" without the orchestra and what happens when that orchestra gets laid in there, is just incredible. It's magic time, so that blend. I think it's achieving the blend of the voices that were used as instruments and the rest of the instruments in the mix that makes all of those "ba-ba's" seem more magical than looking at the page and going (sings flatly) "ba ba ba ba ba ba-ba ba ba ba." What's that? What the hell is that? If you can sing along to it, then it's okay. I can still spell Mississippi because I can sing the song.

PE: Howard, what was it like working with Marc Bolan? That blows my mind. Those are great songs and a great artist.

HK: He was fantastic. He was a wonderful, wonderful human. I truly loved that guy. We had our differences of opinion, certainly, and a big row in the 1970s that almost ended our entire friendship, but it didn't. It didn't end the friendship and I'm lucky and I'm blessed that I knew Marc at the golden point of his life when he was just sailing. Just sailing. I watched him take off and we were aghast at how big he became and how wonderful it was to see him because he didn't change. He was always the same guy to me. He was Mark Feld, so all of the Bolan stuff was just stuff he put on with the top hat.

PE: Your drummer for The Turtles, John Barbata, to me was a fantastic drummer. He just helped that Turtles sound. Would you agree with that?

HK: Absolutely. Jonny was integral in making The Turtles' sound bigger than it was. If any other drummer had been with that band, if the drummer was—not to cast aspersions—had our original drummer, Don Murray, stayed with The Turtles, it wouldn't have been the same group. The songs certainly wouldn't have sounded the same. Those drum fills from hell never would have been there. Barbata, I think, was as good a rock drummer as there ever was. Certainly on pop songs. He had an incredible Buddy Rich-like knowledge of the drums and he never stopped learning. Every night, the cost of that was "uh-oh, here comes the drum solo," but the good news was "here comes the drum solo!" Had it been a tragic drum solo, then it would have been night after night of misery, but they never were. It was always fantastic. At the end of the drum solo, Jonny would dance, dance around his drums and play the rims and stuff and get down on his knees and razzamatazz. It was good ol' showbiz Vaudeville stuff and that's why it worked. It worked because it was formula showbiz stuff.

PE: You and Mark Volman, you're just a pair of guys, but when you get together, you just click and you're so funny. There's not that many bands that have a sense of humor and don't take themselves so seriously. You guys were the greatest, there's no one like you with intelligence and a sense of humor.

CR: Yes. Agreed.

HK: You guys. Thank you, thank you. Unfortunately, senses of humor or sense of humor is not something that is generally rewarded in our culture. Here, anyway. Certainly, it really doesn't go hand in hand much with rock and roll. Since Frank Zappa died, there aren't very many people holding up the torch. When you say rock and humor, most people in this country are going to say, "Yeah, Weird Al," because he's the only guy who even does anything on a Spike Jones kind of level that kids can wrap their heads around. Kids. I say anyone under 75 is a kid to me.

PE: You're before Al. You're on those documentaries and on those films and that's what I'm saying. You guys are like pioneers. There's no question in my mind.

HK: Well, thank you, but pioneers don't get checks. Nobody is writing a check to Gabby Hayes these days. His estate is just "tumbling tumbleweeds." All I ever needed was appreciation. I never needed a check, fortunately, and that is why I could comfortably at this age just retire from the road and just say, "I've done it, mate!" I've never wanted to wind up with my last headline being "Maid Can't Open Holiday Inn Door. Call Security!" That's not it. I don't want to be the Doc Martin shoe that's stuck in the door and they can't come in and there's the maid cart outside. "We can't get 404 to answer." "Well, that's because someone slipped him some Fentanyl last night in his Hawaiian Punch." God knows, but I don't want to be the guy out there that's experimenting with egg dishes and backstage food. I realized this at a concert that I did several years ago, in fact, on the occasion of my 70th birthday, when one of the girls in the crew came out with a cupcake and the two numbers seven and zero stuck into the cupcake with plastic letters and I looked at that and went, "Oh yeah, I can't be doing this. I can't be doing this. I'm 70 years old."

CR: You mentioned Jonny. Great drummer, no doubt. Don Murray passed away. Tim Tucker has passed. Are you in touch with any of the other guys besides Mark Volman and what are your memories of them?

HK: My memories of them are not all that pleasant because in recent years several of those guys have decided that they didn't make enough money fifty years ago, so they're going to see if they can look into our accounts right now and if there's a lawyer somewhere that will say, "Yeah, you're right! I know you're on those records. I saw you on The Ed Sullivan Show. Dammit! You deserve as much as they do! Let's go see what they've got." So that still exists. It existed up until a year and a half ago with a lot of those guys so I don't keep in touch with any of them these days. I never kept in touch with Al Nichol. He's not a party that interests me in his life or his past or his future. He's recently tried to get in touch with me. There's no point. There's just no point. Life's too short.

Some would say that life's too short to ignore him, but I would say just the opposite. Anything I can do to ignore that guy any other way and block him, I really should, especially at this tender time.

CR: About 20 years ago, in 2003, you reunited with Mark, John Seiter and Jim Pons. That was about the closest there was to a Turtles reunion. I think it was a fundraiser.

HK: What was it? You'll have to refresh my memory.

CR: It was September 2003 at the David Center, and it was a fundraiser in New York.

HK: Oh, The David Center. We did that particular event because David was the handi-capable son of Jim Pons, and so it was a very personal cause. Had he not asked personally, I don't think I would have been involved. We have our own charities that we are both into. That was very special, so I'm not surprised that we were all together at the same time then, but I never really put that together as a reunion of any sort. It was just something that we did.

CR: The closest, yeah.

HK: I guess it was the closest. John Seiter, I wish he had the chance in our group to fulfill his dreams, too, because he had lofty ambitions with Spanky and Our Gang. He was a very good drummer. Totally different from John Barbata in style. Jonny was always on top of the kit and he was incredibly, incredibly jacked up. He would be proud of that. He invented Monster Energy Drink whether he knows it or not. He lived it.

CR: Ron Dante's doing a great job with Mark keeping the Happy Together tours alive and The Turtles. You don't miss it? You don't feel like, "Oh, I could have been up there for that particular show?" Any chance you're going to pop in once or twice?

HK: No, there's never a chance I'm going to pop in twice or once. It's not in the cards. I don't see myself coming out and surprising everybody with a cake. I'm not that guy. I don't care. I will never go to see the Happy Together tour because I do have feelings about it. If there's anything that I do miss, it's the shows. I loved the shows. The shows gave back everything else that the rest of the time drained out of me. If it weren't for the recharge, I wouldn't have done it at all. I just can't take the tour bus. God bless Willie Nelson, but let me tell you something, he's out of his mind, and he must have a back from hell because I've lived my life in the back room of those damn tour buses and they're on the wrong side of the wheels. They bounce around like hell. It's like riding on a skateboard. It's no fun. I don't care what's on the television or what's for dinner or who flooded the bathroom last, because it's gonna flood. Those things, as luxurious as they are, are just rolling outhouses.

CR: Let me ask a recording question. *Dirty Duck*. Any unreleased tracks that we will ever see?

HK: I was talking to Mark about it not more than a week ago and we were talking about *Dirty Duck* and I believe that it is going to see the light of day. I believe that we will see *Dirty Duck* coming out or at least to stream this year. I don't think we're going to meet any opposition from Roger Corman's company. I think that anything that turns into money for these guys is going to be well-appreciated after this long absence. They're not going to get any more money from Harry Nilsson's account so I do believe that *Dirty Duck* will see the light of day. I hope it does because there were some great little jazz things that we did with a whole other band. Another great bunch of guys from the Midwest of America who called themselves The Robbs. They were brothers. They used to perform on Dick Clark's *Where the Action Is*, a television show. They were like the house band. These brothers and a cousin. They wound up being our band for an album or two and certainly on the *Dirty Duck soundtrack*. All of it. That was just one of the strangest projects I've ever worked on in my life.

PE: What is your personal favorite Turtles song?

HK: Oooh, my personal favorite, it would have been closest to me, would have been "Marmendy Mill." It would have been a Turtles song, but it turned into a Flo & Eddie song because nobody wanted to listen to anything autobiographical in that band.

PE: You are a true rock and roll legend and you have one of the greatest voices in rock and roll that's going to live on forever and ever.

HK: Thank you. Thank you. Thank you both. My dogs say thank you, too! Thank you, gentlemen.

DISCOGRAPHY

45s:

The Crossfires:
Dr. Jekyll and Mr. Hyde / Fiberglass Jungle—August 1963 (Capco C 104)
One Potato, Two Potato (Three Potato, Four Potato) / That'll Be the Day—February 1965 (Lucky Token LT 112)

The Turtles:
It Ain't Me Babe / Almost There—July 1965 (WW 222)
Let Me Be / Your Maw Said You Cried—October 1965 (WW 224)
You Baby / Wanderin' Kind—January 1966 (WW 227)
It Was a Very Good Year / Let the Cold Winds Blow—1966 (Canadian Quality 1791X)
Grim Reaper of Love / Come Back—May 1966 (WW 231)
So Goes Love / On a Summer's Day—June 1966 (unreleased)
Outside Chance / We'll Meet Again—July 1966 (WW 234)
Making My Mind Up / Outside Chance—July 1966 (WW 237)
Can I Get to Know You Better / Like the Seasons—October 1966 (WW 238)
Happy Together / Like the Seasons—January 1967 (WW 244)
She'd Rather Be With Me / The Walking Song—April 1967 (WW 249)
Guide for the Married Man / Think I'll Run Away—June 1967 (WW 251)
You Know What I Mean / Rugs of Woods and Flowers—July 1967 (WW 254)
She's My Girl / Chicken Little Was Right—October 1967 (WW 260)
Sound Asleep / Umbassa the Dragon—February 1968 (WW 264)
The Story of Rock and Roll / Can't You Hear the Cows—June 1968 (WW 273)
Elenore / Surfer Dan—September 1968 (WW 276)
You Showed Me / Buzz Saw—December 1968 (WW 292)
House On the Hill / Come Over—May 1969 (WW 306)
You Don't Have to Walk in the Rain / Come Over—May 1969 (WW 308)
Love in the City / Bachelor Mother—September 1969 (WW 326)
Lady-O / Somewhere Friday Nite—November 1969 (WW 334)
Teardrops / Gas Money—February 1970 (WW 340) (by The Dedications)
Who Would Ever Think That I Would Marry Margaret / We Don't Want to Party No More—March 1970 (WW 341)
Is It Any Wonder? / Wanderin' Kind—April 1970 (WW 350)
Eve of Destruction / Wanderin' Kind—June 1970 (WW 355)
Me About You / Think I'll Run Away—October 1970 (WW 364)
The Legendary Rhythm Butchers Sampler—1980 (Rhino RNFE 100)
Meat the Rhythm Butchers (Volume 1)—1980 (Rhino RNFE 101)
The Rhythm Butchers Return to the Corral By the Bay (Volume 2)—1980 (Rhino RNFE 102)
Invasion of The Rhythm Butchers (Volume 3)—1981 (Rhino RNFE 103)
Greatest Hits—1982 (Collectables BOX COL B-7)
Turtlesized—1982 (Rhino RNDF 280)
The Rhythm Butchers Sing for Young Lovers (Volume 4)—1982 (Rhino RNFE 104)
The Rhythm Butchers vs. The Zanti Misfits (Volume 5)—1983 (Rhino RNFE 105)
It Ain't Me Babe / Let Me Be—1984 (Rhino Original Masters Series RNOR 4501)
Happy Together / You Don't Have to Walk in the Rain—1984 (Rhino Original Masters Series RNOR 4502)

She'd Rather Be With Me / You Baby—1984 (Rhino Original Masters Series RNOR 4503)
You Know What I Mean / She's My Girl—1984 (Rhino Original Masters Series RNOR 4504)
Elenore / You Showed Me—1984 (Rhino Original Masters Series RNOR 4505)
The Rhythm Butchers on Saturn (Volume 6)—1985 (Rhino RNFE 106)
The Rhythm Butchers Hate You (Volume 7)—1986? (Rhino RNTI 4601)
Happy Together / There You Sit Lonely—April 1987 (Rhino RNOR 74406)
45RPM Vinyl Singles Collection—September 22, 2014 (Manifesto MFO 48030)

Frank Zappa and The Mothers of Invention:
Radio Spots for Frank Zappa's "Chunga's Revenge," Band 1-4—October 1970 (Reprise PRO 432)
Tell Me You Love Me / Will You Go All the Way for the USA?—November 1970 (Bizarre 0967)
Tears Began to Fall / Junier Mintz Boogie—November 1971 (Bizarre 1052)
Magic Fingers / Daddy, Daddy, Daddy—November 1971—(United Artists 50587)

Flo & Eddie (Mark Volman and Howard Kaylan):
Radio Spot for The Phlorescent Leech and Eddie / Goodbye Surprise—1972 (Reprise PRO 533)
Feel Older Now / ?—1972 (Reprise REP 1112)
Goodbye Surprise / Nikki Hoi—September 1972 (Reprise 1113)
Afterglow / The Original Soundtrack from "Carlos and De Bull"—January 1973 (Reprise REP 1142)
Flo & Eddie Meet the Wolfman Part 1 & 2—February 1973 (Reprise PRO 564)
You're A Lady / If We Only Had the Time—June 1973 (Reprise REP 1160)
Let Me Make Love to You / Come to My Rescue Webelos—September 1974 (Columbia 3-10028)
Let Me Make Love to You / Come to My Rescue Webelos—September 1975 (Columbia 3-10204)
Rebecca / Illegal, Immoral and Fattening—December 1975 (Columbia 3-10264)
Elenore / The Love You Gave Away—October 1976 (Columbia 3-10425)
Keep It Warm / Hot—December 1976 (Columbia 3-10458)

LPs and CDs:

The Crossfires:
Out of Control—1981 (Rhino RNLP 019 or Sundazed SC 6062)

The Turtles:
It Ain't Me Babe—September 1965 (WW 111 or WWS 111)
You Baby—April 1966 (WW 112 or WWS 7112)
Happy Together—April 29, 1967 (WW 114 or WWS 7114)
Golden Hits—October 1967 (WW 115 or WWS 7115)
The Turtles Present the Battle of the Bands—November 1, 1968 (WWS 7118)
Turtle Soup—October 1969 (WWS 7124)
More Golden Hits—March 1970 (WWS 7127)
Wooden Head—November 1970 (WW 7133)
Happy Together Again!—November 1974 (Sire SASH 3703 2)
1968—October 1978 (Rhino RNPD 901)
The Best of The Turtles—1981 (Lost Nite LLP 24)
The Turtles Greatest Hits—1982 (Rhino RNLP 160)
The Story of Flo & Eddie and The Turtles—1983 (Rhino RNTA 71998)
20 Greatest Hits—1984 (Rhino RNCD 5160)

Chalon Road—March 1987 (Rhino RNLP 70155)
Shell Shock—March 1987 (Rhino RNLP 70158)
The Best of The Turtles (Golden Archive Series)—1987 (Rhino RNLP 70177)
Turtle Wax: The Best of The Turtles, Volume 2—1988 (Rhino R2 70159)
Lil' Bit of Gold—1988 (Rhino R3 73017)
Lil' Bit of Gold, Volume 2—1988 (Rhino R3 73027)
The Best of The Turtles (Special Editions Series)—1992 (Rhino R2 70127)
The Turtles Featuring Flo & Eddie Captured Live!—November 10, 1992 (Rhino R2 71153)
California Gold—Happy Together Again—1994 (LaserLight 12 380)
Love Songs (Special Editions Series)—1995 (Rhino R2 71873)
Thirty Years of Rock 'n' Roll—September 26, 1995 (LaserLight 15 969)
Solid Zinc: The Turtles Anthology—February 16, 2002 (Rhino R2 78304)
Happy Together: The Very Best of The Turtles—September 28, 2004 (Shout Factory DK 37488)
Turtle Tracks—2006 (FloEdCo 040100)
All Access—March 29, 2008 (FloEdCo 50274)
Save The Turtles: The Turtles Greatest Hits—March 2, 2009 (FloEdCo MFO 48002)
Playlist: The Very Best of The Turtles—March 10, 2016 (Sony 88875093842)
The Complete Original Album Collection—June 22, 2016 (Manifesto MFO 48047)
All the Singles—August 19, 2016 (Manifesto MFO 48040)
The Turtles '66—November 24, 2017 (FloEdCo MFO 48052)

Frank Zappa and The Mothers of Invention:
Chunga's Revenge—October 23, 1970 (Bizarre MS 2030)
Fillmore East - June 1971—August 2, 1971 (Bizarre MS 2042)
200 Motels: Original Motion Picture Soundtrack—October 4, 1971 (United Artists UAS 9956)
Just Another Band from L.A.—March 26, 1972 (Bizarre MS 2075)
Some Time in New York City / Live Jam—June 17, 1972 (Apple SVBB 3392) (by John Lennon and Yoko Ono)
You Can't Do That On Stage Anymore, Volume 1—May 16, 1988 (Rykodisc RCD 10081/82)
You Can't Do That On Stage Anymore, Volume 3—November 13, 1989 (Rykodisc RCD 10085/86)
Freaks and Motherfu#@%!*—July 7, 1991 (Rhino Foo-eee R2 70539)
At the Circus—June 16, 1992 (Rhino Foo-eee R2 71020)
Swiss Cheese/Fire!—June 16, 1992 (Rhino Foo-eee R2 71021)
You Can't Do That On Stage Anymore, Volume 6—July 10, 1992 (Rykodisc RCD 10091/92)
Playground Psychotics—October 27, 1992 (Rykodisc RCD 10557/58)
Carnegie Hall—October 31, 2011 and April 3, 2020 (Zappa VR 2011 1 or ZR 2011 1B)
The Mothers 1970—May 8, 2020 (Zappa ZR 20033)
200 Motels Soundtrack 50th Anniversary—September 24, 2021 (Zappa ZR20037)
The Mothers 1971—January 28, 2022 (Zappa ZR20038)
Live At Fillmore East, June 1971 - 50th Anniversary—January 28, 2022 (Zappa ZR20038-F)
Live at the Rainbow Theatre—January 28, 2022 (Zappa ZR20038-R)

Flo & Eddie:
The Phlorescent Leech and Eddie—September 1972 (Reprise MS 2099)
Flo & Eddie—June 1973 (Reprise MS 2141)
Flo & Eddie Interview with Barry Mann—July 9, 1975 (RCA DJL1 1162)
Illegal, Immoral and Fattening—December 1975 (Columbia PC 33554)
Moving Targets—October 1976 (Columbia PC 34262)
Rock Steady with Flo & Eddie—1981 (Epiphany ELP 4010)

Checkpoint Charlie—1982 (Rhino RNEP 603)
The Winds of Flo & Eddie—1983 (Rhino)
The History of Flo & Eddie and The Turtles—1983 (Rhino RNTA 71998)
Prince Flo & Jah Edward 1—1987 (Rhino RNLP 70079)
The Best of Flo & Eddie—1987 (Rhino RNLP 70134 or RNCD 75880)
The Turtles Featuring Flo & Eddie Captured Live!—November 10, 1992 (Rhino R2 71153)
Dust Bunnies—March 21, 2006 (Intentional/Halogen 61432 41222)
New York "Times" 1979-1994 Live at the Bottom Line—October 20, 2009 (Manifesto 48003)
Shell Shocked—2013 (Audible)

Children's Albums:
The World of Strawberry Shortcake—1980 (Kid Stuff KSS 165)
Strawberry Shortcake in Big Apple City—1981 (Kid Stuff KSS 163)
Strawberry Shortcake Presents Pets On Parade—1982 (Kid Stuff KSS 5024)
Introducing the Care Bears—1983 (Kid Stuff KDP 6016 or KSS 5951)
Let's Dance—1983 (Kid Stuff KSS 5030)
The Care Bears Care For You—1983 (Kid Stuff KSS 5034)
The Care Bears Adventures in Care-a-Lot—1983 (Kid Stuff KSS 5038 or KDP 6019)
A Care Bears Christmas—1983 (Kid Stuff KSS 5040)
Off to See the World—1983 (Kid Stuff KSS 5048)
Castle of the Doomed—1984 (Kid Stuff KSS 5044)
Splash Dance Party—1984 (Kid Stuff KSS 5045)
American Rabbit—The Original Soundtrack—January 17, 1986 (Rhino RNEP 70614)
Gumby—1989 (Buena Vista 6402N)

Backing Vocals:

T. Rex—*T. Rex* (1970)
T. Rex—Electric Warrior (1971)
Steely Dan—Everyone's Gone to the Movies (Demo) (1971)
T. Rex—*The Slider* (1972)
T. Rex—*Tanx* (1973)
Ray Manzarek—*The Golden Scarab* (1973)
Ray Manzarek—The Whole Thing Started With Rock and Roll & Now It's Out Of Control (1974)
Roger McGuinn—*Peace On You* (1974)
David Cassidy—*The Higher They Climb* (1975)
Keith Moon—Two Sides of the Moon (1975)
T. Rex—Futuristic Dragon (1976)
Stephen Stills—*Illegal Stills* (1976)
Alice Cooper—*From the Inside* (1978)
Alice Cooper—*Flush the Fashion* (1980)
Bruce Springsteen—"Hungry Heart" from *The River* (1979)
Blondie—*Autoamerican* (1981)
The Psychedelic Furs—*Forever Now* (1982)
Alice Cooper—*Zipper Catches Skin* (1982)
Paul Kantner—Planet Earth Rock and Roll Orchestra (album) (1983)
Andy Taylor—Thunder (Andy Taylor album) (1987)
Gavin Friday—Each Man Kills the Thing He Loves (1989)
Jefferson Airplane—*Jefferson Airplane (album)* (1989)
Southside Johnny & the Asbury Jukes—*Better Days* (1991)

Ramones—*Mondo Bizarro* (1992)
Duran Duran—*Thank You* (1995)
Johnny Popstar Luv Explosion—*Lizzy the Supermarket Drag Queen* (1999)
Adam Bomb—*New York Times* on Mc Douglas Street & NY Child (2001)

As producers:

The Good Rats—*From Rats to Riches* (1978)
DMZ—*DMZ* (self-titled LP) (1978)

BIBLIOGRAPHY

Barbata, John, *The Legendary Life of a Rock Star Drummer*, DJ Blues Publishing Company, 2007

Bronson, Harold, *The Rhino Records Story: Revenge of the Music Nerds*, Select Books, 2013

Cahan, Andy, *The Most Famous Musician You've Never Heard Of*, independently published, 2020

Kaylan, Howard, *Shell Shocked: My Life with the Turtles Flo & Eddie and Frank Zappa etc…*, Backbeat Books, 2013

Kaylan, Howard, and Mark Volman, *The Story of Flo & Eddie and The Turtles*, Rhino Records, 1983

Pons, Jim, *Hard Core Love: Sex, Football and Rock & Roll in the Kingdom of God*, Waterfront Digital Press, 2017

Sandoval, Andrew, *Solid Zinc: The Turtles Anthology*, Rhino Records, 2003

Sandoval, Andrew, *All the Singles*, Rhino Records, 2016

Turtles: Happy Together, The, Rhino Home Video, 1991

Volman, Mark with John Cody, *Happy Forever: My Musical Adventures with The Turtles, Frank Zappa, T. Rex, Flo & Eddie, and More*, Jawbone Press, 2023

Wacholtz, Larry E, with Mark Volman and Jennifer Wilgus-Fowler, *Off the Record: Your Ultimate Resource for Success in the Music Business*, Thumbs-Up Publishing, 2011, 2013

INDEX

Symbols

10cc 263
1910 Fruitgum Company, The 196

A

Abbey Road Studios 152, 188, 192, 201
Abrams, Casey 43
Adler, Cynthia 228
Aerosmith 86, 264
Agol, Stan 157, 186, 187, 188, 196, 204
A Hard Day's Night 53
Ajaye, Franklyn 239
Alamo, Frank 54, 166, 244
Albana, Vincent 273
Albertine, Charles 213
Allen, Lily 285
Allen, Woody 53, 213
Allison, Jerry 116
Altfeld, Don 46
Ambros, Wolfgang 79
American Spring 225
Anberlin 79
Andreoli, Peter 217, 241
Andrews, Dana 136
Andrews Sisters, The 292
Andy's House 229, 230, 232, 245, 261, 268, 275, 286, 296, 297, 301
Angels, The 181
Angry, The 11, 135, 136
Animals, The 2, 9, 44, 53, 60, 120, 136, 238, 329, 340, 354
Animalympics 263
Anka, Paul 153
Apostle, Chris 126, 215, 219, 227, 228, 232, 233, 234, 265, 270, 271, 276, 294, 295, 298, 328, 383, 415
Applegate, Christina 304, 307, 308, 327
Apple Records 18, 42, 66, 149, 155, 232, 303, 314, 422, 423, 436, 437
Arbogast, Bob 306
Armstrong, R.G. 291
Arnaz, Lucie 54
Arnold, Thomas 164
Arthur Fiedler & the Boston Pops Orchestra 167
Articolo 31 79
Ascot Recorders 76, 95, 120
Asher, Peter 116, 142, 340

Association, The 68, 122, 145, 334, 335, 370, 371, 381, 383, 413
Astor Towers Hotel, The 87, 101
Astronauts, The 93
Audino, John 30, 36, 55, 62, 68, 85, 90, 94, 109, 137, 140
Aufray, Hugues 79
Auger, Bob 159, 172, 173, 181, 184, 189, 194, 197, 199, 202, 205
Avakian, Tristan 250, 270, 298, 384
Aznavour, Charles 301

B

Bacal, Joe 309, 310
Bachman and Cummings 79
Baez, Joan 23, 69, 84
Bailey, Mildred 277
Baker, Roy Thomas 151, 157, 162, 165, 171, 173, 174, 175, 186, 187, 188, 196, 204, 207
Ball, Lucille 52, 53
Banana Splits 6, 91
Band Aid 41
BAP 79
Barbata, John viii, 12, 13, 26, 29, 30, 31, 32, 34, 35, 40, 41, 45, 53, 54, 55, 65, 68, 76, 86, 87, 90, 94, 95, 96, 99, 100, 102, 105, 108, 112, 113, 114, 117, 120, 121, 128, 129, 130, 134, 135, 145, 324, 336, 338, 343, 393, 394, 395, 409, 418, 430, 432
Barber, Dick 199
Barnes, Priscilla 291
Barrett, Aston "Family Man" 224, 244, 255, 265, 272, 273, 277, 280, 281, 285, 288, 290, 293
Barrett, Majel 52
Barretto, Ray 226
Barri, Steve 11, 30, 63, 64, 142, 305
Barry, John 53
Bartel, Paul 239
Bassjackers 54, 166, 244
Batman 269
Baum, Bernie 241
Baxter, Jeff 248, 266, 367
Bay Bops, The 44
Beach Boys, The 2, 10, 32, 73, 77, 84, 97, 115, 225, 232, 240, 241, 257, 350, 358, 360, 371, 413, 414, 427
Beatles, The v, 2, 5, 7, 9, 11, 13, 14, 18, 31, 33, 35, 41, 42, 44, 60, 67, 69, 73, 77, 80, 85, 101, 103, 105, 112, 116, 129, 132, 139, 148,

153, 155, 167, 180, 214, 224, 231, 232, 234, 241, 257, 299, 304, 310, 340, 342, 350, 357, 374, 382, 392, 400, 409, 418, 419, 425, 426, 427, 456
Beaver, Paul 41, 130, 146
Beck, John 74
Bee Gees, The 2, 47, 80, 145
Begley Jr., Ed 239
Behrens, Stanley 307, 308, 311, 312, 313, 315
Belafonte, Harry 23
Bennett, Max 157
Bennett, Paris 181
Benny, Jack 52, 53
Beresford, Steve 285
Bergen, Polly 52, 53
Berlin, Irving 292
Bernal, Carlos 128, 334, 352
Berry, Chuck 74, 340
Berry, Dave 109
Berryhill, Robert 286
Berry, Jan 46
Bertrand, Eddie 286
Biafra, Jello 286
Bickford, Bruce 208
Big Maybelle 197
Big Star 212
Bikel, Theodore 159, 172, 173, 181, 184, 189, 194, 197, 198, 199, 201, 202, 205
Billy J. Kramer & The Dakotas 143
Billy T 225
Biscoe, Eddie 128
Bishop, Joey 15, 52, 53
Bishop, Stephen 128
Bjorn, Anna 239
Blackburn, Lou 55, 105, 112, 134, 145
Black, Jay 64, 348
Black, Jimmy Carl 159, 171, 172, 173, 181, 184, 189, 194, 197, 198, 199, 202, 205, 207, 320
Black Sabbath 51, 60, 180
Blaikley, Alan 245
Blaikley, Howard 62
Blaine, Hal 12, 55, 80, 85, 338, 427
Blair, John 286
Blender, Jeri 291
Blessing, Lynn 55, 86, 301
Blondie 240, 326, 437
Blood, Sweat & Tears 207
Bloom, Lindsay 291
Blue, Ben 52, 53
Blue Oyster Cult 51, 266
BMX Bandits 225
Bobby Comstock and the Counts 181
Boe, Alfie 137

Bolan, Marc 59, 237, 239, 240, 247, 248, 256, 264, 326, 425, 430
Bolger, Ray 313, 320
Bolic Sound 220, 234, 237, 242, 249, 253, 258, 271, 274, 278, 279, 289, 291, 294, 298
Bolton, Michael 79
Bonner, Garry 13, 32, 50, 54, 80, 86, 87, 105, 108, 128, 145, 166, 242, 244
Bonne Villes, The 198
Bono, Sonny 88, 89
Boone, Pat 12, 116, 277, 375, 421
Boone, Steve viii, 413
Botnick, Bruce 32, 53, 54, 55, 80, 85, 86, 96, 102, 105, 108, 117, 122, 135, 145
Botnick, Norman 145
Bottom End, The 210
Bottom Line, The 106, 109, 127, 211, 212, 213, 215, 219, 220, 227, 228, 229, 233, 234, 238, 241, 243, 244, 248, 250, 251, 259, 263, 264, 265, 267, 270, 271, 272, 275, 276, 277, 282, 283, 287, 294, 295, 297, 298, 299, 327, 328, 355, 384, 400, 408, 409, 415, 437
Bowie, David 59, 79, 207, 247, 312
Boy George 269
Brackenridge Brothers, The 224, 244, 255, 265, 272, 273, 277, 280, 281, 285, 288, 290, 293
Bradbury, John 91, 116
Braithewaite, Daryl 212
Bramlett, Bonnie 269
Brandywine Singers, The 23
Brent, Eve 52
Brevette, Tony 290
Bricusse, Leslie 14, 53
Bright, Bette 181
Brightman, Sarah 181
Brisbois, Bud 55, 83, 105, 123, 145
Britz, Chuck 25, 36, 37, 38, 40, 43, 44, 60, 61, 62, 67, 72, 74, 82, 83, 91, 92, 98, 103, 105, 108, 109, 112, 116, 122, 123, 144
Broadway Danny Rose 213
Brody, Marvin 52
Brooks, Jack 250
Brother Phelps 152
Brown, Arthur 195, 208
Browne, Jackson 84
Brown, Errol 224, 244, 255, 265, 272, 273, 277, 280, 281, 285, 288, 290, 293
Brown, James 29, 277
Brown, Jr., Oscar 301
Brown, Larry 115
Brown, Michael 261, 296
Bruce, Bobby 83, 123, 145
Brute Force 66, 155
Bublé, Michael 277

Buchanan, Bob 99
Buckingham, Lindsey 23
Buckinghams, The 371, 383, 384, 416
Buckley, Tim 275, 375, 376, 381
Buddy Holly and the Three Tunes 116
Buffalo Springfield 122
Buffett, Jimmy 255
Burdon, Eric 61, 120, 136, 228, 328, 340
Burke, Johnny 265
Buslowe, Steve 219, 269
Bus Stop 228, 240
Butler, Leslie "Professor" 224, 244, 255, 265, 272, 273, 277, 280, 281, 285, 288, 290, 293
Byrds, The 5, 9, 10, 12, 17, 65, 78, 84, 105, 121, 136, 137, 146, 334, 337, 342, 364, 392, 415, 421

C

Cabot, Sebastian 69, 79
Caesar, Sid 52, 53
Cahan, Andy viii, 117, 210, 213, 214, 216, 218, 219, 221, 222, 223, 226, 229, 230, 231, 232, 239, 240, 242, 245, 246, 248, 251, 252, 253, 255, 256, 257, 260, 261, 262, 263, 264, 266, 268, 269, 273, 275, 276, 278, 279, 280, 282, 284, 285, 288, 289, 291, 292, 296, 297, 301, 307, 308, 311, 312, 313, 314, 315, 316, 319, 320, 326, 354, 368, 381, 401, 408, 410
Calhoun, Roy 115
California Dreaming 221, 273
Callan, Cathy 216, 218, 231, 242, 248, 256, 262, 263, 266, 289
Calvin, John 221
Cannata, Richie 127, 215, 219, 227, 232, 233, 234, 238, 239, 265, 270, 271, 276, 294, 295, 297
Cannon, Freddy 47, 98
Capco Records 40
Captain & Tennille 54, 166, 244
Car 54, Where Are You? 220, 275
Care Bears, The iv, 303, 304, 307, 308, 311, 312, 313, 326, 327, 437
Carey, Timothy 208
Carlin, Fred 273
Carmen, Eric 62, 75, 214, 328, 330
Carnegie Hall 149, 152, 154, 156, 159, 160, 180, 183, 184, 189, 190, 191, 192, 193, 194, 195, 203, 204, 206, 282, 436
Carney, Art 52, 53
Carpenter, John 227, 228, 229, 232, 233, 243
Carson, Johnny 13, 153
Carter, Anita 23
Carter, June 69

Cash, Johnny 69, 137
Casino de Montreux 149, 151, 194
Cassel, Seymour 221
Cassidy, David 225, 329, 437
Caton, Roy 55, 61, 83, 105, 112, 123, 134
Chad & Jeremy 142, 347
Chaikin, Jules 55, 62, 68, 85, 109, 140
Champs, the 29
Changing Times, The 275
Chantoozies 181
Chapin, Miles 239
Chapman, Tracy 234
Charles, Hughie 137, 138
Chavigny, Robert 301
Cheech & Chong 278
Cher 10, 79, 89, 238, 371, 409, 426
Cherokee Studios 224, 252, 258, 260, 269, 293, 300, 320
Chicago 10, 15, 67, 76, 87, 95, 99, 101, 120, 122, 216, 262, 267, 283, 349, 352, 366, 371, 399, 409, 428
Chiffons, The 181
Chin, T. 288
Christie Front Drive 267
Christie, Lou 243
Christopher, Dennis 221
Cihi, Jennifer 167
Clapton, Eric 84
Clark, Dick 10, 12, 81, 128, 400, 433
Clarke, Johnny 281
Clark, Gene 12, 13, 88, 145, 337, 388, 392
Clark, Petula 32, 54, 166, 226, 227, 244
Clash, The 222
Clemons, Clarence 225
Cliff, Jimmy 255
Cohen, Robert "Cricket" 229, 230, 232, 245, 261, 268, 275, 285, 296, 297, 301
Colbert, Stephen 137
Cole, Beccy 69
Collins, Judy 79, 84
Collins, Ray 207
Columbia Records 209, 210, 231, 253, 259, 428, 429, 435, 436
Columbo, Russ 277
Como, Perry 277
Connick, Jr., Harry 292
Conniff, Ray 267
Conrad, Barnaby 221
Cook, Jesse 69
Cooper, Alice 1, 59, 208, 209, 214, 247, 287, 289, 322, 366, 420, 437
Cooper, Dee 291
Cooper, Kim vi, 305, 422
Copyright Control 265, 273

Corea, Chick 292
Corryel, Larry 265
Costa, Nikka 181
Costello, Elvis 226, 227
Count Basie 265
Couture, François 169
Cowell, Simon 89
Cowsills, The 73, 293, 392, 394
Cox, Wally 52, 53
Crack the Sky 88
Craig, Andrew 241, 243, 244, 245, 248, 250, 269, 287, 299
Crawford, Hank 265
Creation, The 79
Crests, The 163, 231
Crickets, The 116
Crimson Discord 43
Crislu, Spencer 152, 167, 170, 176, 184, 188, 190, 201
Criterion Collection 52
Crocker, Glenn 13, 94
Crosby, Bing 265, 277, 292
Crossroads of the World, The 223, 230, 240, 251, 252, 254, 255, 257, 260, 268, 276, 279, 282, 292
Crosswind Singers, The 8, 79, 136
Crystal Sound Recording Studios 31, 50, 66, 80, 116, 147
Crystals, The 238
CSNY 17, 129, 336, 339, 345, 405
Cummings, Bob 82
Cummings, Burton 236
Curtis, Billy 93
Curtis, Jamie Lee 227
Curtis, Sonny 267

D

Dacus, Donnie 248, 266, 367
Dale, Dick 36, 43, 67, 103, 113, 286
Dalley, Robert J. 286
Daly, Jonathan 12, 93
Damned, The 232
Dante, Ron vi, viii, 21, 229, 329, 331, 332, 347, 353, 373, 386, 394, 416, 432
Darlin' 225
Darling, Erik 23
Dave Clark Five, The 53, 147, 354
Davidson, John 54
Davies, Daniel 243
Davies, Dave 62
Davies, Ray 6, 17, 18, 25, 26, 37, 38, 60, 61, 62, 72, 73, 83, 105, 122, 123, 124, 144, 226, 376

Davis, Carlton "Santa" 224, 244, 255, 265, 272, 273, 277, 280, 281, 285, 288, 290, 293
Davis, Douglas 74
Davis, Gary 291
Davis Jr., Sammy 267
Davis, Paul 225
Davis, Skeeter 116
Dawson, Dinky viii, 334
Dawson, Richard 93, 94
Dead End Kids 245
Decca Records 12, 107
Dedications, The 19, 46, 47, 115, 434
Deep Purple 6, 17, 149, 195
De La Soul 146
Delfonics, The 47
Delsener, Ron 156, 160, 193, 203
Delvy, Richard 286
Demon Records 49, 88
Densmore, John 239
Denton, Coby 93
Des Barres, Michael 240
Des Barres, Pamela 199, 208
DeShannon, Jackie 87, 88
Devil Dogs, The 217
DeVoogdt, John 83, 123
Devry, Elaine 52
Diamond, Barry 239
Dick and Dee Dee 23
Dickies, The 43
Dickson, Luther 44
DIIV 79
Diltz, Henry iv, vi, viii, 35, 128, 374, 403
Dino, Kenny 147
Dirty Angels, The 29
Dixie Cups, The 10, 217
Dmitri Vegas & Like Mike 54, 166, 244
Dolenz, Micky 90, 114, 148, 328, 342, 356, 383, 395, 397, 416
Dollar 167, 420
Donaldson, David. *See* Dee Robb
Don and Dewey 74
Donelly, Tanya 226
DonRays, The 40
Doors, The 209, 228
Doucet, Luke 69
Douglas, Bonnie 74
Douglas, Chip vii, viii, 13, 14, 16, 17, 26, 29, 30, 31, 34, 35, 40, 41, 45, 54, 55, 65, 76, 77, 90, 95, 113, 114, 115, 121, 122, 124, 130, 146, 338, 340, 344, 345, 374, 376, 388, 403, 427
Douglas, Deon 93
Douglas, Jack 212, 214, 217, 221, 226, 235, 251, 254, 263, 281, 300
Dow, Caroline 241, 243, 248, 270, 287

Dowe, Brent 290
Down And Dirty Duck 219, 223
Dracula 40, 243, 269
Drake, Nick and Gabrielle 23
Dr. Alimantado 285
Dramatics, The 47
Dr. Demento 154, 272
Drew, Christofer 69
Dr. John 165, 204, 254, 339
Duboff, Steve 73, 275, 361, 362
Duke, George 148, 151, 152, 157, 158, 159, 162, 164, 165, 167, 171, 173, 174, 181, 182, 183, 184, 187, 188, 189, 191, 194, 196, 197, 198, 199, 202, 203, 204, 205, 207, 320, 398
Dunbar, Aynsley 148, 151, 152, 153, 154, 155, 156, 157, 158, 159, 160, 161, 162, 163, 164, 165, 166, 167, 168, 169, 170, 171, 172, 173, 174, 176, 180, 181, 182, 183, 184, 187, 188, 189, 190, 191, 192, 193, 194, 195, 196, 197, 198, 199, 201, 202, 203, 204, 205, 206, 207, 212, 214, 217, 220, 221, 224, 226, 228, 234, 235, 237, 242, 249, 251, 252, 253, 254, 258, 260, 263, 269, 271, 274, 279, 281, 289, 291, 293, 294, 298, 300, 322, 345
Dungeon, The 229, 230, 232, 245, 261, 268, 275, 285, 296, 297, 301
Dunn, Larry 291
Dunsbar, Ainsley 398
Durante, Jimmy 12, 31
Dwight Tunji Trio 22, 39, 44, 47, 60, 64, 65, 73, 95, 142, 143
Dylan, Bob 5, 10, 64, 69, 70, 74, 78, 79, 83, 84, 96, 324, 341, 364, 413

E

Eagles, The 129, 140, 345
Earth Wind & Fire 261
Eastside, Lori 239
Eckstine, Billy 277
Eddie and the Hot Rods 198
Edgewater Inn 180
Edmiston, Walker 228
Edmondson, Bob 55, 62, 68, 85, 109, 140
Edwards, Gail 239
Ehrlich, Jesse 55, 80
Eisner, Eric 121, 122
Ellis, Alton 285
ELO 2, 117, 118, 218, 279
Entwistle, John 382
Epstein, Michael "Eppy" 224, 244, 255, 265, 272, 273, 277, 280, 281, 285, 288, 290, 293
Escape from New York 227, 229, 233, 243, 270, 275
Estrada, Roy 207
Eubanks, Bob 93, 94
Everly Brothers, The 49, 116, 279, 339
Ezrin, Bob 212, 214, 217, 221, 226, 235, 236, 251, 254, 263, 281, 287, 300

F

Fabares, Shelley 64
Fabulous Dawgs, The 29
Faier, Billy 23
Fame, Georgie 285
Farr, Jamie 93, 94
Faryar, Cyrus 35
Fats Mallard and the Bluegrass Fireball 34
Fee, Vicki 93
Feigin, Ted 9, 22, 25, 39, 42, 43, 47, 48, 60, 64, 65, 69, 70, 71, 73, 75, 78, 79, 83, 95, 135, 136, 142, 143, 147, 393
Feldman, Bob 181
Ferguson, Janet 198
Ferry, Anita 307, 308, 311, 312
Ferry, Bryan 69
Fillmore East 54, 149, 152, 153, 154, 158, 159, 160, 161, 163, 164, 165, 166, 167, 168, 169, 170, 174, 176, 177, 178, 179, 180, 183, 184, 188, 190, 191, 192, 195, 196, 201, 202, 203, 282, 436
Filter 54, 166, 244
Fitzgerald, Ella 265
Fitzpatrick, Francis 112, 134
Five Man Electrical Band 140
Flamin' Groovies, The 116
Flatt and Scruggs 69
Fleetwood Mac 84, 333
Foghat 116
Footprint Audio Services 229, 230, 232, 245, 261, 268, 275, 286, 296, 297, 301
Ford, Lita 254
Ford, Mary 277
Forman, David 229, 230, 232, 245, 261, 268, 275, 285, 296, 297, 301
Forte, Fabian 239
Forte, Nick Apollo 212, 213
Four Seasons, The 47, 79
Fowler, Walt 224, 244, 255, 265, 272, 273, 277, 280, 281, 285, 288, 290, 293
Fox, Roy 277
Fraley, Pat 306
Frampton, Peter 254
Francis, Connie 277
Francis, Winston 285
Frank Chacksfield and his Orchestra 267
Franklin, Aretha 197, 254, 265

Fraser, Dean 224, 244, 255, 265, 272, 273, 277, 280, 281, 285, 288, 290, 293
Freddie and The Dreamers 93, 94, 152
Frehley, Ace 254
Friedland, Stephen 66, 155
Frischman, Dan 239
Fritz The Cat 228
Fuller, Dolores 241
Fuller, Jim 286
Fuzztones, The 198

G

Gabrielle Amanda Music, Inc. (BMI). 310
Galik, Denise 239
Gardner, Bunk 207, 307, 308, 311, 312, 313, 315, 320
Gardner, Buzz 207, 307, 308, 311, 312, 313, 315
Garfield, Allen 239
Garfield, Nita 8, 75, 76
Garland, Judy 250, 292
Garner, Erroll 265
Gary Lewis and The Playboys 2, 93, 94, 138, 427
Gaskill, Clarence 277
Gates, David 119, 120
Geffen, David 122, 345
Gershwin, George 238
Giant, Bill 241
Gibb, Andy 283
Gibson, Beau 291
Gibson, Bob 23
Gilmour, David 79
Ginsberg, Arnie 46
Glazer, B. 147
Glitter, Gary 217
Glover,Jim 297
Goffin, Gerry 109
Golder, Barry 115
Gold Star Studios 26, 29, 34, 40, 41, 45, 65, 76, 90, 113, 114, 121, 130, 146
Goldstein. Jerry 181
Gone with the Wind 52, 344
Gooding, Cynthia 23
Good, Jerry D. 228
Goorwitz, Allen. *See* Garfield, Allen
Gordon, Alan 13, 32, 50, 54, 80, 86, 105, 108, 128, 145, 166, 242, 244
Gordon, Barry 306
Gore, Lesley 265
Goth, Mia 274
Gottehrer, Richard 181
Goulding, Graham 263
Gouldman, Graham 262, 263
GQ 285

Grabowski, Norman 93
Grant,Enroy "Tenor" 224, 244, 255, 265, 272, 273, 277, 280, 281, 285, 288, 290, 293
Grass Roots, The 12, 31, 356, 358, 371, 383, 384, 416
Grateful Dead, The 279, 414
Gray, Dobie 93
Gray, Owen 285
Great White 212
Green, Al 167
Green Day 79
Gridley, Judy 199
Griffin, Bessie 35
Griffith, Roni 217
GTOs, The 208
Guess Who, The 236
Guide For The Married Man, A 52, 53
Guidotti, Rick "Squid" viii, 354
Guilbert, Ann Morgan 52
Guthrie, Tyrone 182
Gwynne, Fred 275

H

Hadden, Alfred Cort 215
Haji Mobile Facility, The 223, 230, 240, 251, 252, 254, 255, 257, 260, 268, 276, 279, 282, 292, 301
Halloween 227, 233, 243, 270, 355
Hammett, Dashiel 238
Hampshire, Keith 285
Hand, Terry 9, 82, 92, 112
Hansen, Barry. *See* Dr. Demento
Hanson, Chuck 239
Happening, The 138
Harmony Recorders 35
Harrington, David 208
Harris, Bob 74, 152, 154, 160, 163, 166, 167, 168, 169, 170, 176, 180, 181, 183, 184, 188, 190, 192, 195, 197, 201, 202
Harris, Don "Sugarcane" 74, 157
Harrison, George 41, 208, 222, 231, 253, 268, 269, 276, 394
Harrison, Linda 52
Harrison, Noel 301
Harrison, Rex 53
Harsdhman, Allan 74
Harvey, Adam 69
Harvey, Alex 254
Harvey, George 291
Harvey, Pam 291
Havel, Václav 208
Havens, Richie 269
Hawkes, Greg viii, 332, 384, 398, 411

Hawkins, Coleman 277
Haymes, Dick 292
Heart 6, 220, 270, 310, 382, 401, 437
Heavy Traffic 228
Heller, Ivo 41, 231
Henderson, Bill 239
Hendrix, Jimi 5, 79, 208, 214, 276, 356, 357
Henshaw, William 83, 123
Henske, Judy 19, 285, 286
Herb Alpert and the Tijuana Brass 225
Herb Cohen's studio complex 222, 223, 226, 246, 284
Herman, Cleve 40
Herron, John 212, 214, 217, 221, 226, 235, 251, 254, 260, 263, 269, 281, 293, 300
Hi-C 285
Hightower, Donna 265
Hill, Freddie 112, 134
Hilton, Jim 26, 29, 34, 40, 41, 45, 65, 76, 90, 113, 114, 121, 130, 146
Hinshaw, William 145
Hoier, John 283, 306, 307, 308, 309, 310, 311, 312, 313, 315, 423
Holland, Brian 288
Hollies, The 145, 266, 288, 354
Holly, Buddy 116
Holman, Bill 55, 62, 68, 85, 109, 140
Holmes, Richard "Groove" 265
Holt, Bob 306
Honaker, Michael Alan 291
Honeycombs, The 245
Hopkin, Mary 42, 232, 292
Horne, Lena 277
Horn, Jim 113
Horn, Lew 306
Horten, Rena 93
House of Pain 61, 143
House On Haunted Hill, The 61
Houston, Thelma 197, 254
Howard, Clint 239
Howard, Ken 245
Howard, Rick 229, 230, 232, 245, 261, 268, 275, 285, 296, 297, 301
Howdy Doody 36, 188, 256
Howe, Bones 22, 25, 30, 34, 36, 39, 42, 43, 47, 48, 51, 53, 54, 55, 60, 62, 63, 64, 65, 68, 69, 70, 71, 73, 75, 78, 79, 80, 83, 85, 86, 90, 94, 95, 96, 102, 104, 105, 106, 109, 117, 119, 122, 128, 135, 136, 137, 140, 142, 143, 147, 336
Hudson Brothers, The 238
Humel, Kurt 167
Hunter, Jeffrey 52, 53
Hunter, Jimmy viii, 261, 408
Hunter, Steve 212, 214, 235, 251
Hüsker Dü 267
Hyde, Dick 145
Hyde Park, The 100

I

Ides of March 207
ID Sound Studios 62, 111, 114, 123
Iglesias, Julio 269
Indigo Ranch 225, 244, 255, 265, 272, 273, 277, 280, 281, 285, 288, 290, 293
Ingels, Marty 52, 53
Ink Spots, The 137, 277
Inspiral Carpets 198
Isaak, Chris 116
It's A Mad Mad Mad Mad Mad World 52, 54

J

Jackson, La Toya 288
Jackson, Michael 41
Jaffe, Sam 52, 53
Jagger, Mick 105, 208, 253, 276
Jamal, Ahmad 265
James, Anthony 291
James, Jim 269
James, Tommy 212
Jan and Arnie 46
Jan and Dean 42, 69, 115
Jaws 53
Jebsen, Peter 222, 223, 226, 246, 284
Jeffreys, Garland 198
Jenkins, Bob 26, 41, 108, 113, 130
Jenkins, Katharine 137
Jensen, Karen 93
Jimi Hendrix Experience, The 79
Jim & Jean 297
Jimmi, Bobby 46, 115
Joan Jett and the Blackhearts 267
Joel, Billy 239, 409
Joel Miller 418
John, Elton 216, 240, 256, 269
Johnson, John 112, 134
Johnson, Larry 91, 116
Johnson, Paul 286
Johnson, Plas 113
Johnston, Bruce 225
Jo Jo Zep and the Falcons 225, 429
Jones, Brian 208, 340, 341
Jones, Davy 17, 69, 90, 272, 328, 330, 397
Jones, Dean 18, 130
Joplin, Janis 214
Joseph, Jackie 52, 239

K

Kama Sutra 213, 240, 252, 256, 268
Kaplan, Richard 224, 244, 255, 265, 272, 273, 277, 280, 281, 285, 288, 290, 293
Kasem, Casey 81
Kaye, Danny 282
Kaye, Florence 241
Kazanegras, Alex 223, 230, 239, 251, 252, 253, 255, 257, 260, 268, 276, 279, 282, 292
Keene, Barry 31, 50, 66, 80, 86, 116, 137, 139, 146, 154, 159, 160, 163, 166, 167, 168, 169, 170, 172, 173, 176, 180, 181, 183, 184, 189, 190, 194, 195, 197, 199, 202, 205, 220, 234, 237, 242, 249, 253, 258, 271, 274, 278, 279, 289, 291, 294, 298, 377
Kelley, Ray 83, 123
Kelly, Claire 52
Kelly, Gene 14, 52
Kelly, Luke 226
Keneally, Mike 208
Kesha 69
Kinder, Ford 309, 310
King and I, The 232
King, Carole 109
King, Larry 208
Kingsmen, The 261
Kingston Trio, The 23, 71
Kinks, The 2, 6, 17, 25, 26, 62, 73, 105, 124, 226, 235, 354, 376
Kisselbach, Donnie 126, 215, 219, 227, 232, 233, 234, 250, 265, 270, 271, 276, 294, 295, 298, 360, 384, 400, 401
Klein, Manny 61, 123
KMET 154, 209
Knechtel, Larry 55, 85, 137, 140, 394
Knickerbockers, The 93
Knight, Bobby 55, 105
Knotts, Don 93
Knox, Buddy 26
Kohner, Kathy 286
Koppel, Ted 208
Korn 214
Kornfeld, Artie viii, 73, 275, 361
Kortchmar, Danny 224, 252, 258
Koz, Dave 265
Kraftwerk 210, 223, 326
Krambeck, Dave 14, 15, 68, 87, 99, 100, 101
Kramer, Eddie 180
Krampf, Craig 216, 218, 221, 222, 223, 230, 231, 239, 240, 242, 248, 251, 252, 253, 255, 256, 257, 260, 262, 263, 264, 266, 268, 273, 276, 279, 282, 288, 289, 291, 292, 296, 301, 409
KROQ 209
KTLA-TV 81
Kunc, Dick 157, 186, 187, 188, 196, 204
Kuvo, Kelly vi, 305, 422

L

Lake Shore Drive Holiday Inn 99
Lakeside 167
Lamm, Robert 283
Lane, Ronnie 212
Langdon, Sue Ane 52, 53
Lardner, Lonnie 208
Larson, Joel vii, 12, 137, 140, 393
Laserlight 119
Las Grecas 41, 231
Lasseff, Lee 9, 22, 25, 39, 42, 43, 47, 48, 60, 64, 65, 69, 70, 71, 73, 75, 78, 79, 83, 95, 135, 136, 142, 143, 147, 393
La's, The 116
Last, James 226
Late Night with David Letterman 259
Lauper, Cyndi 244
Lauren, Monica 307, 308, 311
LaVette, Bettye 69
Lawrence, John 93
Leaves, The 13, 18, 19, 84, 418, 421
Lebolt, Dave 219, 269
Led Zeppelin 60, 180, 345, 366
Lee Andrews and the Hearts 115
Lee, Peggy 269
Left Banke, The 211, 262, 296, 331
Leiber, Jerry 241
Leith, Richard 83, 123, 145
Lemon Pipers, The 196
Lennon, John 6, 7, 14, 17, 77, 129, 143, 149, 152, 153, 164, 167, 170, 176, 180, 184, 186, 188, 192, 193, 201, 208, 292, 300, 310, 340, 423, 436
Lenzer, Norm 306
Le Quément, Joëlle 228
Lewis, Forrest 93
Lewis, Jerry 52, 250, 251, 282
Lewy, Henry 74
Liberty Records v, 214, 239, 250
Lickert, Martin 159, 171, 173, 181, 184, 186, 189, 194, 197, 198, 199, 202, 205
Lighthouse 207
Lightning Seeds,The 146
Lind, Bob viii, 39, 363
Lipkin, Steve Barry 31
Lipschultz, Irving 145
Lipton, Leonard 278
Lodge, John 93
Lofton, John 208

Lombardo, Guy 215
London, Bobby 228, 303
London Philharmonic Orchestra, The 199
Lone Ranger, The 36, 92, 108, 109
Long Boards, The 113
Lords of 42nd Street, The 239
Love, American Style 52
Love, Mike 225, 257
Lovin' Spoonful, The 10, 53, 87, 374, 375, 410, 413, 414
Lowe, Jim 111, 114, 123
Lund, Deanna 93, 94
Lyme. *See* Zevon, Warren
Lynne, Jeff 59, 118, 120, 209, 247
Lynn, Vera 12, 137, 138

M

Macainsh, Greg 248
MacColl, Kirsty 226
MacMillan, Alan 216, 218, 231, 242, 248, 256, 262, 263, 266, 289, 366
Madaio, Steve 235, 251, 300
Madey, Brian 307, 308, 311, 312, 313, 315
Malarsky, Leonard 55, 80, 83, 123
Malo 261
Mamas & the Papas, The 10, 101, 142, 334, 336, 352
Manchester, Melissa 181
Manifesto Records 38, 46, 56, 69, 70, 72, 78, 85, 119, 124, 131, 138, 141, 143, 144, 435, 436, 437
Manilow, Barry 213, 268, 332, 373, 386
Mann, Barry 48, 49, 238, 436
Mansfield, Jayne 52, 53
Manson, Charles 208, 222
Manuel, Manny 167
Manzarek, Ray 128, 409, 411, 437
Marbles, The 47
March, Hal 52, 53
Margolis, Bruce 182
Marks, David 286
Marley, Bob 255, 272, 326
Marmalade 80
Marriott, Steve 212
Marsden, Gerry 9, 152
Marshall, Kathy 286
Marshall, Tonie 285
Mars, Ken 306
Martha and the Vandellas 181
Martin, Bill 40
Martin, George 17, 73, 124
Martin, Giles 120
Mart Inn, The 67

Martin, Shane 197
Mathis, Johnny 265, 269
Matthau, Walter 52, 53
Matthews, Brian 30
Matthews, Cerys 23
Mattson, Denver 291
Mawae, Kevin 317
Maximum Breed 285
Mayer, John 306
McCartney, Paul 7, 23, 142, 143, 167, 208, 268, 322, 325, 340, 342, 419, 426
McClelland, Mellisa 69
McClure, Bobby 285
McCorkle, Susannah 292
McCreary, Lew 55, 83, 105, 112, 123, 134
McDougall, Allan 128
McDowell, Malcolm 239
McFarlane, Elaine "Spanky" viii, 15, 128, 352
McGuinn, Roger 136, 145, 392, 437
McGuire, Barry 42
McMahon, Ed 26
McNaughton, Trevor 290
McNeal, Lutricia 146
McNerney, Denny 212, 213, 215, 219, 227, 228, 233, 234, 238, 241, 243, 244, 248, 250, 259, 262, 267, 270, 275, 283, 287, 294, 297, 298, 299
McRae, Carmen 265
Medley, Bill 286
Me First and the Gimme Gimmes 41, 181, 231
Megadeth 269
Mellencamp, John 79
Melodians, The 290
Meloy, Colin 226
Mercury, Freddie 218
Merman, Ethel 292
Michlin, Spence 309, 310
Mighty Diamonds and Ranking Joe, The 255
Mike Douglas Show, The 15, 18, 389
Miles, John 268
Miller, Dick 239
Miller, Lisa 241, 243, 248, 270, 287
Miller, Mitch 265
Miller, Sidney 112, 134
Milli Vanilli 54, 166, 244
Minelli, Liza 250, 292
Miss Mercy 208
Mitchell, Anais 152
Mitchell, Cameron 291
Mitchell, Jim 229, 230, 232, 245, 261, 268, 275, 285, 296, 297, 301
Mitchell, Joni 208, 256, 345, 402
Mitchell, Ollie 83, 123

Mitchell, Randy 229, 230, 232, 245, 261, 268, 275, 285, 296, 297, 301
Modern Lovers, The 198
Modest Mouse 116
Moier, Johann 222, 223, 226, 246, 284
Money, Eddie 262
Monkees, The v, 2, 4, 6, 7, 10, 11, 13, 14, 16, 17, 35, 86, 90, 109, 122, 148, 174, 210, 264, 328, 329, 330, 338, 350, 355, 370, 372, 374, 383, 390, 392, 393, 394, 400, 401, 405, 410, 417, 418, 427, 428, 456
Montenegro, Hugo 54, 166, 244
Montgomery, Wes 265
Moody Blues, The 218
Moon, Keith 59, 199, 209, 247, 437
Moore, Del 282
Morandi, Gianni 41, 231
Morey, Tom 286
Morrison, Jim 228
Morse, Robert 15, 52, 53
Mothers of Invention, The iv, 148, 151, 152, 154, 155, 158, 159, 161, 164, 167, 172, 174, 184, 189, 190, 191, 203, 208, 298, 327, 398, 399, 400, 419, 435, 436
Mothers, The iv, 6, 54, 148, 149, 150, 151, 152, 153, 154, 155, 156, 158, 159, 160, 161, 162, 163, 164, 165, 166, 167, 168, 169, 170, 171, 172, 173, 174, 175, 176, 179, 180, 181, 183, 184, 186, 187, 188, 189, 190, 191, 192, 193, 194, 195, 196, 197, 199, 201, 202, 203, 204, 205, 207, 208, 209, 231, 244, 256, 281, 282, 298, 327, 368, 369, 375, 383, 398, 399, 400, 419, 435, 436
Mott the Hoople 209, 212, 256
Mountain 52, 97, 154, 157, 168, 169, 177, 178, 179, 185, 215, 266, 270, 282, 403, 415
Muller, Romeo 313, 314, 315, 316
Mullins, Michael 291
Mull, Martin 4, 278, 286, 287, 325, 398
Mumford & Sons 226
Mundi, Billy 208
Munro, Matt 277
Munson, Art 286
Murakami, Jimmy 303
Murakami-Wolf Studio 228, 303, 304, 306, 307, 313, 314, 315, 316, 326
Murakami-Wolf-Swenson 303, 304, 306, 307, 313, 314, 315, 316, 326
Murphy, Jimmie 93
Murray, Don 8, 9, 11, 13, 22, 25, 36, 39, 40, 42, 43, 44, 47, 48, 51, 60, 62, 63, 64, 65, 67, 68, 69, 71, 73, 75, 78, 79, 83, 88, 90, 91, 92, 94, 95, 98, 103, 104, 106, 108, 109, 116, 119, 128, 135, 136, 142, 143, 147, 430, 431

Music Explosion, The 197
Music, Lorenzo 306
Mussorgsky, Modest 215
Myers, Charles Samuel 215

N

Nalbandian, Edward 162
Nambo 224, 244, 255, 265, 272, 273, 277, 280, 281, 285, 288, 290, 293
Nash, Graham 116, 128, 336
National Lampoon 228, 303, 376
Nauert, Randy 286
Nelkin, Stacey 239
Nelson, David 126, 215, 219, 227, 232, 233, 234, 238, 241, 243, 248, 265, 269, 271, 276, 287, 294, 295, 297
Nelson, Ricky 84
Nesmith, Michael 4, 13, 16, 122, 123, 389, 393, 395
Neville-Ferguson, Janet 199
Nevison, Ron viii, 216, 218, 231, 242, 248, 256, 262, 263, 266, 289, 366
Newbury, Mickey 23
New Found Glory 69
Newmar, Julie 82
New York Jets, The 19, 242, 421
Nichol, Al 7, 8, 9, 14, 19, 22, 25, 26, 29, 30, 31, 32, 34, 36, 37, 38, 39, 40, 41, 42, 43, 44, 45, 46, 47, 48, 50, 51, 53, 54, 55, 60, 61, 62, 63, 64, 65, 66, 67, 68, 69, 71, 72, 73, 74, 75, 76, 78, 79, 80, 82, 83, 85, 86, 88, 90, 91, 92, 94, 95, 96, 98, 99, 101, 102, 103, 104, 105, 106, 108, 109, 111, 112, 113, 114, 115, 116, 117, 119, 120, 121, 122, 123, 130, 134, 135, 136, 137, 139, 140, 142, 143, 144, 145, 146, 147, 148, 317, 324, 344, 396, 431
Nicks, Stevie 88, 116, 333
Nilsson, Harry 16, 26, 59, 89, 113, 117, 209, 216, 247, 303, 328, 330, 390, 432
Nitzsche, Jack 88, 145, 375
Norman, Chris 88
Norman, Larry 43
Nuckles, Paul 291
Nuttycombe, Gareth 83, 123
Nuttycombe, Wilbert 145
Nye, Louis 52, 53
Nylons, The 54, 166, 244

O

O'Brien, Laurie 306
O'Connor, Glynnis 221
O'Dare, Kathy 291
Offerall, Lucy 198, 199

Ohio Express, The 196
Olmsted Sound Studios 76, 95, 120
Olympics, The 201
O'Malley, Nick 286
Ono, Yoko 6, 17, 112, 149, 152, 153, 167, 170, 176, 178, 180, 184, 185, 186, 188, 192, 201, 202, 256, 282, 436
Orlando, Tony 54, 166, 238, 244
Orlons, The 226
Orrico, Stacie 181
Osibisa 261
Osmond, Donny 54, 166, 244
Outer Limits, The 102
Outsiders, The 25
Overboard 116
Owens, Buck 84

P

Pablo, Augustus 224, 244, 255, 265, 272, 273, 277, 280, 281, 285, 288, 290, 293
Paper Dolls 225
Parker, Ross 137, 138
Parson, Gene 35
Parsons, Alan 382, 416
Parsons, Gram 16, 35
Patsy, The 250
Patto, Mike 285
Paul and Barry Ryan 116
Pauley Pavilion 153, 155, 161, 162, 168, 172, 184
Paul, Les 277
Paul Revere and the Raiders 42, 63, 358, 371
Peake, Donald 112, 134
Pearl 273, 274, 280
Pepper, Art 55, 62, 68, 85, 109, 140
Pepperland 174, 175
Perkins, Bill 55, 85
Perkins, Bob 62, 68, 109, 140
Perkins, Carl 142
Perry, Tom 223, 230, 239, 251, 252, 253, 255, 257, 260, 268, 276, 279, 282, 292
Peter and Gordon 10, 142, 426
Peter, Paul and Mary 23, 278, 325
Peters, Bernadette 292
Petersen, Paul 238
Peterson, Oscar 277
Petty, Norman 116
Petty, Tom 74, 88, 345
Pezman, Steve 286
Philbin, Regis 208
Phillips, Anne 96
Phillips, John 100, 101
Piaf, Edith 301
Piano Guys, The 54, 166, 244

Picardo, Robert 239
"Piknik" VPRO 151, 152, 173, 174, 175, 207
Pine, Robert 93
Pinewood Studios 159, 172, 173, 181, 184, 189, 194, 197, 199, 202, 205
Pink Floyd 210, 213, 214, 423
Pinza, Ezio 89
Pisani, Nick 83, 123
Pitney, Gene 238
Planotones, The 151
Plant, Robert 355
Plastic EP vi, 48, 91, 425
Plastic Ono Band 282
Platters, The 277
Playboy 228, 303
Playten, Alice 221
Pohlman, Ray 55, 61, 83, 105, 123
Poncia, Vince 217, 241
Pons, Jim 6, 13, 15, 18, 19, 20, 25, 26, 29, 31, 32, 34, 37, 38, 40, 41, 45, 46, 50, 53, 60, 61, 62, 65, 66, 67, 72, 74, 76, 77, 80, 83, 85, 86, 87, 90, 95, 96, 99, 100, 101, 102, 105, 108, 111, 112, 113, 114, 115, 116, 117, 120, 121, 122, 123, 128, 129, 130, 134, 135, 137, 139, 144, 145, 146, 148, 151, 152, 153, 154, 155, 156, 159, 160, 161, 162, 163, 166, 167, 168, 169, 170, 171, 172, 173, 176, 180, 181, 182, 183, 184, 188, 189, 190, 191, 192, 193, 194, 195, 196, 197, 199, 201, 202, 203, 205, 206, 212, 214, 217, 220, 221, 226, 234, 235, 237, 242, 249, 251, 253, 254, 255, 258, 260, 263, 269, 271, 274, 279, 281, 289, 291, 293, 294, 298, 300, 317, 324, 344, 345, 378, 389, 391, 418, 432
Poole, George 83, 123
Porter, Cole 250
Portz, Chuck 7, 8, 13, 22, 25, 34, 36, 39, 40, 42, 43, 44, 47, 48, 51, 60, 62, 63, 64, 65, 67, 68, 69, 71, 73, 74, 75, 78, 79, 80, 82, 83, 88, 90, 91, 92, 94, 95, 98, 103, 104, 106, 108, 109, 112, 116, 119, 128, 135, 136, 137, 139, 140, 142, 143, 147, 388
Portz, Matt 47, 104
Power Station 240
Presley, Elvis 23, 147, 241
Preston, Billy 269
Preston, Don 151, 153, 155, 156, 160, 161, 162, 163, 167, 168, 170, 172, 176, 182, 191, 193, 194, 198, 199, 203, 205, 206, 207, 220, 234, 237, 242, 249, 253, 258, 271, 274, 279, 289, 291, 294, 298, 322
Pretty Girls, The 222
Price, Lloyd 265
Price, Vincent 61

Primal Scream 198
Prima Vera 54, 166, 244
Priore, Domenic 286
Proctor, Judy 40
Psychic TV 43
Puckett, Gary viii, ix, 1, 2, 147, 334, 352, 370, 372, 383, 416, 417
Pulp Fiction 98

Q

Quarrymen, The 9, 116
Queen 86, 152, 240, 264, 305, 384, 438
Question Mark and the Mysterians 197, 198
Quiet Riot 212
Quigley, Linnea 239
Quix*o*tic 285

R

Radio City Music Hall 79
Raiders Of The Lost Ark 53
Rainbow Theatre, The 149, 159, 167, 170, 177, 179, 180, 182, 183, 184, 189, 190, 191, 192, 195, 204, 436
Raksin, David 250
Ramocon, Phil 224, 244, 255, 265, 272, 273, 277, 280, 281, 285, 288, 290, 293
Ramones 88, 89, 98, 438
Randi, Don 145
Raspberries, The 2, 62, 75, 86, 264
Ravens, The 116
Ray Barretto y su Charanga Moderna 226
Rayton, Jim 76, 95, 120
RCA Records 61, 83, 111
Rebello, Jason 278
Record Plant, The 157, 186, 187, 189, 196, 204, 212, 214, 216, 217, 218, 221, 226, 231, 235, 242, 248, 251, 254, 256, 262, 263, 264, 266, 267, 281, 289, 300, 366, 368
Records, The 225
Reddy, Helen 18, 261
Red Rockers 43
Reed, Lou 59, 239, 247
Reed, Mike 212, 213, 227, 228, 259, 262, 267, 270, 275
Reed, Phil 216, 218, 221, 223, 230, 231, 239, 242, 248, 251, 252, 253, 255, 256, 257, 260, 262, 263, 264, 266, 268, 273, 276, 279, 282, 289, 291, 292, 296, 301
Reeves, Christopher 53
Reilly, John C. 137
Reiner, Carl 52, 53
Remote, Steve 126, 219, 227, 265, 271, 276, 295
Reprise Records 209, 237
Residents, The 197
Rhino Records vi, 4, 5, 8, 9, 14, 16, 19, 20, 28, 29, 55, 58, 81, 85, 89, 93, 95, 126, 128, 134, 140, 141, 143, 210, 240, 280, 304, 307, 320, 328, 344, 406, 409, 434, 435, 436, 437, 439
Richard, Little 74, 320, 325
Richards, Turley 84
Ridgely, Robert 228
Righteous Brothers, The 238
Rivers, Bob 198
Robb, Dee 224, 252, 258, 260, 269, 293, 300
Roberts, Tanya 221
Robin, Leo 277
Robinson, Alan 61, 123
Rock and Roll Hall of Fame, The 6, 7, 54, 117, 330, 350, 351, 372, 397, 400, 428
Rodgers, Pamela 93
Rodriguez, Sixto 79
Rogers, Roy 121
Rolling Stones, The 2, 65, 79, 104, 145, 180, 254, 354
Rollins, Sonny 292
Roman, Isadore 145
Roman, Murray 208
Romanoff, Michael 52
Ronettes, The 217, 218
Ron Felton Four, The 74
Ronson, Mick 79, 383
Ronstadt, Linda 16, 17, 35, 96, 116, 338, 339, 340, 375, 393
Rossini, Gioachino 108
Rotary Connection 79
Rowles, Gary 212, 214, 217, 220, 221, 226, 234, 235, 237, 242, 249, 251, 253, 254, 258, 260, 263, 269, 271, 274, 279, 281, 289, 291, 293, 294, 298, 300, 322
Roxy Theatre, The 223, 230, 240, 251, 252, 254, 255, 257, 260, 268, 276, 279, 282, 292
Royal Philharmonic Orchestra, The 159, 172, 173, 181, 184, 189, 194, 197, 199, 200, 202, 205
Royer, Rob 273
Ruffin, Jimmy 197
Rumblers, The 113
Rundgren, Todd 326, 382, 402
Russell, Jackie 52
Russell, Leon 254, 339
Ryan, Barry 116, 232
Ryan, Paul 232

S

Saiger, Susan 239
Salt 'n' Pepa 146
Salz-Pfeffer 222, 246, 284

Sandoval, Andrew vi, 38, 86
Sands, Alan 291
Santana 261, 328, 355
Santulis, John 145
Sarstedt, Peter 300
Satan's Pilgrims 198
Saxon, Joseph 55, 80, 83, 123
Scaggs, Boz 116
Schenkel, Cal 164, 208
Schilling, Eric 216, 218, 231, 242, 248, 256, 262, 263, 266, 289
Schlaks, Stephen 147
Schmidt, Marlene 291
Schwartz, Ronald 47
Scott, Erik 216, 218, 221, 222, 223, 230, 231, 239, 240, 242, 248, 251, 252, 253, 255, 256, 257, 260, 261, 262, 263, 264, 266, 268, 273, 276, 279, 282, 288, 289, 291, 292, 296, 301, 408
Scott, Tom 145
SCRAM magazine 305, 422
Searchers, The 84, 88, 89
Sebastian, John 69, 79, 216, 217, 226, 235, 303, 375, 410, 411, 413
Seeger, Pete 23
Seekers, The 23
Seiter, John 19, 20, 25, 31, 37, 38, 46, 50, 60, 61, 62, 66, 68, 72, 74, 80, 83, 85, 99, 101, 102, 105, 111, 114, 115, 116, 122, 123, 129, 130, 137, 139, 144, 146, 162, 230, 317, 338, 377, 380, 420, 432
Selig, Tibor 83, 123
Shadows, The 23
Shana 217
Shandling, Garry 72, 325, 328
Shankar, Ananda 254
Shannon, Del 88
Sheeran, Ed 212
Shelyne, Carole 93
Shepard, Thomas 83, 123
Sheppard, T.G. 54, 166, 244
Sherman, Allan 263, 292
Sherman, Bobby 239, 329
Sherwood, Euclid James 'Motorhead' 198, 199, 207
Shirley, Russ 212, 213, 227, 228, 259, 262, 267, 270, 275
Shoemake, Charlie 145
Short, Bobby 250
Shout Factory 58, 436
Shure, Paul 74, 83, 123
Sigismonti, Henry 83, 123, 145
Silhouettes, The 98
Sill, Judee 18, 74, 75
Silvers, Phil 52, 53

Silvertide 69
Simmons, Jeff 148, 151, 152, 157, 158, 159, 162, 164, 165, 167, 171, 173, 174, 182, 183, 186, 187, 188, 191, 196, 203, 204, 207, 271, 398
Simone, Nina 269
Sinatra, Frank 11, 71, 265, 277, 292, 304, 310, 334
Sinatra, Nancy 69
Sklar, Leland 224, 252, 258
Skyhooks 248, 429
Slade 286, 330
Slick Rick 285
Sloan, P.F. 11, 30, 42, 63, 64, 70, 78, 128, 142, 305
Sly & The Family Stone 297
Small Faces 212
Smith, Bill 44
Smith, Earl "Chinna" 224, 244, 255, 265, 272, 273, 277, 280, 281, 285, 288, 290, 293
Smith, Elliott 269
Smith, Hal 306
Smith, Johnny 265
Smith, Keely 277
Smith, Rick 216, 218, 231, 242, 248, 256, 262, 263, 266, 289
Smith, Robert Weston. *See* Wolfman Jack
Smith, Slim 285
Smith, Warren 224, 244, 255, 265, 272, 273, 277, 280, 281, 285, 288, 290, 293
Smokie 88
Smothers Brothers Show, The 389
Smothers, Tom 128
Sonny & Cher 10, 89, 238
Sound Recorders 32, 53, 54, 55, 62, 68, 76, 85, 86, 95, 96, 102, 105, 108, 109, 112, 117, 120, 122, 134, 135, 140, 145, 218, 222, 240, 261, 288, 306
Spanky and Our Gang 15, 17, 102, 320, 334, 370, 371, 432
Sparks 167, 215, 264, 296
Spazzy 181
Spector, Phil 217, 218, 377
Spickard, Bob 286
Spielberg, Steven 53
Spirit 16, 35, 79, 346, 393
Springsteen, Bruce 1, 6, 219, 220, 240, 326, 332, 401, 402, 410, 437
Sr. Peters, Crispian 275
Stanley, Frank C. 215
Stanley, Helen 115
Stanton, Tom 8, 12, 92, 98, 108, 116
Starr, Edwin 269
Starr, Ringo 59, 121, 194, 198, 199, 207, 209, 247, 248, 328, 330

Star Wars 53
State Farm Show Arena 176, 178, 179, 181, 197
Steele, Billy 218, 222, 240, 261, 288
Steele, Don 27
Stefko, Joe 126, 212, 213, 215, 219, 227, 228, 232, 233, 234, 238, 241, 243, 244, 248, 250, 259, 262, 265, 267, 269, 271, 275, 276, 283, 287, 294, 295, 297, 298, 299, 332, 360, 383, 384, 400, 401
Steiner, Armin 26, 29, 30, 34, 36, 40, 41, 45, 47, 51, 53, 54, 55, 62, 63, 65, 68, 76, 80, 85, 86, 90, 94, 96, 102, 104, 105, 106, 109, 114, 117, 119, 121, 122, 130, 135, 137, 140, 142, 146
Stern, Daniel 239
Stevens, Inger 52, 53
Stevens, Ray 23, 140, 265
Stevens, Shadoe 209, 236, 383
Stewart, Al 79
Stewart, Billy 285
Stewart, Rod 84, 340
Stills, Stephen 128, 153, 427, 437
Stoller, Mike 241
Stone Poneys, The 16, 96
St. Peters, Crispin 275
Strachan, Graeme "Shirley" 242, 248, 266
Stranger Cole and Gladdy 255
Stranglers, The 198
Strawberry Shortcake iv, 6, 59, 247, 303, 304, 305, 311, 312, 313, 314, 315, 316, 326, 327, 328, 355, 358, 422, 423, 424, 437
Streeto, Mike "Ringo" 129
Strijele, Bijele 167
Studio City Sound Recorders 306
Studio Sound Recorders 218, 222, 240, 261, 288
Suicide 198
Sullivan, Big Jim 159, 171, 173, 181, 184, 189, 194, 197, 199, 202, 205
Summer, Dick 282
Sundazed Records 93, 103, 109
Sunset Sound Recorders 32, 54, 55, 86, 96, 102, 105, 108, 117, 122, 135, 145, 212, 214, 217, 221, 226, 235, 251, 254, 264, 281, 300
Sunswept Studios 307, 308, 311, 312, 313, 315
Sunwest Recording Studios 31, 46, 50, 66, 80, 86, 115, 116, 137, 139, 147
Superman 54
Supremes, The 167, 288
Surfaris, The 12, 79
Susman, Todd 221
Sussman, Bruce 213
Swenson, Charles 303
Swinging Medallions, The 47

T

Tarantino, Quentin 27
Taylor, B.E. 54, 166, 244
Taylor, Russi 306, 311, 313
Taylor, Skip 216, 218, 231, 242, 248, 256, 262, 263, 266, 289, 366, 367, 368
Temptations, The 18, 135, 420
Ter-Mar Recording Studios 76, 95, 120
Terran, Tony 55, 61, 105, 123
Terry, Dewey 74
Terry-Thomas 52, 53
Terwilliger, Darrel 83, 123
Texas Detour 219, 222, 240
Thaxton, Lloyd 10, 12, 44, 129, 138, 286, 325
Thomas, B.J. 113
Thompson, Bob 55, 80
Thompson, Uziah "Sticky" 224, 244, 255, 265, 272, 273, 277, 280, 281, 285, 288, 290, 293
Thornton, Billy Bob 210, 229, 230, 232, 245, 261, 268, 275, 285, 296, 297, 301, 330, 331
Thorogood, George 37
Thoroughgood, George 286
Three Dog Night 113, 296
Three Stooges, The 52
Threshold Sound 229, 230, 232, 245, 261, 268, 275, 286, 296, 297, 301
Thrett, Maggie 93
Thunderboys, The 197
Thunders, Johnny 43, 69
Thunes, Scott 208
Thurston, Bobby 285
Tibetan Memory Trick 154, 253, 270, 282
Tomppabeats 285
Tony Orlando and Dawn 54, 166, 244
Toop, David 285
Toots and the Maytals 294
Torme, Mel 54, 166, 244
Tornados, The 43, 113
Torrence, Dean 41, 231
Tortillani 44
Tourneur, Claire 226
Towne, Aline 52
Townsend, Godfrey viii, 332, 382, 401, 415
Townshend, Pete 237, 299
Tracy, Terry 286
T. Rex 6, 212, 237, 240, 256, 264, 437
Trident Studios 157, 171, 174, 175, 186, 187, 189, 196, 204
Tripp III, Arthur Dyer 208
Triscari, Ray 55, 62, 68, 85, 109, 140
Tristan, Dorothy 221
Triumvirat 225
Trobar de Morte 278

453

T.T.G./Sunset-Highland Recording Studios 26, 29, 34, 40, 41, 45, 65, 76, 90, 114, 121, 130, 146, 157, 186, 187, 189, 196, 204
Tucker, Jim 8, 14, 22, 25, 30, 34, 36, 39, 42, 43, 47, 48, 51, 53, 54, 55, 60, 62, 63, 64, 65, 68, 69, 71, 73, 75, 78, 79, 80, 83, 85, 86, 88, 89, 90, 91, 92, 94, 95, 96, 101, 102, 104, 105, 106, 109, 112, 117, 119, 121, 128, 129, 135, 136, 137, 140, 142, 143, 145, 147, 340, 344, 396
Tuff Gong Studios 225, 244, 255, 265, 272, 273, 277, 280, 281, 285, 288, 290, 293, 326
Turner, Ike 220, 234, 237, 242, 249, 253, 258, 271, 274, 278, 279, 289, 291, 294, 298
Turre, Steve 265
Tuttle, Lurene 228

U

U2 146, 240
UB40 294
Underwood, Ian 148, 151, 152, 153, 154, 155, 156, 157, 158, 159, 160, 161, 162, 163, 164, 165, 166, 167, 168, 169, 170, 171, 172, 173, 174, 176, 180, 181, 182, 183, 184, 187, 188, 189, 190, 191, 192, 193, 194, 195, 196, 197, 198, 199, 201, 202, 203, 204, 205, 206, 207, 224, 252, 258, 266, 267, 281, 282
Underwood, Ruth 159, 171, 173, 181, 184, 189, 194, 197, 199, 202, 205, 208
United Records 25, 37, 38, 60, 61, 62, 72, 83, 105, 122, 123, 144
Uriah Heep 266
Utley, Bill 9, 14, 19, 128, 129

V

Vaghan, Sarah 265
Vai, Steve 208
Vale, Jerry 277
Valente, Caterina 250
Vance, Kenny 115, 151
Van Halen 60
Vanilla Fudge 180, 368
Van Ronk, Dave 23
Van Vliet, Don 208
Varèse, Edgard 148, 208
Vee, Bobby 116
Ventures, The 2, 43, 113, 426
Verve Records 148, 297
Vibrations, The 226
Ving, Lee 239
Visceglia, Mike 212, 213, 227, 228, 238, 241, 243, 244, 248, 250, 259, 262, 267, 269, 275, 283, 287, 297, 299

Vogel, Mitch 291
Vogues, The 142, 238, 277
Volman, Sarina-Marie 198

W

Wagner, Dick 235, 263
Wagner, Wende 93
Wailers, The 79, 225
Wakelin, Johnny 255
Wakeman, Dusty 307, 308, 311, 312, 313, 315, 327
Walker Brothers, The 84
Walk In The Sun, A 136
Wallace, Bill 236
Wallace, Cathy 40
Waller, Gordon 142
Walton, Dale 8, 36, 40, 43, 44, 67, 74, 91, 92, 98, 103
Wangberg, Eric 112, 134
War 138, 228, 261
Ward, Walter 201
Warner, Dave 43
Warwick, Dionne 297
Waters, Roger 213, 214
Watres Armory 176, 179
Watson, Johnny "Guitar" 208
Watson Twins, The 146
Wayne, Patrick 291
Webster, Ben 277
Weezer 54, 166, 244
Weiland, Gus 244, 250, 269, 283, 299
Weil, Cynthia 48, 49
Weinberg, "Sticko" Warren 224, 244, 255, 265, 272, 273, 277, 280, 281, 285, 288, 290, 293
Weisman, Ben 241
Weissman, Mitch viii, 415
Wells, H.G. 61
Wenzday 41, 231
Werner, Margot 137
Westchester High School 8, 58, 83, 139, 246
Western Recorders 12, 22, 25, 26, 29, 30, 34, 36, 39, 40, 41, 42, 44, 45, 47, 48, 51, 55, 60, 62, 63, 64, 65, 68, 69, 70, 71, 73, 75, 76, 78, 79, 80, 82, 83, 85, 90, 92, 94, 95, 98, 103, 104, 106, 108, 109, 112, 114, 116, 120, 121, 130, 135, 136, 137, 140, 142, 143, 146, 147
Westheimer, Dr. Ruth 259
West, Kanye 146
What's Up, Tiger Lily? 53
White, Ray 207
White, Vanna 238, 269, 297, 298
White Whale Records 6, 7, 9, 10, 11, 13, 14, 16, 18, 19, 20, 27, 42, 43, 47, 57, 61, 63, 70, 75,

76, 85, 89, 95, 120, 132, 136, 137, 140, 144, 158, 317, 323, 338, 362, 363, 364, 376, 377, 378, 379, 380, 420, 428, 430
Whitney Studios 157, 159, 172, 173, 181, 184, 186, 187, 189, 194, 196, 197, 199, 202, 204, 205
Who, The 2, 25, 60, 105, 249, 267, 299, 366
Wiemeyer, Walter 83, 123
Williams, Andy 269
Williams, John 14, 53, 339
Wilson, Ann 382
Wilson, Brian 115, 225, 257
Wilson, Delroy 224, 225
Wilson, Teddy 277
Wilson, Tom 208
Wing, Albert 224, 280, 283
Winnerbäck, Lars 79
Winter, Alex 208
Winter, Johnny 79, 254
Winter, Kurt 236
Wise, Fred 241
Wissert, Joe 32, 53, 54, 55, 86, 96, 102, 105, 108, 117, 122, 135, 145, 223, 224, 230, 239, 251, 252, 253, 255, 257, 258, 260, 268, 276, 279, 282, 292, 345, 375, 413
Witch Queen 240
WLIR 219
Wolen, Howard 218, 222, 240, 261, 288
Wolen, Lee 76, 95, 120
Wolf, Fred 303, 306
Wolfman Jack 209, 236
Wonder Who, The. *See* Four Seasons, The
Wood, Robert 8, 128, 139
Wood, Roy 59, 209, 247
Woodstock Festival 275
Woronov, Mary 239
Wray, Link 113, 116
Wyman, Bill 208

Y

Yamashita, Tatsuro 225
Yankovic, "Weird Al" 131
Yanovsky, Zal 285, 375
Yarrow, Peter 278
Yester, Jerry viii, 19, 31, 46, 50, 55, 66, 80, 86, 116, 137, 139, 146, 285, 286, 374, 395, 413, 414, 430
Yokus, Shelly 212, 214, 217, 221, 226, 235, 251, 254, 263, 281, 300
Young, Heather 52
Young Rascals, The 79

Z

Zale, Peter 126, 219, 227, 238, 241, 243, 244, 248, 250, 265, 269, 271, 276, 283, 287, 295, 297, 299
Zappa, Carl 208
Zappa, Dweezil 310
Zappa, Frank iv, 1, 6, 8, 19, 20, 45, 54, 75, 132, 134, 149, 151, 152, 153, 154, 155, 156, 157, 158, 159, 160, 161, 162, 163, 164, 165, 166, 167, 168, 169, 170, 171, 172, 173, 174, 176, 180, 181, 182, 183, 184, 186, 187, 188, 189, 190, 191, 192, 193, 194, 195, 196, 197, 198, 199, 200, 201, 202, 203, 204, 205, 206, 207, 209, 230, 231, 244, 249, 274, 278, 282, 298, 299, 303, 320, 323, 331, 368, 375, 383, 398, 399, 400, 419, 420, 422, 431, 435, 436, 439
Zappa, Gail 208
Zappa, Patrice 208
Zevon, Warren 13, 34, 55, 80, 81, 94
Zombie, Rob 275
Zombies, The 285, 324, 325
Zorn, John 285

ABOUT THE AUTHORS

Mark Arnold is a pop culture historian with over 15 books to his credit on subjects ranging from The Monkees, The Beatles, Underdog, Pink Panther, Cracked, Disney, Dennis the Menace, and more. He is currently at work on a book on the history of Mad. He is also the host of the Fun Ideas Podcast.

Contact Mark at funideas.mark@gmail.com.

Charles F. Rosenay!!! is a producer/actor/entertainer/humorist/author who edited a magazine on The Beatles, Good Day Sunshine, for nearly 20 years, and published The Book of Top 10 Horror Lists, The Book of Top 10 Beatles Lists, and True Ghost Stories of Connecticut. Since 1978 Charles has promoted Beatles conventions and festivals, and since 1983 he has been organizing the annual "Magical History Tour" for fans to Liverpool and London during Beatleweek. Charles also hosts the Monkees Interview Show weekends on Monkee Mania Radio (www.Live365.com). For information on the tours to England for Beatles fans, visit the website www.LiverpoolTours.com. For info on any of the books, email LiverpoolProductions@gmail.com.

www.BookOTop10BeatlesLists.com
www.BookOTop10HorrorLists.com
www.ParanormalConnecticut.com

Contact Charles at NotJustHappyTogether@gmail.com

Both authors are working on another music-related project which should also be of great interest to readers of this book. Both authors hope that this book will further the efforts of getting The Turtles into the Rock & Roll Hall of Fame.